Public Budgeting Systems

8th
EDITION

Robert D. Lee, Jr.
The Pennsylvania State University

Ronald W. Johnson
RTI International

Philip G. Joyce
The George Washington University

JONES AND BARTLETT PUBLISHERS
Sudbury, Massachusetts
BOSTON   TORONTO   LONDON   SINGAPORE

World Headquarters

Jones and Bartlett
  Publishers
40 Tall Pine Drive
Sudbury, MA 01776
978-443-5000
info@jbpub.com
www.jbpub.com

Jones and Bartlett
  Publishers Canada
6339 Ormindale Way
Mississauga, Ontario L5V 1J2
Canada

Jones and Bartlett
  Publishers International
Barb House, Barb Mews
London W6 7PA
UK

Jones and Bartlett's books and products are available through most bookstores and online booksellers. To contact Jones and Bartlett Publishers directly, call 800-832-0034, fax 978-443-8000, or visit our website, www.jbpub.com.

Substantial discounts on bulk quantities of Jones and Bartlett's publications are available to corporations, professional associations, and other qualified organizations. For details and specific discount information, contact the special sales department at Jones and Bartlett via the above contact information or send an email to specialsales@jbpub.com.

This publication is designed to provide accurate and authoritative information in regard to the subject matter covered. It is sold with the understanding that the publisher is not engaged in rendering legal, accounting, or other professional service. If legal advice or other expert assistance is required, the service of a competent professional person should be sought.

Production Credits
Executive Editor: David Cella
Acquisitions Editor: Jeremy Spiegel
Editorial Assistant: Lisa Gordon
Production Director: Amy Rose
Production Assistant: Mike Boblitt
Associate Marketing Manager: Jennifer Bengtson
Cover Design: Kristin E. Ohlin
Cover Image: © Inozemtcev Konstantin/ShutterStock, Inc.
Composition: Northeast Compositors, Inc.
Manufacturing Buyer: Amy Bacus
Printing and Binding: Malloy, Inc.
Cover Printing: Malloy, Inc.

Library of Congress Cataloging-in-Publication Data
Lee, Robert D.
  Public budgeting systems / Robert Lee, Ronald Johnson, Philip Joyce. — 8th ed.
    p. cm.
  Includes bibliographical references and index.
  ISBN-13: 978-0-7637-4668-1
  ISBN-10: 0-7637-4668-1
  1. Budget—United States. 2. Budget process—United States. 3. Program budgeting—United States. I. Johnson, Ronald Wayne, 1942- II. Joyce, Philip G., 1956- III. Title.
  HJ2051.L4 2008
  352.4'973—dc22

                          2007008764
6048

Printed in the United States of America
11 10 09 08   10 9 8 7 6 5 4 3

Dedicated to
Ann
and to
Sally
and to
Rita, Christopher, Mariah, and Samuel

CONTENTS

Preface

This is a general book on public budgeting. Its purpose is to survey the current state of the art among all levels of government in the United States. Where their inclusion would be illustrative, we also use examples from other countries and from some nongovernmental organizations. In addition, we emphasize methods by which financial decisions are reached within a system and ways in which different types of information are used in budgetary decision making. We stress the use of program information, since budget reforms for decades have sought to introduce greater program considerations into financial decisions.

Budgeting is considered within the context of a system containing numerous components and relationships. One problem of such an approach is that, because all things within a system are related, it is difficult to find an appropriate place to begin. Although we have divided the text into chapters, the reader should recognize that no single chapter can stand alone. Every chapter mentions some topics and issues that are treated elsewhere in the book.

A discussion of budgeting may be organized in various ways. Historical or chronological sequence is one possible method of organization, although this approach would require discussing every relevant topic for each time period. Another strategy is to arrange topics by level of government, with separate sections for local, state, and federal budgeting. Such an approach again would involve extensive rehashing of arguments and information. Yet another approach is to focus on phases of the budget cycle from preparation of the budget through auditing of past activities and expenditures. Rigid adherence to this approach would be inappropriate, because the budget cycle is not precisely defined and many issues cut across several phases of the cycle. Another approach would be to organize the discussion around the contrast between the technical and political problems of budgetary decision making.

The organization of this book is a combination of these approaches. Chapter 1, *Introduction*, provides a general discussion of the nature of budgetary decision making, including distinctions between private and public budgeting, the concepts of responsibility and accountability in budgeting, the possibility of rationality in decision making, and the nature of budgeting and budget systems. Chapter 2, *The Public Sector in Perspective*, reviews the scope of the public sector, the magnitude of government, the sources of revenues, and the purposes of government expenditures. Budget cycles are the topic of Chapter 3, which summarizes the basic steps in budgeting: preparation and submission, approval, execution, and auditing. Together these chapters provide a basic framework for the remainder of the book.

The next four chapters focus on the budget preparation process. Their purpose is to provide the reader with an understanding of the types of deliberations involved in developing a proposed budget. Chapter 4, *Budgeting for Revenues, Part I*, considers the different sources from which governments obtain their funds, the criteria for evaluating revenue sources, and then specific sources such as income and property taxes. Chapter 5, *Budgeting for Revenues, Part II*, continues the discussion of revenues by considering transaction-based taxes, primarily sales taxes, user fees, and the like. Chapter 6, *Budget Preparation: The Expenditure Side*, discusses early budget reform efforts and contemporary approaches to developing proposals for funding government programs. Chapter 7, *Budget Preparation: The Decision Process*, examines the process of putting together a budget proposal that includes recommended revenue and expenditure levels, and then reviews the types of budget documents that are used in government.

Chapters 8 and 9 deal with the budget approval process. Chapter 8, *Budget Approval: The Role of the Legislature*, provides a general account of the processes used by legislative bodies. Chapter 9, *Budget Approval: The U.S. Congress*, treats separately the special factors and problems associated with congressional budgeting.

The next four chapters concentrate on the execution and audit and evaluation phases of budgeting. Chapter 10, *Budget Execution*, considers the roles played by the chief executive, the budget office, and the line agencies. The chapter treats separately the topics of tax administration, cash management, procurement, and risk management. Chapter 11, *Financial Management: Accounting, Reporting, and Auditing*, presents the basic features of accounting systems and processes, reviews the various types of reports that flow from accounting systems, and explains the types of audits that are conducted. Chapter 12, *Capital Assets: Planning and Budgeting, Analysis, and Management*, examines capital budgeting as a decision process. Decisions about capital budgeting actually occur throughout the budget process, although capital programming occurs during budget execution. Chapter 13, *Capital Finance and Debt Management*, considers the financing of long-term capital investments through debt and equity instruments.

The final two chapters deal with special topics in government budgeting. Chapter 14, *Intergovernmental Relations,* examines the financial interactions among governments, the types of fiscal assistance in use, and possible means of restructuring intergovernmental relationships. Chapter 15, *Government, the Economy, and Economic Development,* surveys the federal government's role in managing the economy and notes the ways that economic conditions affect state and local governments.

The book closes with some brief concluding remarks on themes that can be expected to receive considerable attention from budgeting practitioners and scholars in the next several years. The bibliographic note provides guidance on keeping informed about changes in the field of budgeting.

Overall, this edition retains much of the structure of the seventh edition but gives increased attention to some topics, such as various revenue sources, capital budgeting, and state and local debt management. It also reflects the continuing impact on budgeting of the tragic events that occurred on September 11, 2001, in New York City, Washington, D.C., and a field in rural Pennsylvania and the subsequent wars in Afghanistan and Iraq. Text, tables, and exhibits have been completely updated.

Drs. Lee and Johnson began the *First Edition* as faculty members in the Institute of Public Administration at The Pennsylvania State University. Seven editions later, Dr. Lee is Professor Emeritus of Public Administration and Professor Emeritus of Hotel, Restaurant, and Recreation Management at The Pennsylvania State University. Dr. Johnson is Executive Vice President for International Development at RTI International. With the *Seventh Edition,* Dr. Philip G. Joyce was welcomed, and he continues in this new edition as an integral member of our writing team. He is Professor of Public Policy and Public Administration at The George Washington University.

Our hope is that this new edition will be useful to readers from many backgrounds and with widely diverse purposes.

Acknowledgments

Having gone through seven previous editions, this *Eighth Edition* is necessarily the product of numerous individuals, not just its three authors. We are indebted to colleagues at The Pennsylvania State University, RTI International, and The George Washington University. Professor Joyce was ably assisted in the preparation of this edition by his GWU research assistant, Robin McLaughry. Colleagues and students at other institutions, including a variety of colleges and universities, have provided valuable advice. Practitioners in the United States and many developing countries have helped refine our understanding with real world situations. In preparing the book, we received considerable advice from expert practitioners in the executive and legislative branches of federal, state, and local governments and from their counterparts in nonprofit organizations. The responsibility for the final product, of course, belongs to us alone.

Chapter 1

INTRODUCTION

In what many characterize as the *information age*,[1] it is to be expected that any book dealing with large organizations operating in the world economy would focus extensively on information. This book is about complex governmental institutions that operate in a world economy and society, and its extensive focus on information is no surprise. This book is about budgets, budgeting systems, and budgeting processes; the nature of the decisions that are made; and the processes by which those decisions are made. As we discuss throughout the book, budgeting has always been about information, and budget systems are about gathering the best information available, whether that information be primarily of a technical nature or primarily of a political nature, and bringing that information to bear on decisions about allocating resources to purposes.

Public budgeting involves the selection of ends and the selection of means to reach those ends. It involves the division of society's economic and financial resources between the public sector and the private sector, as well as the allocation of such resources among competing public sector needs. Public budgeting systems are systems for making choices of ends and means. These choices are guided by theory, by hunch, by partisan politics, by narrow self-interest, by altruism, and by many other sources of value judgment including avarice and perceptions of the public interest.

Public budgeting systems work by channeling various types of information about societal conditions and about the private and public values that guide resource allocation decision making. Complex channels for information exchange exist. Through these channels, people process information on what is desired, make assessments of what is or is not being achieved, and analyze what might or might not be achieved. Integral to budgeting systems are intricate processes that link both political and economic values. In making decisions that ultimately determine how resources are allocated, the political process uses sometimes bewildering and often conflicting information about values, about actual conditions, and about possible condition changes. This book is an analysis of procedures and methods—past, present, and prospective—used in the resource allocation process.

This chapter examines some basic features of decision making and budgeting systems. First, some major characteristics of public budgeting are explained through comparison and contrast with private forms of budgeting. Second, the development of budgeting as a means of holding government accountable for its use of society's resources is reviewed. Next, budgets and budgeting systems are defined. Finally, the role of information in budgetary decision making is considered.

▌ Distinctions Regarding Public Budgeting

Budgeting is a common phenomenon. To some extent, everybody does it. People budget time, dollars, food—almost everything. The family hardware store budgets, Wal-Mart budgets, and governments budget. Moreover, important similarities exist in the budgeting done by large public and private bureaucracies.[2]

Budgeting is intended as a mechanism for setting goals and objectives, for allocating the resources necessary to achieve those objectives, for measuring progress toward objectives, for identifying weaknesses or inadequacies in organizations, and for controlling and integrating the diverse activities carried out by numerous subunits within large bureaucracies, both public and private. Budgeting is the manifestation of an organization's strategies, whether those strategies are the result of thoughtful strategic planning processes, the inertia of long years of doing approximately the same thing, or the competing political forces within the organization bargaining for shares of resources. Once resources are allocated through the budgetary process, the organization's strategies become apparent even if they have not been articulated as strategies. Budgeting means examining how the organization's resources have been used in the past, analyzing what has been accomplished and at what cost, and charting a course for the future by allocating resources for the coming budget period. Whether this process is done haphazardly or after exhaustive analyses, whether it is carried out by order of the chief executive officer or requires the extensive input of citizens, it is still budgeting.

Budgeting is also about assigning responsibility for accomplishing the results intended by the executive and legislative actors that ultimately set the public budget. Budgets are executed by individuals generally within large bureaucracies. Budget allocations identify not only the amounts to be spent and the intended purposes of those expenditures, but also the unit within the bureaucracy—and by implication, the individuals managing that unit—responsible for achieving the intended results. In the contemporary age in which much of the value in any process, whether producing a commercial good or producing a public service, is in the information or knowledge applied, responsibility for budget decisions and budget implementation is vastly more complicated. First, the information available to the decision makers, whether they choose to use it or not, is much more extensive. Second, decision-making processes are more highly visible to citizens and other stakeholders. Thus, for practical reasons, and because strong central government controls are politically less feasible than in the past in most countries, budgetary decisions are more decentralized than ever.

Public and Private Sector Differences in Objectives

Resource Availability. Important differences exist between the private and public spheres. In the first place, the amount of resources available for allocation in the budget process varies greatly. Both family and corporate budgeting are constrained by a relatively fixed set of available resources, even if vastly different in size. Income is comparatively fixed, at least in the short run, and therefore outgo must be equal to or less than income. Of course, income can be expanded by increasing the level of production and work, such as a member of the family taking a second job, or temporarily by borrowing, but the opportunities for increasing income are limited.

Governments, on the other hand, are bound by much higher limits. In the United States at least, government does not use nearly all of the possible resources available. Only in times of major crises, such as World War II, has the government of the United States begun to approach the limits of its resources. Then the federal government borrowed an amount that eventually came close to equaling the total production of the economy in a year. Rationing, price controls, and other measures were imposed so as to limit severely private sector consumption and instead allocate most of society's resources to the government. During other times, much is left to the private sector with government using only a fraction of society's work force, goods, and services. In 2005, combined federal, state, and local government receipts amounted to just over 31% of total *gross domestic product* (GDP), with about three-fifths of that being the federal government. That percentage has varied little, from about 25% to about 30% since 1960.[3] Government has the power to determine how much of the society's total resources will be taken for public purposes. Private parties operate within the limits of their ability to acquire resources through their market activities: selling their labor, selling goods, and so forth.

Profit Motive. Another major distinction between private and public budgeting is the motivation behind budget decisions. The private sector is characterized by the profit motive, whereas government undertakes many things that are financially unprofitable. In the private sector, profit serves as a ready standard for evaluating previous decisions. Successful decisions are those that produce profits (as measured in dollars). Some companies, of course, may focus on short-term profits, and others may take a longer-term view, but in the end, failure to achieve a profit or at least break-even means the company goes out of business.

The concept of profit, however, can lead to gross oversimplifications about corporate decision making. Not every budget decision in a private firm is determined by the criterion of making an immediate profit. Sometimes corporations forgo profits in the short run. In the case of price wars, they attempt to increase their share of a given market even if it means selling temporarily at a loss. At other times, they incur large debts and take other apparently unprofitable actions to combat a hostile takeover, an attempt by an outsider to purchase enough stock to exercise control over a corporation's assets. Sometimes their major objectives are to produce a good product and to build public confidence. They have enough confidence in their pursuit of customer service that the result will be sustained, long-run profits. At other times they undertake actions for mainly social motives, wishing to make a contribution to the society that sustains their corporate existence, a concept known as corporate social responsibility (CSR).[4] Still, in private sector firms, revenues must exceed costs over the long run.

Large firms also budget significant resources for research and development (R & D) activities, only a few of which eventually will lead to a product that generates large sales and profits. An R & D division can be evaluated over the long term by how many of its developments contribute to profits, but this kind of evaluation is difficult. Often, the results of R & D are subtle improvements in existing products and measuring the amount of investment relative to the incremental profit gain is impossible. In this regard, private budgeting for R & D is no less difficult than the federal government's support of R & D.

Overall, the evidence is that investing in R & D yields positive returns on that investment.[5] A Congressional Budget Office review of studies estimating the value generated by R & D expenditures noted that although precise achievements are difficult to estimate, R & D spending does yield positive returns.[6] A National Academy of Sciences panel studied five federal agencies' implementation of the Government Performance and Results Act of 1993 to measure the results of their research and development activities. The study noted that the benefits of research are difficult to assess, concluding that "the most effective technique for evaluating research programs is review by panels of experts using the criteria of quality, relevance, and, when appropriate, leadership."[7]

Regardless of the role profit plays in the private sector, government decision making in general lacks even this standard for measuring activities. Exceptions to this generalization are government activities that yield revenues. State control and sale of alcoholic beverages, whether undertaken for profit or for regulation of public morals, can be evaluated, like any other business, in terms of profit and loss. Similarly, the operation of a water system, a public transit authority, or a public swimming pool can be evaluated in business profit-and-loss terms. This does not mean that each of these should turn a profit. After all, operating a public swimming pool may be the result of a decision to provide subsidized recreation to a low-income neighborhood whose residents cannot afford other private recreational alternatives. The budgeting process, however, can be used to assess the operation as a business to clarify the subsidy level and to aid decision makers in comparing costs with those for other public services provided free of direct charge (see Chapter 12).

Nevertheless, the majority of private sector budget decisions pertain to at least long-term profits, and most public sector budget decisions do not. Governments undertake some functions deliberately instead of leaving them to the private sector. Public budgetary decisions, for example, frequently involve allocation of resources among competing programs that are not readily susceptible to measurement in dollar costs and dollar returns. For example, there are no easy means of measuring the costs and benefits of a life saved through cancer research, although the value of future earnings sometimes is used as a surrogate measure of the value of life. The U.S. government undertakes large programs to control or eradicate malaria and other tropical diseases, not based on economic or financial returns, but on a broad concept of the public interest in eradicating diseases that affect low-income populations in developing countries. Nor is there a ready means of clearly separating private incentives from public incentives. For example, although the National Cancer Institute spends millions of public dollars annually on cancer research, the amount is minuscule compared with the amount spent by private companies on research for cancer prevention and treatment.

Just because most public sector activities are not intended to be profitable, it does not mean that business-like measurement of results in relation to costs is useless. Although not susceptible to bottom-line or profit-and-loss measurement, many government programs are able to measure their results in terms of output (efficiency) and outcome (effectiveness). The tropical disease eradication programs undertaken by the U.S. government for reasons of the public interest, for example, can and are measured by the efficiency and effectiveness with which the programs are implemented.[8] Legislation passed in 1993 mandated the use of performance measures to improve the federal government's accountability for the results of its expenditures.[9]

Public and Private Sector Differences in Services Provided

Public Goods. Some government services yield public or collective benefits that are of value to society as a whole, whereas corporate products are almost always consumed by individuals and specific organizations. When Ford Motor Company produces automobiles, persons buying the automobiles use them to meet their own personal needs. When the Departments of Defense and Homeland Security produce a network for preventing nuclear devices from entering the nation's ports, that network benefits the public in general. Economists call these kinds of products and services *public goods*. They have two properties. The first is *nonexcludability*. Once the network is in place, no one can be excluded from its benefits.[10] The second is *nonrivalness*. One person's use of the good or service does not diminish another person's use. For example, a second person can "consume" national defense without lessening the benefits that the first person gets from that public good. Of course, few public products and services qualify as pure public goods, and many goods and services produced by governments are also produced by the private sector. Police protection is a public service, but communities, companies and even individuals also purchase various forms of protection against crime from private security companies.

Externalities. Another class of government services consists of those from which individuals can be excluded but for which the benefits, or costs, extend beyond those who are the immediate targets of the service. When Ford Motor Company sells a car, its stockholders enjoy the benefits of the profits, but those profits do not spill over to society at large. However, when a child is educated through a school system, not only does the child benefit, but society's productive capacity is also enhanced. Many private schools educate children for a profit, and the owners of the schools enjoy the benefits of the profits along with the children and society. However, it seems unlikely that these same for-profit schools would willingly provide equivalent education to all children who cannot make tuition payments. Economists label the benefits that spill over to the rest of society *externalities*. Governments provide at least some services that produce significant externalities because the private sector would provide these only to the extent that profit could be made. Education, if left entirely to the private sector, presumably would be available only to those who could pay, or would be provided in insufficient quantity and quality for the needs of society.

Pricing Public Services. Defining just what is clearly public in nature and determining what the private sector presumably cannot or will not provide is controversial. During the 1980s and 1990s, the federal government cut back on transfers to state and local governments, which also faced more stringent tax and spending limitations inspired by their voters (see Chapter 5). As a consequence, many serv-ices once thought to be exclusively public were converted into private services or to public services provided by private firms on a contract basis.[11] That trend con-tinued when state and local budgets shrank dramatically with the recession that started in 2001–2002, though there is some evidence that smaller jurisdictions or smaller private contracting for public services has waned somewhat, while large contracts seem to be increasing.[12]

This trend advanced throughout many developing countries with public sec-tors even larger than in the United States. The Margaret Thatcher government, in privatizing many formerly public services such as the water utilities throughout the United Kingdom, served as a model for the early 1980s movement in the United States and around the world.

This type of conversion is not a new idea, but public sector budget pressures have changed the landscape to require those who benefit directly from a govern-ment service to pay for its cost (see Chapter 5). For example, in the 1990s the U.S. Coast Guard stopped providing towing services to disabled boats unless a genuine emergency exists; it instead notifies private operators, who charge the cost to the disabled boat captain. That practice has cut back significantly on calls for towing in general, with prices providing a rationing mechanism. What is private and what is public varies over time, and public budgeting is affected by those variations.[13]

Other Public and Private Sector Differences. Whatever objectives, other than profit, that private corporations may have, to stay in business they must seek economic efficiency and obtain the greatest possible dollar return on investments. In con-trast, governments may be intentionally inefficient in resource allocations, under-taking services that the private sector would be reluctant to provide at all. For example, government-financed medical care for the elderly may be inefficient in the sense that other government programs provide greater economic returns to society, but it has been agreed that at least some support should be provided to the elderly. Governments are also charged with other unique responsibilities such as intervention in the economy (see Chapter 15).

Another difference between private and public organizations lies in the clien-tele and the owners of the means of production. In theory, at least, both corpora-tions and governments are answerable to their stockholders and clients. In the private sector, these individuals can disassociate themselves from firms. Their counterparts in the public sector are denied this choice except through the extreme act of emigration. Private stockholders expect dollar returns on their investments, and if they are not satisfied they sell their shares. Because government costs and returns are not so easily evaluated, the electorate has no simple measure for assessing the returns on the taxes they pay, and they have no means to sell their shares, other than to move to another country. Even so, many state and local governments provide annual reports to citizens that are similar in purpose to stockholder reports. These reports emphasize the investments government is making and the benefits citizens are receiving in lieu of profits. Of course the stockholders of corporations and of governments from time to time change management, the latter through regular elections.

Corporate budgetary decision making is usually more centralized than government decision making. Corporations can stop production of economically unprofitable goods such as Oldsmobiles. Given the nature of the public decision-making process, however, governments encounter more difficulty in making decisions both to inaugurate programs and to eliminate them. For example, though there was an apparent large majority consensus for over two decades that the Medicare program that assists the elderly in financing health care should include some form of prescription drug coverage, it was not until 2006 that a program finally was implemented.

Responsible Government and Budgeting

The emergence and reform of formal government budgeting can be traced to a concern for holding public officials accountable for their actions.[14] The "reinventing government" movement represents the most recent manifestation of a rather ancient concern that public officials be held accountable for their actions, though some critics have held that the precepts of reinvention are not new and not necessarily internally consistent.[15] No matter the particular reform terminology in vogue, in a democracy, budgeting is a device for limiting the powers of government. Two issues recur in the evolution of modern public budgeting as an instrument of accountability—responsibility to whom and for what purposes.

Responsible to Whom?

Responsibility to Constituency. Basically, responsibility in a democratic society entails constituents holding their officials answerable, usually through elections. Elected executives and legislative representatives at all levels of government are, at least in theory, held accountable through the electoral process for their decisions on programs and budgets. In actuality, budget documents are not the main source of information for decisions by the electorate. Obviously, most voters do not diligently study the U.S. budget before casting their votes in presidential and congressional elections. However, when the government's share of the total economy grows, it is increasingly clear that voters do hold elected representatives responsible for the overall budget, the budget deficit, and the general performance of the economy. That the electorate holds presidents responsible for the economy was evidenced in 1992 by President George H.W. Bush's defeat in his bid for re-election. Eight years later, the 2000 election showed that even in the midst of a booming economy, many voters were more concerned about apparent ethical and moral lapses in the White House than their happiness with the economy. In 2006, voters indicated great unhappiness with the wars in Afghanistan and Iraq and the overall performance of the presidency by changing the party control in both the House and the Senate. Huge budget deficits seemed to play only a minor role in voter decisions in that election.

State and local governments have specific creditors: the purchasers of bonds issued to finance long-term capital improvements. The interest rates that state and local governments have to pay on their bonds are affected by their ability to provide creditors with convincing evidence of their creditworthiness (see Chapter 13). Hence, financial institutions that purchase bonds and ratings institutions that rate state and local bonds are important constituents to whom these governments are accountable.

Because the public in a large society cannot be fully informed about the operations of government, the United States has used the concepts of *separation of powers* and *checks and balances* as means of providing for responsible government. Power is divided among the executive, legislative, and judicial branches, and each provides some checks on the others. Although the president is held responsible to Congress for preparation and submission of an executive budget, only Congress can pass the budget. Specifically, the U.S. Constitution, in Article 1, Section 9, states that "no money shall be drawn from the Treasury, but in consequence of appropriations made by law. . . ." In most states and many localities, the chief executive has a similar responsibility to recommend a plan for taxes and expenditures. The legislative body passes judgment on these recommendations and subsequently holds the executive branch responsible for carrying out the decisions. Local government practice varies more since some local governments do not have an elected chief executive.

Development of the Executive Budget System. The development of an executive budget system for holding government accountable was a long process that can be traced as far back as the Magna Charta in 1215. The main issue that resulted in this landmark document was the Crown's taxing powers. The Magna Charta did not produce a complete budget but concentrated only upon holding the Crown accountable to the nobility for its revenue actions.[16] At the time, the magnitude of public expenditures and the use of these funds for public services were of less concern than the power to levy and collect taxes. It was not until the English Consolidated Fund Act of 1787 that the rudiments of a complete system were established, and a complete account of revenues and expenditures was presented to Parliament for the first time in 1822.[17]

The same concern in eighteenth-century England for executive accountability was exhibited in other countries. It was carried over to the American experience even prior to the ratification of the Constitution in 1789. Fear of a strong executive branch was evidenced by the failure to provide for such a branch in the Articles of Confederation in 1781. Fear of "taxation without representation" probably explains why the Constitution is more explicit about taxing powers than the procedures to be followed in government spending.

The first decade under the Constitution saw important developments that could have resulted in an executive budget system, but the trend was reversed in subsequent years. The Treasury Act of 1789, establishing the Treasury Department, granted to the secretary the power "to digest and prepare plans for the improvement of the revenue . . . [and] to prepare and report estimates of the public revenue and expenditures."[18] Alexander Hamilton, secretary of the treasury, in interpreting his mandate broadly, asserted strong leadership in financial affairs. Although the Act did not grant the secretary power to prepare a budget by recommending which programs should and should not be funded, such a development might have subsequently occurred.

Instead, Hamilton's apparent lack of deference to Congress strengthened that body's support for greater legislative control over financial matters. To curtail the discretion of the executive branch, Congress resorted to the use of increasing numbers of line items, specifying in narrow detail for what purposes money could be spent.[19] The pattern emerged that each executive department would deal directly with Congress, thereby curtailing the responsibilities of the secretary of the treasury. The budgetary function of the Treasury Department became primarily ministerial. The Book of Estimates, prepared by the secretary and delivered to Congress, could have become the instrument for a coordinated set of budgetary recommendations. Instead, it was simply a compilation of departmental requests for funds. A. E. Buck wrote, "Thus budget making became an exclusively legislative function in the national government, and as such it continued for more than a century."[20]

Modern Executive Budgeting. By the beginning of the twentieth century, changing economic conditions stimulated the demand for more centralized and controlled forms of budgeting. E. E. Naylor wrote that before this time there was little "enthusiasm for action . . . since federal taxes were usually indirect and not severely felt by any particular individual or group."[21] By 1900, however, existing revenue sources no longer consistently produced sufficient sums to cover the costs of government. At the federal level, the tariff could not be expected to produce a surplus of funds, as had been the case. Causes of this growing deficit were the expanded scope of government programs and, to a lesser extent, waste and corruption in government finance. The latter is often credited as a major political factor stimulating reform.

Local government led the way in the establishment of formal budget procedures. Municipal budget reform was closely associated with general reform of local government, especially the creation of the city manager form of government. In 1899, a model municipal corporation act, released by the National Municipal League, featured a model charter that provided for a budget system whose preparation phase was under the control of the mayor. In 1907, the New York Bureau of Municipal Research issued a study, "Making a Municipal Budget," that became the basis for establishing a budgetary system for New York City.[22] By the mid-1920s, most major U.S. cities had some form of budget system.

Substantial reform of state budgeting occurred between 1910 and 1920. This reform was closely associated with the overall drive to hold executives accountable by first giving them authority over the executive branch. The movement for the short ballot, aimed at eliminating many independently elected administrative officers, resulted in governors being granted greater control over their bureaucracies. Ohio, in 1910, was the first state to enact a law empowering the governor to prepare and submit a budget. A. E. Buck, in assessing the effort at the state level, suggested that 1913 marked "the beginning of practical action in the states."[23] By 1920, some budget reform had occurred in 44 states, and all states had a central budget office by 1929.[24]

Simultaneous action occurred at the federal level, and much of what took place there contributed to the reforms at the local and state levels. Frederick A. Cleveland, who was director of the New York Bureau of Municipal Research and who played a key role in national reform, asserted that "it was the uncontrolled and uncontrollable increase in the cost of government that finally jostled the public into an attitude of hostility."[25] In response to this public concern, President Taft requested and received from Congress in 1909 an appropriation of $100,000 for a special Commission on Economy and Efficiency. Known as the Taft Commission, the group was headed by Cleveland and submitted its final report in 1912, recommending the establishment of a budgetary process under the direction of the president. This report was to spur activity at the state and local levels.

The Budget and Accounting Act, which established the new federal system, was not passed until 1921.[26] In the interim, deficits were recorded every year between 1912 and 1919, except for 1916. The largest deficit occurred in 1919, when (largely because of the need to finance World War I) expenditures were three times greater than revenues ($18.5 billion in expenditures as compared with $5.1 billion in revenues). During this period, vigorous debate centered on the issue of whether budget reform would in effect establish a superordinate executive over the legislative branch. In 1920, President Wilson vetoed legislation that would have created a Bureau of the Budget and a General Accounting Office on the grounds that the latter, as an arm of Congress, would violate the president's authority over the executive branch. The following year, President Harding signed virtually identical legislation into law.

Thus, an executive budget system was established, despite a historical fear of a powerful chief executive. In 1939, as a result of recommendations made by President Roosevelt's Committee on Administrative Management (the Brownlow Committee), the Bureau of the Budget was removed from the Treasury Department and placed in the newly formed Executive Office of the President. This shift reflected the growing importance of the Bureau in assisting the president in managing the government. Ten years later, the budgetary task force of the First Hoover Commission on the Organization of the Executive Branch recommended that the Bureau of the Budget be reinstated in the Treasury Department, but the Commission as a whole opposed the recommendation.[27] The Budget and Accounting Procedures Act of 1950 reinforced the trend of presidential control by explicitly granting the president control over the "form and detail" of the budget document.[28] The Second Hoover Commission in 1955 endorsed strengthening the president's power in budgeting as a means of restoring the "full control of the national purse to the Congress."[29] A president, who had full control of the bureaucracy, could be held accountable by Congress for action taken by the bureaucracy.

One of the stated goals of the reform movement was to bring the sound financial practices of business to the presumably disorganized public sector—a goal often expressed by current reformers. Available evidence, however, indicates that business practices were not particularly exemplary at the turn of the century, suggesting that the reforms were largely invented within the public sector rather than being transferred into government from the outside.[30] It remains popular to advocate bringing good business practices to government, but the corporate accounting scandals that revealed false revenue claims in such giants as Enron suggest that private practices are not always exemplary.

Responsible for What?

Revenue Responsibility. The earliest concern for financial responsibility centered on taxes. As indicated above, the Magna Charta imposed limitations not on the nature of the Crown's expenditures but on the procedures for raising revenue. The same concern for the revenue side of budgeting was characteristic of the early history of budgeting in this country. The Constitution is more explicit about the tax power of the government than about the nature or purposes of government expenditures.

Expenditure Control, Management, and Planning. The larger the budget has become, the more the concern has shifted to expenditures. Increasing emphasis has been placed on the accountability of government for what it spends and for how well it manages its overall finances. Expenditure accountability may take several different forms. Budgeting scholar Allen Schick described the focus on accountability in U.S. budgeting as having gone through three stages by the 1960s.[31]

The first stage he characterized as legislative concern for tight control over executive expenditures. The most prevalent means of exerting this type of expenditure control is to appropriate by line item and object of expenditure. Financial audits are then used to ensure that money is, in fact, spent for the items authorized for purchase. This information focuses budgetary decision making on the things government buys, such as personnel, travel, and supplies—the objects of expenditure—rather than on the accomplishments of government activities. In other words, responsibility is achieved by controlling the resources or input side.

Schick's description of the second stage was that of a management orientation, with emphasis on the efficiency of ongoing activities. Historically, this orientation is associated with the New Deal through the First Hoover Commission (1949). The emphasis was on holding administrators accountable for the efficiency of their activities through methods such as work performance measurement. Budgeting by activity achieves accountability by measuring the activities carried out for the money expended.

The third stage of budget reform Schick identified was based on the post-Hoover Commission concern regarding the planning function served by budgets. The traditional goal of controlling resource inputs may be accommodated in the short time frame of the coming budget year. Managerial control over efficiency, although aided by a longer time perspective, also may be accommodated in a traditional budget-year presentation. The planning emphasis focuses on a longer time frame. Many objectives of government programs cannot be accomplished in one budget year. A multiyear presentation of the budget is thus necessary to indicate the long-range implications, both financial and program results, of current budget decisions.

The advent of program budgeting in the 1960s with its focus on multiyear planning and the ultimate results of government programs was the culmination of the planning focus on outcomes that must be measured outside the government itself. Control-oriented information such as objects of expenditure and managerial-oriented information such as the outputs produced by government activities (and the costs to achieve those outputs) do not really require measurement outside the orbit of governmental agencies. A focus on outcomes requires much more extensive information that is not generated by the accounting system. Understanding outcomes requires information about what happens as a result of government expenditures. Typically, these outcomes are achieved only by commitment of resources over many budget years.

Some services provided by government lend themselves well to measures of accomplishment and some do not. Federal responsibilities for defense and foreign policy certainly have visible consequences, but narrowing down to particular budget decisions on expenditures and particular defense or foreign policy outcomes is both conceptually and practically difficult at best. Local government services such as water, streets, solid waste collection and disposal, and so forth are much more susceptible to results measurement. The planning approach epitomized by program budgeting reforms stressed outcome measurement over a multiyear horizon. Are society's ends being achieved as a result of program expenditures?

Financial Management, Financial Condition, and Program Performance. Since those three stages were characterized in the 1960s, additional improvements in using information to ensure responsible government budgeting have become standard practice. Some have suggested that these efforts since the 1960s constitute additional or new stages of budget reform. One author has offered up prioritization, characterized by budget cutbacks in both federal and state government budgeting in the 1980s, as a fourth stage, and accountability, emphasizing performance measurement, as a fifth stage.[32] Another has suggested a similar fourth stage, labeling it limitation, emphasizing the attempts in the 1980s to shrink the federal budget and state taxing and expenditure limitations (see Chapter 4).[33]

While it is clear that budgeting at the federal, state, and local levels continues to change in terms of emphasis and focus, the labeling of additional stages is somewhat in the eye of the beholder. It is difficult to discern a major difference between *limitation* and *control*, for example. It is also clear that some additional budgetary analysis and planning tools have become important in public budgeting systems since the three stages description was first put forward. One of these is performance measurement and performance management, which enhances the ability to budget for the achievement of results. Another is financial management, which entails greater attention to the financial soundness of public sector institutions and new and enhanced tools to measure and report on financial soundness. Measuring financial health and increased use of business-like financial management tools enhances the ability of elected leaders to exert control over resources.

Performance Management. Performance measures associated with work activities and with long-term results are not new, as already noted. However, performance measurement has evolved and expanded since the 1980s. Program budgeting was much more an approach for the executive to gain greater understanding and control over spending by focusing on plans and results. Today, performance measurement and management have a strong emphasis on public reporting on progress and redefining programs based on citizen response to the measured progress. This emphasis on public reporting is a logical extension of the broader concept of *accountability for results* that characterizes budgeting systems, and reforms in budgeting. Newer information tools are focused on external communications. Local government budgeting increasingly focuses on performance budgeting as the major tool for communicating with the public and garnering public support for the budget.[34]

With or without a complete budgetary system overhaul such as program budgeting entails, all levels of government in the U.S., and especially state and local government, typically have extensive performance management systems.[35] The "reinventing government" movement and the National Performance Review of the Clinton administration were two examples of the trend toward more measurement and management of results, but with a much greater emphasis on public reporting.[36] The George W. Bush administration has attempted to build on this progress, but has moved more toward the use of performance measures, with its Program Assessment Rating Tool and the President's Management Agenda.

Performance management emphasizes setting objectives and then motivating managers to be entrepreneurial in their pursuit of those objectives.[37] Of course, since managing growth in government and achieving efficiencies is such a strong focus in performance management, the tools also may be used to shrink programs for other than managerial reasons.[38] Other countries also have given the same emphases to results-oriented or value-driven budgeting as a primary tool in increasing the efficiency and reducing the size of the public sector.[39]

Financial Management. Another feature that has seen heightened focus is on the financial health of the governmental entity or the entire government. There are two facets to this: 1) improved public reporting on the financial condition of government, and 2) a significant focus on the value and condition of long-lived assets such as infrastructure systems. Publicly traded corporations have always had to answer to their stockholders for the financial condition of the corporation and privately held companies at a minimum have to demonstrate sound financial condition to secure debt financing from lenders. But the application of financial management concepts to focus on the financial condition of government agencies was new starting in the late 1980s. The emphasis has been on new tools for measuring the financial condition of government, adapted from private financial and managerial accounting practices, and new mechanisms for ensuring that the government remains in a sound financial position.

One of the motivations behind the concern to hold government accountable for its long-run financial position was the New York City budget crisis of the mid-1970s. Following on the heels of that near-bankruptcy, both financial institutions that purchased municipal bonds and citizens who wondered about their own cities sought to improve the reporting of the long-term financial position of governments.[40] At the time, the general operating budget and related accounting reports often did not reveal the overall financial position of the government entity. Now, virtually every large local and state government in the U.S., as well as the federal government, routinely produce reports, often with much public fanfare on their financial condition.[41]

Fixed Asset Management. Concern at the federal level has led to a much greater emphasis on fixed asset management and increased attention in the annual budget to investments in long-lasting assets. The Governmental Accounting Standards Board Statement No. 34 (GASB 34) requires state and local governments and other public entities to report on their fixed assets (see Chapters 11 and 12). Some government expenditures are really investments in future economic productivity. Others primarily consume resources with little hope of any future payoff. Investment means creating additional productive capacity, such as improving transportation networks that reduce the cost of private sector economic activity through more efficient means of transportation and upgrading education systems that enhance the long-term intellectual ability of students to develop new products and new processes.

All governments budget for these activities, but not all government budgeting systems make explicit the consumption versus investment tradeoffs in budget decisions. The argument can be made that some funds should be diverted away from social welfare programs that fail to produce new capability and toward investment opportunities that stimulate regional and national economic development. While most state and local governments employ formal capital budgeting techniques, federal agencies typically do not, although in specific types of investments such as information technology, formalized capital investment planning and analysis now are required (see Chapter 12).[42]

The notion of stages in budgeting can be overemphasized. Whether one decides ultimately to label trends as new stages, it is clear that there is a stronger emphasis on program and performance measurement and on financial management and reporting with significant efforts and new information tools at all levels of government. Most of the emphasis in this book is on the budget as an instrument for financial and program decision making at all levels of government— federal, state, and local. The one responsibility that most sharply differentiates federal budget decisions from state and local decisions is the federal government's responsibility for the overall state of the economy. The federal budget not only allocates resources among competing programs but it is also an instrument for achieving economic stability and growth (see Chapter 15). The responsibility to use it as an instrument of economic policy has been a part of the federal budgetary process since the Employment Act of 1946.[43]

Budgeting is an important process by which accountability or responsibility can be provided in a political system. As has been discussed, responsibility varies both in terms of the people to whom the system is accountable and in terms of its purposes. Given the various forms of accountability and the types of choices that decision makers have available to them, different meanings can be attached to the terms budget and budgeting system. Depending on the purposes of a budget, decision makers will need different kinds and amounts of information to aid them in making choices. The following sections and subsequent chapters focus on the kinds of information required for different budgetary choices and the kinds of procedures for generating the necessary information.

Budgets and Budgeting Systems

What Is a Budget?

Budget Documents. In its simplest form, a budget is a document or a collection of documents that refers to the financial condition and future plans of an organization (family, corporation, government), including information on revenues, expenditures, activities, and purposes or goals. In contrast to an accounting operating statement, which is retrospective in nature, referring to past conditions, a budget is prospective, referring to anticipated future revenues, expenditures, and accomplishments. Of course, budgets always contain some information about past revenues and expenditures that is consistent with accounting records. Historically, the word *budget* referred to a leather pouch, wallet, bag, or purse. More particularly, "In Britain the term was used to describe the leather bag in which the Chancellor of the Exchequer carried to Parliament the statement of the Government's needs and resources."[44]

The status of budget documents is not consistent across political jurisdictions. In the federal government, the budget has limited legal status. It is the official recommendation of the president to Congress, but it is not the official document under which the government operates. As will be seen later, the official operating budget of the United States consists of several documents, namely, appropriation acts (see Chapters 8, 9, and 11). In contrast, local budgets proposed by mayors may become official working budgets adopted in their entirety by the city councils.[45]

In still other instances, there may be a series of budget documents instead of one budget for any given government. These may include (1) an operating budget, which handles the bulk of ongoing operations; (2) a capital budget, which covers major new construction projects; and (3) a series of special fund budgets that cover programs funded by specific revenue sources (see Chapter 11). Special fund budgets commonly include those for highway programs financed through gasoline and tire sales taxes. In such cases, revenue from these sources is earmarked for highway construction, improvement, and maintenance. As another example, fishing and hunting license fees may constitute the revenue for a special fund devoted to the stocking of streams and the provision of ample hunting opportunities.

The format of budget documents also varies. On the whole, budget documents tend to provide greater information on expenditures than on revenues, which are usually treated in a brief section. On the expenditure side, budgets are multipurpose, in that no single document and no single definition can exhaust the functions budgets serve or the ways they are used. At the most general level, budgets can be conceived of as (1) descriptions, (2) explanations or causal assertions, and (3) statements of preferences or values.

Budgets as Descriptions. Budgets are first descriptions of the status of an organization, whether it is an agency, a ministry, or an entire government. The budget document may describe what the organization purchases, what it does, and what it accomplishes. Descriptions of organizational activity are also common in budget documents. Expenditures may be classified according to the activities they support. For example, a revenue department may be concerned with initial tax collection, taxpayer assistance, and audit/enforcement. Another type of description, organizational accomplishments, states the consequences of resource consumption and work activities for those outside the organization. For example, successful job placements for individuals finishing a vocational rehabilitation program constitute one type of outcome or consequence of a public expenditure. These statements require external verification of the effects of the organization on its environment.

As descriptions, budgets provide a discrete picture of an organization at a point or points in time, in terms of resources consumed, work performed, and external effects. The dollar (or euro or pound sterling) revenues and expenditures, according to these types of descriptions, may be the only quantitative information supplied. Alternatively, information may be supplied about the number and types of personnel; the quantity and kinds of equipment purchased; measures of performance, such as the number of buildings inspected or the number of acres treated; and measures of impact, such as the number of accidents prevented, the amount of crop yield increases, and so forth. Generally, the more descriptive material supplied, the more the organization can be held accountable for the funds spent, the activities supported by those expenditures, and the external accomplishments produced by those activities. Much of the history of budget reform reflects attempts to increase the quantity and quality of descriptive material available both to decision makers and to the public.

Budgets as Explanations. When they describe organizations in terms of purchases, activities, and accomplishments, budgets also at least implicitly serve a second major function—explanation of causal relationships. The expenditure of a specific amount for the purchase of labor and materials that will be combined in particular work activities implies the presumed existence of a causal sequence that will produce certain results. Regardless of how explicit or how vague the budget document or the statements of organization officials may be, budgetary decisions always imply a causal process in which work activities consume resources to achieve goals. Some organizations may have little accurate information about accomplishments, especially public organizations whose accomplishments are not measured in terms of profit and loss. Governments may choose not to be explicit about particular results because they are difficult to measure, politically sensitive, or both. Regardless of the availability of information or the willingness of an organization to collect and use it, the budget is an expression of a set of causal relationships.

Budgets as Preferences. Budgets are statements of preferences. Whether intended or not, the allocation of resources among different agencies, among different activities, or among different accomplishments reveals the preferences of those making the allocations. These may be the actual preferences of a few decision makers, but more often they are best thought of as the collective preferences of many decision makers arrived at through complex bargaining. A preference schedule reflects, if not any one individual's values, an aggregate of choices that become the collective value judgment for the local government, state, or nation.

What Is a Budgeting System?

Systems. Budgeting can best be understood as a kind of system, a "set of units with relationships among them."[46] Budgetary decision making consists of the actions of executive officials (both in a central organization such as the governor's office or the mayor's staff and in executive line agencies), legislative officials, organized interest groups, and perhaps unorganized interests that may be manifested in a generally felt public concern about public needs and taxes. All these actions are related, and understanding budgeting means understanding the interrelationships. Such understanding is best achieved by thinking in terms of complex systems.

A complex social system is composed of organizations, individuals, the values held by these individuals, the norms they act upon, and the relationships among these elements. A system may be thought of as a network typically consisting of many different parts with messages flowing among the parts. The elements of systems interact with each other to produce system results, or consequences, and the network of interactions may produce the same set of results through several different paths, or the same path may from time to time produce different outcomes.[47] Budgeting systems involve political actors, economic and social theories, numerous institutional structures, and competing norms and values, all of which produce outputs in patterns not immediately evident from studying only budget documents.

Budget System Outputs. In a budgetary system, the outputs flowing from the network of interactions are budget decisions, and these vary greatly in their overall significance. Not every unit of the system will have equal decisional authority or power. A manager of a field office for a state health department is likely to have less power to make major budgetary decisions than the administrative head of the department, the governor, or the members of the legislative appropriations committees. Yet each participant does contribute some input to the system. The field manager may alert others in the system to the emergence of a new health problem and in doing so, may contribute greatly to the eventual establishment of a new health program to combat that problem. Modern information technology and the greater emphasis on responsibility at all levels of the organization for achieving results means the lower-level staff in an agency are much more influential than they have been in the past. Even actors not in the formal budgeting system may influence the decisions. For example, doctors and hospitals, who are part of surveillance for early detection of avian flu, in effect are providing inputs to the budgeting system.

Like the outputs of any other system or network, budget decisions are seldom final and more commonly are sequential. Decisions are tentative, in that each decision made is forwarded for action to another participant in the process. This does not mean that all decisions are reversible. Major breakthroughs, such as passage of the Elementary and Secondary Education Act of 1965, which provided substantial federal aid to education, are abandoned only in response to powerful political pressure.[48] The George W. Bush administration's No Child Left Behind Act, which reauthorized major elements of federal assistance to elementary and secondary education, continued most of the key elements of the original 1965 legislation, although giving great emphasis to testing student achievement as a means of ensuring accountability at the classroom level.[49] Likewise, the introduction of prescription drug care into Medicare in 2006 was only after years of debate and proposals. Despite dissatisfaction, eliminating such hard fought programs is nearly impossible. Subsequent budget decisions, therefore, are in large part bounded by previous decisions. The subsequent decisions tend to center on the question of changing the level of commitment—allocating more resources, fewer resources, or different kinds of resources—to achieve desired levels of impact or different types of impact.

System Interconnectedness. Another feature of a system is that a change in any part of it will alter other parts. Because all units are related, any change in the role or functioning of one unit necessarily affects other units. In some instances, changes may be of such a modest nature that their ramifications for other parts of the system are difficult to discern. However, when major budgetary reforms are instituted, they assuredly affect most participants. For example, if one unit in the system is granted greater authority, individuals and organizations having access to that unit have their decisional involvement enhanced, whereas those groups associated with other units have diminished roles.[50] Thus, each individual and institution evaluates budget reforms in terms of how political strengths will be realigned under the reforms.

Information and Decision Making

Types of Information

To serve the multiple functions described in the preceding section, budgeting systems must produce and process a variety of information. Most of the major reforms, whether attempted or proposed, in public budget systems have been intended to reorganize existing information and to provide participants with different types and greater quantities of information. Basically, two types of information exist: program information and resource information. The latter type is more traditional. People are accustomed to thinking of budgets in terms of resources, such as monetary units and personnel. A budget would not be a budget if it did not contain dollar, ruble, or other monetary figures. Similarly, budgets commonly contain data on employees or personnel.

Conventional accounting systems provide much of the information that public organizations use for budgetary decisions. This type of information is limited to the internal aspects of organizations, e.g., the location of organizational responsibility for expenditures and the resources purchased by those expenditures. When the decision-making system incorporates information about the results or implications of programs, one must leave the boundaries of the organization to examine consequences for those outside it. This step requires more extensive and more explicit clarification of governmental goals and objectives (see Chapter 6) and increases the importance of analysis.[51] This feature of budget reforms, such as program budgeting, zero-base budgeting, managing for results, and performance budgeting, with their emphasis on program information and priority setting, has generated the most heat among critics of budget reform.[52]

Decision Making

Much of the criticism of reform has involved the argument that reform of decision-making systems must take into account the limitations on human capabilities to use all the information that might be collected and analyzed. Although sometimes subtle differences distinguish theories of decision making, the various theories can generally be classified into three basic approaches: pure rationality, muddling through or incrementalism, and limited rationality.[53] An early application of these notions to public sector decision making was Graham Allison's study of the Cuban Missile Crisis, *The Essence of Decision*, in which he characterized three models as rational, organizational, and governmental/political.[54] These are descriptive theories as well as prescriptions for how decisions ought to be made.

Rational Decision Making. Decision making according to the pure rationality approach consists of a series of ordered, logical steps. First, all of an organization's or a society's goals are ranked according to priority. Second, all possible alternatives are identified. The costs of each alternative are compared with anticipated benefits. Judgments are made as to which alternative comes closest to satisfying the relevant needs or desires. The alternative with the highest payoff and/or least cost is chosen. Pure rationality theories assume that complete and perfect information about all alternatives is both available and manageable. Decision making, therefore, is choosing among alternatives to maximize some objective function. The rational choice model is built on microeconomics and the notion of the individual actor making an optimal choice to maximize the decision maker's utility.

The applicability of the rationality model is limited, and few argue that it is a description of how ordinary human beings make most decisions. It is most consistent with notions of technical or economic rationality, where objectives can be stated with some precision and the range of feasible alternatives is finite.[55] Also, the model can be of use where accurate predictions of behavior are possible, such as in the private market, where assumptions regarding rational behavior can be used to predict future economic trends.[56]

As a description of how government budgeting works, the pure rationality model is obviously misleading. Meeting the complete requirements of even a few of the steps is impossible. It has been argued that the costs of information are so high as to make it rational to be ignorant; that is, to make decisions on the basis of a limited search and limited information. Some attempts at budget reform have been criticized as attempts to impose an unworkable model, pure rationality, on government financial decision making. The use of program information has been a particular target for criticism.[57] However, this criticism is somewhat misdirected in that it is not so much the information search cost that is limiting, but rather the individual decision maker's perspective. Public budgeting decisions are made in a larger political context with numerous actors involved, a more complicated situation than the clear-sighted approach toward an agreed-upon objective that is the essence of the rational choice model.

Incrementalism. The second approach to decision making, muddling through or incrementalism, has been advocated by critics of pure rationality, such as Charles E. Lindblom, Aaron Wildavsky, and others.[58] According to this view, decision making involves a conflict of interests and a corresponding clash of information which result in the accommodation of diverse partisan interests through bargaining. "Real" decision making is presumed to begin as issues are raised by significant interest groups that request or demand changes from the existing state. Decision making is not some conscious form of pure rationality, but is a process of incrementally adjusting existing practices to establish or reestablish consensus among participants. Alternatives to the status quo are normally not considered unless partisan interests bring them to the attention of the participants in the decision-making process. There is only a marginal amount of planned search for alternatives to achieve desired ends. The decision process is structured so that partisan interests have the opportunity to press their desires at some point in the deliberations. Decisions represent a consensus on policy reached through a political, power-oriented bargaining process.

The most important characteristic of the muddling through, or incrementalist approach, is its emphasis on the proposition that budgetary decisions are necessarily political. Its descriptive appeal is that it more accurately depicts a process in which numerous actors, each with a different point of view, negotiate and bargain for a consensus. The larger the issue, the more difficult it is to achieve consensus for radical change, which results most often in incremental adjustments to the status quo. Whereas a purely rational approach might suggest that budgetary decisions are attempts to allocate resources according to economic or other "objective" criteria, the incrementalist view stresses the extent to which political considerations outweigh calculations of optimality. The strongest critics of many budget reforms have tended to equate those reforms with seeking to establish the pure rationality model or a solely economic model, a description rarely accepted by those proposing budget reforms. As will be seen throughout this book, any "real" budget reform is forced to accommodate the political nature of decision making. In reality, elements of rationalism and incrementalism pervade the budgetary process.[59]

Limited Rationality. The third approach to decision making, a compromise between the other two approaches, is called limited rationality. This model recognizes the inadequacies in the assumptions behind the pure rationality description of decision making as applied to complex problems. While acknowledging the inherent constraints of human cognitive processes, limited rationality does not suggest that a deliberate search for alternative approaches to goal achievement is of no avail. Searching for alternatives is used to find solutions that are satisfactory but not necessarily optimal.

Substantial evidence, cited by some of the giants in budgeting (Wildavsky) and decision making (Lindblom), indicates that many decisions are indeed incremental, and clearly each budget decision does not require a thorough review of all options and careful calculations of the possible outcomes of each option. Yet major decisions that depart dramatically from the past are made from time to time in the budgetary process. Non-incremental change, especially at the macro level addressing major deficits and surpluses do occur.[60] And, of course, major events such as terrorist threats and creating a new agency such as the Department of Homeland Security cause non-incremental change, although the core of federal budgeting did not change significantly after September 11, 2001.[61] Furthermore, decision makers often do attempt to achieve public values and are motivated more by the social and economic problems their agencies must address than by bureaucratic budget maximizing and interest-group pressures.[62]

Limited rationality suggests that large forces are marshalled at times for major change, and incremental adjustments are made at other times for issues that do not generate demand for substantial departure from the status quo. Decision theories do differ in how they view the values that decision making serves and the capacities of decision makers to serve those values. One model assumes virtually no limits on human capacities for processing information, another suggests that decision making should be sensitive only to partisan political interests, and still another attempts to strike a balance between the other models. The history of budgeting and budget reform, we argue, reflects the tensions among these approaches to decision making.

Summary

Public budgeting involves choices among ends and means. Public budgeting shares many characteristics with budgeting in the private sector, but it often requires the application of criteria different from those used by private organizations. Chief among these differences is that few public sector decisions can be assessed in terms of profit and loss. Private sector decisions, on the other hand, ultimately must consider the long-run profit or loss condition of the firm.

Budgeting systems involve the organization of information for making choices and the structure of decision-making processes. Public budgeting systems have evolved as one means of holding government accountable for its actions. Budgetary procedures are developed to hold the government in general accountable to the public, the executive branch accountable to the legislature, and subordinates accountable to their managers. Budgetary procedures also are developed to specify what the executive is accountable for. Concern for the financial solvency of some city governments and the size of the federal budget deficit and total debt have led to reform proposals to use budgeting as a device for holding governments accountable for their long-term financial position. Renewed interest is evident in citizens demanding that governments report regularly on their performance.

Budgetary systems work through information flows. However, each participant in the budgetary process pays selective attention to information. The various theories of decision making advanced differ in terms of how much information decision makers are willing and able to consider. The decision-making approach that seems best to characterize budgetary systems is the limited rationality approach. This approach underlies the discussions throughout this book.

Notes

1. Warsh, D. (2006). *Knowledge and the wealth of nations: a story of economic discovery.* New York: W.W. Norton.

2. Downs, A. (1967). *Inside bureaucracy.* Boston, MA: Little, Brown.

3. U.S. Office of Management and Budget (2007). *Budget of the United States government: fiscal year 2007, historical tables.* Washington, DC: U.S. Government Printing Office, 313.

4. Porter, M. & Kramer, M. (2006). Strategy and society: the link between competitive advantage and corporate social responsibility. *Harvard Business Review, 84,* 78–92.

5. Hsieh, P. et. al. (2003). The return on R&D versus capital expenditures in pharmaceutical and chemical industries. *IEEE Transactions on Engineering Management, 50,* 141–150.

6. U.S. Congressional Budget Office (1993). *CBO staff memorandum: a review of Edwin Mansfield's estimate of the rate of return from academic research and its relevance to the federal budget process.* Washington, DC: U.S. Government Printing Office. Mansfield updated that research in 1998, showing similar results. Mansfield, E. (1998). Academic research and industrial innovation: an update of empirical findings. *Research Policy, 26,* 773–776.

7. U.S. General Accounting Office (2000). *Managing for results: emerging benefits from selected agencies' use of performance agreement.* Washington, DC: U.S. Government Printing Office.

8. U.S. Agency for International Development (2006). *Control of neglected tropical diseases.* Solicitation (M-OAA-GH-06-845) for and subsequent award of Cooperative Agreement (RTI International) to implement the program.

9. Bingman, C. (2006). Proposals for improving GPRA annual performance plans. *Public Budgeting & Finance, 26, Summer,* 143–154.

10. Rosen, H. (2004). *Public finance,* 7th ed. New York: McGraw-Hill.

11. Brooks, R. (2004). Privatization of government services: an overview and review of the literature. *Public Budgeting, Accounting and Financial Management, 16,* 467–491.

12. Rubin, I. (2006). Budgeting for contracting in local government. *Public Budgeting & Finance, 26, Spring,* 1–13.

13. Brown, T. et al. (2006). Managing public service contracts: aligning values, institutions and markets. *Public Administration Review, 66,* 323–331.

14. White, M. (1978). Budget policy: where does it begin and end? *Governmental Finance, 7, August,* 2–9, credits W. F. Willoughby's *The problem of a national budget* with an early (1919) statement of budgeting as a process for holding government accountable.

15. Osborne, D. & Plastrik, P. (1997). *Banishing bureaucracy: the five strategies for reinventing government.* Reading, MA: Addison-Wesley. For the critics' view, see Williams, D. (2000). Reinventing the proverbs of government. *Public Administration Review, 60,* 522–534.

16. Webber, C. & Wildavsky, A. (1986). *A history of taxation and expenditure in the western world.* New York: Simon & Schuster.

17. Burkhead, J. (1956). *Government budgeting.* New York: Wiley, 2–4.

18. Treasury Act (1789). Ch. 12, 1 Stat. 65.

19. Smithies, A. (1955). *The budgetary process in the United States.* New York: McGraw-Hill, 50.

20. Buck, A. (1919). *Public budgeting.* New York: Harper and Brothers, 17.

21. Naylor, E. (1941). *The federal budget system in operation.* Washington, DC: printed privately, 22–23.

22. Burkhead, J. (1956). *Government budgeting,* 12–13.

23. Buck, A. (1919). *Public budgeting,* 14.

24. Burkhead, J. (1956). *Government budgeting,* 23; Willbern, Y. (1967). Personnel and money. In J. Fesler (Ed.), *The 50 states and their local governments.* New York: Knopf, 391.

25. Cleveland, F. (1915). Evolution of the budget idea in the United States. *Annals, 62, November,* 22.

26. Budget and Accounting Act (1921). Ch. 18, 42 Stat. 20.

27. U.S. Commission on Organization of the Executive Branch of the Government (1949). *General management of the executive branch.* Washington, DC: U.S. Government Printing Office.

28. Budget and Accounting Procedures Act (1950). Ch. 946, Title I, part I, 64 Stat. 832.

29. U.S. Commission on Organization of the Executive Branch of the Government (1955). *Budget and accounting.* Washington, DC: U.S. Government Printing Office, ix.

30. Rubin, I. (1993). Who invented budgeting in the United States? *Public Administration Review, 53,* 438–444.

31. Schick, A. (1966). The road to PPB: the stages of budget reform. *Public Administration Review, 26,* 243–258.

32. Tyer, C. & Willand, J. (1997). Public budgeting in America: a twentieth century retrospective. *Journal of Public Budgeting, Accounting and Financial Management, 9,* 189–219.

33. Bartle, J. (2001). Budgeting, policy, and administration: patterns and dynamics in the United States. *International Journal of Public Administration, 24,* 21–30.

34. Tat-Kei Ho, A. & Ya Ni, A. (2005). Have cities shifted to outcome-oriented performance reporting?—a content analysis of city budgets. *Public Budgeting & Finance, 25, Summer,* 61–83.

35. Melkers, J. & Willoughby, K. (2005). Models of performance-measurement use in local governments: understanding budgeting, communication, and lasting effects. *Public Administration Review, 65,* 180–190.

36. National Performance Review (1993). *Mission driven, results-oriented budgeting.* Washington, DC: U.S. Government Printing Office; Thompson, J. (2000). Reinvention as reform: assessing the national performance review. *Public Administration Review, 60,* 508–521.

37. Martin, L. (1997). Outcome budgeting: a new entrepreneurial approach to budgeting. *Public Budgeting and Financial Management, 9, Spring,* 108–126.

38. Gilmour, J. & Lewis, D. (2006). Does performance budgeting work? an examination of the Office of Management and Budget's PART scores. *Public Administration Review, 66,* 742–752.

39. Allen, R. & Tommassi, D. (Eds.) (2001). *Managing public expenditure.* Paris: Organization for Economic Co-operation and Development.

40. Johnson, R. & Lewin, A. (1984). Management and accountability models of public sector performance. In T. Miller (Ed.), *Public sector performance: a conceptual turning point.* Baltimore, MD: Johns Hopkins University Press, 224–250.

41. A good example is Comptroller, State of New York (published annually; see most recent year). *State of New York financial condition report.* Albany, NY: Comptroller's Office of Public Information.

42. U.S. Office of Management and Budget (2002). OMB releases new business reference model to improve agency management. Executive Office of the President: Office of

Management and Budget Press Release. Retrieved July 24, 2002, from http://www.feapmo.gov.

43. Employment Act (1946). Ch. 33, 60 Stat. 23.

44. Burkhead, J. (1956). *Government budgeting, 2.*

45. Powdar, J. (1996). *The operating budget: a guide for smaller governments.* Chicago, IL: Government Finance Officers Association; Bland, R. & Rubin, I. (1997). *Budgeting: a guide for local government.* Washington, DC: International City/County Management Association.

46. Miller, G. (1965). Living systems: basic concepts. *Behavioral Science, 10,* 200.

47. Kendall, K. & Kendall, K. (2004). *Systems analysis and design,* 6th ed. New York: Prentice-Hall.

48. Elementary and Secondary Education Act (1965). P.L. 89–10.

49. No Child Left Behind Act (2001). P.L. 107–110.

50. Jones, L. & McCaffery, J. (1994). Budgeting according to Aaron Wildavsky: a bibliographic essay. *Public Budgeting & Finance, 14, Spring,* 16–43.

51. Administration for Children & Families, U.S. Department of Health and Human Services (2006). *The program manager's guide to evaluation.* Retrieved November 15, 2006, from http://www.acf.hhs.gov/programs/opre/other_resrch/pm_guide_eval/reports/pmguide/pmguide_toc.html.

52. Wildavsky, A. & Caiden, N. (2000). *The new politics of the budgetary process,* 4th ed. New York: Longman Press; Kelly, J. (2003). The long view: lasting (and fleeting) reforms in public budgeting in the twentieth century. *Public Budgeting, Accounting and Financial Management, 15,* 309–326.

53. Brewer, G. & de Leon, P. (1983). *The foundations of policy analysis.* Chicago: Dorsey.

54. Giannatasio, N. (2002). Budget decision making at the grass–roots level. *Journal of Public Budgeting, Accounting and Financial Management, 13,* 48–82, evaluates Allison's decision-making model's applicability to public budgeting at the local level. Allison, G. (1971). *The essence of decision: explaining the Cuban missile crisis.* New York: Harper.

55. The terms technical and economic rationality are the names of two of five basic types of rationality identified by Diesing, P. (1962). *Reason and society.* Urbana, IL: University of Illinois Press.

56. Friedman, M. (1953). *Essays in positive economics.* Chicago, IL: University of Chicago Press.

57. Wildavsky, A. (1979). *Speaking truth to power: the art and craft of policy analysis.* Boston, MA: Little, Brown.

58. Lindblom, C. (1959). The science of "muddling through." *Public Administration Review, 19,* 79–88; Jones, L. (1997). Changing how we budget: Aaron Wildavsky's perspective. *Journal of Public Budgeting, Accounting and Financial Management, 9,* 46–71.

59. Reddick, C. (2002). Testing rival decision-making theories on budget outputs: theories and comparative evidence. *Public Budgeting & Finance, 22, Fall,* 1–25.

60. Reddick, C. (2003). Budgetary decision making in the twentieth century: theories and evidence. *Journal of Public Budgeting, Accounting and Financial Management, 15,* 251–274.

61. Joyce, P. (2005). Federal budgeting after September 11th: a whole new ballgame, or is it déjà vu all over again? *Public Budgeting & Finance, 25, Spring,* 15–31.

62. Reddick, C. (2004). Rational expectations theory and macro budgetary decision-making: comparative analysis of Canada, UK, and USA. *Journal of Public Budgeting, Accounting and Financial Management, 16,* 316–356.

Chapter 2

THE PUBLIC SECTOR IN PERSPECTIVE

One danger of generalizing about the size of the public sector of society is that any single generalization necessarily ignores important information. Although the statement "government is vast" may be valid, it fails to recognize the difficulties in determining what is and is not government or the fact that government is also small in some respects. This chapter describes the size and extent of the public sector, discusses the relative and absolute growth rates of government, and considers the general level of taxes and other revenue sources and the societal functions that these revenues support.

The chapter explores three main topics. The first is the relative sizes of the private and public sectors of society and the reasons for the growth of government. The second is the magnitude of government and the historical growth of local, state, and federal finances. The third section contrasts the purposes of government expenditures with the sources of revenue used by the three main levels of government in the United States.

Relative Sizes of the Private and Public Sectors

Basic to all matters of public budgeting is the issue of the appropriate size of the public sector. This issue is inherently political, not only in the partisan sense but also in the sense that it involves fundamental policy questions about what government should and should not do, and what it can and cannot do. At stake are congeries of competing public and private wants and needs and competing philosophies of the role of the public sector in society. A guiding principle for many of the framers of the Constitution was to keep the central government small to protect individual liberty. However, other early leaders, such as Alexander Hamilton, sought a more activist role for the new government.[1]

Reasons for Growth

Value Questions. The issue of size relates to the values of freedom and social welfare. Keeping government small has been advocated as a means of protecting individuals from tyranny and stimulating individual independence and initiative.[2] On the other hand, critics charge that sometimes reliance on the private sector causes the underfinancing of public programs and the failure to confront major social problems.[3] Some people argue that the wave of corporate scandals that occurred in 2002 (Enron and WorldCom, for example) was in part caused by placing too much faith in an unfettered—or more precisely, deregulated—private sector. Debates over the rise of the welfare and warfare states have been especially acrimonious.

The U.S. political system, of course, is not structured in such a way that any single and overriding decision is made as to the size of this sector. The multiplicity of governments makes it virtually impossible to reach any single decision about overall governmental size. Decisions relevant to size are made in a political context within and between the executive and legislative branches and among the three major levels of government—local, state, and federal. Each set of decisions contributes to an ultimate resolution of the question, but a decision on the appropriate size really results from tallying many individual choices.

Government Responses. Why government expands has been the subject of extended debate.[4] One of the two main reasons is that government is "responsive" to the demands of society. Wagner's law, originally proposed in the 1880s, holds that economic development creates opportunities for new activities that government alone can perform.[5] The second reason is that government has a supposed propensity to be excessive.[6] In this case, government grows as a result of empire building by government bureaucrats, supported by political leaders.[7] Among the numerous factors suggested as stimulating responses from government are the following:[8]

- *The need for collective goods.* Because defense, homeland security, flood control, and some other programs benefit all citizens and cannot be handled readily by the private sector, the government becomes involved. When wars occur, governments grow in size. After the conflict, they tend to remain larger than during the prewar period. Education is another important collective good. Educated people tend to be more productive and increase the total wealth of the society, and the private sector cannot be relied on to provide an appropriate level of public education.

- *Demographic changes.* Increases in total population, newborns, and the elderly stimulate the creation and expansion of government programs.
- *Changes in living patterns.* As the population moves from rural to urban areas, and then from cities to suburbia, demands for government services follow them. Governments must then provide more schools, roads, public utilities, and public safety.
- *Externalities.* Industrial firms, which are concerned mainly with making a profit, may pollute the air and water. Government is expected to control the social costs arising from these private actions.
- *Economic hardships.* Depressions and other negative economic situations stimulate the growth of government.
- *High-risk situations.* When risks are high, the private sector is unlikely to invest large quantities of resources, so government is called upon to support programs. Examples include the development of nuclear energy as a source of electrical power and the creation of the space program. Once the risks of certain aspects of space activity became manageable as a result of government intervention, commercial interests engaged in space research and moved into the launching of private vehicles and satellites.
- *Technological change.* With the advent of new technology, government has provided support, as in the case of roads and airports, to accommodate improved transportation modes and information highways, such as the internet, and to regulate new industries, as in the case of railroads, radio, and television.

These reasons are helpful in explaining why government is necessary and why it has expanded over time. Proposals to expand or contract the scope of the public sector also reflect many political considerations. Principally, any proposal for the expansion of services that results in an increase in taxes is likely to have unfavorable political repercussions. Therefore, the size issue always relates to both government expenditures and revenues (taxes). Decision makers, no matter how crude or approximate their methods of calculating, attempt to weigh the merits of coping with the current situation with the available resources against the merits of recommending new programs that may alleviate problems but at the same time raise the ire of taxpayers. Taxpayer revolts—common since the 1970s— may have had a significant influence in curtailing the growth of government at the state and local levels, although some research suggests that they have just shifted sources of funding to revenue sources that are not covered by tax and expenditure limitations.[9]

Private and Public Sector Boundaries

Major problems are encountered when attempts are made to gauge the sizes of the public and private sectors and to distinguish between one government and another. Government has become so deeply involved in society that one may frequently have difficulty discerning what is not at least quasi-public. Moreover, governments have extensive relationships with each other, to the point where a discussion of any single government becomes meaningless without a discussion of its relationships with other governments.

Statistical data on government revenues and expenditures fail to reflect adequately the size of government. For instance, the entire political campaign process is clearly governmental in that substantial sums of money are spent to elect people to political offices. These funds are not recorded as government expenditures, but nonetheless are "governmental" in nature.[10] Also, the size of government tends to be understated in cases where government activities require relatively little money and personnel but have a substantial impact on the private sector or other governments. This is especially true with respect to regulatory activities, such as the federal government's control of interstate commerce, occupational safety, and environmental health.

Nonexhaustive Expenditures. It can be misleading to rely on revenue and expenditure data for measuring size for another reason. Sometimes the assumption is made that all government expenditures represent a drain on the private economy. In fact, government expenditures can be nonexhaustive as well as exhaustive. Exhaustive expenditures occur when government consumes resources, such as facilities and manpower, that might otherwise have been used by the private sector. Nonexhaustive expenditures occur when government redistributes or transfers resources to components of the society instead of consuming them. Interest payments on the national debt, unemployment compensation, aid to the indigent, and old-age and retirement benefits are major examples of nonexhaustive government expenditures.

Another form of nonexhaustive expenditures is investment for the future, whether for capital facilities or for services, as in education for children. Government aid to small businesses, support of research and development, and similar activities are forms of investment in future economic development. As a result of these kinds of expenditures, the cost of government is actually less than the total dollar figures reported in budgets. Money that is spent by governments will generate future revenue for both society and its governments.

Effects on the Private Sector. Government expenditures have specific effects on industries, occupations, geographic regions, and subpopulations. These effects are especially evident in the field of defense. During the Cold War, clusters of firms and their employees became highly dependent upon defense outlays, resulting in what President Eisenhower in 1961 decried as the military-industrial complex. The case could be made that a dangerous symbiotic relationship developed between the military, with its penchant for new weaponry, and corporations eager to supply such weaponry. Periodic scandals in defense contracting offer seeming confirmation of the fears expressed by President Eisenhower.

The effects of defense are particularly pronounced in regard to employment, despite the downsizing that has occurred since the end of the Cold War. In 2005, civilian employment in the Department of Defense accounted for 0.5% of the private sector labor force and about one-fourth of the federal government's civilian labor force.[11] In addition, in 2005 the federal government employed 1.4 million active duty armed services personnel, including 1.1 million within the borders of the United States or its territories.[12] Total military and civilian employment constituted 1.5% of total U.S. employment in 2005.

The effects of defense expenditures upon the private economy also have been substantial. Defense expenditures account for a significant percentage of jobs in various industries. The creation of defense-related jobs entices people into educational programs that train them to develop the requisite skills. As a result, people are attracted to technical career fields that are dependent upon continued defense spending. These people suffer or flourish based on which policies prevail.

Geographic and Industry Effects. Military research, development, and procurement are of such great magnitude that many specific industries and corporations become quasi-public institutions. In 2004, the Department of Defense spent $269.2 billion in total contracts. Of this amount, $213.7 billion went to business firms in the United States. The remainder was provided to nonprofit or education institutions in the United States, intergovernmental contracts, or work done outside the United States.[13] Defense expenditures greatly influence the private sector—in firms that engage in shipbuilding, aircraft construction, and communications, to name just three examples—and the importance of defense expenditures on the private sector has increased with the recent defense buildup. Besides providers of military equipment, such as Boeing, General Dynamics, General Electric, and General Motors, numerous consulting and research and development firms are dependent on military expenditures. Nondefense contracting firms are similarly dependent, with 60% to 80% of their revenues coming from government contracts.

Employees of these varied private sector firms, judging from their length of service on government projects, are doing work that otherwise would be done (and in many cases, used to be done) by career civil servants. One difference between these contractors and the civil servants that they supplant is that the pay of managerial staff in these firms is often higher than that of similarly trained government employees. Professional salaries, such as for engineers and scientists, tend to be relatively equal, because government must meet private sector salaries to recruit and retain professionals. Another difference is that private sector employees do not constitute a permanent expense to the government. These workers are not protected by civil service laws and are ineligible for government pension benefits. Furthermore, when these workers' services are not needed, government has no obligation to them as it would to its own employees.

The geographic effects of defense expenditures are equally important because they are not uniformly distributed throughout the nation. In 2004, the Department of Defense spent $348 billion. Five states—California, Virginia, Texas, Florida, and Maryland—accounted for $144 billion, or more than 41% of that total.[14] The Department of Defense spent $212 billion for procurement contracts in the same year, with California, Virginia, Texas, Maryland, and Connecticut ranking as the top five recipients and accounting for 43% of all contracts.[15]

Defense, while the most striking example of private dependence upon public outlays, is not the sole example. Highway construction also involves large sums of public money. The employees of construction firms specializing in bridge and highway construction are, in effect, government employees. The same is true for suppliers of road-building equipment. In addition, the 1990s and early 2000s have seen a continued emphasis on contracting out as a means of producing public services. In 2002, there were 8 million individuals employed under federal grants and contracts, up from 7 million in 1999.[16]

In some cases, the impact of government on an industry is greater as a result of what government does *not* do than what it *does* do. The federal government's choice not to tax interest paid on home mortgages, for example, has a far greater effect on the housing industry than all federal expenditures for public housing and redevelopment.

The lack of clear-cut distinctions between the public and private sectors and between one government and another is evident in education. Elementary and secondary education is a function of local school districts, but about half the funds used by these districts come from state governments, with additional funds coming from the federal government and local sources of revenue, primarily the property tax. The states have a primary role in funding public higher education, with important federal support, especially in the form of student aid and research financing. Governments also selectively subsidize private colleges and universities. Private corporations also make important contributions to both public and private schools. In 2002, the U.S. Supreme Court ruled that it is constitutional for governments to use public funds to provide vouchers to parents whose children attend private or parochial schools.[17] This will undoubtedly become another area in which public funds have a substantial effect on private educational activity.

In addition, the level of funding may understate the degree of federal involvement in elementary and secondary education. The federal government can, as a condition of the receipt of federal assistance, insist that state and local governments adopt policies that they might otherwise have chosen not to adopt. The best recent example of this is the federal No Child Left Behind Act, which has attempted to force state and local governments to adopt specific accountability standards in the form of testing requirements.[18] While, under the constitutionally-provided federal system, the national government cannot directly compel states and localities to establish such standards, the threat of the loss of federal funds is sufficient to encourage most to go along with the federal requirements.

Subpopulation Effects. Taxes and expenditures affect different subpopulations in different ways. In the example given earlier of the federal government allowing income tax deductions for interest paid on home mortgages, the middle and upper classes benefit far more than lower-income groups, who typically are renters rather than homeowners. This tax expenditure—namely, the government's not taxing something that could be taxed—has a redistributional effect in favor of the middle and upper classes (see Chapter 4).

Government actions also have important effects on generations, including those who will be born in years to come. Taxing and spending policies can help or harm children (born and unborn) through health and education programs, the working-age population through transportation programs, and the elderly through government-sponsored nursing care and the like. Future generations benefit from government programs that encourage investment in economic development but excessive debts that governments may accumulate may harm these same people in the future.

The Magnitude and Growth of Government

There are many ways to measure the magnitude of government, but dollars and people are generally the easiest measures to apply. By focusing on revenues, expenditures, and numbers of employees, we can use comparable standards in contrasting governments with each other and with private organizations. These measures, then, are the main ones used in this section. While care has been taken in making these comparisons to obtain the most recent and accurate data possible, some of the data here must be considered approximate. A portion of what is reported is a bit more outdated than would be considered optimal because the U.S. Census Bureau has scaled back the data it reports, the frequency of reporting, and the timeliness of the data.

Revenues

One approach to measuring organizations is to consider their revenues or receipts, which allows comparisons among private and public organizations.[19] **Table 2–1** ranks the 25 largest governments and industrial corporations in the world, as measured by revenues. Significantly, 14 of the 25 are governments, with the U.S. federal government ranked first. Three U.S. bureaucracies are included in the list of 25—the federal government and the states of California and New York. It is likely that even more governments would be included on the list, but comparable data on government budgets in India and China were unavailable. The listing is replete with intriguing contrasts. For example, Sweden's government budget is smaller than the budget of California and much smaller than the budget for Wal-Mart.

A similar comparison of only those governments in the United States also demonstrates the significant size of the governmental sector. In a list of the top 50 organizations in the United States, 8 state governments are included (see **Table 2–2**). These states, in order of appearance, are California, New York, Texas, Florida, Pennsylvania, Michigan, Ohio, and Illinois. Ranking ahead of six of these states is New York City.

These statistics dramatically underscore the need for caution in generalizing about governments or private corporations. It is necessary to recognize the important differences in the functions of government and industry and the methods by which these organizations make decisions. Differences also abound within each of these two types of organizations. The services provided and methods of decision making are not identical in the governments of Japan, Germany, and the United Kingdom, nor are they the same in such private corporations as General Motors, IBM, and State Farm Insurance. On the other hand, using the standard of size may provide more insights into the operations of organizations than simply classifying organizations as public or private, national or local, and so forth. Not all industrial firms are like General Motors, nor are all state governments like California's, but perhaps all organizations of any given size, regardless of their private or public character, exhibit some common traits.

Although total revenues or expenditures are useful as approximate guides in measuring the size of government, these data need to be assessed in light of the varied capabilities of societies to support government. Unfortunately, reliable international data are often unavailable. As a consequence, drawing useful comparisons among international organizations is difficult.

Even given these limitations, it is obvious that the U.S. economy is one of the most prosperous in the world. The high per capita gross domestic product (GDP)

Table 2–1	Twenty-Five Largest Governments and Industrial Corporations in the World by Revenues, 2002 (in Billions of Dollars)

Rank	Governments	Revenues	Private Corporations
1	US Federal	1,853.4	
2	Japan	1,265.2	
3	Germany	944.5	
4	France	760.1	
5	United Kingdom	646.6	
6	Italy	570.2	
7	Canada	312.4	
8	Netherlands	283.4	
9	Spain	277.9	
10		246.5	Wal-Mart Stores
11		186.8	General Motors
12		182.5	ExxonMobil
13		179.4	Royal Dutch/Shell Group
14		178.7	BP
15		163.9	Ford Motor
16	Australia	161.1	
17	California	151.2	
18	Sweden	148.6	
19		141.4	DaimlerChrysler
20		131.8	Toyota Motor
21		131.7	General Electric
22	Mexico	127.4	
23		109.4	Mitsubishi
24	New York State	104.5	
25		101.9	Allianz

Sources: U.S. Congressional Budget Office (2007). *The budget and economic outlook: fiscal years 2008-2017.* Washington, DC: U.S. Government Printing Office, 140; Bureau of the Census, U.S. Department of Commerce (2007). *States ranked by revenue and expenditure total amount and per capita total amount.* Retrieved January 27, 2007, from http://www.census.gov/govs/state/02rank.html; Fortune (2003). Fortune global 500. *Fortune, 148, No. 2,* 106; Organization for Economic Co-operation and Development (2007). *Main aggregates of general governments.* Retrieved January 27, 2007, from http://www.oecd.org/wbos/default.aspx? DatasetCode=SNA_TABLE12.

Table 2–2	Fifty Largest U.S. Organizations by Revenues, 2002 (in Billions of Dollars)

Rank	Governments and US Corporations	Revenues
1	**US Federal**	1,853.4
2	Wal-Mart Stores	219.8
3	ExxonMobil	191.6
4	General Motors	177.3
5	Ford Motor	162.4
6	**California**	151.2
7	Enron	138.7
8	General Electric	125.9
9	Citigroup	112.0
10	**New York State**	104.5
11	ChevronTexaco	99.7
12	IBM	85.7
13	Altria Group	72.9
14	Verizon Communications	63.1
15	American Intl. Group	62.4
16	American Electric Power	61.3
17	**New York City**	60.9a
18	**Texas**	60.4
19	Duke Energy	59.5
20	AT&T	59.1
21	Boeing	58.2
22	El Paso	57.5
23	Home Depot	53.6
24	Bank of America Corp.	52.6
25	Fannie Mae	50.8
26	Chase Manhattan Corp.	50.4
27	Kroger	50.1
28	**Florida**	48.5
29	Cardinal Health	47.9
30	Merck	47.7
31	State Farm Insurance	46.7
32	Center Point Energy	46.2
33	**Pennsylvania**	46.2

continues

Table 2–2	Fifty Largest U.S. Organizations by Revenues, 2002 (in Billions of Dollars) (continued)

Rank	Governments and US Corporations	Revenues
34	SBC Communications	45.9
35	Hewlett-Packard	45.2
36	**Michigan**	43.9
37	**Ohio**	43.8
38	Morgan Stanley	43.8
39	Dynergy	42.2
40	McKesson	42.0
41	Sears Roebuck	41.1
42	**Illinois**	41.1
43	Aguila	40.4
44	Target	39.9
45	Proctor and Gamble	39.2
46	Merrill-Lynch	38.9
47	Time Warner	38.2
48	Albertson's	37.9
49	Berkshire Hathaway	37.7
50	Kmart Holding	36.9

Note: This table and all other illustrations in the book were prepared using the most current data available. In the case of Table 2–2, we needed to use comparable data sets for the private and public sectors, resulting in 2002 being the most current year. Unlike governments that are generally stable, corporations can change dramatically in size and consequently their rankings may go up or down sharply within the span of a few years. Changes in corporate rankings reflect their relative successes and failures in sales and also reflect various forms of corporate mergers. For instance, AT&T and SBC are listed separately in the table but subsequently have merged, as have Sears and Kmart. In other words, Table 2–2 is a snapshot in time.

Sources: U.S. Congressional Budget Office (2007). *The budget and economic outlook: fiscal years 2008-2017*. Washington, DC: U.S. Government Printing Office; Bureau of the Census, U.S. Department of Commerce (2007). *States ranked by revenue and expenditure total amount and per capita total amount*. Retrieved January 27, 2007, from http://www.census.gov/govs/state/02rank.html; Fortune (2003). Fortune global 500. *Fortune, 148, No. 2*, 106.

in the United States, $42,047 in 2005, has allowed for both big government and a large private sector.[20] The nation has been able to afford government expenditures equal to about 31.4% of GDP ($13,203 per capita expenditures for the total of all governments in the United States in 2005).[21] This figure, however, is misleading in regards to the size of the public sector in that only about half of the per capita expenditures go toward the purchase of goods and services—the other half is used for transfer payments and interest payments on debt.

Expenditures

Because early records on state and local finance are spotty, federal expenditure data must be used to obtain some overall perspective of the growth of government since the eighteenth century. **Table 2–3** shows federal spending from 1789 through 2011 (estimated). During this period, expenditures rose from only $4.3 million in

Table 2–3	Federal Government Expenditures, Selected Years, 1789-2011 (in Millions of Dollars)

Year	Expenditures	Year	Expenditures	Year	Expenditures
1789-91	4	1885	260	1975	332,332
1800	11	1890	318	1980	590,947
1805	11	1895	356	1985	946,423
1810	8	1900	529	1990	1,253,198
1815	33	1905	567	1995	1,515,837
1820	18	1910	694	2000	1,789,216
1825	16	1915	746	2001	1,863,190
1830	15	1920	6,358	2002	2,011,153
1835	18	1925	2,924	2003	2,160,117
1840	24	1930	3,320	2004	2,293,006
1845	23	1935	6,412	2005	2,472,205
1850	40	1940	9,468	2006*	2,708,677
1855	60	1945	92,712	2007*	2,770,097
1860	63	1950	42,562	2008*	2,813,592
1865	1,298	1955	68,444	2009*	2,921,760
1870	310	1960	92,191	2010*	3,060,875
1875	275	1965	118,228	2011*	3,239,769
1880	268	1970	195,649		

*estimated

Sources: Bureau of the Census, U.S. Department of Commerce (1975). *Historical statistics of the United States: colonial times to 1970*, part 2. Washington, DC: U.S. Government Printing Office, 1114; U.S. Office of Management and Budget (2007). *Historical tables, Budget of the United States Government: fiscal year 2007.* Washington, DC: U.S. Government Printing Office, 53–54.

the first few years to almost $2.5 trillion annually in fiscal year 2005 (bear in mind that an important contributor to this difference is inflation).[22]

The twentieth century has seen important differences in the expenditure patterns of the federal government and those of state and local governments. Federal expenditures have fluctuated most, primarily because of war-related activities. The first year in which federal expenditures exceeded $1 billion was 1865, the peak year of the Civil War. Later, in response to World War I, federal expenditures jumped from $0.7 billion in 1916 to $18.5 billion in 1919, then dropped to $6.4 billion the following year. They also increased from $13.3 billion in 1941, the year the United States entered into World War II, to $92.7 billion in 1945, then declined just after the war. During the Korean War, expenditures rose from $42.6 billion in 1950 to $74.3 billion in 1953, and then dropped to $68.4 billion in 1955, after the war.[23]

In general, the last century has seen a pattern where federal expenditures have risen during wartime and then declined, but not to prewar levels, resulting in a cumulative increase over time. The Vietnam War era, however, departed from this pattern: federal expenditures rose both during and after the war. One of the reasons for the continued high spending from the 1960s onward was the creation and growth of large entitlement programs, such as Social Security, Medicare, and Medicaid. More recently, the Afghanistan and Iraq wars resulted in a noticeable increase in federal spending as a proportion of GDP, and a substantial increase in federal debt (see Chapter 15).

State and local expenditures, on the other hand, have fluctuated less. In 1902, state and local expenditures were $1.1 billion, and they have continued to grow steadily over the past 100 years, with no significant reductions during any period.[24]

Important shifts have occurred in the extent to which the nation relies on different levels of government. At the turn of the century, local governments were by far the biggest spenders, followed by the federal government and then the states. During the Great Depression, federal spending spurted above local expenditures, and the gap has since continued to widen. As of 2004, federal expenditures stood at $2,293 billion[25] compared with $1,406 billion for states and $1,258 billion for local governments.[26] Caution should be exercised in interpreting these numbers, in that each includes intergovernmental transfers—namely, grants from one government to another. Total spending for all governments was $3.9 trillion in 2005, of which $2.5 trillion represented federal expenditures and $1.4 trillion represented state and local expenditures. These last numbers take out the effect of intergovernmental transfers. Therefore, taxes collected at the federal level (for example) but spent at the state or local level are counted as federal spending.[27]

One means of looking at the growth of government over time, while controlling for price changes, is to consider government expenditures as a percentage of GDP. **Figure 2–1** shows that, from 1926 to 2004, the cost of government rose from 12% to 31% of GDP. Increases first occurred in the 1930s due to the Great Depression, and World War II soon after brought expenditures to an all-time high at about half of GDP. A sharp cutback followed in the postwar years, and expenditures dropped to a low of 19% by 1948. The Cold War and the Korean War occasioned another sharp increase in the early 1950s, and—after reductions in military spending in the late 1950s—the Great Society programs and the Vietnam War resulted in increased spending again during the 1960s. Although there has been some year-to-year fluctuation, the percentage of GDP devoted to government has remained relatively stable at between 28% and 34% since 1970.

Figure 2-1 All Government Expenditures as a Percentage of Gross Domestic Product, 1929–2004

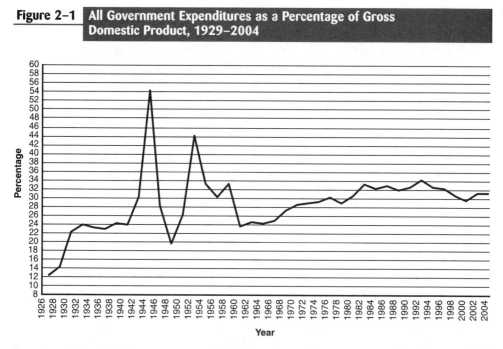

Sources: Bureau of Census, U.S. Department of Commerce (1969). *Historical statistics on governmental finances and employment.* Washington, DC: U.S. Government Printing Office, 1, 36–37; U.S. Council on Economic Advisers (2006). *Economic report of the President.* Washington, DC: U.S. Government Printing Office, 280, 380.

Public Employment

Another way to measure the size and growth of government is to examine trends in the number of government employees. In 1816, there were fewer than 5,000 full- and part-time civilian employees in the federal service. Much more growth in public employment followed the Civil War. In 1871, there were more than 50,000 federal employees, and this number doubled to 100,000 by 1881. The period of fastest growth was from the Great Depression through World War II. In 1931 there were still only 610,000 employees, but by 1945–the peak of the wartime economy –the federal civilian work force had climbed to nearly 4 million. Within a year, however, it was reduced to fewer than 3 million employees, and since then only once (in 1950) has the federal work force dropped below 2 million. Federal civilian personnel averaged approximately 3 million between 1970 and 2000, but decreased to only about 2.7 million by 2005.[28]

Although the size of the federal bureaucracy is extraordinarily large, the government's personnel are geographically dispersed. In 2004, California had 239,000 federal civilian employees, a figure equal to almost half of Wyoming's population. If these employees were all located in one area, they alone, not counting their families, would form a metropolitan area somewhat larger than Baton Rouge, Louisiana, or Reno, Nevada. Federal employees are also numerous in other states, including Texas, with 168,000; Virginia, with 146,000; and Maryland with 133,000.[29] In the 1990s, states such as these became painfully aware of their dependence on federal employment as the government began to downsize the military, since about one of every three federal civilian jobs is in defense.

At the state and local levels, the number of employees has also increased. State employment grew from 3.8 million in 1980 to 5.1 million in 2005.[30] In the same period, local employment increased from 9.6 million to 11.7 million.[31] Significantly, the growth at the local level has been accompanied by a decline in the number of local governments. In 2002, there were almost 88,000 local governments, 30,000 fewer than five decades earlier. This decline is largely attributable to school district consolidation. Since 1972, the number of local governments has been increasing gradually, due mainly to increases in the number of special districts—that is, governments that typically provide a single service such as water provision or recreation services. There were more than 35,000 of these special district governments in 2002.[32]

Sources of Revenue and Purposes of Government Expenditures

Government does not simply get money and spend it in general. Rather, governments obtain revenue from specific sources and spend it on specific public goods and services. The following discussion considers the relationships between income and outgo, i.e., the ways in which revenue is generated and the purposes of government expenditures.

Federal Revenues and Expenditures

The federal government obtains revenues from several different sources. The major source of revenue for the federal government is the individual income tax. In fiscal year 2006, 43% of all federal revenues came from this source. Social insurance taxes (payroll taxes for Social Security and Medicare) accounted for another 35% of the total. Adding in the almost 15% contributed by corporate income taxes, these three sources accounted for 93% of all federal revenues. This distribution represents a substantial shift from the early 1900s, when customs duties and excise taxes were the major revenue sources. These sources now account for 4% of total federal revenues. **Table 2–4** shows a summary of federal revenues and expenditures.

There are two main types of federal spending: discretionary spending, which is provided for through the annual appropriations process, and mandatory spending,

Table 2-4 | **Federal Revenues and Expenditures, 2006 (in Billions of Dollars)**

	Revenues			Expenditures	
Source	**Dollars**	**Percent**	**Source**	**Dollars**	**Percent**
Individual Income	1,044	43.3	Social Security	544	20.5
Corporate Income	354	14.7	Medicare	374	14.1
Social Insurance	838	34.8	Medicaid	181	6.8
Excise	74	3.1	Other Spending	454	17.1
Estate and Gift	28	1.2	Offsetting Receipts	−141	−5.3
Total Taxes	**2,338**	**97.2**	**Total Mandatory**	**1,411**	**53.1**
Customs Duties	25	1.0	Defense	520	19.6
Miscellaneous	44	1.8	Nondefense	496	18.7
Total Receipts	**2,407**	**100.0**	**Total Discretionary**	**1,016**	**38.3**
			Net Interest	**227**	**8.6**
			Total Outlays	**2,654**	**100.0**

Source: U.S. Congressional Budget Office (2007). *The budget and economic outlook: fiscal years 2008-2017.* Washington, DC: U.S. Government Printing Office, 50, 81.

which is provided for through "permanent" law. Discretionary appropriations provide for most of the core functions of government, including the operations of major federal departments. This category accounted for about 39% of all federal spending in 2006, and about half of this amount went for defense. This represents a substantial decline in the relative importance of discretionary spending from 40 years ago. In 1973, 50% of expenditures were discretionary, and the figure was 65% in 1967.[33] Increased defense spending associated with military activities in Iraq and Afghanistan has increased the percentage of the budget accounted for by discretionary spending in recent years, reversing a trend of several decades. As recently as 2001, discretionary spending represented less than 35% of total federal spending.[34]

Mandatory spending (chiefly entitlements) accounted for about 53% of federal spending in 2006. This was a substantial increase in the proportion of the budget that went to mandatory spending since 1970, when the figure was 35%. The major single entitlement—almost 40% of total mandatory spending—is Social Security. The health entitlements (Medicare and Medicaid) together also make up another 40% of all mandatory spending. The expansion of mandatory spending since the mid-1960s (fueled by President Johnson's "Great Society" programs) has increased the proportion of the federal budget devoted to mandatory spending.

The other category of federal spending is net interest. The federal government's spending on interest has increased and decreased, depending on the federal government's reliance on deficit financing. In 2006, it was 8.6% of the budget. In 1995, that figure was 15%.[35] The only way to control net interest expenses is to control the amount of debt issued by controlling deficit spending.

State and Local Revenues and Expenditures

State and local revenues and expenditures are summarized in **Table 2–5**. The first thing to note about state revenues is that almost one-fourth comes from

Table 2–5	State and Local Revenues and Expenditures, 2003-2004 (in Millions of Dollars)				
Source	**State & Local**	**State**	**State Percent**	**Local**	**Local Percent**
Total Revenue	2,435,084	1,586,665	100.0	1,247,463	100.0
General Revenue	1,889,741	1,194,056	75.3	1,094,729	87.8
General Revenue from Own Sources	1,464,058	799,443	50.4	664,615	53.3
Taxes	1,010,277	590,414	37.2	419,863	33.7
Property	318,242	10,714	0.7	307,528	24.6
Sales and Gross Receipts	360,629	293,326	18.5	67,303	5.4
Individual Income	215,215	196,255	12.4	18,960	1.5
Corporate Income	33,716	30,229	1.9	3,487	0.3
Motor Vehicle Licenses	18,709	17,336	1.1	1,373	0.1
Other Taxes	63,766	42,554	2.7	21,213	1.7
Charges and Miscellaneous	435,781	209,029	13.2	244,752	19.6
Utility Revenue	108,357	12,955	0.8	95,402	7.6
Liquor Store Revenue	5,698	4,866	0.3	832	0.1
Insurance Trust Revenue	431,289	374,788	23.6	56,500	4.5
Intergovernmental Revenue	425,683	394,613	24.9	430,114	34.5
From Federal Government	425,683	374,694	23.6	50,989	4.1
From State Government	0	0	0	379,126	30.4
From Local Government	0	19,919	1.3	0	0

continues

Table 2–5	State and Local Revenues and Expenditures, 2003-2004 (in Millions of Dollars) (continued)				
Source	State & Local	State	State Percent	Local	Local Percent
Total Expenditures	2,265,051	1,406,175	100.0	1,257,581	100.0
Intergovernmental	4,721	389,706	27.7	13,720	1.1
Direct	2,260,330	1,016,469	72.3	1,243,861	98.9
Capital Outlay	232,523	85,732	6.1	146,792	11.7
General Expenditures	1,670,671	733,998	52.2	936,673	74.5
Education & Libraries	83,798	181,397	12.9	483,163	38.4
Public Welfare	335,257	291,968	20.8	43,289	3.4
Hospitals	96,551	40,011	2.8	56,541	4.5
Health	63,125	29,608	2.1	33,517	2.7
Employment Security & Veterans' Services	6,183	6,178	0.4	5	0
Highways	118,179	72,194	5.1	45,985	3.7
Other Transportation	23,781	2,783	0.2	20,997	1.7
Police Protection	69,707	9,471	0.7	60,236	4.8
Fire Protection	28,330	0	0.0	28,330	2.3
Corrections	56,521	36,963	2.6	19,558	1.6
Protective Inspection & Regulation	11,498	7,732	0.5	3,766	0.3
Natural Resources	23,299	17,226	1.2	6,072	0.5
Parks and Recreation	30,467	4,571	0.3	25,896	2.1
Housing & Community Development	37,221	4,273	0.3	32,948	2.6
Sewerage	35,535	1,568	0.1	33,966	2.7
Solid Waste Management	20,373	2,952	0.2	17,421	1.4
Governmental Administration	100,742	43,454	3.1	57,288	4.6
Interest on Debt	81,723	33,953	2.3	48,770	3.9
Other	100,143	34,428	2.4	65,716	5.2
Utility Expenditures	155,059	21,676	1.5	133,382	10.6
Liquor Store	4,673	3,924	0.3	749	0.1
Insurance Trust	197,405	171,139	12.2	26,266	2.1

Source: Bureau of the Census, U.S. Department of Commerce (2006). *State and local government finances: 2003-2004.* Retrieved September 30, 2006 from, http://ftp2.census.gov/govs/estimate/04slsstab1a.xls.

other governments, mostly from the federal government. Of the remainder, insurance trust revenue is the largest revenue source, providing 23.6% of all state funds. The majority (80%) of these insurance trust revenues are for employee retirement. Sales and gross receipts taxes account for 18.5% of state government revenue. States obtain another 12.4% from individual income taxes, and 7.2% comes from user charges, such as tuition at state universities.

Not every state taps into each of the varied revenue sources that the states use.[36] Some states have both a sales tax and an individual income tax. Others have only one or the other, with two states (Alaska and New Hampshire) having neither.

Local governments obtain one-third of their money from other governments and the rest mainly through the property tax and other sources. Of all local revenue, 24.6% comes from the property tax. A little less than 30% is obtained from charges, miscellaneous general revenue, and utility fees. While some local governments have income and sales taxes, these sources contribute only about 7.9% of all local revenues in aggregate.[37]

State and local expenditures also follow different patterns. Some expenditures that are important for the federal government are nonexistent in states and localities. For example, neither the states nor their local governments are responsible for defense, postal service, or space exploration. When looking at direct expenditures (that is, expenditures that are actually made directly by the government, as opposed to assistance provided to some other level), public welfare is the largest expense for states, with education spending (primarily for higher education) ranked second. Other significant areas of state expenditure include social insurance, highways, and corrections.

Education spending is by far the largest category of local expenditures. The 38.4% spent on education is more than three times the percentage that is devoted to the second-ranked category, utility expenditure. Other significant areas of expenditure include public safety (police and fire) and hospitals.[38]

Summary

Government is indeed large. The growth pattern of the public sector has been upward, and drawing a definitive line today between the public and private sectors is virtually impossible. If present trends continue, government can be expected to become even larger, albeit at a slower rate, providing more services directly or ensuring the provision of services by regulating the private sector.

Governments in the United States differ in the types of revenue sources used and main areas of expenditure. The federal government relies primarily on personal and corporate income taxes and social insurance taxes. Federal expenditures are concentrated in defense, medical entitlements, and social insurance. States obtain one-fifth of their revenue from the federal government and the remainder largely from sales and individual income taxes. Their expenditures are concentrated in education, social services, and welfare. Local governments, on the other hand, receive one-third of their funds from other governments and one-fourth from property taxes, while their most expensive function is education.

Notes

1. Beer, S. H. (1993). *To make a nation: the rediscovery of American federalism.* Cambridge, MA: Belknap Press; White, L. D. (1948). *The federalists: a study in administrative history, 1789–1801.* New York: Free Press.

2. Friedman, M. & Friedman, R. (1980). *Freedom to choose.* New York: Harcourt Brace Jovanovich; Hayek, F. A. (1945). *The road to serfdom.* Chicago, IL: University of Chicago Press; Drucker, P. & Finer, H. (1945). *The road to reaction.* Boston, MA: Little, Brown.

3. Galbraith, J. K. (1973). *Economics and the public purpose.* Boston, MA: Houghton Mifflin.

4. Musgrave, R. A. & Musgrave, P. B. (1989). *Public finance in theory and practice,* 5th ed. New York: McGraw-Hill; Hyman, D. N. (1996) *Public finance: a contemporary application of theory to policy,* 5th ed. Orlando, FL: Dryden Press; Rosen, H. S. (2005). *Public finance,* 7th ed. New York: McGraw-Hill Irwin.

5. Abizadeli, S. & Basilevsky, A. (1990). Measuring the size of government. *Public Finance, 45,* 359–377.

6. Berry, W. D. & Lowery, D. (1987). Explaining the size of the public sector. *Journal of Politics, 49,* 401–440; Larkey, P. D. et al. (1981). Theorizing about the growth of government. *Journal of Public Policy, 1,* 157–220.

7. Bird, R. (1977). Wagner's law of expanding state activity. *Public Finance, 26,* 1–26; Buchanan, J. M. & Tullock, G. (1977). The expanding public sector: Wagner squared. *Public Choice, 31,* 147–150.

8. Beck, M. (1981). *Government spending: trends and issues.* New York: Praeger; Lewis-Beck, M. S. & Rice, T. W. (1985). Government growth in the United States. *Journal of Politics, 47,* 2–30.

9. Mullins, D. R. & Joyce, P. G. (1996). Tax and expenditure limitations and state and local fiscal structure: an empirical assessment. *Public Budgeting & Finance, 16, Spring,* 75–101; Mullins, D.R. & Wallin, B. (2004). Tax and expenditure limitations: introduction and overview. *Public Budgeting & Finance, 4, Winter,* 2–15.

10. Polsby, N. W. (2004). *Presidential elections,* 11th ed. New York: Chatham House.

11. Bureau of the Census, U.S. Department of Commerce (2007). *Statistical abstract of the United States.* Washington, DC: U.S. Government Printing Office, 322.

12. U.S. Department of Defense (2006). *Active duty military personnel strengths by regional area and by country, March 31, 2006.* Retrieved October 12, 2006, from siadiap.dior.whs.mil/personnel/MILITARY/history/hst0306.pdf.

13. Bureau of the Census, U.S. Department of Commerce (2007). *Statistical abstract of the United States,* 329.

14. Bureau of the Census, U.S. Department of Commerce (2004). *Consolidated federal funds report.* Washington, DC: U.S. Government Printing Office, 23.

15. Bureau of the Census, U.S. Department of Commerce (2004). *Consolidated federal funds report.* Washington, DC: U.S. Government Printing Office, 8.

16. Light, P. C. (2003). *Fact sheet on the new true size of government*, September 5. Retrieved September 15, 2006, from http://www.brookings.edu/gs/cps/light20030905.htm.

17. *Zelman* v. *Simmons–Harris* (2002). 536 U.S. 639.

18. Smith, E. (2005). Raising standards in American schools: the case of No Child Left Behind. *Journal of Education Policy, 20, Number 4*, 507–524.

19. The idea of comparing private and public organizations was suggested by Robert J. Mowitz, then Director, Institute of Public Administration, The Pennsylvania State University.

20. U.S. Council of Economic Advisers (2006). *Economic report of the President.* Washington, DC: U.S. Government Printing Office, 319.

21. Calculated from U.S. Office of Management and Budget (2006). *Budget of the United States government: fiscal year 2007, historical tables.* Washington, DC: U.S. Government Printing Office, 315.

22. U.S. Office of Management and Budget (2006). *Budget of the United States government: fiscal year 2007, historical tables*, 53–54.

23. Bureau of the Census, U.S. Department of Commerce (1975). *Historical statistics of the United States: colonial times to 1970*, part 2. Washington, DC: U.S. Government Printing Office, 1114.

24. Bureau of the Census, U.S. Department of Commerce (1975). *Historical statistics of the United States: colonial times to 1970*, part 2. Washington, DC: U.S. Government Printing Office, 1127.

25. U.S. Office of Management and Budget (2006). *Budget of the United States government: fiscal year 2007, historical tables*, 53.

26. Bureau of the Census, U.S. Department of Commerce (2006). *State and local government finances: 2003–2004.* Retrieved October 10, 2006, from http://ftp2.census.gov/govs/estimate/04slsstab1a.xls.

27. U.S. Office of Management and Budget, *Budget of the United States government: fiscal year 2007, historical tables*, 311.

28. Bureau of the Census, U.S. Department of Commerce (2007). *Statistical abstract of the United States*, 2007, 322.

29. Bureau of the Census, U.S. Department of Commerce (2007). *Statistical abstract of the United States*, 2007, 321.

30. Bureau of the Census, U.S. Department of Commerce (2005). *State government employment and payroll: March 2005, US Summary Table.* Retrieved September 20, 2006, from http://www.census.gov/govs/www/apesst05view.html.

31. Bureau of the Census, U.S. Department of Commerce (2005). *Local government employment and payroll: March 2005, US Summary Table.* Retrieved September 20, 2006, from http://www.census.gov/govs/www/apesloc05view.html.

32. Bureau of the Census, U.S. Department of Commerce (2002). *2002 Census of Governments, volume 1, number 1, Government organization.* Washington, DC: U.S. Government Printing Office, 3.

33. U.S. Congressional Budget Office (2006). *The budget and economic outlook: fiscal years 2007–2016.* Washington, DC: U.S. Government Printing Office, 144.

34. U.S. Congressional Budget Office (2006). *The budget and economic outlook: fiscal years 2007–2016,* 144.

35. U.S. Congressional Budget Office (2006). *The budget and economic outlook: fiscal years 2007–2016,* 52.

36. Bureau of the Census, U.S. Department of Commerce (2006). *State and local government finances by level of government and by state: 2003–2004.* Retrieved October 10, 2006, from http://ftp2.census.gov/govs/estimate/04slsstab1a.xls.

37. Bureau of the Census, U.S. Department of Commerce (2006). *State and local government finances by level of government and by state: 2003–2004.* Retrieved October 10, 2006, from http://ftp2.census.gov/govs/estimate/04slsstab1a.xls.

38. Bureau of the Census, U.S. Department of Commerce (2006), *State and local government finances by level of government and by state: 2003–2004.* Retrieved October 10, 2006, from http://ftp2.census.gov/govs/estimate/04slsstab1a.xls.

Chapter 3

BUDGET CYCLES

Public budgeting systems, which are devices for selecting societal ends and means, consist of numerous participants and various processes that bring the participants into interaction. As described in preceding chapters, the purpose of budgeting is to allocate scarce resources among competing public demands so as to attain societal goals and objectives. Those societal ends are expressed not by philosopher kings but by mortals who must operate within the context of some prescribed allocation process—namely, the budgetary system.

This chapter provides an overview of the participants and processes involved in budgetary decision making. First, the phases of the budget cycle are reviewed. Any system has some structure or form, and budgetary systems are no exception. As will be seen, the decision-making process has several steps. Detailed discussions of these steps are presented in subsequent chapters. The second topic is the extent to which budget cycles are intermingled within government and among governments.

The Budget Cycle

To provide for responsible government, budgeting is geared to a cycle. The cycle allows the system to absorb and respond to new information and, therefore, allows government to be held accountable for its actions. Although existing budget systems may be less than perfect in guaranteeing adherence to this principle of responsibility, the argument stands that periodicity contributes to achieving and maintaining limited government. The budget cycle consists of four phases: (1) preparation and submission, (2) approval, (3) execution, and (4) audit and evaluation.

Preparation and Submission

The preparation and submission phase is the most difficult to describe because it has been subjected to the most reform efforts. Experiments in reformulating the preparation process abound. Although institutional units may exist over time, both procedures and substantive content vary from year to year.

Chief Executive Responsibilities. The responsibility for budget preparation varies greatly among jurisdictions. Budget reform efforts in the United States have pressed for executive budgeting, in which the chief executive has exclusive responsibility for preparing a proposed budget and submitting it to the legislative body. At the federal level, the president has such exclusive responsibility, although many factors curtail the extent to which the president can make major changes in the budget. In parliamentary systems, the prime minister (chief executive) typically has responsibility for budget preparation and submits what is usually called the "government budget" to the parliament.

Preparation authority, however, is not always assigned to state governors and local chief executives. While a majority of governors has responsibility for preparation and submission, some share budget-making authority with other elected administrative officers, civil service appointees, legislative leaders, or some combination of these parties. In parliamentary systems, if a coalition of several parties is necessary to form a government, and the coalition is held together by each of the main parties in the coalition controlling one or more ministries, the prime minister may have very little control over budget preparation. Such was the case with the first government under the Iraq constitution adopted in 2005.

At the municipal level, the mayor may or may not have budget preparation powers. In cities where the mayor is strong—has administrative control over the executive branch—the mayor normally does have budget-making power. This is not necessarily the case in weak-mayor systems and in cities operating under the commission plan where each councilor or commissioner administers a given department. Usually, city managers in council-manager systems have responsibility for budget preparation, although their ability to make budgetary recommendations may be tempered by their lack of independence. City managers are appointed by councils and commonly lack tenure. Even in a city in which the mayor or chief executive does not have budget preparation responsibility, this duty is still likely to be in the hands of an executive official such as a city finance director. Thus, a majority of cities follows the principle of executive budget preparation.

Location of Budget Office. Budget preparation at the federal level is primarily a function of a budget office that was established by the Budget and Accounting Act of 1921.[1] That legislation established the Bureau of the Budget (BOB), which became a unit of the Treasury Department. With the passage of time, the role of the BOB increased in importance. In 1939, it became part of the newly formed Executive Office of the President. Given that the BOB was thought to be the "right arm of the president"—a common phrase in early budget literature—the move out of the Treasury, a line department, into the Executive Office of the President placed the BOB under direct presidential supervision. In 1970, President Nixon reorganized the BOB, giving it a new title, the Office of Management and Budget (OMB). The intent of the reorganization was to bring "real business management into Government at the very highest level."[2]

Information about professional personnel in state budget offices is presented in **Table 3–1**. As of 2005, most professional staff at least had a baccalaureate degree

Table 3–1 | Education of Personnel in State Budget Offices, 2005

	Percent
Level of Education	
High school	2
Two years	1
Baccalaureate	38
Master's	54
Doctorate	4
Total (n = 41 states)	100
University Degree Major	
Public administration	31
Business administration	24
Accounting	13
Economics	8
Other social sciences	8
Other professional majors	6
Mathematics/sciences	3
Liberal arts	3
Humanities	2
Other	2
Total (n = 35 states)	100

Source: Compiled from Burns, R. C. (2006). Unpublished data from Survey of State Budget Offices, 2005. Morgantown, WV: Recreation, Parks, and Tourism Program, University of West Virginia.

and over half had a master's degree or higher. The largest degree field was public administration (31%) followed by business administration and accounting. The professional staff size varied from 5 to 278 employees, with the mean being 30 and the median 20.[3]

Steps in the Preparation Stage. In the federal government, budget preparation starts in the spring, or even earlier for large agencies. Agencies begin by assessing their programs and considering which programs require revision and whether new programs should be recommended. At approximately the same time, the president's staff makes estimates of anticipated economic trends to determine available revenue under existing tax legislation. The next step is for the president to issue general budget and fiscal policy guidelines, which agencies use to develop their individual budgets. These budgets are then submitted in late summer to the OMB. Throughout the fall and into the later months of the year, OMB staff members review agency requests and hold hearings with agency spokespersons. Not until late in the process, usually in November, December, and into January, does the president become deeply involved in the process. It culminates in February with the submission of a proposed budget to Congress.

At the state and local levels, a similar process is used where executive budgeting systems prevail. The central budget office issues budget request instructions, reviews the submitted requests, and makes recommendations to the chief executive, who decides which items to recommend to the legislative body. In jurisdictions not using executive budgeting, the chief executive and the budget office play minor roles. In this type of system, the line agencies direct their budget requests to the legislative body.

Political Factors. The preparation phase, as well as the other three phases in the budget cycle, is replete with political considerations, both bureaucratic and partisan, in addition to policy considerations. Each organizational unit is concerned with its own survival and advancement. Line agencies and their subunits attempt to protect against budget cuts and may strive for increased resources. Budget offices often play negative roles, attempting to limit agency growth or imposing agency budget cuts. Budget offices always are fully conscious of the fact that the chief executive (the governor or mayor, for example) can overrule whatever they propose. All members of the executive branch are concerned with their relationships with the legislative branch and the general citizenry. The chief executive is especially concerned about partisan calculations: Which alternatives will be advantageous to his or her political party? Of course, there is concern for developing programs for the common good, but this concern plays out in a complicated game of political maneuvering.[4]

Fragmentation. One complaint about the preparation phase is that it tends to be highly fragmented. Organizational units within line agencies tend to be concerned primarily with their own programs and frequently fail to take a broad perspective. Even the budget office may be myopic, although it will be forced into considering the budget as a whole. Only the chief executive is unquestionably committed to viewing the budget in its entirety in the preparation phase.

Approval

Revenue and Appropriation Bills. The budget is approved by a legislative body, whether Congress, a state legislature, a county board of supervisors, a city council, or a school board. The important role of the legislature in the United States traces back to the American rebellion against "taxation without representation." For this reason, the "power of the purse" is considered to be a crucial responsibility of the people's representatives. The legislature reviews the executive's budget recommendations and often has access to the original agency budget requests, which enables it to make comparisons. Congress is normally not privy to original budget requests, although ways are often found to obtain this information, such as questions being put to agency representatives in committee hearings. The fragmented approach to budgeting in the preparation phase is not characteristic of the approval phase at the local level. A city council may have a separate finance committee, but normally the council as a whole participates actively in the approval process. Local legislative bodies may take several preliminary votes on pieces of the budget but then adopt the budget as a whole by a single vote.

States, in contrast, separate tax and other revenue measures from appropriations or spending bills. Some states place most or all of their spending provisions in a single appropriation bill, whereas others create hundreds of appropriation bills. Most state legislatures are free to augment or reduce the governor's budget, but some are restricted in their ability to increase the budget. Likewise, many parliamentary systems allow the parliament to modify—but not increase—the government's budget proposal.

At the federal level, the revenue and appropriation processes have been markedly fragmented and involve numerous committees and subcommittees. Not only have revenue raising and spending been treated as separate processes, but the expenditure side is handled in many different major appropriation bills instead of being treated as a whole. Reforms introduced in 1974 attempted to integrate these divergent processes and pieces of legislation, but the system had numerous flaws.[5] Chapter 9 discusses in detail efforts at reforming the congressional budget process.

The legislature holds a series of hearings at which the central budget office and the individual agencies testify. These hearings can be lovefests in which the committees that oversee agencies are eager to recommend increased appropriations for the agencies' programs. Conversely, tensions are common in such hearings. An executive may emphasize the need to restrain expenses, while legislators may seek expansion of various programs and corresponding increases in expenditures. Tensions sometimes are particularly keen between Congress and the president's budget director, especially during periods of divided government in which the president is of one party and Congress is controlled by the other.

In both the preparation and the approval phases, one or two issues often dominate budget deliberations. If a state government is projecting a major decline in revenues due to a weakening of the economy, closing the gap between low revenues and higher expenditures will be a major concern. At the federal level, wrestling with a huge budget deficit was a primary focus in budgeting from the 1980s until the mid-1990s, and may be again with the return of large budget deficits that started in the early 2000s.

Since September 11, 2001, both the president and Congress have been deeply concerned with fighting terrorism on a global scale and increasing domestic security. The result has been huge outlays without comparable revenue increases, turning the budget surpluses of the 1990s into record-breaking deficits. With the budget so badly out of balance, budget proposals considered of highest priority, particularly proposals to fight terrorism and continue the ongoing wars, have been placed in a favored position relative to other priorities in the budget, although there has been little evidence of major cutbacks or the elimination of programs by either the White House or Congress in any part of the budget.

Executive Signature or Veto Powers. The final step of the approval stage is signing the appropriation and tax bills into law. The president, governors, and, in some cases, mayors have the power to veto. A veto sends the measure back to the legislative body for further consideration. Most governors have item-veto power, which allows them to veto specific portions of an appropriation bill but still sign it. In no case can the executive augment parts of the budget beyond that provided by the legislature. The president was given a form of item veto that took effect in 1997, but it was invalidated by the Supreme Court the following year (see Chapter 9).

Execution

Apportionment Process. Execution, the third phase, commences with the beginning of the fiscal year—October 1 for the federal government and July 1 for most state governments. Some form of centralized control during this phase is common at all levels of government and is usually maintained by the budget office. Following congressional passage of an appropriation bill and its signing by the president, agencies must submit to the OMB a proposed plan for apportionment (see Chapter 10). This plan indicates the funds required for operations, typically on a quarterly basis. The apportionment process is used in part to ensure that agencies do not commit all their available funds in a period shorter than the 12-month fiscal year. The intent is to avoid the need for supplemental appropriations from Congress.

The apportionment process is substantively important in that program adjustments must be made to bring planned spending into balance with available revenue. Because an agency most likely did not obtain all the funds requested, either from the president in the preparation phase or from Congress in the approval phase, plans for the coming fiscal year must be revised. To varying degrees, state and local governments also use an apportionment process.

Impoundment. The chief executive may assert control in the apportionment process through an informal item veto known as "impoundment," which is basically a refusal to release some funds to agencies. Thomas Jefferson often is considered the first president to have impounded funds. President Nixon impounded so extensively that it stimulated legislative action by Congress. The 1974 legislation, in a sense, was a treaty between Congress and the White House allowing limited impoundment powers for the president. As will be discussed later, these limited impoundment powers have resulted in very little reduction in spending.

Allotments. Once funds are apportioned, agencies and departments make allotments. This process grants budgetary authority to subunits such as bureaus and divisions. Allotments are made on a monthly or quarterly basis, and, like the apportionment process, the allotment process is used to control spending over the course of the fiscal year. Control often may be extensive and detailed, requiring approval by the department budget office for any shift in available funds from one item to another, such as from travel to wages. Some transfers may require clearance by the central budget office.

Preaudits. Before an expenditure is made, a form of preaudit is conducted. Basically, the preaudit ensures that funds are committed only for approved purposes and that an agency has sufficient resources in its budget to meet the proposed expenditure. The responsibility for this function varies widely, with the budget and/or accounting office being responsible for it in some jurisdictions and independently elected comptrollers being responsible for it in others. Later, after approval is granted and a purchase is made, the treasurer or other responsible official writes a check or makes an electronic fund transfer for the expenditure.

Execution Subsystems. During budget execution, several subsystems are in operation. Taxes and other debts to government are collected. The Internal Revenue

Service (IRS) in the Treasury Department is responsible for this set of tasks at the federal level. Cash is managed in the sense that monies temporarily not needed are invested. Supplies, materials, and equipment are procured, and strategies are developed to protect the government against loss or damage of property and against liability suits. Accounting and information systems are in operation. For state and local governments, bonds are sold and the proceeds are used to finance construction of facilities and the acquisition of major equipment.

Audit and Evaluation

The final phase of the budgetary process is audit and evaluation. The objectives of this phase are undergoing considerable change, but initially the main goal was to guarantee executive compliance with the provisions of appropriation bills, particularly to ensure honesty in dispensing public monies and to prevent needless waste. In accord with this goal, accounting procedures are prescribed and auditors check the books maintained by agency personnel. In recent years, the scope of auditing has been broadened to encompass studies of the effectiveness of government programs.

Location of the Audit Function. In the federal government, considerable controversy was generated concerning the appropriate organizational location of the audit function. In 1920, President Woodrow Wilson vetoed legislation that would have established the federal budget system on the grounds that he opposed the creation of an auditing office answerable to Congress rather than to the president. Nevertheless, the General Accounting Office (GAO) was established in 1921 by the Budget and Accounting Act and was made an arm of Congress, with the justification being that an audit unit outside of the executive branch should be created to provide objective assessments of expenditure practices.

GAO over the years underwent a gradual and major set of changes that led to its name being changed in 2004 to the Government Accountability Office.[6] It obviously retained its initials of "GAO."

GAO Functions. The GAO is headed by the comptroller general, who is appointed by the president, upon the advice and consent of the Senate, for only one term of 15 years. The comptroller general can only be removed by Congress by impeachment or joint resolution. There has never been such an effort, and as of 2006, there had only been seven people in this position since its creation in 1921.

Despite the GAO's title, the organization does not maintain accounts, but rather audits the accounts of operating agencies and evaluates their accounting systems. With major reforms in accounting and auditing undertaken by the executive branch at the direction of Congress, and especially with the creation of independent inspectors general within executive departments and agencies, GAO conducts far fewer audits than it once did.

The GAO provides a variety of other services. It gives Congress opinions on legal issues, such as advising on whether a particular agency acted within the law in some specific instance under consideration. It also resolves bid protests over the awarding of government contracts.

Where GAO has gained major responsibility is in the arena of assessing the results of government programs. Comptroller General David Walker has said that the GAO's "activities [are] designed to determine what programs and policies work and which ones don't. This also involves sharing various best practices and benchmarking information. It means looking horizontally across the silos of government and vertically between the levels of government."[7] This responsibility for evaluating government programs has sometimes led to criticism of the GAO. In particular, some members of Congress have claimed that the office has lost its neutrality and become a policy advocate.

In 2002, the General Accounting Office engaged in a historical conflict with the White House. President George W. Bush had created the National Energy Policy Development Group (NEPDG) to recommend a new energy policy for the government. Vice President Dick Cheney chaired the group. After the group completed its work, the GAO asked to see important records. Of particular concern was the list of companies and individuals from industry that had supplied advice. The energy giant, Enron, had collapsed, leaving many stockholders with huge losses and company employees without retirement benefits. Some suspected that Enron, which had close ties to President Bush before he left Texas for Washington, had exerted undue influence on the design of the energy policy.

The White House refused to release the requested documents, which prompted the GAO to file suit in U.S. district court against Vice President Cheney and the NEPDG.[8] This move marked the GAO's first suit in its history against a high-ranking government official. The GAO contended that taxpayers' dollars were used by the group, and consequently the GAO had a right to know how those dollars were spent. The White House's position was that it had a right to obtain information and advice on a confidential basis and should not be required to release the documents. A U.S. district court ruled that the comptroller general had not been harmed by the withholding of information and therefore lacked standing, namely the right to bring suit.[9] The GAO decided not to appeal the ruling.

State and Local Auditors. At the state and local levels, the issue of organizational responsibility for auditing has been resolved in different ways. The alternatives are to have the audit function performed by a unit answerable to the legislative body, to the chief executive, to the citizenry directly, or to some combination of these. The use of an elected auditor is defended on the grounds that objectivity can be achieved if the auditor is independent of the executive *and* legislative branches. The opposing arguments are that the electorate cannot suitably judge the qualifications of candidates for auditor and that the election process necessarily forces the auditor to become a biased rather than an objective analyst. States primarily use elected and legislative auditors.

Sample Cycle

Figure 3–1 is a sample budget cycle. It is the one used in Pennsylvania where the fiscal year, like most states, begins July 1. As can be seen, preparation begins with budget instructions being issued in August. Pennsylvania also issues Program Policy Guidelines (PPGs), which provide substantive policy guidance to agencies when preparing their budget requests. Submission by the agencies occurs in October followed by budget office analysis and the governor's decisions from October through January. The governor submits the budget to the legislature in February, which deliberates through the spring. The budget is adopted by the legislature by July 1, the beginning of the new fiscal year. Agencies then submit to the budget office what Pennsylvania calls a "rebudget." This is a reworking of their budget requests to reflect what the legislature approved as distinguished from what the agencies requested. The diagram does not show the audit phase that begins at the end of the fiscal year.

Figure 3–1 **Budget Cycle in Pennsylvania**

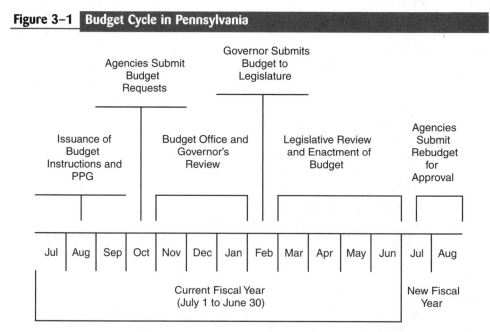

Source: Reprinted from Office of the Budget (2006). *Governor's executive budget, 2006-2007.* Harrisburg, PA: Commonwealth of Pennsylvania, xx.

▌ Scrambled Budget Cycles

Although it is easy to speak of a budget cycle, no single cycle actually exists. Instead, a cycle exists for each budget period, and several cycles are in operation at any given time. The decision-making process is not one that simply proceeds from preparation and submission to approval, execution, and, finally, audit. Decision making is complicated by the existence of several budget cycles for which information is imperfect and incomplete.

Overlapping Cycles

A pattern of overlapping cycles can be seen in **Figure 3–2**, which shows the sequencing of five budget cycles typical of a large state. Only cycle 3 in the diagram displays the complete period covering 39 months. The preparation and submission phase requires at least nine months, approval six months, execution 12 months, and audit 12 months. The same general pattern is found at the federal level, except that the execution phase begins on October 1, giving Congress approximately eight months to consider the budget. As indicated by the diagram, three or four budget periods are likely to be in progress at any point in time.

Budget preparation is complicated particularly by this scrambling or intermingling of cycles. In the first place, preparation begins perhaps 15 months before the budget is to go into effect. Moreover, much of the preparation phase is completed without knowledge of the legislature's actions in the preceding budget period.

Federal Experience. At the federal level, this problem has proved especially thorny. Congress has historically been slow to pass appropriation bills, and the approval phase was rarely completed by the start of the fiscal year when it began July 1. The usual procedure was to pass a continuation bill permitting agencies to spend at

Figure 3–2 Scrambled Budget Cycles

	January	July	January	July	January	July	January	July
Cycle 1	Execution		Audit					
Cycle 2	Approval		Execution		Audit			
Cycle 3		Preparation	Approval	Execution		Audit		
Cycle 4				Preparation	Approval	Execution		
Cycle 5						Preparation	Approval	

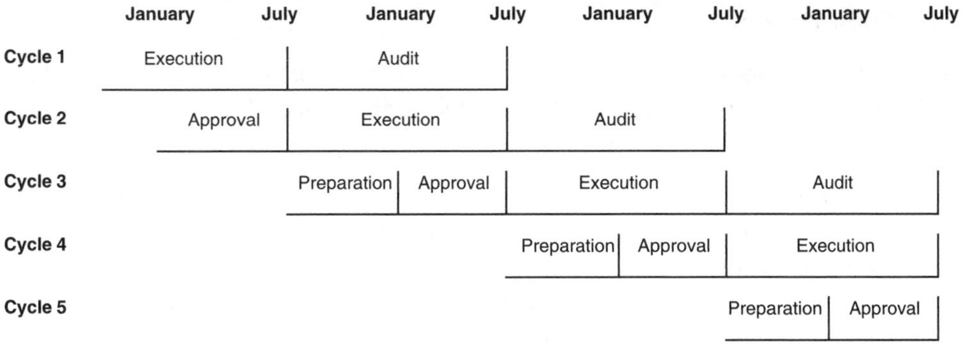

the rate of the previous year's budget while Congress continued to deliberate on the new year's budget. Although the budget calendar adopted in the 1970s gave Congress an additional three months, which was expected to permit completion of the approval phase, agencies' preparation problems for the following year's budget request persisted. In any given year, an agency begins to prepare its budget request during the spring and summer, even as Congress deliberates on the agency's upcoming budget. Despite the additional time granted to Congress to act on the budget, work on the budget was completed on time in only three out of 30 years from the time the new budget calendar went into effect through 2005.[10] This obviously compounds the problem of scrambled budget cycles.

Links Between Budget Phases. While a budget is being prepared, another one is being executed. The budget being executed may be for the immediately preceding budget year, but it can also be for the one before. As can be seen in **Figure 3–2**, in the early stages of preparation for cycle 4 the execution phase is in operation for cycle 2. Under such conditions, the executive branch may not know the effects of ongoing programs but is nevertheless required to begin a new budget, recommending changes upward or downward. Sometimes a new program may be created, and an agency must then recommend changes in the program for inclusion in the next budget without any opportunity for assessing its merits.

Length of Preparation Phase. The cycle, particularly the preparation phase, may be even longer than indicated above, especially when agencies must rely upon other agencies or subunits for information. For example, in preparing the education component of a state budget, a department of education will require budget information and requests from state universities and colleges early to meet deadlines imposed by the governor's budget office. The reliability and validity of data undoubtedly decrease as the lead time increases. Therefore, the earlier these schools submit their budget requests to the state capital, the less likely it is that such requests will be based on accurate assessments of future requirements.

Other Considerations

Besides the factors already mentioned, other issues further complicate budget cycles—most notably, intergovernmental considerations and the timing of budget years.

Intergovernmental Factors. Another problem arises from intermingled budget cycles because the three main levels of government are interdependent. For the federal government, the main problem is assessing needs and finding resources to meet these needs. A state government must assess its needs and those of local governments and must then search for funds by raising state taxes, providing for new forms of taxation by local governments, or obtaining federal revenues. In preparing budgets, governors take into account whatever information is available on the likelihood of certain actions by the president and Congress. For instance, the president may have recommended a major increase in educational programs that would significantly increase funds flowing to the states, but considerable doubt will exist as to whether Congress will accept the recommendation. In such a case, how should a governor shape the education portion of the state budget? The problem is even worse at the local level, which is dependent on both the state and federal governments for funds.

Budget Years. Budget cycles are further complicated by a lack of uniformity in the budget period. Although most state governments have budget years beginning July 1, four states do not: New York's begins April 1; Texas's begins September 1; and Alabama's and Michigan's begin the same day as the federal fiscal year—October 1. Consistency does not even exist within each state. It is common for a state to begin its fiscal year on July 1 but to have to deal with local governments operating with different start dates, such as January 1, April 1, or September 1.

A case can be made for staggering the budget year for different levels of government. This practice might assist decision makers at one level by providing information about action taken at other levels. For example, the federal government might complete action on its budget by October 1. States could then begin a budget year on the following April 1 and local governments on July 1. Under such an arrangement, states could base their budgetary decisions on knowledge of available financial support from Washington. Local governments, in turn, would know the aid available from both Washington and their respective state capitals.

Rearranging the dates for fiscal years is no panacea, however. Information about financial support from other governments is only one of many items used in decision making. Also, any slippage by the legislature in completing its appropriations work by the time a fiscal year begins would void the advantages of staggered budget cycles. In addition, there is no direct translation from appropriations to aid to other governments. Money does not automatically flow to states and communities as soon as Congress passes an appropriation bill. Instead, state and local governments must apply for assistance, a process that typically requires many months.

Annual and Biennial Budgets. Not only is there inconsistency in the date on which budget years begin, but the length of the budget period also varies. Whereas the federal government and most local governments operate under annual budgets, 23 states have biennial (two-year) budgets.[11] Under these systems, a governor typically submits the budget in January, and legislative action is supposed to be completed by June 30. The execution phase runs for 24 months beginning July 1. Such a system violates the once-standard principle of annuality.[12] The argument is that annual budgets allow for careful and frequent supervision of the executive by the legislature and that this approach serves to promote greater responsibility in government. The problem with the annual budget, however, is that little breathing time is available. Both the executive and legislative branches are continuously in the throes of budgeting. The biennial approach, on the other hand, relieves participants of many routine budget matters and may allow greater time for more thorough analysis of government activities.

The 1993 National Performance Review recommended that the federal government adopt biennial budgeting as a means of eliminating "an enormous amount of busy work."[13] The idea continues to hold interest for some reformers (see Chapter 9).[14]

One of the greatest dangers of a biennial system is that it may obstruct—if not prohibit—a prompt response to new conditions. The costs of not being able to adjust to changing conditions may far outweigh any benefits accruing from time saved. This consideration may explain why most of the more populous states are on annual budget systems and why many states with biennial budgets make provision for "reopening" the two-year budget at midpoint.

Still another consideration is whether under "normal" conditions sufficient amounts of new information become available to warrant annual systems. If program analysis were a well-established part of the budgetary process, then conceivably new insights into the operation of programs would continually occur. In such instances, an annual process might be preferable. In other cases in which decision makers operate one year with virtually the same information as was available the preceding year, there seems to be little need for annual budgets. Partially for this reason, proposals have been made for selectively abandoning the annual budget cycle. Under such a system, new programs or proposed changes in existing programs would be submitted in any given year for legislative review, whereas continuing programs would be reviewed only periodically.

Summary

The four phases of the budget cycle are preparation and submission, approval, execution, and audit and evaluation. In general, the first and third phases are the responsibility of the executive branch, and the second is controlled by the legislative branch. The fourth phase in the federal system is directed by the GAO, which is answerable to Congress and not the president, and a set of independent auditors known as inspectors general. Auditing at the state and local levels is normally the responsibility of either independently elected officials or officials who report directly to the legislature.

A standard criticism of budgeting, especially at the federal level, is that the budget is seldom considered in its entirety during its preparation phase. Within the executive branch, only the president and his or her immediate staff view the budget as a whole. Agencies are primarily concerned only with their own portions of the total. The same disjointed approach has been characteristic of the approval phase at the federal level.

Budget cycles are intermingled. As many as four budget cycles may be in operation at any time in a single government. This phenomenon complicates decision making. For example, budget preparation often is forced to proceed without knowledge as to what action the legislature will take on the previous year's budget. Moreover, the interdependent nature of the three levels of government contributes to a scrambling of cycles. One possibility would be conversion to biennial budgets, a practice that is common at the state level.

Notes

1. Budget and Accounting Act (1921). Ch. 18, 42 Stat. 20.

2. Nixon, R. M. (1970). *New York Times, June 11*; Dawes, C.G. (1923). *The first year of the budget of the United States.* New York: Harper and Brothers.

3. Burns, R. C. (2006). Unpublished data from Survey of State Budget Offices, 2005. Morgantown, WV: Recreation, Parks, and Tourism Program, University of West Virginia.

4. Wildavsky, A. & Caiden, N. (2004). *The new politics of the budgetary process,* 5th ed. New York: Longman.

5. Congressional Budget and Impoundment Control Act (1974). P.L. 93–344.

6. Human Capital Reform Act (2004). P.L. 108–271.

7. Walker, D. M. (2002). The role of GAO and other government auditors in the 21st century. Address to the 14th Biennial Forum of Government Auditors, Providence, RI, 2002. Retrieved September 1, 2006, from http://www.gao.gov/cghome/14thbf.html; see Walker, D. M. (2004). Evolving role of public service auditors. Retrieved September 1, 2006, from http://www.gao.gov/cghome/erpsa/.

8. U.S. General Accounting Office (2002). *Decision of the Comptroller General concerning NEPDG litigation.* Retrieved September 1, 2006 from www.gao.gov/cgdecnepdg.pdf#search=%22%22concerning%20NEPDG%20litigation%22%22.

9. *Walker v. Cheney* (2002). 230 F. Supp. 2d 51 (D.D.C.).

10. Streeter, S. (2006). *Continuing appropriations acts: brief overview of recent practices.* Washington, DC: Congressional Research Service, 6.

11. Von Behren, G. & Korfona, P. (2002). *Budget processes in the states.* Washington, DC: National Association of State Budget Officers, 1.

12. Sundelson, J. W. (1935). Budgetary principles. *Political Science Quarterly, 50,* 236–263.

13. National Performance Review (1993). *From red tape to results: creating a government that works better and costs less.* Washington, DC: U.S. Government Printing Office.

14. U.S. General Accounting Office (2000). *Budget process: biennial budgeting for the federal government.* Washington, DC: U.S. Government Printing Office.

Chapter 4

BUDGETING FOR REVENUES: INCOME TAXES, PAYROLL TAXES, AND PROPERTY TAXES

This chapter and the next one describe the principles of taxation and the institutional characteristics of the major revenue sources used by governments. This chapter covers income taxes, payroll taxes, and property taxes, while the next one covers sales taxes, user fees, and gambling revenues. The availability of revenues sets the tone for deciding on the level of expenditures and the decision process for allocating expenditures among competing priorities.

Historically, taxation has been a fundamental concern of the citizenry. Citizens may be less concerned about how government spends its money than about how that money is raised to support programs. The property tax bill, federal income tax filing, and the water bill are more visible events than most of the services citizens receive. The tax bill also almost always seems larger than the value of any individual service, so it is a stark reminder of the cost of government. In developing a budget package, political leaders are always mindful that program initiatives leading to higher expenditures and, therefore, to higher taxes may have negative effects on the possibility of winning reelection to their offices.

This chapter includes two sections. The first section discusses principles of taxation, covering such issues as the adequacy of various revenue sources, equity considerations, economic efficiency concerns, and the ability to collect revenues at a relatively low cost. The second, and longer, section details various revenue sources that rely on income or property as a base, including the individual income tax, the corporate income tax, payroll taxes, and property taxes. The discussion of each of these taxes focuses on such characteristics as their adequacy as a revenue source, their fairness, ease of collection and so forth, and on the mechanics of how the tax base and tax rates are determined.

Principles of Taxation

A chief concern that public officials have for any tax is the extent to which that tax will generate adequate revenue to fund the services provided by the government. The major revenue sources used by governments—income taxes, property taxes, and sales taxes—are used in large part because the number and value of taxable events or the value of the base are so large and therefore have the potential to generate so much income. There are other reasons, aside from the adequacy of revenue, however, to choose one particular revenue source over another. These can include the equity (or fairness) of the revenue source, the extent to which the revenue source distorts economic choices, the cost of administering the tax, and the political feasibility of particular revenue sources.

Adequacy of Revenue

Not all revenue sources have the same potential for growth. In general, as an individual's wealth or income goes up, he or she tends to demand more from government. For this reason, governments should avoid sources of revenue that do not have the potential to grow as fast as income or wealth. In addition, as noted above, some sources of revenue can produce large amounts of income for the government at relatively low rates, because of the sheer size of the tax base. To illustrate these points, consider the federal income tax and taxes on cigarettes. The federal income tax runs off a large tax base, and because of its progressive rate structure, higher levels of income are taxed at higher rates. A tax on cigarettes, on the other hand, runs off a relatively smaller base (sales of cigarettes) and demand for cigarettes does not tend to grow with income. For this reason, the progressive income tax is a much more productive revenue source than the cigarette tax. On the other hand, taxes on cigarette sales do not generate nearly as much controversy among a majority of voters and, therefore, may be more attractive to lawmakers.

In addition to the sheer size of the base, it is important for tax policymakers to take into account the potential of the tax base to respond to changes in tax rates. For many taxes, as tax rates increase, they discourage engaging in the taxed activity. Thus, a higher sales tax increases the price of goods (thus decreasing the amount of goods sold) and high marginal income tax rates may encourage some individuals to choose "leisure" over work, at least at the margin. A recent study confirmed the existence of this relationship between tax rates and the tax base for a range of taxes in North Carolina.[1] Conversely, where demand for a given good is "inelastic" (that is, where demand does not respond to price) an increase in the tax rate is much less likely to discourage consumption. This tends to be true, for example, of the cigarette tax, since many people are addicted to the good in question. The important implication for the adequacy of revenue is that behavioral responses to taxes must be factored in when doing revenue estimates, lest these estimates overstate the amount of revenue that will be generated for a given tax rate.

Equity

As important a question of how much money is going to be raised from a tax is the question of who will pay that tax. In fact, the question of "who pays" is often the central question of taxation. Consider the debate in the 2000 presidential election between George W. Bush and Al Gore. Both candidates, faced with a projection of large and rising budget surpluses, advocated tax cuts. Candidate Bush, however, advocated tax reductions that were more heavily targeted toward higher-income people (who pay the majority of federal income taxes) than candidate Gore, who advocated tax cuts more targeted toward lower-income Americans. The debate here was not about which tax to cut, or even necessarily about how much to cut it, but about who would benefit from those reductions.

There are two general principles of tax equity. The first is the ability to pay principle, which says that the taxpaying capacity of different taxpayers should be taken into account in designing the tax system. The second is the benefit principle, which says there should be some relationship between the benefits received by the taxpayer and taxes paid.

Ability to Pay. Different taxpayers have different levels of income and wealth, and therefore may have different capacities to bear the cost of financing government.[2] One sense of equity relates to the ability to pay principle. A tax should be related to the taxpayer's income or wealth or, more generally, to the taxpayer's ability to pay the tax. A taxpayer who can afford to pay more should pay more. Some consider that equitable. This principle implies that a tax imposes the same loss of utility for each taxpayer, or as economists refer to it, the *equal absolute sacrifice*.[3] Equity has both horizontal and vertical dimensions.

Horizontal Equity. Horizontal equity refers to charging the same amount to different taxpayers whose ability to pay (usually measured by income levels) is the same. If two taxpayers are the same on relevant dimensions, and they pay different levels of tax, that tax would violate the principle of horizontal equity. That can occur, for example, because the way a tax is administered may erroneously identify two taxpayers as being the same, when in fact they are different. This can be a particular problem for the property tax, because the level of tax paid is usually a direct function of assessed values of property. If two parcels are erroneously valued the same, however, when in fact one could sell for more on the market, then these two taxpayers are being treated as if they are the same, when they in fact may be quite different. It is important to note that whether two taxpayers are "the same" is frequently in the eye of the beholder. If two taxpayers have the same level of income, for example, but one is supporting a family of five on that income while the other is a single taxpayer with no dependents, simply differentiating tax paid on the basis of income fails to account for real differences in ability to pay. In this case, a tax that appears to be horizontally equitable may not be at all.

Vertical Equity. While there is nearly universal agreement that horizontal equity should be adhered to, vertical equity is a somewhat harder principle on which to obtain consensus. Put simply, vertical equity has to do with "treating different taxpayers differently." Normally, this implies knowledge of how a given tax affects different people, or income groups, in the society. Vertical equity is normally measured by computing the *effective tax rate*, which is computed by dividing the tax paid by a given individual by some measure of wealth or income. The computation of the effective tax rate can yield conclusions that a given tax, or tax system is:

- *Progressive*, if effective tax rates are higher for higher income taxpayers than for lower income taxpayers;
- *Proportional*, if effective tax rates are essentially the same across different income categories; or
- *Regressive*, if lower income taxpayers experience higher effective tax rates than higher income taxpayers.

Knowing whether a tax is progressive, proportional, or regressive involves knowing more than just the tax rate. For example, a sales tax on purchases seems to treat all taxpayers equally but is often actually regressive in that poorer families may spend a greater proportion of their incomes on taxed items than wealthier families do.

Most people would argue for tax systems that are either proportional or progressive. But even if there is general agreement that a tax system should be progressive (as is generally true for the federal income tax), this does not mean that there is agreement concerning *how* progressive the tax should be. Since debates about progressivity are actually debates about the portion of the tax burden to be borne by different taxpaying groups, they are important and can create substantial controversy.

Overall, the entire U.S. system of revenue, at the national level, is progressive, but that masks some variation by revenue source. While the federal income tax is quite progressive, the payroll tax (for Social Security and Medicare) is actually regressive, because there is an income ceiling above which Social Security taxes are not paid. The revenue system cannot be judged independently of certain government programs. Transfer payments, such as various forms of aid to poor families, are somewhat like "negative" taxes in their effect and increase the progressivity of the tax and transfer system considered together.

A Congressional Budget Office study of the incidence of federal taxes—individual income, social insurance, corporate income, and excise taxes—found that, in 2003, the highest quintile (the one-fifth of households earning the most incomes) experienced an overall effective tax rate of 25% for all federal taxes. This compared to 17.7% in the next highest quintile, and only 4.8% for the lowest quintile. While the individual and corporate income taxes are even more progressive than the overall system, both excise taxes and social insurance taxes tend to be more regressive.[4] Another measure of the level of progressivity of the federal individual income tax is illustrated by the fact that households in the top quintile paid 85% of all income taxes in 2003. This was the main reason that these same taxpayers paid two-thirds of all federal taxes in the same year.[5]

Benefit Received. Another concept to keep in mind is that of benefit received. Some revenue is derived from payments by recipients for services rendered or benefits received. User charges or fees are notable examples, as in municipal parking garage fees, bus fares, and water and sewer charges. People who park in the garage pay for that service. The principle of payment for services results in an efficient allocation of public sector resources, because people will use only the amount of a particular service for which they are willing to pay. This process is similar to the way in which the private market works. That is, the private market produces no more of those goods than people are willing to purchase.

However, if all government services were paid for by fees, some people would be unable to pay and necessarily would be excluded. Elementary and secondary education, for example, is the most expensive local government service. If government provided this service entirely by charging parents and students the cost of providing education, many parents would be unable to send their children to school. This situation would lead to large segments of the society being uneducated and unable to secure employment that required the ability to read, write, and the like. Because of the *spillover effects* (the fact that lack of education would adversely affect others in the society), many government services cannot be appropriately supported solely through user fees.

In addition, the public supports education for equity reasons. Everyone should have access to at least some level of education regardless of their ability to pay for it. Similarly, public goods have positive *externalities*—that is, they benefit all citizens regardless of whether one actually uses the service. Education, for example, benefits the entire community by making it more attractive to businesses making location decisions, and it benefits the entire economy by increasing the productivity of the work force. The benefit received principle simply cannot be applied uniformly to all government services.

Moreover, particular taxes may be structured to permit the overall tax system to better adhere to the benefit principle. For example, the State of Florida has a sales tax but no income tax. This permits substantial taxation of visitors to the state to obtain revenue from individuals who are causing state services to be provided, but might otherwise not pay the cost of any of these services. Tourists would not pay income taxes were the state to have one, yet tourists impose burdens on government services. Therefore, sales taxes help to make tourists pay for the costs they impose. Of course, tourists not only generate costs, but also generate jobs and income for Florida. If the state were to impose what was perceived as onerous sales tax rates, that might drive tourists away to other states.

The problem of nonresident service provisions is also the justification for nonresident income taxes (so-called commuter taxes) in many metropolitan areas, which tax income earned in a jurisdiction, even by nonresidents, as a means of exacting payment from them for services provided.

Economic Efficiency

According to the related concept of efficiency, an efficient tax is one that does not appreciably affect the allocation of resources within the private sector, such as between consumption and saving or among competing items for consumption. Taxes on alcohol, for example, seem to have no appreciable effect on consumption of alcoholic beverages. However, taxes can be used for regulatory purposes, as opposed to purely efficient revenue-raising purposes. Increased taxes on tobacco have been shown to reduce smoking among youth, precisely as intended.[6] Other tax provisions that exclude some items from taxation, such as selected tax deferrals on personal income saved for retirement, are designed to influence behavior and may not be neutral or simply efficient. Tax systems that are progressive can be inefficient and have unintentional consequences. If tax rates are particularly high for wealthy persons, for instance, then the system may encourage them to spend more time on leisure and less on working and earning more income. In many European countries, that effect, encouraging people to spend more time on leisure and less on purely income-earning activities, might be perceived as a positive outcome of the tax.

Tax system design generally tries to consider both equity and efficiency objectives. Use of taxes to regulate behavior, as in increased tobacco taxes, is generally not considered in the overall design of a tax system, but rather is typically legislated separately. Extensive research has focused on how to consider both principles simultaneously while developing optimal tax structures that are designed to achieve an optimal balance between efficiency and equity objectives.[7]

Cost of Administration

Generally, taxes that are expensive to administer should be avoided. Money spent to collect taxes represents a net loss to society, and therefore, the less spent on tax administration, the better. There are a number of specific costs associated with tax collection. Some costs are to the government, some to the taxpayer, and some to an intermediary, such as the shopkeeper who collects the sales tax. The individual income tax, example, may be relatively cheap for the government to administer (given the level of revenue produced), but it can be quite costly for individuals to comply with all of the specific requirements of reporting income and calculating taxes owed. These high compliance costs occur primarily because of the complexity of the tax system. But this complexity, in part, represents the cost of attempting to promote equity. Most of the allowable deductions and credits for the federal income tax, for example, stem from attempts to adjust the tax to allow for individual taxpayer conditions.

On the other hand, there are taxes where the cost of compliance is relatively low, but the cost of initial collection by the government is high. Consider the case of the local property tax. Because the government is obliged to place a value on properties, it needs to expend substantial resources to identify the level of taxes required to be paid and to collect those taxes in the first instance.

In addition to the cost of initial collection, there is the separate cost to the government of enforcement. Enforcement tends to be more difficult and costly in cases where the laws and rules surrounding the revenue source are complex, and where the responsibility for initial collection (for determining the level of tax to be paid) lies with the taxpayer. Thus, the income tax is relatively costly to enforce, while the property tax is much less costly. In the latter case, there is much less room for interpretation by the taxpayer—the amount is not normally in dispute. (Chapter 10, on budget execution, includes a section on tax administration that goes into greater detail on particular techniques and issues.)

Political Feasibility

Even taxes that score well on adequacy, equity, efficiency, and ease of administration still may fall short if they cannot be raised in the current political environment. States without an income tax will probably find it almost impossible to enact one, despite whatever other appeals such a tax may have. Tobacco-growing states probably will find it difficult to raise cigarette taxes, while such taxes may be relatively appealing in states that do not grow tobacco. In fact, it is not surprising that there is wide variation in the per pack tax rates in different states. For example, Virginia and Kentucky, which are major tobacco-growing states, taxed cigarettes at 30 cents per pack in 2005. On the other hand, Rhode Island taxed them at $2.46 per pack and Washington State at $2.03 per pack.[8]

◼ Income, Payroll, and Property Taxes

Many of the major revenue sources used by governments are based on income or wealth—property values being the primary wealth that is taxed in the U.S. to generate revenue. These bases are partially desirable because they are large; a relatively large amount of revenue can be raised at relatively low rates. They are also used because it is easy to adjust the tax to individual taxpayer conditions; that is, those taxpayers with relatively higher incomes have a relatively greater ability to pay taxes. Similarly, taxpayers with a great deal of property wealth may be viewed as having an extraordinary ability to pay, though that is not necessarily true for the elderly, who may have a valuable residence but after retirement have much less income with which to pay the tax. The major revenue sources in this category are the personal income tax, the corporate income tax, the payroll tax (primarily used for Social Security and Medicare), and the property tax.

The Personal Income Tax

The income tax is a relatively recent, but important, addition to the revenue sources used by governments. Until the passage of the 16th amendment to the Constitution, ratified in 1913, the taxation of income was not permitted in the United States. Since that time, the income tax has become the most important revenue source for the federal government, in addition to being an important source for many state and local governments. By tradition and for convenience, state and local income taxes tend to operate in a way that is similar to the federal income tax, albeit with very different rate structures. For this reason, this section describes the structure of the federal income tax system, and then discusses briefly the particular characteristics of state and local personal income tax systems.

Income taxes, in general, have the following structure:

1. The computation of income (in the case of the federal income tax, *adjusted gross income*, or AGI), which is the initial calculation of the tax base.
2. Reductions to adjusted gross income because of individual taxpayer characteristics. These take the form of *deductions* (standard or itemized) or *exemptions* (for the taxpayer and dependents).
3. The application of *tax rates* (graduated in the case of the federal income tax) to taxable income, which is the result of AGI minus deductions and exemptions.
4. Reductions in the tax paid as a result of *tax credits*, which are dollar-for-dollar reductions in taxes paid.

Computing Adjusted Gross Income. Not all income is taxed. In the case of the federal government, decisions have been made about precisely which types of income should be subject to taxation and which should not. Economists have historically embraced a very broad definition of income, called the *Haig-Simons definition*, which defines income as any increase in an individual's potential ability to consume.[9] This includes some of the income used in the federal definition, including salaries, wages, commissions and tips, dividends, interest, rents, alimony, and unemployment compensation. Excluded from the federal definition, however, are most employee benefits (such as employer-provided health insurance and contributions to pension funds), disability retirement, workers' compensation, food stamps, and interest earned on some state and local bonds. This arguably advantages people who have more of the excluded income. For example, two individuals whose adjusted gross income is the same may in fact be not equally well off, if one of them is being provided a subsidy by his employer for health insurance and retirement benefits (not counted in adjusted gross income, and therefore not taxed), while the other is not. For this reason, the more sources of income included in the tax base, the more equitable the income tax. When the base excludes sizable segments of income, vigorous debates immediately arise over whether some interests are receiving undue favoritism as a result of legislative lobbying.[10]

Tax codes also provide for adjustments to gross income that typically have the effect of removing portions of income from the base. For example, the federal tax code excludes expenses for moving to accept a new job, some job-related educational expenses, and some employer-paid business reimbursements. The result of the components of income that are included (above), less these adjustments, becomes the base from which exemptions and deductions are subtracted, or adjusted gross income.

Exemptions and Deductions. Individual exemptions and deductions may further reduce the individual income tax base. Exemptions are reductions to the tax base that literally result from existence. If you file income taxes, you can claim yourself as an exemption. Moreover, however, the more dependents that a taxpayer claims on his or her return, the more exemptions, and therefore, the greater the dollar amount from exemptions. In 2006, the federal exemption was $3,300 for most taxpayers. This means that a married couple filing jointly could claim $6,600 in exemptions. If they had three children, that rose to $16,500. There is one caveat to this. As a result of changes to income tax laws in 1993, the personal exemption is reduced for higher income taxpayers (those who are married filing jointly with incomes greater than $110,000 in 2006, for example) and are eventually phased out entirely.

More important than exemptions for many people are deductions. Each taxpayer is permitted to claim a *standard deduction* without providing any documentation. This standard deduction varies according to the filing status of the taxpayer. In 2006, the standard deduction was $5,150 for a single person, and $10,300 for married people filing jointly (regardless of the number of dependents).

Itemized deductions are much more complicated. These deductions literally attempt to adjust taxable income to reflect differences in individual taxpayer conditions. As such, they can vary widely from one taxpayer to another, but they also require that the taxpayer maintain supporting evidence for the deduction. The main itemized deductions include:

- *Home mortgage interest*—the interest paid on borrowed funds for a taxpayer's first two properties can be deducted from income. This represents an important subsidy for homeowners, and establishes a significant incentive that encourages home ownership. It decreases the progressivity of the federal income tax system, however, since more tax benefits are provided to higher income individuals, a higher proportion of whom are homeowners.[11]
- *Unreimbursed health expenses*—health care expenses, to the extent that they are not reimbursed, may be deducted from income. An important caveat, however, is that only those unreimbursed expenses that exceed 7.5% of adjusted gross income can be deducted. This means that a taxpayer with an AGI of $100,000, and unreimbursed medical expenses of $8,000, could only deduct $500 from his or her taxes.
- *State and local taxes*—many taxes paid to state and local governments are exempt from federal taxation. This includes all state and local income and property taxes, and many vehicle licensing and registration fees. Since 2004, it has also included sales taxes paid (an earlier sales tax deduction had been repealed in 1986), but taxpayers are not permitted to deduct both income taxes and sales taxes. Historically, the real property tax and state income taxes have been the taxes most frequently claimed as deductions from federal taxes.[12]
- *Charitable contributions*—payments made by cash or check to recognized nonprofit organizations are deductible. In addition, items donated to such institutions may also be deducted (provided there is evidence of both the donation and its value), as well as miles driven on behalf of a charity.[13]
- *Business expenses*—particularly for self-employed individuals, a wide variety of business expenses can be deducted. These include the cost of providing for retirement and health benefits, and even a portion of home mortgage costs provided the taxpayer uses the deducted portion of his home solely for business. Even non-self-employed individuals can deduct a variety of expenses, especially related to unreimbursed job costs and certain entertainment expenses. The Internal Revenue Service, however, has been relatively vigilant concerning unwarranted business expense deductions.

These exclusions, inclusions, adjustments, and deductions to the income base are intended to yield income figures for individuals and families that further horizontal and vertical tax equity. These factors together are meant to recognize variations in total income and the circumstances involved in earning that income and meeting living expenses. Individuals earning the same income but having different numbers of family members and expenses will be treated differently, while others with unequal gross incomes ultimately may have the same ability to pay when adjustments and deductions are taken into account.

Rate Structure. The principle of equity is furthered at the federal level by the use of a progressive rate structure. Tax law changes since 2001 have altered tax brackets, reducing the amount of taxes that almost all taxpayers are liable to pay. The federal income tax currently has six tax brackets, which vary from 10% (for the first $15,100 in taxable income for a married couple) to 35% (for taxable income in excess of $336,550 for married taxpayers). It is important to note that the nature of the income tax is such that different portions of income are taxed at different rates. Therefore, even someone with taxable income of $1,000,000 will see the first $15,100 of that income taxed at only 10%. This taxpayer would "experience" each of the tax brackets for various portions of income. **Exhibit 4–1** shows a tax calculation for a hypothetical taxpayer, demonstrating the sequence of taxation, from the calculation of AGI, to taxable income, to tax paid.

Some have proposed a flat rate income tax, or alternatively a national sales tax, to replace the existing federal income tax system. Either of these taxes would likely impose relatively high rates in order to replace the revenue from the existing income tax. In addition, both would be more regressive than the current federal system, although recent research suggests that taxpayers who support such a change do not believe the current system is as progressive as it is, and do not believe that a "reformed" system would be as regressive as it would be.[14]

Tax Credits. Unlike tax deductions, tax credits are dollar-for-dollar reductions in taxes that are applied after all the preceding steps have been completed. Perhaps the largest tax credit is the *earned income tax credit* (EITC), established in 1975. This is a tax credit for the "working poor" and can behave like a *negative income tax*, in that individuals can receive a credit in excess of the tax that they are required to pay. In this case, they receive a check from the government for the amount by which the credit exceeds their liability.[15] Recent research shows that the EITC is heavily used by low-income individuals because it has been around so long, and because it is effectively targeted to low-income individuals.[16] Other tax credits are provided for children (provided that the taxpayer's income is less than $119,000) and for child and dependent care expenses (for example, having a caregiver come into your home to care for a child or an aging relative).

Exhibit 4–1   Example of Computation of the Federal Income Tax in 2006

John and Bernadette Public are a married couple who file their taxes jointly. They have two dependent children. Their adjusted gross income, consisting of $150,000 in salaries and $20,000 in interest, was $170,000 in 2006. They claim a $1,600 tax credit for the care of their dependent children. They itemize deductions, and have three such deductions in 2006: $15,000 in home mortgage interest, $2,000 in state and local taxes, and $1,000 in charitable contributions. The calculation below shows how they compute their federal income tax liability for 2006. The personal exemption (claimed for each of them plus their dependents) is $3,300.

In calculating the Publics' taxes, we first compute their taxable income. Next, we reduce the taxable income by the sum of their itemized deductions (they have chosen to itemize because their itemized deductions exceed the standard deduction) and personal exemptions, to arrive at taxable income. Tax liability is then computed by applying the tax rates from the tax table below to their taxable income (recall that in doing this, different portions of their income are taxed at different rates). Finally, the tax liability is reduced by the tax credit in order to arrive at the total tax paid.

Step 1: Adjusted Gross Income
Salaries—$150,000
Interest—$20,000
Total AGI—$170,000

Step 2: Taxable Income
Adjusted gross income—$170,000
Less: Itemized deductions—$18,000
Less: Personal exemptions—$13,200
Total Taxable Income—$138,800

Step 3: Tax Liability
Total taxable income—$138,800
Calculating tax paid for different components of income:
$15,100*.10=$1,510
$46,200*.15=$6,930
$62,400*.25=$15,600
$15,100*.28=$4,228
Total Tax Liability—$28,268

Step 4: Total Tax Paid
Tax liability—$28,268
Less: Tax credit—$1,600
Total Tax Paid—$26,668

continues

Exhibit 4–1 (continued)

2006 Tax Table: Married Filing Jointly		
If taxable income is over	**But not over**	**Marginal tax rate is**
$0	$15,100	10%
$15,100	$61,300	15%
$61,300	$123,700	25%
$123,700	$188,450	28%
$188,450	$336,550	33%
$336,550	No limit	35%

The Alternative Minimum Tax. The *alternative minimum tax* (AMT) is a feature of the federal income tax system. First introduced in 1969, its intent was to collect taxes from wealthy individuals who might be able to shelter that income from the regular income tax system.[17] The AMT is literally a shadow income tax system. Taxpayers are required to calculate their taxes in two ways—under the regular tax system and the AMT—and are required, in effect, to pay the higher amount.

The AMT has become more controversial in recent years because it applies to more and more taxpayers. The Congressional Budget Office (CBO) estimates that, while 2 million people paid some AMT in 2002, that number will grow to 30 million by 2010.[18] The AMT has expanded its reach for two reasons. First, unlike many of the features of the regular tax system, the parameters of the AMT are not indexed for inflation. Second, because many people are experiencing reduction in taxes under the regular tax system due to the recent tax cuts, they are pushed onto the AMT.[19]

Because more people have been affected by the AMT over time, there has been substantial pressure to reform or eliminate the AMT. This is particularly true because more and more taxpayers who do not consider themselves wealthy are nonetheless paying the AMT. For example, in 2001, only about 5% of taxpayers with incomes between $100,000 and $200,000 paid the AMT. By 2005, that percentage had increased to 80%.[20] Eliminating the AMT, however, would be costly. CBO estimated that abolishing the AMT would result in $645 billion in lost revenue from fiscal year 2005 to fiscal year 2015, representing a loss of roughly 4% in individual income tax receipts over that period.[21]

State and Local Income Taxes. Most personal income taxes levied by the states and local governments are modeled on the federal tax. The states sometimes use the federal base or a modification of it. Some state income taxes, such as Colorado, Illinois, Indiana, and Pennsylvania, are simply a proportion of the federal tax owed. Most states have some kind of graduated rate structure, although the marginal tax rates are uniformly lower than federal marginal rates. California had the highest marginal tax rate (9.3%) in 2006.[22] When the federal government modifies its tax laws, changes inadvertently occur in state taxes. Local income taxes tend to be simple to calculate and involve flat, rather than progressive, tax rates.

Indexing. The federal government and some states use indexing in various forms to adjust income taxes in accordance with changes in price levels. If tax brackets are not altered and prices subsequently rise, then inflation will produce higher tax revenues because rising incomes will place citizens in higher tax brackets without any real increase in buying power. Besides adjusting tax brackets, other indexing techniques include modifying the standard deduction or personal exemption. A controversial issue is the measure of inflation used to adjust tax brackets (and many other revenue and expenditure elements). The consumer price index historically has been used, but many now feel that it overstates inflation, causing taxes to be lower than they should be and, more importantly, causing federal benefit programs to extend benefits greater than should be. We discuss this issue in Chapter 15.

Enforcement. A key income tax issue is enforcement. As noted above, the individual income tax relies heavily on honest self-reporting by taxpayers. Although employers withhold an important proportion of total individual income taxes paid, thereby enforcing tax collection for the Internal Revenue Service (IRS), enforcement remains a problem—and an especially difficult problem when taxpayers think the tax is unfair. Much income is never identified and thus never becomes part of the tax base. A large underground economy operates in which transactions occur in trade, payments in kind, and unrecorded payments in cash never become part of the income tax base. Measuring the size of that invisible economy is naturally difficult, but one study of 17 countries estimated that the underground or shadow economy may range from 10% to 20% of gross domestic product (GDP) in industrialized countries.[23] For the United States, income equal to an estimated 10% of GDP is unrecorded and therefore untaxed.

Tax Expenditures. Revenues that could be, but are not, collected constitute tax expenditures and can aid or hinder attempts to achieve an optimal balance. According to federal law, tax expenditures are "revenue losses . . . which allow a special exclusion, exemption, or deduction from gross income or which provide a special credit, a preferential rate of tax, or a deferral of tax liability."[24]

Tax expenditures are not new. Home mortgage interest payments (on up to two homes) have been deductible from income since 1910, for example. While tax expenditures may exist for any tax, the individual income tax, at the national and state levels, includes by far the largest number of tax expenditures, primarily because of the significant number of permitted deductions from gross income. Numerous exemptions from taxation or deductions from income for corporations have crept into law over the years as well.[25]

The federal budget contains 136 categories of tax expenditures, the largest being exclusion of employer contributions for medical insurance and care, estimated in the fiscal year 2007 proposed budget at more than $146 billion in revenue losses. Home mortgage interest deductions are second, with an estimated 2007 impact of almost $80 billion. Other notable tax expenditures include the exclusion of capital gains from home sales ($44 billion), the child tax credit ($42 billion), exclusion of 401(k) plans ($40 billion), and charitable contributions ($34 billion).[26]

Tax expenditures are not automatically bad. The public policy goal for the home mortgage interest deduction is to encourage and enable individual family home ownership. Exclusion of employer pension and medical insurance contributions is meant to increase savings for pensions and reduce the cost of health care. The housing exemption may help make housing affordable to moderate-income families, but it also benefits more affluent taxpayers and may be of no benefit to low-income families. Is the housing exemption, then, a factor that furthers or detracts from equity?

Since the 1970s, tax expenditures have become an important issue in debates over tax reform. These measures reduce the revenue flowing into government treasuries and can represent "loopholes" for the wealthy. Like the federal government, some state governments routinely report estimates of tax expenditures (see Chapter 6).

Corporate Income Taxes

Taxes on corporate earnings have been defended as appropriate given the size of corporate economic power and the fact that some individuals might be able to escape taxation by "hiding" their income in corporations. On the other hand, corporate income taxes seem to result in double taxation. First a corporation is taxed, and then individuals are taxed on dividends paid on their corporate stock holdings. There have been proposals to replace the corporate income tax with a tax on net business receipts to avoid this double taxation, but these proposals have not attracted much interest. Proposals to exclude dividends from individual income taxation also have been unsuccessful.

Tax Base. Corporate taxes use net corporate earnings as a base. Whereas the individual income tax base basically considers income before expenses, except for some deductions and exclusions, corporate income taxes apply only to net profit after operating expenses. In addition, some deductions are allowed for capital losses, operating losses, depreciation of capital investments, charitable contributions, and expenditures for research and development. How these deductions are applied is often controversial, such as how rapidly a corporation can depreciate capital investments. The federal corporate tax rates gradually increase from 15% to 35%. The United States top corporate tax rates are at the high end of the rates applied in other Organization for Economic Co-operation and Development (OECD) countries, although the majority of these countries had top rates that exceeded 30% in 2003.[27] As a percentage of GDP, receipts from the federal corporate income tax are actually lower than every other OECD country with the exception of Germany and Iceland.[28]

Many states have corporate income taxes as well, although the importance of the corporate income tax has declined at the state level in recent years. In 2002, corporate income taxes accounted for approximately 5% of overall state revenues, about one-half of the level of two decades earlier.[29]

Tax Incidence. The primary issue as regards corporate taxation is who actually carries the burden of corporate taxes. Corporations may be able to increase prices and, in effect, make consumers pay the tax, or they may limit wage increases to workers and, in effect, have them pay the tax. Another option is to take taxes out of profits, thereby reducing dividends for investors. Corporations probably use some combination of these shifts.

An issue involving state corporate taxes is whether they affect decisions to locate and expand operations in one state over another. Legislators and executives in a state government fear that any increase in their corporate income taxes will discourage corporations from locating in the state and encourage others to move out of the state. For example, several states (including Iowa, Massachusetts, Nebraska, and Texas) tax manufacturing companies only on in-state sales. This single-factor business tax apportions the income manufacturers receive into in-state earnings and earnings from out-of-state sales, and taxes only the former. The expectation is that what a state loses in tax revenue it will gain from companies already there expanding their operations in the state and from companies relocating to the state. In Chapter 15 we discuss interstate (and sometimes interlocal) competition with tax incentives and other benefits to attract business investment, sometimes called smokestack chasing.

Payroll Taxes

Insurance trust funds, which are separate accounts set up to hold certain earmarked revenues (see Chapter 11), are financed by means of charges on salaries and wages (the charges are paid by employees, employers, or both). These are typically referred to as payroll taxes, and they are differentiated from income taxes because they are taxes on wages and salaries only, as opposed to more comprehensive taxes on income. These charges are not taxes in as much as they do not generate revenue to be used to pay for services; instead, the programs provide benefits to the people who are covered by them. Employers and employees pay into these systems, and people earn benefit credits through contributions made during their working careers. Social insurance receipts rose as a percentage of GDP from 4.5% in 1972 (as low as 3% in the early 1960s) to 6.5% in 2005.[30]

Social Security and Supplemental Security Income. Social Security is a trust program of vast proportions. Its complexities far exceed the scope of this book. Here we sketch its overall structure.

Three major programs are administered directly by the Social Security Administration. The first, Old Age and Survivors Insurance, is a benefits program for retired workers and their survivors. The second program, Disability Insurance (DI), provides benefits for covered workers who are disabled and cannot work. In 2004, the Social Security Administration paid out benefits to 4.5 million individuals, including 1.9 million retired workers, 800,000 disabled workers, and 1.8 million spouses, children, or survivors of retired or disabled workers.[31] In fiscal year 2004 benefits paid out for Old Age and Survivors Insurance benefits totaled $415 billion. Total benefits for DI in the same year totaled $78 billion.[32]

The third major program under Social Security provides monthly benefits to people who are aged, blind, and disabled. This program is known as Supplemental Security Income (SSI).[33] SSI funds come from general tax revenues, rather than from employer-employee contributions. Unlike DI, SSI does not require work credits for eligibility but does require that recipients be needy. It is possible to qualify for both programs, although qualifying for DI has the effect of reducing SSI benefits. In 2004, 7.1 million people received $37.0 billion in benefits under the SSI program.[34]

Legislation passed in 1983 greatly modified the financing of Old Age and Survivors Insurance to improve the solvency for the long term. Estimates then were that the trust fund would be insolvent before 1990 unless corrective actions were taken. While the increases in both the employer and the employee contribution rates and an increase in the amount of annual income subject to the tax will satisfy the fund's needs for some decades, the consensus is that the program will need revising again, and that the longer reform is postponed, the more dramatic will be the changes required. There are various estimates as to the date at which annual disbursements from the Social Security Trust Fund will exceed annual revenues. The wide variance in estimates is caused by assumptions about retirement age, employment rates that swing with economic fluctuations, and labor force participation rates coupled with population age shifts.

In 2006, the Congressional Budget Office updated its long-term projections for Social Security. These projections indicate that revenues will exceed spending in the Social Security trust funds through fiscal year 2019. Even after that point, however, CBO estimates that Social Security will have enough revenues to cover all scheduled benefits until fiscal year 2046, because of the repayment of funds that the trust funds have loaned to the non-Social Security portion of the federal budget. After 2046, however, unless there is an infusion of funds into the trust funds, Social Security will be unable to pay the full amount of current projected benefits. At that point, benefits could be reduced to match trust fund revenues.[35] For example, if revenues were to come in at 75% of spending, then all benefits would be reduced to 75% of the full benefit level that would be paid under the law. Such a change would inevitably create a political crisis of overwhelming magnitude.

Several issues have fueled the debate over Social Security reform, and the motivations for reform among many groups are not necessarily consistent. First is the issue we might label "violation of trust." This issue is based on an emotional (mis)understanding that the fund is supposed to be a trust fund exclusively for financing Social Security benefits. Many citizens assume that the funds they and their employers contribute to the system are being held in trust, invested much like pension funds to yield the benefits that will be paid out to them in the future. Politicians make a similar claim in their criticisms of Social Security. In reality, each year's payments into the Social Security Trust Fund are used to pay claims to beneficiaries in that year. For some time to come, the payments into the fund will exceed payments to beneficiaries out of the fund. Those excess payments create a surplus in the fund, and that surplus in turn is lent to the U.S. Treasury at the equivalent of the 30-year Treasury bond to finance part of federal spending. The alternative to the Treasury borrowing from the Social Security fund is to force the Treasury to borrow from the U.S. and overseas capital markets. Under such a scheme, the surplus Social Security funds would need to be invested some place rather than sit idle—perhaps the stock market (discussed below)?

Thus, one motivation for reform is the political point of view that the fund should behave as a revolving fund, with proceeds paid into the fund being invested as in most pension funds. That view somewhat naively assumes that private pension funds pay out benefits commensurate with the results of investment of funds paid in. That statement is true of defined contributions plans (retirement plans where individuals pay a set amount into a retirement plan, but are not guaranteed a specific return), but defined benefit plans pay out specific levels of benefits regardless of whether the fund investments are sufficient to meet those benefit payouts. Just as an employer with a defined benefits pension fund is obligated to meet the benefit payouts defined in the plan, from business net profits if necessary, so the federal government is obligated to meet whatever Congress determines will be the benefit structure, first from the trust fund itself and then from other federal revenues as necessary. Unless Congress fails to appropriate funds to meet legislated benefits (if and when the surplus in the fund turns into a deficit) or passes legislation so as to lower benefits, then the trust fund issue really is not an issue. Instead, it is a convenient political football for both parties to kick around.

A second motivation for reform is closely linked to the debates on the federal budget surplus or deficit. Because the fund shows a surplus, and all revenue to the fund counts as part of the federal government's revenue total, the size of the federal deficit is disguised. The more fiscally conservative believe that the practice of using the trust fund surplus to finance part of other spending is inappropriate. The less conservative position was articulated in the Bush administration's 2003 budget, which noted that unlike private "trust" custodians who legally must manage the assets on behalf of the beneficiary, the federal government owns the assets and earnings and can legally change collections, payments, and even the purposes of the funds.[36]

A third issue discussed by advocates for reform is that the funds being paid into Social Security should be earning more than the implicit 30-year Treasury bond rate. The bull market of the 1990s particularly fueled this aspect of the debate, as stocks earned dramatic returns—two and three times the rate of the 30-year Treasury bond. Proposals have been advanced to invest the funds flowing into the trust fund in the stock market, so as to earn higher benefits for future pensioners.

In 1996, the Advisory Council on Social Security, unable to reach a consensus, presented three options for reforming the way Social Security funds are invested. One option, favored by six of the Council's 13 members, was that 40% of the trust fund's money should be invested in the stock market. A second option, favored by two members, recommended that workers put 1.6% of their pay (slightly less than one-third of their own contributions) into personal retirement accounts, with the rest of the employee contributions and all of the employer contributions going into the Social Security Trust Fund as they do now. Individuals would have some say in how the personal retirement accounts would be invested, although Social Security would administer the accounts. The third option, favored by the remaining five members of the Council, would replace the current guaranteed benefit system with a system in which workers would be required to put 5% of their pay into personal accounts, and individuals would bear all the responsibility for determining investments.[37]

In 2001, the Bush administration appointed a new, nonpartisan advisory panel with a prominent Democrat and a prominent Republican as co-chairs.[38] The commission concluded that "Social Security will be strengthened if modernized to include a system of voluntary personal accounts."[39] However, the drastic decline of the stock market between 2001 and early 2003, though not ending discussions of investing Social Security funds in the stock market, greatly diminished the enthusiasm for proposals to invest Social Security funds in the stock market. Although President Bush invested some political capital in trying to encourage the Republican Congress to pass Social Security reforms, including private accounts, early in his second term, Congress was very reluctant to touch Social Security, and Democrats were sharply critical of the plan.[40]

Medicare. In addition to the three main Social Security programs, a fourth one, Medicare, is administered by the Centers for Medicare and Medicaid Services (CMS) in the Department of Health and Human Services. Medicare provides basic health insurance to the elderly, with a separately funded catastrophic coverage component, and is funded by contributions through Social Security, premiums paid by persons covered under the program, and general revenues. Medicare has become one of the major contributors to rapidly rising federal expenditures for health care. Medicare outlays totaled almost $300 billion in fiscal year 2004.[41] In 2002, Congress and the Bush administration passed the Medicare Modernization Act, which established, for the first time, a prescription drug benefit for Medicare that took effect in 2006. Estimates of the ten-year cost of this entitlement expansion ranged from $400 billion to $500 billion.

Reforms that would reduce or control Medicare spending have been discussed, but have not even progressed as far as a presidential proposal, with the notable exception of the failed Clinton health care plan in 1994, which proposed an overhaul of the entire U.S. health care system, including Medicare. In 1997, estimates were that the Medicare trust funds would become insolvent before the end of the decade. That prediction did not materialize, as the payroll tax rate was increased. Reform proposals especially have aimed at reducing the incentives for physicians and hospitals to order expensive treatments for Medicare patients and to reduce the possibilities for fraudulent charges. Holding down reimbursement rates slowed the slide toward a Medicare deficit, and on the agenda for longer-term reform is moving more people into managed care organizations and away from individual physicians.

The combination of the same demographic factors that are driving the Social Security imbalance and the pace of medical care inflation contribute to an even bleaker long-term outlook for Medicare than for Social Security.[42] Almost inevitable is eventually raising the age at which one becomes eligible for Medicare from 65 to perhaps 67. The program's reform is tied up in debates over budget surpluses and deficits. The program's impact on the budget has become so significant that most agree that it can tip the budget into deficit or surplus, especially as the eligible population increases when the baby boom generation becomes eligible.

Medicaid. A fifth program often mentioned in conjunction with these other programs is Medicaid. It does not technically fit under a discussion of payroll taxes since it is funded by federal and state tax revenues as opposed to payroll taxes earmarked for the Social Security Trust Fund. In aggregate, the federal government pays about 57% of the costs of Medicaid, with state and local governments paying the remainder.[43] From 1970 through 2005, total federal Medicaid spending increased from $2.7 billion to almost $183 billion, which represented a fivefold increase in the size of the program as a percentage of GDP (from 0.3% to 1.5%).[44] Medicaid provides medical care to the poor and the medically indigent (persons who are not classified as poor but who cannot afford medical care). Medicaid and SSI are not trust programs as defined earlier, because their funds come from general tax revenues and not revenues earmarked for special trust funds. (For a discussion of Medicaid, see Chapter 14.)

Unemployment Insurance. The second largest insurance trust for state governments is unemployment compensation. This program is administered by the states within a framework imposed by the federal government. A floor on benefits is set nationally, although states have the option of exceeding the floor. The program is supported by payroll taxes paid mainly by employers, although in a few states employees are required to make supplementary payments. It is expected to generate sufficient revenues during prosperous periods to cover payments to unemployed workers during recessionary periods. Sometimes state programs can run into a deficit situation, such as during a sustained recession or occasionally because of temporary timing differences between payments into the funds and payments out. In such cases, the federal government loans money to the states but expects repayment with interest. Obviously, a state with a declining tax base can face severe problems in financing its unemployment insurance program. The economic downturn of the early 2000s underscored this problem for many states.

Workers' Compensation. Another important insurance trust at the state level is workers' compensation, which provides cash benefits to persons who, because of job-related injuries and illnesses, are unable to work. Accidents at work may disable people temporarily or permanently. Poor working conditions can cause physical and mental health problems. In addition to cash benefits, the program pays for medical care and rehabilitation services.

Property Taxes

Taxes on wealth are based on accumulated value in some asset rather than on current earnings from the asset. Real and personal property, financial assets, and equipment are important types of wealth that sometimes are subject to taxation. The wealth tax that is most important in the eyes of taxpayers, however, is the real property or real estate tax. The property tax is the one most reviled by taxpayers, largely because it is regarded by many as the most unfair.[45] This tax is the almost exclusive domain of local governments. Despite forecasts of its demise, the property tax remains the largest single own-source generator of revenue for local governments (it is exceeded only by intergovernmental revenue, as described in Chapter 2), although it has declined in recent years relative to other state and local taxes. It funds almost 75% of locally-raised school district revenues. Courts in at least 17 states, however, have overturned their states' financing systems that relied heavily on local property taxes.[46] The argument is that despite state aid to local school districts, almost sole reliance on the property tax to finance education at the local level means unequal education opportunities across the state (see Chapter 14). The property tax is also the most important source of local own-source revenue for funding urban services in developing countries, although user charges (discussed in Chapter 5) may be a faster growing source of local revenue in the more prosperous emerging market economies.[47]

The justification for using the property tax as the major revenue source for local government is that the services provided by local government supposedly increase the economic value of one's property. It is widely thought that people select their place of residence based on the quality of local schools and other public services. In high-quality service jurisdictions, housing costs are typically higher, reflecting higher costs for delivering services and higher expectations of home buyers for quality services. Property taxes reimburse local government for higher-quality services. The argument goes as follows: If more general taxes, such as the sales tax, were used to finance services that benefit property owners, then property owners would be less aware of the costs of those services and therefore insist on more and higher-quality services. Evidence has been found to support this argument in developing countries, where demand for urban services is much higher in cities that do not use property and other local taxes and charges to finance those services.[48]

The property tax is also less susceptible to tax avoidance than other broad-based taxes because it is clearly visible and is immobile. People can buy goods in other jurisdictions or order goods over the Internet and easily avoid paying sales tax (see the discussion in the next chapter). Property taxes, by comparison, are difficult to avoid. To the extent that they operate as a quasi-price for the public services provided in a given jurisdiction, property taxes are justified on the basis of the benefit principle, as described above. One argument is that homeowners understand that the value of local public services substantially affects the value of their homes, and that they are vigilant in their control of local government largely for that reason.[49]

One way to tie the benefits of services affecting property values to taxes on property is through *tax increment financing* (see Chapter 13 for discussion of bond issues backed by expected tax incremental increases). Tax increment financing has been used in redevelopment of inner cities to capitalize on the economic and financial gains that stem from a major rehabilitation project for a contiguous area usually characterized by urban blight and abandoned properties. Prior to city government action, many property owners in such areas derive no benefits from their properties, and the city is able to collect little or no property tax. A redevelopment project changes conditions so that the property in the redeveloped area attains new value, and the property tax gains from that new value are set aside to pay for financing the redevelopment. Some use also has been made of tax increment financing in rural areas, but it is not as valuable a tool there. Property tax rates are typically much lower in rural areas, land values are more volatile, and investors in bonds to support rural infrastructure tax increment funded projects perceive higher risks.[50]

The main policy issue with the property tax is its regressive nature. Higher-income taxpayers tend to have a larger proportion of their wealth in assets that are not subject to the property tax. As a consequence, these taxpayers generally pay a disproportionately lower property tax (as a percentage of their income) as compared with middle- and lower-income taxpayers, whose only major asset may be their home. For middle- and lower-income taxpayers, most of their wealth is being taxed each year. For renters, the regressive effects of the property tax depend on the extent to which the landlord can pass on the property tax through the rent. For all these reasons, the regressive nature of the property tax fuels controversy. In addition, the property tax is relatively complicated to implement and to maintain. Because the local jurisdiction must establish the tax base (the value of each property within the jurisdiction) rather than basing it on some external objective source, updating the tax base for the property tax is always controversial when carried out.

Tax Base. The base of the real property tax is the assessed value of the land and any improvements on it, such as homes, factories, and other structures. The value is what the property would sell for if placed on the market. Value for commercial and industrial property sometimes is reflected in the income earned by a corporation from the property or facility.

Often the assessed value of property may increase beyond the ability of taxpayers to afford the tax bills. One leading example of this would be in cases where there are rapidly rising property values, and longtime residents (who might not be able to afford to buy their houses in the current market) experience ever-increasing tax bills. These residents may be "property rich" but "income poor." Many states and localities have instituted *homestead exemptions* to address this sort of problem. Under these exemptions, a set initial amount is excluded from assessed valuation. This would tend to benefit those individuals with homes that have lower assessed values, since a higher percentage of the assessed value would be exempt from the property tax for those properties.

Another such issue arises in the case of farmland in metropolitan areas. As metropolitan areas expand and encroach upon farming areas, the value of the land increases even though the use remains unchanged. Situations emerge in which taxes rise beyond what farmers can afford and create a market incentive for the land to be sold and subdivided for homes and other development. All states provide some form of protection for farmland as a means of preserving rural land and discouraging urban sprawl, with reduced tax assessments for farming and other undeveloped land being the most common method. Often these tax breaks are really postponements. If the land is later sold for subdivision and housing at a value much higher than the land's worth as farmland, the seller must then pay back property taxes reflecting the residential use tax rate. As with other tax preferences, property tax reductions to preserve farmland can have unintended consequences. One study of Pennsylvania's program concluded that it preserved land in rural areas where population pressure is light, so the need for preservation is small.[51] Many states also buy the development rights from property owners as a way of preserving land for open space or other purposes.

Many properties are completely tax-exempt in the United States. Federal and state land is normally exempt from local property taxes, for example, although these jurisdictions may make payments in lieu of taxation. Places of worship, such as churches, synagogues, and mosques are tax exempt, as are most parsonages and other related properties. Nonprofit hospitals, YMCAs and YWCAs, nonprofit cemeteries, and the like are usually tax exempt as well.

When tax-exempt properties account for a large proportion of a jurisdiction's potential tax base, the effects of tax exemption can be severe. Some governments have aggressively challenged the tax-exempt status of some nonprofit organizations. The basis for the challenge is that some nonprofit organizations produce for-profit goods and services. Philadelphia, for example, employs a five-part test. To remain exempt from property and other taxes, a nonprofit has to prove that it: "advances a charitable purpose; gives away a substantial portion of its services; benefits people who are legitimate subjects of charity; relieves government of some of its burden; and operates entirely free of profit motives."[52] However, Philadelphia lacks the authority to force those nonprofits that do not meet the tests to pay property taxes. Instead, it asks, with some success, for voluntary payments in lieu of taxes.

A different situation may exist in cases where state governments grant blanket local property tax exemptions. In this case, the state government makes decisions that cost local governments money, and these exemptions may not be directly targeted toward those individuals that most need tax relief. In many such instances, the lost local property tax revenue is replaced by the state government. A study of a homestead exemption program in New York State suggests that there is some evidence that local governments are less efficient in the provision of local public services because those services are funded to a lesser extent by local taxes than by state assistance. The argument here is that, to the extent that state taxes are financing these services, this reduces pressure on local officials to cut back on costs to provide a given level of output.[53]

Assessment. After registering all properties in the taxing jurisdiction, the first major step to generating revenue from the tax is to assess the value of the properties. Local governments do not, in fact, have a direct way of measuring the actual market value of all properties within their jurisdiction. At any given time, the local government can know directly what recent properties have sold for, but this is only a small fraction of all the properties in the registered base. This creates a substantial challenge, in that they need to establish an assessed value for each property absent real information on the sales price of most properties. Many governments use the *market data approach* to assessment. In this method, properties that have not sold are assessed by comparison to similar properties where a market price can be observed. The greatest challenge here is ensuring that properties that are assumed to be comparable are comparable in fact. The probability of doing this can be improved by inspecting individual properties and cataloguing their characteristics, but this is a time-consuming process, particularly if done on an annual basis. Adjustments to property values may be done annually or only once every several years.

While the goal in many jurisdictions is to assess each property at its full market value, in practice many jurisdictions assess parcels at a percentage or fraction of the full market value. The ratio of the assessed value to the market value is known as the *assessment ratio.* A home whose market value is $120,000 would be assessed at only $24,000 if the assessment ratio were 20%. In practice, it should make no difference whether the full value or a fraction of it is used. Fractional assessment simply requires a higher tax rate than market value assessment to produce the same revenue.

Taxpayers may find some psychological solace in fractional assessment, but problems would arise in cases where properties within the same jurisdiction are assessed at different fractions of their market values. This might occur, for example, if reassessments were done of different properties at different times. If some properties are assessed at one percentage of market value and other properties at a different percentage, then the tax burden is no longer proportionate to the value of the property. This is less likely to be an issue where properties are assessed at 100% of market value, particularly because taxpayers are much more likely to know whether their property has been over assessed in this case. Even where the goal is assessing at full market value, fractional assessment may be used to differentiate types of properties. For example, rural property may be assessed at a lower fraction than highly developed property.

Inaccurate and inconsistent assessment practices can cause problems of both horizontal and vertical equity. Horizontal equity problems exist because properties that have the same market value in fact are assessed at different rates, resulting in taxpayers who should be paying the same level of tax paying different levels. Numerous studies have found evidence of horizontal inequity because of lack of data, assessor error, or bias.[54] Vertical equity concerns exist when properties of different market values are assessed at different percentages of those market values. A study found that, in particular, lower-valued houses were assessed at closer to their full market value than higher-valued houses. This means that less affluent taxpayers pay a higher percentage of local property taxes than would be the case were all properties valued at the same percentage of full market value.[55]

For a local government instituting the property tax for the first time, the valuation process is almost overwhelming. Traditional valuation procedures involve comprehensive tax mapping to locate every property. An assessor must visit each property, measuring the foundation to determine square footage, noting construction details, and recording information about the condition of the structure. This type of comprehensive process is now occurring in many developing countries, where property taxes are being newly applied or where existing records are incomplete and largely useless.[56]

For most jurisdictions in the United States, properties have been constructed under building permits that require supplying information about construction details to the local jurisdiction. Periodic inspections of the properties when under construction, conducted by local code enforcement officers or building inspectors, provide additional information. A database, then, can be devised using existing building records and information about sales of properties when deeds are transferred. As new structures are built, they can be added to the database.

Exhibit 4–2 shows a property tax valuation system in Orange County, North Carolina, that is considered a model for the country. Techniques such as those used in Orange County help to foster a perception of fairness among taxpayers. Property owners conclude that they are paying their fair share and are not being

| Exhibit 4–2 | **Property Tax Valuation in Orange County, NC** |

Orange County, North Carolina, has what is considered a model property tax valuation system. It is fully computerized and includes diverse information about each property in the county. Besides information about the location of each lot, the size of the structure, and the number of baths, a drawing of the lot and the location of the structure on it are included in the computerized file and can be displayed onscreen. Of course, printed maps of properties are available as well.

Characteristics of Properties

- Property address
- Plot map and reference to deed register
- Area of lot (square footage)
- Occupancy (single-family dwelling, two-family, multifamily)
- Size of dwelling (square footage of living space)
- Number of structures
- Number of stories of each structure
- Basement, slab, or crawl space
- Foundation construction method
- Exterior construction method
- Roof type and roofing materials
- Number of rooms
- Number of bathrooms
- Number of bedrooms
- Year built
- Number of fireplaces
- Interior finish
- Floor type
- Built-in appliances
- HVAC system
- Special features (spas, etc.)
- Landscaping
- Land topography
- Utility connections
- Paved or unpaved driveway
- Last sale price and date

Source: Extracted from Office of the Tax Assessor (2002). Orange County database. Hillsborough, NC: Orange County.

overcharged while other taxpayers are being undercharged. If these equity considerations are met, then the likelihood of a taxpayer revolt is minimized. However, it does not make the property tax popular, as it is likely that it is the most hated tax in the country.

Tax Rates. Property tax rates are a percentage of assessed value. The rate is expressed in mills, with one mill being one-tenth of one percent. As applied to property taxes, a one-mill rate yields $1 of revenue for every $1,000 of assessed value. A property tax rate of 68.5 mills as applied to a $120,000 property assessed at 20% of market value would yield $1,644 (120 × 0.2 × 68.5 = 1,644).

Local jurisdictions often determine the annual property tax rate by calculating backward from projected expenditures minus other revenues. The property tax increase then is expected to make up the budget gap. The community's decision makers simply determine how many additional mills will be needed to close the gap. Of course, attempts are made to avoid such tax increases by keeping expenditures as low as considered possible. The process of adjusting the tax rate to match expenditure requirements probably accounts for the great popularity of the property tax among local officials. This tax is one over which officials have considerable control, unlike other taxes that depend on the economy (income and sales taxes) or intergovernmental aid.

Many local governments in areas of rapidly increasing property values have found that they are able to accommodate budgetary increases above the base level at declining property tax rates. In most of these cases, the rate of assessment increase exceeds the percentage of rate reduction, thus resulting in a rising tax bill. The key decision for any local government involves how often to reassess properties. With the housing boom of the 1990s and 2000s, substantial incentives have existed to reassess properties frequently in order to take advantage of increasing property values and therefore be able to produce increasing levels of revenue at declining property tax rates. This may result from increased demands on the part of citizens for additional services, or by desires by government officials to expand government.[57]

With the cooling of the real estate market starting in 2006, many local governments found that their ability to maintain revenues with declining, or even stable, tax rates was compromised.

Circuit Breakers. As taxes rise, some property owners may encounter considerable difficulty in paying their tax bills and may even be forced to sell their homes and move into rental housing. To alleviate this problem, several states use *circuit break-er* systems that set a limit on taxes, particularly for low-income elderly persons. A qualified homeowner pays an amount up to the limit, and the state pays any additional amount owed. Often a state bases the limit on some income criterion: when property taxes exceed a specified percentage of the taxpayer's income, the state pays the difference.[58]

Personal Property. Besides taxing real property, some jurisdictions tax personal property. For individuals, such property includes furniture, vehicles, clothing, jewelry, and the like. Intangible personal property includes stocks, bonds, and other financial instruments such as mortgages. For corporations, personal property includes equipment, raw materials, and items in inventory. Taxes on personal property are unpopular and subject to considerable evasion.

Taxing and Spending Limitations. Although citizens seemingly have had little opportunity to affect taxes and spending other than through the process of selecting elected representatives, 1978 changed all that. In that year, California voters approved Proposition 13, an initiative that limited the property tax rate to 1% of market value. That provision by itself would have required a rollback in taxes, but an additional provision further cut taxes. Property assessments were to be returned to their values in 1975, when property was considerably less expensive.

Although tax limitation measures were not new, Proposition 13 began a new era in which government officials were forced to consider taxpayer reaction and to limit taxes and spending.[59] Many state and local governments followed California's lead during the late 1970s and early 1980s by passing statutory limits or, in some cases, adding restrictions to state constitutions. California voters approved Proposition 4 in 1979, which limited both state and local government expenditures. In the following years, restrictive measures were adopted in about half of the states. Massachusetts, which had come to be known as "Taxachusetts," gained notoriety in 1980 as a result of its passage of Proposition 2½. This measure required that local governments reduce taxes by 15% each year until they equaled 2.5% of market value.[60]

"By 1990, 21 states had enacted potentially binding limitations and 13 had enacted nonbinding limitations on the finances of their local governments."[61] The elections of 1994 and 1996 brought more conservative control to many state legislatures and ushered in a new round of tax limitation proposals.[62] Oregon, Colorado, and Missouri also passed tax or spending limitations in the mid- to late 1990s.

The original stimulus behind what came to be known as the taxpayers' revolt was the sharp rise in property values and, consequently, tax bills, but a more generally negative attitude emerged—the attitude that government officials have an insatiable appetite for spending. Besides taxing too much, governments allegedly use the revenues to interfere needlessly in the lives of citizens and the operations of corporations. Property taxes remain one of the most criticized forms of taxation. This is probably because of dissatisfaction with the results school systems are producing, which are funded almost entirely by the property tax.[63] The result has been several types of tax and expenditure limitations. One review classified them into five categories:

1. Overall property tax limitation (for example, limit to maximum annual percentage increase)

2. Specific property tax limitation (for example, limit on use of property tax to finance education)

3. Property tax levy limit (for example, ceiling on amount of tax)

4. General revenue or general expenditure increase limit (for example, limit annual expenditure increase to a specific limit)

5. Property tax assessment increase limit (limit on the assessed value increase)[64]

Most of these limitations focus on the property tax specifically, but the fourth (overall revenue or expenditure limits) is more broadly restrictive, and can apply at the state as well as the local level. Taxpayers' concerns have caused many state and local governments to increase communication with the public on what is accomplished with tax dollars and how taxes are kept to a minimum. Minnesota, for example, enacted a law requiring the construction of an overall index calculating the cost of everything residents pay to the government as a percentage of personal income. Not only are taxes included, but so are all fees, charges, and any other payment to government. The index is kept for different state departments and individual local governments so that citizens throughout the state can compare their own government with others and with limitation guidelines.[65]

The effect of these limitations has varied, but in most cases local governments made up for the revenue loss through other sources, usually non-general-revenue sources. In some cases, state governments almost immediately made up for the shortfall.[66] Overall, spending may have declined in some jurisdictions but not enough to show up in aggregate figures for individual states. There is some evidence, however, that these limitations are more constraining on local property taxes in the long run than in the short run.[67] The main effects seem to have been fivefold.

First, state legislatures and local governments are much more reluctant to initiate new programs and especially to propose tax increases or new taxes. In the case of new programs, this is presumably because there is more uncertainty surrounding the affordability of these programs in the future. The reluctance to impose tax increases probably relates to knowledge of the underlying disposition of taxpayers toward these increases in states with tax and expenditure limitations (TELs).

Second, combined with major cutbacks in federal aid to states and localities in the 1980s, the limitation movement set these governments on an imaginative hunt for alternative finance measures. The significantly greater use of impact fees, discussed earlier, and other direct charges to those benefiting from services was an outgrowth of the tax revolt.

Third, states provided increased financial assistance to hard-pressed local governments. For example, when Michigan ran into problems with property tax funding for education, the state increased the sales tax and, in turn, used state funds for formerly local education funds. A more explicit example is Oregon's experience with Ballot Measure 5, which required the state to replace lost property tax revenue with state aid, thus shifting many of the fiscal effects of the initiatives to the state government.[68] Sometimes that state aid has come at a price—namely, various strings attached by states for their aid. One simple example is that local governments were forbidden by Oregon from giving their employees salary increases greater than those given to state employees.

Fourth, overall expenditures have been cut somewhat and some services have been reduced, either in quality or quantity, as a means of curbing spending.[69] Essential services such as law enforcement and fire protection have been maintained, albeit at decreased levels. Budget problems forced cutbacks in maintenance of buildings and purchase of new vehicles and equipment.[70] Overall, however, tax and expenditure limitations did not materially change the relative amounts that state and local governments spend on government functions.[71] Some evidence indicates that spending cuts have produced long-term quality decline, at least in some services. For example, public school student performance has declined in several states that have imposed expenditure limitations, even after controlling for a number of other possible influences.[72]

Fifth, tax and expenditure limitations have had differential effects on the capacity of local governments to rely on local property taxes to deliver services. A nationwide study found that these limitations do not offer a uniform constraint across jurisdictions, but rather represent a greater constraint for some than others. In the case of both general purpose governments (cities or counties) and school districts, there is significant variation across these jurisdictions within single metropolitan areas. In particular, the effects seem to be "greatest within counties comprising the urban core and those with relatively more disadvantaged populations."[73]

Summary

Governments use numerous revenue sources to support their operations, with taxes obviously being one of the most important types. In devising a tax system, governments need to consider the adequacy of the tax revenue being produced, the equity of the tax system (on both ability to pay grounds and on the basis of who benefits from local public services), economic efficiency, collectibility, and political feasibility. Taxes on personal and corporate income are important sources of income for the federal government and state governments. They are highly complex taxes, and the personal income tax in particular is usually adjusted to individual taxpayer conditions. Payroll taxes are typically used to finance particular services, and are earmarked for those purposes. By far the largest payroll taxes are for Social Security and Medicare. The property tax, which is the largest tax for local governments, is heavily influenced by assessment practices, which can substantially affect the equity and the production of the tax. The use of property taxes is constrained by the imposition of constitutional or statutory limitations.

Notes

1. Walden, M. (2003). Dynamic revenue curves for North Carolina taxes. *Public Budgeting & Finance, 23, Winter*, 49–64.

2. Magner, N., Sobery, J. S., & Welker, R. B. et al. (1998). Tax decision making in municipal governments: citizens' reactions to outcomes and procedures. *Journal of Public Budgeting and Financial Management, 9*, 552–570.

3. Burgat, P. & Jeanrenaud, C. (1996). Do benefit and equal absolute sacrifice rules really lead to different taxation levels? *Public Finance Quarterly, 24*, 148–162.

4. U.S. Congressional Budget Office (2005). *Effective federal tax rates: 1979 to 2003.* Washington, DC: U.S. Government Printing Office.

5. U.S. Congressional Budget Office (2005). *Historical effective tax rates: 1979 to 2003.* Washington, DC: U.S. Government Printing Office, 4–5.

6. Chaloupka, F. J. & Grossman, M. (1997). Price, tobacco control policies and smoking among young adults. *Journal of Health Economics, 16*, 359–373.

7. McClure, C. E., Jr. & Zodrow, G. R. (1994). The study and practice of income tax policy. In J. M. Quigley & E. Smolensky (Eds.), *Modern public finance*. Cambridge, MA: Harvard University Press, 185.

8. Urban Institute-Brookings Tax Policy Center (2006). *Cigarette Rates 2001–2006.* Retrieved January 22, 2007, from http://www.taxpolicycenter.org/TaxFacts/ TFDB/TFTemplate.cfm?Docid=433.

9. Nelson, S. C. & Cronin, J. (2006). Adjusted gross income. In J. Cordes, R. Ebel, & J. Gravelle (Eds.), *Encyclopedia of taxation and tax policy*. Washington, DC: The Urban Institute Press, 3.

10. Pollack, S. (1996). *The failure of U.S. tax policy: revenue and politics.* University Park, PA: Pennsylvania State University Press.

11. Green, R. (2005). Mortgage interest deduction. In J. Cordes, R. Ebel, & J. Gravelle (Eds.), *Encyclopedia of taxation and tax policy*. Washington, DC: The Urban Institute Press, 260–261.

12. Maguire, S. (2005). State and local tax deductibility. In J. Cordes, R. Ebel, & J. Gravelle (Eds.), *Encyclopedia of taxation and tax policy*. Washington, DC: The Urban Institute Press, 367–370.

13. Randolph, W. (2005). Charitable deductions. In J. Cordes, R. Ebel, & J. Gravelle (Eds.), *Encyclopedia of taxation and tax policy*. Washington, DC: The Urban Institute Press, 51–53.

14. Slemrod, J. (2006). The role of misconceptions in support for regressive tax reform. *National Tax Journal, 59*, 57–75.

15. Dowd, T. (2005). Distinguishing between short-term and long-term recipients of the earned income tax credit. *National Tax Journal, 58*, 807–828.

16. Dickert-Conlin, S., Fitzpatrick, K. & Hanson, A. (2005). Utilization of tax credits by low-income individuals. *National Tax Journal, 58*, 743–785.

17. Weiner, D. (2006). Alternative minimum tax. In J. Cordes, R. Ebel, & J. Gravelle (Eds.), *Encyclopedia of taxation and tax policy*. Washington, DC: The Urban Institute Press, 11.

18. Holtz-Eakin, D. (2005). The individual alternative minimum tax. Statement before the Subcommittee on Taxation and IRS Oversight, Committee on Finance, United States Senate, May 23.

19. Holtz-Eakin, D. (2005). *The individual alternative minimum tax, 2*.

20. Holtz-Eakin, D. (2005). *The individual alternative minimum tax, 5*.

21. Holtz-Eakin, D. (2005). *The individual alternative minimum tax, 2*

22. Tax Policy Center (2006). State individual income taxes (tax rates for tax year 2006). http://www.taxpolicycenter.org/TaxFacts/TFDB/content/PDF/state_incomerates.pdf.

23. Light on the shadows (1997). *The Economist, 343, May 3*, 63–64.

24. Congressional Budget and Impoundment Control Act (1974). P.L. 93–344, 88 Stat. 297, 299.

25. Gravelle, J. G. (2006). Tax expenditures. In J. Cordes, R. Ebel, & J. Gravelle (Eds.), *Encyclopedia of taxation and tax policy*. Washington, DC: The Urban Institute Press, 406–408.

26. U.S. Office of Management and Budget (2006). *Budget of the United States government, fiscal year 2007, analytical perspectives*. Washington, DC: U.S. Government Printing Office, 296–297.

27. U.S. Congressional Budget Office (2005). *Corporate income tax rates: international comparisons*. Washington, DC: U.S. Government Printing Office, 22.

28. U.S. Congressional Budget Office (2005). *Corporate income tax rates: international comparisons, x*.

29. Cornia, G., Edmiston, K., Sjoquist, D., & Wallace, S. et al. (2005). The disappearing state corporate income tax. *National Tax Journal, 48*, 115–138.

30. U.S. Congressional Budget Office (2006). *Historical budget tables.* Retrieved November 1, 2006, from http://www.cbo.gov/budget/historical.pdf.

31. U.S. Social Security Administration (2006). *Annual statistical supplement to the Social Security Bulletin.* Washington, DC: U.S. Government Printing Office, 6.1.

32. U.S. Social Security Administration (2006). *Annual statistical supplement to the Social Security Bulletin,* 4.1–4.4.

33. Daly, M. C. & Burkhauser, R. V. (2000). *The supplemental security income program.* San Francisco, CA: Federal Reserve Bank of San Francisco.

34. U.S. Social Security Administration (2006). *Annual statistical supplement to the Social Security Bulletin,* 7.2–7.3.

35. U.S. Congressional Budget Office (2006). *Updated long-term projections for Social Security.* Retrieved November 5, 2006, from http://www.cbo.gov/ftpdocs/72xx/doc7289/06-14-LongTermProjections.pdf.

36. U.S. Office of Management and Budget (2003). *Budget of the United States government: fiscal year 2003, analytical perspectives.* Washington, DC: U.S. Government Printing Office, 351.

37. American survey: the pensions conspiracy (1996). *The Economist, 341, December 14,* 20, 27–28.

38. Duka, W. (2001). AARP's Deets sees flaws in Social Security panel. *AARP Bulletin, 42, June,* 19.

39. The President's Commission to Strengthen Social Security (2001). *Strengthening Social Security and creating personal wealth for all Americans.* Washington, DC: U.S. Government Printing Office. Retrieved January 22, 2007, from http://www.csss.gov/reports/Final_report.pdf.

40. Barshay, J. & Wayne, A. (2005). 10 signs the Bush Social Security plan is dead (for now). *Congressional Quarterly Weekly Report, 63,* 2696.

41. U.S. Congressional Budget Office (2006). *Historical budget data.* Retrieved January 22, 2007, from http://www.cbo.gov/budget/historical.pdf.

42. U.S. Congressional Budget Office (2005). *The long-term budget outlook.* Washington, DC: U.S. Government Printing Office, 27–38.

43. Marron, D., Acting Director, U.S. Congressional Budget Office (2006). *Medicaid spending growth and options for controlling costs.* Testimony before the Special Committee on Aging, United State Senate, 2.

44. U.S. Congressional Budget Office (2006). *Historical budget data.* Retrieved November 1, 2006, from http://www.cbo.gov/budget/historical.pdf.

45. Fisher, G. W. (1996). *The worst tax? a history of the property tax in America.* Lawrence, KS: University Press of Kansas.

46. Fischel, W. A. (2002). School finance litigation and property tax revolts: how undermining local control turns voters away from public education. *Developments in school*

finance: fiscal proceedings from the annual state data conference, July 1999 and July 2000. Washington, DC: National Center for Education Statistics, 79–127.

47. Johnson, R. W. & McCullough, J. S. (1996). Case study on urban local government finance. Paper presented at the Asian Development Bank seminar on Urban Infrastructure Finance in Asia. Research Triangle Park, NC: Research Triangle Institute, April 17.

48. Bahl, R. W. & Linn, J. F. (1992). *Urban public finance in developing countries.* New York: Oxford University Press; Bird, R. M. (1992). *Tax policy and economic development.* Baltimore, MD: Johns Hopkins University Press.

49. Fischel, W. (2001). Homeowners, municipal corporate governance, and the benefit view of the property tax. *National Tax Journal, 54,* 157–173.

50. Petersen, J. E. (2000). TIFs in the hinterlands. *Governing, 13, August,* 68.

51. Kelsey, T. W. & Kreahling, K. S. (1996). Preferential tax assessments for farmland preservation: influence of population pressures on fiscal impacts. *State and Local Government Review, 28,* 49–57.

52. Lemov, P. (1995). Tin-cup taxation: local governments are pressuring nonprofits to chip in to cover the costs of the services they use. *Governing, 8, October,* 25–26.

53. Eom, T. & Rubenstein, R. (2006). Do state-funded property tax exemptions increase local government efficiency? An analysis of New York State's STAR program. *Public Budgeting & Finance, 26, Spring,* 66–87.

54. Allen, M. & Dare, W. (2002). Identifying determinants of horizontal property tax inequity: evidence from Florida. *Journal of Real Estate Research, 24,* 153–164.

55. Allen, M. (2003). Measuring vertical property tax inequity in multifamily property markets. *Journal of Real Estate Research, 25,* 171–184.

56. Zorn, C. K. et al. (2000). Diversifying local government revenue in Bosnia-Herzegovina through an area-based property tax. *Public Budgeting & Finance, 20, Winter,* 63–86; Kelly, R. (2000). Designing a property tax reform strategy for sub-saharan Africa: an analytical framework applied to Kenya. *Public Budgeting & Finance, 20, Winter,* 36–51.

57. Stine, W. (2005). Do budget maximizing public officials increase the probability of property reassessment? *Applied Economics, 37,* 2395–2405.

58. Monk, D. H. (1990). *Educational finance: an economic approach.* New York: McGraw-Hill, 158–160.

59. Rueben, K. (2000). The impact of initiatives on state and local government finance. *Municipal Finance Journal, 20,* 20–25; Hoene, C. (2004). Fiscal structure and the post-proposition 13 fiscal regime in California's cities. *Public Budgeting & Finance, 24, Winter,* 51–72.

60. Ladd, H. F. & Wilson, J. B. (1983). Who supports tax limitations: evidence from Massachusetts' proposition 2½. *Journal of Policy Analysis and Management, 2,* 256–279; Moscovitch, E. (1985). Proposition 2½. *Government Finance Review, 1, October,* 21–25;

Wallin, B. (2004). The tax revolt in Massachusetts: revolution and reason. *Public Budgeting & Finance, 24, Winter*, 34–50.

61. Mullins, D. R. & Joyce, P. G. (1996). Tax and expenditure limitations and state and local fiscal structure: an empirical assessment. *Public Budgeting & Finance, 16, Spring*, 75–101.

62. Gold, S. D. (1996). State tax cuts of 1995: is something new afoot? *Public Budgeting & Finance, 16, Spring*, 3–22; National Association of State Budget Officers (1997). *1996 state tax initiatives.* Retrieved January 22, 2007 from http://www.nasbo.org/Policy_Resources/Taxes_Fees/taxib.html.

63. Bradbury, K. L. et al. (1998). School quality and Massachusetts enrollment shifts in the context of tax limitations. *New England Economic Review, July/August*, 3–20.

64. Mullins, D. & Joyce, P. (1996). Tax and expenditure limitations and state and local fiscal structure, an empirical assessment. *Public Budgeting & Finance, 16, Spring*, 77.

65. Minnesota Budget Project (2006). *Minnesota tax burdens: who pays and how much?* Retrieved January 20, 2007 from, http:// www.mncn.org/bp/incid01.htm.

66. McGuire, T. J. (1999). Proposition 13 and its offspring: for good or for evil? *National Tax Journal, 52*, 129–138.

67. Dye, R. et al. (2005). Are property tax limitations more binding over time? *National Tax Journal, 58*, 215–225.

68. Thompson, F. & Green, M. (2004). Vox populi? Oregon tax and expenditure limitation initiatives. *Public Budgeting & Finance, 24, Winter*, 73–87.

69. Brown, T. (2000). Constitutional tax and expenditure limitation in Colorado: the impact on municipal governments. *Public Budgeting & Finance, 20, Fall*, 29–50.

70. King-Meadows, T. & Lowery, D. (1996). The impact of the tax revolt era state fiscal caps: a research update. *Public Budgeting & Finance, 16, Spring*, 102–112.

71. Joyce, P. G. & Mullins, D. R. (1991). The changing fiscal structure of the state and local public sector: the impact of tax and expenditure limitations. *Public Administration Review, 51*, 244–245.

72. Downes, T. A. & Figlio, D. N. (1999). Do tax and expenditure limits provide a free lunch? Evidence on the link between limits and public sector service quality. *National Tax Journal, 52*, 113–128.

73. Mullins, D. (2004). Tax and expenditure limitations and the fiscal response of local government: asymmetric intra-local fiscal effects. *Public Budgeting & Finance, 24, Winter*, 111–147.

Chapter 5

BUDGETING FOR REVENUES: TRANSACTION-BASED REVENUE SOURCES

In addition to the income, payroll, and wealth-based taxes covered in Chapter 4, governments raise revenue from a number of sources that are based on largely voluntary transactions. The largest and most important of these is the general retail sales tax. There are also a number of sales taxes levied on specific goods, including taxes on luxury goods such as expensive automobiles, so-called "sin taxes" on liquor and cigarettes, and benefit-based excises on items such as motor fuel. Governments also have expanded their use of fees and charges, many of which are used to finance related services. Over the past 30 years the use of lotteries and games of chance as a revenue source for state governments has mushroomed. Although having grown over the years, neither charges nor gambling revenues represent a primary source of revenue for general-purpose governments, although many special districts get the majority of their revenue from charges.

This chapter reviews each of these revenue sources, discussing their applications and the political and economic issues raised by them. In doing so, we discuss how these revenue sources stack up relative to the criteria identified in Chapter 4. At the conclusion of the chapter, we describe the important process of revenue estimating as it applies to revenue sources in general.

▮ Retail Sales and Other Consumption Taxes

Sales taxes are one of the most important sources of revenue for state governments. Forty-five of the 50 states (all but Alaska, Delaware, Montana, New Hampshire, and Oregon) levy a general sales tax, and it is the largest state-generated source of revenue for many of them.[1] All states have at least some selective sales taxes. Overall, the general and selective sales taxes account for more than 18% of total state general revenues from all sources. User charges are the second largest single general revenue source at 13%, followed closely by the income tax, which accounts for about 12% of general revenues. However, all taxes account for just more than 50% of state general revenues. If one looks at the sales tax as a proportion of tax revenues only, sales taxes account for 36% of state tax revenue.[2]

There are two types of sales taxes. The general sales tax is a tax on all (or most) consumed goods and sometimes services. Specific sales taxes are taxes on a particular type of good or service. There are also two varieties of sales tax. *Ad Valorem* taxes are levied as a percentage of the purchase price of an item. If an item subject to a sales tax costs twice as much as another item subject to a sales tax, the tax paid is twice the amount as well. General sales taxes are *ad valorem* taxes.

Unit taxes, on the other, hand, are levied per unit of the item sold, without regard to price. This means that more expensive brands are taxed at the same level as less expensive brands. Gasoline, or cigarette, or liquor taxes, are usually unit taxes, since taxation is based on the gallons (in the case of gasoline or liquor) or packs (in the case of cigarettes) sold. One implication of the type of tax is that the production from *ad valorem* taxes, for obvious reasons, tends to rise as prices increase, while unit taxes yield relatively flat revenues.

General Sales Taxes

The general sales tax is the largest revenue source for state governments, and is used by many local governments as well. Many state governments raise as much as one-fourth to one-third of state tax revenue from this source. Some states raise as much as one-half. Sales tax revenues result from the level of the tax base and the rates applied to that base.

Tax Base. While all three levels of government rely on some form of consumption tax, state governments are the most dependent, particularly on retail sales taxes. The base of any consumption tax is a product or class of goods (sometimes services) whose value is measured in terms of retail gross sales or receipts. The base is a function of which products and services are included and excluded. All states except Illinois exempt prescription medicines (Illinois taxes these at a lower rate of 1%), and 29 of the 45 states with sales taxes exclude food, except for that sold in restaurants, delis, or other specialty foods sold in grocery stores.[3] Some states have opted for reducing the sales tax rate on food compared to other taxed items, rather than eliminating it altogether.

Other commonly excluded items are clothing, household fuels, soaps, and some toiletries. Some items may be exempt from the general sales tax only because they are subject to another sales tax. Cigarettes, gasoline, and alcoholic beverages are examples of specific goods exempted from the general sales tax for this reason. States generally are not precluded from levying two taxes on one sale. Such double taxation may occur, for example, when a general sales tax and a specific sales tax are placed on cigarettes and alcoholic beverages.

The justification for these commodities' exemptions is typically that they make the sales tax less regressive, to the extent that the nontaxed items are necessities. The clearest case is food, where lower-income persons spend a larger percentage of their income on this commodity than higher-income persons. This same justification applies to the exemption for prescription and other medicines.[4] Tax exemptions for clothing are less clear on vertical equity grounds, although some states exempt only a portion of the cost of a given article of clothing (the first $100, for example) in an effort to offset this problem.

The most notable items not included in most sales tax bases are services, such as the professional services of doctors and lawyers, dry cleaners, or accountants. A Council of State Governments study found that consumption expenditures for tangible goods are less than those for services. States that exclude services from the sales tax base may forgo considerable revenue, depending on the distribution between the "goods" and "services" economy in that state.

However, applying the sales tax to services is so unpopular that few states have implemented that option. Only three states (Hawaii, New Mexico, and South Dakota) tax most services.[5] In fact, when the State of Florida passed a law that applied the sales tax to services in 1986, it was forced to repeal that tax the next year when citizens and affected interests "discovered" the tax.[6]

The largest current issue regarding the application of the sales tax concerns the ability of states to tax mail-order or Internet sales. As more and more commerce has switched from traditional retail outlets to mail-order or Internet outlets, state and local governments have lost substantial revenue because of the difficulty in enforcing the use tax (a tax paid by the purchaser on items where sales tax was not paid at purchase). **Exhibit 5–1** discusses the issues surrounding the taxation of these mail-order or Internet sales.

Tax Rates. State sales tax rates vary from as low as 2.9% (Colorado) to as high as 7% (Mississippi, Rhode Island, and Tennessee).[7] To avoid levies of a fraction of a cent, bracket systems are used in which a set amount is collected regardless of the

Exhibit 5–1 **Taxation of Mail Order and Internet Sales**

States currently have only limited authority to tax mail-order sales and have been lobbying Congress to pass legislation allowing full taxation. The reason is a simple one. Mail-order sales vastly increased starting in the 1980s and constitute a potentially lucrative source of revenue.

U.S. Supreme Court interpretations of the due process and interstate commerce clauses have been fairly restrictive on states' ability to tax interstate sales. A 1967 case (*National Bellas Hess, Inc.* v. *Department of Revenue, State of Illinois*) concluded that a mail-order firm had to have a substantial nexus of business in a state in the form of a physical presence. A 1992 case (*Quill Corporation* v. *North Dakota*) relaxed the so-called nexus doctrine, holding that the due process clause of the Constitution does not bar enforcement of North Dakota's use tax on the Quill Corporation, but on other grounds it still refused to overrule *Bellas Hess*.[1]

An additional complication is the growth of sales through cable and satellite television and other electronic commerce. Use of the Internet as a mechanism to place orders shipped interstate has become a significant mode of commerce and it will continue to grow as more users gain access to electronic sources. One estimate put national losses from the failure to tax Internet sales nationwide at almost $11 billion in 2003. States with relatively large revenue losses, according to this estimate, included California ($1.5 trillion), Texas ($932 million), New York ($849 million), and Florida ($753 million).[2] Although the principle has not been tested in any court case so far, Internet commerce is being treated the same as interstate mail-order and phone sales. Recent research demonstrates a small, but statistically significant, relationship between the state sales tax rate and the propensity of consumers to purchase online, with higher sales tax rates leading to more online spending.[3]

There are a number of significant policy problems raised by the mail-order and Internet sales issue. First, as noted above, is the sheer magnitude of the revenue loss. This puts those states with only a sales tax at a significant disadvantage compared to states with both an income and a sales tax, or only an income tax. Second, there is the problem that it creates for traditional "bricks and mortar" businesses, whose costs—rent, for example—are higher than for online businesses, and who must include the tax in the cost of the price of their goods. Third, to the extent that some taxpayers can avoid paying the sales tax through Internet or mail-order purchasing, the tax burden is shifted to those who do not engage in these kinds of transactions. To the extent that traditional sales fall more heavily on lower-income individuals without access to the Internet, this would tend to make the sales tax more regressive.

In 1998, Congress passed the Internet Tax Freedom Act and extended the law in 2004 by passing the Internet Tax Non-discrimination Act.[4] That Act placed a moratorium on taxing Internet sales, and Congress appointed an Advisory Commission on Electronic Commerce to deal with the issue.[5] The Commission deadlocked without effectively solving the problem. In its wake, some states have taken matters into their own hands. Michigan and North Carolina attempt to tax Internet purchases by asking taxpayers filing individual income tax returns to

continues

Exhibit 5–1 | **Taxation of Mail Order and Internet Sales (continued)**

report on goods purchased from out of state through on-line sources, but have not created any enforcement mechanisms.

More generally, state governments have joined together through the National Governors Association to create the Streamlined Sales Tax Project. This project intends to simplify and make consistent across the states the application and administration of the sales tax. Success with this approach might overcome judicial objections to requiring retailers to collect sales taxes for all 45 states, each of which has a different system, as an undue burden.[6] Some research suggests that, under some circumstances, firms might have incentives to comply voluntarily with the collection of sales tax on Internet sales. The authors of this study, however, were not sanguine about the ability of states to simplify tax administration sufficiently to create widespread voluntary compliance.[7]

[1]Coleman, H. A. (1992). Taxation of interstate mail-order sales. *Intergovernmental Perspective 18, Winter,* 9–14; *National Bellas Hess, Inc.* v. *Department of Revenue, State of Illinois* (1967). 386 U.S. 753; *Quill Corporation* v. *North Dakota* (1992). 504 U.S. 298.

[2]Sparks, C., McCoskey, M., & Alvis, J. (2004). Can internet sales be taxed? *Public Finance and Management,* 4, 126.

[3]Alm, J. & Melnik, M. (2005). Sales taxes and the decision to purchase online. *Public Finance Review, 33,* 184–212.

[4]Internet Tax Freedom Act (1998). P.L. 107–75; Internet Tax Non-discrimination Act (2004). P.L. 108–435.

[5]Goolsbee, A. & Zittrain, J. (1999). Evaluating the costs and benefits of taxing internet commerce. *National Tax Journal, 52,* 413–428.

[6]Swope, C. (2000). E-tax outrage turns into action. *Governing, 13, September,* 86.

[7]Cornia, G., Sjoquist, D., & Walters, L. (2004). Sales and use tax simplification and voluntary compliance. *Public Budgeting and Finance, 24, Spring,* 1–31.

specific sale. For example, a 5% tax might yield five cents on any purchase starting at 81 cents or 90 cents. With computers and electronic scanners at checkout counters in stores, determinations can be quickly made as to whether an item is taxable and how much tax, if any, should be charged.

Many states permit a separate local sales tax on top of the state sales tax. Local sales tax rates vary widely, from a low of only 0.25% in Mississippi to a high of 7% in Alabama. Local sales taxes are typically collected by the state and remitted to the local treasury.

Sales taxes are regarded as regressive in that higher-income consumers typically have more discretionary income and may spend it on items not subject to sales taxes. As noted above, the more the base of the sales tax excludes necessities (such as food and prescription drugs) and includes luxury or nonessential goods and services, the less regressive the tax is likely to be.

This regressive nature of the sales tax may represent a somewhat counterintuitive result, since sales taxes almost always employ a single rate (as opposed to the federal income tax, for example, which has graduated rates). Even though sales taxes are levied on a flat rate basis, however, this does not mean that the sales tax is a proportional tax. Quite to the contrary, the vertical equity implications of the tax are substantially dependent on the portion of an individual's income that is spent on taxed items.

Consider a case where one taxpayer earns $50,000 in income and spends $40,000 of that on items subject to the sales tax, while a second taxpayer earns $80,000 and spends $60,000 of that on tax items. The first taxpayer will pay $2,000 in tax ($40,000 times 5%), which represents an effective tax rate of 4% ($2,000/$50,000). The second taxpayer pays more in tax ($3,000, or $60,000 times 5%), for an effective tax rate of 3.75% ($3,000/$80,000). Even if the sales tax rate is 5% for each taxpayer, the lower-income taxpayer will have a higher effective tax rate than the higher-income taxpayer. Thus a tax that appears proportional may actually be regressive. As noted above, the exemption of necessities such as food and drugs tend to have the effect of making the tax less regressive and even progressive in some cases.

The general sales tax continues to be a relatively popular and widespread form of taxation, but state and local governments increasingly see threats to the sales tax as a revenue source, for several reasons. First, as noted in **Exhibit 5–1**, the threat to the productivity of the tax resulting from sales to remote vendors is a real one. Second, the trend is toward more services (that tend not to be taxed) and fewer goods (that are subject to the tax), which impacts the productivity of the tax. Third, legislatures have had a tendency in recent years to provide tax exemptions (in particular, in the form of tax "holidays" to encourage shopping in the state during specific time periods such as the weekend before school starts) that have questionable results but impose substantial revenue losses. For these reasons, one noted sales tax expert is concerned about the viability of the sales tax as a revenue source, and sees those states that rely heavily on the sales tax as having a more difficult time keeping pace with demands for services.[8]

The Value-Added Tax. Increased concerns about the robustness of the U.S. tax system, especially the intergovernmental system of taxation and revenue transfers (see Chapter 14), have led some to advocate adoption of a value-added tax (VAT).[9] The United States is one of the few industrialized countries without a VAT. As its name implies, a VAT is a consumption tax on the value added by producers and distributors at every stage in the production, distribution, and sales process. Interest in the VAT in the United States seemed to peak in the early 1990s. Proposed during the 1992 election by then-candidate Bill Clinton, the VAT did not get serious attention in Congress. During recent presidential campaigns, it has not been mentioned at all, but has instead been superseded by various candidates' proposals for fundamental income tax reform, including various flat-tax alternatives. Tax professionals argue that it is superior to many other forms of consumption taxation, but it just has not generated much enthusiasm in the United States.[10]

Selective Sales Taxes

Selective sales taxes are normally referred to as *excise taxes*. There are three general categories of excise taxes: luxury excises, sumptuary excises, and benefit-based excises. They differ according both to the specific types of sales that are taxed and according to the fiscal or social goals of the tax.

Luxury Excises. These excise taxes are levied on items that are "uniquely or predominantly consumed by the rich" meaning that the act of purchasing the good itself is considered to be evidence of an extraordinary ability to pay taxes.[11] At one time, federal excise taxes were levied on a wide range of luxury goods, such as jewelry, yachts, and expensive automobiles. The logic of these taxes rests on the assumption that the purchase of such goods is prima facie evidence that the consumer can afford the tax. The overall effect of these taxes, then, is to make the tax system more progressive. Luxury excise taxes tend not to exist at the state level, and the federal luxury tax has ebbed and flowed according primarily to political factors. The most recent experience with federal luxury taxation was under the Omnibus Budget Reconciliation Act of 1990, when luxury taxes on boats (over $100,000), automobiles (over $30,000), airplanes (over $250,000), and furs and jewelry (over $10,000) were imposed. These taxes proved unpopular, however, and all have since been repealed.[12]

There are some problems created by luxury excises. One problem is that the definition of what is a "luxury" is in no way fixed. That is, a watch is not a luxury, but an "expensive watch" may be. A car is not a luxury, but an "expensive car" may be. The problem, of course, is that there is no standard definition for "expensive" so any definition used is by necessity somewhat arbitrary. Some families may have a need to purchase a more expensive car in order to accommodate their family. For a single person, the purchase of such a vehicle may be a luxury. Thus, the definition of a luxury item is clearly open to debate and interpretation.

Another issue with luxury excises is that they can create distortions between taxed and untaxed goods. The luxury tax itself changes the relative price of the luxury item compared to items that are not subject to the tax. This means that tax policy is discriminatory against these luxury items relative to other goods that may be purchased. This has the effect of discouraging, at the margin, purchases of these items, which has the related effect of disadvantaging retailers and producers of luxury goods, perhaps to the point of driving them out of business. In 1990, a new federal luxury tax on yachts was criticized as bankrupting yacht producers and sellers, although it was difficult to evaluate the appropriateness of that claim since the imposition of the tax occurred virtually simultaneously with the economic recession of the early 1990s.

Sumptuary Excises. These sales taxes are regulatory in nature. Taxes on alcohol and tobacco have been justified as deterring people from consuming these commodities. In reality, the evidence suggests that the demand for these products is relatively *inelastic*, casting doubt on whether taxes discourage usage. These items tend to be relatively demand inelastic in large part because they are addictive in nature. Therefore, a smoker is unlikely to stop smoking, or even cut back, because of higher taxes on a pack of cigarettes.

In the 1990s, a substantial tax increase on tobacco was proposed as an important source of financing for federal health care reform. The rationale was that smokers are one of the major sources of health care insurance utilization and that those who create those costs should be the ones to pay taxes to fund them—a sort of reverse benefit principle. The proposal, however, did not get serious review in Congress. Nevertheless, some states have substantially increased tobacco taxes both as a revenue measure and as a health regulatory measure. As noted earlier in this chapter, large increases in tobacco taxes have reportedly discouraged youth from smoking.

Sumptuary excises, regardless of their regulatory nature, tend to be somewhat regressive, for two reasons. First, there is a tendency toward greater alcohol and cigarette consumption among lower-income groups than higher-income groups. Second, and perhaps even more important, since these taxes are unit taxes instead of ad valorem taxes, effective tax rates are higher for lower-priced brands. While this is likely less of an issue for cigarettes (because the price difference between brands is not great) it is a much larger issue for alcoholic beverages, where there is a huge price range for bottles of wine or spirits (or even six-packs of beer). As an example, if the tax on wine amounted to 50 cents per bottle, this would represent a 10% tax on a $5 bottle, but only a 2% tax on a $25 bottle.

There is a federal alcohol beverage tax, and many states levy liquor taxes as well. Both federal and state alcohol taxes are levied on a unit basis. In fiscal year 2004, the federal tax was $13.50 per gallon of distilled spirits, $18 per 31-gallon barrel of beer (or $0.58 per gallon), and $1.07 per gallon of table wine.[13]

Table 5–1 shows the state tax rates for both the cigarette tax (per pack of cigarettes) and the tax on distilled spirits (per gallon) in 2006. Several things are

Table 5–1	State Excise Tax Rates, 2006 (As of January 1, 2006)

State	Cigarette[a]	Distilled Spirits[b]	Gasoline[c]
Alabama	$0.43	SC	$0.18
Alaska	$1.60	$12.80	$0.08
Arizona	$1.18	$3.00	$0.18
Arkansas	$0.59	$2.50	$0.23
California	$0.87	$3.30	$0.18
Colorado	$0.84	$2.28	$0.22
Connecticut	$1.51	$4.50	$0.25
Delaware	$0.55	$5.46	$0.23
Florida	$0.34	$6.50	$0.15
Georgia	$0.37	$3.79	$0.15
Hawaii	$1.40	$5.98	$0.16
Idaho	$0.57	SC	$0.25
Illinois	$0.98	$4.50	$0.20
Indiana	$0.56	$2.68	$0.18
Iowa	$0.36	SC	$0.21
Kansas	$0.79	$2.50	$0.24
Kentucky	$0.30	$1.92	$0.19
Louisiana	$0.36	$2.50	$0.20
Maine	$2.00	SC	$0.26
Maryland	$1.00	$1.50	$0.24
Massachusetts	$1.51	$4.05	$0.21
Michigan	$2.00	SC	$0.19
Minnesota	$1.23	$5.03	$0.20
Mississippi	$0.18	SC	$0.18
Missouri	$0.17	$2.00	$0.18
Montana	$1.70	SC	$0.27
Nebraska	$0.64	$3.75	$0.27
Nevada	$0.80	$3.60	$0.25
New Hampshire	$0.80	SC	$0.20
New Jersey	$2.40	$4.40	$0.15
New Mexico	$0.91	$6.06	$0.19
New York	$1.50	$6.44	$0.24
North Carolina	$0.30	SC	$0.30
North Dakota	$0.44	$2.50	$0.23
Ohio	$1.25	SC	$0.28

continues

Table 5-1	State Excise Tax Rates, 2006 (As of January 1, 2006) (continued)		
State	**Cigarette[a]**	**Distilled Spirits[b]**	**Gasoline[c]**
Oklahoma	$1.03	$5.56	$0.17
Oregon	$1.18	SC	$0.24
Pennsylvania	$1.35	SC	$0.31
Rhode Island	$2.46	$3.75	$0.31
South Carolina	$0.07	$2.72	$0.16
South Dakota	$0.53	$3.93	$0.22
Tennessee	$0.20	$4.40	$0.21
Texas	$0.41	$2.40	$0.20
Utah	$0.70	SC	$0.25
Vermont	$1.19	SC	$0.20
Virginia	$0.30	SC	$0.18
Washington	$2.03	SC	$0.31
West Virginia	$0.55	SC	$0.27
Wisconsin	$0.77	$3.25	$0.33
Wyoming	$0.60	SC	$0.14
District of Columbia	$1.00	$1.50	$0.23

[a]Tax per pack of cigarettes.

[b]Tax per gallon of distilled spirits.

[c]Tax per gallon of gasoline. Diesel fuel and gasohol may have different rates.

Notes: SC=State Controlled; distilled spirits sold directly by the state and not taxed. All figures rounded to the nearest whole cent.

Source: Compiled from Council of State Governments (2006). *The Book of the States.* Table 7.14. Lexington, KY: Council of State Governments, 371.

notable from this table. First, while every state taxes cigarettes, the cigarette tax varied widely from state to state. South Carolina had the lowest tax in the nation, at only seven cents per pack, while Rhode Island's cigarette tax was 35 times that level, at $2.46 per pack. Overall, there were 18 states with a tax of more than $1.00 per pack, and seven states with taxes of 30 cents per pack or less. Distilled spirits showed substantial variation but not as much as cigarettes, with a range of $1.50 (Maryland) to $12.80 (Alaska). In 18 states, the state sells liquor directly thus earning the majority of revenue from direct profit rather than from taxation.

One of the arguments in favor of liquor taxes is that they reduce alcohol consumption. Studies have shown that heavy and moderate drinkers tend to reduce their consumption in response to higher taxes, since these taxes affect the price of a fifth of liquor, a bottle of wine, or a six-pack of beer. Young and underage drinkers are thought to be particularly responsive to price. The tax, then, is thought to assist in helping these individuals to recognize the external costs that their drinking has on society.[14]

Benefit-based Excises. These taxes are justified on the basis of the benefit received concept discussed in Chapter 4. The assumption here is that the tax should be levied on individuals who cause particular services to be provided, and that the proceeds from the tax should go to finance that particular service.

Motor vehicle fuel taxes are the classic case. In most states and for the federal government, revenues from taxes on gasoline and diesel fuels are used for transportation purposes. This includes road and bridge construction and maintenance, as well as mass transportation in many cases. The argument here is a simple one. Those individuals who purchase more motor fuels tend to use the highways more than those who purchase a lesser amount of motor fuels. To the extent, then, that the motor fuel tax is used to finance these transportation services, the result is that a greater portion of the cost of financing these services is borne by users. Further, the greater the service consumption, the more the tax paid. Even in cases where gasoline taxes are used to finance mass transportation, the argument holds, since encouraging use of mass transportation creates benefits for drivers who are driving on roads that are less congested.

Taxes are typically levied on different types of motor fuels, such as gasoline, diesel, and gasohol. **Table 5–1** also includes a column showing the tax rates for gasoline only. As with the excise taxes discussed earlier, gasoline tax rates differ from state to state, although the range here is much narrower, from a low of 8 cents (Alaska) to 33 cents (Wisconsin). The tax rates in the vast majority of the states (45 out of 51, including the District of Columbia) fall somewhere between 15 and 30 cents per gallon.

Other such excises include taxes on airline tickets. The revenues from these taxes are used to maintain airports and airport security.

▮ User Charges

All governments have user charges, and almost all public sector functions are partially supported by user charges. As noted earlier, user charges and fees for services are the fastest growing state and local revenue source. For example, admission fees are charged to national and some state parks and to local tennis courts, other recreational facilities, and exercise and athletic programs. Some elementary and secondary schools charge for textbooks, and higher-education institutions charge tuition. Hospitals, transit systems, water and sewer operations, and refuse collection revenues come mainly from fees and charges. Some jurisdictions own electric and telephone facilities, which they finance through user fees. Police departments charge fees for fingerprinting and special assignments, such as patrolling at sports events.

Rationale for Charges and Fees

The employment of user charges to raise revenues is based on the principle that citizens ought to pay for the cost of public services as a control on the amount of services produced. The more technical argument for their employment holds that the amount of a service provided is closer to the *optimal level of service*, as determined by consumer preferences, when the cost of service is borne directly by the consumer.[15] If the cost of a service is part of general taxes, then citizens tend to demand more of that service than they are actually willing to pay.

At the federal level, the growth in user charges and fees began with the Reagan administration's opposition to tax increases. With massive annual federal deficits and a president opposed to raising taxes, federal agencies in need of additional revenues selectively considered fees as an alternative. The philosophy of federal user charges, that "the service, sale, or use of Government's goods or resources provided by an agency to specific recipients be self-sustaining," is expressed in Office of Management and Budget Circular A-25.[16] During and following the budget surplus years of the late 1990s, presidents have found it financially useful and politically acceptable to increase user fees while holding taxes steady or even cutting taxes. President Bush's fiscal year 2007 budget proposed new or expanded user fees that would have resulted in almost $50 billion in additional revenue between fiscal year 2007 and fiscal year 2011.[17]

Types of Charges

Fees vary in the extent to which they are voluntary. Charges for entrance into a museum or a municipal swimming pool clearly are voluntary. Other leisure options are available if citizens prefer not to pay for these public services. On the other hand, charges for sewers and trash collection usually are mandatory. If a municipal sewer system exists, citizens normally have no choice but to use it and pay the requisite fee. The largest federal user fees are levied by the U.S. Postal Service. These charges may be considered partially voluntary in that alternatives for at least some postal services exist. Other services lie between these extremes. Paying a bus or subway fare may be voluntary, but for many people without other transit options the fees are required. Differentiating between a mandatory fee and a tax is difficult.

The federal government collected $185 billion in user charges in fiscal year 2005. **Table 5–2** lists the most common of these fees. By far the largest of these were charges collected by the Postal Service, which totaled $68 billion. Other large user charges were those collected for Medicare Part B insurance premiums ($39 billion), federal employee insurance premiums ($10 billion), Tennessee Valley Authority sales of energy ($8 billion), customs and immigration charges ($6 billion), and recreation and other fees by the Department of the Interior (also $6 billion). Taken

Table 5–2	Major Federal User Charges, Fiscal Year 2005

Department/Agency	Description	Millions of Dollars
Receipts:		
Corps of Engineers	Harbor Maintenance Fees	1,048
State	Immigration, Passport, Consular Fees	911
Miscellaneous	Other Charges	1,452
Discretionary Offsetting Collections and Receipts:		
Defense	Commissary and Other Charges	8,934
Homeland Security	Transportation Security and Other	2,044
Security and Exchange	Regulatory Fees	1,665
State	Passport and Other Charges	1,605
Commerce	Patent and Trademark, Weather, etc.	1,596
Treasury	Commemorative Coins and Other	1,550
Health and Human Serv.	FDA, Medicare and Medicaid, etc.	1,377
Energy	Various Energy and Power Charges	785
Miscellaneous	Other Charges	1,703
Mandatory Offsetting Collections and Receipts:		
U.S. Postal Service	Fees for Postal Services	68,504
Health and Human Serv.	Medicare Part B and Other	39,854
Personnel Management	Employee Health and Retirement	10,298
Tennessee Valley Auth.	Sale of Energy	7,806
Homeland Security	Customs, Immigration, and Other	6,196
Interior	Recreation and Other	5,584
Energy	Sale of Energy, Nuclear Disposal	4,709
Labor	Insurance Premiums—Private Pensions	2,519
Agriculture	Crop Insurance and Other	1,880
Veterans Affairs	Life Insurance and Other	1,682
Defense	Commissary Surcharge and Other	1,090
Miscellaneous	Other Charges	10,430
Grand Total		***185,222***

Source: Compiled from U.S. Office of Management and Budget (2006). *Budget of the United States government, fiscal year 2007, analytical perspectives.* Washington, DC: U.S. Government Printing Office, 274.

together, these six types of charges represent $137 billion of the total $185 billion in user charges, or almost three-fourths of the total.[18]

The federal government classifies user charges into two categories. One category is for offsetting collections, which are credited against particular accounts as offsets to spending (for example, charges for entering national parks credited against National Park Service spending). The second one is offsetting receipts, which are not credited toward any particular account but are treated, in effect, as general revenues.[19]

State and local governments also generate substantial user charges. In fiscal year 2004, state governments in aggregate collected $115 billion in user charges. Of this amount, more than $63 billion (55%) was for higher education, primarily for tuition and room and board. The other large user charge area was hospitals at $26 billion (23%). States also collect charges for (toll) highways, natural resources and recreation, and numerous other activities, but none of these other individual categories accounts for more than 5% of total state charges. Local governments collected $174 billion in charges in the same year, with hospitals as the largest single area ($46 billion, or 26%). Other significant local charges were for sewerage ($34 billion, or 20%), housing and community development ($33 billion, or 19%), and parks and recreation ($26 billion, or 15%). The aforementioned four categories accounted for 80% of all local charges.[20]

Some fees are continuous, whereas others are applied only for special occasions. Transit fares and sewer and water charges are examples of continuous fees. Special-occasion charges include a building permit fee that a contractor has to pay preparatory to erecting an office building. Although many jurisdictions use general tax revenues to repave and improve streets, other communities levy special assessments on the property owners whose streets will be improved. Similarly, when a community installs a sewer system for the first time, property owners are assessed connection or hook-up fees. These charges are calculated on a front footage basis—namely, the number of linear feet that a lot faces or fronts a street. User charges increasingly are being seen as effective revenue sources for social and human services as well.

Special assessments are used in more general ways to support municipal services. Firms that construct new office buildings in a city may have an option to provide on-site parking or pay a fee that is used to construct municipal parking facilities. Cary, North Carolina, finances much of the cost of extending streets, water, and sewer lines, and expanding parks in new developments through the imposition of impact fees on developers. Other communities use impact fees to fund low- and moderate-income housing and environmental programs.

User charges have had a limited role to play in financing local education services, despite the fact that education is the largest area of expenditure at the local level. Fees for school lunches represent the single case where substantial use has been made of charges to recover costs for local public services. Other fees that could be charged, but often are not, are for services such as transportation, textbooks, or activities. The authors of a 2002 study argued that education fees could be expanded substantially, particularly for auxiliary services (services over and above the basic educational market basket), including such services as transportation, after-school care, and other services beyond the scope of a typical K-12 curriculum. The argument for charging for these services is usually made on the basis of efficiency. That is, the argument is that parents are more likely to demand careful accounting for the costs of these services if they are required to pay these costs. This will have the effect of reducing overall costs for those services.[21]

Charges and Tax Subsidies

Although user charges can be substantial, they often fail to cover the costs of the services they support. Entrance fees to a municipal swimming pool usually do not provide adequate funds to operate the pool. Therefore, tax revenues are used. An important example of such a subsidy is in the operation of municipal transit systems. If transit fares were set high enough to generate the required operating revenues, the rates would be so high that poor commuters could not afford to use the system and higher-income commuters would shift to alternative modes of travel—private vehicles and taxicabs. Pricing policies for some services can be quite complicated, making it difficult to determine whether the actual costs are fully recovered by the tariff structure.[22] Furthermore, recovery of the capital cost of constructing facilities such as swimming pools and transit systems would increase the cost still more than just fees to recover operating costs. However, the failure to include capital cost recovery in user charges also likely leads to underinvestment in capital facilities, or significant subsidy from the general fund, at the expense of all taxpayers.

Subsidies aid all who use a service. If transit fares remain artificially low because of a tax subsidy, then both the wealthy and the poor who use the system benefit, though the wealthier could certainly afford to pay for the service. Alternative mechanisms include providing free service to the poor, such as free bus tokens, or setting fees on a sliding scale. For example, a government-operated mental health clinic might charge poor and moderate-income families little or nothing for services while charging higher-income families at a rate that covers costs.

Some local governments that own profitable utilities, such as public electricity companies and sometimes water enterprises with substantial industrial customers, use utility fee revenue to decrease the taxes otherwise needed to finance other, unrelated services. For those local governments owning such profitable enterprises, the overall cost of other government services to citizens is often lower per capita than for other comparable local governments.[23] Caution is in order, however, before one automatically assumes that local governments should seek to become utility owners. The sometimes hidden costs of diverting public management talent to the operation of an essentially private business could adversely affect the municipality's overall management efficiency, although that may be difficult to quantify.

Besides the various revenue sources discussed so far, there are still others that can be mentioned only briefly here. Governments operate revolving loan programs that produce revenue as borrowers make principal and interest payments. Licenses are issued that usually require fees. The purpose of these fees may be to cover costs (for example, building permit fees are used to pay the salaries of building inspectors) or to raise revenues beyond costs. Charitable contributions constitute another revenue source, such as gifts to municipal hospitals, county nursing homes, state universities, and the like.

Borrowing also must be mentioned, not literally as a revenue source, but as a temporary means to obtain revenue while waiting for other revenues to enter the city or state coffers. As will be seen later in discussions of congressional budgeting and budget execution, the federal government's budget is often out of balance, and deficits are routinely financed through the issuance of debt instruments. State and local governments sometimes obtain revenues through borrowing to cover short-term cash flow problems. These governments borrow on a long-term basis to fund capital projects such as highways and government buildings (see Chapter 13).

Lotteries, Casinos, and Other Forms of Gambling

For the past 40 years in the United States, state governments have increasingly operated lotteries and other games of chance in an effort to raise revenues. In addition, more and more states have permitted casino gambling and slot machines over recent years, and have taxed and regulated these activities. Governments had taxed gambling activities, such as horse and dog racing, for many years, but with the advent of lotteries beginning in the 1960s the states became more directly involved in the operation of games of chance.

Lotteries and Gambling

Since 1963, when New Hampshire began the first modern state lottery, all but 13 states have launched lottery programs. In 2004, states generated $15 billion in net revenue from all lottery games.[24] This represented just under 2% of overall state revenues from their own sources (that is, excluding grants and other intergovernmental revenues).

There is wide variation from state to state in the importance of the lottery as a revenue source. The State of New York raised almost $2 billion from the lottery in 2004, or 3.5% of its own-source general revenue of $58 billion. Other large states varied substantially, with California at about 1% and Massachusetts at 5%. Some small states raise substantial sums from the lottery. The states of West Virginia and Rhode Island each raised 8% of their own-source general revenue from lotteries in 2004, and Delaware raised 7%.[25]

Revenues generated from the programs can vary considerably from year to year, depending upon lottery activity in adjacent states, the size of jackpots, and the extent to which a lottery has "matured" and lost the public's interest. State lottery revenues rose rapidly in the late 1980s and early 1990s, then leveled off by mid-decade. In recent years, there has been a resurgence in interest due in part to very large, multi-state payouts and the serious state fiscal trouble resulting from the economic down-turn of the early 2000s. Still, the big increase in lottery sales came between 1985 and 1995, when sales more than tripled. In the decade since 1995, lottery sales have increased by approximately 50%, or close to the rate of inflation over that period.[26]

Still, even with all of this activity, the lottery is not a significant revenue source for most states. Recent research not only demonstrates that lotteries do not raise much revenue, but provides evidence that the revenue that is raised from the lottery often comes at the expense of revenues from other sources, especially sales and excise taxes. Put simply, either taxpayers may substitute spending on the lottery for other spending subject to the sales tax, or politicians may feel less pressure to raise taxes from other sources because of the revenue generated by the lottery.[27]

Lotteries can be regressive in that lower-income individuals are more likely to participate than middle- and upper-income individuals.[28] A review of the research on lotteries consistently found the lottery to be among the most regressive "taxes" at the state level. This same article went a step further and argued that, in states with lotteries, the regressive nature of the tax contributed to the concentration of wealth toward higher-income taxpayers.[29] A partial exception to this trend was found in the high-stakes "Powerball" game, where, for higher jackpots, the lottery tends to become significantly less regressive, suggesting that higher-income people are willing to play the lottery if the potential returns are high enough.[30] The regressive nature of the lottery is considered particularly problematic given the substantial effort—in the form of advertising—that is made by states to convince citizens to play the lottery. It should be noted, however, that the odds against winning substantial sums from playing the lottery are astronomically high.

In addition to their regressive nature, one factor that distinguishes lotteries from other forms of taxation is their relatively high administrative costs. According to data from the U.S. Census Bureau, in 2004, out of the total money spent on lottery tickets, 61% of those funds went back to lottery players in the form of prizes, 33% went to the state in net revenue, and the remaining 6% went for administrative costs.[31] This means that, given conventional ways of calculating administrative costs of taxes (administrative costs as a percentage of revenue), the lottery, at 18%, is a very expensive tax to administer. This tax costs so much to administer primarily because of the high cost of advertising. Again, as noted above, there is no other tax where the government expends so much time and money trying to convince people to pay it.

Recently, there have been calls to privatize lotteries in some states, with private firms "buying" the right to operate the lottery and reap annual profits in exchange for a one-time payment to the state which could then be used either for immediate spending (on capital improvements, for example) or to produce an annual revenue stream. **Exhibit 5–2** discusses this phenomenon.

Casino Gambling

In addition to lotteries, a number of states have legalized casino gambling and other forms of amusements, such as slot machines. While in 1988, legalized casino gambling existed only in Nevada and New Jersey, by 2002, 28 states had Native American casinos, and 11 states had non-Native American casinos. These two types of casinos operate substantially differently. In the case of Native American casinos, states negotiate with tribes for the state "take" of casino revenues. In cases of non-Native American casinos, taxes are levied on gross receipts or adjusted gross receipts (gross receipts less winnings). Some states use a flat scale, while others use an adjusted scale. States also raise money from licensing fees and fees for gaming devices, such as slot machines. Chapter 14 discusses the intergovernmental aspects of casino gambling, namely the relationships between states and Native American tribes.

Most states raise little or no money from amusement taxes. In 2002, there were only nine states that raised more than $100 million in revenues from these taxes. Although in some states, such as Louisiana, casino gambling has cut into state lottery revenues, other states are generating significant revenues from such ventures. Illinois has found casino gambling and lottery revenues to be reinforcing, earning more than $1.2 billion in net revenues in 2002.[32] Some other states receive substantial support from amusement taxes, including the obvious leader, Nevada (home of Las Vegas and Reno), which generated $739 million in amusement taxes in 2002, or 13% of total own-source revenues in that year. Other significant contributions from amusement taxes came in Louisiana (4.4%), Indiana (4%), Mississippi (2.7%), and Iowa (2.2%). Nationwide research suggests that, while there is significant "cannibalization" of lottery revenues from casinos, states as a whole seem to benefit, from a revenue perspective, from having both lotteries and casino gambling.[33]

Overall, however, the enthusiasm for tax and economic benefits from lotteries, casinos, and other legalized gambling has waned somewhat, except in those states where neighboring states seem to be attracting residents of nonlottery states to cross state borders to purchase lottery tickets. For example, one argument often used in 2002 in North Carolina to support a lottery proposal was the amount of money that North Carolina residents were spending in the neighboring Virginia and South

Exhibit 5–2   Privatizing State Lotteries

Since 1963, when the first modern state lottery was started by the State of New Hampshire, lotteries have been a growth industry. The advent of computerized lottery games, such as the Lotto, has expanded substantially the market for, and the profitability of, lotteries. In those states with lotteries, they returned $15 billion in revenue to state coffers in 2004.

This growth has not gone unnoticed by private entrepreneurs, who have recently begun to covet lottery largesse for themselves. Responding to this interest, at least two midwestern states were actively considering selling their state lotteries to private firms in 2007. These firms, in exchange for guaranteed payments to the states, would gain the exclusive ability to market and sell lottery tickets in the states.

Illinois Governor Rod Blagojevich first proposed selling his state's lottery in the spring of 2006, and continued to propose it during his 2006 gubernatorial reelection campaign.[1] In January of 2007, Blagojevich took the first steps toward privatizing the lottery. Under the proposal, the new owners would give the state several billion dollars up front (the Governor's earlier estimate was that the state might receive as much as $6 billion) in exchange for receiving the right to all revenue and profit for 75 years.[2] Mitch Daniels, the governor of neighboring Indiana, proposed his own privatization of that state's Hoosier Lottery. Under the Daniels proposal, a private firm would pay more than $1 billion in order to gain a 30 year right to sell lottery tickets.[3]

The stated benefit of lottery privatization is to get the state out of the business of marketing and selling lottery tickets in exchange for providing an influx of cash that can be used to provide state services. In both the Illinois and Indiana cases, the proposed revenue would be dedicated to education, which is the stated beneficiary of current lottery proceeds in these states. Illinois expects the sale to provide elementary and secondary education with an estimated $650 annually over 18 years. Indiana, on the other hand, proposed that the funds from the lottery sale be used for college and university scholarships and loans.

Opponents of lottery privatization raise at least two cautionary concerns. First, there is the possibility that the states will be selling these assets for less than they may be worth. This would have the potential effect of costing the states hundreds of millions (in the case of Indiana) or even billions (in Illinois) of dollars of revenue in the future. Second, some express concerns that private lottery operators will market the games more aggressively toward the poor and gambling addicts, which states have been somewhat reluctant to do as matter of public policy.[4]

[1] Bellandi, D. (2006). Blagojevich says state could get more money by privatizing lottery. *Associated Press state and local wire.* Retrieved January 23, 2007, from http://web.lexis-nexis.com.proxygw.wrlc.org/universe/document?_m= 7f31fe756f82363a6f.4845691a4b40eb&_docnum=1&wchp=dGLbVtb-zSkVA&md5= e07f7e9c38137cd4eccb5d17f8e873d1.

[2] Duhigg, C. & Anderson, J. (2007). Illinois is putting lottery on block for quick payoff. *New York Times*, January 23. Retrieved January 23, 2007, from http://www.nytimes.com/2007/01/23/business/23lottohtml.

[3] Hinnefeld, S. (2006). Governor Daniels proposes privatizing lottery, using profits on higher education. *Bloomington Herald-Times.* Retrieved January 23, 2007, from http://web.lexis-nexis.com.proxygw.wrlc.org/universe/document?_m= 7f31fe756f82363a6f4845691a4b40eb&_docnum=2&wchp=dGLbVtb-zSkVA&md5= 073b938da312b1adfb7c3ce8d0d99a46.

[4] Duhigg & Anderson (2007).

Carolina lotteries. The state of Pennsylvania recently introduced slot machines, an action that arguably could have been influenced by the existence of casinos in neighboring New Jersey. The economic benefits in terms of employment and increased tax revenues have been less than expected, though definitely positive. Hard evidence of social consequences has been difficult to find, although anecdotally opponents of legalized gambling argue that the social costs exceed the economic benefits.[34]

One of the selling points often used to market the lottery and other forms of gambling revenues is that their proceeds will be used to support spending for some specific (usually popular) policy area. For example, many states earmark lottery revenues, or other gaming revenues, for education or senior citizen programs. It is frequently difficult, however, to make the case that this earmarking actually leads to a net increase in funding for these areas. In cases where funds are dedicated to education, for example, lottery earmarking may simply have the effect of freeing up other revenues that would have been spent on education to be used for other purposes.[35] This is because of the *fungibility* of revenues, given that some sources can be substituted for others without increasing spending for particular programs (see Chapter 14). In some states where lottery earnings are earmarked exclusively to support education, state legislatures have cut other state education spending by commensurate amounts.[36] An exception was found to this general rule in Georgia, where lottery revenues have stimulated additional spending in the areas advertised by lottery proponents. According to the authors of this study, this occurred because of the specific structure of the earmark, the transparency of the budget process, and the commitment of the governor to increase funds rather than substitute them.[37]

Pari-mutuel Wagering Taxes. In addition to lottery and amusement taxes, some states allow betting on athletic competitions, primarily horse racing (although some states also have legalized dog racing and jai-alai). These are more similar to amusement taxes than lotteries in the sense that the activity is not operated by the state, but is rather regulated and taxed by the state. Nationwide, pari-mutuel taxes generated only $302 million in 2002. This represented only 0.04% of total own-source revenue for states in that year. Only California ($42 million), New York ($38 million), and Florida ($32 million) raised more than $20 million in that year, but in each of these cases the revenue from this source made an inconsequential contribution to state revenues.

Revenue Estimating

Turning to the full scope of revenues, the subject matter of this chapter and the previous one, little imagination is required to appreciate the importance of revenue estimating. If a government is required to have a balanced budget, as state and local governments are, then accurate revenue forecasts become critical. Estimates that are too high can create major crises during the execution phase, at which time expenditures must be cut so as not to exceed revenues. Low estimates also cause problems, in that programs may be needlessly reduced at the beginning of the fiscal year.

Deterministic Models

Perhaps the easiest method of revenue forecasting involves deterministic models that manipulate the revenue base and tax rate to produce a desired level of revenue. Property tax forecasts are deterministic in that a government can adjust assessments and tax rates to meet desired revenue levels. The main problems to address in such forecasting are the extent that (1) overall property values will rise or possibly decline, (2) new properties will be added to the tax rolls, and (3) old and deteriorating properties will fall into default. Deterministic models are useful for revenue sources over which a jurisdiction has substantial control. They are not useful for taxes on such items as personal income and retail sales, which depend on economic conditions.

Simple Trend Extrapolations

Both formal and informal trend extrapolations are used in revenue estimating. In an informal situation, an assumption may be made that a particular revenue source will increase by 5% because that is what has occurred for the last several years. In most cases, of course, revenues do not increase or decrease by a set percentage or remain constant. Revenue growth may increase on average by 5%, but in some years the growth may be 10% and in others only 1 or 2%. Given this information, what percentage estimate should be used for the upcoming budget year?

One method of dealing with this problem is to use *simple linear regression*, a statistical technique that fits a straight line to a series of historical data. The formula used is $y = mx + b$. In the equation, y, the forecast revenue, is a function of a coefficient m multiplied by a known value x plus a constant b. In the formula, m is the slope of the straight line, x is the actual revenue generated the previous year, and b is a scale factor that adjusts for orders of magnitude differences between values. Computer software is readily available for making the appropriate calculations, but such projections also can be made using simple calculators.

The straight-line calculation of linear regression, however, may not parallel the actual historical series. The fit of the regression can be gauged by calculating the correlation coefficient known as R. When the data are random, R is 0.00. The closer R is to 1.00, the more likely it is that the regression accurately forecasts revenue.

Besides linear regression, other techniques exist for smoothing out fluctuations in a historical series into a straight line. The method called *moving averages* calculates an average value for each point in the historical series. Starting with a series of, say, 8 years, the revenues for years 1, 2, and 3 are averaged. This average becomes the new smoothed value for year 2. Then actual values for years 2, 3, and

4 are averaged to create a new "smoothed" year 3. Similar averages are calculated for the remaining years. A variant of this technique weighs the most recent years more heavily than the early years in calculating the moving average, on the grounds that recent years are better predictors.

Underlying these techniques is the premise that the future will be like the past. The purpose of any projection technique is to reduce historical information to a discernible pattern and then extend that pattern into the future. One way of testing how well the technique works is to "predict" several recent time periods and compare those predictions with what actually occurred. Most local governments, except large cities, still rely on one form or another of *trend extrapolation*. Chesterfield County, Virginia, adds the expert judgment of the county government's program managers, business leaders, state tax experts, and expertise from the Federal Reserve Bank of Richmond convened in a semi-annual forum to discuss underlying trends. This addition of expert judgment allows the county to adjust the results of trend extrapolation methods.[38] Evidence suggests that when used in combination with other tools, trend extrapolations produce reliable estimates for local governments.[39] Extrapolation methods are not helpful when there are significant and abrupt changes in economic conditions such as the rapid economic decline that began in late 2000, causing rapid reversal from state and local budget surpluses to severe fiscal pressures.

Econometric Models

Several types of econometric techniques for forecasting revenues exist.[40] One of the most popular is *multiple regression*. In multiple regression models, independent variables are sought that can serve as predictors of revenue yield. The assumption is that a linear relationship exists between each predictor and the dependent variable of forecast revenue. Another assumption is that each independent variable is unrelated to the others. A model for sales tax receipts might include the independent variables of population, personal income, and the consumer price index. As each of these variables increases, revenues increase.

Multiple predictor variables are used in *simultaneous equation models* (multiple regression models rely on a single equation). In simultaneous equation models, individual equations relate each independent or predictor variable to the revenue to be forecast. These individual equations are solved simultaneously. The advantage of simultaneous equation models is that, unlike multiple regression models, they do not assume that each predictor variable is independent of each other predictor variable. Because many of the variables one would use to make a revenue forecast would be expected to be related to each other, the simultaneous equation approach is both more realistic and computationally more valid.

Revenue forecasts can be made using *microsimulation models* that are dependent on large databases manipulated by computers. Individual taxpayers and corporations are included in the models and exhibit behavior changes in response to projected changes in the economy, tax laws, price levels, personal income, and the like. The models use data based on the historical performance of actual taxpayers in the jurisdiction.

All of these models necessarily use variables that are sensitive to changes in economic conditions. Sales and income tax receipts rise and fall according to economic trends. Many user charges are affected, too. When people are unemployed, they curtail their use of public transportation, parking facilities, museums, and zoos. Therefore, these models are most vulnerable with regard to the assumptions made about future economic trends. Also critical are basic demographic shifts. Changing population patterns due to shifting birth rates and migration can undermine the effectiveness of forecasting models that previously had shown themselves to be extremely accurate.[41] Projecting national trends is extremely difficult, and state and local trends are no easier to predict, especially given that each subnational jurisdiction has its own economic characteristics and is influenced by national trends.

Politics

Revenue estimating has its political aspects. Presidents, governors, and mayors are loathe to forecast economic hard times and low revenue levels. Political executives tend to campaign for election in part on the promise that they will strive for economic growth. Presidents have the additional problem that the forecast of a recession may be a self-fulfilling prophecy. State and local executives must limit expenditures to available revenue. Pessimistic estimates force executives to make difficult choices as to where to cut programs so as to reduce overall expenditures. In general, there seems to be a tendency to underestimate revenues more often than to overestimate them. Apparently, politicians feel the political risks of underestimating and producing a surplus at the end of the year are less dire than the consequences of overestimating and having to make program cuts or raise taxes unexpectedly during the year.[42] Since revenue estimates can rarely, if ever, be guaranteed to come true, establishing *contingency reserves* or *rainy day funds* may be a useful method of protecting against possible shortfalls and the political problems that ensue from them (see Chapter 10).

◼ Summary

Some revenue sources, instead of being taxes on income or wealth, are taxes on individual transactions. Among these are general and specific sales taxes, user charges, and revenue raised from games of chance, such as lotteries. These revenue sources have in common that they are levied on a more or less voluntary basis. That is, individuals have relatively more "choice" in whether they engage in the transaction or pay the tax.

The general sales tax is the largest single revenue source for state governments, and is also used by many local governments. The tax is levied on sales made at the retail level. Many states exclude particular transactions from the tax base. Among the most frequent exclusions are food and prescription drugs. By and large, these exclusions make the tax less regressive, since they are necessities and thus tend to represent a larger percentage of total spending for lower-income taxpayers than for higher-income taxpayers. In recent years, the viability of the sales tax has been threatened by the increased spending by consumers from remote vendors, including both mail-order sales and sales over the Internet. States and local governments lack a reliable way to collect taxes on these transactions.

Sales taxes are also levied on particular types of transactions. There are three general categories of these selective sales, or excise, taxes. First, luxury excises are levied on items (such as boats or luxury automobiles) the purchase of which is viewed as evidence of an extraordinary taxpaying ability. Second, sumptuary excises (so-called "sin" taxes) are levied on items such as cigarettes and liquor, ostensibly to discourage consumption of these goods that are thought to cause harm to both the individual who consumes them as well as society as a whole. Third, benefit-based excises operate as a quasi-price by taxing individuals and then using the proceeds of those taxes to finance benefits used by the specific taxpayers on whom the tax is levied. A classic example of this is gasoline taxes used to finance transportation, especially highways.

Increasingly, governments charge citizens directly for their purchase of individual services, or have dedicated revenue from charges for particular spending programs or functions. In this way, government services can be made to resemble market transactions. User charges have been growing at all levels of government, and include such varied items as federal postal service fees, state university tuition, and local water and sewer fees.

Many state governments rely on revenue from gambling to finance a portion of state government services. While most states do not raise much money from gambling, games of chance have been a growth industry for states. There are substantial differences between lotteries and other forms of gaming revenue. In the case of lotteries, the games are operated directly by the government, with games marketed, tickets sold, and proceeds paid directly to state coffers. In the case of other games of chance, such as casino gambling, the games are not operated by the state but are taxed by the government. Casino gambling has been on the increase in recent years, including both Native American and non-Native American components.

Regardless of the revenue source, it is obviously important for any government to be able to forecast revenues accurately. A wide variety of estimation methods is used by governments for revenue forecasting. Deterministic models manipulate the tax base and tax rates to achieve a given level of desired revenue. Trend extrapolations may also be used, and these may either represent relatively simple forecasts or more complicated predictions based on more sophisticated methods, such as multiple regression. Among the most sophisticated of these are microsimulation models that rely on numerous variables to forecast revenues. Political factors play a significant role in revenue forecasting, particularly when a chief executive decides that a given level of revenue requires that particular assumptions be used. Presidents, governors, and mayors also tend to assume that their policies will result in positive economic growth, which can introduce somewhat of an optimistic bias into revenue forecasting.

Notes

1. Brookings-Urban Tax Policy Center (2006). *State general sales tax rates, 2006.* Retrieved November 7, 2006, from http://www.taxpolicycenter.org/TaxFacts/TFDB/Content/PDF/state_sales_tax.pdf.

2. Hoffman, D. (Ed.) (2002). *Facts and figures on government finance*, 36th ed. Washington, DC: Tax Foundation, 178; Fischel, W. A. (2002). School finance litigation and property tax revolts: how undermining local control turns voters away from public education. *Developments in school finance: fiscal proceedings from the annual state data conference, July 1999 and July 2000.* Washington, DC: National Center for Education Statistics, 79–127.

3. Brookings-Urban Tax Policy Center (2006). *State general sales tax rates, 2006.* Retrieved November 7, 2006, from http://www.taxpolicycenter.org/TaxFacts/TFDB/Content/PDF/state_sales_tax.pdf.

4. Due, J. & Mikesell, J. (2005). Retail sales tax, state and local. In J. Cordes, R. Ebel, & J. Gravelle (Eds.), *Encyclopedia of taxation and tax policy*. Washington, DC: Urban Institute Press, 337.

5. Due, J. & Mikesell, J. (2005). Retail sales tax, state and local. In J. Cordes, R. Ebel, & J. Gravelle (Eds.), *Encyclopedia of taxation and tax policy*, Washington, DC: Urban Institute Press, 337.

6. The Government Performance Project: Florida (2003). *Governing.* Retrieved November 7, 2006, from http://www.governing.com/gpp/2003/gp3fl.htm.

7. Brookings-Urban Tax Policy Center (2006). *State general sales tax rates, 2006.* Retrieved November 7, 2006 from http://www.taxpolicycenter.org/TaxFacts/TFDB/Content/PDF/state_sales_tax.pdf.

8. Mikesell, J. (2004). The prospects for general sales taxation in American state and local government finance: challenges for a fiscal workhorse unready for the new millennium. *Journal of Public Budgeting, Accounting and Financial Management, 16*, 63–79.

9. Rivlin, A. M. (1992). *Reviving the American dream: the economy, the states and the federal government.* Washington, DC: Brookings Institution.

10. Zodrow, G. R. (1999).The sales tax, the VAT, and taxes in between—or, is the only good NRST a "VAT in drag"? *National Tax Journal, 52*, 429–442.

11. Davie, B., updated by D. Zimmerman (2005). Luxury taxes. In J. Cordes, R. Ebel, & J. Gravelle (Eds.), *Encyclopedia of taxation and tax policy*. Washington, DC: Urban Institute Press, 245–247.

12. Davie, B, updated by D. Zimmerman (2005). Luxury taxes. In J. Cordes, R. Ebel, & J. Gravelle (Eds.), *Encyclopedia of taxation and tax policy*. Washington, DC: Urban Institute Press, 245–247.

13. Pogue, T. (2005). Alcohol beverage taxes, federal. In J. Cordes, R. Ebel, & J. Gravelle (Eds.), *Encyclopedia of taxation and tax policy*. Washington, DC: Urban Institute Press, 5.

14. Pogue, T. (2005). Alcohol beverage taxes, federal. In J. Cordes, R. Ebel, & J. Gravelle (Eds.), *Encyclopedia of taxation and tax policy*. Washington, DC: Urban Institute Press, 5.

15. Johnson, R. W. & McCullough, J. S. (1996). Case study on urban local government finance, Paper presented at the Asian Development Bank Seminar on Urban Infrastructure Finance in Asia. Research Triangle Park, NC: Research Triangle Institute.

16. U.S. Office of Management and Budget (1993). *Circular A-25.* Retrieved January 21, 2007, from http://www.whitehouse.gov/omb/circulars/a025/a025.html.

17. U.S. Office of Management and Budget (2006). *Budget of the United States government, fiscal year 2007, analytical perspectives.* Washington, DC: U.S. Government Printing Office, 276–277.

18. U.S. Office of Management and Budget (2006). *Budget of the United States government; fiscal year 2007, analytical perspectives.* Washington, DC: U.S. Government Printing Office, 274.

19. Richardson, P. (2005). Offsetting collections and receipts. In J. Cordes, R. Ebel, & J. Gravelle (Eds.), *Encyclopedia of taxation and tax policy*. Washington, DC: Urban Institute Press, 280–81.

20. Bureau of the Census, U.S. Department of Commerce (2006). *State and local government finances by level of government and by state, 2003–2004.* Retrieved November 15, 2006, from http://www.census.gov.govs/estimate/0400.uss._1.html.

21. Wassmer, R. & Fisher. R. (2002). Interstate variation in the use of fees to fund K-12 public education. *Economics of Education Review, 21,* 87–100.

22. Foster, B. D. & Fujita, G. (2000). Rate setting for municipal utilities: Detroit's combined sewer overflow facilities. *Government Finance Review, 16, June,* 33–40.

23. Khan, A. & Stumm, T. J. (1994). The tax and expenditure effects of subsidization by municipal utility enterprises. *Municipal Finance Journal, 15,* 68–81; Stumm, T. J. & Khan, A. (1996). Effects of utility enterprise fund subsidization on municipal taxes and expenditures. *State and Local Government Review, 28,* 103–113.

24. Bureau of the Census, U.S. Department of Commerce (2006). *Income and apportionment of state-administered lottery funds: 2004.* Retrieved November 16, 2006, from http://ftp2census.gov/govs/state/04lottery.pdf.

25. Calculations by author from Bureau of the Census, U.S. Department of Commerce (2006). *Income and apportionment of state-administered lottery funds: 2004* and *State and*

local government finances by level of government and by state: 2003–2004. Retrieved November 16, 2006, from http://ftp2census.gov/govs/state/04lottery.pdf and www.census.gov/govs/www/estimate04.html.

26. Calculations by author from Bureau of the Census, U.S. Department of Commerce (2006). *Income and apportionment of state-administered lottery funds: 2004*. Retrieved November 16, 2006, from http://ftp2census.gov/govs/state/04lottery.pdf.

27. Fink, S., Marco, A., & Rork, J. (2004). Lotto nothing? The budgetary impact of state lotteries. *Applied Economics, 36*, 2357–2367.

28. Clotfelter, C. T. & Cook, P. J. (1990). On the economics of state lotteries. *Journal of Economic Perspective, 4, Fall*, 105–119.

29. Freund, E. & Morris, I. (2005). The lottery and income inequality in the states. *Social Science Quarterly, 86*, 996–1012.

30. Oster, E. (2004). Are all lotteries regressive? Evidence from the Powerball. *National Tax Journal, 57*, 179–187.

31. Bureau of the Census, U.S. Department of Commerce (2006). *Income and apportionment of state-administered lottery funds: 2004*. Retrieved November 16, 2006, from http://ftp2census.gov/govs/state/04lottery.pdf.

32. Bureau of the Census, U.S. Department of Commerce (2006). *Statistical abstract of the United States, 2006*. Washington, DC: U.S. Government Printing Office, 283.

33. Elliott, D. E. & Navin, J. (2002). Has riverboat gambling reduced state lottery revenue? *Public Finance Review, 30*, 235–247.

34. U.S. General Accounting Office (2000). *Impact of gambling: economic effects more measurable than social effects*. Washington, DC: U.S. Government Printing Office.

35. Gribbin, D. & Bean, J. (2006). Adoption of state lotteries in the United States, with a closer look at Illinois. *The Independent Review, 10*, 360.

36. Spindler, C. J. (1995). The lottery and education: robbing Peter to pay Paul? *Public Budgeting & Finance, 15, Fall*, 54–62.

37. Lauth, T. & Robbins. M. (2002). The Georgia lottery and state appropriations for education: substitution or additional funding? *Public Budgeting & Finance, 22, Fall*, 89–100.

38. Stegmaier, J. & Reiss, M. (1994). The revenue forum: an effective low-cost, low-tech approach to revenue forecasting. *Government Finance Review, 12, April*, 13–16.

39. Grizzle, G. & Klay, W. (1994). Forecasting state sales tax revenues: comparing the accuracy of different methods. *State and Local Government Review, 26*, 142–152.

40. Cirincione, C. et al. (1999) Municipal government revenue forecasting: issues of method and data. *Public Budgeting & Finance, 19, Spring*, 26–46.

41. Mullins, D. R. & Wallace, S. (1996). Changing demographics and state fiscal outlook: the case of sales taxes. *Public Finance Quarterly, 24*, 237–262.

42. Rodgers, R. & Joyce, P. (1996). The effect of underforecasting on the accuracy of revenue forecasts by state governments. *Public Administration Review, 56*, 48–56.

Chapter 6

BUDGET PREPARATION: THE EXPENDITURE SIDE

By the mid-2000s, the federal government's Office of Management and Budget (OMB) was using its Program Assessment Rating Tool (PART) throughout the government to help determine the strengths and weaknesses of programs and to assist in allocating resources in the budgetary process. State and local governments similarly were widely using program information in their budget processes. These were the outgrowth of changes that began in the early 1900s. Budgeting had come a long way.

In the budget preparation phase, important decisions about expenditures are made simultaneously with decisions concerning revenues. The two general types of information relevant for budgeting are program and resource information (see Chapter 1). Program information consists of data on what government does and what those activities accomplish. Resource information consists of the inputs necessary to perform those activities. The inputs include dollars, facilities, equipment, supplies, and personnel, and have been a long established feature of budgetary systems. The use of program information, on the other hand, has slowly emerged as an integral part of budgeting.

The critical argument relating to these two types of information is that they must be considered in combination if budgeting is to be a sensible process of allocating resources. The budget is expected to relate the accomplishments of government to the resources available. The history of budgetary reform can be viewed as a struggle to create such budget systems.

This chapter examines the various approaches used in assembling the expenditure side of budgets, with the following chapter considering the political concerns of budget preparation. The first section of this chapter discusses early reform efforts. The second section describes the types of program information used to varying degrees in budget systems. The last section explores the numerous budget systems that have been used, including performance, program, zero-base, and hybrid budgeting systems.

Early Developments

As noted in Chapter 1, budgeting can focus on expenditure control, management of resources, and planning for future allocation decisions.[1] While the development of these three emphases has been sequential over time to some extent, they are not rigidly fixed to specific time periods, and both the management and planning phases have involved greater utilization of program information. Not only is there a blurring of distinctions between these stages in terms of the dates of their popularity, but use of planning coupled with program information also was advocated at least as far back as the early part of the twentieth century. By planning we are specifically referring to an effort to associate means with ends in an effort to attain goals and objectives in the future.

Program Information

1910–1939. Before the establishment of the federal budgetary system, budgeting often was advocated as a means of allocating resources to obtain program results.[2] Two of the most notable proponents were President Taft[3] and the 1912 Taft Commission on Economy and Efficiency. At one point in its report, the Commission stated, "In order that he [the administrator] may think intelligently about the subject of his responsibility he must have before him regularly statements which will reflect *results in terms of quality and quantity*; he must be able to measure quality and quantity of results by units of cost and units of efficiency"[4] (emphasis added). Although there was an obvious interest in economizing—in saving dollars—there was also an interest in obtaining the best return in program terms for resources spent.[5]

Other important spokespersons for program results in budgeting in the 1910s included Frederick A. Cleveland[6] and William F. Willoughby.[7] The 1920s and 1930s brought more proponents for program results being included in budgets including Lent D. Upson,[8] A. E. Buck,[9] Wylie Kilpatrick,[10] and the 1937 President's Committee on Administrative Management.[11] A. E. Buck's classic, *Public*

Budgeting (1929), admittedly lacked a strong program information orientation, but Buck did express interest in reforms that would concentrate on measuring the products of government activities.

1940–1960. Although the use of program information and planning was advocated throughout the first four decades of the twentieth century, this issue received far greater attention beginning in the 1940s. V. O. Key, Jr., challenged previous budgetary literature as largely mechanical and criticized it for failing to focus on the "basic budgeting problem" of comparing the merits of alternative programs: "On what basis shall it be decided to allocate X dollars to activity A instead of activity B?"[12] The 1949 Commission on the Organization of the Executive Branch of the Government, commonly known as the First Hoover Commission, recommended that the federal budget be "based upon functions, activities, and projects: this we designate as a performance budget." Budgeting should be in terms of "the work or the service to be accomplished."[13]

More proponents of the same viewpoint emerged in the 1950s. Noted scholars included Verne B. Lewis,[14] Frederick C. Mosher,[15] Catheryn Seckler-Hudson,[16] and Arthur Smithies.[17] The Second Hoover Commission supported the recommendations of its predecessor.[18] Smithies suggested the use of program information in budgeting as a primary means of improving both executive and legislative decision making. Jesse Burkhead's *Government Budgeting* (1956), while basically descriptive rather than normative, devoted considerable discussion to performance and program budgeting.[19]

By the 1950s the use of program information in budgeting had become a mainstream reform issue. At the same time, another school of thought led by Charles E. Lindblom, Aaron Wildavsky, and others, challenged the budget reform movement on the grounds that political decision systems were not readily adaptable to program planning. Lindblom advanced the "muddling through" model of decision making (see Chapter 1) that ran counter to budgetary reform efforts. Wildavsky was to become the most outspoken skeptic of the feasibility of using program information in budgeting. In 1969 he concluded, "No one knows how to do program budgeting."[20]

Nonbudgetary Developments

An alternative school of thought led by David Novick, Charles J. Hitch, Roland McKean, and others, was rooted in a set of theoretical and technological fields that developed after World War II. These fields and technologies were highly compatible with the budget reform movement and served as the theoretical foundation for planning-programming-budgeting (PPB) systems attempted in the 1960s. Of central importance were the following six conceptual fields and technologies:[21]

1. Operations research, a technique that involves specifying objectives, designing a model representing the situation under investigation, and collecting and applying relevant data.[22]

2. Economic analysis, a process of determining whether benefits exceed costs of a current or contemplated program.[23]

3. General systems theory, an approach that focuses on how components of a system relate to one another.[24]

4. Cybernetics, the science of control and communication.[25]

5. Information technology, the methods by which data are manipulated to produce information suitable for analysis and supportive of the decision-making process.[26]

6. Systems analysis, an eclectic form of analysis that draws upon the previous five items.[27]

These fields and technologies were developed outside of the budget reform movement but were highly compatible with it. The six constituted the theoretical and technological foundation for what became the PPB system in the Department of Defense in the 1960s.

The reform efforts from the early 1900s to 1960 that emphasized the use of program information, coupled with this series of other nonbudgetary developments, constitute the foundation for more recent budget system innovations and for contemporary budget systems.

▉ Structuring the Request Process

Except in the smallest organizations, a central budget office alone cannot prepare a budget. As noted in Chapter 3, budget preparation begins with the almost simultaneous amassing of supporting information in the operating agencies and the issuance of budget instructions from a central budget office.

The information developed at this stage depends partially on how each agency chooses to make its case and partially on the way decisions are expected to be made within an organization. If only dollar requests are prepared, obviously no information will be available with which to make judgments on program effectiveness. On the other hand, a central budget office may not necessarily use program information in its deliberations even if it requires its submission. Still another factor determining what information will be prepared is the known information demands from other budget participants, most notably, the legislative body. Much data may be amassed, not because the agency or the chief executive has any intention of using them for decision purposes, but simply because each year the legislative body demands that information.

Preparation Instructions

Budget preparation practices vary considerably within agencies. Different degrees of participation by field office staff and other line personnel occur, but while such variation exists, the overall process is guided by a set of instructions issued by a central budget office of a government.

At the federal level, such instructions are contained in OMB Circular A-11, Preparation, Submission, and Execution of the Budget. This document, issued annually, contains considerable detail about most aspects of federal budgeting and, counting text and supporting illustrations, runs more than 800 pages in length. The sections specifically pertaining to budget preparation and submission cover about 220 pages. The circular is available on the Internet, and agencies can submit much of their budget requests through a computer template system.[28] **Table 6–1** indicates the vast array of materials that agencies must submit. Much of this information is mandated by various statutes, such as performance information being required by the

Table 6–1	Selected Materials that Federal Agencies Must Submit as Part of Their Budget Requests

Section Title of OMB Circular A-11	Description
Summary of Requirements	Overview of materials they must submit
Performance Information Requirements	Link program data used for strategic planning and other activities with budget data in accordance with Budget and Performance Integration (BPI) Initiative
Compliance with Administrative Policies and Other General Requirements	Confirm that budgets comply with President's spending levels, President's Management Agenda, and other requirements
Personnel, Compensation, Benefits, and Related Costs	Estimate expenditures for employee pay and benefits
Estimates Related to Specific Types of Programs and Expenditures	Estimate expenditures for construction, leases of capital assets, hospitals, advisory committees, and tax expenditures
Basic Justification Materials	Summarize justification of programs, employment levels, any agency restructuring, grant programs, and performance indicators and performance goals

continues

Table 6–1	**Selected Materials that Federal Agencies Must Submit as Part of Their Budget Requests (continued)**

Section Title of OMB Circular A-11	Description
Information on Financial Management	Submit information on in-house financial activities, contracting, and grants, and auditing of activities
Information Technology and E-Government	Report information technology spending and efforts to expand public access to information through technology (e-government)
Rental Payments for Space and Land	Show expenditures for rental of buildings, other structures, and land
Budget Data System	Overview of MAX budget system, which provides computer support for the budget process
Development of Baseline Estimates	Overview of preparing baseline estimates
Policy and Baseline Estimates of Budget Authority, Outlays, and Receipts	Project budget authority, outlays, and receipts for future years based on existing laws (current services projections)
Program and Financing	Report budget authority, obligated expenses, outlays, compliance with rescissions, and other financing by program activity
Object Classification	Submit information about personnel, contractual services, acquisition of assets, and grants and fixed charges
Character Classification	Report expenditures as to whether they are investments or non-investments and whether they provide funding to state and local governments
Estimating Employment Levels and the Personnel Summary	Estimate the full-time equivalent (FTE) of personnel by program activity
Special Schedules	Provide balance sheets that summarize financial transactions
Budget Appendix and Print Material	Indicate appropriations language and provide narrative statements about program activities

Source: Adapted from U.S. Office of Management and Budget (2006). Preparation, Submission, and Execution of the Budget, Circular No. A-11. Retrieved July 28, 2006, from http://www.whitehouse.gov/omb/circulars/a11/current_year/a_11_2006.pdf.

Government Performance and Results Act of 1993.[29] (Explanations of various items in **Table 6–1** are provided in other chapters.)

Table 6–2 provides a comparable summary of budget preparation instructions for New York State. One striking characteristic is the attention devoted to capital expenditures, such as monies for the purchase of land, buildings, and large pieces of equipment.

Instructions such as those contained in Circular A-11 and New York State's budget instructions include forms to be completed, reducing uncertainty among agencies as to what the budget office expects of them. Typically, a calendar will be provided explaining when requests are due for submission to the budget office and indicating

Table 6–2	Selected Materials That New York State Agencies Must Submit as Part of Their Budget Requests

Subject	Description
Commissioner's Statement	Indicate agency's mission, funding requirements, and changes requested
Agency Summary Recapitulation	Show appropriations by fund type, aid to localities, capital projects, and debt service
Program Recapitulation	Summarize current appropriations by program/fund and show requested changes
Miscellaneous Receipts	Report miscellaneous receipts
State Operations and Aid to Localities	Provide expenditures by objective classification and report aid to localities
State Operations Request for Replacement/Additional State Vehicles	Indicate request for vehicles including type of vehicle and type of fuel
State Operations Nonpersonal Services	Submit information on all equipment and real property that requires installment payments out of state bond proceeds
Special Revenue Funds—Federal	Report existing and new federal grants
Reappropriations of Current Appropriations in Force	Request reappropriation when an existing appropriation will not be expended by its expiration date
Commissioner's Capital Plan Overview	Report major changes in five-year capital plan
Capital Projects Summaries	Provide detailed data on capital projects
Non-Highway and Highway Appropriation Request	Request approval of new capital projects
Capital Commitments	Report expected dollar value of contracts expected to be awarded
Capital Projects Codes	Supply departmental and budget codes for each capital project
Capital Maintenance Plan Report	Provide overview of plans for maintenance of capital
Description of Maintenance Projects	Show detailed information about planned maintenance projects
Requested Maintenance Appropriations, Reappropriations, and Disbursements	Request approval of maintenance appropriations
Summary of Capital Assets	Indicate age, useful life, and value of agency assets
Summary of Maintenance Plan Evaluations	Supply narrative discussing the evaluation of plans to maintain agency assets

Source: Adapted from New York State Division of the Budget (2006). *Budget Request Manual.* Retrieved July 27, 2006, from http://www.budget.state.ny.us/brm/item2.html.

a period when agencies may be called for hearings with the budget office. The instructions, then, determine the type and amount of information that will be required of the agencies, although the budget office may request additional information from particular agencies. In the case of the federal government, Circular A-11 describes a two-step process. The circular is released in the summer and agencies have varying deadlines to submit their requests. Then the agencies receive feedback, or "passback," on their proposals and must submit revised and more detailed requests using the computer support system. This second stage occurs in November, leading up to the president's submission of the budget to Congress after the first of the year.

No matter what the jurisdiction, standard items can be found in virtually all budget instruction manuals. Where appropriate, agencies are asked to submit revenue data (e.g., an agency operating a loan program with a revolving fund). Most of the instructions, however, concentrate on expenditures. The expenditures are keyed with the accounting system, using objects of expenditures such as personnel and supplies (see Chapter 11). There also may be detailed breakouts on the number of persons in a given unit, their job titles, and their current salaries. The instructions usually allow for the agencies to provide narrative statements to justify their requests.

Separate sets of instructions may be provided for the operating and capital fund budgets. Instructions for the latter, which are used extensively at the state and local levels, are meant primarily for requests on major fixed assets such as buildings and equipment (see **Table 6–2**). Federal agencies are required to separate out their investments in fixed assets, although no distinctions are made between investments in assets, or capital, and operating or current expenses when Congress appropriates funding for the agencies (see Chapter 12).

Program Information

Budget systems are making increased use of program information. Therefore, preparation instructions specify which types of program data are to be supplied. The measures typically will have been negotiated between the budget office and the agencies before budget preparation time. In other words, when the agencies receive the request instructions, they already know what program information they need to submit. Determining what information to collect and present in budget requests is of concern at all levels of government in the United States and abroad. As of the mid-2000s, the umbrella term used to describe the overall field of program information was *performance measurement*.[30] Such measurement is seen as a means for holding agencies accountable for the expenditure of tax dollars and other public resources.

Social Indicators. Of the variety of program information, social indicators are the broadest or most general type. These measures of the physical, social, and economic environments are intended to reflect what sometimes is called *quality of life*.[31] The percentage of the work force unemployed broken out by age, sex, race, and income constitutes a set of important social indicators. Other commonly used social indicators gauge family stability/broken homes, income for individuals and families, and health-related topics such as infant mortality. Measures of this type are useful in assessing past and current trends and provide decision makers with some insights into the need for programs.

Rarely are social indicators used as measures of program performance because they are so broad as to defy demonstrating causal linkage between a specific program expenditure and a change in one of these indicators. But they are important in identifying the problems on which government may need to focus.

One volunteer network in the Seattle area has developed 40 such indicators to determine whether the region is maintaining "sustainability"—namely, preserving its "cultural, economic, environmental and social" conditions. In the 1990s, the group found that the region was declining in sustainability in such areas as wetlands, energy use, and children living in poverty.[32] In the 2000s, the City of Seattle strove for sustainability while at the same time fostering development.[33]

One limitation of the Seattle measures, as well as other social indicators, is their lack of direct linkage with any given government service, meaning that the indicators are of little use for making yearly budget decisions. Children live in poverty as a result of many factors and no government program alone could be expected to solve the problem.[34] At the same time, social indicators about communities in a state may give rise to decisions about how to help each of the communities in need.[35]

Outcomes. Measures of more direct relevance to budgeting are outcomes, also called impacts. Measures of this type concentrate on *effectiveness*—whether desired effects or consequences are being achieved. When a government action has affected "individuals, institutions [or] the environment," an impact has occurred.[36] In the case of employment, an outcome measure might be the average earnings of nonwhite men who completed a job training program or, even more narrowly focused, the average increase in hourly earnings after completion of the program compared with prior earnings. Such a measure needs to be assessed carefully because earnings may have increased in a given time period mainly as a result of inflation or an upturn in the economy. Outcomes can be seen as a method of gauging the value of government services or determining whether expenditures are accomplishing what decision makers wished to achieve.

One approach may be to think of some outcomes as "raw" and others as "adjusted." Raw outcomes might be various measures of performance by school children on a standardized achievement test. Adjusted measures might take into account the children's characteristics, their families' socioeconomic background, and the neighborhoods in which they live.[37]

Sometimes myths or doctrines lead to problems in the selection of impact measures. For example, in providing funds to police departments, the assumption is often made that crime will be controlled. This assumption leads to the selection of crime rates as impact measures despite the fact that police have only limited control over crime.

Outputs. In contrast with outcome measures, output measures reflect the immediate products or services being provided. Returning to the employment example, the number of graduates of the training program would be the output. The percentage of persons enrolled who graduate, or the completion rate, can be calculated from year to year. Such measures are far easier to calculate than many impact measures because the data sources are within the organization. One needs simply to keep accurate records of who enrolled and who graduated. Impacts, on the other hand, are external. From this example, if we look at earnings of graduates, a monitoring or follow-up system for the graduates is necessary to obtain the appropriate outcome data.

Similarly, a program to spray for malaria is easy to measure in terms of the number of households sprayed, because the agency responsible for spraying keeps track of the output. But it may be a different part of the same agency, or sometimes a different agency, that measures health status, the presumed intended outcome.

When it is known that a relationship exists between outputs and outcomes, then allocating resources may be straightforward. For example, measles inoculations are known to prevent the disease; therefore, allocating funds for the inoculations is warranted, presuming a disease threat exists. In the case of small pox, vaccination programs ceased when the disease was basically eradicated.

One drawback of using output measures alone is that an erroneous assumption can be made about causal relationships. Focusing on the graduation rate of a job training program makes sense only if it is known that training improves employability. Unless data are collected to verify anticipated results (i.e., a higher rate of employment at the end of the job training), the program is being maintained without outside corroboration of its goal.

Outputs, then, may encourage *suboptimization*, or the improvement of operations for attaining subobjectives, while risking the possibility of moving away from larger values. If the job training program was ineffective but the emphasis was placed on outputs, then decision makers would focus attention on increasing the quantity of outputs and at reduced unit costs without realizing that the expenditures were altogether ineffective. In order to avoid this suboptimization problem, the U.S. Office Management and Budget expects agencies to use outcome measures and requires special justifications when agencies recommend using only output measures.[38] Please see **Exhibit 7–3** in Chapter 7 for a demonstration of the use of output and outcome measures for fire prevention and investigation in the City of Detroit.

Activities and Workload. Activities are the work that is done to produce outputs. The total hours of instruction could be a measure for a job training program, or the measure might be more tightly focused, such as hours of instruction in lathe operations. Activities are sometimes measured as workload. The number of applications processed and the number of enrollees in a program are both workload measures. If the number of applicants increases even though enrollments are kept constant because of space limitations, the workload will still increase, because more applications must be screened. Both activities and outputs are far easier to measure than impacts, a factor that contributes to the extensive use of the former in budgeting and more limited use of the latter.

Productivity. A term having many different meanings is *productivity*.[39] This term is sometimes used to cover virtually all forms of program measurement. A different approach is to limit the concept of productivity to comparisons of resource inputs and work. Ratios are typically used for productivity measurement, such as the total cost of a job training program divided by the number of graduates yielding an average cost per graduate. If average cost remains constant from one year to another despite increases in salary rates and various supplies, then the assumption is that the unit is more productive. OMB Circular A-11 provides that agencies should report gains in *efficiency*, which is sometimes a synonym for productivity.

Productivity measures often require extensive recordkeeping. If a group of employees together performs several different activities, then a reporting system is needed to account for the hours committed to each activity by each employee. This accounting is sometimes accomplished by means of daily report forms. State and local police often must submit daily reports on hours spent patrolling, investigating, testifying in court, and report writing itself. Less complicated systems may use weekly, monthly, or quarterly report forms. On the cost side, accounting systems need to capture nonpersonnel expenditures related to activities.

Need. A final type of measure gauges the need for a program. The need measure indicates the gap between the level of service and the need for it. In the case of the job training program, one need measure would be the number of persons who are without adequate job skills and, therefore, require training.

In discussing need, we have come full circle back to social indicators, prompting a few words of caution. We have relied here on several examples to show differences among types of measures, but it should be understood that the differences might not always be so obvious. For example, the dollar value of fire damage in a city might be considered a social indicator, an impact of the fire department, and an indicator of fire service need.

Using Program Measures. A major challenge facing any budget system is deciding how to use these diverse types of information. Which types of information will be used, in what combination, and to what extent? An initial temptation is to decide to use every imaginable measure of government operations. Such an approach is doomed to failure. If carefully and thoroughly executed, it would produce massive amounts of data that could not be comprehended by decision makers. Indeed, such data produce what is called "noise" rather than information.

Reformers for decades have been concerned that budgeting keep its focus on the missions of government and on the goals and objectives to be achieved. Osborne and Gaebler's popular work *Reinventing Government* stresses the need to keep mission primarily in mind when making decisions in government.[40] *Mission* refers to the fundamental reasons why a government program exists. Although scholars and practitioners in the field of budgeting have yet to reach any consensus on what constitutes a goal as distinguished from an objective, one approach is to think of goals as broadly stated ideal conditions, such as the absence of crime. *Goals*, under this definition, are unlikely to be achieved but function as desired states that governments can continuously work toward attaining. *Objectives*, on the other hand, are more focused and immediate, and impact data are used to gauge whether a program is moving toward achieving its objectives. A jurisdiction might focus on reducing burglaries and could specify a quantitative target for the future, such as a 10% reduction in burglaries. In setting goals and objectives, decision makers must understand that some desired results can be achieved in a comparatively short period, such as a year, whereas other results will require many years of effort to achieve.[41]

The program measures that agencies develop may be a reflection of their overall types of missions. One research team suggested four mission types may exist: distributive, redistributive, regulatory, and market emulators.[42] *Distributive* encompasses the provision of services such as defense and transportation. *Redistributive* refers to making transfer payments, as with rent subsidies, and programs targeted at special groups, such as health benefits for the needy. *Regulatory*, as the term suggests, concentrates on control, such as controlling would-be air polluters or controlling food producers as a means of protecting the nation's food supply. *Market emulators* are those government operations that are run like a business, such as public utilities. Operations such as municipal golf courses, parking garages, and institutions of higher education may operate somewhat like businesses.

The OMB recognizes seven types of programs and then expects program measures to be derived in conformance with the key characteristics of these types.[43] **Table 6–3** shows that the types are direct federal, competitive grant, block/formula grant, regulatory-based, capital assets and service acquisition, credit, and research and development. The table provides illustrative federal programs for each type.

Selecting measures for any given program depends on perceptions about the program's mission. Individuals may differ widely on what they consider to be a specific program's mission. In a broad sense, the vision one has of a program is related to one's perception of what the public interest is. In a narrow sense, individuals may have specific expectations of what government programs should accomplish. Renters may want a city housing program to focus

Table 6–3   Typology of Federal Programs and Agencies

Program Type	Description	Example
Direct Federal	Services provided primarily by federal employees	State Department's Visa and Consular Services program
Competitive Grant	Competition used to award grants to state and local governments, organizations, and individuals	Health Centers at the Department of Health and Human Services
Block/Formula Grant	Formula used in awarding grants to state and local governments and other entities	Department of Energy's Weatherization Assistance program
Regulatory-Based	Rulemaking and enforcement used to accomplish mission	Environmental Protection Agency's Mobile Source Air Pollution Standards and Certification program
Capital Assets and Service Acquisition	Goals accomplished by acquisition of "land, structures, equipment, and intellectual property" or purchase of services	Navy Shipbuilding
Credit	Goals served by providing loans, loan guarantees, and direct credit	Export-Import Bank's Long Term Guarantees program
Research and Development	Knowledge creation and its application	Solar System Exploration program of National Aeronautics and Space Administration

Source: Compiled from U.S. Office of Management and Budget (2006). *Program assessment rating tool guidance no. 2006-02*, 6.

on affordable rental housing, while homeowners may be largely concerned with city policies that will protect property values and keep taxes low. Owners of rental properties, in contrast, may be chiefly interested in achieving substantial returns on their financial investments. Ultimately, the success of many, if not most, government programs will be evaluated in terms of several measures rather than only one or two. The need to use multiple measures makes analysis of a program's achievements more challenging than if a single measure is used.

Interpreting measures, especially social indicators and impacts, poses an additional problem. Because conditions in society result from a wide assortment of variables, isolating government's contribution to any given situation is difficult. One of the most difficult tasks in developing program measures is to select those that reflect what a particular government accomplishes. The federal government faces considerable challenges in this arena, because national programs are carried out through a variety of means, such as through multiple federal agencies, state and local governments, and nonprofit organizations. If a given program is successful, to what extent is the success due to partial funding by a particular federal agency?[44]

Choosing among Program Results. Inevitably some tradeoffs occur when trying to decide among programs. Consequently, *equity* becomes a concern: are different segments of the citizenry benefiting according to some standard of fairness? The perceived severity of a problem to be addressed by government enters into such deliberations, such as the perception that a community has a major illegal drug problem or that the nation must address the problem of conquering acquired immune deficiency syndrome (AIDS). In both of these examples, a tempering factor is whether government programs are able to use infusions of resources effectively. Large budget allocations for combating drugs or AIDS will not necessarily resolve these problems.

Governments are at a disadvantage in making these difficult choices in comparison with private corporations, which have the profit motive as their primary concern. Put simply, a private corporation will invest in those product lines that are expected to yield the highest rate of return on investments. Governments utilize some combination of the types of program information discussed here but cannot readily convert them into a single measure of profit. Instead, they must choose among disparate commodities such as fire protection, air pollution reduction, and public transit. Making comparisons may help in this situation. Where government actions such as physical capital investments can be measured more easily on the cost and result side with a common metric—monetary—then a single measure of return on investment comparable to private sector metrics can be and is used (see Chapter 12).

Systems of Budgeting

If the central budget office simply instructed agencies to request budgets for the coming year, the result most likely would be several different types of responses based on different assumptions about the coming budget year. One agency might respond by requesting what it felt was needed. Another might respond in light of what resources it thought were available, resulting in a much lower request. Others might use combinations of these and other approaches. The consequences would be budget requests based on varied assumptions and these requests would require different reactions by the budget office. To avoid such disparities in the assumptions made by requesting agencies, budget instructions often provide guidance to agencies.

Preparation Assumptions

Current Services Budgeting. One type of guidance is to assume essentially no change in programs. A department's current budget is considered its base, and any increases are to be requested only to cover additional operating costs, such as increased costs for personnel, supplies, and so on. An assumption is made that the government is committed or obligated to continue existing programs. Often, this base approach has been used only implicitly, but since the 1960s and 1970s many governments have had their budgets explicitly indicate levels of commitment for agencies and programs.

The federal budget has included current services estimates since the 1970s. For the federal government, current services estimates are frequently referred to as "baseline" budget estimates. A baseline budget, like a current services budget, estimates the effects of continuing current tax and spending policies into the future. Chapter 7 presents a variety of samples from budget documents, including baseline estimates for the federal government.

Nonprofit organizations sometimes consider the base, or current services, budget to be last year's budget less specific projects that were intended to have a starting and stopping point. Other special projects may be included in the new budget request, but the baseline total budget does not include the costs of projects that have been completed in the previous year. For example, a youth nonprofit organization might have received a three-year grant for after-school programming for teens. The grant money, since it is temporary, would not be considered part of the base and would be budgeted accordingly. Explicitly determining the current commitments is difficult because programs often are created without any forthright statement of commitment. In the easiest cases, there is an obligation to serve all claimants on the system. School districts, for example, are obligated to serve all eligible children. Therefore budget requests from units within the school district would be based on the expected number of enrolled children. In other cases, the commitment may be in terms of the level of service, specifically outputs and workload. Using job training as an example again, the unit could have a commitment to maintain the same number of graduates or, alternatively, the same number of students. Budgeting, then, can be seen as adding increments to or subtracting them from the base.

Fixed-Ceiling Budgeting. An alternative to the current commitment approach is fixed-ceiling budgeting. Under this system, a dollar limit is set government-wide, then factored into limits for departments, bureaus, and other subunits. The advantage is that budget requests are created that do not, when totaled, exceed the desired ceiling. The disadvantage is that some organizational units may receive inadequate funding and others may be overfunded in terms of program priorities. This imbalance can result from the unavailability of adequate information about program requirements when limits are set. Fixed-ceiling budgeting is most useful during periods of stability, although fixed-ceiling approaches are used quite frequently by governments to encourage line agencies to make fewer expenditure demands during periods of fiscal stress.

A weakness of both the base and fixed-ceiling approaches is that by themselves they offer no suggestions for program changes. If the budget office and chief executive have only these types of budget requests, they lack information about alternative resource allocations. In response to this lack of information, several "what-if" approaches to budget requests have been devised. These approaches ask agencies to develop alternatives by asking, for example, "what if more dollars were available?" or "what if program improvements were to be made in specific areas?"

Open-Ended Budgeting. One of the most common what-if approaches is open-ended budgeting. The question is asked, "what if resources were available to meet all anticipated needs?" This approach is sometimes called "blue sky" budgeting in which the sky is the limit in requesting new funds. Agencies are expected to ask for what they think they need to deal with problems assigned to them. Open-ended budgeting should not be confused with the absence of guidance, in which some agencies might request "needed" funds and others might ask for lesser amounts. The advantage of the open-ended approach is that it brings perceived needs for services to the surface. The open-ended budget, in contrast with the current services budget, can serve as the basis for discussions of preferred funding levels. The disadvantage is that open-ended requests may exceed the economic and political capabilities of the jurisdiction, making the requests seem like fanciful wish lists.

Performance Budgeting

A flurry of budget reform activity aimed at bringing greater program data into the budget decision-making process occurred in response to the First Hoover Commission (1949), which proposed the use of performance budgeting. In response to the Commission's recommendation, Congress specifically provided in the National Security Act Amendments of 1949 that performance budgeting be used in the military.[45] The following year saw passage of the Budget and Accounting Procedures Act, which in essence required performance budgeting for the entire federal government.[46] State and local governments followed suit.

Among federal, state, and local agencies, performance budgeting was geared mainly toward developing workload and unit cost measures of activities. For the postal service, the number of letters that could be processed by one employee was identified. Armed with this knowledge and an estimate of the number of letters to be processed, postal officials could calculate the personnel required for the coming budget year.[47] In the name of performance budgeting, the Department of Defense in 1950 adopted a single set of budget categories that were applied to all services. These categories, most of which were still in use in the 2000s, included personnel, maintenance and operation, and research and development.

Although reconstructing the past is difficult, little evidence suggests that performance budgeting ever became the basis upon which decisions were made in federal, state, or local budget processes. Nevertheless, some lasting effect is evident. Performance budgeting did introduce on a wide scale the use of program information in budget documents as well as the use of performance information for various purposes. Both program and performance information gained increasing attention in later years.

Planning-Programming-Budgeting and Program Budgeting

The origin of the term *planning-programming-budgeting* is uncertain. Mosher used it in his 1954 book on Army program budgeting.[48] During the early 1960s in the Department of Defense, PPB stood for program package budgeting, because a package was presented in terms of the resource inputs (personnel, equipment, and so forth) and outputs.[49] By 1965, when President Lyndon Johnson extended the system to civilian agencies, PPB had come to mean planning-programming-budgeting. It should be recognized that planning and programming are not distinct from each other but differ only in degree. They have been defined as follows:

> *Planning* is the production of the range of meaningful potentials for selection of courses of action through a systematic consideration of alternatives.
>
> *Programming* is the more specific determination of the manpower, material, and facilities necessary for accomplishing a program.[50]

Today, PPB is generally used to refer to a series of budgetary reform efforts in the 1960s. The terms program budgeting and performance budgeting are more generic and apply to systems intended to link program costs with results.

Defense. There are several reasons why PPB started in the Department of Defense. Probably the most important one was that, despite having the authority to manage the military, the secretary of defense did not have the necessary management support. Secretary Robert S. McNamara in 1961 had the determination to initiate change. In coming to the Pentagon, he brought with him several people from the RAND Corporation who earlier had done extensive work related to program budgeting. David Novick of RAND published reports in the 1950s recommending such a system for the Department of Defense.[51] The key person for program budgeting under McNamara was Charles J. Hitch, who became assistant secretary of defense (comptroller). McNamara, Hitch, and others made use of the development of operations research, computers, and systems analysis, all of which were complementary to the mainstream of budgetary reform.

The central component of the Department of Defense system is the Future Years Defense Program (FYDP), which projects costs and personnel according to missions or programs. The programs form the *program structure*, a classification system that begins with broad missions and factors them into subunits and activities. The structure groups like activities together regardless of which branches of the service conduct them, thereby allowing for analyses across organizational lines. The major programs within the FYDP have been:

- Strategic forces
- General-purpose forces
- Intelligence and communications
- Airlift and sealift
- Guard and reserve
- Research and development
- Central supply and maintenance
- Training, medical, and other general personnel activities
- Administration and associated activities

- Support of other nations
- Special operations forces

Changes in the FYDP are accomplished by the Office of the Secretary of Defense issuing guidance, to which the services respond by preparing *program objective memoranda*, which contain budget proposals for modifying the FYDP.[52] The program objective memoranda suggest programmatic and resource incremental changes to the base established in the FYDP. In addition to this elaborate process, the Department of Defense undergoes a Quadrennial Defense Review every four years, following the presidential election.[53] While the PPB system is organized around programs, Congress has continued to appropriate funds for defense based on object classifications, with the main ones including military personnel; operation and maintenance; procurement; research, development, test, and evaluation; and military construction.

In 1995, the Commission on Roles and Missions of the Armed Forces, created by the National Defense Authorization Act for Fiscal Year 1994, issued a wide-sweeping set of recommendations, including a call for a major overhaul of the defense budget process. Earlier, the National Performance Review (NPR) had suggested changes in the process, but the 1995 Commission made recommendations that would fundamentally revise the system.[54] The report stated, "The current PPB system reexamines the entire multiyear defense program annually, uses too many people, takes too long, goes into too much detail, and leaves little time for reflection and creativity." [55] Despite much discussion during the Clinton administration, the defense decision-making system remained largely unchanged and was passed to the George W. Bush administration in 2001.

The most far-reaching changes in defense planning and budgeting since the inception of PPB system were initiated under Defense Secretary Donald Rumsfeld particularly during George W. Bush's second term.[56] The reforms merged the once separate program and budget review processes, allowing for some streamlining of the system.

Federal Civilian Reforms. Turning to the civilian side of government, use of PPB by federal agencies was announced in 1965 by President Johnson, who had been impressed with the Department of Defense budget system. This action sparked massive reform efforts throughout all levels of government in the United States.

The federal civilian system was intended to be similar to the Department of Defense model. Multiyear plans, known as program and financial plans, were to be devised for each department. Changes were to be made through the submission of program memoranda. However, by 1969, when Richard M. Nixon became president, PPB had not been fully implemented by the civilian agencies. In 1971, OMB relieved agencies of the duty to prepare program and financial plans and program memoranda. As a major budget system, PPB was allowed to die quietly.[57]

A study conducted by the Bureau of the Budget (now OMB) found six factors that characterized the more successful efforts to introduce PPB:[58]

1. The number of analysts was sufficient.
2. Analysts were well qualified.
3. Analysts had formal access to agency heads and managers.
4. Analysts had informal access.
5. Agency heads and managers gave strong support for use of analysis.
6. Analysis was viewed as a valuable tool by agency heads and managers.

This study and others found that lack of understanding of and commitment to program budgeting on the part of leadership tended to deter success, as did an agency's general "underdevelopment" in the use of analytic techniques. Agencies administering "soft" social programs had difficulty devising useful program measures. Bureaucratic infighting also reduced the chances of successful implementation. These findings are instructive for any government that undertakes to restructure the operations of its budget system.

State and Local Reforms. The use of PPB did not revolutionize state and local decision making in the 1960s any more than it revolutionized federal decision making. Most of the states that experimented with PPB emphasized the development of program structure, multiyear plans, and program memoranda, while only a few concentrated on analysis as their main thrust. By the mid-1970s, the emphasis had swung away from the structural features of PPB to the use of measures of effectiveness and efficiency and program analysis. In the 1960s, many states and municipalities took only cautious first steps and established no timetable for completion of the installation process. Others began the effort on a pilot basis, attempting PPB in one department before expanding its use.

By the close of the 1960s, it was difficult to identify many ongoing PPB systems at the state and local levels. The reasons for failure or lack of major success were similar to those already mentioned for federal agencies. State and local governments usually did not have sufficiently sophisticated management practices to be able to undertake the expected transformation. Additionally, people simply expected too much to result from conversion to PPB and did not realize the financial and administrative costs associated with the conversion. Legislative bodies often showed little support for the new budget system, and this fact was interpreted by some as legislative hostility toward change.[59]

Change, however, did occur as a result of efforts to introduce PPB systems. Perhaps the biggest single achievement was that governments began to make greater use of program information in budgetary decision making, albeit information largely of the output variety.[60]

Zero-Base Budgeting

Zero-base budgeting (ZBB) is another form of "what-if" budgeting. "Traditional" ZBB—that is, not the type used by the federal government during the Carter administration—asks, "What if a program were to be eliminated?" Rather than assuming that a base exists, the approach asks what would happen if a program were to be discontinued. Each program is challenged to justify its very existence in every budget cycle.

Early Use. The U.S. Department of Agriculture engaged in an experiment with ZBB in the early 1960s, and the results were disappointing.[61] ZBB, it was found, wasted valuable administrative time by requiring the rehashing of old issues that had already been resolved. The system was unrealistic, since many programs were mandatory within the political arena and could not be dismantled no matter how compelling the available data and analysis. Decision makers within the agency could not adequately review the excessive paperwork that was generated.

The disadvantage of ZBB is analogous to that of open-ended budgeting. Both approaches make basically unrealistic assumptions. Whereas open-ended budgeting assumes unlimited resources, the zero-base approach assumes that decision makers have the capacity to eliminate enough programs to justify the time spent in evaluating them. In reality, the political forces in any jurisdiction are such that few programs in any given year can be abandoned. For this reason, ZBB may be better applied to selective programs in any one year rather than government-wide. A cycle of reviews can be established such that some programs are thoroughly reviewed each year using ZBB, and all programs are reviewed in any five-year period.

The 1970s. Zero-base budgeting gained new popularity in the 1970s.[62] Much attention focused on Georgia and its governor, Jimmy Carter, who subsequently brought a new version of ZBB to the federal government upon becoming president in 1977.[63] The Carter administration's version had three major characteristics:[64]

1. *Decision units* were identified for which budget requests, called decision packages, were to be prepared. Approximately 10,000 of these were prepared each year.
2. Alternative funding levels were used for each package:
   - The *minimum level*, which entailed providing services below present levels;

- The *current level*, which maintained existing services and reflected increased costs for personnel, supplies, and the like; and
- An *enhancement level*, which provided for upgraded services.
3. Alternative funding levels of decision packages were to be ranked by importance.

The ZBB experiment at the federal level was criticized on several counts. The most frequently heard complaint related to the amount of time required to prepare requests and the corresponding deluge of paperwork. The ZBB system, contrary to what President Carter had promised, did not require agencies to justify every tax dollar they received. Administrators puzzled over how a minimum level below current operations could exist when the statute under which an agency operated specified benefits, as in the case of Social Security.

Rarely did ZBB eliminate unnecessary programs, curtail their growth, or result in reassigning priorities among programs.[65] In some isolated instances, savings were achieved by funding programs at the minimum level, but that produced agency resentment. Administrators of these programs saw themselves as being punished because they had identified how their programs could operate with less than the current budget. More often, however, the system was seen as involving excessive paperwork that ultimately had little or no impact on policy making. Shortly after President Reagan took office in January 1981, the new administration announced that ZBB would no longer be practiced.

The experience at the state and local levels was comparable to that of the federal government. Although ZBB initially seemed to hold great promise, ultimately it was abandoned, even if some governments continued to describe their budget systems as founded on the concept.

One observation was that ZBB efforts in the 1970s were doomed because of the immense amount of data that needed to be processed with technology that would seem ancient compared with today's standards. An extension of such reasoning is that today's technology may make possible ZBB and other reforms that failed in earlier times.[66]

Strategic Planning and Guidance

Planning. Some governments, in part following the lead of private sector organizations, have engaged in strategic planning efforts, which focus attention on missions, goals, and objectives.[67] In strategic planning, options are identified and chosen in light of fundamental values and purposes. Annual budgeting is then used to allocate resources according to the established priorities. Some have called budget systems that use strategic planning and performance measurement *performance-based budgeting* (PBB).[68] Performance-based budgeting is not to be confused with performance budgeting (mentioned earlier). Performance-based budgeting differs, as did program budgeting, in that it focuses on results rather than on workload or activity.

Strategic planning can be an extremely time-consuming process in which various plans, often presented in great detail, are drafted, reviewed, and then modified. This process usually involves developing an overall plan and then revising the plan annually to reflect new information and revised priorities. Comparisons can be drawn here with the Department of Defense's FYDP, mentioned earlier. The process of devising and revising plans is sometimes considered as valuable as the actual written plans themselves, in that the process fosters extensive thinking within a government about its core values in serving the citizenry.

Policy and Program Guidance. A less ambitious but nevertheless useful approach is to provide broad policy guidance or more narrowly focused program guidance to departments and agencies before they begin to prepare their budget requests. At the federal level, the OMB often instructs specific agencies regarding which program funding proposals are likely to receive favorable review and instructs them to prepare issue papers on specific programs for which concern exists about the efficacy of resource utilization. Some state and local budget offices provide program guidelines that indicate to agencies the concerns of their governors or mayors, namely, the issues that have high priority for the coming budget year.

In response to such guidance, agencies prepare detailed program requests. A discussion of the range of available alternatives is likely to take place, possibly with detailed costing and the expected results of each. Where guidance is not directed at any one agency, two or more may submit competing requests, each attempting to show how its proposed alternative would deal with a problem. For example, both the city police and the recreation departments might submit budget proposals for dealing with juvenile gangs.

The advantage of such guidance is that agencies prepare requests that are likely to be favorably received by the chief executive and are spared many hours of needless work in preparing requests that are fated for rejection. Policy or program guidance, however, does not ensure executive approval of agency requests. The requests may be rejected simply because of inadequate funds or because the arguments for the proposed changes fail to persuade decision makers.

Other Budgeting and Management Systems

Numerous other budgeting and management systems exist. These include management by objectives, total quality management, and managing for results.

Management by Objectives. Workload is often the focus of management by objectives (MBO) and other participative management techniques that were developed in the 1950s and 1960s.[69] Although many diverse activities have been carried out in government under the rubric of MBO, a common theme tends to be prescribing objectives for organizational units, managers, and workers in terms of the work they are expected to accomplish. Participative management systems such as MBO emphasize involvement of all strata of the bureaucracy in the development of objectives.

Total Quality Management or Continuous Quality Improvement. Total quality management (TQM)—also called continuous quality improvement—is not a budget system but, as envisioned by its creator, W. Edwards Deming, is a management system that focuses on the end products or results of organizations.[70] Available space does not allow a thorough discussion of TQM, but it should be noted that the system relies heavily on program measurement and that one of Deming's 14 TQM recommendations is to avoid management by objectives. The latter management system is seen as setting quotas for workers rather than empowering them to think creatively and allowing them to achieve results that might well be beyond any expected quotas.

Managing for Results. A term that gained popularity in the U.S. after 2000 is *managing for results* (MFR). The term may have its roots in the United Kingdom, Australia, and New Zealand. A key factor in MFR efforts is that managers must be held accountable for their operations *and* must have the authority to get done whatever tasks are required.[71]

Multiyear Requests

All budget requests are multiyear in that they at least cover the current year plus the coming budget year and probably the past year as well. States with biennial budgets obviously have multiyear requests. One issue is whether budget requests should extend beyond the budget year and, if so, how a multiyear perspective is to be included in the budget. The argument for multiyear requests is simple: Without looking beyond the budget year, commitments of resources may be made that were never intended. This argument applies particularly to proposed expansions and new programs (see Chapter 12).

Time Horizons. In theory, the time horizon of a budget request should be geared to the life cycle of each program. This life cycle is clearest in specific projects or programs that have an obvious beginning and conclusion. A weapons system is one of the best examples. The cycle begins with research and concludes when the system is judged to be obsolete.

On the other hand, many government programs have no foreseeable conclusion. The need for education, roads, law enforcement, recreation, and the like will always exist. Each may have unique properties that suggest possible time horizons. Given the length of time required to design and construct schools, projections of several years are needed. Multiyear requests can reveal when roads will require major repairs, redesigns, and expansions. Indeed, the necessity for multiyear planning is often part of the justification for the separate capital budgeting processes pursued by many governments (see Chapter 12).

Because an appropriate life cycle for multiyear requests often is not obvious, an arbitrary set of years may be imposed. The most common is the budget year plus the four succeeding years, known as a five-year projection. Making projections beyond five years is difficult because of the many unknowns. Using the road example, it may be largely unknown what the typical commuting pattern will be 10 or more years from now. Further, political leaders have limited incentives to focus on costs or benefits that occur many years in the future, because these future costs and benefits will likely arise outside of their electoral window.

Cost and Program Projections. Assuming they can be made, projections can be limited to finances or can include program data projections. The state of the art tends to limit projections to finances, showing anticipated future financial requirements. When program impacts and outputs are projected, the requests show what resources will be needed in future years as well as the benefits that will be accrued.

Multiyear projections using cost and program data can prove helpful in coping with severe economic conditions. Where program reductions are necessary, agency requests can illustrate the consequences over a longer time period. Cuts in an agency's budget made this year may seem essential but produce undesirable future consequences. To live within available revenues, a city may reduce its road maintenance program, with no noticeable reduction in road quality in the first year. However, by the second or third year following these cuts, the city may have a road network of substantially lower quality than before, and that in turn can lead to more costly capital investments to rehabilitate the road network.

Use of Budget Techniques

Hybrid Techniques. Many of the techniques discussed here can be used in combination to form hybrid systems. ZBB, for example, can be used selectively for some agencies undergoing intensive review even as others use a fixed-ceiling approach. A government may use fixed-ceiling budgeting to allocate monies among major departments but then allow each department to use *entrepreneurial* budgeting, namely, allocating funds within the department with only a minimum of control from the central budget office.[72] *Target-base budgeting* is also sometimes used. In this type of budgeting, agencies prepare budget requests based on fixed ceilings but then may propose budget increases above the ceilings.[73] Governments can use a current services budget in conjunction with priority listing of decision packages in an approach akin to the Carter administration's version of ZBB. The base approach can be combined with open-ended budgeting, in which agencies request funds for what they perceive to be their needs. Program guidance can be linked with priority listings.

Federal Initiatives—National Performance Review. Upon taking office in 1993, President Clinton established the National Performance Review (NPR) under the direction of Vice President Gore. The NPR's initial report, issued in 1993, contained a host of recommendations intended to streamline all aspects of the government.[74] Prompted by the work of this group, President Clinton issued Executive Order 12862 in 1993, requiring that federal agencies devise *customer service standards,* intended to establish levels of performance by agencies. The executive order instructed agencies to determine what services customers demand and what complaints customers have, and to allocate resources—make budget decisions—based on customer satisfaction.

The NPR, which continued through President Clinton's second term, became known as the National Partnership for Reinventing Government and had as its focus the *reengineering* or *reinvention* of government. The intent was to redesign processes carried out by agencies so as to improve their efficiency and effectiveness. Such reengineering efforts continue to the present.[75] *Benchmarking* was an important component in which best practices elsewhere, whether in government or the private sector, were identified and used as a guide for revising how government operates.[76] As NPR reported, benchmarking was "stealing shamelessly" from the best, as in the case of the Social Security Administration learning about toll-free telephone service from American Express, AT&T Universal Card, Citibank, and the like.[77] Other aspects of NPR included an emphasis on regulatory reform and seeking opportunities for privatizing government services.

At the end of the Clinton administration in 2001, those involved in NPR claimed great results. Savings were said to amount to $137 billion.[78] Others, including the U.S. General Accounting Office, said that NPR had not been as successful as some had claimed.[79] When George W. Bush became president, he allowed NPR to fade into history.

Customer satisfaction surveys continue today.[80] The American Society for Quality, the University of Michigan's Ross School of Business, and the CFI Group have developed the American Customer Satisfaction Index that has been used in gauging satisfaction with services in both the private and public sectors. Some of the 2005 results for government are reported in **Table 6–4**. As can be seen, government as a whole received a score of 67.1 on a scale of 100. This score was in the same range as previous years dating back to 1998. Local satisfaction was 65.9, and

Table 6–4	American Customer Satisfaction Scores for Public Sector, Local Government, Federal Government, and Selected Customer Segments, 2005

	Customer Segment	Score
Public Administration/Government		67.1
Local Government		65.9
	Police Service/central city (metro)	60.0
	Police Service/suburban (metro)	68.0
Federal Government		71.3
Center for Medicare & Medicaid Services, Health and Human Services	Medicare recipients	76.0
National Weather Service, Commerce	Users of weather services	84.0
General Services Administration	Users of Federal Supply Service	77.0
Small Business Administration	Applicants for Disaster Recovery Assistance	66.0
Internal Revenue Service, Treasury	All individual tax filers	64.0
Internal Revenue Service, Treasury	Large and midsize business corporate tax filers	48.0

Source: Compiled from American Society for Quality, University of Michigan Ross School of Business, and CFI Group (2006). ACSI Scores. Retrieved October 31, 2006, from http://www.theacsi.org/government/govt-public.html and /www.theacsi.org/government/govt-05.html.

federal satisfaction was 71.3. **Table 6–4** shows just a small sampling of agencies and their customers. The table shows, for instance, that while individual taxpayers on a whole gave the Internal Revenue Service (IRS) a score of 64, the IRS received a score of only 48 from large and midsize corporate taxpayers. Another example of citizen surveys comes from the U.S. General Services Administration which announced plans in 2006 to launch a survey asking citizens about how federal agencies serve the public and about preferred methods of being served.[81]

Federal Initiatives—Government Performance and Results Act. Occurring coincident with the NPR was congressional passage of the Government Performance and Results Act (GPRA, pronounced "gip-ra") of 1993 and the law's ensuing implementation.[82] This law resulted from a congressional and presidential concern about "waste and inefficiency" in government and "insufficient articulation of program goals and inadequate information on program performance." It is based on the premise that agencies (1) need to define their missions and desired outcomes, (2) measure performance, and (3) use the performance information to revise programs.[83] All aspects of GPRA are under the direction of the OMB and the Chief Financial Officers (CFO) Council, consisting of the top financial officers of major federal agencies.[84] OMB Circular A-11, which instructs agencies on how to prepare their budgets, provides guidance on the implementation of GPRA.

Federal agencies were required to have strategic planning processes and plans in place by the end of fiscal 1997. According to OMB Circular A-11, plans must cover at least six years—the budget year plus the next five future years. Plans must show agency mission, strategic goals, and means and strategies planned for achieving goals. Updates and revised plans must be submitted to the president (i.e., OMB) and Congress at least every three years. **Figure 6–1** illustrates the

Figure 6–1   **Implementing GPRA: Key Steps and Critical Practices**

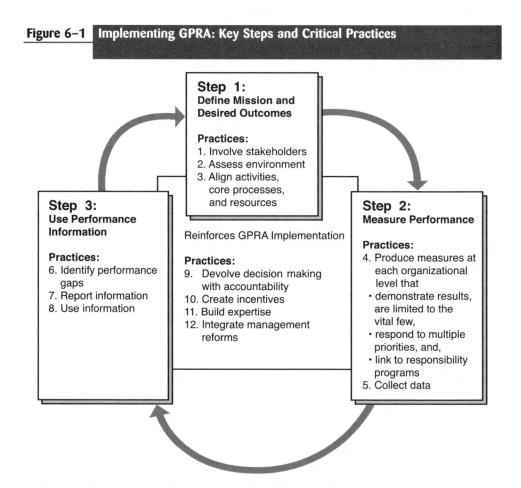

Source: Reprinted from U.S. General Accounting Office (1996) *Executive guide: Effectively implementing the Government Performance and Results Act.* Washington, DC: U.S. Government Printing Office, 10.

GPRA system in which mission and desired outcomes lead to performance measures, and the use of performance information helps redefine missions and desired outcomes.

Beginning with fiscal year 1999, annual performance plans were prepared as outgrowths of the multiyear strategic plans. The OMB did not prescribe a specific format for the annual plans, but Circular A-11 gives agencies overall guidance for what information the plans must contain.

Given the diversity of agencies within the federal government and the immensity of the task of implementing GPRA, unevenness in the quality of the annual plans was inevitable.[85] In its review of the first draft plans, GAO said that "a significant amount of work" needed to be done for agencies to meet GPRA's requirements.[86] Goals were said to be vague, such as the Veterans' Affairs' goal to "improve benefit programs." Objectives and goals as stated often could not be measured. Social Security, for instance, said it aimed "to promote valued, strong, and responsive social security programs." The OMB's own plan was criticized for such weaknesses as failing to show a clear results orientation of goals and objectives and failing to show how the unit's strategies would move toward the attainment of goals and objectives.[87]

Federal Initiatives—George W. Bush's Management Agenda. In his first year in office, President Bush announced a five-prong president's management agenda (PMA). The items are human capital, competitive sourcing, financial performance, E-government, and budget/performance integration (BPI). The last item is easily understood given the above discussion. Program information is inextricably linked with the budget process. Indeed, if a program has an approved annual performance budget, it may serve in lieu of an annual program plan. The budget/performance integration component has been called the linchpin of the management agenda, since without an effective budgeting and performance management system the other four parts of PMA are most likely to fail.[88]

Regarding the other items, the topic of human capital has received considerable attention. Congress passed the Chief Human Capital Officers (CHCO) Act of 1992, which gave federal agencies greater discretion in managing their human resources, including developing and training workers.[89] A major interest of reformers was linking pay with performance.[90]

Competitive sourcing focuses upon competition for government contracts (see Chapter 10). Financial performance concentrates on government accounting and auditing (see Chapter 11). E-government is concerned with improving service delivery through information technology.[91]

The PMA, which is steered by the President's Management Council, rates departments on each of these five areas. "Green" is for success. "Yellow" is for mixed results. "Red" is for unsatisfactory. In 2006, for example, the Treasury

Department received "greens" on human capital and competitive sourcing, "yellows" on E-government and budget/performance integration, and "red" on financial performance. OMB received no "greens," "yellows" on human capital and E-government, and "reds" on competitive sourcing, financial performance, and budget/performance integration. In contrast, the Labor Department received "greens" on all five items. The National Science Foundation (NSF) and the Social Security Administration (SSA) both received four "greens." NSF's and SSA's weak area was competitive sourcing ("red" and "yellow" respectively).[92]

PMA not only rates departments' status on the five areas but also rates their progress on each. For example, while the Agriculture Department in 2006 received only one "green," which was for its operations involving human capital, with the other factors being three "yellows" and one "red," the department received all "greens" on its progress.[93]

Besides federally administered rating systems and scorecards, there have been private initiatives in this area. One project conducted between 1999 and 2002 found some impressive examples of results-based management in places such as the U.S. Coast Guard and the National Weather Service, both of which received "A" grades. It also found that units such as the Immigration and Naturalization Service and the Bureau of Indian Affairs deserved "D" grades. The overall average across the federal government was a "B minus."[94]

Federal Initiatives—Program Assessment Rating Tool. The Program Assessment Rating Tool (PART) is the system that the George W. Bush administration introduced to evaluate systematically the operations of government and to move forward budget reform. The reform was in keeping with the mainstream of budget reform, bringing to bear greater program information to the allocation of scarce resources. "Performance budgeting" is the term used to describe what was used, but this should be distinguished from the performance budgeting of the 1950s.

The PART process is used "to assess the performance of federal programs and to drive improvements in program performance."[95] The starting point for the PART was the identification of 1,000 programs in the federal budget. In 2003, the Bush administration pledged to evaluate 200 of these programs each year for five years. Thus, at the end of the five-year period, the president's budget would have included analyses of all 1,000 programs. The key goals of the PART are to identify which of these programs work and how well they work. The clear intent of this is to inform the budget formulation process in the executive branch.

PART consists of a series of mainly yes-or-no questions that agencies must answer about their programs. There are four groups of questions:

1. *Program Purpose and Design:* to assess whether the program's purpose and design are clear and sound [20 %],

2. *Strategic Planning:* to assess whether the program has valid long-term and annual measures and targets [10%],

3. *Program Management:* to rate the program's management, including financial oversight and program improvement efforts [20%], and

3. *Program Results/Accountability:* to rate program performance on measures and targets reviewed in the strategic planning section and through other evaluations [50%].[96]

Exhibit 6–1 is a sample of the detailed guidance that the Office of Management and Budget provides for agencies in using the PART. As noted earlier, the emphasis is on outcome measures and not outputs. The guidance requires at least one efficiency measure as well. Of particular significance is that an agency and its corresponding resource management office (RMO) within OMB must agree on measures or the answer to the question is an automatic "no." OMB guidance suggests this is a "collaborative" process, but some agencies undoubtedly have felt the heavy hand of OMB in rejecting measures they preferred and advocating measures less favorable to the agencies' budget reviews.

The PART process occurs prior to budget submission. Agencies complete their PARTs and submit them to the budget office for review in the spring.[97] Feedback is given in July, with agencies then making revisions in their PARTs. OMB has instituted a consistency check in an effort to insure that all agencies are treated alike, since some had thought they received harsher treatment than others. In August, agencies may appeal to a board over whether OMB actions were within its own PART guidelines.[98] Why might appeals be made? Because given whatever measures were devised and the answers to the various questions in PART, agencies' programs may receive unfavorable ratings that the agencies think are unwarranted.

After scoring and weighting the four groups of questions, overall PART scores are tabulated. Programs are ultimately judged to be effective (85 to 100), moderately effective (70 to 84), adequate (50 to 69), or ineffective (0 to 49). When a program fails to have approved long-term and annual performance measures, the program automatically receives a rating of "results not demonstrated." This last category includes programs that possibly are ineffective and programs that may be effective but for which suitable measures have not been developed.

OMB has created a website devoted exclusively to the Program Assessment Rating Tool: ExpectMore.gov.[99] The site is a one-stop source for OMB guidance and memoranda on PART. Links are provided to agency's programs and their PARTs along with their ratings. For example,

• The State Department's program for refugee admissions to the U.S. was rated "effective"

Exhibit 6–1   **Question on Annual Performance Measures in Program Assessment Rating Tool**

Does the program have a limited number of specific annual performance measures that can demonstrate progress toward achieving the program's long-term goals?

Purpose: To determine whether a limited number of annual performance measures have been identified that directly support the long-term goals evaluated in Questions 2.1 and 2.2. The measures should be logically linked to the long-term goals in a manner that enables them to demonstrate progress toward achieving those long-term goals.

Elements of Yes: A Yes answer needs to clearly explain and provide evidence of each of the following:

 ✔ A limited number of discrete, quantifiable, and measurable annual performance measures have been established for the program.

Question 2.3: Quick Tips	
Answer Options	Yes, No
Question Linkages	If No on 2.1, must provide explanation of how annual performance goals contribute to long-term outcomes and purpose to get Yes on 2.3.
Additional Guidance	Block Grant R&D Capital Assets and Service Acquisition

 ✔ Annual performance measures adequately measure the program's progress toward reaching the long-term goals evaluated in Questions 2.1 and 2.2. The explanation must clearly state how the outcomes help achieve the long-term goals of the program.

 ✔ Annual performance measures focus on outcomes. Measures may focus on outputs if the program can adequately justify why it is unable to define satisfactory quantifiable outcome measures. The justification for not adopting outcome measures and the explanation of how output measures show progress toward desired outcomes must be clearly presented in the explanation and/or evidence sections.

The annual performance measures may be those developed by the agency to comply with GPRA (Government Performance and Results Act), if the performance measures meet the criteria listed above.

Elements of No: A No answer must be given if the agency and OMB have not reached agreement on measures that meet PART requirements.

Programs must have at least one efficiency measure as part of their annual measures. Credit for efficiency measures is given in Question 3.4.

Source: Reprinted from U.S. Office of Management and Budget (2006). *Guide to the Program Assessment Rating Tool (PART)*, 25. Retrieved August 1, 2006, from http://www.whitehouse.gov/omb/part/fy2006/2006_guidance_final.pdf.

- The Transportation Department's FAA aviation safety program was rated "moderately effective"
- FEMA's disaster relief and recovery program was judged to be "adequate"
- AmeriCorps' National Civilian Community Corps was rated "ineffective" and
- The Agriculture Department's national school lunch program was rated "results not demonstrated." One should keep in mind that this rating could well mean the program was effective but suitable measures had not been devised.

Figure 6–2 shows the cumulative results of the PART process from 2002 through 2005. In 2002, only 234 programs were evaluated whereas the number climbed to 793 by 2005. As can be seen from the figure, the number of programs rated "results not demonstrated" steadily declined over time. In 2002, the figure was 50%, and that dropped to 24% by 2005. Programs rated effective or moderately effective combined accounted for about 40% to 45% in 2004 and 2005, respectively.

In 2006, the President's Management Council shifted direction somewhat to emphasize successes over specific grades. The council reported that acceptable performance measures had been identified in 90% or more of the programs in the Departments of Defense, Education, Energy, State, and Transportation, and in

Figure 6–2 | **Cumulative PART Scores for 2002 through 2005**

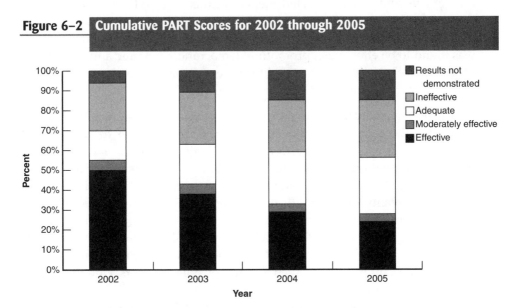

Source: Compiled from U.S. Office of Management and Budget (2006). *PART refresher training.* Retrieved October 31, 2006, from http://www.whitehouse.gov/omb/part/training/2006_refresher_training.pdf.

such agencies as the Environmental Protection Agency, the U.S. Agency for International Development, and the Office of Personnel Management. Treasury lagged at 74% and Housing and Urban Development at 71%.[100]

The report further noted progress had been achieved in developing efficiency measures. Again, 90% or more of the programs had such measures in Education, Interior, Justice, Labor, State, and Transportation.

Although no comprehensive analysis has been conducted on the effects of the Program Assessment Rating Tool, some conclusions can be drawn. First, PART has undoubtedly forced agencies to be mindful about how they need to justify their programs through specific measures. At the same time, OMB has not sought to use PART results as a weapon to slash underachieving programs. The administration specifically addressed the "myth [that] PART is just a way for the administration to terminate programs it doesn't like." The President's Management Council said:

> The Administration wants programs to work. The primary purpose of the PART is to make sure that federal programs live up to their congressionally-mandated intent and are effectively managed to provide the best value for taxpayers. The PART is rarely the only basis for program termination proposals. If a program is ineffective, it may well need more money.
>
> There are numerous examples of programs rated effective that received budget cuts and programs rated ineffective that received more funding. For example, although the Office of the Coordinator of U.S. Assistance to Europe and Eurasia (Support for East European Democracy/Freedom Support Act) was found to be effective at promoting democratic, economic and other types of reform, its budget was proposed for reduction because Romania, Bulgaria, and Croatia graduated from U.S. assistance.[101]

One expert has described the process as "performance-informed budgeting."[102] While the term "performance budgeting" might seem to suggest that budget decisions are based on performance, this alternative term suggests that performance information aids decision makers but that use of such information is tempered by a variety of factors that include assessments of the quality of information and the reality of the political environment. Still, PART may well have influenced budget decisions. One study found that PART scores were related to OMB budget recommendations, particularly for small and medium sized programs.[103] Another study found that PART enhanced OMB's control over the budget, which is important in that the agency is responsible for overseeing the budget on behalf of the president.[104]

OMB has applied PART intensively to basically all federal agencies and programs, which has had the effect of creating immense workloads for agencies and the budget office, itself. The argument can be made that the budget office staff has been spread too thinly to be able to cope adequately with PART. On the other hand, the process has driven home an idea that undoubtedly some agencies preferred to ignore or hoped would go away: programs need to be evaluated by outcome measures and budget allocations need to be made accordingly.[105] In 2005, the Government Accountability Office concluded, "It is not clear that PART has had any significant impact on authorization, appropriations, and oversight activities to date"[106] On the other hand, GAO did report that year on a select group of federal agencies that had used performance information to enhance their operations.[107]

PART has received comparatively little attention from Congress, and there have been concerns that OMB did not consult with units in Congress over the selection of program measures.[108] If the measures developed for PART are not what members of Congress consider important, then PART's results are likely to go ignored. For instance, one observer suggested that the federal program, Even Start, in the Department of Education, was created by Congress to improve adult literacy, but the department has focused its attention on measuring the achievement of general equivalency diplomas (GEDs) instead.[109]

Federal Initiatives—The Problems of Measurement. Applying performance budgeting to all aspects of government is difficult, regardless of whether PART or some other methodology is used. For instance, there is no easy method for determining how much defense is enough. The problem is that defense is mainly a matter of deterrence and preparedness. The military is expected to have sufficient strength to deter an attack by a potential aggressor and to be sufficiently prepared for war or other emergencies if they do occur. The deterrent strategy is working when no attack has been launched. Preparedness, on the other hand, can be tested only in real combat and other military situations. When the nation is not fighting a war or deploying troops in emergency situations at home or abroad, it is difficult to prove conclusively that the nation is or is not sufficiently prepared.

Once military troops are called to action, there are obvious problems in gauging their success. On May 1, 2003, President George W. Bush, aboard the USS Abraham Lincoln, announced the end of major combat operations in Iraq.[110] He stood before a banner that proclaimed "Mission Accomplished." Yet years later, war continued in Iraq, and the government seemingly had no easy way of extricating itself from the situation. There were hosts of questions raised as to how to bring about stability in that war-torn nation so that efforts to rebuild would be successful.[111]

The civilian sector is equally prone to problems of outcome measurement. Hurricanes Katrina, Rita, and Wilma of 2005 are noticeable examples of how federal, state, and local government agencies and private organizations, most noticeably the American Red Cross, can be called upon for disaster relief. The suffering inflicted by these storms on the residents of New Orleans and throughout the Gulf Coast brought to attention the inadequacies of disaster responses, no matter how thorough program measures may have existed for the U.S. Federal Emergency Management Agency (FEMA) and comparable state and local bodies.[112]

State Techniques. States are moving toward requiring performance measurement as part of their budget processes, and many states have demonstrated commitments to revising their budget system to use program information in decision making. One study found that 33 state legislatures prescribed the use of performance measurements, and another 17 state administrative or executive officers prescribed their use.[113] The U.S. Government Accountability Office selected five state governments and studied them carefully as examples of how performance information is being used. The states were Arizona, Maryland, Texas, Virginia, and Washington.[114]

Various surveys of state budget offices shed light on state budgetary practices. A study in 2005 found that about half of the states (48%) provided policy guidance in writing in budget preparation and a quarter (27%) provided program guidance in writing. Almost all of the states (97%) required agencies when requesting approval of new programs or revisions in existing programs to submit data on estimates of program effectiveness. About half of the states (47%) used a current services budget, and 68% used priority ranking. Somewhat less than half (42%) said they used fixed ceilings expressed in dollars.[115]

Other surveys have shed additional light on state techniques. One study found that 10 states used performance measures and then tied appropriations to the measures: Arkansas, Hawaii, Illinois, Louisiana, New Hampshire, New Jersey, Texas, Virginia, Washington, and Wisconsin.[116] Intriguingly, a survey of state executive and legislative budgeters found disagreement in eight states regarding whether performance-based budgeting (PBB) had been implemented. These states were Alabama, Georgia, Idaho, Minnesota, New Hampshire, Ohio, Vermont, and Washington. Nine states reported not implementing PBB, and 29 states reported implementing PBB.[117] On the plus side, the vast majority of the respondents said that PBB had improved their understanding of state government operations (82%). On the minus side, a substantial majority said the system had increased their workload (75%). More than half (61%) said that PBB could not be traced to even some changes in appropriations.[118]

The Government Performance Project (GPP), an activity sponsored by the Pew Charitable Trusts and conducted by a consortium of researchers and journalists, has been studying management capacity in both state and local governments. Using a letter-grade system, the project found a wide range of performance in managing for results in 1999, 2001, and 2005. The GPP, as currently constituted, grades states in their management of money, people, infrastructure, and information. The information category focuses a great deal of attention on the availability and use of performance information in state governments. The most recent results in 2005 identified Louisiana, Missouri, Utah, Virginia, and Washington as the top performers in their use of information for management. Each of these states received grades of "A-." The lowest rated states were Hawaii and South Dakota with "D" grades. The study found that more states are making use of performance information for budgeting and for managing their day-to-day activities than in the past, but that the use of performance information for budgeting very often does not extend to legislative use of performance data in allocating resources.

The 2005 project had a redesigned format, and rather than surveying for managing for results, the project team surveyed more generally about the handling of state monies. Factors that were rated within the money category were long-term outlook, budget process, structural balance (revenues and expenditures), contracting/purchasing, and financial controls and reports.[119] On the money scorecard, the top states were Minnesota (A-), Utah (A), Virginia (A-), and Washington State (A-). The 50-state average was a grade of B-. The states' low grades in large measure were attributable to forced cutbacks in spending, including budgetary analysis, due to revenue shortfalls that stemmed from economic hard times.[120]

There is reason to question whether report cards over-simplify matters and whether they provide useful information to consumers, whether the users are the general public or government decision makers, such as legislators.[121] On the other hand, governments may well embrace management reforms partially in pursuit of improved ratings. The GPP has received extensive publicity, and low grades for a state not only are embarrassments but may have political repercussions. As a consequence, states may strive to improve their management so as to improve their ratings.

Local Techniques.   Use of program information at the local level is more limited than at the state level, but there are signs of progress.[122] A mid-1990s study of members of the Government Finance Officers Association found that 51% of local governments still used line-item budgeting.[123] Performance budgeting and zero-base/target-base budgeting were used by 2% to 3%, while program budgeting was used by 10% of the local governments. Thirty-five percent reported using a hybrid system. In contrast, a survey of city and county administrators and budgeters done in the early 2000s found performance measurement to be "pervasive."[124] Another study of 21 cities documented "clear progress toward outcome-oriented performance measurement."[125]

In addition to grading the states, the Government Performance Project graded the nation's largest cities and counties on several factors, including managing for results.[126] The highest-ranked city in 2000, with an "A," was Phoenix, Arizona. "A-" cities were Austin, Indianapolis, Milwaukee, and San Diego. The lowest-graded cities, with scores of "D+," were Buffalo and New Orleans. Milwaukee, which had a high grade, has attracted attention as to how a city can undergo comprehensive management and budget reform.[127] More recently, Atlanta has won recognition for its "Atlanta Dashboard" system which is a performance management system designed to identify the effectiveness of city programs.[128]

At the county level, the Government Performance Project assigned the highest grades for managing for results in 2002 to Fairfax, Virginia; Maricopa, Arizona; and San Diego, California, with "A-" grades. Not only did Fairfax and Maricopa perform well on managing for results, but these counties were the only ones in the study of 40 major counties to receive an average grade of "A-" for all five subject areas including financial management, capital management, human resources, and information technology plus managing for results. The lowest-rated county was Nassau, New York, receiving an "F." Other low ranking counties were Allegheny, Pennsylvania ("D"); Anne Arundel, Maryland ("D+"); San Bernardino, California ("D"); and Westchester, New York ("D+").[129] Since 2002, the GPP has ceased evaluating local governments, focusing all of its resources on state government evaluations.

While performance measurement clearly has gained ground among cities and counties, the use of program information in decision making may be more limited. A study of counties found that of those reporting usage of performance measurement in budgeting, 78% said measures were used in preparing departmental budget requests, 68% said measures helped county commissioners review the executive budget, and 80% said measures were used for monitoring the efficiency and effectiveness of services.[130] A study of cities and counties found that administrators had doubts about the extent that program measurement was being used in decision making.[131]

Techniques in Other Nations. Efforts to include performance measurement in budgeting are common in other countries. In the mid-1990s, New Zealand was said to be furthest along in developing a resource allocation system that relied heavily upon quantified performance.[132] Australia, Canada, and the United Kingdom received worldwide attention when they embarked on performance measurement projects as a means for curtailing budget deficits and for holding government agencies accountable for achieving results.[133] Local governments in the United Kingdom have undergone a performance management initiative known as "Best Value."[134] A survey of local governments in the Australian state of Victoria found that 50% of the respondents thought budget reforms changed attitudes in favor of planning and 47% thought the reforms influenced resource allocations.[135] Singapore has made extensive use of performance information and is increasing its emphasis on outcome measures. However, Singapore, while using program information in budgetary decision making, does not attempt to link directly performance and budget data.[136] In contrast, the Australian government has been on a crash course for linking accrual financial data with performance measures.[137] A study of five governments in Canada, England, and the United States found performance reporting was being used in strategic planning and agency decision making.[138]

Management reforms, including those in the budgeting arena, in Australia, New Zealand, the United Kingdom, and, to a lesser extent, Canada, have been called the *New Public Management* (NPM).[139] Over time, this movement has spread throughout Europe, especially into Austria, Germany, and Switzerland. NPM has reached the United States from the standpoint of scholars trying to understand what constitutes NPM, whether it has accomplished anything in other countries, and whether it is on the upswing or downswing. It should be noted, at a minimum, that NPM is more than a budgeting reform. It typically covers myriad other changes, including privatization and increased flexibility for managers.

Reasons for Adopting Reforms

Why do some governments adopt budget reforms while others do not—or adopt them at a slower pace?[140] Researchers have identified several factors:

- Fiscal stress caused by the inability of governments to finance all programs at what seems to be a minimal standard stimulates searches for alternative budget techniques. Improved budgeting is seen as a means for improving the "health" of the government and the economic health of the economy.[141] On the other hand, when fiscal stress becomes severe, governments may simply attempt to cope through a crisis rather than improving their ability to manage themselves.
- Governments search for techniques that facilitate dealing with the knottiest of problems and provide them with the sense of being in control of current and future operations. Emphasis is on increasing the efficiency and effectiveness of operations. The concern is to link programmatic goals with results.[142] When an agency is under pressure from higher-level decision makers about its effectiveness and even existence, the agency may initiate budget changes using performance measures on its own as a means of strengthening its position in the political-administrative arena.[143]
- Government structure is sometimes important. Local governments with professional managers are more likely to adopt program and performance budgeting than are those with strong mayor systems.[144]
- Having an elected and appointed political leadership that is committed to budget reform is another important ingredient, because reforms that are generated exclusively from lower levels in the bureaucracy are unlikely to be effective. Leadership not only must be committed but must also have the leadership skills necessary to forge ahead.[145]
- Governments need trained professional staffs and computer capabilities to undertake many budget reforms.[146] Involvement by employees and incentives for their involvement may increase the chances for success.[147]

Agencies led by "prospectors" as distinguished from "defenders" and "reactors" may be more likely to introduce performance management and be successful in the endeavor.[148] Any such changes that are undertaken should be expected to take time. Expectations of quick results are likely to lead to disappointments.

- A desire on the part of legislators for enhanced information as an aid in exercising oversight of the executive branch is another important factor.[149] On the other hand, when the budget structure and appropriations are not aligned with performance information, the legislature may send a signal to the executive branch that performance is not all that important.[150]

- Legal requirements, such as the 1993 federal legislation instructing agencies to prepare strategic and annual performance plans, and other mandates and incentives are important.

- Another potential influence of major proportions relates to professions. The professional accounting field has shown interest in mandating that accounting systems be linked to program measurement. The Governmental Accounting Standards Board (GASB) is moving toward possibly adopting a requirement that governments link *service efforts and accomplishments* to their accounting systems.[151] GASB is in stage five of a six-stage cycle, with the last stage being consideration by the board for taking action.[152] The Government Finance Officers Association, in opposing the GASB proposal, favors a voluntary system and maintains that the GASB, as an accounting organization, would overstep its bounds and area of expertise were it to require service efforts and accomplishments reporting.[153]

- Involvement of customers/citizens in the process has been identified as facilitating the adoption and use of performance measurement in budgeting.[154]

This listing is in no way exhaustive but simply illustrates some of the factors that can be important in whether a government successfully implements some form of budget reform that is results-oriented.

Impediments to Reform

Perhaps one of the most difficult barriers to reform is overcoming the past. So-called new management practices arise with great frequency. Governments may feel pressure to jump on the most current bandwagon, but then later they jump from that bandwagon to another. Any person involved in policy making and administration can easily become cynical about the prospects for any new management practice actually being implemented. Experienced administrators inevitably question whether the latest technique will have any real effect upon how decisions are made and what outcomes they produce.

Other factors that complicate or deter reform include the following:

- Major difficulties can be expected in setting goals and measures and gaining acceptance of those goals.[155] For example, environmental and conservation interests hold differing views on which goals the U.S. Forest Service should pursue.[156] This lack of clarity would be much less of a problem for an agency such as the U.S. Weather Service, which operates with the luxury of an agreed-upon mandate—to forecast the weather in an accurate and timely manner.
- Another concern is whether strategies lead to accomplishment of goals. Do the efforts of the U.S. Citizenship and Immigration Services really influence the influx of illegal aliens entering the United States?[157] Is an integrated comprehensive approach to strategic planning possible?[158]
- More generally, producing believable data presents a major problem. Simple errors can occur in collecting and tabulating data. Organizations may be tempted to falsify or misrepresent their accomplishments. For example, road crews in Houston seemingly inflated their numbers when reporting how many potholes they filled. If a pothole was large, it might be reported as five potholes.[159] Data need to be valid (measures are appropriate) and verified (completeness, accuracy, consistency, and the like).[160]
- Agencies have overlapping missions, and consequently any outcomes or impacts may actually result from several agencies' work. Managing for results suggests prospects for collaboration across agencies but can work in the other direction, leading to battles over administrative "turf."[161]
- Measuring the accomplishments of regulatory agencies is particularly challenging, and much of what the federal government does is of a regulatory nature.[162] The regulatory units are located both in departments, such as the Food and Drug Administration in the Department of Health and Human Services, and in stand-alone bodies, such as the Securities and Exchange Commission and the Federal Communications Commission.
- Obtaining accurate data in a uniform format and on a timely basis can be a nightmare for federal agencies that depend upon information from state and local governments and private enterprises. The same problem arises for state agencies in obtaining data from local governments.
- Some governments have used adjusted performance measures that attempt to take into account the extent to which external factors (i.e., those outside of an organization's control) influence outcomes. These techniques are themselves subject to criticism.[163]
- Linking program data with cost data is complicated by the limited abilities of accounting systems and inconsistencies across accounting systems (see Chapter 11). Accounting systems may track financial transactions in formats

that do not match up well with the needs of a program manager. Comparisons between units may be thwarted because the units use different accounting system rules.

- The lack of incentives can doom efforts to use performance measurement in budgeting. If high-level executives and legislators show little or no interest in using performance data for decision making, lower-level administrators will consider data collection and program planning to be merely a paper exercise.[164] Equally as troublesome is holding executives and managers accountable for results but not giving them the means to accomplish the desired outcomes. Due to revenue declines, budgets may be cut, but departments may be expected to accomplish what was originally planned.

- Managers often find it unpleasant, if not downright repulsive, to have their operations compared with operations in other departments or in other governments. Yet, benchmarking is frequently regarded as a desirable technique. As discussed earlier, benchmarking involves comparing one's operations with those of others. Serious problems of comparison arise in that governments operate in different environments, may measure their activities differently, and may account differently for their use of resources. Therefore, a city roads department will be wary of comparing its operations with those of other cities, unless there are assurances that variations are taken into account, such as variations in weather, amount of traffic, and terrain.[165] Benchmarking holds the prospect of being able to compare schools as to which are performing better in educating children but in doing so threaten those who run the schools. The federal government's No Child Left Behind Act, for example, requires testing of individual students to hold teachers and administrators accountable for educational outcomes. Citizen satisfaction can be measured across governmental boundaries, such as determining whether one community is more satisfied with its recreation services than other communities.[166]

If all of these problems were not enough, additional factors could become influential. The public sector routinely borrows management ideas from the private sector, and one that is emerging is the "balanced scorecard," developed and popularized by Robert S. Kaplan and David P. Norton.[167] Its underlying premise is that the private sector has been too focused on the "bottom line" of profit and loss and needs to be concerned with other matters, such as customer satisfaction and employee satisfaction. While public sector performance measurement often includes customer satisfaction, employee satisfaction may be of limited concern. The balanced scorecard suggests that government should step back and rethink how it measures its activities and results.

Finally, the question must be asked whether budget reforms aimed at fostering performance management have any bearing on global rethinking about the purposes of government and how those purposes or goals are pursued.[168] Yes, budget systems may be tied with strategic planning, but do these systems address in any real sense fundamental questions about government and draw attention to key issues, such as immigration, terrorism, international trade imbalance, and the like?

Summary

One of the main themes running through budgetary literature has been the need to use the budgetary process as a vehicle for planning. In particular, this need has facilitated an attempt to incorporate program data into the system along with resource data, such as dollar and personnel costs.

During and after World War II, a set of theoretical fields and technologies emerged that had a great influence on budgetary reform. These include operations research, economic analysis, general systems theory, cybernetics, computer technology, and systems analysis.

Budget requests are prepared by agencies in accordance with instructions provided by the central budget office. In addition to data on finances and personnel, request instructions increasingly require program data, including social indicators, impacts, outputs, workloads, and activities, as well as data on the need or demand for services. Productivity measures are used to relate resource consumption, as measured in dollars and personnel, to the work accomplished and the product of that work.

Budget request manuals take varied approaches to providing guidance on how agencies should request resources. These approaches include current commitment, fixed-ceiling, and open-ended budgeting. Reform efforts since the 1960s have focused on PPB systems, or more generally program budgeting, as well as on zero-base budgeting. Strategic planning and policy and program guidance also have proved popular. Current emphasis is on performance measurement. Governments tend to use hybrids of these systems.

Notes

1. Schick, A. (1966). The road to PPB: The stages of budget reform. *Public Administration Review, 26,* 243–258.

2. Williams, D. W. (2004). Evolution of performance measurement until 1930. *Administration & Society, 36,* 131–165.

3. Taft, W. H. (1912). *Economy and efficiency in the government service.* House Doc. No. 458, 16.

4. Commission on Economy and Efficiency (1912). *The need for a national budget.* House Doc. No. 854, 4–5.

5. Williams, D. W. (2003). Measuring government in the early twentieth century. *Public Administration Review, 63,* 643–659.

6. Cleveland, F. A. (1915). Evolution of the budget idea in the United States. *Annals, 62,* 15–35.

7. Willoughby, W. F. (1918). *The problems of a national budget.* New York: Appleton.

8. Upson, L. D. (1924). Half-time budget methods. *Annals, 113,* 69–74.

9. Buck, A. E. (1929). *Public budgeting.* New York: Harper and Brothers.

10. Kilpatrick, W. (1936). Classification and measurement of public expenditures. *Annals, 183,* 19–26.

11. President's Committee on Administrative Management (1937). *Report.* Washington, DC: U.S. Government Printing Office.

12. Key, V. O., Jr. (1940). The lack of a budgetary theory. *American Political Science Review, 34,* 1138–1144. See Light, P. C. (2006). The tides of reform revisited: patterns in making government work, 1945–2002. *Public Administration Review, 66,* 6–19.

13. Commission on Organization of the Executive Branch of the Government (1949). *Budgeting and accounting.* Washington, DC: U.S. Government Printing Office, 8.

14. Lewis, V. B. (1952). Toward a theory of budgeting. *Public Administration Review, 12,* 42–54.

15. Mosher, F. C. (1954). *Program budgeting: theory and practice with particular reference to the U.S. Department of Army.* Chicago: Public Administrative Service.

16. Seckler-Hudson, C. (1952). Performance budgeting in the government of the United States. *Public Finance, 7,* 327–345.

17. Smithies, A. (1955). *The budgetary process in the United States.* New York: McGraw-Hill.

18. Commission on Organization of the Executive Branch of the Government (1955). *Final report to Congress.* Washington, DC: U.S. Government Printing Office; Commission on Organization of the Executive Branch of the Government (1955). *Budgeting and accounting.* Washington, DC: U.S. Government Printing Office.

19. Burkhead, J. (1956). *Government budgeting.* New York: Wiley, 133–182.

20. Wildavsky, A. (1969). Rescuing policy analysis from PPBS. *Public Administration Review, 29,* 193.

21. The early thinking on this topic was suggested by Robert J. Mowitz, Director of the Institute of Public Administration, The Pennsylvania State University.

22. Churchman, C. W. et al. (1957). *Introduction to operations research.* New York: Wiley.

23. For an early survey of the economic analysis field, see Prest, A. R. & Turvey, R. (1965). Cost-benefit analysis: a survey. *Economic Journal, 75,* 683–735.

24. Von Bertalanffy, L. (1951). General system theory: a new approach to unity of science. *Human Biology, 23,* 303–361.

25. Wiener, N. (1956). *The human use of human beings.* Garden City, NY: Doubleday.

26. Ouchi, W. G. (1970). A short history of the development of computer hardware. In T. L. Whisler (Ed.), *Information technology and organizational change,* Belmont, CA: Wadsworth, 129–134.

27. Fisher, G. H. (1966). *The analytical bases of systems analysis.* Santa Monica, CA: The RAND Corporation.

28. U.S. Office of Management and Budget (2006). Preparation, submission, and execution of the budget, circular A-11. Retrieved July 25, 2006, from http://www.whitehouse.gov/omb/circulars/a11/current_year/a11_toc.html.

29. Government Performance and Results Act (1993). P.L. 103-62.

30. Hatry, H. P. (1999). *Performance measurement: getting results.* Washington, DC: Urban Institute; Walters, J. (1998). *Measuring up: governing's guide to performance measures for geniuses (and other public managers).* Washington, DC: Congressional Quarterly; Klitgaard, R. & Light, P.C. (Eds.) (2005). *High-performance government: structure, leadership, incentives.* Santa Monica, CA: RAND Corp; U.S. Government Accountability Office (2005). *Performance measurement and evaluation: definitions and relationships.* Washington, DC: GAO.

31. See the *Social Indicators Research* journal.

32. Sustainability Seattle (1998). *Indicators of sustainability community.* Seattle: Sustainability Seattle.

33. Department of Planning and Development, City of Seattle (2006). *Sustainable communities.* Retrieved July 25, 2006, from http://www.seattle.gov/dpd/GreenBuilding/SustainableCommunities/Overview.

34. Aristigueta, M. P. et al. (2001). The role of social indicators in developing a managing for results system. *Public Performance & Management Review, 24,* 254–269.

35. Murphey, D. A. (1999). Presenting community-level data in an "outcomes and indicators" framework: lessons from Vermont's experience. *Public Administration Review, 59,* 76–82.

36. Mowitz, R. J. (1970). *The design and implementation of Pennsylvania's planning, programming, budgeting system.* Harrisburg, PA: Commonwealth of Pennsylvania.

37. Rubenstein, R. et al. (2003). Better than raw: a guide to measuring organizational performance with adjusted performance measures. *Public Administration Review, 63,* 607–615.

38. U.S. Office of Management and Budget (2006). *Program assessment rating tool guidance no. 2006-04.*

39. See current issues of *Public Performance and Management Review,* a quarterly journal.

40. Osborne, D. & Gaebler, T. (1992). *Reinventing government: how the entrepreneurial spirit is transforming the public sector.* Reading, MA: Addison-Wesley; Osborne, D. & Plastrik, P. (1997). *Banishing bureaucracy: the five strategies for reinventing government.* Reading, MA: Addison-Wesley; Rondinelli, D. A. & Cheema, G. S. (Eds.) (2003). *Reinventing government for the twenty-first century: state capacity in a globalizing society.* Bloomfield, CT: Kumarian.

41. Spicer, M. (2004). Public administration, the history of ideas, and the reinventing government movement. *Public Administration Review, 64*, 353–362; Kim, P. S. et al. (2005). Toward participatory and transparent governance: report on the sixth global forum on reinventing government. *Public Administration Review, 65*, 646–654.

42. Whicker, M. L. & Mo, C. (1998). Impact of agency mission on agency budget strategy, paper presented at the national conference of the Association for Budgeting and Financial Management, Washington, DC.

43. U.S. Office of Management and Budget (2006). *Program assessment rating tool guidance no. 2006-02*, 4–6.

44. Whitaker, G. P. (2004). Mutual accountability between governments and nonprofits. *American Review of Public Administration, 34*, 115–133; Page, S. (2004). Measuring accountability for results in interagency collaboratives. *Public Administration Review, 64*, 591–606; U.S. Government Accountability Office (2005). *Results-oriented government: practices that can help enhance and sustain collaboration among federal agencies.* Washington, DC: GAO.

45. National Security Act Amendments (1949). Ch. 412, 63 Stat. 578.

46. Budget and Accounting Procedures Act (1950). Ch. 946, 64 Stat. 832; U.S. General Accounting Office (1997). *Performance budgeting: past initiatives offer insights for GPRA implementation.* Washington, DC: U.S. Government Printing Office.

47. Schick, *The road to PPB*, 252–253.

48. Mosher, *Program budgeting*, 34–47.

49. Massey, R. J. (1963). Program packages and the program budget in the Department of Defense. *Public Administration Review, 23*, 30–34.

50. Novick, D. (1965). The Department of Defense. In D. Novick (Ed.), *Program budgeting: program analysis and the federal budget.* Cambridge, MA: Harvard University Press, 91.

51. Novick, D. (1956). *Efficiency and economy in government through new budgeting and accounting procedures.* Santa Monica, CA: RAND Corporation.

52. Jones, L. R. (1991). Policy development, planning, and resource allocation in the Department of Defense. *Public Budgeting & Finance, 11, Fall*, 15–27; U.S. General Accounting Office (2004). *Future Years Defense Program: actions needed to improve transparency of DOD's projected resource needs.* Washington, DC: GAO.

53. U.S. Department of Defense (2006). DoD releases QDR to chart way ahead to confront future. Press release. Retrieved July 31, 2006 from http://www.defenselink.mil/news/Feb2006/20060203_4104.html.

54. National Performance Review (1993). *Creating a government that works better and costs less: Department of Defense.* Washington, DC: U.S. Government Printing Office.

55. Commission on Roles and Missions of the Armed Forces (1995). *Directions for defense.* Washington, DC: U.S. Government Printing Office.

56. Jones, L. R. & McCaffery, J. L. (2005). Reform of the planning, programming, budgeting system, and management control in the U.S. Department of Defense: insights from budget theory. *Public Budgeting & Finance, 25, Fall*, 1–19.

57. Schick, A. (1973). A death in the bureaucracy: the demise of the federal PPB. *Public Administration Review, 33*, 146–156.

58. Harper, E. L. et al. (1969). Implementation and use of PPB in sixteen federal agencies. *Public Administration Review, 29*, 634.

59. Casselman, R. C. (1973). Massachusetts revisited: chronology of a failure. *Public Administration Review, 33*, 129–135.

60. Sallack, D. & Allen, D. N. (1987). From impact to output: Pennsylvania's Planning-Programming-Budgeting System in transition. *Public Budgeting & Finance, 7, Spring*, 38–50.

61. Wildavsky, A. & Hammann, A. (1965). Comprehensive versus incremental budgeting in the Department of Agriculture. *Administrative Science Quarterly, 10*, 321–346.

62. Phyrr, P. A. (1973). *Zero-base budgeting: a practical management tool for evaluating expenses*. New York: Wiley.

63. Lauth, T. P. & Rieck, S. C. (1979). Modifications in Georgia zero-base budgeting procedures: 1973–1981. *Midwest Review of Public Administration, 13*, 225–238.

64. U.S. General Accounting Office (1979). *Streamlining zero-base budgeting will benefit decision making*. Washington, DC: U.S. Government Printing Office.

65. Schick, A. (1978). The road from ZBB. *Public Administration Review, 38*, 177–180.

66. Metzgar, J. & Miranda, R. (2001). Bringing out the dead: can information technology resurrect budget reform? *Government Finance Review, 17, April*, 9–14.

67. Rabin, J. et al. (Eds.) (2000). *Handbook of strategic management*, 2nd ed. New York: Marcel Dekker; Poister, T. H. & Streib, G. (2005). Elements of strategic planning and management in municipal government: status after two decades. *Public Administration Review, 65*, 45–56.

68. Willoughby, K. G. & Melkers, J. E. (2000). Implementing PBB: conflicting views of success. *Public Budgeting & Finance, 20, Spring*, 105–120.

69. Odiorne, G. (1965). *Management by objectives*. New York: Pitman; Poister, T. H. & Streib, G. (1995). MBO in municipal government: variations on a traditional management tool. *Public Administration Review, 55*, 48–56; Antoni, C. (2005). Management by objectives: an effective tool for teamwork? *International Journal of Human Resources Management, 16*, 174–184.

70. Deming, W. E. (1928). *Quality, productivity, and competitive position*. Cambridge, MA: Massachusetts Institute of Technology Center for Advanced Engineering Study; McLaughlin, C. P. & Kaluzny, A. (Eds.) (2006). *Continuous quality improvement in health care: theory, implementations, and applications*, 3rd ed. Sudbury, MA: Jones and Bartlett; Mukhopadhyay, M. (2005). *Total quality management in education*, 2nd ed. Thousand Oaks, CA: Sage.

71. Moynihan, D. P. (2005). Goal-based learning and the future of performance management. *Public Administration Review, 65*, 203–216; Moynihan, D. P. (2006). Managing for results in state government: evaluating a decade of reform. *Public Administration Review, 66*, 77–89.

72. Kobrak, P. (1996). The social responsibilities of a public entrepreneur. *Administration and Society, 28,* 205–237.

73. Rubin, I. S. (1991). Budgeting for our times: target base budgeting. *Public Budgeting & Finance, 11, Fall,* 5–14.

74. National Performance Review (1993). *From red tape to results: creating a government that works better and costs less.* Washington, DC: U.S. Government Printing Office.

75. U.S. Government Accountability Office (2006). *2010 Census: redesigned approach holds promise but Census Bureau needs to annually develop and provide a comprehensive project plan to monitor costs.* Washington, DC: GAO.

76. For a discussion of benchmarking, see Folz, D. H. (2004). Service quality and benchmarking the performance of municipal services. *Public Administration Review, 64,* 209–220.

77. National Performance Review (1995). *Common sense government: works better and costs less.* Washington, DC: U.S. Government Printing Office, 59–60.

78. Lunney, K. (2001). NPR director touts reinvention's results. *Govexec.com.* Retrieved July 31, 2006, from http://www.govexec.com/dailyfed/0101/010901m1.htm.

79. U.S. General Accounting Office (1999). *NPR's savings: claimed agency savings cannot all be attributed to NPR.* Washington, DC: U.S. Government Printing Office.

80. Callahan, R. F. & Gilbert, G. R. (2005). End-user satisfaction and design features of public agencies. *American Review of Public Administration, 35,* 57–73.

81. U.S. General Services Administration (2006). USA Services launches citizen services survey. Press release. Retrieved October 31, 2006, from http://www.gsa.gov/Portal/gsa/ep/contentView.do?contentType=GSA_BASIC&contentId=21472&noc=T.

82. Government Performance and Results Act (1993). P.L. 103–62.

83. U.S. General Accounting Office (1996). *Effectively implementing the Government Performance and Results Act.* Washington, DC: U.S. Government Printing Office; Long, E. & Franklin, A. L. (2004). The paradox of implementing the Government Performance and Results Act: top-down direction for bottom-up implementation. *Public Administration Review, 64,* 309–319.

84. See CFO website. Retrieved on July 31, 2006 from http://cfoc.gov/textonly/about.cfm.

85. Bingman, C. F. (2006). Proposals for improving GPRA annual performance plans. *Public Budgeting & Finance, 26, Summer,* 143–154.

86. U.S. General Accounting Office (1997). *Managing for results: critical issues for improving federal agencies' strategic plans.* Washington, DC: U.S. Government Printing Office.

87. Posner, P. L. & Mihm, J. C., U.S. General Accounting Office (1998). *Managing for results: observations on OMB's September 1997 strategic plan,* testimony before House committee on Government Reform and Oversight, U.S. Congress.

88. Joyce, P. G. (2003). *Linking performance and budgeting: opportunities in the federal budget process.* Washington, DC: IBM Center for the Business of Government.

89. Chief Human Capital Officers Act (2002). P.L. 107-296; U.S. Government Accountability Office (2005). *Human capital: observations on agencies' implementation of the Chief Human Capital Officers Act.* Washington, DC: GAO.

90. Burke, B. (2005). The human side of managing for results. *American Review of Public Administration, 35,* 270–286; U.S. Government Accountability Office (2004). *Human capital: principles, criteria, and processes for governmentwide federal human capital reform.* Washington, DC: GAO; Meier, K. J. et al. (2006). Management activity and program performance. *Public Administration Review, 66,* 24–36.

91. U.S. Office of Management and Budget (2005). *Expanding e-government.* Retrieved August 1, 2006, from http://www.whitehouse.gov/omb/budintegration/expanding_egov_2005.pdf. See West, D. M. (2005). *Digital government: technology and public-sector performance.* Princeton, NJ: Princeton University Press; Mandel, J. (2006). E-government scores improve slightly on latest management score card. *Govexec.com.* Retrieved August 2, 2006 from www.govexec.com/dailyfed/0806/080106m1.htm.

92. U.S. Office of Management and Budget (2006). *Results.gov.* Retrieved November 1, 2006, from http://www.whitehouse.gov/results/agenda/fy06q3scorecard.pdf.

93. U.S. Office of Management and Budget (2006). *Results.gov.* Retrieved November 1, 2006, from http://www.whitehouse.gov/results/agenda/fy06q3scorecard.pdf.

94. Laurent, A. (2002). Management counts. *Government Executive, 23, May,* 8–16; Treverton, G. F. (2004). The state of federal management. *Government Executive, January.* Retrieved August 1, 2006, from http://www.govexec.com/features/0104/0104s1.htm.

95. U.S. Office of Management and Budget (2006). *Guide to the Program Assessment Rating Tool,* 1. Retrieved August 1, 2006, from http://www.whitehouse.gov/omb/part/fy2006/2006_guidance_final.pdf.

96. U.S. Office of Management and Budget (2006). *Guide to the Program Assessment Rating Tool,* 11–12.

97. U.S. Office of Management and Budget (2006). *2006 PART schedule.* Retrieved August 1, 2006, from http://www.whitehouse.gov/omb/part/fy2006/attach_b_schedule.pdf.

98. U.S. Office of Management and Budget (2006). *Guidance on appeals process for 2006 PARTs.* Retrieved August 1, 2006, from http://www.whitehouse.gov/omb/part/guidance/part_guid_2006-5.pdf.

99. U.S. Office of Management and Budget (2006). *ExpectMore.gov.* Retrieved August 1, 2006, from http://www.whitehouse.gov/omb/expectmore/.

100. President's Management Council (2006). *Giving the American people more for their money.* Retrieved November 1, 2006, from http://www.whitehouse.gov/results/agenda/06_Results_Report.pdf.

101. President's Management Council (2006). *Facts about the president's management agenda.* Retrieved November 1, 2006, from http://www.whitehouse.gov/results/agenda/PMA-MythFact20061003.html.

102. Joyce, P. G. (2003). *Linking performance and budgeting: opportunities in the federal budget process.*

103. Gilmour, J. B. & Lewis, D. E. (2006). Assessing performance budgeting at OMB: the influence of politics, performance, and program size. *Journal of Public Administration Research and Theory, 16,* 169–186.

104. Dull, M. (2006). Why PART? The institutional politics of presidential budget reform. *Journal of Public Administration Research and Theory, 16,* 187–215.

105. U.S. Government Accountability Office (2005). *Performance budgeting: PART focuses attention on program performance, but more can be done to engage Congress.* Washington, DC: GAO.

106. U.S. Government Accountability Office (2005). *21ˢᵗ century challenges: performance budgeting could help promote necessary reexamination.* Washington, DC: GAO.

107. U.S. Government Accountability Office (2005). *Managing for results: enhancing agency use of performance information for management decision making.* Washington, DC: GAO.

108. U.S. Government Accountability Office (2005). *Performance budgeting.*

109. Mandel, J. (2006). OMB program assessments viewed as flawed budget tool. *Govexec.com.* Retrieved November 1, 2006, from http://www.govexec.com/dailyfed/0406/040406m1.htm.

110. Bush, G. W. (2003). *President Bush announces major combat operations in Iraq have ended.* Press Release. Retrieved July 31, 2006 from www.whitehouse.gov/news/releases/2003/05/20030501-15.html; Bash, D. (2003). White House pressed on 'mission accomplished' sign. *CNN.* Retrieved July 31, 2006, from http://edition.cnn.com/2003/ALLPOLITICS/10/28/mission.accomplished/.

111. Government Accountability Organization (2006). *Rebuilding Iraq: governance, security, reconstruction, and financing challenges.* Washington, DC: GAO.

112. U.S. Government Accountability Office (2006). *GAO's preliminary observations regarding preparedness, response, and recovery.* Washington, DC: GAO; U.S. Department of Homeland Security, Office of the Inspector General (2006). *A performance review of FEMA's disaster management activities in response to Hurricane Katrina.* Retrieved July 31, 2006, from http://www.dhs.gov/interweb/assetlibrary/OIG_06-32_Mar06.pdf.

113. Melkers, J. & Willoughby, K. (2004). *Staying the course: the use of performance measurement in state governments.* Washington, DC: IBM Center for the Business of Government. Retrieved August 2, 2006, from http://www.businessofgovernment.org/pdfs/MelkersReport.pdf. See Willoughby, K. G. (2004). Performance measurement and budget balancing: state government perspective. *Public Budgeting & Finance, 24, Summer,* 21–39.

114. U.S. Government Accountability Office (2005). *Performance budgeting: states' experiences can inform federal efforts.* Washington, DC: GAO.

115. Burns, R. C. (2006). Unpublished data from Survey of State Budget Offices, 2005. Morgantown, WV: Recreation, Parks, and Tourism Program, University of West Virginia.

116. Jordan, M. M. & Hackbart, M. M. (1999). Performance budgeting and performance funding in the states: a status assessment. *Public Budgeting & Finance, 19, Spring*, 68–88.

117. Willoughby, K. G. & Melkers, J. E. (2000). Implementing PBB: conflicting views of success. *Public Budgeting & Finance, 20, Spring*, 85–120.

118. Melkers, J. E. & Willoughby, K. G. (2001). Budgeters' views of state performance-budgeting systems: distinctions across branches. *Public Administration Review, 61*, 54–64.

119. Government Performance Project (2005). How we grade: a look inside the GPP. *Governing.com*. Retrieved August 2, 2005, from http://www.governing.com/gpp/2005/how.htm.

120. Barrett, K. & Greene, R. (2005). Grading the states '05: the year of living dangerously. *Governing.com*. Retrieved August 2, 2006, from http://www.governing.com/gpp/2005/intro.htm and http://results.gpponline.org/Documents/ DOCTYPE_STATESUMSIDEBAR_127_1_0_2.pdf.

121. Coe, C. K. & Brunet, J. R. (2006). Organizational report cards: significant impact or much ado about nothing? *Public Administration Review, 66*, 90–100.

122. Kelly, J. M. & Rivenbark, W. C. (2003). *Performance budgeting for state and local governments*. Armonk, NY: M.E. Sharpe.

123. O'Toole, D. E. et al. (1996). Current local government budgeting practices. *Government Finance Review, 12, December*, 25–29.

124. Melkers, J. & Willoughby, K. (2005). Models of performance-measurement use in local governments: understanding budgeting, communication, and lasting effects. *Public Administration Review, 65*, 180–190.

125. Ho, A. T. & Ni, A. Y. (2005). Have cities shifted to outcome-oriented performance reporting? A content analysis of city budgets. *Public Budgeting & Finance, 25, Summer*, 61–83.

126. Barrrett, K. & Greene, R. (2000). Grading the cities: a management report card. *Governing, 13, February*, 22–88.

127. Hendrick, R. (2000). Comprehensive management and budgeting reform in local government: the case of Milwaukee. *Public Productivity & Management Review, 23*, 312–337.

128. Edwards, D. & Thomas, J. C. (2005). Developing a municipal performance-measurement system: reflections on the Atlanta Dashboard. *Public Administration Review, 65*, 369–376; City of Atlanta (2006). *Atlanta Dashboard*. Retrieved August 3, 2006, from http://www.atlantaga.gov/mayor/dashboard.aspx.

129. Barrett, K. & Green, R. (2002). Grading the counties 2002. *Governing.com*. Retrieved August 3, 2006, from http://www.governing.com/gpp/2002/gp2intro.htm; http://www.governing.com/gpp/2002/gp2grade.htm.

130. Wang, X. (2000). Performance measurement in budgeting: a study of county governments. *Public Budgeting & Finance, 20, Fall*, 102–118.

131. Melkers, J. & Willoughby, K. (2005). Models of performance-measurement use in local governments: understanding budgeting, communication, and lasting effects. Public Administration Review, 65, 180.

132. Organization for Economic Cooperation and Development (1995). *Budgeting for results: perspectives on public expenditure management*. Paris: Organization for Economic Cooperation and Development, 55.

133. U.S. General Accounting Office (1995). *Managing for results: experiences abroad suggest insights for federal management reforms*. Washington, DC: U.S. Government Printing Office.

134. Harris, J. L. (2000). Best value and performance management: lessons learned from the United Kingdom. *Government Finance Review, 16, August*, 27–33.

135. Kluvers, R. (2001). An analysis of introducing program budgeting in local government. *Public Budgeting & Finance, 21, Summer*, 29–45.

136. Working Party of Senior Budget Officials, Organization for Economic Cooperation and Development (2006). *Budgeting in Singapore*. Retrieved August 2, 2006, from http://appli1.oecd.org/olis/2006doc.nsf/43bb6130e5e86e5fc12569fa005d004c/d7169 edc120eedfac125717f004e128a/$FILE/JT03209867.DOC.

137. Kelly, J. & Wanna, J. (2004). Crashing through with accrual-output price budgeting in Australia: technical adjustment or a new way of doing business? *American Review of Public Administration, 34*, 94–111.

138. Cunningham, G. M. & Harris, J. E. (2005). Toward a theory of performance reporting to achieve public sector accountability: a field study. *Public Budgeting & Finance, 25, Summer*, 15–42.

139. Barzelay, M. (2001). *The new public management*. Berkeley, CA: University of California Press; Page, S. (2005). What's new about the new public management? Administrative change in the human services. *Public Administration Review, 65*, 713–727; Pollitt, C. et al. (Eds.) (2007). *The new public management in Europe: adaptations and alternatives*. New York: Palgrave.

140. Forrester, J. P. & Adams, G. B. (1997). Budgetary reform through organizational learning. *Administration and Society, 28*, 466–488; Fernandez, S. & Rainey, H. G. (2006). Managing successful organizational change in the public sector. *Public Administration Review, 66*, 168–176.

141. Walters, J. (2000). Raising Alabama. *Governing, 14, October*, 28–32.

142. U.S. General Accounting Office (1999). *Managing for results: opportunities for continued improvements in agencies' performance plans*. Washington, DC: U.S. Government Printing Office.

143. Barzelay, M. & Thompson, F. (2006). Responsibility budgeting at the Air Force Materiel Command. *Public Administration Review, 66*, 127–138.

144. Lu, H. & Facer, II, R. L. (2004). Budget change in Georgia counties: examining patterns and practices. *American Review of Public Administration, 34*, 67–93.

145. U.S. General Accounting Office (2000). *Managing for results: federal managers' views show need for ensuring top leadership skills*. Washington, DC: U.S. Government Printing Office; Klitgaard, R. & Light, P. C. (Eds.) (2005). *High-performance government: structure, leadership, incentives*. Santa Monica, CA: RAND Corporation.

146. Ingraham, P .W. et al. (2003). *Government performance: why management matters.* Baltimore, MD: Johns Hopkins University Press.

147. Boyne, G. A. et al. (2004). Toward the self-evaluating organization? An empirical test of the Wildavsky model. *Public Administration Review, 64,* 463–473; Swiss, J. E. (2005). A framework for assessing incentives in results-based management. *Public Administration Review, 65,* 592–602.

148. Andrews, R., Boyne, G. A., & Walker, R. M. (2006). Strategy content and organizational performance: an empirical analysis. *Public Administration Review, 66,* 52–63.

149. Mihm, J. C., U.S. General Accounting Office (2001). *Using GPRA to assist oversight and decisionmaking,* testimony before the House Subcommittee on Government Efficiency, Financial Management and Intergovernmental Relations. Washington, DC: U.S. Government Printing Office.

150. U.S. Government Accountability Office (2005). *Performance budgeting: efforts to restructure budgets to better align resources with performance.* Washington, DC: GAO.

151. Governmental Accounting Standards Board (1994). *Concepts Statement No. 2: service efforts and accomplishments reporting.* Norwalk, CT: Governmental Accounting Standards Board; Epstein, P. et al. (2005). *Government service efforts and accomplishments performance reports: a guide to understanding.* Norwalk, CT: Governmental Accounting Standards Board.

152. Governmental Accounting Standards Board (2006). *GASB project—general information.* Retrieved August 2, 2006, from http://www.seagov.org/sea_gasb_project/index.shtml.

153. Government Finance Officers Association (2002). *Public policy statement: performance measurement and the Governmental Accounting Standards Board.* Retrieved August 3, 2006, from http://www.gfoa.org/services/policy/gfoapp2.shtml#ppbud8.

154. Yang, K. & Holzer, M. (2006). The performance-trust link: implications for performance measurement. *Public Administration Review, 66,* 114–126; Berman, B. J. (2006). *Listening to the public: adding the voices of the people to government performance measurement and reporting.* New York: Fund for the City of New York; Epstein, P. D. et al. (2006). *Results that matter: improving communities by engaging citizens, measuring performance, and getting things done.* Hoboken, NJ: Jossey-Bass.

155. Nicholson-Crotty, S. et al. (2006). Disparate measures: public managers and performance-measurement strategies. *Public Administration Review, 66,* 101–113.

156. Peckenpaugh, J. (2001). Linking performance goals to budgets won't be easy, experts say. *Govexec.com.* Retrieved August 3, 2006, from http://www.govexec.com/dailyfed/0301/032201p1.htm.

157. U.S. General Accounting Office (2000). *Managing for results: challenges agencies face in producing credible performance information.* Washington, DC: U.S. Government Printing Office.

158. Roberts, N. (2000). The synoptic model of strategic planning and the GPRA. *Public Productivity & Management Review, 23,* 297–311.

159. Graves, R. (2001). Pothole crew's reports scrutinized by officials. *Houston Chronicle*. Retrieved August 3, 2006, from http://www.chron.com/CDA/archives/archive.mpl?id=2001_3299070.

160. U.S. General Accounting Office (1999). *Performance plans: selected approaches for verification and validation of agency performance information*. Washington, DC: U.S. Government Printing Office.

161. Simeone, R. et al. (2005). A systems approach to performance-based management: the national drug control strategy. *Public Administration Review, 65,* 191–202.

162. U.S. General Accounting Office (1999). *Managing for results: strengthening regulatory agencies' performance management practices*. Washington, DC: U.S. Government Printing Office.

163. Brooks, A. C. (2000). The use and misuse of adjusted performance measures. *Journal of Policy Analysis and Management, 19,* 323–328.

164. U.S. General Accounting Office (2001). *Managing for results: federal managers' views on key management issues vary widely across agencies*. Washington, DC: U.S. Government Printing Office; Bourdeaux, C. (2006). Do legislatures matter in budgetary reform? *Public Budgeting & Finance, 26, Spring,* 120–142.

165. Ammons, D. N. et al. (2001). Performance-comparison projects in local government: participants' perspectives. *Public Administration Review, 61,* 100–110.

166. Van Ryzin, G. G. et al. (2004). Drivers and consequences of citizen satisfaction: an application of the American Customer Satisfaction Index Model to New York City. *Public Administration Review, 64,* 331–341; Swindell, D. & Kelly, J. (2005). Performance measurement versus city service satisfaction: intra-city variations in quality? *Social Science Quarterly, 86,* 704–723.

167. Kaplan, R. S. & Norton, D. P. (1996). *The balanced scorecard*. Boston, MA: Harvard Business School Press; Kaplan, R. S. & Norton, D. P. (2001). *The strategy-focused organization*. Boston, MA: Harvard Business School Press; Smith, R. F. (2007). *Balanced scorecard and business process management: focusing processes on strategic drivers*. Hoboken, NJ: Wiley & Sons.

168. U.S. Government Accountability Office (2005). *Strategic budgeting: risk management principles can help DHS allocate resources to highest priorities*. Washington, DC: GAO.

Chapter 7

BUDGET PREPARATION: THE DECISION PROCESS

Budget preparation is like a giant juggling act. Many balls are tossed up into the air—some by agencies, some by the budget office, some by the chief executive, and some by others—and surprisingly each year they do not all come crashing down. Instead, a proposed budget comes out of this dizzying assortment of taxing and spending initiatives.

Preparing a budget in an executive budget system involves having agencies prepare requests and then assembling those requests; however, the process involves much more. Indeed, the request process is simple compared with the difficult task that remains—making decisions on the recommended levels for revenues and expenditures. Is a tax increase needed? What programs should be expanded and what programs should be reduced? In systems that do not centralize budget preparation in the executive, the same concerns prevail. A legislative committee or a joint group of executives and legislators may be responsible for weighing the citizens' joint demands for increased services and possibly lower taxes and for proposing a budget package that balances these competing demands.

This chapter includes two sections. The first section considers how a proposed executive budget is assembled. Deliberations on the revenue and expenditure sides of the budget are examined. The second section reviews the products of budget preparation, namely, the various types of budget documents and their formats.

◼ Decisions on Budget Requests

Budget preparation involves participation by a variety of individuals and organizations, which have myriad values regarding taxing and spending. In an *executive budget system*, the chief executive has the overall responsibility for the preparation process. Numerous other actors play roles as well, including the central budget office and other units such as the treasury office. Not all governments have executive systems. Many county governments do not have a county executive or manager, for example. As a consequence, their budgets are prepared jointly by several different executive and legislative officials. In other systems, such as some local governments in Russia, finance departments have reporting responsibilities to both the mayor and the legislative council. Municipal finance officers and/or treasurers sometimes are appointed by the central government, such as in Ukraine.

Legislators or their staffs may be involved in budget preparation. On occasion, state legislative staff members may be allowed to attend executive budget hearings that review the proposed budgets of line agencies. This practice helps the legislative branch become aware of the budget proposals being developed and the rationales behind these proposals prior to the budget actually reaching the legislature. In small local governments, budget preparation may be a relatively fluid process that is characterized by close links between executive and legislative officials. Even when legislative officers are not involved, their views on taxing and spending are taken into account. For example, a mayor will think twice about recommending a budget increase for a program when it is known that perhaps two-thirds of city council has serious doubts about the program's worth.

In some other systems, such as in Egypt, agencies make their recommendations to a minister of finance, who has the final decision-making authority but is not subject to significant legislative review. Subunits of other ministries, without the presence of their superiors, may be called to defend budget requests before the finance ministry, creating a situation in which heads of ministries may have only limited input into their budgets.

Concerns of the Chief Executive

The chief executive—president, governor, mayor, county executive, and the like—may have official responsibility for budget preparation, but usually will have only limited direct involvement until the later stages of preparation. This system allows the chief executive time to take care of other duties. Having the budget office and other units, such as treasury, involved early in the process provides for the application of professional administrative talent in analyzing problems and options that will later come before the chief executive for review. A professional budget staff endeavors to take preliminary actions on budget requests that are in keeping with the policy objectives of the chief executive, thereby allowing the chief executive to avoid dealing with minor problems and reserving time to deal with major ones.

Strategic Concerns. The chief executive needs to convey to the departments, bureaus, and offices involved, and especially to the central budget office, a sense of priorities so that effort is not needlessly wasted on proposals that will later be rejected. Several concerns arise, with a major one at the national level being the overall philosophy of the role of government in contemporary society. What is the overall public interest, and how large should the public sector be in the total economy? Parallel questions at the regional (state or province) and local (city, county, or school district) levels are usually related to a few key issues such as the quality of the education system, the condition of roads or other infrastructure, and taxes, especially the property tax.

Another concern for many chief executives is the effect that the budget may have on the economic environment. Cities, counties, states, and the national government are concerned about budgetary influences on the economy. For local and state chief executives, their concern tends to focus on whether current or proposed taxes will deter businesses from locating or expanding operations in their jurisdictions. Perhaps equally important is the quality of government services. While school districts and special districts may have little or no official role in economic development, the quality of education, water systems, sewers, and so on are critical in the location decisions of corporations. The national government has these same concerns and others as well, including international implications and price stability (see Chapter 15).

The chief executive sets ground rules on policies and program priorities. A president conveys an overall sense of priorities to the Office of Management and Budget (OMB) regarding national security and domestic spending and a sense of priorities within each of these categories. Election campaign promises are important in that chief executives usually attempt to pursue the objectives outlined in their bids for voter approval. For many chief executives, the budget serves as a vehicle for strategic planning for the government. For example, President George W. Bush wanted to advance his faith-based initiative in which religious organizations would be enlisted to help combat social problems. That initiative was eclipsed by the disasters of September 11, 2001. His administration subsequently placed much greater emphasis on homeland security concerns and combating terrorism globally.

Program priorities also can be viewed from the perspective of achieving some degree of social justice or equity (see Chapter 15 discussion of equity and equality).[1] While space constraints prohibit any extensive discussion of what constitutes social justice, it can be said that budget deliberations include an overall assess-ment of how different segments of the society will benefit or be burdened by gov-ernmental actions. One way of viewing this situation is to think of government as redistributing income among the various segments of society. Funding one set of programs at a high level obviously will benefit those programs' clients. If, for example, the elderly benefit from a program, then the young do not. Providing income maintenance checks to the needy redistributes money from the middle and upper classes to the poor. Redistribution also occurs through tax measures, including tax expenditures, such as the policy of not taxing home mortgage inter-est payments (see Chapter 4). Proposed tax cuts are always debated in part based on whether the direct beneficiaries will be upper-, middle-, or lower-income indi-viduals and households.

A major concern of most states and particularly southern and western border states is social justice as it pertains to illegal immigrants. When taxes are high, and available revenues cannot keep pace with funding needs, one view holds that ille-gal aliens should be denied access to government services like health care and var-ious social services. Complaints from citizens arise in such instances as when most mothers giving birth at the Los Angeles County Hospital are illegal aliens.[2] Providing free services to illegal immigrants is seen by many people as imposing an unfair burden on taxpayers.

Another suggestion whose popularity is growing is that budgeting should be concerned with its generational effects—the extent to which current actions will improve or harm the conditions that older, younger, and future generations must confront.[3] For example, the federal government has reported generational effects in terms of taxes and transfers.

Today, science plays a major role in strategic decision making, namely what scientific information can be brought to bear on problems? For example, what is the threat of mad cow disease to the U.S. beef industry and the health of the pub-lic and what roles should federal, state, and local governments play in fighting the disease?[4] How likely is an avian flu pandemic and what actions should govern-ment be taking? Is the evidence persuasive, as most scientists would say, that the world is facing massive problems due to global warming or is the evidence still inconclusive as the George W. Bush administration maintained?[5]

Budget preparation also uses to some extent available program analyses.[6] *Cost-effectiveness analyses* measure outcomes in quantitative but nonmonetary form. For example, a study might focus on the number of students who achieve or exceed the standard on end-of-grade achievement tests. *Cost-benefit analyses* measure outcomes in monetary form, thereby allowing for the development of ratios or other measures of the extent to which returns exceed costs, or vice versa. For example, cost-benefit analysis might estimate the dollar value of rehabilitating people with narcotics addictions. Benefits would include reduced health care costs for the addicts, possibly reduced crime that would have been caused by the addicts, increased taxes paid by the addicts who were now able to work, and the like. If the benefits derived are equal to or greater than the costs, then the program can be said to be a good investment (a ratio of 1.0 or greater).

A 2005 survey of state budget offices offers insight into the use of analysis in state budget preparation. According to the survey, 60% of the offices said they conducted effectiveness analysis of programs and 70%, productivity analysis. They also reported that 62% of their post auditors, such as the auditor general offices, conducted program analysis. As for decision making, 26% said effectiveness analysis was used substantially in decision making, and another 67% said it was used somewhat. Comparable figures for productivity analysis were 26% and 70%.[7]

Issues exist over how best to use analysis in decision making. Who conducted the analysis and can the results be trusted? If an agency evaluated its own program, are the results believable or was the analysis designed in such ways as to produce favorable results? For example, what items were included as costs and what ones as benefits? If costs are minimized and benefits maximized, the resulting cost-benefit ratio is likely to be well above the 1.0 level. When the analyses are considered valid, questions remain. If results from a program analysis are discouraging, should that be used to cut an agency's budget or to increase the budget so as to get better performance? At the federal level, how can the OMB best use results from its Program Assessment Rating Tool (PART) (see Chapter 6)?[8]

Surplus or Deficit? The dynamics of decision making are greatly affected by whether a current services budget would be expected to yield a surplus or a deficit. In other words, if current revenue sources and spending patterns continue, will a surplus or a deficit result? In budget preparation, the projection of a budget deficit becomes an overriding issue that cannot be ignored. For state and local governments, chief executives are often required to submit balanced budgets, so any projections of a deficit must be resolved.[9] For the federal government, deficits loomed so large between 1981 and the mid-1990s that most discussions about the budget seemed to focus on how to reduce the deficit. Instead of being concerned with which alternatives were more likely to bring positive results in the operation of a program, decision makers worried almost exclusively about the cost of the alternatives and their potential for increasing or decreasing the deficit. Deficits can incapacitate decision makers, who presume they are unable to deal with society's problems for lack of funds. Deficits in the mid-2000s, however, were not the main focus of election campaigns and annual budgetary decision making.

In the latter half of the 1990s and into 2000, a robust national economy great-ly altered budgetary decision making. Federal, state, and local governments expe-rienced surpluses as incomes rose and people paid greater income taxes and, at the state level, sales taxes.[10] These surpluses are seen as producing *slack*, allowing decision makers some flexibility.[11] The federal government used some of its addi-tional resources to pay down a portion of the national debt. Probably most gov-ernments used some of their surpluses to create new programs or enhance exist-ing ones. Other approaches were to cut taxes and to put some of the surplus monies into rainy day funds (Chapter 10). Exercising fiscal discipline is difficult during surplus times. There is a temptation to act as though surpluses will con-tinue indefinitely, when that surely is not the case.[12]

By 2001, budgetary decision making had flip-flopped from being oriented toward surpluses to being oriented toward deficits. The economy weakened and eventually entered a recession, resulting in a sharp decline in revenues at all lev-els of government. By January 2002, 39 states had officially declared budget short-falls and other states soon followed suit.[13] To some extent, the states may have cre-ated problems for themselves by overspending and reducing revenue through tax cuts during the budget surplus years. By the mid-2000s, there had been a dramat-ic turnaround for most states, with 42 reporting surpluses in 2006.[14]

The situation was even more complicated at the federal level. When President Bush came into office in January 2001, he succeeded in getting Congress to enact a tax cut. The administration's position was that the cut would help stimulate the economy, but critics contended that it simply worsened the budget situation by reducing revenues.

The events of September 11, 2001, changed everything. All sorts of expendi-tures were justified on the grounds of fighting terrorism at home and abroad. The U.S. Department of Homeland Security was created in 2002 and involved one of the most extensive reorganizations in the history of the federal bureaucracy.[15] Other actions that influenced deficit spending were tax cuts and disaster assis-tance spending in the aftermath of the 2005 hurricane season. The federal budget inevitably went into a deficit mode and great uncertainty arose as to when the sit-uation might be reversed. (See Chapter 9 for additional details on federal budget-ary politics.)

Tactical Concerns. In addition to a "philosophical" approach to taxation and expenditures, the chief executive conveys a tactical view. An assessment must be made of political reactions to any possible proposed tax increase or cut. Of course, increases are more likely to produce negative reactions than are tax cuts.

For governors and the president, intergovernmental relations constitute an important component of budget preparation deliberations. Presidents may prefer, where possible, to carry out policies through state and local governments rather than directly through federal agencies. Likewise, governors may prefer to work through local governments. Mandating that state and local governments deliver services, adopt standards, or otherwise implement federal programs is seen by some as a way of achieving a federal policy goal without paying for it. These *unfunded mandates* are extremely unpopular with governors, state legislatures, mayors, and city councils (see Chapter 14).

Another set of considerations involves relationships with the legislative body. Stated simply, the chief executive assesses the chances of various recommendations receiving the approval of Congress, the state legislature, or the city council. Executives must decide whether to push for proposals that will meet with certain opposition from some legislators in alliance with interest groups. In making such calculations, chief executives do not recommend only policies likely to be approved. A doomed recommendation may be put forth as a means of preparing the legislature to approve the proposal in some future year, or the chief executive may be strongly committed to a proposal despite legislative opposition. An executive may want to score political points by advocating a proposal that has no chance with a legislature controlled by another political party, then using the no-vote in subsequent elections.

There was speculation in 2002 that President Bush took a somewhat hands-off approach on the budget with Congress because, in part, he wanted to avoid any skirmishing that might harm his high public approval rating that had resulted from the handling of the September 11, 2001, crisis.[16] His approval rating, nevertheless, plummeted after his 2004 re-election as the end of the war in Iraq seemed nowhere in sight and with the perceived federal bungling of hurricane disaster relief in 2005. Congress then appeared much more likely to oppose the president's policies. President Bush, in general, was not particularly confrontational in his relations with Congress. His first veto came in 2006, about five and a half years after taking office, when he vetoed a bill that would have expanded government funding for stem cell research.[17]

Perceived citizen preferences regarding service and tax levels constitute another consideration. Chief executives have a keen sense for what the general citizenry and interest groups desire. What services do citizens demand and what are they willing to pay for those services through either taxes or fees? Results from national and state polls are watched in an effort to identify important trends. Some cities conduct surveys of citizens and hold public hearings at which citizens may testify as a means of identifying prevailing attitudes about existing and desired services.

In preparing a budget for the upcoming fiscal year, the executive must also consider the current budget. Supplemental appropriations are standard at the federal level. Supplemental appropriations, simply called supplementals, are when an agency's budgets are selectively augmented during the fiscal year to meet unanticipated needs. As Chapter 10 explains, supplementals became the standard means for providing spending authority for the wars in Afghanistan and Iraq. These supplemental appropriations may throw the existing budget out of balance (or further out of balance) as the president and the budget office begin preparing a deficit budget for the next fiscal year. This kind of situation can play into the hands of the president's political opponents.

Revenue Deliberations

Revenue Estimates. Central to deliberations on the revenue side of budget preparation are revenue estimates.[18] Chapter 5 dealt with some of the technical problems associated with revenue estimating. Here we note that several important bureaucratic considerations apply. Sometimes revenue estimating is assigned to the organization responsible for collecting revenues, most often a treasury or revenue department. Such an arrangement may place that unit in competition with the budget office because the two may offer different revenue projections. The budget office may be essentially forced into developing a budget package that is perceived to be unnecessarily constrained because of an estimate that anticipates little or no growth in revenue or even a downturn in revenue collections. This problem is especially troublesome in some developing countries where the local treasurer is a central government appointee. At the federal level, the revenue-estimating function is handled jointly by OMB, the Council of Economic Advisers, and the Treasury Department. The Congressional Budget Office makes independent revenue estimates for congressional consideration.

Taxing Limitations. Since the 1970s, taxing limitations have constituted a major consideration at the state and local levels.[19] Government officials, in assembling a budget proposal, may be constrained by having to present a balanced budget that allows for no increases in tax revenues. Limited in their ability to increase revenues, decision makers sometimes are forced to fund programs at less than optimal levels and even may have to cut programs.[20].

During the first year of President George W. Bush's administration, some members of Congress proposed "triggers" for tax cutting. Although not enacted, the idea was that some automatic trigger would be placed in law that would reduce taxes either to stimulate the economy or to reduce an excessively large surplus. President Bush opposed the concept, preferring that tax cuts take effect regardless of the level of the surplus or deficit.[21]

Balanced Budgets. For state and local governments, revenue estimating is particularly critical because of the standard requirement that they have balanced operating budgets. Indebtedness is possible but is typically used only for capital investments and other selected expenses. If a budget is built on revenue estimates that are too high, crises will ensue during execution as the government attempts to bring expenditures down so as to balance them against actual revenues. As noted in Chapter 4, one of the reasons for the popularity of the property tax among revenue departments, but not taxpayers, is that in the short run, revenue from the property tax is easily forecast and budget shortfalls can be made up by resetting the property tax rate. Of course that may be constrained by previous voter approved limitations and may be the end of incumbents' political careers.

In addition to legal restraints, the bond markets impose some budgetary discipline on state and local governments. Some states or localities may lack structural balance between revenues and spending or may resort often to extraordinary means to bring budgets into balance. Such jurisdictions may experience lower bond ratings and higher borrowing costs, creating strong incentives for sound fiscal management (see Chapter 13).

Although most states have requirements for a balanced budget, the requirements are not uniform across all states. In the first place, "balance" means that expenditures may not exceed revenues, but not all available revenues must be appropriated and spent. Coverage is not all-inclusive, and trust funds and capital expenditures are often excluded.[22] Consequently, as little as half of all state funds may be covered by the balanced budget requirement. Balancing requirements also vary as to when they apply in the budget process, such as when the budget is presented to the legislature or when it is adopted. Similar variations are found at the local level.

Achieving balance in a state budget is a political process. The obvious alternatives are to seek revenue increases or impose spending decreases, but balance can also be attained through other means. Budget reserves, rainy day funds, or savings from previous years may be drawn upon to cover expenditures.[23] It is possible that some governments may continue spending at high levels when helped by rainy day funds, at a time that budget cuts are really needed. Sometimes payments from one fiscal year may be shifted to the next, even though resources are actually used in the earlier year. Political leaders use this technique and others to make budgets appear to be balanced when the opposite is true.

Elimination of tax expenditures can yield additional revenues without officially raising tax rates. For instance, adding products or services to the list of items subject to a state sales tax can increase revenues. Decision makers are concerned with whether each tax expenditure serves any major public purpose, and all tax expenditures are particularly subject to challenge when revenues are needed to balance a budget.[24]

One commonly used alternative to raising taxes is raising user fees or adding new fees. A school district might consider imposing new or higher fees on student parking, school trips, lost textbooks, and physical education. Of course, there are limits on how much can be realistically collected from such fees. Could the new fee revenue cover a projected revenue shortfall and alleviate a need for a tax increase?

Budget gimmickry also is used during economic boom times. By estimating revenues to be lower than are most likely to occur, decision makers later in the year can "discover" that a budget surplus exists and then use the money for some combination of tax relief and new spending.

Tax earmarking often constrains efforts to balance budgets without necessarily helping the programs officially decreed to be beneficiaries.[25] Receipts from state lotteries, for instance, are often earmarked for such good causes as public education or aid to senior citizens. Available evidence indicates that programs with such earmarked revenues do not receive proportionately greater overall funding than other programs or than before the lottery was enacted. Indeed, earmarking is sometimes used as an excuse for not providing more funds to a program, because it is expected to operate within available revenue from the earmarked source. The supposed program that benefits from a lottery, then, may receive no greater funding than it would have without the lottery. Earmarking in effect "Balkanizes" governments' finances and can greatly hamper efforts to resolve budget problems when revenues decline, because monies are compartmentalized and cannot be treated as part of the total resources available for creating an overall balanced budget.[26]

In addition, revenue gaps are sometimes closed with public employee pension monies. A government may simply not make its full contribution to the employee pension funds or may even have the freedom to withdraw monies in an effort to balance the budget. Typically, financial penalties must be paid for such actions, including negative reactions by the financial markets for municipal bonds issued by jurisdictions engaging in such practices. More subtle methods involve adjusting actuarial assumptions. By making an assumption that retired employees will die comparatively early in life, fewer dollars will be needed to cover expected retirees when benefit levels are predetermined. Also, by assuming that investments on retirement monies will result in comparatively high returns, more dollars will become available to cover expected retirement benefits and the government will need to contribute less to the retirement fund.[27] One study found that in 2003, seven states reduced their contributions to pension funds in order to close their budget gaps.[28]

Another revenue source used by the states is the money received from the negotiated settlement with the tobacco industry. After states filed suit for compensation for the costs they incurred through treating smokers, tobacco companies agreed to pay the states billions of dollars. States used this money for a variety of purposes, including antismoking campaigns to discourage people from starting to smoke and to encourage smokers to quit. When budget crunches arose, the states turned to these monies for budget balancing purposes as well.[29]

Whereas the decision makers responsible for state and local budgeting spend substantial time and energy balancing their budgets, the situation is quite different at the federal level. Whether to require a balanced federal budget has long been a controversial issue, but a law requiring an annually balanced budget has yet to be adopted (see Chapters 9 and 15).

One general rule of thumb is that one-time revenues should not be the basis upon which long-term commitments are made.[30] If a state's tobacco settlement funds are seen as consumable rather than continuing over time, then that state should not build into the budget expansion of programs or create new programs with these monies since their eventual consumption will result in budget problems. Similarly, if a federal grant to a local government is used in part to create jobs, then workers hired under the grant need to be made aware that their jobs will no longer exist once funding ceases.

Spending Deliberations

Entitlements and Other Commitments. Much of the spending side of any budget is determined in advance of budget preparation deliberations. Interest on the debt must be paid and prior commitments to employees, such as set levels of contributions to retirement plans, must be met. Entitlement programs that guarantee benefits to various groups, such as the needy, the elderly, and the ill, determine much of the spending side of a budget, where the amount spent is a function of the numbers of people qualifying for various programs, and the amount each would be paid under existing law. Increased spending for these entitlements is often pegged to increases in the consumer price index, which has been criticized as overstating the rate of inflation (see Chapter 15). Nevertheless, as long as a law is mandated to use the consumer price index, budget makers must use its projected increases as the basis for calculating entitlement costs.[31]

Organizational Competition. Just as central administrative organizations compete in trying to influence revenue decisions, so organizations vie with one another on the spending side of the budget. At the top level of a government, personalities become important. The roles of various participants at the federal level depend upon a president's administrative style, his or her confidence in the abilities of key figures, and the roles that these figures seek for themselves. A president is not obligated to rely on the advice of any individual and may seek guidance from anyone inside or outside government.

The international policy arena includes many participants, such as the president's national security advisor, the State Department, the Department of

Defense, the National Security Agency, and the Central Intelligence Agency (CIA), and each may resist major exercise of control by the central budget office. In addition, the National Security Council (NSC) exists to advise the president on "domestic, foreign, and military policies relating to national security."[32] The NSC is headed by the president and includes among its members the vice president and the secretaries of state and defense. The director of the CIA and the chair of the Joint Chiefs of Staff serve as statutory advisers to the council. Also included is the president's national security advisor.

The Office of Management and Budget is notably not part of the National Security Council, although it can be invited to meetings at the president's discretion. OMB can be eclipsed in this arena, performing the largely routine function of assembling budget materials rather than influencing how much money is to be allocated to defense and foreign affairs and for what purposes.

Since the disasters of September 11, 2001, all governments have struggled to devise appropriate methods for intelligence gathering and responding to potential threats against national security. In 2005, President George W. Bush created an office of Director of National Intelligence, better known as the Intelligence Czar.[33] This office has responsibility for coordinating intelligence gathering by the Department of Homeland Security, the Federal Bureau of Investigation, the Central Intelligence Agency, and the Drug Enforcement Administration. These organizations together have been described as a "confederacy of warring states."[34] The extent to which OMB plays a role in budget decision making in this arena depends upon a president's proclivities. Given that this structure is comparatively new and has existed under only one president, there is no publicly known role that OMB plays in the intelligence and security arena of policy making.

In the domestic arena, the competition is also fierce. Cabinet officers seek to gain acceptance and financial support for their agencies' programs. Central advisers to the president are other contenders for attention. In addition to advice provided by the White House Office staff, advice is available from the Domestic Policy Council, the National Economic Council, and the Council of Economic Advisers. At these high levels of government as well as elsewhere throughout the government, heated debates occur over such topics as Social Security and health care funding.[35]

Some have suggested that at this level of government, but also at lower levels, misrepresentation and other ethically questionable behaviors prevail.[36] The competitive nature of budgeting may emphasize self-interest, both personal and collective, to the detriment of the public interest. As C. W. Lewis notes, "The process depends on and rewards deceit."[37] Agencies may misrepresent their situations to budget offices—for example, by claiming dire consequences unless budgets are increased for programs that are highly visible and favored by the public. At a higher level, political leaders may deceive the public—for example, by downplaying the importance of budget deficits and rationalizing the need for greater spending on pet projects even though the budget is out of balance. Financial managers, in serving their political bosses, often are ethically stressed during times of budget crises.[38]

Budget Office Roles. The central budget office has numerous roles to perform. Not only does it recommend policies on spending, but it participates in the review of legislative proposals, economic policy, administrative regulations, evaluation of programs, collection of data by agencies, and agency management studies and management improvement efforts (see Chapter 10). When OMB examines an agency's budget request, all of these forces come into play. Agency budget proposals will be seen in the context of what legislative changes will be necessary, what regulatory actions will be required by the agency, and whether the agency is perceived as well managed.

Agency Expectations and Deliberations. In approaching the budget process, including the preparation phase, agencies have expectations about what constitutes success. Until the latter half of the 1970s, success often was measured in terms of budget increases approved by the executive and ultimately by the legislative body. This approach of adding increments to a base has since been discarded in many locales. Where taxing and spending limits have been imposed at the state and local levels, agencies have been forced instead to concentrate on defending their bases and minimizing the extent of cuts imposed on their budgets. The period from the late 1970s to the early 1990s has been dubbed the decremental age.[39]

By the time a budget request reaches the central budget office, an extensive series of discussions has been completed within the line agency. In large agencies having several layers of organizational units, those at the bottom will have attempted to persuade their superiors to approve requests for additional funding. The force being exerted from the top downward tends to be negative—in the sense that pressure is applied to limit the growth of programs and the corresponding rise in expenditures. This does not mean that there is simply a set of petitioners and a set of rejecters who do battle within each agency or department. Middle managers up through department heads are required to take positive and negative positions, rejecting many of the proposals brought to them by subordinates and, in negotiating with their superiors, advocating those proposals that they accept.

Part of the influence within an agency is a function of superior levels attempting to determine what is likely to be salable to the budget office and the chief executive. Agencies are aware that they are likely to get less than they request. Therefore, they will avoid requesting too little, but will not ask for exorbitant sums unless an open-ended budget system is in use.

The amount eventually requested by a department is necessarily a function of the type of budget system in place. As discussed in Chapter 6, some systems provide for a base budget and then permit requests for additions to that base. Others use a current services budget and require that an agency include information about possibly funding activities below and above the current services level. Some budget systems may require reductions. For example, President Clinton issued Executive Order 12837 in 1993, requiring federal agencies to segregate their administrative expenses from other budget items and to reduce these expenses (when adjusted for inflation) each year through fiscal 1997. The executive order was intended to force agencies to improve their productivity—that is, to meet their statutory mandates to provide services but with reduced resources.

Sometimes across-the-board cuts may be imposed during budget preparation, although, as was noted in Chapter 6, those can be far more harmful to some agencies than others and result in harm to the clients of the agencies that suffered reduced funding. Prioritization, therefore, is sometimes used. Washington State has used a combination of across-the-board cuts and priority funding.[40]

Budget Office and Agency Relations. Just as the interplay within an agency is extensive and vociferous during budget preparation, so is the interplay between the central budget office and the agencies. The central office, serving as the agent of the chief executive, must assert a unifying influence over the diverse interests of administrative units. These, on the other hand, can be expected to favor greater autonomy. Operating departments and agencies will, of course, favor the advancement of their particular programs (seeking greater funds or defending programs against cuts), while the budget office usually will be forced to say no to program growth and even sometimes to say yes to cutbacks.

When the budget office receives agency budget submissions, analysts or examiners are assigned to review these documents. The examiners serve as the main link between the budget office and line units. These professionals must balance a variety of factors, such as being expected to be thorough but having limited time available for their work, and being sensitive to political matters but serving professional values.[41] With the passage of time, examiners gain considerable knowledge about their agencies, providing substantive expertise within the budget office. They often become advocates for the agencies they review and frequently even shift their employment to an operating agency. Still, the accusation is commonly made by the agency officials that budget analysts are not program-oriented and are insensitive to the needs of operating units. Legislative analysts also may be part of the budget development process, particularly in state governments.[42] Sometimes budget office analysts may consult informally with legislative analysts during the preparation phase. In some governments, legislative analysts are permitted to attend sessions when budget office analysts meet with representatives of line agencies regarding their budget proposals.

The structure of budget offices varies from government to government and from time to time. One key concern is whether the central function of examining agency budget requests should be integrated with other functions, notably management functions (discussed in Chapter 10), program analysis, and planning. The argument for their integration is that it gives budget analysts much broader exposure to the operations of government and enhances the analysts' opportunities to make valuable inputs into budget deliberations. The argument against integration is that all too often budget examination activities take top priority, leaving all other activities on the sidelines.

The desire to better integrate the management and budget functions of OMB led to a reorganization, called "OMB 2000," under Director Alice Rivlin.[43] The purpose of this reorganization was to try to better integrate management improvements into the budget process. Since this reform, the budget review function at OMB has been organized into four resource management offices (RMOs):

1. Natural resources (including agriculture, energy, science, and space)

2. National security (including international affairs)

3. Human resources (including education, health, and labor)

4. General government (including housing, justice, transportation, and treasury)

Each resource management office is responsible for budgeting, management, and planning/policy issues within its particular arena.

Budget office discussions with agencies involve how services are to be delivered to the citizenry, as well as the funding for those services. The deliberations include whether services should be provided directly by agencies, by private corporations or other governments operating under contract with government, or through some combination of these and other modes.

The nature of the dialogue between the budget office and the agencies hinges in large measure on the extent to which the latter consider the former to be an important ally or an opponent. Only minimal information can be expected from an agency that is suspicious of the central budget office. A common concern is that an agency will not release data that could be used to its detriment. On the other hand, if an agency can win the confidence and support of the examiner, then it in effect gains a spokesperson for its program on the chief executive's staff.

The budget office holds hearings with agency representatives. Whereas earlier in the process the examiners may have contacted agencies by phone, e-mail, facsimile, or in person to clarify detailed items included in requests, hearings tend to focus on broader concerns. The budget office must decide whether agencies can accomplish what they propose and whether the anticipated accomplishments are worth seeking. The burden of proof rests with the agencies. The operating agency that has a reputation for requesting excessive sums and for overpromising on results will be suspect.

At the same time, winning budget office approval does not guarantee success for the agency. The resistant or recalcitrant agency may, indeed, be able to increase the caution with which the examiner makes recommendations to reduce the agency's budget. At the federal level, the significance of OMB action is mitigated by the fact that Congress is a very strong legislature that guards jealously its power to pass appropriations. It has been suggested that opposition by the budget office to any agency's request for funds may sometimes be helpful in winning legislative support.

The agencies, not the Office of Management and Budget, have had major responsibility for defending their budget requests before Congress, and therefore the OMB's utility to the agencies has been greater in the preparation phase than in the approval phase of the budget cycle. Some organizational units, such as the Federal Bureau of Investigation (FBI) in the 1950s and 1960s and the National Institutes of Health more recently, have been able to secure extensive support within Congress, thereby providing them with some autonomy vis-à-vis their departments and OMB. Of course, agencies, including the FBI, can fall out of favor when their heads lose public and congressional confidence, making the agencies more vulnerable to OMB control. Beginning in the 1980s, OMB gained greater responsibility for explaining and defending the president's budget before Congress. This role, however, often was negative in the sense that the main task was to explain how and why reductions should be made in agencies' budgets.[44]

Legal requirements and court decisions may force increases in expenditures and preclude some decision making by agencies and the central budget office. For instance, state government mandates may require local governments to establish recycling programs for solid waste. Federal officials may require a city to upgrade its sewage treatment facilities. Federal and state court decisions may force a state government to expand prison facilities to accommodate increased numbers of prisoners or may overturn programs. Court cases may be filed against governments, forcing them to spend considerable sums on legal representation. Such suits may be filed by private citizens or corporations or by one government against another.

Budget Office Recommendations. The response of the budget office to agency requests is, in part, a function of the office's assessment of its own powers and responsibilities in relation to the operating agencies and other central units. Few would deny to a budget office the ministerial or bookkeeping functions of assembling requests and carrying out the mechanical duties of designing, tabulating, and overseeing the printing of the budget. At the same time, how many additional responsibilities the budget office has depends largely on the competition from other units and the management style of the chief executive.

In an executive budgeting system, the chief executive has the final say on what to recommend to the legislative body. Thus, the budget office attempts to formulate recommendations thought to be in keeping with the executive's priorities. As part of the calculation of what to recommend, it assesses the chances of agencies making direct appeals to the chief executive, or in the extreme case to the legislature, and thereby overturning the budget office's recommendations. If this strategy—making an end run around the budget office—is successful, it can severely weaken the budget office's role. If an agency knows it can get what it wants by appealing directly to the chief executive or the legislature, the agency is likely to consider the budget office as merely a bookkeeper that can be largely ignored. Normally the budget director will communicate to the chief executive the importance of keeping the budget office in the loop and resisting unilateral appeals from agencies.

As a staff unit of the chief executive, the budget office is expected to develop recommendations that are compatible with executive priorities. On the other hand, as professionals, budgeters have a responsibility to report to the chief executive their views on the worthiness of programs. To report that a given program is operating well simply because the chief executive wants to hear that message does a disservice. So does recommending severe budget cuts to the chief executive when the budget office knows that these cuts could have devastating results on the affected programs. *Neutral competence* has been proposed as the appropriate role for the budget office: The office should retain its professional approach in developing its budget recommendations but simultaneously should develop recommendations in tune with executive priorities.[45]

As the budget is being developed by the budget office and when it is released, the budget office may engage in a public relations campaign that is intended to reach not only the public but also administrative agencies. At the federal level, the OMB director may issue press releases, hold press conferences, appear on Sunday television talk shows, and speak before such groups as the National Press Club. In this way, the budget director communicates on a broad scale the priorities of the administration and in effect warns agencies to beware of pushing for other priorities.

Downsizing, Rightsizing, and Spending Cutbacks

For many government programs, the 1980s marked the beginning of a new era that continued into the 1990s, an era of downsizing, rightsizing, and spending cutbacks. A brief respite from this trend occurred in the second half of the 1990s and into 2000 when a robust economy produced budget surpluses and eased some pressure on cutbacks. The ensuing recession brought a return to cutback management.

Government sometimes has been viewed as bloated by years of excessive budget increases, and the response has been to reduce the size of operations. Whether this process is called downsizing or rightsizing, the result is the same. Agencies must try to provide the same or even more services with fewer personnel and other resources.

Fiscal Stress. State and local governments experience periods of both short and prolonged fiscal stress or distress.[46] Some of these governments' problems derive from extended declines in their economies. Other problems stem from a temporary lack of robustness in the national economy. When the economy slumps, state and local sales and income tax revenues fall. So-called Rust Belt states, especially Michigan, Ohio, and Pennsylvania, face a different set of economic woes, namely, a long-term erosion in their tax bases. Additional fiscal stress sometimes is caused by major reductions in aid from the federal government. During the 1980s, the national government permanently reduced funding of many grant programs and totally eliminated general revenue sharing (see Chapter 14). During the recession of the early 2000s, state revenues fell sharply, and the states responded by cutting their expenditures—not only their direct expenditures but also grants to their respective local governments, most notably school districts.[47]

The tax revolt movement discussed in Chapter 4 imposed additional constraints on spending. In some instances, a jurisdiction's economy may have been vibrant, but the government was precluded from taxing that economic base to the extent it perceived was needed to fund government programs.

Cutback Management. In response to their financial problems, governments sometimes engage in cutback management, retrenchment, downsizing, or rightsizing.[48] Governments in other countries experience similar problems.[49] Also, sometimes retrenchment programs are undertaken not because of fiscal stress but because of the preferences of the political leadership, that is, a desire on the part of officials to reduce the size of government.

The tactics used to deal with a budget shortage depend in part upon its perceived duration. If the shortage is considered to be short term, perhaps lasting only for the current year, then modest adjustments can be made, such as imposing temporary cuts on programs and drawing on budget reserves or rainy day funds.

When long-term budget retrenchment is seen as necessary, then decision makers must manage the immediate problems of the current and upcoming budget years and anticipate problems in future years. Where budget cuts must be imposed several years in a row, then decision makers must be prepared to make extraordinarily difficult choices. Sometimes across-the-board cuts are ordered. These uniform cuts can have the effect of inappropriately freezing current priorities in place rather than taking a hard look at which lower-priority programs deserve larger reductions or even terminations.

Which budget cuts will be made ultimately hinges on the extent to which various groups in the society will suffer from program reductions or eliminations. Budget cuts are less likely to be imposed on groups that are politically organized and vocal than on other, less visible groups. Applying the budget knife to programs for the elderly is often politically dangerous, for instance, whereas cutting programs for the poor, who tend to be politically less active, may seem "safer" for decision makers. In relatively homogeneous communities, budget cutback procedures do not pit one segment of the community against another.

Budget Office Roles During Cutbacks. When jurisdictions confront fiscal stress, the decision process initially tends to be centralized. After all, without central instruction to begin a process of cutting, agencies might well submit budget requests based on unrealistic assumptions. The central budget office, working with the chief executive, attempts to instruct departments as to priorities for funding. Efforts are made to avoid across-the-board cuts in all programs because such an approach can cause severe harm to essential services.

If programs are set aside as immune from budget cuts, they may have few incentives to be efficient in their spending. Moreover, achieving the level of budget reductions needed to balance a budget may be impossible if many key programs are protected from cuts. This problem existed at the federal level during the Reagan administration, where Social Security and the Department of Defense were protected from cuts. Similarly, in the George W. Bush administration, defense and homeland security spending was viewed by many as exempt from serious budget review in light of the wars in Iraq and Afghanistan and post-September 11, 2001, domestic security concerns.

In a retrenchment environment, agencies normally can expect budget office approval of no more than their projected current services budgets. In other situations, the central budget office may provide specific budget ceilings to each department. These figures, which most likely are below the current services levels, are used in preparing budget requests. This process has all the strengths and the weaknesses of fixed-ceiling budgeting. Where such approaches are taken, the process of cutting often starts earlier in the calendar than in a budget situation where growth predominates.[50] More time may be needed to determine which programs will be cut than to introduce new programs or expand existing ones, although some governments may find themselves in crisis situations in which cuts must be imposed immediately to avert a collapse of their financial situation.

Legislative Roles. If legislative preferences can be identified at the beginning of budget preparation, then cuts can be planned that are ultimately likely to meet with legislative approval. Some communities have used confidential questionnaires and other techniques for soliciting legislative input when budget cutting must be part of the preparation phase. Members of local legislative bodies, however, may prefer not to reveal their preferences until later, when more is known about the options for cutting and about citizens' attitudes. Of course, legislatures are not always on the "cutting" side of the budget process, in that sometimes legislatures are in the position of restoring cuts proposed by the executive.

Items to Cut. When reductions in expenditures become necessary, certain standard areas are considered. One of them is personnel costs. Because much of any government's operating budget covers personnel costs, it is difficult to make any appreciable reduction in expenditures without reducing personnel numbers. Holding down general pay increases for workers is a common practice, although this technique can make compensation for government jobs noncompetitive with that for private sector jobs. Commonly used techniques for reducing personnel expenditures include delaying filling vacant positions, leaving other positions empty as they become vacant, and, if necessary, laying off workers. Financial incentives may be offered to senior workers to encourage them to retire early. Nonpaid furloughs of one day per week may be required of all employees, and, depending on legal restrictions, some workers may be required to accept pay cuts. Governments must be cautious in instituting personnel and other cutbacks because intergovernmental aid can be reduced accordingly, especially if grants include matching provisions.

Equipment and facilities are other areas in which cutting can occur. Decisions may be made to delay the purchase of major equipment and to defer maintenance, such as postponing the repair of city-owned sidewalks, roofs on government buildings, and potholes in city and state roads. The savings here can be short-lived: The failure to repair a roof, for example, might result in water damage costing many thousands of dollars. There may be a tendency to use the deferred maintenance approach on less visible facilities, especially water and sewer lines, although highways and bridges have suffered notably due to state and local fiscal problems.

In so-called tight budget periods, major emphasis is given to making operations as efficient as possible. The expectation is that organizational units should be able to operate with fewer resources while maintaining existing service levels. On the other hand, no single agency is eager to relinquish resources through increased efficiency if other agencies are not compelled to take the same route. Each agency is fearful of being the first to show how savings can be accomplished in its operations. This same attitude prevails in the approval phase among legislators, who are not eager to agree to budget cuts in their favored programs even though it is well understood that major cuts will be necessary.

Governments sometimes allow agencies to carry forward unspent money into the next fiscal year. This technique is seen as giving agencies incentives to use their resources efficiently. In a cutback period, however, the budget office and the legislature may be tempted to cancel out any carryover monies. Agencies mindful of such possible action, then, may avoid carrying forward any monies during economic recessions.

Budget cutting creates havoc, low morale, and some inefficiency in agencies. Personnel rightfully become concerned that their positions will be eliminated in the agency's budget request. Political appointees in an agency may be at odds with career personnel over which activities are essential and which are expendable. Some budget cuts necessitate agency reorganization, which disrupts operations. Uncertainty in funding can require stretching out the completion of projects. Defense is a major example of this problem, where changes in project schedules can result in billions of dollars of increased costs.

Budget Systems and Cutbacks. A final consideration regarding cutback budgeting is how the various budget systems discussed in Chapter 6 assist in retrenchment efforts. As already noted, central budget offices use variations on fixed-ceiling budgeting to indicate to agencies what funding levels are acceptable in the budget preparation process. Perhaps most other budget systems have been developed on the stated or unstated premise that budgets will increase from year to year and, therefore, these budget systems are less central to decision making when budget cuts must be imposed. At the same time, program budgeting and various forms of zero-base budgeting in theory should be highly useful in budget-cutting situations. During prosperous times, budgeting may be largely a process of considering possible incremental additions to the budget bases of programs. During declining times, the process may become one of subtracting increments from the base.

Final Preparation Deliberations

The chief executive becomes most active in the budget preparation phase during its final weeks, a frustrating period for the budget office. Decisions are seemingly reached but then may be reversed. The chief executive may instruct the budget office to include an agency's proposed change in the budget but later reject the proposal after considering revenue estimates. The chief executive may tentatively decide to recommend tax increases and then reverse that decision. Materials prepared during evenings and weekends by the budget office may find their way to the paper shredder as decisions are changed. The process may seem haphazard—and it probably is in many respects—but it is necessarily complicated because of the numerous factors being evaluated simultaneously.

A common complaint about the preparation phase is that only the chief executive and the director of the central budget office consider the budget as a whole. An organizational unit within a department or agency is concerned primarily with its own piece of the budget, and the same is true of a department vis-à-vis other departments and the rest of the budget. Even within the central budget office, budget examiners focus mainly on one or a few segments of the budget and not on the total package. The chief executive, assisted by the budget director, must pull together pieces of information and intelligence provided by various sources into a set of decisions that can be defended as a whole. The budget that is to be submitted to the legislative body is the chief executive's creation.

The decision process necessarily involves tradeoffs. A $1 million increase in a city police department's budget means there is that much less available for other departments in the government. A one-mill increase in property taxes makes more money available to provide services that citizens want but at the same time may anger those same citizens who face an increase in their tax bills. Planning personnel layoffs may seem a reasonable choice for avoiding tax increases, but will layoffs be imposed on all agencies, including highly visible units such as the police and fire departments? Chief executives take seriously the justifications that agencies make for increasing budget amounts or for avoiding budget cuts, and perceptions about the effectiveness of agencies' programs and activities influence executive decisions in the preparation phase of budgeting.

In this final stage of preparation, the chief executive must decide to what extent to include initiatives that may be ill-received by the legislature. For example, with the end of the Cold War and the advent of global terrorism, the Defense Department has insisted on the need to transform itself. The argument is made that the military needs to invest in new technologies and scrap old ones. Closing unneeded military bases is part of this argument, but it runs counter to the interests of key members of Congress, who want to preserve bases in their jurisdictions. The president, then, must decide what to include in the budget on this sensitive matter, balancing the needs of national security with the reality of politics. Sustained combat operations also rapidly speeds up the need for equipment replacement, spare parts, and in every war, new threats are identified that lead to research and development (R&D) expenditures for new technologies and tools to defeat the threats, such as the need to defeat or reduce damage from improvised explosive devises (IEDs).

Chief executives often include items in their budgets that they do not wholeheartedly support, because they know that the legislature is likely to fund the initiatives in any event. In this type of situation, an executive may include the item to get a more realistic picture of ultimate expenditures and budget tradeoffs.

█ Budget Documents

The final product of the preparation phase of budgeting is a budget document (or documents) that contains the decisions reached during the months of agency requests and executive reviews. The budget at this point is only a proposal, a set of recommended policies and programs set forth by the chief executive. It remains a proposal until the legislative body acts on it.

Number and Types of Documents

The budget for any government may consist of one or several documents. Small jurisdictions often have one-volume budgets, whereas larger governments usually package their budgets in several volumes. The size of a jurisdiction's budget, as measured in receipts or expenditures, does not always determine the size of its documents, however. Documents are printed on different sizes of paper and vary considerably in their graphics. Some volumes contain mainly text and tables, while others include charts, graphs, photographs of citizens and government buildings, and magazine-style articles on special topics—for example, nursing home care for the elderly.

The preparers of budget documents are paying increasing attention to making the documents more "user friendly," reflecting the fact that these documents are expected to communicate the proposals contained within not only to technical budget analysts but also to executive and legislative political leaders, the news media, and the general citizenry. Budget documents often include glossaries that define technical terms in everyday language. Explanations are provided as to how tables should be read. Sections are sometimes color-coded and tabbed or have markings on page edges to help readers find the topics of interest to them. Since 1984, the Government Finance Officers Association has given its Award for Distinguished Budget Presentation to more than 1,000 state and local governments.[51]

A government may produce one main document as well as one or more additional documents. A *budget-in-brief* may be prepared for general consumption that places emphasis on graphics and readability. The government can enhance its documents' interest to general readers by using attractive formats made possible by the widespread availability of affordable desktop publishing computer software. Of course, many governments have their budgets online, which increases their accessibility. Nashville has an online *Citizen's Guide to the Metro Budget*.[52]

Federal Documents. In some years, the federal government publishes numerous budget documents. In other years, it provides far fewer documents. The main budget document is the *Budget of the United States Government*,[53] which is backed up by a second and much larger document—the *Budget Appendix*.[54] In addition to preparing these documents, OMB prepares *Analytical Perspectives*, which provides more detailed information about specific aspects of the budget.[55] The content of this document varies over time but often includes discussions of crosscutting programs, such as homeland security, economic assumptions that are the foundation for the budget, budget reform proposals, and the current services budget. *Historical Tables* provides multiyear financial data on a variety of subjects.[56]

OMB produces other important documents, such as budget circulars (for example, Circular A-11 discussed in Chapter 6) and annual publications covering procurement and the midyear status of the budget. Some documents may be prepared for a few years but then are replaced or superseded by other documents. For instance, sometimes separate annual volumes have been prepared that describe the policy initiatives being advocated by the president and the information being collected by federal agencies. OMB's website provides links to other documents it issues as well as a discussion of other sources of budget-related information.[57] In the past several years, the OMB website has included a great deal of information on federal management issues, including agency performance relative to the standards established under the President's Management Agenda, and the review of federal programs under the Program Assessment Rating Tool (PART) (see Chapter 6).

The *Economic Report of the President* is prepared by the Council of Economic Advisers and is released at about the same time as the other main budget documents. The report discusses expected economic trends for the coming fiscal year and is the basis upon which the president's economic policy is formulated. The economic assumptions reflected in this report are used for estimating revenues and expenditures for the budget year.

The Treasury Department has an extensive publishing program and produces several documents specifically related to budgeting. The *Combined Statement of Receipts, Outlays, and Balances of the United States Government* reports on the financial condition of the government (see Chapter 11).[58] The *Treasury Bulletin*, issued quarterly, reports information about the economy, government receipts and outlays, and federal debt.[59] This document provides details on the various forms of federal securities. In addition to these documents, the Treasury Department publishes monthly and daily reports on the government's financial transactions and separate reports on trust funds, such as the unemployment, highway, and disability insurance trust funds.

Other Specialized Documents. Governments sometimes publish specialized budget-related documents in addition to those already mentioned. Some states and many local governments publish capital budgets, showing planned construction projects and major pieces of equipment to be purchased (see Chapter 12), and some publish separate volumes on personnel.

The federal government and some states publish discussions of tax expenditures, which are losses in government revenue due to tax provisions that exempt some items from taxation or provide favorable tax rates. In its annual publication *Analytical Perspectives*, OMB provides an extensive discussion of the effects of various tax provisions on receipts, namely how these provisions create tax expenditures (see Chapters 4 and 5). Massachusetts annually publishes a separate volume on tax expenditures.[60] **Exhibit 7–1** illustrates how tax expenditures in Pennsylvania are aimed at creating jobs. If the state chose to revoke these provisions, several millions of dollars presumably would flow into the treasury. On the other hand, the presumption is that the tax provisions help create jobs which more than pay for themselves in increased income-tax payments by wage earners.

Budget Messages. Another feature of budget documents is the budget message, in which the chief executive highlights the major recommendations in the budget. This message sometimes is presented orally to the legislature. The president's budget message is included in the *Budget of the United States Government* itself. State governments vary widely in this regard, with some having no message and others having lengthy ones, sometimes as long as 100 pages. State and local jurisdictions occasionally publish their budget messages as separate documents. **Exhibit 7–2** presents the budget message for Cape May County, New Jersey.

Approved Budgets. Some jurisdictions publish their approved budgets (i.e., budgets that reflect action taken by the legislative bodies). North Carolina, for example, publishes a *Post-Legislative Budget Summary*. The federal government does not provide such a volume.

Coverage

Budget documents vary with regard to the extent of their coverage. All report information about government receipts and expenditures. Likewise, intergovernmental transactions are reported. A state budget highlights the funds it receives from the federal government and the funds it provides local governments within the state. Issues arise over how much detail to provide on these items.

State and Local Budgets. Confusion is common in the handling of funds in budget documents. State and local governments are major users of special funds, which basically are financial accounts for special revenue sources, such as the Casino Revenue Fund in New Jersey, and which can be used only for specific purposes. A jurisdiction's general fund consists of revenue that can be used for all functions of the government. These different types of funds are discussed elsewhere in this book in conjunction with accounting issues (Chapter 11), but here we note that many jurisdictions have a general fund budget document plus one or more documents for special funds. One result of having separate budgets can be confusion over the size of the total budget and the amount spent by any given agency, because the agency may be receiving support from several funds.

The Federal Budget. The coverage issue at the federal level is similar. Until the late 1960s, there were really three types of federal budgets: the administrative budget,

Exhibit 7-1 **Pennsylvania Tax Expenditure, Job Creation Tax Credit, 2003-2010**

Description   A tax credit is available to businesses and individuals creating and sustaining jobs. The tax credit equals $1,000 per job for each year in the approved term and may be applied to the corporate net income tax, capital stock/foreign franchise tax, insurance premiums tax, gross receipts tax, bank and trust company shares tax, mutual thrift institution tax, title insurance company shares tax, personal income tax, or any combination thereof. The total amount of funds for tax credits available in a year is $22.5 million.

Purpose   This tax credit encourages job creation and preservation in the Commonwealth.

Administrative   Costs to administer the Job Creation Tax Credits are borne by the
Costs   Department of Community and Economic Development and the Department of Revenue. Estimated costs for both departments total $0.2 million per year.

(Dollar Amounts in Millions)

Estimates	2003-04	2004-05	2005-06	2006-07	2007-08	2008-09	2009-10
	$ 22.5	$ 22.5	$ 22.5	$ 22.5	$ 22.5	$ 22.5	$ 22.5

Beneficiaries   Approximately 110 companies doing business in Pennsylvania benefit from this tax expenditure

Source: Adapted from Office of the Budget, Commonwealth of Pennsylvania (2006). *Governor's executive budget, 2006-2007*. Harrisburg, PA: Commonwealth of Pennsylvania, D8.

Exhibit 7–2 **2006 Budget Message, Cape May County, New Jersey**

On behalf of the Cape May County Board of Chosen Freeholders, I am pleased to offer the county budget for the Year 2006. This year's budget marks the sixth straight year of a significant cut in the county tax rate. It also represents the eleventh straight year we have either cut the rate or kept it at a zero increase—continuing to give us the best tax record of all of the twenty-one counties in the state.

The budget cuts the tax rate close to three and a half cents bringing the rate to seventeen cents. This cut continues the trend of making history as the new lowest recorded rate for Cape May County—surpassing the historical lows of the last three years.

Also achieving another milestone—this budget restricts the new tax levy on municipalities to the new revenue generated from new construction for the fourth straight year. As we've stated when we introduced this concept to Cape May County government, not only is this self-imposed CAP significantly less than the state would allow us to spend—it is genuinely the best approach to truly reduce the tax burden—beyond tax rates—to real tax dollars.

We believe our efforts in keeping the new tax levy no higher than new revenues reflects genuine tax reform. The State Cap would have allowed us to raise the tax levy on municipalities $11.5 million. Our self-imposed CAP kept this amount to $1.9 million representing the precise amount of new revenue from new construction.

That being said, we suspect this year may reach equilibrium in this approach. Even though our county may witness a greater amount of real construction growth, we may see less actual revenue generated because of the substantial cuts in the tax rate.

Again this year—another important component of the budget is our focus on how we spend—how we save—and how we invest—our surplus. Our continuing skyrocketing ratable base coupled with our prudent management of county dollars has generated almost thirty six million dollars in surplus.

This year we will use close to sixteen million dollars to support our budget. Besides helping fund the services of county government—we will again be paying for one-time capital expenditures and investing in reserve accounts.

After appropriating this sixteen million dollars—we will have a balance of slightly under twenty million dollars. As this budget is being introduced—we are exploring the most practical and beneficial way that we can use some of this surplus to help support municipal capital projects throughout the county.

Our primary responsibility is to retain an appropriate amount of surplus to protect county services and county taxpayers now—and well into the future. At the same time—we are looking at developing an innovative and effective program that will allow us to assist local municipalities for one-time capital improvement costs if it will not jeopardize the county's current and future financial integrity.

The specific overview breakdown of this year's budget in rounded-off dollars is as follows:

1. The Total County Budget for the Year 2006 is $124 million compared to the adopted 2005 Budget of $117 million. Operating expenses account for $3.6 million of this increase. An additional $1.9 million in Group Health Insurance costs represents the largest amount of this operating expense increase.

continues

Exhibit 7-2 **2006 Budget Message, Cape May County, New Jersey (continued)**

Total Salary and Wages for all contract obligations as well as new and replacement positions account for the additional $2.8 million in this year's budget increase. Twenty-three new positions were added to strengthen and expand the needs of county residents.

Of these new positions—thirteen are offset by new revenues and ten pertain to public safety.

2. The amount of monies to be raised by property taxes to support the Year 2006 Budget is $75 million compared to $73 million for the year 2005. This is a $1.9 million increase. The amount of revenue other than property tax used to support the budget is $49 million. An additional $200,000 of surplus over last year will be used for this year's budget.

3. The budget uses approximately 44% of our surplus. Specifically $15.9 million of the available $35.8 million while reserving $19.9 million.

4. The County equalized tax rate for the Year 2006 will be 17.13 cents per $100.00 of assessed value, compared to 20.61 cents in the year 2005 providing for taxpayer relief in the amount of 3.48 cents. Although it will vary depending on the ratio of assessed value to true value in each of the County's sixteen municipalities; an average property assessment of $100,000.00 will see a reduction in county taxes from $206.12 to $171.30.

5. The total amount of estimated ratables for the Year 2006 is $43.8 billion compared to $35.4 billion in the year 2005. This is an $8.3 billion or a 23.5% increase.

These are the highlights of this year's budget. I believe it continues to exceptionally serve both the residents and visitors of Cape May County. It sustains our outstanding tax record while keeping our services among the finest in the state. It saves for the future — and it accommodates the increasing demands and responsibilities of county government.

The Year 2006 Budget complies with the New Jersey "CAP" Law, which limits a property taxation increase to 2.5% in the year 2006. Public Hearing on the Budget will be held on February 28, 2006 at 4:30 P.M. in the Freeholders Meeting Room at the County Administration Building. Public comment and recommendations are welcome. Besides being on hand at the Office of the Clerk of the Board at the Administration Building, all financial documentation pertaining to this proposed budget is accessible on the county web site at capemaycountygov.net

In closing—as always—I would like to personally thank my fellow Freeholders as well as all of the department heads, county employees and the budget team for their commitment to county government and their hard work and professionalism in working with the Freeholders in preparing this budget.

And again this year, I most importantly want to express the Board's genuine appreciation to the citizens of Cape May County for giving county government both the opportunity and the resources to serve you. Thank you.

Freeeholder Director Daniel Beyel

Source: Reprinted from Cape May County, New Jersey (2006). *Budget message.* Retrieved October 26, 2006, from http://www.capemaycountygov.net/FCpdf/2006%20Budget%20HTML012406%2Ehtm.

the consolidated cash statement, and the federal sector of the national income accounts. Using three types of budgets resulted in much confusion. Because each type had a different coverage, total revenues and expenditures varied from one to another, leading to different statements of budget surpluses and deficits. Different pictures of federal finances—gloomy or bright—could be painted by choosing to discuss one budget statement and ignoring the other two. In response to this problem, President Johnson in 1967 appointed the President's Commission on Budget Concepts, whose eventual recommendation for a unified budget was incorporated into the budget document beginning with fiscal year 1969.[61]

In the revised format, all federal agencies and programs are included, with some important exceptions noted below. Receipts, budget authority (appropriations), outlays (expenditures), and the resulting deficit or surplus are shown. Information is supplied for the means of financing the deficit and about the size of the federal debt.

Since adoption of the unified budget, important changes have occurred. One trend was toward greater use of moving some items out of the reported budget totals, what is known as *off-budget totals*. Congress determined what was off-budget, which varied somewhat from year to year. The U.S. Postal Service, for example, was moved off-budget, because it was expected to operate like a business, largely independent of the government. Other federal entities were removed from the budget because they operated largely with revolving funds rather than annual appropriations and made direct loans to the public. For example, the Rural Telephone Bank, the Federal Financing Bank, and the U.S. Synthetic Fuels Corporation were placed off-budget. The Gramm-Rudman-Hollings Act of 1985, however, required that all federal entities be placed on budget, with some exceptions. As of the mid-2000s, Old Age and Survivors Insurance, Disability Insurance, and the Postal Service were off-budget. Determination of what is and is not included in the budget totals is almost exclusively a political decision.

Government-sponsored enterprises are neither on-budget nor off-budget. The same is true for the Board of Governors of the Federal Reserve System. These transactions that are not in the budget are normally described as "nonbudgetary."

Alternative Budget Presentations. The decades of debate about how best to present the overall budget of the federal government have made clear that probably no single format is ideal. As a result, OMB attempts to satisfy the needs of different participants in the budget process by presenting information in a variety of formats. The exact coverage of the *Budget of the United States Government* varies from year to year. The document may show outlays divided into mandatory and discretionary categories, along with revenues and the deficit or surplus. Mandatory outlays include deposit insurance, federal retirement, Medicaid, Medicare, and the like. An alternative presentation is sometimes provided using national income and product accounts (see Chapter 15). Presentations may be based on a format suggested by the GAO or on one similar to a typical state government format. The budget may be displayed so as to highlight its effects upon various age groups or generations. Although the federal government does not have a capital budget, a presentation usually is provided to show federal investment expenditures as distinguished from operating costs.

Coverage—The Special Case of Credit and Insurance Liabilities

In assembling a proposed budget, both obvious and not-so-obvious expenditures must be anticipated. Much of any budget will be committed to funding the operations of government, either for direct services provided by the government's departments or through grant programs, as in the case of state aid to local school districts. Monies also must be set aside for making payments on the principal and interest for any outstanding debt. As is discussed in subsequent chapters, sustained federal budget deficits have yielded an increasingly large total federal debt that requires massive interest payments every year—so massive that they now constitute one of the most important components of federal expenditures. In addition to debt accumulated through borrowing by the U.S. Treasury Department, federal debt has grown through borrowing by federal agencies such as the U.S. Postal Service and the Tennessee Valley Authority.

Beginning in the late 1980s, political leaders, public administrators, leaders in private financial institutions, and the citizenry became painfully aware that the federal government had other liabilities that until then had seemed innocuous or almost nonexistent.[62] Hundreds of savings and loan institutions failed, forcing the federal government to meet its financial commitments to depositors. The Resolution Trust Corporation was established, as a temporary agency, to manage the resources of thrifts going into receivership at a staggering cost to taxpayers. Further liabilities were encountered when the government had surviving banks acquire many of the failed thrifts.[63]

Types of Liabilities. Appreciating the nature of government liabilities is difficult due to the complex nature of the institutions involved. At least three methods for differentiating these institutions and the programs that they administer are possible: (1) the ownership of the institution, (2) the purpose that it serves, and (3) the type of service that it provides.

Figure 7–1 indicates how ownership can vary from an agency within a regular department of government, to a separate government corporation, such as the Rural Telephone Bank, to a government-sponsored enterprise, such as the Federal National Mortgage Association (Fannie Mae), and finally to a privately owned

Figure 7-1 | **Comparison of Public and Private Entities**

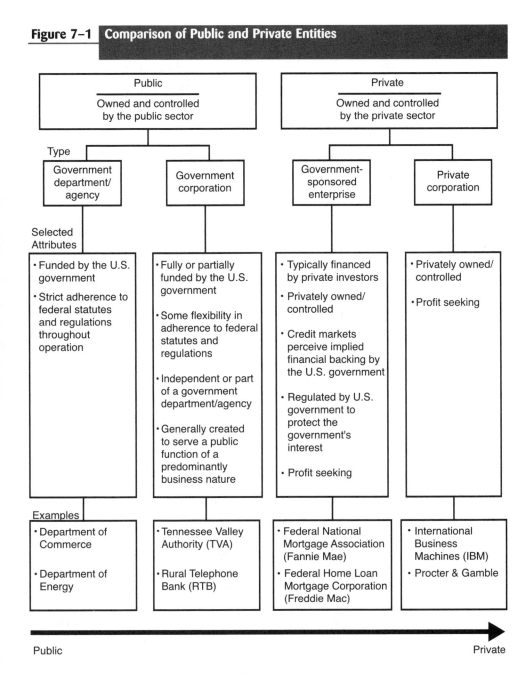

Source: Reprinted from U.S. General Accounting Office (1995), *Government corporations: profiles of existing government corporations.* Washington, DC: U.S. Government Printing Office, 5.

corporation. As the figure illustrates, a government corporation is owned by the public but may be only partially funded by government, may be largely independent of any government department, and is usually created for a business purpose. A *government-sponsored enterprise* is a "federal chartered, privately owned, for-profit corporation designed to provide a continuing source of credit nationwide to a specific economic sector."[64] As might be expected, institutions in this obscure realm do not always fit nicely into one of the four categories suggested by **Figure 7–1**. Indeed, Congress has recognized in legislation that some government corporations have mixed ownership, including the Federal Deposit Insurance Corporation (FDIC) and Amtrak.[65]

A second way of viewing these institutions is to consider them in terms of the purposes that they serve. They bolster and foster growth of the financial system of the nation, housing, education, agriculture, and the like.

A third approach is to consider the methods the institutions use in serving these purposes. Here, four approaches are used, as outlined in **Table 7–1**. As can be seen, the instruments used and the consequent categories of liabilities are direct loans, guaranteed loans, insurance, and government-sponsored enterprises.

Before discussing these instruments, we should note that other major liabilities are omitted from the table, such as the costs of environmental clean-up of nuclear weapons production plants, defense installations that are being closed both in the United States and overseas, and other federal agency facilities. Other exclusions include federal research and development centers, such as the RAND Corporation, which are primarily the creations of the Departments of Defense and Energy, and congressionally chartered, nonprofit corporations, such as the American Red Cross.

Direct loans involve operations at home and abroad. Monies are available to help farmers acquire homes, electrify their farms, and engage in overseas commerce. International operations include loans to support the defense and economic development of other nations and to stimulate the growth of the private sectors in these countries. Immense political risks exist with such instruments, because a change in a government may lead to the renunciation of previous commitments to repay loans. In other situations, developing countries may be too poor to repay loans so that these become de facto grants.

Guaranteed loans entail agreement by the government to pay loans when customers default. A major segment of the housing mortgage market in the United States is backed by federal government loan guarantees. The category has also included student loans, which have had a history of high rates of default.[66] In the international arena, the federal government has guaranteed billions of dollars of loans made by U.S. financial institutions to developing countries under the former

Table 7–1	Long-Term Federal Government Obligations and Risks

1. Direct Loans
   - Federal Student Loans
   - Farm Service Agency (excluding CCC), Rural Development, Rural Housing
   - Rural Utilities Service and Rural Telephone Bank
   - Housing and Urban Development
   - Export-Import Bank
   - Public Law 480—Agriculture
   - Agency for International Development
   - Commodity Credit Corporation
   - Federal Communications Commission
   - Disaster Assistance
   - Veterans Administration Mortgage
   - Other Direct Loan Programs
2. Guaranteed Loans
   - Federal Housing Administration Mutual Mortgage Insurance Fund
   - Veterans Administration Mortgage
   - Federal Family Education Loan Program
   - Federal Housing Administration General/Special Risk Insurance Fund
   - Small Business
   - Export-Import Bank
   - International Assistance
   - Farm Service Agency (excluding CCC), Rural Development, Rural Housing
   - Commodity Credit Corporation
   - Maritime Administration
   - Air Transportation Stabilization Program
   - Government National Mortgage Association
   - Other Guaranteed Loan Programs
3. Insurance
   - Deposit Insurance—Federal Deposit Insurance Corporation
   - Pension Guarantees—Pension Benefit Guaranty Corporation
   - Disaster Insurance—flood, crop
   - Insurance against Security-Related Risks—terrorism, airline, war

continues

Table 7-1	Long-Term Federal Government Obligations and Risks (continued)

4. Government-Sponsored Enterprises
   - Federal National Mortgage Association (Fannie Mae)
   - Federal Home Loan Mortgage Corporation (Freddie Mac)
   - Farm Credit System
   - Federal Home Loan Banks

Source: Adapted from U.S. Office of Management and Budget (2006). *Analytical perspectives, budget of the United States Government, fiscal year 2007.* Washington, DC: U.S. Government Printing Office, 65–97.

Housing Guaranty Loan Program and other programs such as the Development Credit Authority.

Federal insurance programs cover deposits in financial institutions and private pension deposits. While the huge bank failures of the 1980s have been mopped up, bank failures continue to occur.[67] Pension guarantees present other problems. Corporate failures, as in the case of Enron, leave pensioners and employees with credits into pension plans that lack adequate financial backing. The Pension Benefit Guarantee Corporation deals with these problems, with the support of the federal government. Other programs include crop insurance for farmers.

Government-sponsored enterprises are another potential source of liability. The institutions listed in **Figure 7–1**, including Freddie Mac and Fannie Mae, involve largely secondary credit markets, in which these institutions purchase debt instruments, such as mortgages, and in turn release funds to lending institutions for further loan activity.[68] Questions have been raised whether government reaps many benefits from the advantages it bestows on these entities and whether the bonuses enjoyed by their executives are warranted, especially when some have been involved in scandals, as was the case of Fannie Mae.[69]

Federal Liability Reforms. Efforts are under way to bring some clarity to what liabilities the government has, and proposals exist for reforming this immense area of finance. The concerns about such liabilities are not new but rather date back to 1945, when Congress passed the Government Corporation Control Act.[70] At the time, there was concern that government corporations were operating without sufficient guidance and control by the government. The argument can be made that, despite the numerous revisions Congress has made in the law over the years it remains inadequate in controlling these major institutions.

The Financial Institutions Reform, Recovery, and Enforcement Act of 1989 dealt with failed thrift institutions and required the General Accounting Office (now the Government Accountability Office [GAO]) to investigate the financing of government-sponsored enterprises.[71] The GAO has designated some programs, such as farm loan programs, as "high risk."[72] The GAO's intent is to train attention on those programs that have the potential for creating large economic losses for the government.

The Federal Credit Reform Act of 1990 required the government to upgrade its accounting for credit programs.[73] OMB issued Circular A-129 (1993, rev. 2000), which provides a uniform set of procedures for agencies engaged in loan programs, both direct and guaranteed. The procedures indicate how agencies should estimate the costs of loans and loan guarantees, a function that is difficult to accomplish. The purpose of Circular A-129 is to reduce risks and place the federal government's credit operations on a better financial foundation. Agencies that guarantee loans must estimate potential defaults and include those estimates in their current appropriations requests. This requires the annual costs of credit programs to represent the present value of the long-term costs to the federal government. This reform places potential defaults in direct competition with current spending requests, a practice expected to make decision makers more cautious in extending loans and loan guarantees.

It has proved difficult, however, to obtain reliable estimates of these long-term costs, because of the uncertainty associated with forecasting the long-term liabilities associated with a given program.[74] On the other hand, the Treasury Department makes estimates of country risk for some agencies such as the Development Credit Authority, and then the U.S. Agency for International Development has little problem in calculating the appropriation it needs to cover any potential default.

Efforts are now under way to improve the collection of debts rather than simply writing off bad debts. The Debt Collection Improvement Act of 1996 strengthened the government's ability to retrieve monies owed.[75] Agencies may refer bad debts to private collection companies and may share information with one another in locating those borrowers who are in arrears.

These significant changes, however, have not addressed the main issue, namely, what should be the federal government's responsibilities in this area and how can liabilities and risks be curtailed? One line of criticism states that the federal government has been too generous. Fostering a credit market is important to national economic growth, but should the federal government have such a major role?

Credit programs subsidize risk-taking on the part of individuals and corporations. When the federal government provides full backing for a venture, then it assumes 100% of the risk. Crop insurance, for example, is available at comparatively low cost to farms. Only about one in four farms uses the insurance, however, because when droughts, floods, and other conditions destroy crops, the government usually passes legislation that fully covers all damage. Similarly, were government to cover all of the damage from hurricanes and their related floods, then there would be little incentive to purchase insurance. The hurricane seasons in the mid-2000s, especially that of 2005 and Hurricanes Katrina and Rita, underscored the fact that the government was not about to cover all associated costs from storms and that property owners needed to purchase insurance.

Prescriptions for reform, therefore, tend to favor increasing the risk of the private sector and decreasing that of the public sector. Such action was taken in 1996 with the passage of the Student Loan Marketing Association Reorganization Act, which provided for the privatization of Sallie Mae (student loans) and Connie Lee (college construction loans).[76] Connie Lee was converted to a private entity in 1997 and Sallie Mae in 2004.[77] In 2005, Congress passed the Terrorism Risk Insurance Extension Act which extended coverage available through the Treasury Department.[78]

Another reform theme insists that structural changes should bring greater coordination among the various institutions involved and greater oversight of their operations. It may be desirable to have a single regulatory body that would oversee many government-sponsored enterprises and related institutions. An oversight board specifically dedicated to this function might be more energized than OMB, which must oversee the operations of these varied institutions as well as all of the regular departments and agencies of the government. President George W. Bush in his Fiscal 2007 and 2008 budgets recommended that Congress create a special regulator for government-sponsored enterprises, especially in the housing field.[79]

Although one line of concern insists that credit and insurance institutions have become burdensome on government, perhaps suggesting that they should be totally privatized, the reality is that they serve important functions. Proposals exist for creating still more of these bodies. Government corporations have been proposed for air traffic services, management of petroleum reserves, and development of national infrastructure.

State and Local Governments. Similar liability and risk problems exist at the state and local levels. The Governmental Accounting Standards Board has prescribed how these governments should report risks and insurance (see Chapter 11). Potential losses can be due to "torts; theft of, damage to, or destruction of assets; business interruptions; errors or omissions; job-related illnesses or injuries to employees; acts of God; and any other risks of loss assumed under a policy or participation contract issued by a public entity risk pool."[80] Torts are civil wrongs that occur independent of contract, as when a city refuse truck accidentally backs into a person's vehicle and causes personal harm and property damage. Among the greatest liabilities of state and local governments are their pension systems, which are sometimes actuarially unsound.

Information Displays

Revenues. Budget documents present both revenue and expenditure data. The coverage of receipts or revenues usually is substantially less extensive than the coverage of expenditures. Budgets show receipts from taxes, such as individual and corporate income taxes; from user charges, such as water service fees; and from other governments, such as state grants to local government. **Table 7–2**, taken from a Tennessee budget, shows the state, federal, and other revenues that support the state's military-style boot camp for non-violent criminal offenders. Budget documents also typically discuss proposed changes in tax laws, especially proposed tax rate changes. For the federal government, some revenues are treated as expenditures. OMB treats receipts generated by an agency in the form of user fees as an *offsetting collection* and deducts them from outlays rather than treating the amount as revenue.

Expenditures. The bulk of the budget document is devoted to the expenditure side of government finance, with the main classification usually based on organizational unit. Each department presents a budget within which subunits are given separate treatment. A generally uniform format is used for each subunit, including a brief narrative description of the subunit's responsibilities and functions. Narratives contained in the federal *Appendix* also contain proposed appropriations language that may be quite specific—for the Commodity Futures Trading Commission's budget of nearly $127 million, not more than $3,000 was to be used for "official reception and representation expenses."[81]

In addition to the narrative are various tabular displays. Expenditures are reported by object classes, such as personnel, equipment, and travel (see Chapter 11). These financial tables may be primarily for informational purposes or they may later be incorporated into the appropriation bill. When this practice is used, the legislative body is said to have adopted a *line-item budget*, which reduces the president's, governor's, or mayor's flexibility in executing the budget.

Personnel. The main component of an operating budget often consists of salaries, wages, and employee benefits. For that reason, budget documents sometimes include specific information about personnel. The Tennessee table just noted includes a break-out of expenses between payroll and other operating expenses. **Table 7–3** shows how personnel information can be provided in great detail. The

Table 7–2   Base and Improvement Budget, Wayne County Boot Camp, Tennessee, 2004–2007

The Wayne County Boot Camp is a minimum security special alternative incarceration unit. The boot camp program is a highly disciplined, military-style training program combined with various treatment programs. Eligible offenders are those convicted of non-violent crimes with sentences of six years or less (longer for most drug offenses). In 1997, a 300 bed minimum-security annex opened to house technical probation and parole violators who were temporarily housed at Tennessee Correctional Work Center and other minimum-security inmates. Occupant capacity is 450.

	Actual 2004–2005	Estimated 2005–2006	Base 2006–2007	Improvement 2006–2007	Recommended 2006–2007
Full-time	155	155	155	0	155
Part-time	0	0	0	0	0
Seasonal	0	0	0	0	0
Total	155	155	155	0	155
Payroll	5,971,000	6,273,300	6,273,300	0	6,273,300
Operational	2,831,700	3,398,800	3,461,400	103,000	3,564,400
Total	$8,802,700	$9,672,100	$9,734,700	$103,000	$9,837,700
State	8,464,200	9,329,600	9,392,200	103,000	9,495,200
Federal	0	0	0	0	0
Other	338,500	342,500	342,500	0	342,500

Performance Information
   Standard: Increase the GED completion rate
      Measure: GED pass rate

	Actual 2004–2005	Estimated 2005–2006	Base 2006–2007	Improvement 2006–2007	Recommended 2006–2007
	85%	86%	88%	0	88%

   Standard: Reduce the rate of incidents (per 100 inmates)
      Measure: Institutional incident rate (per 100 inmates)

	29.32	31.20	31.00	0	31.00

   Standard: Reduce the rate of employee turnover
      Measure: Correctional officer turnover rate

	7%	5%	5%	0	5%

Source: Compiled from Division of Budget (2006). *Performance-based budget, fiscal year 2006–2007.* Nashville, TN: State of Tennessee, 91–92.

Table 7-3   Selected Personnel, Department of Information Technology, City of Seattle, 2004–2006

		2004 Actuals		2005 Adopted		2006 Endorsed		2006 Proposed	
	F/P	Pos.	FTE	Pos.	FTE	Pos.	FTE	Pos.	FTE
Accountant, Principal	F	1	1	1	1	1	1	1	1
Accounting Technician II	F	3	3	3	3	3	3	3	3
Accounting Technician III	F	2	2	2	2	2	2	2	2
Computer Operator, Lead	F	3	3	3	3	3	3	3	3
Computer Operator, Senior	F	2	2	2	2	2	2	2	2
Computer Operations, Supervisor	F	2	2	2	2	2	2	2	2
Information Technology Professional A	F	17	17	17	17	17	17	19	19
Information Technology Professional B	F	43	43	47	47	47	47	45	45
Information Technology Professional C	F	23	23	23	23	23	23	28	28
Information Technology Specialist	F	1	1	1	1	1	1	1	1
Information Technology Systems Analyst	F	24	24	20	20	20	20	20	20
Information Technology Technical Support	F	1	1	0	0	0	0	0	0

Source: Reprinted from Finance Department (2006). *2006 proposed budget.* Seattle, WA: City of Seattle, 621.

table shows some of the jobs in the City of Seattle's Department of Information Technology. Full- and part-time positions are noted along with the number of positions and their full-time equivalent. **Table 7–4** shows budget changes for personnel and other expenses for fire-rescue in the City of San Diego. Carefully studying the table will give the reader a sense of the effort in calculating such budget tables and how they might be used by decision makers, both executive and legislative.

Budget presentations sometimes show for the past fiscal year the budgeted amounts and actual amounts, for both receipts and expenditures. This information is important in understanding the accuracy with which the government is able to estimate its revenues and keep its expenditures within budgeted amounts.

Current Services. Governments sometimes provide current services budget data, which are intended to show decision makers what receipts and expenditures will be without any changes being made in tax laws, other revenue sources, and spending levels. **Table 7–5** shows current services projections for the federal government from 2005 through 2011. In addition to receipts, the table reports outlays subdivided into discretionary spending and mandatory or entitlement spending. It also shows the differences between on-budget and off-budget receipts and outlays for each year. The off-budget surplus is due to the Social Security system bringing in more revenue than it pays out. This phenomenon will be reversed when the baby boom generation starts to draw Social Security, unless rates are substantially increased or benefits are cut.

Program Information. Since World War II, program data have become increasingly common in the budget documents of most governments. Federal program data are presented in the *Appendix* volume of the *Budget of the United States Government*, but only for a small number of agencies, and the information tends to be presented in terms of workload or outputs rather than impacts. **Table 7–6** illustrates the workload of the Food Safety and Inspection Service of the U.S. Department of Agriculture. The table shows the numbers of different types of plants inspected and the millions of pounds of meat and eggs inspected.

With regard to state governments, about half reported in 2005 that their documents contained effectiveness and productivity measures for half or more of their respective agencies. Another quarter reported coverage for some or a few agencies. Only 13% said this type of information was lacking in their budgets.[82]

While the extent of program data in the federal budget has remained largely unchanged for decades, the budget's format was changed to give it a more programmatic thrust starting with the budget for fiscal year 2003. In particular, the budget was organized according to departments. Within each department, a long narrative discussion was provided.

Table 7-4 General Fund Budget Changes, Fire-Rescue, City of San Diego, California, 2007

	Salary and Benefit Adjustments[1]	Supplemental Information[2]	Vacancy Savings[3]	Non-Discretionary[4]	Restructure/ Transparency[5]	Other Department Adjustments[6]	Total
Positions		10.30				9.73	20.03
Personnel Expenses	$3,918,614	$4,170,538	$(11,231,800)			$9,411,603	$6,268,955
Non-Personnel Expenses		$1,100,000		$(729,807)	$1,629,458	$1,089,696	$3,089,347
Total	$3,918,614	$5,270,538	$(11,231,800)	$(729,807)	$1,629,458	$10,501,299	$9,358,302

[1]Adjustment to reflect the annualization of the Fiscal Year 2006 negotiated salary compensation schedule, negotiated salaries and benefits, changes to average salaries, and other salary and benefit compensation.

[2]Adjustments to include expenditures and revenues that have not been included in the budget over the past years. Information includes all supplemental positions, personnel expenses, non-personnel expenses, and revenues that existed in fiscal Year 2006 and are expected to continue in Fiscal Year 2007.

[3]Adjustments that reduce the funding of personnel expenses due to vacant and/or underfilled positions, salary step savings, and any other circumstances that might contribute to personnel expense savings. The vacancy savings adjustments do not reduce positions.

[4]Adjustments to reflect expenses that are determined outside of the departments' direct control; however, departments are consistently reminded to conserve these expenditures when appropriate and possible. Examples of these adjustments include utilities, insurance, rent, and information technology.

[5]Adjustments to reflect the new structure of the City [from council-manager to strong mayor] to improve the focus of resources and allow clearer accountability.

[6]Adjustments to reflect other budget requests, such as additions, reductions, restorations, annualizations of new facilities and transfers.

Source: Compiled from Office of Independent Budget Analysis (2006). *Proposed annual budget, fiscal year 2007*. San Diego, CA: City of San Diego, 35, 38.

Table 7–5 **Current Services Estimates, Baseline Category Totals, U.S. Budget, 2005–2011 (in Billions of Dollars)**

	2005	2006	2007	2008	2009	2010	2011
Receipts	2,154	2,301	2,444	2,597	2,729	2,901	3,064
Outlays:							
Discretionary:							
DoD-Military	473	480	440	438	445	456	472
Homeland security	30	32	34	35	35	36	38
Other discretionary	465	486	488	484	493	498	507
Subtotal, discretionary	968	998	962	957	973	990	1,017
Mandatory:							
Social Security	519	550	581	612	645	683	723
Medicare	294	338	390	405	429	457	500
Medicaid and SCHIP[1]	187	198	205	219	234	251	270
Other mandatory	320	365	319	340	359	371	390
Subtotal, mandatory	1,320	1,451	1,495	1,575	1,668	1,762	1,883
Net interest	184	219	244	266	284	298	310
Total outlays	2,472	2,669	2,701	2,798	2,925	3,050	3,210
Unified deficit	-318	-367	-257	-201	-196	-149	-146
On-budget	-494	-549	-449	-416	-428	-402	-420
Off-budget	175	182	192	216	233	252	274
Memorandum							
BEA[2] baseline deficit	-318	-367	-305	-266	-244	-230	-127
Do not extend emergencies	--	--	45	67	76	82	86
Correct growth rates for pay	--	--	2	3	3	3	3
Remove special rule for administrative expenses of selected programs	--	--	--	--	--	--	1
Extend certain tax provisions	--	--	-1	-8	-37	-14	-119
Related debt service	--	--	1	4	6	9	11
Current baseline deficit	-318	-367	-257	-201	-196	-149	-146

[1]State Children's Health Insurance Program

[2]Budget Enforcement Act

Source: Reprinted from U.S. Office of Management and Budget (2006). *Analytical perspectives, budget of the United States Government, fiscal year 2007.* Washington, DC: U.S. Government Printing Office, 360.

Table 7–6	Food Safety and Inspection Service Activities, U.S. Department of Agriculture, 2005–2007

	2005 Actual	2006 Estimate	2007 Estimate
Federal inspected establishments:			
Slaughter plants	113	112	110
Processing plants	3,993	3,990	3,995
Combination slaughter and processing plants	908	906	902
Talmadge-Aiken plants	361	360	355
Import establishments	130	130	130
Egg plants	71	70	69
Other plants	674	670	655
Federal inspected and passed production (millions of pounds):			
Meat slaughter	45,633	45,700	45,700
Poultry slaughter	55,324	55,400	55,400
Egg products	4,300	4,300	4,300

Source: Reprinted from U.S. Office of Management and Budget (2006). *Appendix, budget of the United States Government, fiscal year 2007.* Washington, DC: U.S. Government Printing Office, 87.

In the case of the budget for the Department of Education for fiscal year 2007, information was given about progress made in implementing the No Child Left Behind Act, increasing America's competitiveness in the international arena through improved education, and enhancing the performance of special education students. The budget gave an update on the department's progress on the president's budget and performance integration initiative. The budget frankly noted that the department had had major problems in identifying performance measures and that progress had been achieved in correcting these problems. Following the narrative was a table organized somewhat along program lines and providing three years of financial information (past year, current year, and budget year). The detail about specific organizational units within the department, such as the Office of Innovation and Improvement, was provided in the budget's *Appendix.*

Program Structure. An alternative to arranging the budget document by organizational unit is to arrange it by program structure. The structure consists of a number of broad programs that are subdivided into more narrowly focused subprograms, which are themselves subdivided. Terminology varies, but one approach divides programs into program categories, which are divided into subcategories and then into elements.

The federal government does not have a program budget but has used broad functional classifications to summarize the budget: national defense, natural resources and environment, agriculture, transportation, and the like.[83] The functional classifications are useful for highlighting the changing character of government expenditures over time, such as changes in the proportion of the budget committed to social services, but these classifications are not linked explicitly to program descriptions, specific agency activities, or appropriation decisions by the Congress.

Using a program structure for the main outline of a budget has both advantages and disadvantages. On the positive side, the budget shows how the activities of different programs relate to each other, regardless of the agency location of the activities, since they are juxtaposed with one another in the document. As a result of being placed in the same program, agencies are forced to recognize their dependence on each other and the need for cooperation. For example, a city transportation department and police department must acknowledge that they both influence traffic safety.

On the negative side, the "pure" program structure type of budget disperses parts of agencies throughout the budget, making it difficult to identify the budget for any one agency. One solution to this problem is known as *crosswalking*, in which information organized by program is reconfigured into an organizational format. Crosswalking, while a successful technique when computer technology is employed, is cumbersome and may force a government to produce two budgets— a program budget and an agency budget.

Analytical Perspectives of the federal budget has a section on crosscutting programs, which selectively crosswalks some government agencies into programmatic configurations. For example, the fiscal 2007 budget provided a lengthy section on homeland security that discussed the relevant roles of many federal agencies in this area besides the Department of Homeland Security.

It is possible to reach a compromise between these two methods. A budget can be divided into major programs first, such as the protection of persons and property program and the human services program, and then each program can show the departments within it.

Table 7–7, derived from the Illinois budget, shows selected program measures reported for higher education as a whole, not for specific institutions within the state. These crosscutting measures include enrollments, degrees granted, the racial/ethnic composition of the student body, and average costs per student credit hour.

Table 7–7	Selected Higher Education Performance Measures, State of Illinois, 2003–2007

	Actual FY 2003	Actual FY2004	Actual FY2005	Estimated FY2006	Projected FY2007
Total fall enrollment, all sectors and levels	781,190	799,216	801,548	805,608	807,000
Total degrees granted, all sectors and levels	149,865	55,196	163,589	169,800	177,000
Percent of degrees granted by race/ ethnicity:					
Black, Non-Hispanic	11.5%	11.6%	11.7%	11.7%	11.8%
Hispanic	6.9%	6.7%	6.9%	7.0%	7.2%
White, Non-Hispanic	67.0%	66.1%	65.8%	65.7%	65.6%
All Other	14.6%	15.6%	15.6%	15.6%	15.4%
Average net instructional cost per credit hour					
Community colleges ($)	191.09	193.16	195.00	199.00	203.00
Public universities ($)	279.19	281.99	284.00	288.00	293.00

Source: Compiled from Office of Management and Budget (2006). *Illinois state budget book, fiscal year 2007.* Springfield, IL: State of Illinois, 6–11.

Exhibit 7–3 provides information on fire prevention and investigation in the City of Detroit. The table reflects concerns over the city being plagued with house and vehicle fires caused by arsonists. Besides providing a description of the fire prevention and investigation program and its goals and major initiatives, the budget provides output measures, such as the number of inspections; outcome indicators such as arson convictions; and efficiency measures, such as percent of billing collections.

Program Revisions. Chief executives often wish to use the budget to highlight the programmatic initiatives they are recommending to their respective legislative bodies. Budget documents frequently contain sections that set forth themes that summarize the major recommendations being made. The Pennsylvania budget for fiscal 2006–2007 had eight themes, including "Challenges Met, Promises Kept and a Better Pennsylvania," "Making Government Work Smarter," and "Investing in Our Children, Investing in Our Future."

Exhibit 7–4 illustrates how Pennsylvania displayed recommended program revisions in the budget. The exhibit provides a sample of what is a lengthy narrative about the revision on "Investing in Our Children." Next, data are supplied for several program measures beginning with the budget year of 2006–07 and ending

Exhibit 7–3 **Fire Prevention and Investigation Activity, City of Detroit, 2003-2007**

Activity Description: Fire Prevention and Investigation
   The role of the Fire Marshal Division is to enforce all laws and ordinances governing fire prevention, protection, public education investigation, providing protection of life and property to the citizens of Detroit.

Goals:
1. Increase the effectiveness of building inspections, thereby eliminating fire hazards in a timely manner.
2. Continue to increase arson convictions through vigorous investigations and prosecution.
3. Reduce the number of fire-related injuries and deaths through public education programs.
4. Identify new billable services for billing purposes, thereby increasing revenue.

Major Initiatives for FY 2005–06 and FY 2006–07:
   The passing of the Vehicle Arson Law by the State of Michigan has and continues to be successful in lowering vehicle fires. The law requires that all owners of vehicles that burn be interviewed by a Fire Investigator.

Type of Performance Measure List of Measures (Selected)	2003–04 Actual	2004–05 Actual	2005–06 Projection	2006–07 Target
Outputs: Units of Activity Directed Toward Goals:				
48 hour facilitation of information records request	90%	90%	95%	100%
Number of fire inspections	15,200	13,000	14,000	10,000
Investigations	2,620	2,5151	2,763	2,840
Warrants issued	144	103	125	140
Arson arrests	120	95	130	150
Public and private buildings inspected	6,500	5,993	6,200	6,500
Community group training				
	995	975	1,050	900
Outcomes: Results or Impacts of Program Activities				
Percent of incendiary fires not investigated	48%	46%	49%	51%
Arson convictions	55	27	40	55
Efficiency: Program Costs Related to Units of Activity				
Percent of billing collections	75%	65%	65%	75%
Service fees collections ratio—Licenses and Permits				
	100%	70%	70%	90%
Activity Costs (000)	$7,050	$8,714	$8,225	$6,272

Source: Compiled from Budget Department (2006). *2006–2007* Executive budget. Detroit, MI: City of Detroit, 24–2, 24–3.

Exhibit 7–4 Pennsylvania Program Revision: Investing in Our Children, 2004–2011

Over the past three years the Commonwealth has joined the ranks of states that are leading the nation in ensuring that every child has access to high-quality education by instituting systemic strategies that are building a foundation for early school success and academic achievement. …

To ensure economic success for our future work force and for our state, the Commonwealth must prepare all of its students with solid critical thinking skills and with a strong background in reading, math and science. This Program Revision recommends a total of $382.1 million in new education funding.

Program Measures	2004–05	2005–06	2006–07	2007–08	2008–09	2009–10	2010–11
Elementary schools upgrading science curriculum							
Program Revision	0	0	150	150	150	150	150
High schools with Internet-equipped laptop computers on student desks							
Program Revision	0	0	100	200	300	400	501
Additional children receiving Head Start services							
Program Revision	0	0	1,540	5,990	8,990	11,990	11,990
Additional children receiving Early Intervention services							
Program Revision	0	0	2,347	3,497	4,748	6,036	7,363
School districts receiving Accountability Block Grant funds							
Program Revision	0	0	501	501	501	501	501
Additional schools participating in Project 70							
Program Revision	0	0	30	30	30	30	30
Additional students earning college credit before high school graduation							
Program Revision	0	0	3,000	4,000	5,000	6,000	7,000

continues

Exhibit 7–4   Pennsylvania Program Revision: Investing in Our Children, 2004–2011 (continued)

Program Revision Recommendations (Dollar Amounts in Thousands)

Program	Amount	Description
Dual Enrollment Payments	$2,000	To provide resources to school districts to assist 3,000 additional students earn college credit as they complete their high school graduation requirements
Basic Education Funding	$224,609	To provide a 5 percent increase for basic education programs and to continue foundation funding to assist school districts in boosting spending toward the statewide foundation level.
Pennsylvania Accountability Grants	$50,000	To provide flexible block grant resources for proven programs to help school districts attain or maintain academic performance targets.
Head Start Supplemental Assistance	$15,000	To provide resources to federal Head Start providers to expand programs to 1,540 additional children.
Science: It's Elementary	$10,000	To provide resources for hands-on learning equipment and intensive teacher training to elementary schools that commit to upgrading their science curriculum.
Classrooms for the Future	$20,000	To provide resources for core-subject high school classrooms in 100 high schools to acquire an Internet-equipped laptop computer on each student desk and multi-media technology at the teacher's fingertips.
Teacher Professional Development	$10,200	To provide resources to assist teachers to integrate technology into lessons and daily activities, improve career counseling, increase accountability, and improve teacher quality.
Special Education	$38,123	To provide a 4 percent increase for special education programs.
Early Intervention	$7,907	To provide resources to implement a new funding methodology that establishes a benchmark payment per child for program services and to expand early intervention services to 2,347 additional children from ages three through five.
High School Reform	$4,300	To provide grants to school districts to transform high schools by increasing the rigor of academic programs and enhancing post-secondary opportunities for students.
Program Revision Total	$382,139	

continues

Exhibit 7–4 Pennsylvania Program Revision: Investing in Our Children, 2004–2011 (continued)

Recommended Program Revision Costs by Appropriation (Dollar Amounts in Thousands)

	2004–05	2005–06	2006–07	2007–08	2008–09	2009–10	2010–11
Dual Enrollment Payments	$0	$0	$2,000	$2,000	$2,000	$2,000	$2,000
Basic Education Funding	0	0	224,609	224,609	224,609	224,609	224,609
Pennsylvania Accountability Grants	0	0	50,000	50,000	50,000	50,000	50,000
Head Start Supplemental Assistance	0	0	15,000	15,000	15,000	15,000	15,000
Science: It's Elementary	0	0	10,000	10,000	10,000	10,000	10,000
Classrooms for the Future	0	0	20,000	20,000	20,000	20,000	20,000
Teacher Professional Development	0	0	10,200	10,200	10,200	10,200	10,200
Special Education	0	0	38,123	38,123	38,123	38,123	38,123
Early Intervention	0	0	7,907	7,907	7,907	7,907	7,907
High School Reform	0	0	4,300	4,300	4,300	4,300	4,300
Total	0	0	$382,139	$382,139	$382,139	$382,139	$382,139

Source: Compiled from Office of the Budget (2006). *Governor's executive budget, 2006–2007.* Harrisburg, PA: Commonwealth of Pennsylvania, E14.19, E14.22, & E14.23.

four years later with 2010–11. What this segment of the exhibit lacks is any base data. For example, the exhibit shows the number of high schools that would receive internet-equipped laptop computers on student desks but does not show how many schools already had such.

The next section of **Exhibit 7–4** shows specific revisions and dollar amounts. The funding for helping high school students to earn college credits is presented along with funding for special education and early intervention education. Finally, the exhibit presents recommended funding levels for the budget plus four additional years. The recommended future-year levels are constant, reflecting no anticipated increase in expenses due to inflation. These funding levels might be questioned considering that the program measures anticipate increases in outputs, such as the additional children receiving early intervention education tripling between 2006–07 and 2010–11. Would this be possible to achieve with funding levels constant?

Future Years. Budget reformers have tended to advocate multiyear projections as a method for helping decision makers understand the long-term implications of policy and program issues.[84] However, given the uncertainty of the future, one might expect few governments to attempt to make projections beyond the budget year or biennium. Perhaps somewhat surprisingly, the use of multiyear projections has increased. A longitudinal study of state budgeting found that while only 2% of the states responding in 1970 said they projected effectiveness measures in budget documents, 37% reported they made such projections in 2005. Comparable figures for the use of productivity measures were 8% and 38%, respectively. These 2005 figures, however, were lower than the results of the 2000 survey, perhaps suggesting states have retrenched in their use of future-year projections.[85]

Decision makers always calculate how their actions will affect the future so including projections in budgets seems appropriate. However, these projections easily can be faulty. The tax cuts recommended by President Bush and adopted by Congress in 2001, as it was discovered, did not yield the revenue surpluses that had been projected.

Space Limitations. Not all available program and resource information can be presented in budget documents without making the documents unwieldy. The budget formats of some jurisdictions rigidly prescribe allowed space, for example, one page for each bureau, program, or activity. This type of format may increase the readability of the document. Its disadvantage is that not all subunits are of equal importance, in terms of either budget size or political interest. Therefore, many jurisdictions use more flexible formats, providing more information on some agencies and programs and less information on others. With this type of format, larger agencies commonly receive more extensive coverage because they are more complex and engage in more varied activities. Agencies that are particularly popular or unpopular may receive more extensive coverage regardless of their size.

With the widespread use of computer technology, the space problem can be eased somewhat with some information being made available only in electronic format. Some budget offices provide their most detailed information only by CD-ROM or on their websites.

▌ Summary

In beginning the preparation phase, the chief executive conveys to agencies some sense of priorities, either formally in writing or by more subtle means. The executive's view of the role of government in society is indicated to agencies, along with more specific priorities.

The revenue side of the budget is examined carefully, especially because state and local governments are generally prohibited from having operating budgets that exceed available revenues. Requiring the federal government to balance its budget annually is a proposal that has gained considerable acceptance but has not been put into law (see Chapter 9).

Budget preparation begins in agencies and involves extensive debate. Similar debate develops between agencies and the central budget office, which in turn must compete with other central staff units. Because little formal authority is granted to a central budget office, it must always be concerned with being overruled by the chief executive.

The 1980s ushered in a new era in budgeting, where the focus was on budget cutbacks rather than program expansion. Fiscal stress, taxing and spending limitations, and an increase in anti-big government attitudes among political leaders have resulted in retrenchment efforts. A respite in cutbacks occurred in the second half of the 1990s, when the booming economy produced budget surpluses. With the recession of the early 2000s, cutback management returned.

Decision makers have come to realize that they can be forced to deal with immense problems associated with credit and insurance liabilities. The collapse of hundreds of federally backed thrift institutions amply demonstrated the risks that are involved.

The product of the preparation phase is a budget or a set of budget documents that reflect executive decisions on policies and programs. The federal government has what is called a unified budget. Revenue and expenditure data are treated in all budgets, but the latter receive much more extensive treatment. One common budget format has a structure based on organizational units and includes supporting narratives and tabular displays that present costs, personnel, and program data.

Notes

1. Hampton, G. (1999). Environmental equity and public participation. *Policy Sciences, 32,* 163–174; Rubin, M. M. & Bartle, J. R. (2005). Integrating gender into government budgets: a new perspective. *Public Administration Review, 65,* 259–272; Midgley, J. (2005). *Women and the U.S. budget: where the money goes and what you can do about it.* Gabriola Island, BC: New Society Publishers.

2. Mathesian, C. (1994). Immigration: the symbolic crackdown. *Governing, 7, May,* 52–57.

3. Williamson, J. et al. (2003). Generational equity, generational interdependence, and the framing of the debate over Social Security reform. *Journal of Sociology and Social Welfare, 30,* 3–14; Gokhale, J. & Smetters, K. (2003). *Fiscal and generational imbalances: new budget measures for new budget priorities.* Washington, DC: AEI Press.

4. Beck, M. et al. (2005). Public administration, science, and risk assessment: a case study of the U.K. bovine spongiform encephalopathy crisis. *Public Administration Review, 65,* 396–408.

5. See Gore, A. (2006). *An inconvenient truth: the planetary emergency of global warming and what we can do about it.* Emmaus, PA: Rodale Press and *An inconvenient truth,* documentary movie featuring A. Gore (2006). Hollywood, CA: Paramount Classics; Bush Disses Global Warming Report (2002). *CBS News.* Retrieved August 10, 2006 from http://www.cbsnews.com/stories/2002/06/03/tech/main510920.shtml.

6. Weimer, D. L. & Vining, A. R. (2004). *Policy analysis: concepts and practice,* 4th ed. Upper Saddle River, NJ: Pearson Prentice Hall; Royse, D. et al. (2006). *Program evaluation: an introduction.* Belmont, CA: Thomson Brooks/Cole.

7. Burns, R. C. (2006). Unpublished data from Survey of State Budget Offices, 2005. Morgantown, WV: Recreation, Parks, and Tourism Program, University of West Virginia.

8. U.S. Government Accountability Office (2005). *Program evaluation: OMB's PART reviews increased agencies' attention to improving evidence of program results.* Washington, DC: GAO.

9. Balanoff, H. R. & Pinto, C. W. (1999). What do you do when your city is looking at a million-dollar deficit in the current fiscal year? *Public Productivity & Management Review, 23,* 83–88.

10. Rubin, I. (2003). *Balancing the federal budget: eating the seed corn or trimming the herds?* New York: Chatham House.

11. Hendrick, R. (2006). The role of slack in government finances. *Public Budgeting & Finance, 26, Spring,* 14–46.

12. Posner, P. L. & Gordon, B. S. (2001). Can democratic governments save? Experiences of countries with budget surpluses. *Public Budgeting & Finance, 21, Summer,* 1–28.

13. Pattison, S. (2002). Fiscal state of the states, presentation at the national conference of the Association for Budgeting and Financial Management, Washington, DC.

14. Eckl, C. (2006). *State budget actions: FY 2005 and FY 2006.* Denver, CO: National Council of State Legislatures.

15. Homeland Security Act (2002). P.L. 107-296.

16. Collender, S. (2002). Backing off. *Govexec.com.* Retrieved August 8, 2006, from http://www.govexec.com/dailyfed/0102/012302bb.htm.

17. First Bush veto maintains limits on stem cell use (2006). *New York Times, July 19.* Retrieved October 25, 2006, from http://www.nytimes.com/2006/07/20/ washington/20bush.html?ex=1311048000&en=706eb16610c12416&ei=5088&partner= rssnyt&emc=rss.

18. Cornia, G. C. et al. (2004). Fiscal planning, budgeting, and rebudgeting using revenue semaphores. *Public Administration Review, 64,* 164–179.

19. Mullins, D. R. & Wallin, B. A. (2004). Tax and expenditure limitations: introduction and overview. *Public Budgeting & Finance, 24, Winter,* 2–15; Mullins, D. R. (2004). Tax and expenditure limitations and the fiscal response of local government: asymmetric intra-local fiscal effects. *Public Budgeting & Finance, 24, Winter,* 111–147.

20. James, F. J. & Wallis, A. (2004). Tax and spending limits in Colorado. *Public Budgeting & Finance, 24, Winter,* 16–33.

21. Collender, S. (2001). Trigger happy. *Govexec.com.* Retrieved August 8, 2006, from http://www.govexec.com/dailyfed/0301/032801bb.htm.

22. Hou, Y. & Smith, D. L. (2006). A framework for understanding state balanced budget requirement systems: reexamining distinctive features and an operational definition. *Public Budgeting & Finance, 26, Fall,* 22–45.

23. Joyce, P. G. (2001). What's so magical about five percent? A nationwide look at factors that influence the optimal size of state rainy day funds. *Public Budgeting & Finance, 21, Summer,* 62–87.

24. Jen, K. I. (2002). Tax expenditures in Michigan: a comparison to federal findings. *Public Budgeting & Finance, 22, Spring,* 31–45; Brixi, H. P. et al. (2004). *Tax expenditure: shedding light on government spending through the tax system.* Washington, DC: World Bank.

25. Rushton, M. (2005). Support for earmarked public spending on culture: evidence from a referendum in metropolitan Detroit. *Public Budgeting & Finance, 25, Winter,* 72–85.

26. Anderson, S. H. & Smirnova, N. V. (2006). A study of executive budget-balancing decisions. *American Review of Public Administration, 36,* 323–336.

27. Schneider, M. & Damanpour, F. (2001). Determinants of public pension plan investment return. *Public Management Review, 3,* 551–573; Peng, J. (2004). Public pension funds and operating budgets: a tale of three states. *Public Budgeting & Finance, 24, Summer,* 59–73.

28. Willoughby, K. J. (2005). Unpublished data from Government Performance Project. Atlanta, GA: Georgia State University.

29. Johnson, C. L. (2004). The state of the tobacco settlement: are settlement funds being used to finance state government budget deficits? *Public Budgeting & Finance, 24,* Spring, 113–125.

30. Ingraham, P. W. et al. (2003). *Government performance: why management matters.* Baltimore, MD: Johns Hopkins University Press, 34.

31. White, J. (1998). Entitlement budgeting vs. bureau budgeting. *Public Administration Review, 58,* 510–521; Chowdhury, M. J. A. (2004). Poverty and entitlement: concepts— a review of literature. *Journal of Social Studies, No. 104,* 49–66.

32. National Security Act (1947) and Amendments (1949). 50 U.S.C. § 401–402.

33. White House (2005). President congratulates America's first director and deputy director of national intelligence, news release. Retrieved August 8, 2006, from http://www.whitehouse.gov/news/releases/2005/05/20050518.html.

34. Weiner, T. (2006). The world: intelligence turf, a guide. *New York Times Archives.* Retrieved August 8, 2006, from http://query.nytimes.com/gst/fullpage.html?res=9B01EEDB143EF937A25756C0A9609 C8B63.

35. Rivlin, A. & Sawhill, I. (Eds.) (2005). *Restoring fiscal sanity, 2005: meeting the long-run challenge.* Washington, DC: Brookings Institution.

36. Jones, L. R. & Euske, K. J. (1991). Strategic misrepresentation in budgeting. *Journal of Public Administration Research and Theory, 1,* 437–460; Peterson, P. G. (2004). *Running on empty: how the Democratic and Republican Parties are bankrupting our future and what Americans can do about it.* New York: Farrar, Straus and Giroux.

37. Lewis, C. W. (1992). Public budgeting: unethical in purpose, product, and promise. *Public Budgeting and Financial Management, 4,* 667–680.

38. Miller, G. J. et al. (2005). How financial managers deal with ethical stress. *Public Administration Review, 65,* 301–312.

39. Schick, A. (1983). Incremental budgeting in a decremental age. *Policy Sciences, 16,* 1–25.

40. Government Performance Project (2003). *Washington: money.* Retrieved October 25, 2006, from http://results.gpponline.org/StateCategoryCriteria.aspx?id=139&relatedid=2.

41. Goodman, D. & Clynch, E. J. (2004). Budgetary decision making by executive and legislative budget analysts: the impact of political cues and analytical information. *Public Budgeting & Finance, 24, Fall,* 20–37; Lidman, R. & Sommers, P. (2005). The "compleat" policy analysts: a top 10 list. *Public Administration Review, 65,* 628–634.

42. Hoffman, K. U. (2006). Legislative fiscal analysts: influence in state budget development. *State and Local Government Review, 38,* 41–51.

43. U.S. General Accounting Office (1995). *Changes resulting from the OMB 2000 reorganization.* Washington, DC: U.S. Government Printing Office.

44. Stockman, D. A. (1986). *The triumph of politics: how the Reagan revolution failed.* New York: Harper & Row; Wildavsky, A. & Caiden, N. (2004). *The new politics of the budgetary process,* 5th ed. New York: Pearson/Longman.

45. Heclo, H. (1975). OMB and the presidency: the problem of "neutral competence." *Public Interest, 38*, 80–98.

46. Feiock, R. C. et al. (2001). Political conflict, fiscal stress, and administrative turnover in American cities. *State and Local Government Review, 33*, 101–108; Kloha, P. et al. (2005). Developing and testing a composite model to predict local fiscal distress. *Public Administration Review, 65*, 313–323.

47. Reschovsky, A. (2004). The impact of state governmental fiscal crises on local governments and schools. *State and Local Government Review, 36*, 86–102.

48. Willoughby, K. J. & Lauth, T. P. (2003). Cutback management in Georgia: state agency responses to Fiscal Year 1992 budget reductions. *Public Administration and Public Policy, 103*, 377–392.

49. Kraan, D. J. (2001). Cutback management in the Netherlands. *Public Budgeting & Finance, 21, Summer*, 46–61.

50. Schick, A. (1986). Macro-budgetary adaptations to fiscal stress in industrialized democracies. *Public Administration Review, 46*, 124–134.

51. Government Finance Officers Association (2006). *Distinguished Budget Presentation Award.* Retrieved August 9, 2006, from http://www.gfoa.org/services/awards.shtml#budgetawards.

52. Metropolitan Government of Nashville and Davidson County (2006). *Citizen's guide to the metro budget.* Retrieved October 25, 2006, from http://www.nashville.gov/finance/management_and_budget/CB2006/flash/.

53. U.S. Office of Management and Budget (2006). *Budget of the United States Government, fiscal year 2007.* Retrieved August 9, 2006, from http://www.whitehouse.gov/omb/budget/fy2007/budget.html.

54. U.S. Office of Management and Budget (2006). *Appendix, budget of the United States Government, fiscal year 2007.* Retrieved August 9, 2006, from http://www.whitehouse.gov/omb/budget/fy2007/appendix.html.

55. U.S. Office of Management and Budget (2006). *Analytical perspectives, budget of the United States Government, fiscal year 2007.* Retrieved August 9, 2006, from http://www.whitehouse.gov/omb/budget/fy2007/pdf/spec.pdf.

56. U.S. Office of Management and Budget (2006). *Historical tables, budget of the United States Government, fiscal year 2007.* Retrieved August 9, 2006, from http://www.whitehouse.gov/omb/budget/fy2007/pdf/hist.pdf.

57. U.S. Office of Management and Budget (2006). *Website.* Retrieved August 9, 2006, from http://www.whitehouse.gov/omb/.

58. U.S. Treasury Department (2006). *Combined statement of receipts, outlays, and balances of the United States Government.* Retrieved August 9, 2006, from http://www.fms.treas.gov/annualreport/.

59. U.S. Treasury Department (2006). *Bulletin.* Retrieved August 9, 2006, from http://www.fms.treas.gov/bulletin/index.html.

60. Department of Revenue, Commonwealth of Massachusetts (2006). *Tax expenditure budget, fiscal year 2007*. Retrieved August 9, 2006, from http://www.dor.state.ma.us/Stats/TEB/TEB2007.pdf.

61. President's Commission on Budget Concepts (1967). *Report*. Washington, DC: U.S. Government Printing Office, 1085.

62. Committee on the Budget, U.S. House of Representatives (1991). *Hidden exposure: the unfunded liabilities of the federal government: hearing*, 102nd Cong. 1st sess. Washington, DC: U.S. Government Printing Office.

63. Feldman, R. (1996). How weak recognition and measurement in the federal budget encouraged costly policy: the case of "supervisory goodwill." *Public Budgeting & Finance, 16, Winter*, 31–44.

64. U.S. General Accounting Office (1991). *Government-sponsored enterprises: a framework for limiting the government's exposure to risk*. Washington, DC: U.S. Government Printing Office.

65. Government Corporations. 31 U.S.C. § 9101.

66. U.S. General Accounting Office (2001). *Student loans: direct loan default rates*. Washington, DC: U.S. Government Printing Office.

67. Ennis, H. M. & Malek, H. S. (2005). Bank risk of failure and the too-big-to-fail policy. *Economic Quarterly* (Federal Reserve Bank of Richmond), *91, No. 2*, 21–44.

68. U.S. General Accounting Office (2004). *Government-sponsored enterprises: a framework for strengthening GSE governance and oversight*. Washington, DC: U.S. Government Printing Office.

69. Lucas, D & Torregrosa, D. (2004). *Updated estimates of the subsidies to the housing GSEs*. Washington, DC: U.S. Congressional Budget Office; Kosar, K. R. (2005). *Government-sponsored enterprises (GSEs): an institutional overview*. Washington, DC: U.S. Congressional Research Service; Shin, A. (2006). Fannie Mae gives regulator its review of executives' bonuses. *Washington Post, October 24*. Retrieved October 25, 2006, from http://www.washingtonpost.com/wp-dyn/content/article/2006/10/23/AR2006102301127.html.

70. Government Corporation Control Act (1945). Ch. 557.

71. Financial Institutions Reform, Recovery, and Enforcement Act (1989). P.L. 101-73.

72. U.S. General Accounting Office (2001). *Major management challenges and program risks: Department of Agriculture*. Washington, DC: U.S. Government Printing Office.

73. Federal Credit Reform Act (1990). P.L. 101-508, as part of the Omnibus Budget Reconciliation Act.

74. Phaup, M. (1996). Credit reform, negative subsidies, and FHA. *Public Budgeting & Finance, 16, Spring*, 23–36.

75. Debt Collection Improvement Act (1996). P.L. 104-34; also see Federal Debt Collection Procedures Act (1990). P.L. 101-647.

76. Student Loan Marketing Association Reorganization Act (1996). P.L. 104-208, 2009-275, as part of the Omnibus Consolidation Appropriations Act (1997).

77. U.S. Department of Treasury (2004). *Treasury announces successful privatization of Sallie Mae*. Retrieved August 8, 2006, from http://www.treasury.gov/press/releases/js2173.htm; Corder, J. K. & Hoffman, S. M. (2004). Privatizing federal credit programs: why Sallie Mae? *Public Administration Review, 64*, 180–191.

78. Terrorism Risk Insurance Extension Act (2005). P.L. 109-144.

79. U.S. Office of Management and Budget (2006). *Analytical perspectives, budget of the United States Government*, 71–74; U.S. Office of Management and Budget (2007). *Analytical perspectives, budget of the United States Government*. Washington, DC: U.S. Government Printing Office, 73–76.

80. Governmental Accounting Standards Board (1989). *Accounting and financial reporting for risk financing and related insurance issues*, Statement No. 10. Norwalk, CT: Financial Accounting Foundation.

81. U.S. Office of Management and Budget (2006). *Appendix*, 1118.

82. Burns, R. C. (2006). Unpublished data from Survey of State Budget Offices, 2005.

83. U.S. Office of Management and Budget (2006). *Historical Tables.*

84. Jameson Boex, L. F. et al. (2000). Multi-year budgeting: a review of international practices and lessons for developing and transitional economies. *Public Budgeting & Finance, 20, Summer*, 91–112.

85. Lee, R. D., Jr. & Burns, R. C. (2000). Unpublished data from survey of state budget offices, 1975 through 2000. University Park, PA: The Pennsylvania State University; Burns, R. C. (2006). Unpublished data from survey of state budget offices, 2005.

Chapter 8

BUDGET APPROVAL: THE ROLE OF THE LEGISLATURE

The tradition of legislative "power of the purse" is perhaps as strong in the United States as in any other country. This means that the struggle over the budget has only begun when the budget document goes to the legislative body. Executive budget preparation at the state and federal levels will have consumed months, but the product of the process is simply a proposal. The distinction between preparation and approval is alluded to by the phrase, "the executive proposes and the legislature disposes." The process of legislative disposition is often not pretty. Like the federal government (see Chapter 9), for example, New York State has chronic difficulties adopting a budget on time. The fiscal year 2005 budget was signed into law four-and-a-half months after the fiscal year began. This difficulty stems from not only the inability of the legislature to get along with the governor, but the inability of the two legislative houses to work together.[1]

The process in the U.S. differs from that used in parliamentary governments such as the British one, in which the executive and legislative functions are controlled by the same political party. In such systems, the approval phase is largely pro forma. Parliaments generally can alter the government's budget but often are prohibited from increasing it. Party discipline generally ensures that the changes made by a parliament are typically minor. In the United States, in contrast, the legislative body may approve a budget that diverges in important respects from the budget proposed by the executive. A recent study by the International Monetary Fund characterized 28 countries in terms of the relative budgetary powers of the legislature. This study ranked the U.S. as the one with the most legislative budgetary power, far ahead of the Westminster countries (notably Great Britain and Australia), but also more powerful than others, such as Germany, Mexico, and

Spain.[2] While this study was focused on national governments, the tradition of legislative independence in the U.S. tends to apply to states and localities as well.

In this chapter, major emphasis is given to the similarities in the approval phase across levels of government—local, state, and federal. The next chapter focuses exclusively on Congress, because that body is unique in the American political system and has unique budgetary roles, procedures, and problems.

This chapter has three main sections. The first discusses the parameters that constrain how legislative bodies operate and the processes used in approving government budgets. The second section examines the legislative budget process itself, including relationships between the legislative and executive branches, and the procedures used by the legislature. The third discusses the changing role of the legislature as an overseer of the executive branch.

▊ Constraints on Legislatures

General Characteristics of Legislatures

Legislative bodies—city councils, school boards, state legislatures, and Congress—sometimes have had a reputation for being relatively weak, ineffective bodies, but that perception has changed in recent times. Legislative bodies at all levels of government are reasserting their authority to set policy and are taking measures to increase their ability to wield the powers granted to them. There are certain underlying trends and characteristics that affect the environment for legislative deliberation on the budget. These include:

- the role of the legislature as, first and foremost, a representative body,
- trends in how legislators are selected for their jobs, and
- the movement toward limiting legislative terms.

Representation of Interests. Both socioeconomic and political diversity influence legislative behavior. At the national level, Congress must deal with a broad range of issues and associated interest groups. States tend to be less diverse and tend to have fewer interest groups that press their preferences upon legislatures. This situation can allow for a relatively small number of interests to influence legislation.[3] The concentration of influence can be even greater at the local level, as in the case of a town that is dominated by a single employer.

Citizen initiatives, allowable in many states, constitute another set of parameters that can have major impacts on the legislative bodies responsible for approving budgets.[4] Under the initiative process, citizens have the power to initiate changes, often by making amendments to state constitutions. If citizens become dissatisfied with tax rates, as was frequently the case in the 1970s, voters may approve new limits on taxes that force jurisdictions to cut tax rates and spending.

The news media are also important influences on legislatures. The media bring issues to the public's attention, help frame those issues and their solutions, and focus attention on legislatures in their efforts to resolve issues. However, newspapers, local radio and television stations, and news networks vary in their abilities to understand complex budget matters and to convey information to the public.[5] As a consequence, the media can be important sources of misinformation as well as information regarding public budgeting and finance. Though there is still a decidedly higher proportion of young adults than any other age group that uses the web as a basic source of information, the web is a rapidly increasing source of both information and misinformation for everyone. Individuals can create their own blogs, and there is considerable volunteerism creating opinions and information on the web. Sources like Wikipedia publish unvetted information on a large array of topics, though it is often difficult in these websites to distinguish fact from opinion or error.

A responsibility—if not the chief responsibility—of legislators is to represent their constituents. Decisions on the budget can have major positive and negative effects on a legislator's constituents and on the legislator's prospects for re-election. Although a legislator may generally favor reduced government spending, one common exception arises with any budget reduction proposed for the legislator's district. Positive budget decisions—increases in government spending or fending off possible decreases in spending—are seen by every office-holder as essential for gaining re-election, that itself is seen as of paramount importance. Some research suggests that not all public preferences are for decreased spending and that decisions about capital spending are more important to voters in local elections than current operating expenditures.[6]

Legislative Apportionment. How the duty of representation is met is influenced by how legislators are elected to their jobs. In the 1960s, the U.S. Supreme Court ruled that state legislatures must draw district lines that are proportional to population. The effect of this ruling has been to apportion legislative election districts on a population basis and to reduce substantially what was once over-representation of rural interests and to increase representation of urban and suburban areas in states.[7]

Local governments are undergoing similar changes. City councils are changing from using at-large seats because this procedure tends to result in under-representation of minority interests. Instead, the movement is toward single-member districts based on neighborhood populations, or a combination of these and at-large seats.[8] Legislative bodies are increasingly diverse in terms of gender and minority representation, although the distinct influence that women and minority legislators have on the legislative process is uncertain.

Race is of great concern regarding how district boundaries are drawn. In an earlier time when efforts were made to deliberately under-represent the interests of minorities, boundaries were drawn such that minority neighborhoods were carved into small segments and then apportioned to several districts. This approach ensured that a minority candidate would never be elected to represent any of the districts. In contemporary times, efforts have been made to help ensure minority representation by drawing boundaries to encircle minority neighborhoods. The Supreme Court has held through a series of rulings that when race becomes the dominant factor in deciding on district boundaries that action is a violation of the Equal Protection Clause of the Fourteenth Amendment.[9] The result has been considerable confusion when state legislatures have redrawn district boundaries for their own election districts or for congressional districts.

Beyond any racial justification for redistricting, however, there is the pure political motivation for drawing or redrawing district lines. In an infamous case in advance of the 2004 election, then-House Majority Leader Tom Delay aggressively pursued the redrawing of Texas congressional boundaries in a way that would make it easier for the Republican Party to keep its majority in Congress. Democratic legislators attempted to thwart this effort by fleeing the state in an effort to prevent a vote occurring on this plan. Ultimately the U.S. Supreme Court upheld the redrawn Texas districts as constitutional, but questionable ethical behavior by Delay in his pursuit of the new congressional boundaries led to his resignation from the Congress.[10]

Redistricting plans are frequently challenged in courts for any number of reasons, and federal courts have been very active in ruling on state redistricting plans.[11] Some plans are viewed as being unfair to minorities or as over-representing them.[12] The U.S. Supreme Court, for example, that had initially found that the State of North Carolina violated the Constitution because it used race as a "predominant factor" in redrawing its congressional boundaries, later overruled a state court decision that a subsequent redrawing of the boundaries was racially (rather than politically) motivated.[13] In short, the Court seems now to be content to side with boundaries that are redrawn primarily for partisan political reasons, even if the result is a district that consists mostly of minority people where one had not existed before.[14]

Term Limits. A related concern regarding legislators is that they not become so entrenched in their positions that they lose a sense of responsibility to the citizens who elected them. One response to this concern has been a move to impose term limits that curtail the number of years a person may serve.[15] The limits typically involve consecutive years of services, such as no more than two terms of four years in a state senate and no more than six terms of two years in a state house. Limits also can be on a lifetime basis, such as limiting the total number of years a person may serve in the house or senate for one's entire life. As of 2006, six states had lifetime limits for membership in their state legislative bodies.[16]

Term limits have been proposed at all levels of government, and many governments now have such limits. Many large cities, such as New York City, Los Angeles, and Philadelphia, along with smaller cities such as Honolulu, Fargo, and Spokane, have term limits.[17] There are currently legislative term limits on the books in 16 of the 50 states. By 2008, these limits will have forced legislators to retire in every one of these 16 states.[18] As for the federal government, the Supreme Court has ruled that term limits to be imposed on Congress must be carried out through a constitutional amendment.[19]

Term limits are, as one might imagine, controversial. One view is that the reform has led to more women and Latinos being elected. In 1997, members of the California Assembly chose the state's first-ever Latino speaker, a feat that would have been highly unlikely without term limits.[20] More broadly, the advocates of term limits argue that term-limited representatives are more likely to embrace the ethic of the "citizen-legislator" as opposed to a careerist politician that may lose touch with his or her constituency.

Term-limits reform has its downside. Political bodies are automatically denied the experience that can be gained only from long years of service in a legislature. People do not automatically change their family doctors and dentists every six years, so why should they do so with their elected representatives? Effective representatives presumably should be retained in office, while ineffective ones should not be re-elected. Reducing the length of time that someone may stay in office may deter some more-qualified people from running for office in the first place. Term limits, in addition to denying a legislative body experienced legislators, may also increase the influence of staff who know vastly more about particular issues than inexperienced members. In fact, given the complexity of government, many legislators find that their learning curve has just reached a peak at about the time that their legislative career is drawing to an end.

A study sponsored by the National Conference of State Legislatures concluded, after a detailed comparison of states with term limits to those without, that term limits have led to inexperienced lawmakers, polarized legislatures, and a shift in the balance of power toward the executive branch. The same study concluded that these costs have not come with the associated benefits of greater representative diversity.[21] To counter this problem, some states have established "training" and "mentoring" programs for new legislators to try to increase their effectiveness.[22] Citizens may support term limits less because of any dissatisfaction with their representatives and more because of a general cynicism about government itself.[23]

Factors Affecting Legislative Decisions

Beyond these general characteristics of legislative bodies that affect their selection and tenure in office, there are other factors that tend to influence the manner in which they deliberate on the budget. Legislatures tend to differ from each other in terms of many of these characteristics, such as the extent of fragmentation, the role of party leadership, the amount of time available to legislate, and the availability of staff. The capacity to legislate—and consequently to budget—is heavily influenced by these factors.

Fragmentation. An overriding characteristic of state legislatures and Congress is fragmentation in budgeting. Constitutionally-imposed bicameralism divides the legislature into two chambers, a house and a senate, that seek to establish their own identities and powers but which must be coordinated if a budget is to be approved. Local governing bodies, in contrast, usually are unicameral and do not face this fragmentation problem. Fragmentation also is apparent within each chamber of a legislative body and between the executive and legislative branches.

Political parties can serve as a unifying force between branches, between legislative chambers, and within chambers. According to conventional practice, whichever party wins a majority of seats in a chamber controls the leadership positions, has a majority of its members on each committee, and has each committee chaired by a member of the party. In theory, if the Democrats hold a majority of the seats in a state senate, then the Democratic Party has control of that chamber in handling all legislative matters. Sometimes a ruling party may have the narrowest possible majority or no majority at all. In 2005, the Iowa Senate and the Montana House were each evenly divided between Republicans and Democrats.[24] The 2006 midterm congressional election left the Senate with a 51 to 49 Democratic majority, one so narrow that a single party switch or the death or resignation of a single Democratic senator could result in Republican control of the body.

Political Party Leadership. In the United States, political parties are weak, meaning that party leadership cannot control their own party members by telling them how to vote. On any given issue there may be no guarantee that all or even most of the party's members will vote as a block. Many members of the legislative body, especially those who have gained seniority through numerous re-elections, are not always amenable to supporting the policies pursued by their party's leadership, whether in the legislature or in the executive branch. Further, in term-limited legislatures, the assistance that leaders can offer rank-and-file members with re-election is much less important. For this reason, leaders do not have as much to offer these members in exchange for toeing the party line. In addition, regional differences sometimes trump partisan differences. In the Illinois Senate, for instance, a Republican from the Chicago area may be as likely to vote with a Chicago Democrat on some issue that affects the Chicago area as to vote with a Republican from "downstate" Illinois. Studies have also found evidence that interpersonal ties influence legislators' votes independent of partisanship.[25] In a situation where party control is weak, leaders must try to persuade members to win their votes, unlike in earlier times when legislative leaders may have ruled with iron fists.[26]

Parties attempt to exert influence on their legislators by providing or withholding privileges or by taking party positions in caucuses. Legislative leaders have different levels of institutional control over rank-and-file members. They may, for example, differ substantially in terms of their ability to appoint members to key committees or to provide resources.[27] Republicans in a state house of representatives, for example, will meet periodically to develop party positions on issues and then attempt to exert their influence on party members to vote accordingly. The positions approved in caucus meetings do not always coincide with the views of the party's leadership.

The situation is further complicated by the fact that the two chambers can be controlled by different parties. Even if both are controlled by one party, the chief executive might be of another party. In 2006, for example, 29 states had divided governments in which the governor, the lower legislative chamber, and the upper legislative chamber were not all controlled by the same political party.[28] This condition is sometimes seen as leading to gridlock, which is one oft-cited cause for the inability of government to deal with pressing problems. While gridlock has a negative connotation, however, it should be noted that "checks and balances" (which leads to gridlock) is a principle firmly ingrained in the political philosophy of the United States and its citizens. Divided government, as will be seen in this chapter and later ones, should not be considered the sole explanation of why governments sometimes fail to address major problems.[29]

Legislative Committees. The extensive use of legislative committees is essential in that acting as a committee of the whole is impractical, but committee structures add to fragmentation. Committees become little legislatures in their own right.[30] Given that the U.S. House of Representatives has 435 members and the Senate has 100 members, a committee structure is inevitable. Among the states, New Hampshire has the largest legislature, with 424 members, and Nebraska the smallest, with 49 members in its single chamber. In 42 of the 50 states there are at least 100 legislators.[31]

In a bicameral legislative body, legislation is handled by parallel committees in each chamber. These committees report out bills that are acted upon by the full membership of the house and senate. When differences exist in the two bills, a conference committee is usually appointed, which reports a revised bill that again is acted upon by both houses. The conference committee consists of members from the two committees that prepared the legislation. Once the chambers have passed identical bills, the legislation is ready for signing or vetoing by the governor or president.

At the local level, where unicameralism prevails, a budget committee often assumes the main responsibility for reviewing and amending the executive's proposed budget and for submitting a set of recommendations to the full legislative body, such as a city council or school board.

Committees that continue on a permanent basis are known as standing committees, whereas ad hoc committees are usually created to deal with specific problems and are then disbanded. Most standing committees consist of selected members of one house of a legislature, but standing committees can be joint in nature, consisting of selected members from both chambers. State legislatures usually have 15 to 20 standing committees in each chamber. In 2005, the range was eight (Maryland Senate) to 46 (Minnesota House).[32]

Legislators seek to serve their district's or state's interests by gaining appointment to appropriate legislative committees. Someone from a farming community may seek appointment to a state senate's agriculture committee. A member of the U.S. House of Representatives from a district that includes major military installations may seek appointment to the Armed Services Committee to help ensure that military funds continue to flow into the district. Similarly, members of the House and Senate will seek appointment to key subcommittees (organized in line with key constituencies, i.e., defense, agriculture, transportation, and so forth) of their chamber's appropriations committee.[33]

Availability of Time. How a legislative body operates is greatly influenced by whether it continues in session throughout the year. City councils usually hold meetings once, twice, or even more times per month throughout the year. Congress is in session much of each year except for holidays and recesses during election periods.

State legislatures vary widely. While about a dozen states have no limits on the length of legislative sessions, the rest control whether the legislature can meet each year, for how many days, and whether the legislature may call itself back into session after adjournment. The legislatures in California, Illinois, Iowa, Michigan, New Jersey, New York, North Carolina, Ohio, Oregon, Pennsylvania, Rhode Island, South Carolina, Vermont, and Wisconsin hold sessions that are not limited as to their length, and thus may run during much of the year.[34] When legislatures have time limitations, procedural limits are used to "budget" the available time. For example, a common practice is to set a cutoff date for the introduction of bills, as late submission would carry deliberations beyond the required adjournment.

Similarly, time limits are set on the budget process. Some states allow their spending and taxation committees only a few weeks to consider their relevant portions of the budget, while other states allow 20 or more weeks. In some states, the entire budget approval process must be completed by the legislature within six weeks or less. Other states allow 20 weeks, 30 weeks, or even more.

A major problem facing Congress is not that it has limits on the time that it may be in session, but rather that it has difficulty approving the budget within the available time (see Chapter 9). This problem, while it may exist for some states and localities (such as New York, as indicated in the beginning of this chapter), is much more the exception than the rule. The reason for this relative timeliness for states and localities may be more that they face a separate external force that does not exist at the national level. They may discover that the failure to enact bills on time can have an adverse effect on bond ratings and, therefore, increase borrowing costs. Indeed, in 2004 when the State of Virginia budget talks resulted in a dispute over whether to raise taxes to address a budget shortfall, one factor cited in bringing both parties successfully to the table was the possibility that such a shutdown would likely cost Virginia its highly valued AAA bond rating.[35] That would translate into higher borrowing costs, amounting to millions of extra dollars over the years.

Compensation and Staff. Closely associated with time limits on legislatures is the issue of compensation for their members. Annual compensation is low in many states. For example, in 2005, Arkansas, Indiana, Mississippi, Nebraska, New Hampshire, North Carolina, Rhode Island, South Carolina, South Dakota, Texas, and West Virginia paid their legislators $15,000 or less.[36] In these states and others, however, members might be eligible for per diem payments, travel expenses, and other payments. Nevertheless, pay for state legislators overall is low, so most legislators need other income sources, such as from law practices or other alternative employment, in order to make ends meet. In contrast, members of Congress earn incomes and receive other benefits, such as travel expenses, that allow the legislative job to be a full-time occupation. One of the most important forms of compensation afforded members of Congress is generous pension benefits that can be an incentive for continuing to stand for re-election. Fees for speeches and other appearances are lucrative for some legislators, although these are generally prohibited to be paid to members of Congress.

Staffing is another factor that influences legislative behavior. Staff dedicated to assist legislators presumably can help them perform more effectively and reduce their reliance on the executive branch and lobbyists for information. Although local legislators, such as county commissioners or city council members, rarely have sizable staffs at their disposal, Congress does. So do many state legislatures, although some states have small staffs. A predominantly rural state, such as Wyoming, will have a legislative staff numbering less than 100, while a large state, such as New York, will have a staff numbering in the thousands. These personnel serve individual members, committees, and persons holding leadership positions, as in the case of the speaker of a state house of representatives. In addition, some legislative staff units serve a variety of individuals and committees in both chambers. The Congressional Budget Office (CBO) is a notable example of such a unit, but many states have similar legislative budget offices. California's Office of the Legislative Analyst, in fact, is one of the most highly regarded of such offices, and served as a model for the development of the CBO at the national level. Since the 1960s, staffs in state legislatures and Congress have greatly increased their professional training. Many staff members now have graduate degrees, including doctorates.

Legislative fiscal committee staffs provide a host of services. For example, most state legislatures' fiscal committee staffs conduct fiscal research studies, prepare reports on revenues and taxes, and prepare reports on expenditures and the budget. Other important staff functions include making revenue projections, analyzing budget trends during the fiscal year, and preparing reports on economic conditions. States also differ as to whether they maintain separate fiscal staffs for each house or one joint legislative fiscal office that serves both houses.[37]

A study published in 2000 identified the following as the most "professional" of state legislatures: Alaska, California, Florida, Illinois, Michigan, New York, Ohio, and Pennsylvania. This study measured professionalism according to several factors. Those legislatures judged to be the most professional were those with the highest level of compensation, those that spent the greatest number of days in session annually, and those that spent the most money on staff and other services.[38] Professionalism, however, is no guarantee of a smoothly operating legislature, as has been evident in such states as California and New York. One view is that professionalism attracts better-informed individuals who inevitably clash with one another, yielding conflict that is not necessarily productive.[39]

The Legislative Budget Process

This section examines what happens to the executive budget when it reaches the legislature. Legislatures are not integrated wholes but rather consist of numerous subunits, and this section considers how the executive branch relates to those subunits, especially to the two legislative chambers and their committees.

General Relations Between the Branches

The executive and legislative branches of government in the United States are typically said to be coequal.[40] The separation of powers—in this case, between the executive and legislative branches—is a fundamental feature of U.S. governments. Since political power tends to be a somewhat "zero-sum" game, the two branches tend to be wary of possible diminution of their powers and may seek strategies for demonstrating their independence. Confrontations between the two are sometimes akin to tests of strength with each branch showing it is not subservient to the other.

Authority. In earlier days, the legislature was considered to be responsible for setting policy. Today, both the legislative and executive branches are inextricably engaged in policy making. Conflicts arise, not over whether the executive should be involved in policy making, but rather to what extent and in what ways. The movement toward executive budget systems has placed the executive four-square in the policy-making process, because the preparation of budget proposals by the executive is, in effect, the drafting of proposed policies. Congress, state legislatures, and city councils have often found themselves in the position of having to react to executive recommendations instead of formulating policy. To demonstrate their independence, then, legislators may feel a compulsion to alter a proposed budget no matter how compatible its recommendations are with their own preferences.

Not all governments have executive budgeting systems. In some governments, budgeting powers overlap between the branches. In others, legislatures dominate the budgeting process. In fact, in a study of 13 states in terms of their budget practices, only three were characterized as states where the executive is dominant, while four were judged as states where the legislature is dominant. In the rest, budgetary power was viewed as relatively equal between the branches.[41] Regardless of the distribution of powers, tensions will exist between the branches of government.

Constitutional and legal constraints greatly affect the extent of executive and legislative powers in budgeting. The Budget and Accounting Act of 1921 and comparable legislation at the state level have granted substantial budgetary powers to the president and governors. Yet, in some states, the governor must share budget-making authority with other relatively independent executive officers or legislative bodies. In most states, the legislature is free to adjust the governor's budget either upward or downward, but in three states, Maryland, Nebraska, and West Virginia, the legislature has limited or no authority to appropriate amounts above those recommended by the governor.[42]

Relationships between the branches change over time. Changes in political leadership have both short- and long-term effects. When a new executive takes office, inevitable discontinuities occur during the transition period that can last from a few weeks to months.[43] In addition, personalities and the political clout of leaders influence executive–legislative relations. The election of a highly popular political leader in the legislature can lead to diminished executive powers. A newly-elected governor who is more assertive than his or her predecessor, may succeed in demanding that the legislature yield some of its budgetary powers. When either the executive or the legislative branch changes its partisan makeup (as occurred, for example, in the late 1990s, when several southern states elected Republican legislatures for the first time since Reconstruction, or in 1995 when the U.S. House was taken over by the Republicans for the first time in 40 years), it can create a period of instability while new relationships are forged. In periods of fiscal crisis and other challenging times, the executive may tend to garner greater budgetary powers at the expense of the legislature.[44]

Constituency Differences. The legislative and executive branches have different constituencies and, as a result, have different perspectives on the budget. One common interpretation has been that the chief executive, being elected by the jurisdiction's entire constituency, has a broader perspective on the budget. A governor will attempt to satisfy the diverse needs of citizens throughout the state. Legislative bodies, on the other hand, have been seen as consisting of parochial individuals who may be less impressed with government-wide problems and, therefore, more likely to cut budgets. The legislature, then, is seen as a protector of the treasury and as a budget cutter.

A competing view of legislative bodies is that, in their desire to represent constituents, they tend to be eager to spend resources far beyond what is financially sound and that, while the requirement for a balanced budget keeps that desire to spend in check at the state and local levels, few constraints are evident at the national level. *Pork barrel*, a basic term of U.S. politics, refers to legislatively approved government projects that are aimed at helping home districts and states.[45] In fact, some prominent political scientists have suggested that pork barrel spending and constituent casework (intervening on behalf of constituents with administrative agencies) have become more valued than legislating because they offer a more certain path to re-election.[46] A standard complaint of pork barrel projects is that they have limited utility beyond winning votes for legislators seeking re-election. The item veto, discussed below, may help to reduce the wastefulness of pork barrel spending.

Factors Constraining Legislative Deliberations on the Budget

Members of the legislature or their staff often participate in budget preparation deliberations by the executive branch. When the budget reaches the legislature, it may contain relatively few surprises in terms of proposals being advanced because many of the key legislators already will be familiar with the budget's main proposals. Legislative involvement during preparation can help build support for executive budget recommendations. In addition to the political and institutional characteristics discussed previously, the deliberation of any legislature is constrained by some factors outside of its control, such as the state's economic environment and the effect of previous budget decisions. Operating within those constraints, the legislature then makes the decisions necessary for the chief executive's budget proposal to become law.

Economic and Political Environment. As with all human enterprise, legislative bodies must operate within a set of parameters that greatly constrain how they approve the budgets. One of the most important constraints is the economic environment both in the short and the long term. How a legislative body approaches the task of passing a budget is influenced greatly by whether a surplus of revenues is projected or whether sizable cuts must be made to bring expenditures down to meet anticipated reductions in revenues. Further, the legislature is constrained by whether the political environment would permit additional revenues to be raised, whether the level of revenues under current law represents a revenue ceiling, or even whether tax cuts have already been promised.

Previous Decisions. Before a local legislative body commences considering the budget, many decisions already will have been made. As explained in previous chapters, the state will have imposed a variety of mandates. A school district will be told how many days it must operate in a school year, possibly what the minimum salaries should be for teachers at different levels, and what courses must be taught. More than half of a school district's budget typically comes from state aid, that greatly reduces what the school district can decide on its own. The state also will have imposed limits on the taxation and borrowing authority for each type of local government and may deny taxing power to some jurisdictions, as is sometimes the case with special districts.

Whether the legislative body is Congress, the state legislature, or a local legislature, many decisions already will have been made before legislative deliberations begin. Entitlement laws that provide open-ended benefits to individuals, such as guaranteed payments to all persons qualifying for disability benefits under Social Security, greatly curtail what Congress can do in a given year. Programs such as Medicaid, where many rules that affect state and local costs have been made by the federal government, may seem uncontrollable at the state or local level. Additionally, courts force legislative bodies to take actions, such as legislatures having to revise state funding formulas for school districts to comply with court orders (see Chapter 4). If tax increases must be approved by voters, as is sometimes the case with sewer taxes on property, and voters reject proposed increases, then the sewer board may be faced with finding revenues in some other forms, such as raising monthly or quarterly sewer fees.

The Legislature Adopts the Budget

The legislative budget process typically involves several sequential types of actions:

- Committee action, where committees, or sometimes subcommittees, hold hearings and collect other information on proposed agency budgets, and then use their expertise to draft bills that reflect their judgment concerning funding levels for programs and agencies under their jurisdiction;
- Action by the legislature as a whole, which must vote on proposals coming out of committees, frequently modify those proposals, and resolve differences that usually exist between the branches; and
- Action by the chief executive, whose assent is often necessary (and always necessary at the state and federal levels) in order for any budget legislation to have the force of law.

While the process is sequential, actions are simultaneous. Several committees work simultaneously on bills but report out on them at various times. Committees work on bills at the same time the full chambers act on others and the executive considers signing or vetoing others.

Committee Action. Legislatures—especially in a large government with many responsibilities—are not typically in a position to deal with the budget in a unified way. Frequently when a budget reaches a state legislature or Congress, the document is divided into numerous pieces and sent to committees. Proposals that require new substantive legislation to implement them will be sent to substantive standing committees. These committees exist for areas such as environmental protection, education, recreation, welfare, and, at the federal level, defense and international relations. For programs to be implemented, these committees must report bills that will be approved eventually by the two chambers of the legislature. Legislation of this type authorizes the existence of programs, while appropriations provide the necessary funding.

While deliberations proceed on these substantive matters, other committees deal with the financial aspects of the budget. A regular practice is to assign taxing and other revenue matters to one group of committees and spending or appropriations to another. Appropriations may be handled at the full committee level, or in subcommittees, each of which provides appropriations for a portion of the government.

Coordination problems and terrain battles among committees are common. A person typically achieves the position of chair of a committee by serving on the committee for a long time and, once made chair, is unlikely to look favorably on threats to the committee's powers. Nevertheless, some coordinating mechanisms are essential to ensure that realistic budgets are adopted. For example, if separate revenue and expenditure committees are free to act independently, then there may be little relationship between how much revenue comes into the government and how much is spent.

It was precisely this situation that led the federal government to enact the Congressional Budget and Impoundment Control Act of 1974, creating the Budget Committees and budget resolution to better coordinate action on the budget (see Chapter 9). The budget resolution, that is under the jurisdiction of the Budget Committees, sought to address the fragmentation of the budget process at the federal level by requiring Congress to vote on the whole budget, rather than considering it only in pieces. This type of fragmentation may be less likely to occur at the state and local levels, particularly in smaller and less complex governmental units. Local governments are particularly unlikely to have particular budget committees.

Hearings. In local governments with elected boards or councils, hearings and budget reviews are typically conducted with the entire legislative body present. Directors of city or county departments are asked to defend budget proposals in the same way that similar officials defend their budget requests at the state and national levels. The public, however, may be more involved in local budget issues at a much greater level of detail than is the case for national or state budgets, because citizens are likely to be more knowledgeable about local issues and more directly affected by the budget.[47] In fact, specific provision for direct citizen input into the budget process is a common feature of local government budgeting.[48]

While an executive budget system provides the chief executive with control over budget preparation, there is no guarantee that all units within the executive branch will subscribe fully to the budget's recommendations. The chief executive will not be uniformly in support of all portions of the budget. Some recommendations will have been approved because of political considerations. Typically, the chief executive will single out a few major recommendations for which approval is sought, with other recommendations being considered low priority. The budget office will be expected to make general presentations on the overall recommendations contained in the budget even though it may be lukewarm toward many of those recommendations. Hearings may be held by budget or appropriations committees, or for the legislative body as a whole, in an effort to discern the overall fiscal and policy direction implied in the budget.

More detailed hearings with executive branch agencies, however, typically dominate the budget process. In advance of these hearings, executive branch agencies may be requested to provide *budget justification* documents to legislative committees with jurisdiction over the budget. These documents may simply be the sections of the chief executive's budget that deal with the agency, or agencies may be required to present budget data in an entirely different format than was included in the executive budget document. Agencies usually know in advance what data the committees want and in what formats and prepare accordingly during the budget preparation phase.

Hearings may generate more heat than light. It is normally the responsibility of executive branch officials to defend the chief executive's agency-by-agency budget recommendations to the legislature. The heads of the agencies in a strong executive system are the appointees of the chief executive and have an obligation to defend the budget recommendations, even though higher funding levels may be preferred.[49] Agency representatives, however, may have little enthusiasm for defending budget proposals that call for deep cuts in programs. As a result, agencies attempt to calculate the extent to which they can reveal their preferences for greater resources to the spending committees in the legislature and still remain "faithful" to the chief executive. They do not always calculate correctly. In 2002, President George W. Bush's appointed civilian head of the Army Corps of Engineers, former Representative Mike Parker, was fired for being a bit too honest in his responses to questions from Congress about the adequacy of the Corps' budget.[50] Agencies also seek to head off any budget cuts being contemplated by the appropriations committee and are willing to engage in conflict if necessary to protect their budgets.[51]

During the approval phase, central budget offices may have responsibility for exercising some control over agencies that might seek to garner financial support beyond what the executive is recommending to the legislature and may serve as a major negotiator for the executive in sensitive discussions with legislative leaders. Since the early 1980s, the Office of Management and Budget (OMB) has played a much more prominent role in legislative relations. This role includes activities not just of the OMB director, but also of individual budget examiners.[52]

Strategies. Regardless of what level of government is considered, executive–legislative relationships inevitably can be characterized as cat-and-mouse games, although it is not always clear who is the cat and who is the mouse. Strategies are devised in each branch to deal with the other. On the executive side, an almost ubiquitous strategy is to cultivate clientele who will support requests for increased funding. Agencies are sensitive to where they locate buildings and other facilities. A new facility in a key legislator's district may gain the support of that legislator. Agencies pursue such strategies continuously as a matter of course.[53]

Contingent strategies, on the other hand, are limited to particular situations. No comprehensive cataloging of them is possible because they vary from agency to agency and from circumstance to circumstance. They arise out of perceptions of what is possible in a given budget period. In growth periods, when revenue surplus or slack is evident, agencies may seek to expand existing programs or gain approval for the creation of new ones. Even when revenues are scarce, agencies whose areas are favored by the chief executive may seek expansion, as occurred with defense and homeland security in the aftermath of the September 11, 2001, terrorist attacks. Sometimes obtaining approval for a new program may be easier than obtaining approval for expansion of an existing one. Executives and legislators alike prefer being able to take credit for creation of a new program over simply improving an existing one.

A ploy used by supporters of programs may be to start a new project with a small appropriation, get the legislature accustomed to the program, and then seek much greater appropriations in subsequent years. This tactic has been referred to as the "camel's nose" strategy. Under this imagery, the majority of the "camel" (the new program) is outside the tent, and thus obscured from view. The camel's nose is visible, but the nose represents a small percentage of the total camel (the eventual cost of the program). The assumption is that once the first part (the nose) of the program is funded, funding for the rest (the remainder of the camel) will follow.[54]

When funds are less plentiful, one strategy is to defend programs against cuts and to maintain what is called the base. An agency's existing budget is often regarded as the base, with the budget process adding or subtracting increments to the base. Agencies have been known to warn that the slightest of budget cuts would necessarily diminish popular programs and thereby erode electoral support of legislators.

When cuts are perceived as inevitable, often because of declining tax revenues, one strategy is to minimize cuts in the base and to obtain fair share funding. An agency will argue, on the one hand, that its programs are essential and should not be cut at all. On the other hand, it will insist that, if cuts must be made, they be no greater than cuts imposed on programs in other agencies.

Strategies used by proponents of government programs can be highly situational. A thorough study of the strategies used by federal agencies in dealing with OMB and Congress catalogued 35 different strategies used at various times. These included some that have been well documented in the budgeting literature, such as establishing earmarked funding sources, portraying the disastrous consequences of failing to spend money, and stressing the needs of a particular group that will be served. They also include many more arcane strategies that have been less well documented: establishment of a government-sponsored enterprise, creation of a loan guarantee program, establishment of a tax expenditure (see Chapter 4), and leasing instead of purchasing a capital asset.[55] There are, in short, many different "tools" available to governments to satisfy the desire for social action. Increasingly, these tactics involve less direct means than government expenditures, for strategic as well as substantive reasons.[56] Some changes in the budget process, such as federal credit reform (see Chapter 11), have occurred specifically to lessen the incentives to provide resources through less direct and apparently less costly means.

While various strategies may be influential there are limits to their effectiveness. Legislatures are influenced by personal values and committee role expectations as well as by agency budget strategies and presentations. Agency strategies may also backfire and create negative feelings on the part of members of the appropriations committees, perhaps because they suspect they are being exploited.

In response to agency pressure, legislators devise a number of strategies for dealing with their budgetary responsibilities. A major problem is the capacity of agencies to produce vast amounts of information in support of their requests— more information than the legislature can process. Legislative strategies may be seen as methods to simplify complex choices.

For example, an appropriations committee or subcommittee may find it difficult, if not impossible, to decide rationally if $83.6 million is the exact amount that should be granted to an agency. As a consequence, legislators in appropriations committees may look for other ways to determine what should be granted an agency. They may place much of the burden for calculation on the executive branch and demand that an agency justify its need for certain funds in response to probing questions. Detailed questions, that to outsiders may seem petty and trivial, are designed to determine how much confidence the subcommittee can place in the executive's stewardship of public funds. Legislators have "discernible patterns" in their line of questioning, suggesting that they have their own strategies for dealing with different agencies and that these strategies depend in part upon changes in fiscal conditions.[57] How the various strategies affect the outcomes of appropriations is uncertain and no doubt varies among jurisdictions and over time.

Fiscal Notes. One important mechanism that has been adopted is the requirement that fiscal notes be developed for most draft legislation reported out of legislative committees. A fiscal note is a report that addresses the current and future costs of implementing a proposed bill. It may include analysis of the purpose of the legislation, the proposed sources of funding, and the impact on other governments, as in the case of a state law affecting local government budgets.

Fiscal notes are typically prepared by legislative staff. At the state level, appropriations committees often have this responsibility. At the federal level, the Congressional Budget Office (CBO) prepares fiscal notes to any bill that is reported out of a House or Senate Committee. CBO is required to estimate the cost of the proposed legislation to the federal government relative to the baseline, that is the estimate of costs under current law. It also estimates the costs of legislation to state and local governments. The Unfunded Mandates Reform Act of 1995 requires that Congress consider the possible financial effects of draft legislation on state and local governments and creates hurdles to considering legislation that does not include an estimate of potential unfunded mandates (see Chapter 14).[58]

The fiscal note is intended to help decision makers be better informed about the implications of draft legislation. For example, if a proposal provides for revising a state program for teenagers to include 13-year-olds, whereas only those 14 years old and older are currently included, the revision could greatly increase the number of clients served and heighten the demand on resources. Fiscal notes also are prepared for revenue proposals, as in the case of forecasting the extra income that would be generated by increasing a state sales tax by one percentage point.

Fiscal notes are particularly important at the state and local levels, where balanced budgets are required. Indeed, the revenue estimates prepared by the chief executive, coupled with any fiscal note on proposed revenue increases, will greatly influence what spending programs the legislature will be able to approve. While nearly all states require that fiscal notes be prepared,[59] the content and thoroughness of fiscal notes varies widely from state to state. Some states, for example, require that fiscal notes be prepared for tax expenditure proposals (see Chapter 4), while others do not.[60] The failure to prepare thorough fiscal notes may be a function of short deadlines that are impossible to meet and the lack of qualified staff in sufficient numbers to prepare the notes.[61]

In addition to fiscal notes, other mechanisms are devised to link together the work of committees and ensure that "reasonable" budgets are developed. Some states have used a system by which lump-sum amounts are assigned to program areas, and these funds then are distributed among programs within each area by standing committees and reported back to the appropriations committee for inclusion in their budget bills. Congress uses a variation of this approach. Local governments generally have less of a coordination problem because most of the budget work is handled by a single committee.

The Committee Adopts the Budget. Once committees have gathered and processed all of the information collected as a part of the hearing process, they turn to drafting and approving the budget legislation itself. This is best seen as the starting point for later legislative deliberations on the budget. The initial committee proposal can be quite influential, depending on how much interest or power the rest of the legislature has to amend bills after they emerge from committee. From the perspective of executive branch agencies and interest groups, it is highly desirable to receive favorable budget treatment in draft committee legislation.

Obtaining Overall Legislative Approval. All of the previous activity implies that legislative action is taking place in one committee of the legislature. In a bicameral legislative system all of the previous activity takes place not in one set of legislative committees, but in committees in both chambers. Since differences almost always exist between the two legislative chambers, a bicameral system complicates the ultimate approval of the budget. Another complicating factor is that there may be multiple committees with jurisdiction over legislation that affects the budget. Thus, many different bills may be required in order to finally pass the entire budget.

One set of considerations from both the executive and the legislative branch perspectives involves the relative roles of the two chambers. At the federal level, the Constitution (Article I, Section 7) requires that revenue or tax bills begin in the House of Representatives—in particular, the Ways and Means Committee. Until the 1974 reform legislation, the normal procedure was for the Senate Finance Committee to wait until the House completed action before taking up the tax bill. Appropriations were handled in a similar manner, although the practice was based on custom and not the Constitution. Appropriation bills began in the House and later were referred to the Senate. Under that system, strategists were able to concentrate their attentions on first one committee and then another and on one chamber and then the other as the legislation worked its way through Congress. Since 1974, the House and Senate have simultaneously commenced work on the budget.

In either legislative house, once the budget or a component of the budget has been approved by the appropriate committee, it is considered by the relevant house where that committee is housed. The overall house may or may not substantially revise or amend the budget as approved by the relevant committee depending on the rules of that particular legislature. In some legislatures the practice is for quite substantial amendment of committee proposals, whereas in others there is a great deal of deference to the approved committee budgets.

One factor that influences legislative deliberations on the budget is the relative roles played by the two legislative chambers. Where appropriations are handled sequentially (that is, beginning in the lower chamber and then moving to the upper chamber), the two chambers tend to take on different roles. Since a House of Representatives tends to have more members than a Senate, a House appropriations committee tends to have more members than its counterpart in the Senate. As a result, House committee members can specialize in segments of the budget, whereas senators must attempt to become informed on a larger number of areas and consequently may be viewed as amateurs. Members of the Senate committee, on the other hand, might consider themselves to have a broader awareness of total budget needs than House members. Also, given the sequencing of one chamber acting followed by the other, the House appropriations committee tends to focus on the proposed budget, whereas the Senate committee focuses on what the House did to the proposed budget.[62]

A vital and complicating factor in bicameral systems is the necessity to resolve the inevitable differences that result from the deliberations of the two legislative bodies. Almost invariably, because of the difference in constituencies between the branches or because the branches may be controlled by different political parties, a conference committee or some other institution will be required to work out these disputes. The conference committee process is often a delicate balancing act where the members attempt to draft legislation that can gain enough votes in each chamber without costing votes of members who may find that their preferred project or funding level did not survive in conference.

Chief Executive Action on the Budget. Once a revenue or expenditures bill has passed the legislature, it typically (at least in states and in the federal government) will go to the chief executive for approval. Deadlock between the branches is a common phenomenon. When the two cannot agree on a budget, commuters can be greatly inconvenienced due to shutdowns in public transit, welfare recipients can be forced to eke out an existence without their checks, and public employees may have to endure payless paydays. Balanced budget requirements at the state and local levels, while imposing fiscal discipline, can lead to delays in adopting budgets because neither the executive nor legislative branch wishes to take the first step toward compromise lest it be viewed as a sign of weakness. In 1992, California state government operated for months without a budget, during which time employees were issued scrip rather than dollars.

Budget offices commonly perform a clearinghouse function by reviewing all proposed legislation and bills that have been passed by the legislature and forwarded to the chief executive for signing. OMB Circular A-19, Legislative Coordination and Clearance, prescribes for federal agencies that they submit to OMB an annual set of proposals for legislation.[63] If these proposals are not submitted in time for consideration during budget preparation, then they are excluded from the president's budget and therefore not endorsed by the president and his administration. Circular A-19 provides that when Congress passes a bill, OMB distributes copies of the enrolled bill to affected agencies for their comments. The agencies must respond promptly, either endorsing or opposing the enrolled bill, to be considered within the president's limit of ten days. If the president does not act within the ten days (including holidays but excluding Sundays), the bill automatically becomes law.

Item Veto. Once appropriation and revenue bills are adopted by the legislature, the approval phase is not completed. In more than 40 states, governors have item-veto power, that permits reductions in amounts that have been appropriated. In some cases, governors may eliminate selected language in appropriation bills that can have substantial effects on policy. State legislatures may seek to override these vetoes. Usually a two-thirds vote is required for an override. As with the general veto power, the threat of the item veto may be as important as its eventual use, in that legislators may avoid including some measures in an appropriation bill on the assumption they would be excised eventually by the governor.

The item veto has three uses:[64]

1. It allows chief executives to keep total expenditures within the limits of anticipated available revenue.

2. The executive can reduce or even eliminate funds for projects or programs considered to be unworthy. The item veto can help curtail the excesses of pork barrel projects mentioned earlier.

3. The veto can be used for partisan purposes. This kind of use often occurs in situations where the governor is of one political party and one or both chambers of the legislature are of another party.

Studies have found that the item-veto power sometimes, but not always, has a negative effect on spending. This is especially true for pork barrel highway projects and can be particularly important when at least one chamber is under the control of a political party that differs from the governor's party.[65] From a practical standpoint, the item veto allows action by the governor without forcing the legislature to react unless it chooses to do so. Indeed, legislators may be privately pleased to have the governor veto some projects that were included in an appropriation bill to satisfy strong lobbying pressure. In spite of the constitutional foundations underlying state item vetoes, state courts have been very active in interpreting their application and these court decisions have had substantial effects on the "reach" of a governor's item-veto power.[66]

At the federal level, the president has always been able to exercise the standard veto power, meaning that he can veto an entire appropriation bill. When this power is exercised, the House and Senate may override the veto by a two-thirds vote. Should the veto be sustained, the legislation is referred back to the committee for further review. The disadvantage of the veto power for both Congress and the president is that much time and energy may be consumed in redrafting the legislation and negotiating an agreement between the two branches.

Every president since Ulysses S. Grant, including President George W. Bush, has requested the item-veto power or a variant of it.[67] In 1996, Congress granted that wish by passing the Line Item Veto Act.[68] The law, ultimately declared unconstitutional by the Supreme Court in 1998, is discussed in Chapter 9, which deals with congressional budget processes.[69]

Legislative Oversight

Not only are the executive and legislative branches typically separated in U.S. governments, but each branch is also provided with powers that can be used to limit the powers of the other. The basic structure of this checks-and-balances system is set forth in the U.S. Constitution, state constitutions, and city charters. However, constitutional and statutory provisions must be implemented on a daily basis, and the extent to which one branch limits the other may fluctuate over time. In this section, we consider the increasing interest being given to the legislative body's oversight of executive operations.[70]

Influences on Oversight. When revenues are limited and the demands for expenditures are seemingly limitless, legislators perceive a need for greater efficiency and effectiveness in government operations. Such perceptions increase the interest in oversight operations, that in turn increases the pressure on administrative agencies to improve their operations while curtailing or even reducing expenditures. Agencies are required to provide masses of information to legislative committees to support their quest for ferreting out mismanagement and saving taxpayers' dollars.[71]

There are, of course, other reasons for the current legislative oversight movement. Financial crises in major cities have contributed to the interest in oversight. The Watergate scandal during the Nixon administration and subsequent scandals and abuses of government funds by federal agencies have stimulated interest in greater legislative oversight. A turnover in the party controlling the legislature, especially if it happens to both chambers and the new legislature is of a different party than the chief executive, can substantially increase oversight activities. This happened with the Democratic party takeover of both the House and Senate after the 2006 congressional election. Legislators have not been immune from their own scandals, raising the question of whether they have the appropriate credentials to oversee executive branch operations.

Legislators may be sincerely interested in using government to alleviate societal problems. Frustrated by what is perceived as inept administration, they are attracted to the idea of expanding their oversight roles in the hope of improving government operations. Of course, oversight of the executive branch can also provide an opportunity for legislators to score political points. In fact, legislatures have often been criticized for engaging in oversight designed to take an agency to task for some particular perceived offense, rather than using this opportunity to attempt to understand programs in detail so that they can be reformed constructively.

This legislative interest in oversight occurs at a time when executives feel increasingly frustrated with their own efforts to control public bureaucracies. Elected executives often complain that they lack the authority needed to control and redirect agencies. Merit systems that protect civil service employees are often cited as weakening executives and protecting lazy and incompetent employees from disciplinary actions. Tensions exist between the White House and Congress over control of the chief financial officers in federal agencies, with the White House seeing the officers as a means of exerting executive influence and Congress being concerned with extending its oversight function (see Chapter 11).[72]

Methods. Legislative oversight can be performed using numerous methods. Legislation that provides authorizations, revenues, and appropriations constitutes one set of methods. Other familiar devices are laws that prescribe the structure of executive agencies and personnel policies regarding hiring, promotion, and dismissal. An informal type of oversight occurs when a legislator or a legislative staff member contacts an agency about specific day-to-day operations. Although legislators may have no official power to command any action by an agency, their wishes will be treated carefully and with some urgency by agency personnel. Oversight is important in advise-and-consent proceedings in which a senate committee screens a nominee for an executive position. Commitments made by a nominee in response to questions asked during such nomination hearings can influence that person's actions once in office.

Legislative investigations and just the simple threat of investigation are other instruments of oversight. A legislative committee chair may greatly influence an agency by suggesting that investigative hearings will be scheduled unless certain practices are changed within the agency.

Greater specificity of legislative intent is being used to reduce executive discretion. In the past, ambiguous language was used as a deliberate tool for delegating responsibilities to the executive and increasing executive flexibility in carrying out policies. The opposite is common today. State legislatures attempt to establish legislative intent through the use of wording contained in line items, footnotes, and concluding sections to appropriation bills; the use of committee reports; and the use of letters of intent delivered to the governor.

Legislatures often find it difficult to enforce legislative intent. What if an agency stays within the legal prescriptions of legislative intent but violates its spirit? The punitive action of cutting the agency's budget often is not possible. Citizens benefiting from agency programs would be harmed as well as the agency itself. Therefore, the main punitive alternative may be to impose more restrictions on the agency, such as making legislative intent more explicit, specifically pro-hibiting various practices, and increasing the number of line items in the agency's budget to hamstring its flexibility.

The legislature may also attempt to enforce legislative intent by requiring agencies to collect and provide specific information to the legislature. This prac-tice denies agencies the tactic of confessing ignorance about their own programs If legislation indicates that an agency is to collect specific data, the agency will be expected to deliver it at designated times every year.

Congress often adopts appropriation bills that have detailed language. In par-ticular, the foreign assistance program is said to be hamstrung by crosscutting leg-islative requirements built into appropriations. For example, appropriations spec-ify how much each country will receive. In addition, appropriations specify the amounts that will be spent on programs such as child survival, population, the environment, and natural resources. Executives of the Agency for International Development must plan their expenditures within a matrix that links programs with nations even though more flexible planning might better serve foreign poli-cy objectives.

Sunset Legislation and Zero-Base Budgeting. Another type of oversight mechanism consists of sunset legislation coupled with zero-base budgeting (see Chapter 6). Programs are authorized to exist for a given period, after which they expire (the sun sets on them). Before a program's expiration date, an agency may be required to present a zero-base budget indicating the achievements of the agency's program and the projected consequences if the program is not renewed. Depending on how these proposals are implemented, they can provide greater leverage for the legis-lature. For these reasons, sunset legislation is used widely by state legislatures.

Information and Analysis. Program budgeting and analysis constitute another approach to legislative oversight. Legislatures are increasingly demanding impact and output data from agencies. Such demands have reinforcing effects on chief executives' efforts to install program budgeting. At the federal level, the Government Performance and Results Act of 1993 and President George W. Bush's initiative to better integrate budgeting and performance measurement are expected to result in increased programmatic information being presented to Congress as well as to the president (see Chapter 6).

Tensions exist over which organizational units should conduct analyses. Legislatures have sometimes given little attention to oversight, and the function has fallen to audit agencies that at the state level are often headed by independ-ently elected auditors. When legislative bodies later develop their own analytic capabilities, turf issues arise.[73] Virginia's Joint Legislative Audit and Review

Commission and Florida's Office of Program Policy Analysis and Government Accountability are examples of state legislative analysis units.[74]

At the federal level, the Government Accountability Office (GAO) has an extensive ongoing research agenda that examines the full gamut of government programs.[75] The fact that the GAO works for Congress often brings it into conflict with the executive branch. The most high-profile recent case involved the GAO's desire to obtain records of Vice President Cheney's contacts with outsiders in the process of developing the administration's energy policy. This issue became particularly salient politically after the collapse of Enron, which had ties to some high-ranking officials in the Bush administration.[76] The White House, however, maintained executive privilege and the requested documents and names were not provided to the GAO.

Information technology also makes possible greater legislative oversight. Congress and state legislatures have developed their own information systems that allow them to tap into a variety of databases, including those maintained by agencies. The application of this technology is limited by the quality of data being maintained. Computer hardware and software cannot compensate for agency neglect in collecting important information.

Legislative Veto. Legislatures are making increased use of their power to veto proposed executive actions. For instance, an agency may be granted authority to issue regulations, but a stipulation in the legislation can require the agency to obtain legislative approval prior to implementing the regulations.[77] Depending on the governing legislation, a proposed action can be vetoed by a vote in either house or both houses of a legislature, or it can be implemented only with a vote of approval from both houses. Sometimes legislative committees have veto powers. More than 40 state legislatures exercise some form of legislative veto over executive agency regulations.[78]

The legislative veto is used as a means of furthering policy. Legislative intent is served presumably by allowing the full legislature or designated committees to oversee executive implementation. The veto process can steer executive agencies away from actions that are contrary to what the legislature wishes to see implemented.

Not surprisingly, executives have a less positive view of legislative vetoes. The process often delays implementation of actions because the legislature is assured a given number of weeks to consider whether to support or veto a proposal. These vetoes are seen as giving authority to legislatures to meddle needlessly in the details of administration and, more significantly, to infringe upon the constitutional administrative powers of the executive.

A crisis seemed to develop in 1983 when the Supreme Court handed down one of its most controversial decisions in *Immigration and Naturalization Service v.*

Chadha.[79] The case dealt with congressional veto power involving the deportation of aliens. What was significant was not that the Court struck down that legislative veto, but rather that it struck down most, if not all, such vetoes at the federal level. The Court's reasoning was simple: The Constitution provides for the House and Senate to set policy subject to veto by the president and does not allow for the opposite procedure.

Following the *Chadha* decision, Congress did not rush to adopt statutory measures or seek constitutional revisions that would reinstate the legislative veto. Instead, it dealt with matters as they arose and, in some instances, largely ignored the Court's ruling. For example, subsequent appropriation bills have included legislative vetoes. In 1996, Congress passed the Congressional Review Act, that provides a form of legislative veto of agency draft regulations (see Chapter 10).[80]

Oversight Limitations. While numerous methods of oversight are available, the organizational locus of oversight remains a problem because of the fragmentation discussed earlier. A coherent approach to oversight is not possible when committee powers overlap. Every federal agency must deal with at least one (and often more) substantive committee plus the Appropriations Committee and the Budget Committee (discussed in Chapter 9) in each chamber of Congress. That is six committees at a minimum, not counting subcommittees. These committees may disagree with each other and may not have the backing of the full legislative body. Turf battles among committees are routine. For instance, the Chief Financial Officers Act of 1990 (see Chapter 11), by creating chief financial officers in agencies, enhanced the oversight powers of the House Government Reform and Oversight Committee and the Senate Governmental Affairs Committee at the expense of the Appropriations Committees.[81]

One approach to overcoming fragmentation might be to concentrate oversight in a staff unit of the legislature. For example, GAO at the federal level could be given greater oversight responsibilities. GAO already attempts to assist in establishing the oversight agenda for Congress. In fact, prior to the 2006 election, Comptroller General David Walker sent a letter to congressional leaders from both parties recommending an oversight agenda for the new Congress, regardless of which party was in control.[82] Another option would be to give oversight duties to committee staffs. The problem with these suggestions is that they tend to conflict with legislators' desire to have staffs act in subordinate and inferior capacities. For a staff unit to evaluate a program enacted by the legislative body, to find the program inadequate, and to suggest means of improving it is likely to be viewed by many legislators as an affront to their authority in setting policy. For this reason, legislative analytic units tend to be cautious in program analysis and tentative in reaching conclusions and recommendations.

A final limitation on oversight is the priorities that legislators set for themselves. Re-election is always paramount, and legislators often regard oversight activities as not contributing appreciably to their prospects for winning voter approval. In that sense, the limited oversight role performed by legislatures is seen as a completely rational response to the incentives facing them. If voters are more supportive of legislators who initiate new programs than of those who serve as watchdogs over the executive branch, legislators will respond accordingly.

Summary

A variety of factors constrain the budgetary role of legislatures. First and foremost, legislatures are representative bodies. As such, they are constrained by the methods through which individual members are selected, and often by limits on their terms. In addition to these constraints, there are others that affect how they make budget decisions. The factors that may affect how legislatures budget include the extent of fragmentation, the role of party leadership, the amount of time available to legislate, and the availability of staff.

When the budget reaches the legislature, the availability of revenue greatly influences how the legislature approaches budget approval. Previously reached decisions, such as established entitlement programs, limit action, as do numerous socioeconomic and political factors, such as the influence of interest groups. The budget is approved through the work of substantive standing committees, appropriations committees, and revenue or finance committees. These committees hold hearings and produce draft legislation that is then considered by each legislative house. In interacting with these committees, agencies use numerous strategies in seeking approval of their budgets. An administrator's initial objective may be to obtain increased funding for a program. If that is not possible, then the administrator will concentrate on protecting the base and preventing budget cuts beyond those that constitute a fair share. Fiscal notes have become important tools for tracking the financial implications of proposed legislation. Once the legislature adopts the budget, it is sent to the chief executive for approval. In many states, chief executives make use of the item veto to strike individual projects or activities from the legislative budget.

Legislative oversight has become increasingly popular. Prior legislative approval of some administrative decisions may be required. Legislative investigative hearings serve the oversight function, along with detailed specification of legislative intent. Sunset legislation and zero-base budgeting are other oversight techniques.

Notes

1. Grading the states: 2005 (2005). *Governing, Special issue, February*, 75.

2. Lienert, I. (2005). Who controls the budget: the legislature or the executive? *IMF Working Paper.* Washington, DC: International Monetary Fund.

3. Keefe, W. J. & Ogul, M. S. (2000). *The American legislative process: Congress and the states*, 10th ed. Upper Saddle River, NJ: Prentice-Hall.

4. Kurfirst, R. (1996). Direct democracy in the sunshine state: recent challenges to Florida's citizen initiative. *Comparative State Politics, 17, August*, 1–15.

5. Swoboda, D. P. (1995). Accuracy and accountability in reporting local government budget activities: evidence from the newsroom and from newsmakers. *Public Budgeting & Finance, 15, Fall*, 74–90.

6. MacManus, S. (2004). "Bricks and Mortar" politics: how infrastructure decisions defeat incumbents. *Public Budgeting & Finance, 24, Spring 2004*, 96–112.

7. *Baker v. Carr* (1962). 369 U.S. 186; *Reynolds v. Sims* (1964). 377 U.S. 533.

8. *Reno v. Bossier Parish School Board* (1997). 520 U.S. 471.

9. *Shaw v. Reno* (1993). 509 U.S. 630; *Miller v. Johnson* (1995). 515 U.S. 900; *Shaw v. Hunt* (1996). 517 U.S. 899; *Bush v. Vera* (1996). 517 U.S. 952.

10. Lane, C. & Balz, D. (2006). Justices affirm GOP map for Texas. *Washington Post, June 29*, A1.

11. Federal court involvement in redistricting litigation (2001). *Harvard Law Review, 114*, 878–901; Bates, R. P. (2005). Congressional authority to require state adoption of independent redistricting commissions. *Duke Law Journal, 55*, 333–372; Fromer, J. C. (2005). An exercise in line-drawing: deriving and measuring fairness in redistricting. *Georgetown Law Journal, 93*, 1547–1622.

12. *Abrams v. Johnson* (1997). 521 U.S. 74; *Lawyer v. Department of Justice* (1997). 521 U.S. 567.

13. *Hunt v. Chromartie* (2001). 532 U.S. 234.

14. Savage, D. G. (2001). High court flexible on redistricting. *State Legislatures, 27, June*, 21.

15. Sundquist, J. L. (1992) *Constitutional reform and effective government.* Washington, DC: Brookings Institution, 144–198.

16. Info about term limits (2006). Retrieved August 1, 2006, from http://www.termlimts.org/Current_Info/current_infor.html.

17. Term limits across America (2006). Retrieved August 1, 2006 from http://www.termlimitslorg.

18. Info about term limits (2006). Retrieved August 1, 2006, from http://www.termlimts.org/Current_Info/current_infor.html.

19. *U.S. Term Limits, Inc. v. Thornton* (1995). 514 U.S. 779.

20. Katches, M. & Weintraub, D. M. (1997). The tremors of term limits. *State Legislatures, 23, March*, 21–25.

21. Term limits erode effectiveness of legislative branch, new study finds. Retrieved August 22, 2006, from http://www.ncsl.org.

22. Greenblatt, A. (2001). Term limits: crash course. *Governing, November*. Retrieved January 20, 2007, from http://www.governing.com/archive/2001/nov/term.txt.

23. Karp, J. A. (1995). Explaining public support for legislative term limits. *Public Opinion Quarterly, 59*, 373–391.

24. Council of State Governments (2006). *Book of the states, 2006 edition.* Lexington, KY: Council of State Governments, 72–73.

25. Arnold, L. W., Deen, R. E. & Patterson, S. C. (2000). Friendship and votes: the impact of interpersonal ties on legislative decision making. *State and Local Government Review, 32*, 142–147.

26. Jewell, M. E. & Whicker, M. L. (1994). *Legislative leadership in the American states.* Ann Arbor: University of Michigan Press.

27. Clucas, R. A. (2001). Principal-agent theory and the power of state house speakers. *Legislative Studies Quarterly, 26, May*, 319–338.

28. Storey, T. (2006). 2005 legislative elections and partisan control. *Book of the States, 66.*

29. Cox, C. W. & Kernell, S. (Eds.) (1991). *The politics of divided government.* Boulder, CO: Westview Press.

30. Goodwin, G., Jr. (1970). *The little legislatures: committees of Congress.* Amherst: University of Massachusetts Press; Deering, C. & Smith, S. (1997). *Committees in Congress.* Washington, DC: CQ Press.

31. Council of State Governments (2006). *Book of the states*, 72–73.

32. Council of State Governments (2006). *Book of the states*, 119.

33. Gryski, G. S. (1991). The influence of committee position on federal program spending. *Polity, 23*, 443–459.

34. Council of State Governments (2006). *Book of the states*, 68–71.

35. Bonded (2006). *Richmond Times-Dispatch, March 5*. Retrieved August 21, 2006, from http://www.timesdispatch.com.

36. Council of State Governments (2006). *Book of the states*, 84–86.

37. Chadha, A. et al. (2001). The consequences of independence: functions and resources of state legislative fiscal offices. *State and Local Government Review, 33, Fall*, 202–207.

38. King, J. D. (2000). Changes in professionalism in U.S. state legislatures. *Legislative Studies Quarterly, 25, May*, 327–343.

39. Mahtesian, C. (1997). The sick legislature syndrome. *Governing, 10, February*, 16–20.

40. Loftus, E. (1994). *The art of legislative politics.* Washington, DC: Congressional Quarterly Press, 61–75; Gill, J. (1995). Formal models of legislative/administrative interaction: a survey of the subfield. *Public Administration Review, 55*, 99–106.

41. Clynch E. J. & Lauth, T. P. (Eds.) (1991). *Governors, legislatures, and budgets: diversity across the American states.* New York: Greenwood Press.

42. National Conferences of State Legislatures (2006). *Legislative budget procedure: a guide to appropriations and budget processes in the states, commonwealths and territories.* Retrieved August 21, 2006, from http://www.ncsl.org/programs/fiscal/ibptabls/index.htm.

43. O'Lessker, K. (1992). The new president makes a budget: from Eisenhower to Bush. *Public Budgeting & Finance, 12, Fall,* 3–18.

44. Clynch, E. J. & Lauth, T. P. (Eds.) (1991). *Governors, legislatures, and budgets.*

45. Payne, J. L. (1991). *The culture of spending: why Congress lives beyond our means.* San Francisco, CA: ICS Press.

46. Fiorina, M. (1989). *Congress: keystone of the Washington establishment*, 2nd ed. New Haven: Yale University Press.

47. Bland, R. L. & Rubin, I. S. (1987). *Budgeting: a guide for local governments.* Washington, DC: International City/County Management Association.

48. Ebdon, C & Franklin, A. (2006). Citizen participation in budgeting theory. *Public Administration Review, 66,* 437–447.

49. Dobel, J. P. (1995). Managerial leadership in divided times. *Administration and Society, 26,* 488–514.

50. Rosenbaum, D. (2002). Official forced to step down after testifying on budget cut. *New York Times, March 7,* A22.

51. Johnson, C. M. (1992). *The dynamics of conflict between bureaucrats and legislators.* Armonk, NY: M. E. Sharpe.

52. Johnson, B. (1989). The OMB budget examiner and the congressional budget process. *Public Budgeting & Finance, 9, Spring,* 5–14.

53. Wildavsky, A. & Caiden N. (2000). *The new politics of the budgetary process*, 4th ed. New York: Longman, 47–55, 59–64.

54. Wildavky, A. (1988). *The new politics of the budgetary process.* Glenview, IL: Scott Foresman and Company, 115.

55. Meyers, R. T. (1994). *Strategic budgeting.* Ann Arbor: University of Michigan Press.

56. Salamon, L. T. (2002). *The tools of government: a guide for the new governance.* Baltimore, MD: Johns Hopkins Press.

57. Stanford, K. A. (1992). State budget deliberations: do legislators have a strategy? *Public Administration Review, 52,* 16–26.

58. Unfunded Mandates Reform Act (1995). P.L. 104-4.

59. Council of State Governments (2006). *Book of the states,* 109–110.

60. Snow, D. R. (1999). Do legislative procedures affect tax expenditures? *Journal of Public Budgeting, Accounting and Financial Management, 11,* 357–385.

61. Kelly, J. M. (1994). Fiscal noting reconsidered: the experience of the states with mandate cost estimation. *Public Budgeting and Financial Management, 6,* 1–27.

62. Fenno, Jr., R. F. (1966). *The power of the purse: appropriations politics in Congress.* Boston, MA: Little, Brown; Horn, S. (1970). *Unused power: the work of the Senate Committee on Appropriations.* Washington, DC: Brookings Institution.

63. U.S. Office of Management and Budget (2006). *Legislative coordination and clearance, Circular A-19.* Retrieved August 24, 2006, from http://www.whitehouse.gov/omb/circulars/a019/a019.html#purpose.

64. Abney, G. & Lauth, T. P. (1985). The line-item veto in the states. *Public Administration Review, 45,* 372–377; Lauth, T. P. (1996). The line-item veto in government budgeting. *Public Budgeting & Finance, 16,* 97–111.

65. Alm, J. & Evers, M. (1991). The item veto and state government expenditures. *Public Choice, 68,* 1–15; Berch, N. (1992). The item veto in the states: an analysis of the effects over time. *Social Science Quarterly, 29,* 335–346; Thompson, P. & Boyd, S. R. (1994). Use of the item veto in Texas, 1940–1990. *State and Local Government Review, 26,* 38–45.

66. Lee, Jr., R. D. (2000). State item veto legal issues in the 1990s. *Public Budgeting & Finance, 20, Summer,* 49–73.

67. Bellamy, C. (1989). Item veto: dangerous constitutional tinkering. *Public Administration Review, 49,* 46–51; Sundquist, J. (1992). *Constitutional reform and effective government,* 281–294.

68. Line Item Veto Act (1996). P.L. 104-130.

69. Joyce, P. G. (1998). The line item veto act: after the Supreme Court decision, what's next? *Public Budgeting & Finance, 18, Winter,* 3–21.

70. Aberbach, J. B. (1990). *Keeping a watchful eye: the politics of congressional oversight.* Washington, DC: Brookings Institution; Evans, D. (1994). Congressional oversight and the diversity of members' goals. *Political Science Quarterly, 109,* 669–687.

71. Lewis, B. J. & Ellefson, P. V. (1996). Evaluating information flows to policy committees in state legislatures. *Evaluation Review, 20,* 29–48.

72. Lawrence, C. C. (1991). New chief financial officers straddle branches of power. *Congressional Quarterly Weekly Report, 49,* 2286–2287.

73. Walton, K. S. &. Brown, R. E. (1990). State legislators and state auditors: is there an inherent role conflict? *Public Budgeting & Finance, 10, Spring,* 3–12.

74. Joint Legislative Audit and Review Commission, Commonwealth of Virginia (2006). *Website.* Retrieved August 24, 2006, from http://jlarc.state.va.us/; Office of Program Policy Analysis and Government Accountability, State of Florida (2006). *Florida Monitor.* Retrieved August 24, 2006, from http://www.oppaga.state.fl.us/default.asp.

75. Havens, H. S. (1990). *The evolution of the General Accounting Office: from voucher audits to program evaluations.* Washington, DC: U.S. Government Printing Office; National Academy of Public Administration (1994). *The roles, mission and operation of the U.S. General Accounting Office.* Washington, DC: U.S. Government Printing Office.

76. Denniston, L. (2002). GAO sues for access to Cheney records. *Boston Globe, February 23,* A1.

77. Gibson, M. L. (1992). *Weapons of influence: the legislative veto, American foreign policy, and the irony of reform.* Boulder, CO: Westview Press.

78. Council of State Governments (2006). *Book of the states,* 129–130.

79. *Immigration and Naturalization Service v. Chadha* (1983). 462 U.S. 919.

80. Congressional Review Act (1996). P.L. 104-121.

81. Jones, L. R. (1993). Counterpoint essay: nine reasons why the CFO Act may not achieve its objectives. *Public Budgeting & Finance, 13, Spring,* 87–94.

82. Pulliam, D. (2006). GAO to recommend oversight priorities for next Congress. *GovExec.* Retrieved October 23, 2006, from http://govexec.com/story_page.cfm& articleleid=35311&dcn=e_gvet.

Chapter 9

BUDGET APPROVAL: THE U.S. CONGRESS

The preceding chapter examined the budget approval process across levels and types of government. This chapter examines the special case of Congress, which is of unique importance in the U.S. governmental system and has unique procedures. Whereas Chapter 8 emphasized similarities among governments, this chapter considers the special budgetary processes used by Congress and the problems it faces. In the process, it discusses the peculiarities of the federal budget process in general.

The chapter has four sections. The first section reviews the historical development of the modern budget process, from the passage of the Congressional Budget and Impoundment Control Act of 1974 to the deficit-based budget process reforms embodied in the Gramm-Rudman-Hollings reform and the Budget Enforcement Act of 1990. The second section reviews the timetable for the resulting budget process, from presidential budget submission to budget resolution to committee action, including reconciliation, authorizations, and appropriations. The third section chronicles the movement of the federal budget from deficit to surplus and then back to deficit again, by discussing the Omnibus Budget Reconciliation Act of 1993, the Balanced Budget Act of 1997, and developments during the George W. Bush administration (including the tax cuts and the wars that have been fought since the terrorist attacks of September 11, 2001). The last section discusses a variety of possible reforms to the budget process.

▉ Evolution of the Federal Budget Process

The federal budget process has evolved over the past eight or nine decades as it has been used to achieve particular objectives and to solve particular problems. For that reason, understanding this history is crucial to demystifying the budget process. Most of the current procedures result from two laws: the Budget and Accounting Act of 1921 and the Congressional Budget and Impoundment Control Act of 1974. In addition, there were a number of deficit-based budget reforms (such as Gramm-Rudman-Hollings and the Budget Enforcement Act) that were enacted in the 1980s and 1990s. The first of these laws, the Budget and Accounting Act of 1921, was discussed in Chapters 1 and 7. It had three main purposes. First, it created a requirement that the president submit a budget to Congress each year. Prior to the Budget and Accounting Act, federal agencies submitted their budget estimates directly to Congress. Second, it created the Bureau of the Budget (now the Office of Management and Budget) to assist the president in preparing the budget.[1] Third, it created the General Accounting Office (now the Governmental Accountability Office—see Chapter 8), initially to help control agency spending but later to do programmatic and performance audits of federal agencies and programs.[2]

The Congressional Budget and Impoundment Control Act of 1974

Congress, like the legislatures discussed in the previous chapter, conducts its work in committees. Subcommittees are especially important in the appropriations process. One group of committees, as explained in Chapter 8, has responsibility for substantive legislation. These committees develop authorizing legislation, which establishes departments and agencies and the programs they operate. An authorization provides a dollar amount as a ceiling for spending. Approval to commit the government to spend, however, is given through the appropriation process.[3]

Another set of committees provides the wherewithal for the government to operate.[4] The Ways and Means Committee in the House and the Finance Committee in the Senate fashion legislation that generates revenue for the government. In addition to being responsible for tax legislation, these committees are responsible for some substantive measures, such as Social Security and Medicare. They handle legislation permitting increases in the federal debt. Such legislation is necessary because the government typically accumulates debt by spending more than it collects in revenues. Raising the debt is a sensitive matter because members of Congress fear that their votes for debt increases can be cited by their political rivals as evidence of fiscal irresponsibility.

The Ways and Means Committee includes about 40 of the 435 members of the House, and the Finance Committee includes about 20 of the 100 members of the

Senate. The number of seats held by each party on the committees is generally proportional to total party membership in the chambers.

Discretionary, or non-entitlement, spending is under the aegis of the Appropriations Committee in each house.[5] There are more than 60 members on the House committee and approximately 30 on the Senate committee. The spending side of the budget is currently divided among 12 subcommittees in the House and an identical number in the Senate that report out appropriation bills. Appropriations permit agencies to commit the government to expenditures, with some spending occurring in subsequent budget years as a result of contracts signed in the current year.

Starting in the 1940s, two major problems with this process became abundantly clear. First, because Congress dealt with the budget through a variety of bills, the budget was handled piecemeal, making it difficult to set overall comprehensive policy. Second, the piecemeal approach meant that various subcommittees, committees, and the two chambers had to exercise discipline over themselves to complete their work in time for the beginning of the fiscal year.

When appropriation bills are not passed on time, agencies financed through the appropriations process no longer have the funds to operate and are forced to shut down. To avoid this situation, Congress passes one or more continuing appropriation bills (often called continuing resolutions). These bills permit the affected agencies to operate for a specified time period, usually spending at the same level as they did in the just-completed fiscal year. Typically, no new programs can begin spending while the agency is operating under a continuing resolution, even if budget savings have been achieved by having proposed in the budget elimination of other programs or reduction in size of other programs. When the federal government's fiscal year began on July 1, it was common for many or most appropriation bills not to have cleared Congress by the deadline, and agencies often operated for an entire fiscal year with continuing rather than regular appropriations.

Early Reforms and the Emergence of Backdoor Spending. Congress first attempted to deal with these problems by passing the Legislative Reorganization Act of 1946.[6] The law allowed Congress to agree on an overall budget package before detailed tax and spending bills were developed and approved. In 1947, the House and Senate could not reach agreement. In 1948, the chambers reached agreement and ignored it. The law's requirement for an overall budget was ignored in subsequent years.[7] Next, Congress experimented with using a single omnibus appropriation bill as a means of controlling total spending. The process seemed to work well for fiscal year 1951, but neither the Appropriations Committees nor the White House supported its continuation.[8]

During the 1960s and 1970s, the situation was complicated by what became known as backdoor spending, in which spending authority was provided outside of the appropriation process.[9] Backdoor spending may take several forms, including direct actions by substantive committees, such as contract authorizations that allow agencies to commit the government to spend and later may force the Appropriations Committees to provide the necessary funds. Substantive committees have given agencies borrowing authority, which allows them to borrow from the Treasury and spend debt receipts. Entitlement programs (Medicare and Medicaid, for example) that provide direct or mandatory spending constitute the main form of backdoor spending in that the government obligates itself to provide benefits to all qualifying applicants.

The effect of backdoor spending was that virtually all committees in Congress came to play important roles in financial decisions with no mechanism existing to coordinate their diverse activities. Many observers and participants believed that the budget was becoming increasingly uncontrollable, meaning that, barring any major readjustment in commitments to programs, much of the budget could not be altered in a given year. Contributing to this situation were multiyear government contracts with government suppliers, multiyear grants to state and local governments, entitlement programs, and interest on the national debt.[10]

As a means of controlling spending, President Nixon vetoed appropriation bills on the grounds that they included too much spending, but that action pleased neither Congress nor the agencies that were covered by the bills. Later in his administration, Nixon went ahead and signed the bills but refused to spend all of the money, a process known as impoundment. The lack of a coordinating mechanism for the budget, combined with a desire to limit impoundments, led to passage of the Congressional Budget and Impoundment Control Act of 1974.[11]

The 1974 Budget Reform. The 1974 reform legislation had many objectives.[12] One objective was to provide Congress with a means for controlling the budget as a whole, namely, linking appropriation bills with each other and linking these with revenue measures. Controlling the budget as a whole was seen as essential if Congress was to influence economic policy. Resolving conflict between Congress and the president was another important objective that required dealing with the impoundment problem. Members of Congress wished to assert their policy-making role vis-à-vis the presidency. A process was needed by which Congress could complete its work on the budget by the beginning of the fiscal year.

Taken as a whole, the Budget Act of 1974 had four main effects. First, it created a new mechanism, the budget resolution, to express the overall will of Congress on budget issues. Second, it created the Budget Committees to marshal the budget resolution through Congress. Third, it created the Congressional

Budget Office, a new agency intended to provide Congress with information on the budget and the economy. Finally, it established a new procedure for dealing with presidential impoundments.[13]

The Budget Resolution. Under the procedures established by the Budget Act of 1974, Congress would adopt a concurrent budget resolution that established the overall outline of the budget (a concurrent resolution is an action that is taken by both houses of Congress that does not require the president's signature). The resolution would represent a "blueprint" for the budget, showing aggregate budget numbers—revenues, budget authority (the authority to commit the government to spend money), outlays (the actual spending of funds out of the Treasury), the overall target (budget deficit or surplus, if any), and government debt.

Following passage of the concurrent resolution in the spring, Congress then reverted to its old procedures. Committees in Congress needed to adopt individual pieces of legislation affecting revenues and spending within the constraints imposed by the budget resolution. Subcommittees of the Appropriations Committees considered specific appropriation bills, and the revenue committees considered their portion of the budget. To allow for accommodating changes in policy, a second resolution was to be adopted by September 15. That resolution could be used for *reconciliation*, a process in which committees were instructed to adjust spending and revenue measures upward or downward to conform to the overall budget plan. The beginning of the fiscal year was shifted from July 1 to October 1, thereby giving Congress three additional months for its annual budgetary work.

The Budget Committees. To provide for coordination among the various components of Congress, the 1974 law established House and Senate Budget Committees, whose members are representatives from the chambers' leadership and relevant committees—the four major money committees and the substantive committees that provide authorizations. As of 2007 (the beginning of the 110th Congress), there were 39 members on the House Budget Committee and 23 on the Senate Budget Committee. The Budget Committees were to serve two functions. First, they had jurisdiction over the development of the budget resolution itself, putting them in the center of macro-level budget policy. Second, they were to serve as watchdogs, making sure that legislation was not substantially at variance with the resolution, although they lacked authority to overrule other committees. The resolution could be enforced through points of order, which would make legislation not consistent with the resolution more difficult to enact.

The Congressional Budget Office. The law also provided Congress with additional staff support by creating the Congressional Budget Office (CBO) to serve as overall staff to the Budget Committees, the other four money committees, and any other committees or individuals in Congress that need assistance in the area of budgeting. CBO's charge was to serve Congress in a nonpartisan manner, presenting "just the facts." Given that charge, CBO decided that it would refrain from providing policy recommendations. It was to play three main roles:

1. Developing the budget baseline (a current services estimate) that would prove to be the starting point for the resolution;
2. Estimating the costs of proposed legislation; and
3. Conducting policy research on issues before Congress.[14]

The CBO currently has a staff of about 230. It had seven directors from its creation through this writing: Alice Rivlin, Rudolph Penner, Robert Reischauer, June O'Neill, Dan Crippen, Douglas Holtz-Eakin, and Peter Orszag, who was named director in early 2007.

Impoundment Control. Prior to the passage of the 1974 legislation, the Nixon administration claimed it was simply following in the footsteps of virtually every president since Thomas Jefferson in deciding not to spend all of the funds that were appropriated.[15] The Anti-Deficiency Act of 1950, allowing the executive to establish agency reserves in the apportionment process (see Chapter 10), was used as further justification for impounding monies.[16]

Not only did the Nixon administration use impoundment to control total spending, but the process also was used to halt spending on grant programs that the president wanted consolidated into block grants (see Chapter 14). Several court suits were filed, which generally were decided in favor of releasing funds, but the Supreme Court never addressed the issue of whether the president has the constitutional power to impound monies.

The Congressional Budget and Impoundment Control Act represented a compromise between the legislative and executive branches, albeit one that the Nixon administration was forced to accept. Two forms of impoundments were permitted: rescissions and deferrals. When in the judgment of the president part of or all funds of a given appropriation were not needed, a *rescission* proposal (a proposal to cancel budget authority already provided) was to be made to Congress. The rescission would not take effect unless approved by Congress within 45 working days. The other type of impoundment, deferral, was a proposal to delay obligations or expenditures. Like rescissions, deferral proposals had to be submitted to Congress, but they became effective unless either the House or the Senate passed a resolution disapproving them.

The impoundment process was dealt a major blow by the Supreme Court in *Immigration and Naturalization Service v. Chadha* (1983), which prohibited most uses of the legislative veto (see Chapter 8).[17] In effect, the 1975 law had given the president a form of item veto coupled with a legislative veto, in which Congress had an opportunity to veto actions taken by the president, but those provisions were nullified by the *Chadha* decision. The president, then, has been forced to request congressional action on policy rescissions and deferrals. The *Chadha* decision did not deal with the constitutionality of the item veto, a topic addressed later in this chapter.   '

The Arrival of Large Deficits, 1981–1985

The Budget Act of 1974 established procedures and institutions to govern priority-setting in Congress, but was largely silent concerning budget outcomes. That is, no assumptions were made about the appropriate size of the federal budget or budget deficit. The focus of the budget process changed substantially in the 1980s, however, largely in response to the unprecedented large deficits ushered in during the administration of President Ronald W. Reagan.[18] Reagan came into office in January 1981 following a major victory at the polls during the previous November. The 1980 election created a phenomenon not seen since the 83rd Congress of 1953: the Senate dominated by a Republican majority, the House remaining under the control of the Democrats, and a Republican president. Reagan submitted a set of budget proposals that provided for severe budget cuts in domestic programs, a shift toward the use of block grants to state and local governments (see Chapter 14), an increase in defense spending, and a massive set of cuts in the personal income tax that became law in the Economic Recovery Tax Act of 1981.[19] Although the House of Representatives was under the control of the Democrats, Reagan was so popular that few political leaders dared to speak out against his recommended policies.

During the early Reagan years, OMB began to play an increasingly important role.[20] Previously, it had the job of making overall presentations on the budget before congressional committees, but the defense of specific recommended appropriations was left to the affected departments. After Reagan's election, major realignments in policies were being recommended on both the revenue and the expenditure sides of the budget, and the defense of these recommendations became the job of OMB.[21]

The Deficit. A cloud soon developed that ended the euphoria of early 1981, as the budget deficit began to grow at an alarming rate.[22] As early as 1983, Reagan budget director David Stockman famously (and accurately) predicted "$200 billion deficits as far as the eye can see."[23] The administration had championed the 1981 massive tax cuts as a means of stimulating the economy and thereby increasing revenues. Though there was a supporting theoretical tradition in economics long before the 1981 tax cuts, 1980–81 was the first time that supply side economics specifically led to change in tax law, namely tax cuts were expected to produce such stimulative effects on the economy that growth in the economy would more than make up for the lost revenue from the cuts. The economy was stimulated, but not enough to avoid large deficits. Subsequently, Congress used various tactics to escape having to vote on budget resolutions that would show the budget badly out of balance. Members wanted to avoid voting directly on increases in the federal debt by embedding the provision in an overall budget package. The debt limit had to be raised to $1.1 trillion in 1981 and $2.1 trillion in 1985.

Stalemate. Substantive issues were partially to blame for Congress's inability to adhere to the prescribed timetable. During these years, President Reagan took a firm stand on priorities. He wanted the tax cuts that had been approved in the 1981 law, wanted a buildup in defense capability, insisted that programs such as Social Security be protected from budget cuts, and at the same time sought a balanced budget.[24] All of those objectives simply could not be met simultaneously. If the budget were to be brought into balance by reducing its unprotected areas, which included an array of social programs such as Aid to Families with Dependent Children, decimation of the remaining part of the federal government would be required. As a consequence, a stalemate between the president and Congress developed, with the two occasionally reaching agreement on actions that only marginally improved the situation.

Reconciliation. As noted earlier, reconciliation was intended to provide in one resolution directed guidance to committees on how they should alter authorizing, taxing, and spending legislation. The process was envisioned as coming at the end of the budget approval phase. However, in the years following the 1974 reforms, the House and Senate Budget Committees were reluctant to use reconciliation because it would have been seen as an infringement on the domains of powerful committees and as a personal affront to the committee chairs.

The reconciliation process was used for the first time in 1980, the last year of the Carter administration, and from that time forward it became a prominent feature of congressional budgeting.[25] Significantly, reconciliation was used early in the 1981 approval process, with the bill clearing Congress in July rather than in September, as originally intended. Early action was needed to give affected committees sufficient time to adhere to the reconciliation instructions, such as reducing amounts in a given appropriation bill. The current use of reconciliation is discussed below as a part of the discussion of the general budget timetable.

Controllability and Policy Making. The deficit situation during the 1980s imposed constraints on Congress in regard to what it could and could not fund. The Reagan administration proposed numerous program cuts that were unpopular in

Congress. While Congress had every right to reject the president's recommendations, in rejecting the proposed savings and trying to avoid adopting a budget more out of balance than that recommended by the president, Congress was forced to find offsetting measures to raise revenues, cut expenditures, or both. The result was a tendency to impose across-the-board budget cuts on programs. As a consequence, programs became smaller and smaller. Advocates of programs struggled to maintain the existence of programs no matter how small they might become. "Staying alive" became an objective, as it would be extremely difficult to revive a program once cut out of the budget. Continuing resolutions became the norm, which created substantial uncertainty for federal agencies and recipients of government funds. Deficits continued to grow, as there was a large structural imbalance between revenues and spending.

The Gramm-Rudman-Hollings Era, 1985–1990

The situation came to a head in the latter part of 1985. Democrats agreed with Republicans and representatives agreed with senators that the deficit situation had become intolerable. The White House did not exhibit the same level of concern but concurred that something should be done to remedy the situation.

By October 1, 1985, the beginning of the fiscal year, not a single appropriation bill had cleared Congress. A stopgap continuing appropriation bill was passed to keep the government operating. The budget resolution had been adopted on August 1 despite the official deadline of May 15. By November, both the stopgap appropriation bill and the debt-limit ceiling were expiring, forcing another stopgap appropriation bill and an increase in the debt ceiling to be rushed through Congress.

Enactment of the Law. It was in this politically charged atmosphere that Congress adopted the Balanced Budget and Emergency Deficit Control Act of 1985.[26] The chief authors were Senators W. Philip Gramm (Republican of Texas), Warren B. Rudman (Republican of New Hampshire), and Ernest F. Hollings (Democrat of South Carolina). As an indication of how Congress had changed, both Gramm and Rudman were serving their first terms in the Senate. In an earlier time, only more senior senators would have authored legislation of such importance.

The main objective of Gramm-Rudman-Hollings was simple: to reduce the size of the budget deficit annually until expenditures were in balance with revenues. Target figures were set, and if the president and Congress could not reach agreement on a budget package that met the target figure for a given fiscal year, then automatic across-the-board reductions in expenditures were to occur—a process known as sequestration. Senator Rudman described the law as "a bad idea whose time has come."[27]

Legal Challenge and Revision. As soon as the law was enacted, it was challenged in court. The case was brought on appeal to the Supreme Court, which ruled in July 1986 that one key provision violated the Constitution.[28] The comptroller general, who headed the General Accounting Office and as such is an officer of Congress, was found to have been granted executive powers in violation of the Constitution.

After much debate, Congress, in September 1987, adopted the Balanced Budget and Emergency Deficit Control Reaffirmation Act, which modified the original Gramm-Rudman-Hollings legislation.[29] In the interim between the Supreme Court's ruling and the 1987 revisions, the Republicans lost control of the Senate in the November 1986 elections. When Congress convened in January 1987, the Democrats controlled both chambers while the White House was still occupied by President Reagan.

Timetable. Gramm-Rudman-Hollings, as amended, provided a new timetable for Congress to act on the budget and set new target figures for annual budget reductions until the budget was supposed to be balanced in fiscal 1993. The Gramm-Rudman-Hollings process began with the president's submission of the budget in early January. Provisions were made for calculating a baseline, which is analogous to current services calculations. The baseline projects budget authority, outlays, revenues, and the resulting unified budget deficit or surplus for the budget year and subsequent ones. Congress then was to prepare its budget resolution in response to the president's recommendations. Reconciliation was to be completed in June, after which the president was to prepare a midsession budget due in July.

Sequestration. Gramm-Rudman-Hollings created a new procedure—called sequestration—that was to impose budget reductions if the procedures were not followed. Some cuts were to be taken from appropriated spending and some from mandatory spending. Of the appropriated cuts, half were apportioned to defense and the other half to domestic programs. On the mandatory side, special rules applied to some domestic programs, such as Medicare and guaranteed student loans. The rules generally limited the severity of sequestration. Other programs, projects, and activities (PPAs) were totally protected from sequestration. These included the basic retirement program under Social Security, Aid to Families with Dependent Children, civil service retirement funds, and the like. The budgets of Congress and the courts were subject to sequestration.

Gramm-Rudman-Hollings was overtaken by events in 1987. Less than a month after Congress passed the Reaffirmation Act of 1987, the stock market crashed. On Tuesday, October 19, the Dow Jones Industrial Average dropped 23% (508 points), a greater drop than the 13% decline on October 28, 1929.[30]

The crash, as would be expected, startled private and public sector leaders. Although a feared depression did not materialize, the situation served as a catalyst to force an agreement on budget deficit reduction. In November, a two-year agreement was reached by the president and Congress on cutting the deficit, but by no means eliminating it. After four stopgap measures, Congress on December 22 passed a huge continuing appropriation bill, along with a reconciliation bill, for the remainder of the fiscal year.

Gramm-Rudman-Hollings and the 1987 budget accord contributed to the trend toward centralization mentioned earlier. Both provided for decision making to be handled by central players, with lesser figures being told what the parameters of the budget would be.

The 1980s closed without Gramm-Rudman-Hollings having appreciably affected the overall budget deficit situation of the government.[31] In fact, the Gramm-Rudman-Hollings targets were routinely met by basing presidential budgets and congressional budget resolutions on unrealistically optimistic economic assumptions. Nothing in the act required the president and the Congress to do anything when (invariably) these projections did not come true.

The 1990 Budget Summit and the Budget Enforcement Act

President George H. W. Bush was elected in 1988 and almost immediately faced a rapidly deteriorating budget outlook. While the process limped along under the Gramm-Rudman-Hollings act during 1989, by late summer 1990 the budget situation had reached another crisis stage. If Congress were to live within the constraints imposed by Gramm-Rudman-Hollings, it would have required a massive reduction in the deficit in a single year. Because this result was not credible or possible, political leaders of both parties became convinced that another approach to deficit reduction was necessary. A budget "summit" was held between Bush administration officials and key members of Congress in late 1990, which ultimately resulted in the passage of the Omnibus Budget Reconciliation Act of 1990 (OBRA 1990). OBRA 1990 included a combination of revenue increases, reductions in mandatory spending, and budget enforcement procedures estimated to reduce cumulative deficits by almost $500 billion between fiscal year 1991 and fiscal year 1995.[32]

The Budget Enforcement Act. The Budget Enforcement Act (BEA), which was established by Title XIII of OBRA 1990, provided for a new budget process that officially only temporarily replaced Gramm-Rudman-Hollings. The 1990 law shifted emphasis away from fixed annual targets for the budget deficit. In effect, it was based on the premise that Congress had little control over the total annual deficit and that the emphasis should therefore be on those areas over which control was possible. Entitlement program expenditures were allowed to fluctuate according to shifts in the eligibility pools. The law also exempted the budget from emergencies. The Persian Gulf War and the bailout of failed savings and loan institutions were to fall under this heading.[33] Spending limits, or caps, were set for the discretionary portion of the budget. These caps were considered to be reductions in the deficit because they did not allow discretionary spending to grow as fast as inflation.

The Budget Enforcement Act established so-called *firewalls* for discretionary spending, separating the three areas of defense, international aid, and domestic spending. Spending caps were set for each area for fiscal 1991, 1992, and 1993, and overall budget caps were set for 1994 and 1995. The significance of the firewalls was that each area was protected from possible budget cuts in response to budget increases in one of the other areas. For instance, the rules prevented defense advocates from trying to avoid cuts by proposing extra cuts in domestic programs. When the Soviet Union crumbled and Eastern European nations dismantled their communist governments, the existence of a single cap after 1994 allowed the targets to be reached through cuts in the defense budget: the "peace dividend."

The BEA also created a *pay-as-you-go* (PAYGO) process affecting laws governing revenues and entitlement programs. The PAYGO system required that, in a given Congress, the overall effect of policies that would expand entitlement spending or decrease revenues relative to the baseline should be deficit-neutral. In practice, it was intended to focus attention not only on the cost of the policy change but also on tradeoffs with existing tax or spending programs. PAYGO gave an advantage to those programs already budgeted and made difficult the inclusion of new or expanded initiatives. The Budget Enforcement Act, along with its parent the Omnibus Budget Reconciliation Act of 1990, were successful inasmuch as they limited the growth in programs, but they were not intended to eliminate the annual deficit and had no such effect. The laws successfully kept the budget process under control through the 1992 presidential election, a primary objective of many political leaders. Members of Congress came to the realization that whatever proposals they wished to advance, a price was to be placed on them. Neither tax cuts nor spending increases could be advocated without taking into account their effects on the overall deficit. The 110th Congress upon taking office in 2007 vowed to reinstate a PAYGO approach to counter a return to large budget deficits.

■ The Resulting Congressional Timetable

When put together, these four laws—the Budget and Accounting Act, the Budget Act of 1974, Gramm-Rudman-Hollings, and the BEA—had by 1990 prescribed the rules and the timetable for enacting the federal budget each year. As will be discussed in a subsequent section, neither Gramm-Rudman-Hollings nor the BEA are currently in effect. Gramm-Rudman-Hollings was effectively superseded by the

Table 9–1 Federal Budget Process Timetable, Fiscal Year 2007

Date	Action to Be Completed
Between the first Monday in January and the first Monday in February	President transmits the budget
Six weeks later	Congressional committees report budget estimates to Budget Committees
April 15	Action to be completed on congressional budget resolution
May 15	House consideration of annual appropriation bills may begin
June 15	Action to be completed on reconciliation
June 30	Action on appropriations to be completed by House
July 15	President transmits mid-session review of the budget
October 1	Fiscal year begins

Source: Reprinted from U.S. Office of Management and Budget (2006). *The budget system and concepts, budget of the United States Government, fiscal year 2007: analytical perspectives.* Washington, DC: U.S. Office of Management and Budget, 381.

BEA, and the BEA itself was allowed to expire by Congress and President Bush after Fiscal Year 2002. At this point, therefore, the Budget and Accounting Act of 1921 and the Congressional Budget Act of 1974 are the remaining controlling budget process laws.

This section of the chapter summarizes the steps in the budget process as a chronology of events. Each year, the budget process begins (not quite in earnest, but it begins) with the president's budget submission in early February. It continues (with luck) only until October 1, with all appropriations enacted prior to the start of the fiscal year. More frequently, the process continues beyond October 1, as one or more bills fail to become law by the statutory deadline. **Table 9–1** shows the timetable for budgetary action as applied to the fiscal year 2007 budget process.

Submission of the President's Budget Request

As noted in Chapter 6, chief executives submit their budget proposals hoping that the legislature will "rubber stamp" the plans, but expecting (except in cases where the legislature is very weak) that significant changes will be made. Congress is an extremely strong and professional legislative body, so the president's budget is viewed as only the "first shot" in what is almost invariably an annual budgetary war.

The law provides that a president submit his budget to Congress no later than the first Monday in February. In practice, this schedule has been met except for cases where new presidents have just taken office on January 20. In this case, OMB normally submits current services estimates by the February deadline, and the new president submits policy proposals, in the form of amendments to the budget, within two months.

The Budget Resolution and Reconciliation

Congress responds to the president's budget request by producing its overall plan for the budget, in the form of its budget resolution. As noted earlier, the budget resolution, created as a coordinating mechanism by the 1974 Budget Act, serves as the overall blueprint for the budget. It also may result in reconciliation, an optional process used to make changes in revenues and mandatory spending.

The Budget Resolution. Under the current timetable, Congress is to complete work on the budget resolution by April 15 of each year. The groundwork for the development of the budget resolution is typically done by the Congressional Budget Office, whose annual report *The Budget and Economic Outlook* presents baseline budget estimates 10 years into the future.[34] This is designed to give Congress a reasonable idea of the starting point for its deliberations. The budget resolution ultimately includes aggregate budget targets (total revenue, total budget authority, and the like), functional budget targets, and allocations of budget authority and revenue authority to congressional committees. Committees are not permitted to exceed these targets—called Section 302(a) allocations—and face procedural points of order on the House and (particularly) Senate floor if they attempt to do so.[35]

The budget resolution, in practice, is a tricky annual spring ritual in which the House and Senate Budget Committees must each work with other committees and members to forge an agreement that will withstand later challenges as the details of the budget are prepared. In many years, the budget resolution has not been adopted by the statutory deadline because of difficulties in reaching agreement within one house or (in particular) between both houses. An extreme version of this problem would be the failure to adopt a budget resolution at all. For example, no budget resolution was enacted for the following fiscal years: 1999, 2003, 2005, and 2007.[36] The current budget timetable provides that, if Congress has not enacted a budget resolution prior to May 15, the appropriations committees can begin to act on appropriation bills without any limits that would have been imposed by the budget resolution.

Reconciliation. Reconciliation, an optional procedure, has been used since 1980 primarily during years when some major change is anticipated affecting either mandatory spending or revenues. When the procedure is used, reconciliation instructions are included in the budget resolution that will tell committees to produce legislation that has the effect of reducing spending and increasing revenues.[37] At least six major observations can be made about the use of reconciliation.

1. The size and complexity of these bills defy individual comprehension. When these bills are assembled, even the members of the originating committees may not be familiar with all the details spread across hundreds of pages.

2. Large bills are open invitations to pork barrel politics. Some members will succeed in adding pet projects or programs that, if required to stand by themselves for approval, might not be accepted by Congress.

3. Large bills place presidents at a distinct disadvantage in that they must either accept or reject the bills in their entirety. On the other hand, reconciliation bills differ from appropriations in that they do not need to pass, and Congress has sometimes been hard-pressed to get the president to go along with them on reconciliation.

4. Large bills are compatible with congressional desires to avoid blame. Members of the House or Senate cannot be held accountable for their votes supporting any one aspect of a bill, because they can say they felt compelled to vote for the bill even though it admittedly was flawed in numerous respects.

5. The use of large bills and Congress's preoccupation with budgeting in the 1980s contributed to centralization of decision making at a time when Congress had been democratized. Power was redirected to those members of Congress most closely associated with the budget process. Further, because reconciliation bills cannot be filibustered, some have argued that they changed the operations of the Senate in a way that no longer gives sufficient protection to legislative minorities.[38] In fact, the protections offered by reconciliation caused the George W. Bush administration to use reconciliation bills as a means to ease passage of its legislative agenda (including tax cuts, which were passed as a result of reconciliation) without the normal hurdles that such changes would face, particularly in the Senate.[39]

6. Sometimes members of the Appropriations Committees have expressed concern that their powers are diminished through the reconciliation process, which is under the direction of the Budget Committees. In reality, reconciliation involves other members of Congress besides those who serve on the House and Senate Budget Committees. In working out a conference bill between the two chambers, the numerous subconference committees created include conferees who are not members of either the House or Senate Budget

Committees. Nevertheless, the Appropriations Committees see the situation as centralizing power in the hands of the Budget Committees.

The Authorization Process

Theoretically, federal programs must be authorized and appropriated. Authorizations play an important role in federal budgeting. They establish or change federal programs, and they create the terms and conditions under which those programs operate. Authorizations can be provided for one year (as is common for defense programs), for multiple years (Congress passes an agriculture authorization—or "farm bill"—every four to five years), or permanently (many mandatory spending programs). In the case of mandatory spending programs, authorizations provide spending directly. Major entitlement programs are authorized and appropriations are provided simultaneously. An entitlement such as Social Security, for example, is created by an authorization and the authorization itself creates the obligation for the federal government to spend money that goes to program beneficiaries.

For discretionary spending, the authorization does not provide the appropriation directly, but rather creates a program that may or may not later be funded in the appropriations process. These authorizations typically include what are called "authorizations of appropriations," which are intended to provide guidance to the appropriations committees but are not binding on them. In fact, the appropriations committees routinely enact appropriations for programs that have no authorization at all. In fiscal year 2006, Congress appropriated $159 billion for programs whose authorizations had expired.[40]

The Appropriations Process

While the reconciliation process is optional and the authorization process does not happen for all programs in all years, there is nothing optional or episodic about the process of enacting annual appropriations. In fact, enacting the regular appropriations bills is the only budget action that Congress has to take each year. Without appropriations, federal agencies cannot pay staff or contractors and cannot deliver basic benefits. For this reason, in most years the main focus of the budget process is on the fate of appropriations. The appropriations process itself involves several kinds of activities, including action in subcommittee, action in committee, action by the full House and Senate, conference committee action, and negotiation with the White House.

Subcommittee and Committee Action. Both the House and the Senate have Appropriations Committees. Historically, the Appropriations Committee in each house was divided into 13 subcommittees, which do the substantive work of crafting the detailed bills that fund each individual budget account. Each subcommittee produces a bill that funds various cabinet departments and (sometimes) related agencies. The number of subcommittees changed in 2005, when a rather contentious reform of the process created some disconnect between the House and the Senate subcommittee structure. As a result, the House had only 10 subcommittees while the Senate had 12. This reform was allegedly driven by the desire of House Majority Leader Tom Delay (Republican of Texas) to put NASA in a more favorable position by not having to compete for resources in the same appropriation bill with the Department of Veterans Affairs.[41]

Prior to the creation of the Department of Homeland Security which among other things consolidated some previously independent agencies as well as pulled functions out of other departments into the new department, agencies' funding appeared in only one of the appropriations acts. Congress has not yet, and may not, realigned its subcommittee structure and its appropriations process with the executive reorganization. As a result, some agencies have appropriations in more than one appropriations act.

With the takeover of Congress by the Democrats in 2007, more changes were made in the makeup of committee jurisdictions. The legislative branch, which had been handled by the full committee in the House, was once again given subcommittee status in both houses. The Transportation and Treasury subcommittee was once again broken up, with separate subcommittees for Transportation, Housing and Urban Development and Related Agencies, and Financial Services and General Government. Once again this will mean that both houses will have parallel committee structures, a move that is designed to make the appropriations process run more smoothly. **Table 9–2** lists the jurisdiction of the subcommittees

Table 9–2	Appropriations Subcommittees in Houses of Congress, 2007

Agriculture, Rural Development, and Related Agencies
Commerce, Justice, and Science
Defense
Financial Services and General Government
Energy and Water
Homeland Security
Interior and Related Agencies
Labor, Health and Human Services, Education, and Related Agencies
Legislative Branch
Military Construction and Veterans Affairs
State, Foreign Operations, and Related Programs
Transportation, Housing and Urban Development

(that is, which federal agencies and programs are financed by which subcommittee) in the House and the Senate. The jurisdictional arrangements shown in the table reflect the 2007 change in jurisdictions.

As noted earlier, the Appropriations Committees receive a 302(a) allocation as a part of the budget resolution. It effectively tells the committees how much money they have to divide up in aggregate. At an early stage of the process, the committees divide these allocations by subcommittee. These Section 302(b) allocations tell Congress how much money will be available to divide among the various agencies funded as a part of each subcommittee's bill. In other words, the 302(a) allocations establish the size of the appropriated pie, while the 302(b) suballocations tell each subcommittee how large a slice it will have.

After the suballocations have been set, the subcommittees work to produce appropriation bills. Appropriation bills become law in the same way that other bills become law. They must ultimately be passed by both houses in identical form and approved by the president. For appropriation bills, getting to this point involves a lengthy process:

- *Subcommittee action*—where hearings are held (see Chapter 8) and initial allocations are made to each account in each appropriation bill. Each subcommittee is headed by a chairperson who exercises substantial influence over the operations of agencies under the subcommittee's jurisdiction. In fact, the subcommittee "chairman's mark" represents the starting point for deliberations on the appropriation bill, and the bill is considered by the full committee under a process know as the "mark-up," where amendments to the bill are considered in the subcommittee.

- *Full committee action*—where typically the actions of the subcommittee are ratified with very little change.

- *Floor action*—where procedural limitations in each house restrict what amendments may be proposed, and where amendments that add money normally need to be offset by reductions.

- *Conference action*—where selected members of appropriations subcommittees in each house convene to work out differences between bills.

- *Presidential action*—where the president exercises his constitutional authority to approve or veto appropriation bills.

The process of getting through these steps is time-consuming, and often one or more appropriation bills does not become law prior to the beginning of the fiscal year. There were only three years between 1977 and 2006 when all appropriations cleared Congress prior to the start of the fiscal year.[42] In a recent example,

Congress failed to complete 10 of the 12 fiscal year 2007 appropriation bills before adjourning in October 2006. The new Democratic Congress, in an unprecedented move, decided to enact a continuing resolution to cover the rest of the government for the entirety of fiscal year 2007, with the stated goal of giving the new Congress time to focus on the fiscal year 2008 appropriations process.

Appropriations can be a source of great conflict within Congress, or between Congress and the administration. Perhaps the clearest recent case of this conflict was between President Clinton and Congress in 1995 and 1996, leading to two separate lengthy government shutdowns. This case is discussed in more detail in the next section. There is every chance, however, that the conflict between President Bush and the Democratic Congress may be equally acrimonious. Even though both sides have pledged to eliminate the deficit by fiscal year 2012, it is probable that any agreement on how to achieve that goal will not be easy to reach.

Another source of conflict in the appropriations process has to do with items that are added to the budget by Congress but were not in the president's budget. The incentives facing Congress and the president lead them to pursue different types of priorities. While not confined to the appropriations process, "pork barrel politics" (see Chapter 8) is perhaps most visible in the appropriations process. The pursuit of these special-interest priorities has led to the effort to provide the president with the line-item veto, as discussed in the last section of this chapter.[43]

From Deficit to Surplus to Deficit, 1991–2007

The Omnibus Budget Reconciliation Act of 1990, while it did not promise a balanced budget, was projected to put the budget on a path to that budgetary promised land. But, while a CBO analysis done immediately after the passage of OBRA 1990 projected a deficit of only $29 billion by fiscal year 1995, an analysis done only 13 months later projected a deficit in excess of $200 billion by mid-decade.[44] This deterioration resulted from the effects of economic recession, not because of any policy actions. It meant, among other things, that the deficit was a salient issue in the 1992 presidential campaign, which saw the election of Bill Clinton. The same election also featured the strong showing of third-party candidate Ross Perot, who was able to garner enough votes that Clinton was elected with only 43% of the popular vote. Because many of Perot's supporters had been advocates of greater deficit reduction, both political parties needed to appeal to these voters by embracing deficit reduction as a policy goal.[45]

Coming into office in January 1993, President Clinton attempted to follow through on his campaign promise to bring the budget deficit under control. In fact, the Clinton administration embraced deficit reduction as a top priority only after it failed to gain congressional approval of a proposed stimulus package to bolster a weak economy. Critics, who claimed the package was unnecessary because the economy was already on the rebound and because the government could not afford more spending at a time when the deficit was high, were successful in defeating the proposal in the Senate. The administration then turned its attention to a comprehensive deficit reduction proposal.[46]

The 1993 Budget Agreement

The Omnibus Budget Reconciliation Act of 1993, adopted in August 1993, was approved by the narrowest of margins: 218 to 216 in the House and 51 to 50 in the Senate (Vice President Gore cast the tie-breaking vote).[47] The measure was passed without any Republican votes (neither on the reconciliation bill nor on the budget resolution that preceded it) and with considerable pressure applied by Republican members to have their Democratic colleagues join them in the opposition. The Clinton administration knew that the vote would be close, so the White House lobbied members with great intensity. As a result, all members had ample opportunity to be involved in the process of adopting the budget, unlike in earlier situations, such as in 1990, when the rank and file complained that the leadership had made all of the decisions.

The 1993 law included four types of actions:

1. Tax increases, particularly increases in individual income taxes for the wealthiest Americans, gasoline taxes, and corporate taxes;

2. Spending cuts, notably cuts in Medicare, Medicaid, and defense, but in other programs as well;

3. Spending increases, such as for empowerment zones, which are designated urban and rural areas that are provided with increased services to attract business; and

4. Tax expenditures, such as tax credits for lower-income workers and tax incentives for businesses operating in empowerment zones.

Overall, the law was expected to shrink, but in no way eliminate, the deficit. The spending caps and the PAYGO process from the Budget Enforcement Act were revised and extended through fiscal 1998.[48] Annual deficits under the law were expected to approach $200 billion. Because nearly $500 billion in deficits was to be eliminated over five years, the debt was expected to increase by "only" $1.1 trillion over that same period. The total deficit reductions were expected to be equal to or somewhat less than the reductions that resulted from the Budget Enforcement Act of 1990. If the administration wanted to tackle the budget deficit in earnest, then another round of spending cuts and tax increases would be necessary. Further, the budget would need to be revisited if the president and Congress could reach agreement on a plan for revising health care and its financing, a high priority of the first Clinton administration and one that failed to win congressional approval.

The 1995–1996 Debacle

The November 1994 elections set up a situation ripe for intense executive–legislative conflict that would benefit few, harm many, and add to the skepticism of the citizenry about the worthiness of government and its political leaders. The elections produced victories for the Republicans, giving them the control of both the Senate, which had been under Republican control for six years during the Reagan administration, and the House of Representatives, which had not been under Republican rule for 40 years. The House's new Speaker, Newt Gingrich (Republican of Georgia), had championed a Contract with America in the elections. Gingrich, along with a sizable group of newly elected Republican members, felt deeply committed in legislating the various components of the contract.[49] Their extensive package of proposals included a balanced budget amendment to the Constitution, the line-item veto, and the requirement of a three-fifths majority vote to raise taxes. The new House majority was also committed (at least on paper) to shrinking the size of domestic government.

The new Republican Congress and the Democratic president found themselves on an unavoidable collision track. The Republicans managed to produce a reconciliation bill in spring 1995 that included substantial reductions in many federal programs, including a $270 billion reduction over seven years (from the baseline) for Medicare spending.[50] This proposal was projected to result in a balanced budget by fiscal year 2002. When Congress sent this bill to President Clinton, however, he vetoed it as "extreme." Congress responded by holding appropriation bills hostage until or unless Clinton capitulated on reconciliation. In particular, Congress insisted that the president come up with his own balanced budget plan using the more conservative budget estimates of the Congressional Budget Office, rather than the more optimistic Office of Management and Budget projections.

When the president refused to do this to the satisfaction of Congress, the resulting "train wreck" led to portions of the government being forced to shut down for two extended periods (November 14 to 19, 1995; and December 16, 1995, to January 8, 1996).[51] People were inconvenienced in innumerable respects, such as not being able to visit the Grand Canyon and not being able to obtain a passport for overseas travel. While the government continued to distribute Social Security payments, processing was halted on new applications for benefits. Businesses in Washington, DC, which relied on patronage from business travelers and tourists, were hurt financially as people stayed away from the city.

Eventually, the congressional Republicans capitulated. There was no reconciliation bill and a compromise was reached on discretionary spending that did not cut appropriations by as much as was desired by the Republicans. All participants were eager to have the battles resolved, if for only a short period, to avoid having this situation continue into the 1996 presidential election. As it was, Republicans probably were blamed by the electorate for the shutdowns and overall chaos, partially explaining their losses in the House of Representatives, albeit not enough to lose control, and the win by President Clinton in his bid for re-election.[52]

The 1997 Balanced Budget Act

January 1997 ushered in the 105th Congress, with a new collective mindset, and was the beginning of President Clinton's second and final term in office. The congressional leadership realized that a balanced budget could not be achieved without Clinton's support, as it would be virtually impossible to gain enough votes to override any presidential veto. A balanced budget would inevitably involve budget cuts, which are always unpopular with anyone affected by them. As a consequence, Republicans were eager for a bipartisan budget agreement as a means for spreading the blame for cuts in programs. President Clinton, who had earlier championed the idea of a balanced budget, may well have seen 1997 as an opportunity to achieve this goal and consequently to enhance his record of achievement. Working behind the scenes were a group of largely conservative Democrats in the House, who billed themselves as the "Blue Dogs," eager to find some middle-road compromise that would avoid elimination of programs as a budget reduction effort and yet bring spending under control to balance the budget.[53]

In May 1997, President Clinton and the Republican leadership in Congress agreed on the outline for a package of decisions that was supposed to balance the budget by 2002.[54] The agreement was followed by passage of two key laws—the Balanced Budget Act and the Taxpayer Relief Act—both of which were signed by President Clinton at a special ceremony on August 5, 1997. The Balanced Budget Act was an immense piece of legislation covering such topics as food stamps, housing, communications, welfare, education, civil service retirement, and much, much more. The Taxpayer Relief Act provided tax benefits for college education, capital gains tax cuts, family tax credits for children, and other relief measures.[55] Cuts in domestic programs were included, and Medicare expenditures were shaved back. Although spending for Medicaid, which serves the needy, was reduced, the cuts were not as severe as some had advocated.

The Balanced Budget Act made permanent the requirement that budget resolutions cover a five-year period. Discretionary spending limits, to be enforced through sequestration, were extended through fiscal year 2002, as were PAYGO requirements.

The Arrival—and Disappearance—of Surpluses

The Balanced Budget Act projected that the federal budget would move into surplus in fiscal year 2002. The sustained growth of the economy that continued into the late 1990s merely accelerated this timetable. Fueled in large part by increases in federal revenues (which grew by an average of 8.4% per year between fiscal years 1995 and 2000), the budget surplus arrived a full four years earlier than had been projected. The federal government ran a unified budget surplus of $69 billion in fiscal year 1998. The surplus, which was the first since fiscal year 1969, grew to $129 billion in 1999 and to $236 billion in 2000.[56] Attention then turned from the question of "How do we get rid of the deficit?" to "What do we do with the surplus?"

George W. Bush assumed the presidency in January 2001. Within a month after he had taken office, both CBO and OMB projected cumulative surpluses of $5.6 trillion between fiscal years 2002 and 2011.[57] Three competing uses of the surplus were debated in the spring of 2001. One group wanted to use the surplus to pay down the debt as quickly as possible. A second group advocated spending the surplus on key domestic programs, including (in particular) a prescription drug benefit for Medicare. A third group advocated a tax cut. Many supported a combination of these three approaches.

Ultimately, the Economic Growth and Tax Relief Reconciliation Act (EGTRRA), a tax cut estimated to amount to $1.3 trillion over 10 years, was enacted by Congress in June 2001.[58] The tax cut alternative was given substantial legs by Federal Reserve Board Chairman Alan Greenspan, who reversed his earlier opposition to tax cuts in light of the large projected surpluses.[59] The bill created a new 10% tax bracket, redefined the 15% bracket, and effected a gradual reduction in other marginal rates. By fiscal year 2006, the rates for the other brackets were to be 25%, 28%, 33%, and 35%. In addition, the act phased in a number of other changes, such as repealing the current restrictions on itemized deductions and personal exemptions, doubling the child tax credit (to $1,000) over a 10-year period, and phasing out the estate tax over a 10-year period. All estate and "generation-skipping" taxes will be repealed by 2010.[60]

The estimate of $1.3 trillion tax cut understates its magnitude, since various provisions were "turned off" in later years so as not to exceed the allowable cost of the tax cut under reconciliation. The CBO estimated that, if some future Congress and future president do not allow these provisions to expire (which seems likely), this action would add another $440 billion to deficits through 2012, and almost $2.3 trillion to deficits through 2017.[61]

The tax cut is one of several factors that have contributed to a substantially deteriorating budget outlook for the federal government.[62] Revenues and spending were affected by the continuing weakness of the economy in 2001. Further, the terrorist attacks of September 11, 2001, occasioned a response that will have continuing budgetary ramifications. This response included not only the remediation of the immediate effects of the attacks, but also a domestic and international response. On the domestic front, Congress and the president created the

Department of Homeland Security (DHS) which combined a great many agencies that had been in separate departments under a single agency. In addition, costly wars in Afghanistan and Iraq were justified on the basis of a continued war on terrorism. In 2007, CBO estimated that these military actions had cost $503 billion over five years, with no clear end in sight.[63] Finally, an extremely severe hurricane season in 2005 resulted in horrific death and destruction in the Gulf Coast area, occasioning an unprecedented federal disaster relief effort.

Table 9–3 shows the trend in deficits and surpluses for the federal government from fiscal year 1985 through fiscal year 2006. The table clearly demonstrates the rise in the deficit, the movement toward surpluses after 1997, and the return of the deficit after 2002.

By January 2007, the Congressional Budget Office had released a revision of its budget outlook that underscored just how much the fiscal situation had deteriorated since January 2001. In this forecast, CBO estimated that the federal budget would experience cumulative surpluses, in the amount of $628 billion for the period of fiscal year 2007 to 2017.[64] This forecast is quite likely to be optimistic, since CBO's budget projections must assume "current law," and current law does not include some likely changes in policy that would make the deficit outlook worse.

Table 9–3 | **Federal Deficits and Surpluses, Fiscal Year 1985 to Fiscal Year 2006 (in Billions of Dollars)**

Fiscal Year	Surplus or Deficit	Fiscal Year	Surplus or Deficit
1985	−212	1996	−107
1986	−221	1997	−22
1987	−150	1998	69
1988	−155	1999	125
1989	−153	2000	236
1990	−221	2001	128
1991	−269	2002	−158
1992	−290	2003	−378
1993	−255	2004	−413
1994	−203	2005	−318
1995	−164	2006	−248

Source: Compiled from U.S. Congressional Budget Office (2007). *The budget and economic outlook: fiscal years 2008–2017*. Washington, DC: U.S. Government Printing Office, 141.

Table 9–4	**Projected Federal Deficits, Fiscal Years 2007–2017, Under Baseline and Alternate Scenarios (in Billions of Dollars)**		

Fiscal Year	Baseline Projection	Tax Changes[1]	Tax Changes/Freeze Discretionary[2]
2007	−172	−184	−184
2008	−98	−172	−155
2009	−116	−200	−160
2010	−137	−242	−177
2011	−12	−277	−184
2012	170	−195	−73
2013	159	−259	−106
2014	185	−277	−90
2015	208	−289	−75
2016	192	−365	−102
2017	249	−362	−59
2007–2017	628	−2822	−1365

[1]Assumes extension of the Bush tax cuts, extension of other tax provisions scheduled to expire, and reform of the Alternative Minimum Tax.

[2]Assumes tax changes from previous column, and assumes that discretionary appropriations are frozen at 2007 levels, meaning that no adjustments for inflation would be added after 2007.

Source: Calculated from U.S. Congressional Budget Office (2007). *The budget and economic outlook: fiscal years 2008–2106.* Washington, DC: U.S. Government Printing Office, xii, 16, 17.

This imbalance is illustrated in **Table 9–4**, which shows CBO's projections of future deficit under alternate scenarios. The table compares the baseline cumulative surplus forecast of $628 billion to two other scenarios. The first assumes changes in tax law to make permanent the Bush tax cuts and various other expiring tax cuts, and to reform the Alternative Minimum Tax (AMT—see Chapter 4). Under this forecast, these surpluses become cumulative deficits of $2.8 trillion over the 2007–2017 period. The second alternate scenario assumes all of these tax changes, but their effect is moderated somewhat by assuming that discretionary spending is frozen at the level of spending in 2007, thus permitting no increases for inflation or program expansions in the future. Under this scenario, cumulative deficits would total $1.4 trillion over this same 11-year period. Clearly there are many other possible scenarios, but this comparison would seem to indicate that the likelihood of the budget being balanced on its own without policy changes is remote indeed.

There has been very little movement to address this fiscal imbalance in the short-or the long-term. In the immediate term, the urgency of the war on terrorism has moved fiscal discipline to the back burner. While from the mid-1980s to the late 1990s the norm of the balanced budget prevailed, no similar fiscal target has emerged to replace it. The budgetary impact of the terrorist attacks has been largely to drive budgetary considerations underground. Until some consensus is reached on a norm to replace "the balanced budget" as a macrobudgetary goal, the process is likely to remain adrift.[65] The fact that the discretionary spending caps and the PAYGO process were allowed to expire after fiscal year 2002 is an indication of the change in the attitude toward deficit reduction. There are those who believe that reinstituting these strictures would go a long way to solve the budget problem, but it is likely that without a preceding commitment to fiscal discipline, reinstituting these procedural devices would have little effect.[66]

As further evidence of the lack of interest on the part of the president and Congress in deficit reduction, consider the fact that president George W. Bush proposed a modest five-year reduction of $65 billion in mandatory spending savings (less than 1% below the baseline level of mandatory spending over those five years) in his fiscal year 2007 budget. While the House-passed budget resolution assumed $6.8 billion in mandatory savings, the Senate-passed budget resolution included not one dollar of those savings.[67] A glimmer of hope seemed to emerge in early 2007 when the new Democratic Congress and President Bush each pledged to propose policies that would balance the budget by fiscal year 2012. In the past, getting from the outlines of such an agreement to the specific policies that would be necessary to make it a reality has proved a difficult journey.

The short-term problems pale in comparison to the long-term fiscal imbalance faced by the country. Because of demographics and increased costs, the major entitlement programs—Social Security, Medicare, and Medicaid—have highly uncertain fiscal futures. Since Social Security and Medicare represents transfers between current workers (who pay the payroll taxes) and current retirees (who receive the benefits financed by those taxes), the impending retirement of the baby boomers will have a substantial effect on the finances of these programs. In 2005, CBO projected that the number of workers per Social Security beneficiary would decline from 3.3 at that point to only 2.1 by 2030.[68] At the same time, individuals are living longer, thus receiving benefits from these programs for a longer period of time. Further, medical care inflation across the economy as a whole is on the rise, and if it continues unabated this will have a substantial effect on the future costs for the government's health care programs. Put together, under CBO's intermediate long-term forecast these programs almost double their draw on the federal budget (as a percentage of GDP) between 2005 and 2030[69] (see Chapter 15 for more discussion of federal debt).

Proposals to reform the programs to address these problems—from President Clinton's health care reform proposal in 1994 to President Bush's calls for Social Security reform in 2005—have gone nowhere. There is general agreement, however, on two things. First, that the status quo is unaffordable. Second, that the longer the nation waits to act, the more draconian the necessary actions will be.

Proposed Reforms and Their Prospects

Congress, the president, and the nation face a complex set of interwoven problems. The overall fiscal picture is much brighter today than it was in the mid-1990s, but tremendous uncertainty remains concerning budget priorities and the proper role of government. The current budget process seems dysfunctional, with the most basic tasks, like the adoption of a budget resolution, proving elusive in a number of recent years. Given this, it is reasonable to ask what changes might be made to the budget process, and even whether the whole idea of establishing a congressional budget process was doomed from the start.[70]

The movement of the budget from deficit to surplus and back to deficit again has policy makers struggling to establish the correct goals for the budget. In addition, the nation faces what is perhaps a fundamental, and expensive, shift in priorities to confront threats to security both at home and abroad. In the short run, the aftermath of September 11 seems to have given the Defense Department a blank check. However, a perennial question is: How much defense is enough? Defense policy must be rethought given the absence of the threat of nuclear attack by Russia, the potential threat of terrorism, and the instability in particular regions of the world, especially the Middle East. At the same time, the budget faces a lurking fiscal time bomb, associated with the government's entitlement programs.[71] Further, the practice at least through 2007 of funding all of the Iraq and Afghanistan war and reconstruction efforts through supplementals takes the executive budget process out of the picture as well. The budget process of the Department of Defense (DoD) is regarded as one of the most effective processes for detailed and close examination of the costs of various defense strategies, but the hundreds of billions in supplementals largely avoided those processes. Even the equipment replacement requirements for the combat arms groups that by 2007 had become critical, and normally are readily handled through the DoD budgeting process and the regular congressional defense appropriation process, escaped the usual scrutiny and review in both the executive and legislative branches.

Can Congress better organize itself to deal effectively with this daunting set of problems?[72] If Congress's primary role is to set policy and provide leadership in furthering the nation's interests, then do means exist for improving the processes of that august body to help it meet its responsibilities? Since the budget process is at the very center of policy making, it attracts much attention from reformers and raises fundamental questions. For example, how should power be distributed between the leadership and the individual members? Placing power in the hands of those in leadership positions can help facilitate decision making, but at the same time can subjugate the voices of individual members who have been chosen by their voters to represent them.[73] How should responsibilities be distributed between new members and those with seniority? How should power be shared by the two chambers of Congress? To what extent should or must Congress delegate powers, such as the power to sequester funds, to the president and to others in the executive branch of government?[74]

These questions of process cut to the core of any congressional member's future. For example, getting appointed to the "right" committee—any committee in a position to address the needs of one's home district—is considered critical, and any plan to reorganize the committee structure is necessarily regarded as threatening. One view is that Congress will never be able to deal with fundamental problems as long as campaign funds must be obtained largely through contributions from constituent organizations. Those organizations are likely to donate substantial funds only on the condition that members provide pork barrel spending and other immediate benefits.

Budget process reform proposals are hardy perennials in Congress. Many members, convinced that the current process is fundamentally broken, propose changes in budget procedures or institutions as solutions to fiscal problems. There are many more of these proposals than can be catalogued on these pages, but among the most common are reforms that would give the president a line-item veto, would amend the Constitution to require a balanced budget, would reorganize Congress as it deals with the budget, and would convert Congress to a biennial budget process.

The Item Veto

As discussed in Chapter 8, most governors have item-veto power, allowing them to reduce or eliminate line items in appropriation bills. The president of the United States has historically lacked such power. The power could be provided in a statute or, as many would advocate, in an amendment to the Constitution. Thomas Jefferson may have been the first president to refuse to spend money appropriated by Congress, and Ulysses S. Grant may have been the first president to ask for the item-veto power.[75]

Pros and Cons of the Item Veto. One of the main justifications cited for the item veto is that the president needs the authority to reduce or eliminate funding of pork barrel projects that have little merit other than pleasing specific constituent groups of individual members of Congress. However, what constitutes excesses in spending is necessarily a function of one's values and priorities, and the executive branch is not immune from advocating spending for programs and projects of questionable utility. One aspect that is clearly not a purpose of the item veto is to reduce the budget deficit. The spending cuts that might be made by a president would be unlikely to have any appreciable effect on total spending.[76]

Critics of the item veto contend that it gives the president an unwarranted increase in power, allowing for presidential policy preferences to supplant congressional preferences. If a president needed to muster senatorial votes for an initiative, he could privately threaten to item-veto favored projects of individual senators. When the White House was controlled by one political party and Congress by the other, White House priorities might prevail. One can speculate that if Presidents Reagan and George H. W. Bush had been able to wield item-veto power, then several agencies and programs would have been eliminated, such as the Economic Development Administration, the Appalachian Regional Commission, and urban mass-transportation formula grants.

The Rescission Process. Procedures, as initially established by the Congressional Budget and Impoundment Control Act of 1974, provide that the president submit packages of proposed rescissions in appropriations enacted by Congress. Congress has 45 days in which it is in session to approve each package or approve its own set of cuts. Before adopting an appropriation bill, Congress is made aware of what items are likely to be cut by the president. Presidential priorities are reported to Congress through budget submissions and statements of administration policy, which indicate White House opposition to provisions in draft appropriation bills. Similarly, congressional intentions also are provided to the administration, through the OMB, during the budget mark-up process, and the White House has an opportunity to comment and give feedback to the subcommittees marking up the bill. After appropriations, when the president does propose rescissions, a consistent pattern has been that Congress makes greater cuts than recommended by the president, albeit using a different set of priorities to determine which items will be cut.[77]

Enhanced Rescission and the Line Item Veto Act. After decades of debate, the Republican-controlled Congress enacted the Line Item Veto Act (LIVA) of 1996, which was part of the Contract with America. The act took effect in January 1997, giving President Clinton a tool to use against Congress during the 1997 legislative session. A general consensus exists that a "true" item-veto power could be provided to the president only through a constitutional amendment and, therefore, the 1996 law is best viewed as enhanced rescission power. The 1996 law explicitly recognized that many "earmarks" (another name for pork barrel items) are listed not in the legislation itself (an appropriation bill or a tax bill, for example) but in committee reports accompanying those bills. Significantly, then, the LIVA gave the president power to cancel three types of provisions: (1) new items of discretionary spending (found either in appropriation bills or in committee reports accompanying these bills as well); (2) new entitlements or increased entitlements; and (3) tax provisions that would benefit 100 or fewer individuals or corporations. The president was required to veto an entire item and not just reduce an amount, and he could not veto existing entitlement programs and other forms of mandatory spending. Any savings achieved through this process could not be reappropriated for other purposes but rather would be used to reduce the budget deficit. This lockbox provision was important to those who wanted the veto power to be used for deficit reduction. The law had a sunset provision, withdrawing this power from the president on January 1, 2005.[78]

In an effort to circumvent the Supreme Court's ban on legislative vetoes (see the earlier discussion of the *Chadha* decision), the 1996 measure provided a convoluted form of veto. The president was to submit a set of proposed budget cuts. Congress then had 30 calendar days, during a time when it is in session, to consider passing a disapproval bill. If Congress did not act, the proposed vetoes would take effect. The disapproval bill would be on an expedited schedule but would go through the standard procedure of passage in both houses and, most likely, a conference committee procedure for working out the differences between the houses. The president could then either sign or veto the disapproval bill. A veto of the disapproval bill would mean he was standing behind his original set of decisions to cut items in the budget. Congress could override the president's veto only by a two-thirds vote.

The item veto was first used by President Clinton to cut three items from the Balanced Budget Act of 1997 and the Taxpayer Relief Act of 1997, just five days after signing these laws. The vetoes covered (1) tax shelters for financial service companies, (2) a Medicaid provision that specifically would benefit New York State and New York City, and (3) a tax benefit that would go to a small number of agribusinesses, including large corporations that in his view did not need such a tax advantage. Clinton noted that many items were protected from his veto on the grounds that the White House had an obligation to act in good faith in retaining items that had been explicitly approved as part of the bargaining process with the Republican-controlled Congress.[79] He agreed with suggestions from the press that the vetoed items were relatively minor but noted that he expected more significant vetoes to arise when appropriation bills began to reach his desk for approval.

President Clinton also used the line-item veto power in the appropriations process. By far the most aggressive use of this power was on the military construction appropriation bill, where he cancelled 38 projects totaling $287 million.

Congress used the procedures contained in the act to pass a disapproval bill, which was ultimately vetoed by President Clinton. His veto was overridden by Congress, thereby restoring funding for these projects. Clinton was much more restrained in his use of the veto on other appropriation bills, canceling only $190 million in total budget authority from those other 12 bills.[80]

The Line Item Veto Act included a section for judicial review, allowing for members of Congress and others to file suit in the U.S. District Court for the District of Columbia, with its decision being appealable directly to the Supreme Court. Well before President Clinton had an opportunity to use this new set of powers, the law was challenged in court by Senator Robert C. Byrd (Democrat of West Virginia), who had been the law's most outspoken critic, calling it "a malformed monstrosity."[81] The district court agreed with Byrd that the law had unconstitutionally delegated congressional powers to the president. That decision was appealed to the Supreme Court, which ruled on a procedural rather than substantive basis. In *Raines v. Byrd* (1997), the Court decided that Byrd and others lacked standing, a condition in which the party bringing suit must show that an injury has occurred or is about to occur.[82] The Court found that an injury had not occurred, as the president had not yet exercised the new power granted to him. Standing was said to be especially important in cases involving conflict between two branches of the government, in this case, between Congress and the president.

Ultimately, the constitutionality of the Line Item Veto Act was challenged on its merits by individuals with standing who had suffered injury as a result of its application. In late 1997, two suits were brought: one by the City of New York and the other by the Snake River (Idaho) Potato Growers over Clinton's cancellation of items in the Balanced Budget Act and the Taxpayer Relief Act, respectively. The law was found unconstitutional in U.S. District Court, and in 1998, the Supreme Court, in a 6 to 3 decision, sided with the District Court in the case of *Clinton v. City of New York*.[83] The Court ruled that the act ran afoul of the Presentment Clause of the Constitution, because it permitted the president to unilaterally unmake law that had been made by both houses of Congress in concert with the president. The majority argued that providing the president with the kind of power envisioned in the act would require an amendment to the Constitution. Thus, the Line Item Veto Act was relegated to a one-year experiment—a blip on the federal budgeting radar screen.[84]

Subsequently, President Bush has proposed that he be granted a reduced form of line-item veto authority through what is referred to as "expedited rescission." Under this proposal, a president would be guaranteed a vote on rescission proposals that he proposed, and individual items would be subjected to an "up-or-down" vote on the Senate or House floor. The presumption is that these items would be subject to greater scrutiny, making it harder for the more egregious pork barrel projects to survive.[85] The House of Representatives passed a version of the president's proposal in June 2006.[86] The Senate did not follow suit, and Senate Budget Committee chair Judd Gregg (Republican of New Hampshire) acknowledged that the president's line item veto legislation would fall short of achieving support among all Republicans, admitting that "eight or nine on my side" would be unlikely to support the bill.[87]

Thus, as of this writing, the president still lacks any form of line-item veto authority other than the narrow authority to propose rescissions granted by the 1974 law. According to CBO testimony, this power has done little to reduce spending over time. Between 1976 and 2006, presidents have proposed approximately $73 billion in total rescissions, representing about one-half of one percent of the almost $15 trillion in discretionary budget authority legislated over that time. Further, Congress actually enacted only about one-third of these proposed rescissions.[88]

Proposed Balanced Budget Requirement

A persistent proposal has been for the federal government to adopt a balanced budget requirement.[89] Proponents typically refer to the successful use of this requirement at the state level—all states except North Dakota currently require some form of balanced budget.[90] Note that balanced budget requirements in most states do not preclude borrowing for capital investments, and few state budgets are annually balanced when both current and capital expenditures are taken into account. Many states also have limitations on revenue raising and spending, stemming from the Proposition 13 movement of the 1970s.

A major concern regarding implementation of a balanced budget requirement at the federal level is that the measure might impose unwarranted restrictions in times of economic hardship or national security emergencies.[91] Some form of override mechanism must be included for situations when the federal government needs to spend more to counteract economic recessions and to wage war. For the override to occur, both houses might be required to have votes of 60%, two-thirds, or a majority of all members (rather than a majority of those voting).

Having some set of enforcement mechanisms is regarded as essential for successful implementation, although such mechanisms do not exist at the state level, where the balanced budget process is regarded as generally successful. The states, however, have an externally imposed imperative for bringing revenues and expenditures into structural balance: Failing to do so would have an adverse effect on their bond ratings and borrowing costs.

Skeptics of congressional abilities to reach agreement on a balanced budget fear that Congress would resort to "smoke and mirror" techniques that merely give the illusion of a balanced budget. Such devices might include overestimating revenues to be collected and moving some expenditures off-budget so that they would be excluded from official total spending. These are, of course, precisely the kinds of tricks that resulted under Gramm-Rudman-Hollings, the federal government's prior failed experiment with fixed deficit targets. Attempting to prohibit such practices by outlawing them in the constitutional amendment would be cumbersome, and creative minds might always be able to find loopholes in the amendment's language. In addition, detailed provisions in the amendment could create an inflexibility that later might prove detrimental to the nation's best interests.

Critics of the balanced budget proposal contend that it would unduly enhance the powers of the president. A typical requirement of balanced budget proposals is that the president would have to submit a balanced budget, thereby setting the agenda from which Congress might have little latitude to veer. One line of reasoning states that for the proposal to be effective, an item veto for the president would be essential. Another criticism is that an annually balanced budget is not an appropriate goal for federal fiscal policy. The federal government has routinely, and appropriately, engaged in deficit spending during times of recession or when it needed to deal with other emergencies.[92]

Once the budget moved from deficit to surplus in 1998, the interest in a balanced budget amendment waned. But with the reemergence of budget deficits and the potential search for a new consensus for an overall goal of fiscal policy, members of Congress have begun to propose such an amendment again. Representative Ernest Istook (Republican of Oklahoma) is the leading proponent in the House, having sponsored the amendment with 113 other colleagues in 2006.[93]

Proposed Congressional Reorganization

A perennial topic of discussion in Congress is how it could better organize itself to fulfill its responsibilities, especially its budget responsibilities. Important changes did occur as a result of passage of the Legislative Reorganization Acts of 1946 and 1970 as well as other reorganizations that affected either the House or the Senate.[94]

Committees. One typical proposal is to reduce the number of congressional committees and subcommittees. These various bodies create problems in coordination, because their domains often overlap and subject areas are needlessly segmented among committees and subcommittees. Power becomes diffuse, and setting overall policy is complicated by the split jurisdictions. The greater the number of committees, the greater the number of committee assignments members have, meaning that they can easily be scheduled to attend two or more committee meetings at the same time. This problem is even more acute in the Senate, where 100 members must handle the same work that is done by the 435 members in the House.

The large number of committees and subcommittees poses problems for the executive branch as well as for Congress. Agency administrators complain that valuable time is wasted in having to prepare for and testify before these panels. The defense area is particularly subject to comprehensive congressional involvement, with Defense Department officials having to testify before dozens of committees and subcommittees.

The size of committee membership is a related concern. Memberships are often large because members want to be placed on committees of relevance to their home districts and states. However, the larger the committee size, the greater the number of committees on which members serve and the greater the number of meetings they are unable to attend. The result is a proxy system in which another member, often the chair, casts votes for absent members on the committee.

Although considerable agreement may exist that Congress needs to reduce the number of committees and subcommittees, the task is difficult. Chairing one of these committees provides power, prestige, and perquisites, so any chairperson or other senior member on the committee is likely to defend continuance of the committee and repel efforts to diminish the committee's powers.[95] Members in both houses have historically sought seats on committees dealing with the various aspects of the budget, as a means of gaining power over congressional actions.

One controversial suggestion has been that the budget process could be streamlined by eliminating the two Appropriations Committees and assigning their duties to the committees that handle authorizations. Rather than appropriation bills emanating from one committee, they would arise from the standing substantive committees in each chamber. Critics of this proposal contend that such a reform would worsen the budget situation, because the Appropriations Committees are far more likely to restrict government spending than the substantive committees, which are often seen as having been captured by the executive branch agencies that they oversee. Further, the Appropriations Committees currently wield great power, and they vigorously oppose any efforts to reduce that power. They would not be abolished without a fight.

Other committee-related proposals involve reconfiguring the House and Senate Budget Committees, and possibly even merging them into a joint committee. Another option would be to eliminate these committees on the grounds that they have merely added to the complexity of congressional budgeting, and have recently failed to accomplish their major objective in any event. During the nine years between fiscal year 1999 and fiscal year 2007, Congress four times failed to adopt a budget resolution, which is the primary task of the budget committees.

Leadership. Strengthening the powers of the Speaker of the House is another possible reform of how Congress conducts its business.[96] One recommendation is to increase the Speaker's power in determining who chairs committees and how long they retain these roles. Increased power would enhance the abilities of the Speaker to coordinate the diverse components of the chamber and develop a unified set of policies but might stifle the independence of individual members.

Term Limits. Growing interest in limiting the length of time a member may serve continuously in Congress is evident.[97] Imposing term limits, as noted in Chapter 8, is seen as a way to remove encrusted members who have lost touch with the real world and infuse "new blood" into the system. However, term limits by themselves would not resolve the serious financial problems facing the government. Term limits, if imposed, would need to be applied to all members. If only some states adopt this approach, their members will have less seniority than those in other states and consequently will have less influence on policy making. In 1995, the Supreme Court ruled that states could not impose qualifications for federal offices beyond what was contained in the Constitution.[98] The Court rejected the view that the Reserve Powers Clause of the Tenth Amendment gave states the power to set term limits on congressional elections. The Republicans in Congress have sought to initiate a constitutional amendment that would set term limits but have been unable to gain the necessary two-thirds vote. In the meantime, many individuals who run for Congress impose voluntary limits on their service. There have been numerous cases, however, of lawmakers reneging on these pledges, and there is little evidence that they are punished at the polls for doing so.[99]

Biennial Budgeting

One frequently mentioned proposal is to change over to a biennial budget.[100] Since Congress has such difficulty acting on a budget, why not simplify the problem by requiring action only every other year? The idea of moving the federal government from an annual to a biennial process is not a new one. Representative Leon Panetta (Democrat of California) introduced the first bill proposing such a change in 1977, and the proposal has been more or less an annual entry in the budget reform sweepstakes since then. Most biennial budgeting proposals would have the president submit his budget biennially and would also feature biennial budget resolutions and appropriations.

Perhaps the high-water mark for biennial budgeting came in 1993, when both the Joint Committee on the Organization of Congress and Vice President Gore's National Performance Review recommended that the federal government adopt a biennial timetable for the process. Despite this long history of support, however, no bill to create a biennial process has ever passed either the House or the Senate.[101] The most recent proposal for biennial budgeting is included as one of several budget reforms in Senate Budget Committee Chair Judd Gregg's *Stop Over Spending (SOS) Act* in 2006. Gregg himself, however, has not backed biennial budgeting in the past.[102] The key supporter of biennial budgeting in the Senate, Senator Pete Domenici (Republican of New Mexico), alleged in 2006 that biennial budgeting legislation was approaching a filibuster-proof majority in the Senate.[103] Once again, however, Congress adjourned in 2006 without enacting any bill in either house that would establish a biennial budget process.

Proponents of biennial budgeting argue that the current annual process features repetitive votes on many fiscal issues that eat up valuable committee and floor time. For example, there may be three votes on the budget for defense: one associated with the budget resolution, one associated with the annual defense authorization bill, and one on the annual defense appropriations bill. Second, in a related issue, supporters note that time spent on budgeting cannot be spent on other activities, particularly detailed oversight of federal programs. In particular, these advocates of a biennial process indicate that the need for Congress to review agency performance under the Government Performance and Results Act necessitates spending more time on such detailed oversight. Third, supporters point to the dismal record of Congress and the president in enacting annual appropriation bills prior to the start of each fiscal year. Finally, executive branch officials decry the time-consuming nature of the annual process from their perspective. The sequence of developing an agency budget request, having that budget undergo review by the Office of Management and Budget and the president, and justifying the budget to Congress is continuous in an annual process.[104]

There are also numerous arguments offered by opponents of biennial budgets. First, the federal government has a rather checkered history of budget forecasting. Producing a budget every two years would increase the probability that budgets would be based on erroneous information. A two-year budget resolution adopted in April, for example, would be adopted a full 30 months before the end of the second fiscal year of the biennium. The agencies would have begun developing their budgets for that fiscal year at least 10 months prior to the passage of the budget resolution, or more than three years from the end of the second fiscal year of the biennium. Second, opponents argue that the benefits of biennial budgeting (decreased time on budgeting, more time for oversight) are overstated. The biennial process may degenerate into an annual process, given the uncertainties associated with budgeting for a $2 trillion enterprise (Congress already engages in an annual process of adopting supplemental appropriations) and the likelihood that Appropriations Committee members will want to act on the budget every year. Third, an increase in oversight under biennial budgeting would occur only if the current lack of oversight results from a lack of time. Opponents argue that even if members of Congress had more time to do oversight, they would not be likely to do more of it simply because they do not have any incentives to do so. Understanding more about how federal programs work in great detail is not politically sexy, nor does it offer any specific benefits in terms of helping members get re-elected.[105]

Other Proposed Revisions in the Budget Process

While the previously mentioned changes have been the most frequently debated, they are by no means the only reform proposals put forth. One whole set of reforms, to include more performance information in the budget process, is discussed in Chapter 6. Another reform, to bring more accrual accounting concepts to the federal government, is discussed in Chapter 11. At least four other reforms are also worthy of discussion—automatic continuing resolutions, making the budget resolution into a joint resolution, capital budgeting, and sunset provisions for federal programs.

Automatic Continuing Resolutions. Under this proposed reform, the institution of automatic continuing resolutions for appropriations would become another possible strategy. If Congress failed to pass an appropriation bill, the agencies affected would operate with a continuing appropriation without Congress's having to act. Since congressional failure to act on the budget in a timely fashion has become the norm, the obvious advantage of an automatic continuing resolution is that it would eliminate the crisis handling of appropriation bills. The disadvantage of the proposal is that incentives for Congress to adopt regular appropriation bills would be reduced.[106]

Joint Budget Resolutions. A more far-reaching proposal would eliminate the concurrent nature of budget resolutions, which do not require presidential signature, and substitute a joint resolution or law to be signed by the president.[107] In effect, budget summitry would be employed at the outset of the budget process. The hope is that the president and key congressional leaders would develop an annual budget resolution that all would support, thereby helping to ensure more timely action as the details of the budget are worked out at a later time. Budget summits bind all participants so that a president who endorsed a summit agreement could not later renege when Congress passed appropriation bills in conformance with the agreement. The down side of a joint budget resolution is that conflict would be "front loaded." Obtaining the agreement of both houses without having the president involved has often proved difficult. Allowing the president to have a veto over the budget resolution might be the practical equivalent of ensuring that no budget resolution will occur in many years.[108]

Capital Budgeting. Adoption of a capital budgeting system is yet another possibility. It is advocated as a way of helping to put the deficit into perspective, because it would show that much of federal spending is of an investment nature and not simply annual consumption. However, the federal budget has very little investment in it, if one excludes major defense systems and intergovernmental transfers to state and local governments for infrastructure (see Chapter 12 for discussion of the pros and cons of capital budgeting). Capital budgeting presumably would encourage better planning of expenditures. On the negative side, capital budgets could be used to downplay the true magnitude of federal budget deficits and total debt. More and more of the budget could be "capitalized" as a method of making desired spending appear to be less costly. Further, if a balanced budget constitutional amendment were adopted, Congress most likely would move capital expenditures off-budget, just as states permit indebtedness for investments but not for operating expenses.[109]

Sunset Provisions. As noted in Chapter 6, proposals for zero-base budgeting were justified in large part by the incremental nature of the budget process, and programs, once created, tend to live forever. A relative of zero-base budgeting is *sunset review*, which puts government programs on a set timetable for review and possible abolition. Under separate bills introduced by Representative Todd Tiahrt (Republican of Kansas) and Representative Kevin Brady (Republican of Texas), commissions would be established, similar to the base closing commissions of the 1990s, to review specified federal programs and recommend possible reorganization, expansion, or abolition. While the commissions under the Tiahrt bill would be more ad hoc, the Brady bill would establish a standing commission that would review each agency at least once every 12 years. While supporters of the bills trumpet them as being able to root out inefficient and ineffective programs, skeptics wondered whether the commissions would be susceptible to politicization.[110]

Summary

Congress has an elaborate system for approving the budget. An authorization process exists independently of appropriations. Meanwhile, the House Ways and Means Committee and the Senate Finance Committee have power to deal not only with tax measures but also with some spending. The Appropriations Committees in the two houses operate by developing a series of bills through subcommittees.

The current budget process resulted from two main laws. The Budget and Accounting Act of 1921 prescribes the president's budget process. The Congressional Budget and Impoundment Control Act of 1974 attempted to deal with several problems, including congressional tardiness in adopting the budget, impoundments, and piecemeal handling of the budget. A budget resolution process, Budget Committees, and the Congressional Budget Office were established. Two other laws were passed in the 1980s and 1990s in an attempt to control the deficit. The Gramm-Rudman-Hollings law was a failed attempt to bring the deficit under control. Later efforts that coupled "budget summits" with a new change in process, codified in the Budget Enforcement Act, have proved much more successful. Both of these laws, however, were allowed to expire by 2002.

The resulting budget process has several stages. First, the president submits his budget on or before the first Monday in February. Congress then adopts a budget resolution that establishes a blueprint for the budget. Committee action follows the constraints established by the budget resolution. In some years, reconciliation bills, which make changes to government revenue and entitlement legislation, are enacted. In each year, much of the budget process focuses on the fate of the regular appropriation bills.

During the presidency of Bill Clinton, the budget finally moved from deficit into surplus. The improvement in the budget outlook resulted from a series of legislative actions coupled with the continued strong growth of the economy (fueling an increase in federal revenues). Fiscal year 1998 was the first year since 1969 that the federal government had a budget surplus. These surpluses lasted through fiscal year 2001, but in 2002 a combination of a tax cut advocated by President George W. Bush, a weakening of the economy, and the after effects of the terrorist attacks of September 11, 2001, signaled the return of deficits. These deficits are projected to increase for the immediate future, and the long-term prospects for the federal budget are not good, largely because of the outlook for the major entitlement programs—Social Security, Medicare, and Medicaid. In early 2007, the new Democratic Congress and President Bush both pledged to adopt policies that would balance the budget by fiscal year 2012.

Numerous proposals exist for further revising how the federal government adopts the budget. Major proposals include giving item-veto power to the president, passing a constitutional amendment requiring that the budget be balanced, restructuring congressional committees, and moving the government to a biennial budget cycle. Other proposals involve establishing automatic continuing resolutions, changing the concurrent budget resolution to a joint resolution or law, separating the budget into capital and operating components, and creating a sunset review for federal programs.

Notes

1. Tompkin, S. (1998). *Inside OMB: politics and process in the President's budget office.* Armonk, NY: M. E. Sharpe.
2. Hughes, J. (1998). General Accounting Office. In J. M. Shafritz (Ed.), *International encyclopedia of public policy and administration.* Boulder, CO: Westview Press, 969–972.
3. Fisher, L. (1987). *The politics of shared power: Congress and the executive,* 2nd ed. Washington, DC: Congressional Quarterly Press, 91–217; Schick, A. (2000). *The federal*

budget: politics, policy, process, 2nd ed. Washington, DC: Brookings Institution, 105–240.

4. Manley, J. (1970). *The politics of finance: the House Committee on Ways and Means.* Boston, MA: Little, Brown.

5. Fenno, Jr., R. (1966). *The power of the purse: appropriations politics in Congress.* Boston, MA: Little, Brown; Shuman, H. (1992). *Politics and the budget: the struggle between the President and the Congress*, 3rd ed. Englewood Cliffs, NJ: Prentice-Hall; Wildavsky, A. & Caiden, N. (2000). *The new politics of the budgetary process*, 4th ed. New York: Longman.

6. Legislative Reorganization Act (1946). Ch. 753.

7. Fisher, L. (1973). *Experience with a legislative budget (1947–1949)*; Senate Committee on Government Operations, *Improving Congressional control of the budget: hearings, Part 2*, 93rd Cong., 1st sess. Washington, DC: U.S. Government Printing Office, 237–239.

8. Wallace, R. (1959). Congressional control of the budget. *Midwest Journal of Political Science, 3*, 151–167.

9. Kim, S. (1968). The politics of a congressional budgetary process: "backdoor spending." *Western Political Quarterly, 21*, 606–623; Schick, A. (1973). Backdoor spending authority in Senate Committee on Government Operations, *Improving Congressional control over the budget: a compendium of materials*, 93rd Cong., 1st sess. Washington, DC: U.S. Government Printing Office, 293–302.

10. Schick, A. (1980). *Congress and money.* Washington, DC: The Urban Institute Press.

11. Congressional Budget and Impoundment Control Act (1974). P.L. 93–344.

12. Fisher, L. (1985). Ten years of the Budget Act: still searching for controls. *Public Budgeting & Finance, 5, Fall*, 3–28.

13. Schick, A. (2000). *The federal budget*; Joyce, P. & Reischauer, R. (1992). Deficit budgeting: the federal budget process and budget reform. *Harvard Journal on Legislation, 29*, 429–453.

14. Crippen, D. (2002). *Informing legislators about the budget: the history and role of the U.S. Congressional Budget Office.* Speech to parliamentary officials of the OECD. Washington, DC, June 7.

15. Fisher, L. (1970). The politics of impounded funds. *Administrative Science Quarterly, 15*, 361–377.

16. Anti-Deficiency Act (1950). Ch. 510, §3, 34 Stat. 49.

17. *Immigration and Naturalization Service* v. *Chadha* (1983). 462 U.S. 919.

18. Joyce, P. (1996). Congressional budget reform: the unanticipated implications for federal policy making. *Public Administration Review, 56*, 317–325.

19. Economic Recovery Tax Act (1981). P.L. 97-34.

20. Johnson, B. (1984). From analyst to negotiator: the OMB's new role. *Journal of Policy Analysis and Management, 3*, 501–515; Johnson, B. (1989). The OMB budget examiner

and the congressional budget process. *Public Budgeting & Finance, 9, Spring*, 5–14; Tompkin, S. (1998). *Inside OMB.*

21. Stockman, D. (1986). *The triumph of politics: how the Reagan revolution failed.* New York: Harper & Row.

22. LeLoup, L. & Hancock, J. (1988). Congress and the Reagan budgets. *Public Budgeting & Finance, 8, Fall*, 30–54.

23. A plea from David Stockman (1983). *Washington Post, April 20*, A20.

24. Ippolito, D. (1990). *Uncertain legacies: federal budget policy from Roosevelt through Reagan.* Charlottesville, VA: University Press of Virginia.

25. Doyle, R. (1996). Congress, the deficit, and budget reconciliation. *Public Budgeting & Finance, 16, Winter*, 59–81.

26. Balanced Budget and Emergency Deficit Control Act (1985). P.L. 99-177, Title II; Havens, H. (1986). Gramm-Rudman-Hollings: origins and implementation. *Public Budgeting & Finance, 6, Fall*, 4–24; LeLoup, L. et al. (1987). Deficit politics and constitutional government: the impact of Gramm-Rudman-Hollings. *Public Budgeting & Finance, 7, Spring*, 83–103.

27. Rudman, W., as quoted in Wehr, E. (1985). Congress enacts far-reaching budget measure. *Congressional Quarterly Weekly Report, 43*, 2604.

28. *Bowsher v. Synar* (1986). 478 U.S. 714; Symposium: *Bowsher v. Synar* (1987). *Cornell Law Review, 72*, 421–597.

29. Balanced Budget and Emergency Deficit Control Reaffirmation Act (1987). P.L. 100-119, Title I.

30. Metz, T. et al. (1987). Stocks plunge 508 amid panicky selling. *Wall Street Journal, October 20*, 1.

31. Schier, S. (1992). *A decade of deficits: Congressional thought and fiscal action.* Albany, NY: State University of New York Press; Thelwell, R. (1990). Gramm-Rudman-Hollings four years later. *Public Administration Review, 50*, 190–198.

32. U.S. Congressional Budget Office (1993). *The economic and budget outlook: fiscal years 1994–1998.* Washington, DC: U.S. Government Printing Office, 85.

33. The Budget Enforcement Act was a component of Omnibus Budget Reconciliation Act (1990). P.L. 101-508 (1990); Joyce, P. & Reischauer, R. (1992). *Deficit budgeting.*

34. U.S. Congressional Budget Office (2006). *The budget and economic outlook: fiscal years 2007–2016.* Washington, DC: U.S. Government Printing Office.

35. Schick, A. (2000). *The federal budget*, 105–138.

36. Dennis, S. (2006). House adopts budget, setting up floor action on appropriation bills. *CQ Today*, May 17.

37. Doyle, R. (1996). *Congress, the deficit, and budget reconciliation.*

38. Dauster, W. (1998). The monster that ate the United States Senate. *Public Budgeting & Finance, 18, Summer*, 87–93.

39. Collender, S. (2001). Repeated reconciliation. *Government Executive*. Retrieved January 10, 2001, from http://www.govexec.com/dailyfed/0101/011001bb.htm.

40. U.S. Congressional Budget Office (2006). *Unauthorized appropriations and expiring authorizations*. Washington, DC: U.S. Government Printing Office.

41. Lilly, S. (2005). Does rearranging appropriations panels make any sense? *Roll Call, January 27*.

42. Streeter, S. (2006). *Continuing appropriations acts: brief overview of recent practices*. Washington, DC: Congressional Research Service, 6.

43. Dennis, S. & Higa, L. (2006). Conservatives frustrated in earmarks crusade. *CQ Today, June 14*. Retrieved August 30, from http://oncongress.cq.com.

44. U.S. Congressional Budget Office (1990). *The 1990 budget agreement: an interim assessment*. Washington, DC: U.S. Government Printing Office; U.S. Congressional Budget Office (1992). *The economic and budget outlook: fiscal years 1993–1997*. Washington, DC: U.S. Government Printing Office.

45. Woodward, B. (1994). *The agenda: inside the Clinton White House*. New York: Simon and Schuster.

46. Woodward, B. (1994). *The agenda: inside the Clinton White House*. New York: Simon and Schuster.

47. Omnibus Budget Reconciliation Act (1993). P.L. 103-66.

48. Oak, D. (1995). An overview of adjustments to the Budget Enforcement Act discretionary spending caps. *Public Budgeting & Finance, 15. Fall*, 35–53.

49. Bader, J. (1996). *Taking the initiative: leadership agendas in Congress and the "Contract with America."* Washington, DC: Georgetown University Press; Gimpel, J. (1996). *Legislating the revolution: the Contract with America in its first 100 days*. Boston, MA: Allyn and Bacon.

50. Joyce, P. & Meyers, R. (2001). Budgeting during the Clinton presidency. *Public Budgeting & Finance, 21, Spring*, 1–21.

51. Meyers, R. (1997). Late appropriations and government shutdowns: frequency, causes, consequences, and remedies. *Public Budgeting and Finance, 17, Fall*, 25–38.

52. Joyce, P. & Meyers, R. (2001). *Budgeting during the Clinton presidency. Public Budgeting & Finance, 21, Spring*, 1–21.

53. Shear, J. (1996). The tale of the dogs. *National Journal, 28*, 18–22.

54. Hager, G. (1997). Clinton, GOP Congress strike historic budget agreement. *Congressional Quarterly Weekly Report, 56*, 993, 996–997.

55. Balanced Budget Act (1997). P.L. 105-33 (1997) and Taxpayer Relief Act (1997). P.L. 105-34.

56. U.S. Congressional Budget Office (2001). *The budget and economic outlook: fiscal years 2003–2012*. Washington, DC: U.S. Government Printing Office, 158.

57. U.S. Congressional Budget Office (2001). *The budget and economic outlook: fiscal years 2003–2012*, xiv; U.S. Office of Management and Budget (2001). *A blueprint for new beginnings*. Washington, DC: U.S. Government Printing Office, 185.

58. Economic Growth and Tax Relief Reconciliation Act (2001). P.L. 107–16.

59. Berry, J. (2001). Greenspan supports a tax cut. *Washington Post, January 26*, A1.

60. Nitschke, L. & Boudreau, W. (2001). Provisions of the tax law. *Congressional Quarterly Weekly Report, 59, June 9*, 1390.

61. U.S. Congressional Budget Office (2007). *The budget and economic outlook: fiscal years 2008-2017*. Washington, DC: U.S. Government Printing Office, 16.

62. For an early take on the reasons for this deterioration, see Gale, W. & Orszag, P. (2003). Fiscal follies: the real budget problem and how to fix it. *The Brookings Review, 21*, 7–11.

63. U.S. Congressional Budget Office (2007). *The budget and economic outlook: fiscal years 2008-2017*, 7.

64. U.S. Congressional Budget Office (2007). *The budget and economic outlook: fiscal years 2008-2017*, xii.

65. Joyce, P. (2005). *Federal budgeting after September 11th*: A whole new ballgame, or is it deja vu all over again? *Public Budgeting & Finance, 25, Spring*, 15–31.

66. Joyce, P. (2005). Federal budgeting after September 11th; Senate Committee on the Budget (2006). Eating more ice cream causes crime rates to rise. *The Informed Budgeteer, June 29*, 1.

67. Dennis, S. (2006). Comparing House and Senate budget resolutions. *Congressional Quarterly Weekly Report, 64*, 1405.

68. U.S. Congressional Budget Office (2005). *The long-term budget outlook*. Washington, DC: U.S. Government Printing Office.

69. U.S. Congressional Budget Office (2005). *The long-term budget outlook*, Washington, DC: U.S. Government Printing Office, 4, 10.

70. Meyers, R. & Joyce, P. (2005). Congressional budgeting at age 30: Is it worth saving? *Public Budgeting & Finance, 26, Special Issue*, 68–82.

71. U.S. Congressional Budget Office (2002). *The looming budgetary impact of society's aging*. Washington, DC: U.S. Government Printing Office.

72. Rieselbach, L. (1993). *Congressional reform: the changing modern Congress*. Washington, DC: Congressional Quarterly Press.

73. Sinclair, B. (1995). *Legislators, leaders and lawmaking: the U.S. House of Representatives in the post-reform era*. Baltimore, MD: Johns Hopkins University Press.

74. Marini, J. (1992). *The politics of budget control: Congress, the presidency and the growth of the administrative state*. Washington, DC: Crane Russak.

75. Gryski, G. S. (1991). The influence of committee position on federal program spending. *Polity, 23*, 443–459.

76. U.S. General Accounting Office (1992). *Line item veto: estimating potential savings*. Washington, DC: U.S. Government Printing Office.

77. Letter from Anthony H. Gamboa to The Honorable Thad Cochran and the Honorable Robert C. Byrd (2005). *Updated rescission statistics, fiscal years 1974-2005*. Washington, DC: U.S. Government Accountability Office.

78. Line Item Veto Act (1996). P.L. 104-130; Joyce, P. & Reischauer, R. (1997). The federal line-item veto: what is it and what will it do? *Public Administration Review, 57*, 95–104.

79. W. J. Clinton (1997). Remarks by the president on the line item veto. August 11. Retrieved December 11, 1997, from http://www.whitehouse.gov.

80. Joyce, P. (1998). The line-item veto experiment: after the Supreme Court ruling, what's next? *Public Budgeting & Finance, 18, Winter*, 3–22.

81. Byrd, R., as quoted in Taylor, A. (1996). Congress hands president a budgetary scalpel. *Congressional Quarterly Weekly Report, 54*, 866.

82. *Byrd* v. *Raines* (1997). 6 LW 2660 (DDC); *Raines* v. *Byrd* (1997). 521 U.S. 811 (1997).

83. *Clinton* v. *City of New York* (1998). 524 U.S. 417.

84. Joyce, P. (1998). *The line-item veto experiment.*

85. Statement of Donald B. Marron before the United States Senate, Committee on the Budget, May 2, 2006.

86. A veto in the Senate? (2006). *Wall Street Journal, July 28*, A14.

87. Cohn, P. (2006). Chances poor for line-item veto legislation. *Govexec.com.* Retrieved August 25, 2006, from http://www.govexec.com/dailyfed/0706/072006dam2.htm.

88. Statement of Donald B. Marron, May 2, 2006.

89. Hager, G. (1997). Country comes full circle on balancing the budget. *Congressional Quarterly Weekly Report, 55*, 278–285.

90. Hou, Y. & Smith, D. L. (2006). A framework for understanding state balanced budget requirements systems: re-examining distinctive features and an operational definition. *Public Budgeting & Finance, 26, Fall*, 22–45.

91. Kiefer, D. W. et al. (1992). *A balanced budget constitutional amendment: economic issues.* Washington, DC: Congressional Research Service.

92. U.S. Congressional Budget Office (1993). *The economic and budget outlook: fiscal years 1994–1998.*

93. Rep. Istook leads drive for balanced budget amendment (2006). *U.S. Fed News.* Retrieved August 25, 2006, from http://web.lexis-nexis.com.

94. Legislative Reorganization Act (1946). Ch. 753; Legislative Reorganization Act (1970). P.L. 91-510.

95. Shear, J. (1996). Power loss. *National Journal, 28*, 874–878.

96. Mann, T. & Ornstein, N. (1993). *Renewing Congress: a second report.* Washington, DC: Brookings Institution.

97. Garrett, E. (1996). Term limitations and the myth of the citizen legislator. *Cornell Law Review, 81*, 623–697.

98. *U.S. Term Limits, Inc.* v. *Thornton* (1995). 514 U.S. 779.

99. Kapochunas, R. (2006). One promise that's safe to break: the term limit pledge. Retrieved August 29, 2006, from *CQ Today, March 24*, http://oncongress.cq.com/display.do?dockey=/cqonline/prod/data/docs/html/news/109/new.

100. Meyers, R. (1988). Biennial budgeting in the U.S. Congress. *Public Budgeting & Finance, 8, Summer*, 21–32.

101. Joyce, P. (2000). Testimony before the Subcommittee on Legislative and Budget Process, Committee on Rules, United States House of Representatives, *Biennial budgeting: a tool for improving government fiscal management and oversight, March 20*, 268–274; National Performance Review (1993). *From red tape to results: creating a government that works better and costs less.* Washington, DC: U.S. Government Printing Office.

102. Allen, J. (2006). Sen. Judd Gregg fills budget bill with a host of reforms. *The Hill, June 14*, 3.

103. Allen, J. (2006). Biennial budgeters hopes rise. *The Hill, February 28*, 3.

104. Joyce, P. (2000). Testimony before Subcommittee on Legislative and Budget Process.

105. Joyce, P. (2000). Testimony before Subcommittee on Legislative and Budget Process.

106. H.R. 853, Comprehensive Budget Process Reform Act, Reported in House August 1999.

107. Meyers, R. (1990). The budget resolution should be a law. *Public Budgeting & Finance, 10, Fall*, 103–112; Meyers, R. (1994). *Strategic budgeting.* Ann Arbor, MI: University of Michigan Press.

108. Fulton, A. (2000). Budget reform bill faces opposition in House. *Congress Daily, May 16*.

109. U.S. General Accounting Office (1998). *Budget issues: budgeting for capital.* Washington, DC: U.S. Government Printing Office.

110. Mandel, J. (2006). Panel debates competing bills to "sunset" federal programs. Retrieved August 2, 2006, from http://www.govexec.com/dailyfed/0706/071906m2.htm.

Chapter 10

BUDGET EXECUTION

Once the budget has been approved, the execution phase of the budget cycle begins. Of course, at the federal level it is common for many agencies to enter the execution phase with only a continuing resolution to spend at the previous year's rate rather than to spend under a new appropriation (see Chapter 9). This same practice sometimes occurs at the state level. In contrast, local governments usually are required by state law to complete the budget approval phase by the beginning of the new fiscal year.

This chapter has five sections. The first section deals with interactions between the central budget office and the line agencies. Then four subsystems of the execution phase are discussed—tax administration, cash management, procurement, and risk management.

Budget Office and Agency Relations

As would be expected, relationships—both direct and indirect—are extensive between the central budget office and the line agencies during the execution phase of the budget. In this section, we examine these relationships as they pertain specifically to the budget. We then consider a variety of other activities that bring the budget office into contact with agencies.

Interactions on Budgeting

Execution is the action phase of budgeting, in which the plans contained in the budget are put into operation. Every budget either explicitly or implicitly contains plans for the work to be done and the achievements to be made. Execution, then, involves converting those plans into operations. During this phase, budget office personnel gain important insights into the operations of agencies and this knowledge later becomes important during the next round of budget preparation.[1]

Legislative Intent. The legislature provides some indication of legislative intent through a variety of mechanisms, some legally binding and some advisory. Legislative intent is what the legislators had in mind when creating and funding programs. Legislative intent begins with the creation of a governmental unit and programs for it to administer. For example, a state legislature will have created a unit for special education and one or more programs for that unit to administer. Congress goes the additional step of passing authorization legislation that may specify specific dollar amounts to be spent, although as was seen in Chapter 9, those amounts serve as ceilings and usually wait to be funded through appropriation bills. Besides these provisions are a host of other legal requirements pertaining to legislative intent. The Government Accountability Office has a manual known as the "Red Book" that discusses these requirements.[2]

Agencies prefer *lump-sum* appropriations, meaning monies that are in one overall pot and not broken into smaller ones. In the example of special education, the legislature can appropriate for that category as a whole or for specific types of disabilities, such as special education for people with hearing impairments, sight impairments, and the like. The amounts could be further specified by the type of service provided to each of these target groups.

The legislative intent contained in authorizing and appropriating legislation is by definition legally binding during budget execution, but beyond these is a grey area of legislative intent. Bills reported out for full house consideration are accompanied by committee reports that explain what provisions were considered and why the committees are recommending specific provisions. These reports can run to tens or even hundreds of pages in length.

When a bill is debated on the floor of the house and senate at the federal and state levels, members of the relevant committees will speak about the bill's provisions as will other members. These presentations may be aimed at persuading colleagues to vote for the bill as reported and without unwelcome amendments, but certainly of equal importance is getting into the official record the intent of the bill's framers.

In some cases, legislative units issue further reports about bills after their passage. In other words, after an appropriation bill is passed, a legislative unit may prepare a summary report explaining its interpretation of what transpired when the full legislative body adopted the bill.

Except for two critical factors, statements contained in committee reports, statements made from the house and senate floors, and statements made in reports subsequent to passage of bills lack much legal status regarding legislative intent.

First, these statements have the effect of putting the budget office and the affected agencies on notice of what is expected in the implementation of the laws. To ignore these informal provisions, an agency runs the risk of raising the ire of legislators, people who may have the power to cut their budgets next year or to hamstring them with specific provisions in law.

The second factor involves legal challenges. Some laws and how they are administered are challenged in court by private citizens, state and local governments, interest groups, and even legislators themselves. Courts in deciding legislative intent first turn to the statutes involved and use a "plain language" interpretation. In other words, how does the law read using standard usage of the English language? If ambiguities remain, then courts turn to the unofficial forms of legislative intent, namely committee reports before passage, floor debates, and committee reports after passage.

Both legislators and executives realize that language in authorizing legislation and appropriations needs to be worded somewhat generally so as to provide flexibility over time. An authorization law might be valid for five years, ten years, or indefinitely. The appropriation will be valid for one year or two in states with biennial budgets. As time passes, executive agencies need flexibility to adapt to changes in their environments and therefore need flexibility in the laws under which they operate. This flexibility, then, creates an opening for further decision making at the onset of the new fiscal year. Once an agency's appropriation is passed by the legislature, the agency is not simply in the position of routinely commencing administration with its new funding.

Apportionments and Allotments. At the state and federal levels, an apportionment process is used in which line agencies submit plans to the central budget office for how appropriated funds will be used. The plans often indicate proposed expenditures for each month or quarter of the fiscal year. Office of Management and Budget (OMB) Circular A-11 governs this process at the federal level. According to OMB, "Apportionment means a distribution made by OMB of amounts available for obligation in an appropriation or fund account into amounts available for specified time periods, program[s], activities, projects, objects, or any combinations of these. The apportionment amount limits the obligations that may be incurred."[3]

A primary purpose of apportionment is to ensure that agencies spend at a rate that will keep them within limits imposed by their annual appropriations.

Another purpose is to guide agencies so that the desired program accomplishments are achieved. As A-11 indicates, "The apportionment also identifies meaningful program reporting categories that agencies will report obligations against. . . ." The apportionment plan, therefore, should seemingly be linked closely with performance plans, although that is not always the case. Agencies should be required to defend their proposed apportionment plans in terms of the work that they expect to accomplish over the course of the fiscal year. A third purpose may be to guide agencies in using resources efficiently. At the federal level, agencies use Standard Form 132 to submit their apportionment plans, that OMB then approves, modifies, or disapproves. Spending cannot begin until approval is granted.

The budget office may require modification of agency proposals and eventually approves apportionments for each agency. Following the approval of apportionments by the budget office, allotments are made within departments. This process grants expenditure authority to subunits. At the local level, this process may be relatively informal, while the process is complicated at the federal level where allotments may be divided into suballotments and allocations.

In the apportionment process, chief executives and their budget offices have greater power to deny authority than to grant authority to agencies. The executive cannot approve apportionments for projects prohibited in the appropriation but may be able to reduce or eliminate some appropriated items. As noted in Chapter 9, presidents have impounded appropriated funds. Another executive means of denying spending authority is to exercise the item veto, that is common among the states and also is used in some local governments.

Initial Planning. At the outset of the fiscal year, agencies must accommodate differences between the actual appropriations and the original requests for funding. In addition, some substantive changes may be specified in the appropriations, or an informal understanding may have developed between an agency and legislators over how a program will be redirected.

For agencies that were fortunate enough to obtain increased funds for improving or expanding existing programs or for new programs, the budget office plays a key role. Mindful that the legislature will expect a detailed reporting of how these funds were used, the budget office exercises oversight in implementing the program revisions or new programs.

Control of Agencies. From the perspective of the central administration, agencies must live within their budgets. Otherwise, the budget process becomes an empty exercise. Therefore, various controls are imposed upon agencies, including the *preaudit*. After approval of an apportionment plan and granting an allotment, an agency still is not free to spend but rather must submit a request to obligate the government to spend resources. The request is matched against the unit's budget to determine whether the proposed expenditure is authorized and whether sufficient funds are available in the agency's budget.

Several different units may carry out the preaudit function. Not only the budget office, but also an accounting department, may be involved. At the state and local levels, independent comptrollers, controllers, or auditors general often have preaudit responsibilities. These officials have the duty of providing another, presumably independent, check on financial transactions.

In the case of an agency proposing to hire new staff, not only will the usual preaudit procedure be used, but a central personnel office also may review the request. Such a review, known as *personnel complement control*, is used in part to avoid increasing personnel commitments and corresponding increases in budget requirements over what has been appropriated.

Midyear Changes. As the year progresses, the budget office conducts reviews of agency operations. One all-too-common problem is that the need or demand for services far exceeds the funds appropriated. Such conditions are known at the outset of the fiscal year, with allotment plans being used in effect to ration services across the year. In other situations, the need or demand may rise unexpectedly and sharply during the year. That may prompt a request for a supplemental appropriation from the legislative branch. In other circumstances, the budget office will work with agencies to stay within funding limits.

Each summer the Office of Management and Budget issues the *Mid-Session Review of the Budget* that discusses economic trends and the ways in which these trends are affecting receipts, spending patterns, the activities of credit programs, and whatever other procedures are in place to attempt to limit the budget deficit. The Congressional Budget Office (CBO) issues monthly budget reviews and then in mid-summer updates its *Budget and Economic Outlook*. These reports cover some of the same ground as the OMB mid-session document. The Treasury Department issues a *Monthly Treasury Statement of Receipts and Outlays of the U.S. Government* that is another tool for tracking government finances during budget execution.

Midyear crises may arise because of an unfavorable revenue situation. Government budgets that depend heavily on a single commodity export, like Venezuela's budget, that relies on oil, may experience significant fluctuation during the year as the world price of the commodity fluctuates. In the United States, a downturn in a state's economy can have devastating effects on sales tax and income tax receipts, forcing across-the-board cutbacks in spending, as happened in the recession of 2001–2002. Because personnel costs usually are the largest single item in operating budgets, these costs must be curtailed when revenue receipts fall below projected levels. Personnel hiring freezes are common in government.

Another, more extreme, technique is to furlough employees. Some governments have expected all employees to share in the solution by working and being paid for, a four-day week rather than a five-day week, thereby creating a 20% savings. Depending on the chief executives' authority, they may be able to cut back on agency spending to bring outgo in line with income or they may need approval from the legislature to take such action.

The September 11, 2001, terrorist attacks on the World Trade Center and the Pentagon, followed by the spread of anthrax through the mail system, had enormous impacts on budgets at all levels of government. Decision makers ordered increased security for airports, bridges, water systems, and the like. Health officials at all levels of government stepped up activities to be prepared for possible widespread bioterrorism. The Defense Department began a war on the Taliban regime in Afghanistan and sent troops to Yemen and the Philippines, resulting in expenses not previously anticipated in the department's budget. These threats to the health and safety of society had to be met and necessarily forced the midyear approval of major budget changes.

The 2001 catastrophes pushed the then-weak economy into a recession, resulting in decreased revenues at a time when the need for government spending had risen sharply. State governments found themselves having to rework their budgets as a result of massive revenue shortfalls. Meanwhile, Congress had to pass supplemental appropriations to authorize increased spending for federal agencies in the thick of the fight against terrorism.

As the wars in Afghanistan and later Iraq waged on into the second Bush administration, funding of these massive efforts was handled through supplemental appropriations rather than regular appropriations. The administration took the position that even though it was known that vast sums would be needed in these endeavors, the specific needs could not be forecast at regular budget time and therefore were left to be handled through supplementals. Additionally, recovery from the 2005 hurricane season was handled through this method. **Table 10–1** lists defense funding legislation for the War on Terrorism from 2001 through 2006. Note that supplementals dominate the table.

When an agency wishes to shift existing resources to meet new needs during the fiscal year or when an agency receives a supplemental appropriation, it must prepare a revised apportionment or reapportionment plan. The budget office then has an opportunity to exercise some guidance over how the agency will spend its monies. This process is sometimes known as *budget revision* or *rebudgeting*.

Just because a government is experiencing a downturn in revenues and needs to cut expenditures, it does not mean there will be no need for supplemental appropriations. In other words, budget increases and decreases occur simultaneously during budget execution. Some agencies' budgets of necessity may be augmented while others are cut to try to make up the difference.[4] For example, many

Table 10–1	Defense Funding Provided for the War on Terrorism, 2001–2006* (in Billions of Dollars)		
Appropriations		**Date**	**2001–2006**
2001 Emergency Supplemental, Appropriations Act for Recovery from and Response to Terrorist Attacks on the United States		September 2001	$13.6
Department of Defense and Emergency Supplemental Appropriations for Recovery from and Response to Terrorist Attacks on the United States		January 2002	3.5
2002 Supplemental Appropriations Act for Recovery from the Response to Terrorist Attacks on the United States		August 2002	14.0
Department of Defense Transfers in 2002 from Regular Appropriations		Not Applicable	0.3
Department of Defense Appropriations Act, 2003		October 2002	6.4
Consolidated Appropriations Resolution, 2003		February 2003	10.0
Emergency Wartime Supplemental Appropriations Act, 2003		April 2003	62.8
Department of Defense Transfers in 2003 from Regular Appropriations		Not Applicable	1.1
Department of Defense Appropriations Act, 2004		September 2003	–3.5
Emergency Supplemental Appropriations Act for Defense and for the Reconstruction of Iraq and Afghanistan, 2004		November 2003	65.2
Department of Defense Appropriations Act, 2005		August 2004	24.9
Department of Defense Transfers in 2004 from Regular Appropriations		Not Applicable	1.6
Emergency Supplemental Appropriations for Defense, the Global War on Terror, and Tsunami Relief Act, 2005		May 2005	75.9
Department of Defense Transfers in 2005 from Regular Appropriations		Not Applicable	1.5
Department of Defense Appropriations Act, 2006		December 2005	50.0
Emergency Supplemental Appropriations Act for Defense, the Global War on Terror, and Hurricane Recovery, 2006		June 2006	66.1
Total			$393.3

* Data are for defense funding only and exclude international affairs funding for the war on terrorism.

Source: Adapted from U.S. Congressional Budget Office (2006). *Table: Defense funding provided for the war on terrorism, 2001–2006*. Washington, DC: CBO. Retrieved October 27, 2006, from http://www.cbo.gov/ftpdocs/75xx/doc7506/GWOT_Tables_2006_08.pdf.

state government departments may have their budgets trimmed, while the state's labor department budget is being augmented to cope with an increased caseload of unemployed workers.

Throughout the execution phase, which by definition is the entire fiscal year, budget analysts play critical roles. Here leadership in the budget office is essential, since left on their own, analysts will vary greatly among one another as to how they operate. Some may perform more of a control function, focusing largely on financial numbers and trying to keep agencies in check. Other analysts may be more oriented toward the substantive content of the programs that they oversee, attempting to assert influence over the content of agency operations and not being content with mere number crunching to keep budgets on track with apportionment plans.[5] Therefore, the role of the budget director and other top staff members is critical in orchestrating a coherent approach to budget execution.

During the execution phase, agencies are required to supply periodic reports on their budgets. At the federal level, quarterly reports are required by law (Standard Form 133). Also cabinet departments and some independent agencies must supply outlay reports that are used to monitor trends in budget deficits or surpluses.

End-of-Year Spending. As the fiscal year approaches its end, agencies will attempt to zero out their budgets. An agency having unexpended funds at the end of the fiscal year may be considered a prime candidate for cuts in the upcoming budget. Agencies with budget surpluses at the end of the year may have their budget bases reduced in the next fiscal year. Also, unexpended or unencumbered funds often lapse at the end of the budget year. From the agency's perspective, it is a now-or-never situation for spending the available money. Another factor is that an agency may have delayed some expenditures, saving a portion of its budget for contingencies. This delay results in a spurt in expenditures at the end of the year, with some spending being highly appropriate and other spending being utterly wasteful. Congress has reduced this last-minute spurt by limiting the proportion of an agency's funds that may be spent in the final quarter of the fiscal year.

An alternative is to allow surplus funds to be transferred to the agency's new budget without requiring a reappropriation. Some jurisdictions allow this kind of transfer within limits, such as a small percentage of each unit's total budget.[6] Advocates of an entrepreneurial spirit in government argue that agencies should be rewarded for efficiency by being allowed to carry over funds into the next fiscal year. The National Performance Review recommended that agencies be able to carry as much as 50% of their internal operations budgets into the next fiscal year.[7]

Reorganizing, Downsizing, Privatizing, and Outsourcing

The Taft Commission on Economy and Efficiency is best known for its 1912 report recommending the establishment of a federal budget process under the direction of the president. The title of the commission is significant in that a primary goal was a better use of government resources (see Chapter 1). More than nine decades later, the same concerns of the Taft Commission remain prevalent at all levels of government. Incentives for economy and efficiency are created by taxing and spending limitation measures, by fiscal stress or distress resulting from the erosion of tax bases of many jurisdictions, and by the increased popularity of a form of conservatism dedicated to reducing the role of government in society.

Budget offices historically have played central roles in examining the structures of departments and agencies, with an eye toward possible reorganization as a means for increasing the efficiency of operations. In addition to structural arrangements, budget offices often seek improvements in management processes as a means of garnering savings. Outside experts are used, as was the case in the Grace Commission during the Reagan administration. The commission, whose full title was the President's Private Sector Survey on Cost Control, consisted of chief executive officers from private corporations.[8] The National Performance Review (NPR), during the Clinton administration, was an in-house effort to improve all aspects of government and recommended the reorganization of several government offices and the elimination of others. The Office of Management and Budget was deeply involved in all of these efforts, although its participation was not always synchronized with NPR efforts. When the Department of Homeland Security was created in 2002, OMB played a key role in orchestrating the massive reorganization of units from various federal departments into the new department.[9]

A phenomenon that gained special momentum in the 1980s and continued since is that of cutback management, downsizing, or "rightsizing" (see Chapter 7). Much of the focus of such efforts is on reducing government employment, with the budget offices often in charge of implementing such initiatives. At the federal level, the Clinton administration adopted the NPR's recommendation to reduce personnel levels. The George W. Bush administration initially supported cutbacks by recommending major reductions in the supervisory ranks of government workers and by outsourcing government jobs to the private sector. However, in reducing the ranks of government employment, the government denied entry into the federal workforce to younger workers, and the average age of workers climbed. Subsequently, the administration faced a deluge of retirements that would rob the bureaucracy of experienced talent. OMB included as part of the budget preparation process a requirement that agencies specify target reductions in personnel and show how they planned to meet these targeted figures, but this practice was later dropped. Defense Department downsizing over the years has included closure of numerous installations as well as a "drawdown" in personnel. The White House subsequently recognized in the human capital section of the *President's Management Agenda* that a cost had been paid for the years of cutbacks.[10]

Downsizing and rightsizing and similar efforts may be aimed simply at reducing the size of government on the assumption that the bureaucracy is bloated and that cutbacks are possible without really altering the level of service. Other efforts to reduce the size and role of government may be based on the premise that certain functions are necessary but that most likely are not well run and could be performed better by the private sector. One option to achieve this reduced role of government in favor of the private sector is *privatization*. While definitions vary, the core of any definition of privatization or privatizing is the reassignment of government activities to the private sector. Privatization typically involves the selling of government assets to the private sector and turning the operation of these facilities over to private companies. For example, in the United Kingdom during the administration of former Prime Minister Margaret Thatcher, British Overseas Airways Corporation became a private company and some public water companies were sold off. Privatization is sometimes coupled with close regulation, namely, while a company is privately owned, it must continue to comply with extensive government regulations.

The delivery of governmental services can be carried out to a considerable degree with the cooperation of private for-profit and nonprofit enterprises. A common mechanism used for this is *contracting* or *outsourcing*, in which a private firm provides a product or service at an agreed quantity, quality, and price. Other means of encouraging private sector involvement in the provision of public services include grants, loan guarantees, tax expenditures, social regulation, and government corporations. Outsourcing of government services is intended to increase government efficiency and reduce government spending. It should be kept in mind that outsourcing may result officially in a reduction in the number of government employees, but that many private sector employees will have jobs only because of government contracting. Outsourcing can be used for so-called business services such as janitorial housekeeping, but also for more fundamental basic services such as water, roads, prisons, and the like.[11]

Although the procedures used in contracting are reviewed later in this chapter, we note here that OMB Circular A-76, Performance of Commercial Activities, provides for a review process to determine when activities of the government should be contracted out. Two main criteria apply: that the activity be a "commercial" one and not "governmental," and that the cost be lower in the private sector than in government. Examples of commercial activities include guarding public buildings and providing cafeterias for employees. Policy-making activities are not to be contracted out.

Contracting out has at least two types of supporters. One group wants to increase the efficiency of government operations through utilization of the private sector.[12] Circular A-76 uses an efficiency standard, namely, contracting out should be used when the unit cost for a service is lower outside of government than inside it. The second group adheres to the view that the population is better served if service delivery is left, where possible, to the private sector. These advocates of outsourcing contend that government should be proactive in seeking opportunities for turning over functions to the private sector.

Although critics contend that sometimes too much faith is placed in private enterprise and that outsourcing supports non-unionized firms that pay low wages, private sector contracting has become a familiar form of service delivery in the United States and abroad.[13] Contracting out is routinely used for such services as refuse pickup and towing of illegally parked vehicles. Private sector firms under government contract now handle services once thought to be exclusively the responsibility of the public sector, such as welfare services and the operation of prisons. Ports are being largely privatized, and there has been discussion of outsourcing both the air traffic control function and Social Security, namely having private companies operate these activities for the government.[14]

Several lessons have been learned as governments have ventured into outsourcing, with one of the most important being the need to conduct a thorough analysis before taking the plunge.[15] There is a need to consider whether cost efficiencies will be attained, whether the private firm will be held accountable for its performance, whether any cost efficiency is attained at the expense of quality, and whether equity or fairness in treating citizens and employees will be achieved.[16] Another important question is whether companies in the market can provide the agreed-upon services in a timely fashion and can respond to unforeseen problems that may arise. Do any legal barriers prohibit privatizing a given service? And what liability risks may be created by having a private firm deliver a government service?

The analysis needs to include projected costs for monitoring a firm in its delivery of a service. A government must be able to assure itself that a firm is abiding by its commitments and be able to respond when citizens complain about a service. Part of the monitoring process includes determining whether the cost savings that were predicted in the original analysis did, indeed, materialize. Some local governments that contract out for solid waste collection also retain some capacity inside government. In a given city, waste is collected in some areas by private contractors and in some areas by city employees. That way the city retains some capability if the private service provider does not live up to its obligations, and it ensures that there will be at least one competitor if only one private firm ventures a bid.

A dogmatic stance that services should be contracted out wherever possible is unwarranted in that government may well be able to provide some services at costs lower than private firms can deliver. Competitive bidding on contemplated outsourcing projects can include not only private firms but government agencies as well. Phoenix, Arizona, and Fort Lauderdale, Florida, have been leaders in developing and using this approach.[17] Contracting out to private firms to operate a school system also has been adopted in some jurisdictions, both to save money and to improve student performance on testing programs. The evidence as to whether school districts are getting what they intended is uncertain. Further, a mix in service delivery may be more cost-effective than strict outsourcing. In other words, any given service may be delivered in a cooperative arrangement that includes a combination of government agencies, for-profit firms, and nonprofit organizations.

The aftermath of the September 11, 2001, catastrophes is instructive. One patently obvious fact was that airport security had been breached so that terrorists were able to commandeer and crash four airliners. To that point in time, security had been the responsibility of private companies whose expenses were paid by the airlines. There was consensus that this private sector system failed abysmally and that government involvement was warranted. A vigorous debate ensued in Congress between Democrats, who wanted the government to take over airport security, and Republicans, who wanted the government to oversee private security operations. The decision ultimately was to convert airport screening jobs to the public sector under the direction of the new Transportation Security Administration.

Management Controls

Budget offices have been assigned a variety of management-related duties beyond the core activities of assembling proposed budgets and overseeing their execution. For instance, budget offices may be partially responsible for establishing standards to be used in accounting systems (OMB Circular A-127). Of course, other units such as the Government Accountability Office (GAO) at the federal level also play major roles in this area. Information systems and procurement are other important areas in which budget offices have key roles. Procurement is discussed later in this chapter.

Some budget offices have responsibility for studying agency procedures and for recommending or prescribing new procedures. These organization-and-management (O&M) studies can recommend changes in the department's management processes.

Budget offices set ground rules for many of the routine activities of line organizations. For example, limitations are set for paying employee travel costs. Centrally imposed standards also circumscribe the use of consulting services.

Some budget offices are charged with performing a legislative clearinghouse function. Before an agency may endorse a proposal for new or revised legislation, the proposal must be vetted through the budget office. This practice helps ensure that what is proposed is consistent with the views of the chief executive, both substantively and financially (see OMB Circular A-19).

Because corruption in government often involves finance, budget offices sometimes have major responsibility for protecting the government against fraud, waste, and abuse of government resources. The Inspector General Act of 1978 created relatively independent inspector general offices in major federal departments and gave these offices responsibility for investigating possible cases of fraud and other wrongdoing. The inspectors general meet as the President's Council on Integrity and

Efficiency, which is chaired by the OMB.[18] In addition, agency-appointed inspectors general meet as the Executive Council on Integrity and Efficiency. This body includes representatives of independent agencies, such as the Federal Trade Commission and the Corporation for Public Broadcasting. The President's Council was active in ferreting out fraud in the aftermath of Hurricanes Katrina and Rita in 2005.[19]

The OMB also oversees agency compliance with the Federal Managers' Financial Integrity Act of 1982, which requires safeguarding financial systems, particularly accounting and payroll, from fraud.[20] OMB Circular A-123, which is used to implement the law, was revised in 2004 and took effect in 2006. The circular emphasizes that managers should be held accountable for producing government services that yield desired results as well as for providing these services free of fraud and abuse of resources. Similar controls are established at the state and local levels.[21] In the private sector, following such major corporate failures as Enron, the Sarbanes-Oxley Act applies (see Chapter 11). One provision of this multifaceted law is a strict requirement on internal controls.[22]

Presidents frequently assign OMB responsibility for improving the management of government operations. In 2001, his first year in office, President George W. Bush issued the *President's Management Agenda*.[23] Three of the five government-wide initiatives in the agenda were specifically related to budgeting: competitive sourcing (contracting), improving financial performance (correcting errors in government payments, see Chapter 11), and integrating budgeting and performance (see Chapter 5). The other two were strategically managing human capital and expanding electronic government. To implement the management agenda as well as other management initiatives, President Bush reconstituted the President's Management Council, a body that had been created by President Clinton in 1993. The council consists of chief operating officers (COOs), who have the status equal to that of deputy secretary. In other words, these COOs are expected to have authority to implement management reforms within their respective units.

To bring pressure to bear on departments and agencies, OMB initiated a scorecard system using "traffic light" grading on the five initiatives of the management agenda (see Chapter 6). President Bush asked Congress in 2001 to pass two bills related to management of agency operations. The first, the Freedom to Manage legislation, would expedite congressional action in reviewing presidential requests to amend or eliminate statutory provisions that present barriers to efficient management. The contention was that some statutory provisions were well intentioned when originally passed but had outlived their usefulness. The second bill, the Managerial Flexibility Act, would ease many restrictions imposed by personnel management systems. Agencies would have greater flexibility in recruiting workers, compensating them (including the use of bonuses), and retaining workers.[24] Although neither bill was approved by Congress, they highlight what some executives consider solutions in improving federal management.

Another function of OMB is to deal with alleged instances of post-employment conflicts of interest in which former government employees may be illegally benefiting from their previous experience in government or their new employers may be illegally benefiting from inappropriate contacts. Of course, OMB is not the sole central agency responsible for handling problems in this area. Other important offices include the Office of Personnel Management, the Merit Systems Protection Board, the Department of Justice, and GAO. In the matter of employee conflict of interest, the chief legal counsel of the agency usually evaluates whether a former employee's activity is inappropriate when contacting the agency.

OMB, along with the Council on Environmental Quality (CEQ), which is a unit of the Executive Office of the President, is responsible for devising means for cleaning up environmental conditions on federal land. Extensive environmental pollution exists on military installations, facilities of the National Aeronautics and Space Administration, and other federal properties. More generally, OMB and CEQ oversee agencies in their preparation of comprehensive Environmental Management Systems.[25]

Agencies must report to OMB on several other matters. According to law, OMB must be given reports on agency activities and expenditures pertaining to crime control and drug control. Agencies must report on how they are complying with the Federal Advisory Committee Act of 1972, Executive Order 12838 (1993), and Circular A-135 (1994), that require agencies to reduce their use of advisory committees.[26] The premise here is that while the government benefits from external advice, such advice often costs more than it is worth.

Besides these areas mentioned, budget offices may have some responsibility for other management controls over agencies. For example, budget offices may be involved in implementing government-wide affirmative action plans. Some states have right-to-know laws that require employers, both public and private, to inform their employees whether they are working with hazardous materials. Measures aimed at reducing dangerous conditions obviously have budgetary implications. Budget offices may have some responsibilities in implementing freedom-of-information laws.

Control of Information Collection, Quality, Security, and Dissemination

Budget offices are heavily involved in government collection and dissemination of information. A chief concern is that government agencies heap huge burdens on individuals and corporations, and in the case of the federal government, on state and local governments in requiring them to submit information. The Paperwork Reduction Act (PRA), originally passed in 1980 and thoroughly rewritten in 1995, provides an elaborate process by which the federal government handles information.[27] The process is under the supervision of OMB's Office of Information and

Regulatory Affairs (OIRA). The law is implemented by OMB Circular A-130. Each department is required to have a Chief Information Officer (CIO), appointed by the department head and directly accountability to the head. These officers meet periodically as the CIO Council.[28]

The Paperwork Reduction Act, as its title suggests, requires agencies to reduce the information collection burdens that they impose. Agencies are required to calculate the thousands of "burden hours" that the collection process demands of those required to submit information to them. Each year OMB publishes an *Information Collection Budget*. The document indicates both reductions and increases in burden hours. For instance, an agency may have made an administrative decision to cut back on some of the information it collected for a specific program, but that same agency may have decided to increase its collection of other information.

Despite efforts to cut paperwork, the federal government has increased its information collection as is shown in **Table 10–2**. The table shows information for 2004, 2005, and 2006 for all federal departments and the three independent agencies that impose the largest burden hours—the Environmental Protection Agency, the Federal Trade Commission, and the Securities and Exchange Commission. As can be seen from the table, the Internal Revenue Service within the department of Treasury is by far the largest demander of information, accounting for about 75% of all information collected. OMB estimated that between 2004 and 2006, 95% of the increases in burden hours came from recently enacted statutes requiring the collection of information and not from agency decisions to collect increasing amounts of information.[29] The Medicare Prescription Drug Program (P.L. 108-173) and the CAN-SPAM Act (P.L. 108-187), aimed at limiting unsolicited commercial e-mail, were singled out as particularly burdensome.

Any new collection of information must be approved by OIRA, but before that can occur, an agency must go through an elaborate analytic process. Factors to consider include the importance to the agency in collecting the information (the practical utility of the information), a realistic assessment of the burden imposed on those who would be required to submit the information, and a determination that the information does not exist already in some other form or in another agency. The agency might be expected to implement a pilot program as a means of evaluating the collection process and the utility of the information collected. Once all of this activity is completed, the agency must post a notice about the proposed collection process in the *Federal Register* and then go through a period in which it accepts comments from the public. The CIO of an agency must review and certify the proposal. Only after these steps are completed may the proposal be submitted to OIRA. That office can reject the agency's proposal on grounds such as that the information is nonessential, that the information already exists, that the process would impose an undue burden, or simply that the proposed forms are unacceptable. After OMB approves a proposal, it must be posted once again in the *Federal Register*.

Table 10–2 Information Collection Totals for Federal Government Departments and Selected Agencies, Fiscal Years 2004, 2005, and 2006 (in Millions of Hours)

Department/ Agency	2004	2005	2006—Expected changes due to	
			Agency Action	New Statutes
Total	7,971.18	8,412.27	5.86	31.93
Total without Internal Revenue Service	1,604.34	2,012.75	8.10	31.93
Agriculture	89.12	84.47	0.60	−1.80
Commerce	14.11	15.22	4.17	0.00
Defense	52.78	52.81	0.03	0.00
Education	41.48	41.53	−0.10	0.53
Energy	3.39	3.13	−0.06	—
Health and Human Services	277.49	539.90	8.34	4.48
Homeland Security	80.51	84.87	−1.41	2.57
Housing and Urban Development	27.21	25.68	−0.04	0.15
Interior	7.43	7.91	1.18	0.02
Justice	14.58	13.12	0.06	—
Labor	164.21	166.12	0.39	—
State	32.51	35.57	−0.02	—
Transportation	250.79	253.15	−7.72	0.08
Treasury				
Internal Revenue Service	6,366.83	6,399.53	−2.24	—
Other Treasury	39.35	35.46	−0.05	—
Veterans Affairs	5.87	5.88	0.47	0.08
Environmental Protection Agency	142.36	143.94	1.16	0.00
Federal Trade Commission	71.43	72.55	0.03	—
Securities and Exchange Commission	166.32	171.77	0.01	—

Source: Adapted from U.S. Office of Management and Budget (2006). *Information collection budget of the United States Government, fiscal year 2006.* Washington, DC: OMB, 5. Retrieved October 27, 2006, from http://www.whitehouse.gov/omb/inforeg/icb/fy2006_icb_report.pdf.

At any point in time, OIRA has many agency proposals under review, and action may take up to several months on each. One example of the type of approval that must be sought is the Department of Agriculture's proposal for increasing the number of responses from the private sector from 500 to 1,000 for the Trade Adjustment Assistance for Farmers program. The proposal required a doubling of the burden hours from 7,000 to 14,000.[30] Surveys are seen as particularly burdensome and to the end of reducing their harmful impact, OMB has issued specific guidance on their design and approval.[31]

The Government Accountability Office (GAO) has been critical of the PRA process.[32] Posting of the draft collections twice in the *Federal Register* has been seen as accomplishing little. CIOs have been criticized for not reviewing their agencies' proposals with the care that is needed. Similarly, OMB's reviews may be more *pro forma* than real.

In addition to controlling the collection of information, OIRA regulates the quality of information. Its authority in this area was strengthened in 2000 by a provision in its appropriation. The rider is the Federal Data Quality Act, commonly called the Information Quality Act.[33] OMB subsequently published "Guidelines for Ensuring and Maximizing the Quality, Objectivity, Utility, and Integrity of Information Dissemination by Federal Agencies."[34] Agencies, including OMB, also have published quality guidelines for the information that they disseminate.

Another concern for the Office of Management and Budget in this area is the use of electronic signatures as a way of eliminating paperwork. The Government Paperwork Elimination Act of 1998 required federal agencies to have their most important forms online by 2003 and stated that individuals and corporations could submit such forms electronically and verify their authenticity through electronic signatures.[35]

The process of disseminating information also is of concern. OMB provides guidance so that the dissemination process does not invade the privacy of citizens or reveal trade secrets of corporations. Circular A-130 provides guidance on when and how much agencies may charge for their information. The Paperwork Reduction Act requires that information be made available in a timely fashion.

Since September 11, 2001, a major concern is that information not be disseminated that could be used by terrorists, such as information about nuclear power plants that could be used to create a nuclear catastrophe. Terrorism also could come in the form of computer hackers destroying major databases. Earlier, Congress had passed the Government Information Security Reform Act of 2000 that gave OMB responsibility for increasing computer security.[36] In 2002, Congress passed the Federal Information Security Management Act.[37] The law aims to protect the government's information and support systems, including computer hardware and software. The Office of Management and Budget and the

National Institute of Standards and Technology, an arm of the Commerce Department, have responsibility for the law's implementation. In 2004 alone, the government spent over $4 billion for upgrading its information security.[38]

OMB has other important roles in the information arena. The office influences how much information is collected by controlling agencies' budgets, particularly those agencies whose primary mission is information collection. If budgets are cut for the Census Bureau in the Commerce Department or the Bureau of Labor Statistics in the Labor Department, the immediate results are less information being collected or being made available to the public. An agency might collect information but lack the staff needed to make it available in usable form, whether in paper, electronic, or another format.

Information security has been particularly troublesome. Some cases are well publicized, such as the theft of a Veterans Administration laptop and hard drive in 2006 that contained information on 26.5 million individuals. Yet, many other cases go unreported, and indeed, agencies may be unaware that their data have been compromised. Electronic filing of tax returns pose important challenges in safeguarding the security of data.[39] The Government Reform Committee of the House of Representatives gave the government an overall grade of D+ for its information security practices.[40]

Enterprise Architecture and E-government

The term *enterprise architecture* (EA) has become widely used throughout the public and private sectors and refers in general to a framework for how business processes within an organization should relate to one another. Major emphasis is given to information technology for linking these processes. The term is defined in OMB Circular A-130, Management of Federal Information Resources, as follows:

> An EA is the explicit description and documentation of the current and desired relationships among business and management processes and information technology. It describes the "current architecture" and "target architecture" to include the rules and standards and systems life cycle information to optimize and maintain the environment which the agency wishes to create and maintain by managing its IT portfolio. The EA must also provide a strategy that will enable the agency to support its current state and also act as the roadmap for transition to its target environment.[41]

The federal enterprise architecture (FEA) initiative was launched in 2002 and has several objectives. A key objective of course is to improve management practices that in turn work toward achieving mission outcomes. An FEA objective is to reduce redundancy in information systems, and another is to further information sharing within the federal government and among all levels of government. Improved information technology is seen as working toward a citizen-centered government.[42]

Protecting the privacy of individuals and organizations is central to information management. OMB is responsible for overseeing this aspect of information management and works with the CIO Council, mentioned above.[43] The office has provided guidance on such matters as information sharing among agencies. On the one hand, there is a desire to share information so as to avoid two or more agencies collecting the same information and thereby increasing the paperwork burden on individuals. On the other hand, privacy can be violated when information sharing is not handled with suitable safeguards.

Electronic-government or *E-government* is of central concern in this arena. The E-government Act of 2002 empowered OMB to work with federal departments and agencies in using electronic media to interface with the public.[44] Information technology can be and is used in data sharing with the public, procurement, the regulatory process, and the issuance of grants and their administration. OMB has directed attention at several "lines of business" for E-government including improved financial management and human resources management.[45] One study found *FirstGov* (renamed *USA.gov*), the intended one-stop location for searching federal websites, to be the best E-government example at the federal level.[46] Treasury was ranked 5th, IRS 6th, the Congressional Budget Office 21st, and OMB 53rd. The top states were Texas, New Jersey, Oregon, Michigan, and Utah. In world rankings, Korea, Taiwan, and Singapore were the top nations in E-government followed by the United States in fourth place.[47]

OMB planned to shift information technology support for financial management systems away from the model of each agency having a stand-alone enterprise toward cross-government service centers operated by federal entities or the private sector. Organizations would be selected for such IT work on a competitive basis (see A-76 below).[48]

Executive Order 13392, Improving Agency Disclosure of Information, was issued in 2005 by President George W. Bush. As its title suggests, the order is intended to enhance the public's access to information, specifically through the Freedom of Information Act (FOIA) of 1966.[49] FOIA provides a mechanism by which requests can be made of federal agencies for information contained in records systems. The government can deny access for a variety of reasons, such as for national security and law enforcement. The 2005 executive order required agencies to designate Chief FOIA Officers and to create FOIA improvement plans so as to foster "citizen centered" and "results oriented" systems.[50]

The Federal Funding Accountability and Transparency Act of 2006 requires the government to create an extensive search engine and database accessible to the public.[51] The new system, under the direction of the Office of Management and Budget, will provide information about most government grants, loans, and contracts in excess of $25,000 and is to be operational by 2008. The law did not address the widely recognized problem of existing databases having missing or erroneous data. Data often are unavailable on a timely basis.[52]

Control of Regulations

In addition to providing relief from paperwork, budget offices may be responsible for providing regulatory relief to businesses and governments. Critics of regulations view them as imposing needless expenses on corporations, that in turn pass these costs on to consumers, or to taxpayers in the case of state and local governments. On the other hand, one should keep in mind that regulations are issued pursuant to statutes and that both the regulations and the statutes presumably have important public purposes, such as ensuring the safety of a polio vaccine or the nation's food supply.

The regulatory process occurs at all levels of government and has its champions and critics at all levels.[53] Few would argue that all government regulations are worthless, but regulations can be questioned over their utility considering the costs that they impose on individuals, corporation, and other governments, as in the case of federal regulations affecting state and local governments.

Beginning in the Reagan administration, OMB was given increased powers over the regulatory process, and those powers have been greatly expanded in subsequent years. Part of this movement has probably had political motivations in which presidents have sought to show their concern for keeping a potentially runaway bureaucracy in check. In 2001, President George W. Bush, acting through his White House Chief of Staff, imposed a moratorium on the regulatory process on his very first day in office.[54] The official reason cited was to give new Bush appointees in the departments an opportunity to review the regulations that were in the pipeline. Another reason was concern over the flurry of regulations that had been released at the end of the Clinton administration. After the suspension period, some regulations were permanently canceled and others were allowed to go into effect.

A central line of reasoning is that thorough analysis is needed to determine whether regulations should be issued and then whether they should be retained. The current executive order governing this field at the federal level is 12866, issued in 1993 by President Clinton. President George W. Bush amended that order in 2002 by issuing Executive Order 13258. Orders 12866 and 13258, coupled with the Paperwork Reduction Act of 1995 (discussed earlier), give OIRA a veto power over most agency regulatory activity. Executive Order 13422, issued by President Bush in 2007 and amending 12866, extended OIRA's scope to cover agencies' "guidance documents" that interpret regulations. The order also required that each federal agency have a presidential (political) appointee in charge of its respective regulatory process. Proponents saw this provision as helping to bring agencies into conformance with administration policies, while critics saw the provision as politicizing the regulatory process.

Executive Order 12866 provides for a regulatory planning and review process under OIRA. Each year agencies must submit to OIRA their proposed plans for revising, issuing, and rescinding regulations. Any proposals for new or revised regulations must be evaluated in terms of their costs and benefits. When OMB rejects a regulation, it is sent back to the agency in the form of a "return letter." The OMB also may send a "prompt letter" that need not be in a response to a submission by an agency but rather suggests that an agency has a problem with its regulations and offers suggestions for improvement.

A major thrust for reformists has been the idea that regulations should exist only if their benefits outweigh the costs they impose on society. Circular A-4, Regulatory Analysis, provides ground rules for the conduct of evaluations so that some degree of standardized procedures exist from one agency to another.[55] Executive Order 13422 requires an agency to make a determination of "specific market failure" that warrants agency intervention through the issuance of a regulation. Agencies are required to estimate the "combined aggregate costs and benefits" of all of their regulations as distinguished from measuring the costs and benefits of selected, individual regulations.

There are major technical and political issues over what gets counted as a cost and what as a benefit. The budget office was charged by the Regulatory Right-to-Know Act of 1999 with reporting to Congress on the "annual costs and benefits (including quantifiable and nonquantifiable effects) of federal rules and paperwork."[56] OMB estimated that between 1995 and 2005 it reviewed regulations that together had annual costs ranging between $37 billion and $44 billion and benefits ranging between $94 billion and $449 billion.[57]

Adopting a regulation or revising an existing one is an extremely complicated process in the federal government. OMB has identified nine basic steps that include drafting the regulation, publishing it in draft form, obtaining public comments, preparing it in final form, obtaining OMB approval, and publishing it in final form.[58] In addition, several other laws and executive orders may apply. If a regulation affects state and local governments, then analysis must be conducted to determine the financial implications of the regulation. This is in accord with the Unfunded Mandates Reform Act of 1995 (see Chapter 14).[59] A draft regulation may be required to undergo special analysis of its impact on federalism as required by Executive Order 13132.

Sometimes interest groups are said to play too key of a role in rulemaking, such as the lobby interests located on K Street and elsewhere in Washington, DC.[60] Other times, the argument is made that rulemaking should be less adversarial and that government agencies should cooperate with those being regulated in the writing or rewriting of regulations. The Negotiated Rulemaking Act of 1990 works in this direction.[61]

Major efforts are underway to increase what is referred to as government "transparency" by placing increasing amounts of regulatory information on government websites and not only placing that information but making it readily accessible through navigation devices. OMB has teamed with the General Services Administration in creating the website of *RegInfo.gov*.[62] The site contains the government's current and past regulatory plans and agendas. It has links to the *Federal Register*, which contains draft and final rules, and to the *Code of Federal Regulations*, which houses current regulations organized by subject. The other important website in this regard is *Regulations.gov*.[63] This site, created by the Environmental Protection Agency and 23 other federal agencies, provides easy access to all documents that are open for public comment and allows searching of regulations by subject. This site is commonly referred to as the Federal Docket Management System, allowing for a one-stop shopping location for regulations.[64] All of these efforts are part of E-rulemaking and E-government.[65]

Controversy often arises over the fact that many regulations are written for large entities and, as a result, small organizations experience major burdens in attempting to comply with the regulations. In response to that view, Congress passed the Regulatory Flexibility Act of 1980 and made important changes in the law in 1996 through passage of the Small Business Regulatory Enforcement Fairness Act.[66] The 1980 law encourages the use of flexible regulations that require lesser amounts of information from smaller entities, including small businesses and local governments. The 1996 law, supplemented by Executive Order 13272 issued in 2002, instructs agencies to prepare guides to show small businesses how they can comply with regulations. The Small Business Administration was assigned the role of ombudsman in assisting small businesses when they encounter regulatory problems with agencies. In the name of "regulatory relief," agencies may selectively waive the application of regulations to small businesses and waive penalties when these businesses violate the regulations. When small businesses think an agency has failed to comply with the law, they may file suit, claiming the regulation in question is invalid. Compliance with the law has "varied across agencies, within agencies, and over time."[67]

The 1996 law also includes within it the Congressional Review Act.[68] This law provides a form of legislative veto of administrative regulations. Before a proposed rule can take effect, it must be submitted to Congress. Congress then has 60 days, excluding days when it is in recess for four days or more, to review the regulations and can pass a joint resolution disapproving or vetoing the regulations. The president may veto the resolution, and Congress may consider overriding the president's veto. The Government Accountability Office, in a ten-year review of the law, found that the mere threat of congressional disapproval of regulations may have deterred agency rulemaking somewhat, but in general concluded that presidential oversight through OMB was more significant than congressional oversight.[69]

The Truth in Regulating Act of 2000 strengthened congressional influence over the regulatory process. When Congress receives an "economically significant rule, a chairman or ranking member of a committee of jurisdiction of either house of Congress may request the Comptroller General of the United States to review the rule."[70] The Comptroller General, who heads the GAO, has up to six months to submit a report on the proposed rule.

Given all of the items discussed here—reorganization, management controls, control of information, enterprise architecture and E-government, and control of regulations—some observers have suggested that such management tasks are too great to be left to budget offices. One suggestion is to create a separate office of management that would have nonbudgetary duties ranging well beyond what OMB currently has. The argument against creating an office of management hinges mainly on the fact that the issues addressed have budgetary implications and to assign them to a different agency would automatically create coordination problems.

In addition to relations between the central budget office and the line agencies, several other subsystems are in operation during budget execution. Taxes and other debts must be collected, the cash needs of the government must be met, items must be purchased, and the vulnerability of the government to loss of property and other problems must be managed. These topics are discussed next.

▮ Tax Administration and Debt Collection

Tax administration, which is discussed here, and cash management, which is discussed in the next section, are two functions that usually are under the same administrative officer, typically a secretary of treasury or revenue. Having the two functions linked together administratively facilitates sharing information. The cash manager uses information generated by the tax administrator. At the federal level, the Treasury Department handles these tasks. While Chapters 4 and 5 discuss the nature of various taxes, here we consider how those taxes are administered over the course of the fiscal year.

Besides taxes, numerous other revenue sources must be administered. User charges are common at all levels of government. State lotteries have become important sources of revenue. Administrators responsible for lotteries focus on marketing to increase sales. As the dollar value of sales increases, the unit cost of administration declines. Governments loan billions of dollars, and loan payments frequently are delinquent. Therefore, debt collection is of great import.

Main Steps

Tax administration has four main steps:

1. Determining the objects or services to be taxed. Using the local property tax as an example, parcels of land and structures, along with their owners, must be identified.

2. Applying the tax. In the case of the property tax, this is an annual process. In contrast, sales tax calculations are made each time a sale occurs. Governments make property tax calculations, and bills are sent to property owners. Individuals have the responsibility to calculate their own income taxes.

3. Collecting the revenues. Funds are paid either directly to the government, as in the case of a corporation's paying income tax, or through a third party, as in the case of employers' remitting individual income tax withholdings to the government.

4. Enforcing the law. Audits are conducted selectively of taxpayers to verify compliance, and some taxpayers are prosecuted for tax evasion.

Tax administration is less concerned with the policy issues of tax equity (see Chapter 4) and more concerned with generating the revenue that is expected and with gaining compliance from the vast majority of taxpayers.

Organizational Structure

In response to extensive criticism of the IRS extending over decades, Congress passed the Internal Revenue Service Restructuring and Reform Act of 1998.[71] The law instructed the commissioner to reorganize the agency to reflect the types of taxpayers rather than continue with its then-existing structure organized around geography—nation, region, and district. This "modernization" effort was aimed at achieving a balance between meeting taxpayers' needs and having taxpayers comply with the tax laws. The agency has six operating divisions: (1) Wage and Investment for individual taxpayers, (2) Large and Mid-Size Business, (3) Small Business/Self-Employed, (4) Tax Exempt and Government Entities, (5) Tax Compliance, and (6) Professional Responsibility.[72] The latter office is responsible for licensing "enrolled agents" who represent clients in tax cases before the IRS. The office has authority to disbar these agents as well as licensing them. In addition to restructuring, IRS has initiated other reforms, such as updating work processes and procedures, improving data management, strengthening its customer focus, and improving its use of performance measures.[73]

Another important structural change made by the 1998 legislation was to move the Office of the Chief Inspector out of the IRS and redesignate it as the Treasury Inspector General for Tax Administration (TIGTA). This office is in addition to the Inspector General for Treasury and is responsible for ferreting out fraud and abuse in IRS, promoting efficient and effective administration of the tax laws, evaluating the security of IRS technology, and protecting IRS workers from corrupt influences.

The same law created the Internal Revenue Service Oversight Board.[74] This permanent body consists of nine members, six of whom are not employed by the government. These individuals plus one government employee are appointed by the president. The other two members are the Treasury Secretary and the Commissioner of the IRS. The board has the power to review and approve strategic plans prepared by IRS and to review and approve budget requests before they are forwarded to the president.

Enforcement

Numerous tax enforcement measures are used, and well-trained and ethical personnel are essential for effective enforcement practices.

- The IRS verifies mathematical accuracy through the use of optical scanning. Proper design of forms and clearly written instructions contribute to improved taxpayer accuracy in filing returns.
- Tax return information supplied by individuals is compared with information supplied by banks and employers.
- Governments share computer-based data to compare information on income being reported (or not reported).[75]
- Taxpayer services are provided to help in preparing tax returns. Services may be available at designated government offices, at other facilities, by telephone, and online.[76]
- Governments draw samples of taxpayer returns to audit. Regression models are designed to identify cases that are most likely to involve noncompliance with the tax laws.
- One of the most common groups singled out for tax auditing includes individuals and corporations for which "leads" have been given. Undercover operations may be used in these situations.
- Delinquent accounts are investigated, as are accounts in which taxpayers have stopped complying altogether.
- Some taxpayers are prosecuted in court, depending on the "seriousness" of the cases and the availability of resources to pursue the cases in court.

- Special enforcement is reserved for sources of illegal income, such as gambling, prostitution, narcotics, and, more generally, organized crime.

Any government must decide how many resources to commit to these various activities and how resources should be distributed among them. The IRS has been criticized for not having a firm idea of the relative yield in tax revenue generated from these activities. Performance measures are needed to determine the relative merits of these activities.[77] Decisions must be made not only about the type of activity to conduct, but also about the distribution of tax enforcement resources across different forms of taxes. For example, a state needs to decide how many resources to commit to tax cheating on personal income, corporate income, and motor fuels taxes.[78]

Complaints often arise that some taxpayers are being audited more intensively that others. Increased auditing may be warranted where it is known that certain types of taxpayers are more likely to cheat on their returns than others. Politics also come into play. Sometimes special audit attention is given to people filing for earned income tax credits in which the claim is made that their incomes are so low that they owe little or no taxes.

A component of the objective of having taxpayers comply with the law is having them report all taxable income. Failure to report income results in less money being paid in taxes. The difference between what taxpayers pay and what they should pay is known as the *tax gap*. The Internal Revenue Service estimated the initial tax gap for tax year 2001 to be $345 billion, but with follow-up enforcement, that was reduced to an estimated $290 billion. The tax gap for corporate federal taxes exceeded $30 billion.[79] In 2006, the Treasury Inspector General for Tax Administration issued a report that documented the failure of IRS and a prime contractor to develop a web-based system for fraud detection.[80] The report estimated that $318 million were paid out that year in fraudulent claims. This gap between taxes owed and taxes paid is critical considering the budget in the mid-2000s was grossly out of balance and was considered to be structurally out of balance for the long-term, meaning that improvements in economic conditions could not be expected to eliminate the budget deficit.[81]

Determining compliance/noncompliance with the tax laws is a difficult task. If the IRS or any other tax agency knew that taxpayers were not complying, the agency would seek to collect the delinquent taxes owed. Noncompliance data by nature, therefore, are estimates that are necessarily imprecise. The IRS for a time used a system of super-audits that required a sample of taxpayers to substantiate every item on their tax returns, but these were determined to be ineffective in detecting unreported income and identifying unauthorized or fraudulent claims for tax deductions and tax credits.

Greater revenue can be achieved through a variety of means, including *levies* on government payments and *abatement* programs. With regard to levies, government sometimes is in the situation of making payments to taxpayers—both individuals and corporations—for one purpose, while those entities are simultaneously in arrears on their taxes. Levies can be imposed to recoup the taxes owed.[82] As for abatements, tax administration offices may have the authority to negotiate payments from taxpayers and forgive some taxes that are owed. Abatement programs may obtain revenues from sources that otherwise would have paid nothing or almost nothing. On the other hand, attempts to negotiate tax payments can have the unintended consequence of forcing taxpayers into bankruptcy. Liens can be placed against properties as a means of forcing the payment of taxes. The IRS Restructuring and Reform Act provided new guidance to the agency on liens, levies, and the seizure of property.

Another consideration is that tax administration would be far less complicated if tax laws were less complicated. Of course, the reason for their complexity is simple. Tax laws are replete with specific conditions to take into account the specific conditions of taxpayers. Some countries have tax withholding systems that free most taxpayers from the onerous task of preparing and filing tax returns. If tax laws were simplified, people would be better able to calculate their tax bills and would have less opportunity to cheat, and tax agencies would need to spend far less than current levels on tax administration.[83] Tax simplification, however, if carried out, needs to be done in such manner as to be revenue neutral. The reform if only for simplification purposes should neither raise nor reduce tax revenues and should not shift tax burdens from one segment of society to another. Tax simplification might well unintentionally harm various segments of society that are currently protected by existing tax law provisions. The alternative view is that simplification would close tax loopholes that inappropriately benefit special interests.

Beginning in the 1980s, *tax amnesty* became popular as a means of retrieving unpaid state taxes. Amnesty programs became especially popular during the 2001–2002 recession, when states were particularly in need of revenue, and continued into the mid-2000s.[84] Taxpayers who were delinquent in their income taxes could file returns during a specified time period in a state without fear of prosecution. The taxpayers, however, were expected to pay all back taxes and interest. The amnesty programs have been successful in getting many taxpayers back on the tax rolls. One possible drawback is that taxpayer compliance declines somewhat following an amnesty program, suggesting that taxpayers feel that government is likely to be less vigilant in ferreting out evaders after having enticed many people to return to the tax rolls. Also, taxpayer evasion is related to tax rates—as tax rates increase, evasion increases. Evasion can be related to perceptions of fairness. If people think the tax system is unfair, they are likely to evade paying taxes owed.

Tax administration usually focuses upon generating revenue but on occasion includes distributing revenue. In 2001, Congress passed a tax rebate program that resulted in considerable expense for both the rebates and their administration. Individual taxpayers received $300 each, while heads of households received $500 and married couples filing jointly received $600.

Technology in Tax Administration

It should come as no surprise that technology is playing increasingly important roles in tax administration:

- Besides routine recordkeeping, computers are used for drawing samples for tax auditing and for cross-checking information between different sources.
- Many businesses are required to make federal tax payments through the Electronic Federal Tax Payment System.[85]
- State and local governments electronically submit federal income tax and Social Security withholdings.
- Answers to frequently asked questions (FAQs) pertaining to tax laws are commonly available on government home pages on the Internet.
- Some local governments have automated tax systems that can make withdrawals for property taxes from taxpayers' bank accounts, providing that taxpayers preapprove such withdrawals.
- In some jurisdictions, taxpayers use the telephone or online services to pay their taxes.
- Some governments accept credit and debit cards for payment of taxes, fees, parking tickets, and the like. The cards, of course, are possible only because of today's computer technology.
- Some states accept electronic fund transfers for corporations making tax payments.
- Electronic auctions are used by governments to sell delinquent tax properties.
- Auditors on field assignments use portable computers, some with wireless (Wi-Fi) Internet connections. Computers can be used to manage tax cases, providing on any one case a variety of information and prompting the case manager with reminders about the status of the case.

- Tax office employees can work at home on secure tax files using high-speed access to networks.[86]

One of the most important developments in this area relates to online tax filing and payments. The IRS Restructuring and Reform Act mandated the rapid development of electronic filing. In 2001, the Internal Revenue Service unveiled its Electronic Federal Tax Payment System–Online Service for use by individual taxpayers and businesses.[87] This system is much more user-friendly than the system originally developed for businesses. By the mid-2000s, about 70% of all taxpayers filed electronically.[88] As the deadline for filing tax returns in 2006 approached, the IRS website recorded 3,237 visits per second, many of which were tax filings.[88]

The conversion of various aspects of tax administration from paper files to computer systems or from one computer system to a more advanced one can result in problems for both tax administrators and taxpayers. The IRS became well aware of this problem starting in the late 1980s, as it engaged in a multibillion-dollar Tax Systems Modernization project.[89] In the late 1990s, the IRS halted much of its modernization work after spending $3.4 billion[90] and developed a new plan that relied more heavily upon a prime contractor for modernizing the agency's operations. Congress, painfully aware of the deficiencies in IRS technology and the false and expensive starts made in updating the technology, created a special Information Technology Investment Account.[91]

By the mid-2000s, the Internal Revenue Service continued to struggle with adapting information technology to meet the agency's complex needs. The IRS was experimenting with the use of "business rules engine" codes for scanning tax returns for possible fraud.[92] The agency's Information Technology Asset Management System had a variety of modules directed at meeting its diverse needs. Problems persisted, such as in 2006 when a faulty computer system may have allowed for the paying out of $300 million in fraudulent tax refunds.[93]

Tax administration involves several personnel-related problems. Some of these are discussed in **Exhibit 10–1**. Should tax administration personnel be immune from government-wide layoffs, because they typically generate far more revenue than they are paid? What is the best mix of training for these employees? How can ethical behavior be fostered?

Intergovernmental Relations in Tax Administration

There are intergovernmental aspects to tax administration. As already noted, some governments share information with each other to help detect noncompliance with tax laws. Local governments sometimes work together in joint billing, such as when a county, city, and school district prepare a single bill for property taxes. Tax provisions of governments are sometimes linked to each other, so that the calculation of

Exhibit 10–1 Personnel in Tax Administration

Tax administration involves several personnel-related problems, with one being the sheer number of employees. As long as tax recordkeeping and tax filing use paper-based processes to some extent, treasury departments need large numbers of employees, especially at tax filing time (often April 15). Even with the conversion to online filing, personnel are still needed, especially for auditing and investigating tax returns. Because these employees typically generate far more revenue than their salaries, the argument can be made that such units should be immune from budget cuts that result in furloughing employees. Nevertheless, treasury departments often are expected to suffer with all other departments when across-the-board layoffs occur.

Treasury departments often encounter difficulties in training their workers. One of the most common forms of training is for new employees to be instructed by senior ones. If senior employees are used to train new employees then important resources are diverted away from the main duty of collecting revenue. Probably few tax offices carefully analyze the resources they commit to training and the benefits derived.[1]

Opportunities abound for unethical and illegal activities by employees.[2] As the IRS has improved its computer operations, employees have gained wide access to the tax files of most private citizens, and some employees have been found browsing out of curiosity through the income tax returns of prominent citizens. In response, Congress passed the Taxpayer Browsing Protection Act of 1997.[3] In other instances, employees have been able to have tax refund checks illegally sent to themselves. Other employees may have important conflicts of interest, such as reviewing tax returns of corporations in which they have financial holdings. To avoid these conflicts or reveal their existence, governments require treasury and other employees to file financial disclosure statements that show their financial investments.

Congress, in passing the 1998 IRS Restructuring and Reform Act, made several changes in personnel management at the IRS. Management was given greater flexibility in personnel matters, incentives were provided for encouraging people to resign or retire, and the agency was directed to improve its training operations. Among the most controversial components of the law are what IRS employees refer to as the "Ten Deadly Sins." Any employee found to have committed just one sin must be fired, unless the IRS commissioner specifically intervenes. The "sins" include not getting the proper signatures when a taxpayer's home is to be seized for back taxes, threatening a tax audit for personal gain, or threatening a personal enemy with an audit. Hundreds of IRS agents have been fired because of the law and thousands more have been subjected to lengthy investigations. On the one hand, these "sins" have encouraged employees to work more conscientiously and particularly to avoid abusing taxpayers. On the other hand, the "sins" have caused morale problems among workers.[4]

High standards need to be expected of employees and also of managers, namely that management needs to treat workers fairly. In one instance, the IRS was ruled to have unfairly passed over 1,400 employees for promotions.[5] While the ruling was a victory for workers, the situation most likely was cause for many employees to be disgruntled and unmotivated.

---

[1]U.S. Government Accountability Office (2005). *Tax administration: IRS needs better strategic planning and evaluation of taxpayer assistance training.* Washington, DC: GAO.

[2]Van Blijswijk, J. A. M. et al. (2004). Beyond ethical codes: the management of integrity in the Netherlands Tax and Customs Administration. *Public Administration Review, 64*, 718–727.

[3]Taxpayer Browsing Protection Act (1997). P.L. 105-35.

[4]Friel, B. (2002). Treasury asks Congress to make IRS "Ten Deadly Sins" less deadly. *Govexec.com.* Retrieved August 17, 2006, from http://www.govexec.com/dailyfed/0202/020702b1.htm; Yancey, R. (2004). *Confessions of a tax collector: one man's tour of duty inside the IRS.* New York: Harper Collins.

[5]Rutzick, K. (2006). IRS finds 1,400 employees unfairly passed over promotions. *Govexec.com.* Retrieved August 17, 2006, from http://www.govexec.com/dailyfed/0406/041406r1.htm.

one government's tax is based on the calculation of another government's tax. This fact can unintentionally create policy and administrative problems. For example, changes in the federal income tax laws can affect provisions in state taxes, necessitating adjustments in those laws. The tax package adopted by Congress in 2002 mandated federal tax cuts that resulted unintentionally in state tax cuts, unless the states adjusted their laws accordingly. The federal government and the states have cooperated somewhat in tax administration. As noted earlier, governments may expect tax and Social Security holdings to be submitted electronically. When a local government submits state income tax withholdings by check, the local government can be fined for failing to meet state requirements for electronic filing.

Debt Collection and Taxpayer Rights

One of the biggest debts owed government is taxes, but individuals and corporations also may owe several other types of debt to government. Loans, both direct and guaranteed, result in some defaults. Federal credit programs exist for college students, low-income housing, ship construction, development in other nations, and small businesses recovering from disasters, to name only a few. Various other business transactions with government result in debts, including farmers owing on crop insurance payments and foreign countries owing on purchases of agricultural commodities. Fines are another form of debt owed to the government, as in the case of a corporation being fined for not meeting environmental standards for its mining operations.

The National Performance Review recommended that agencies be allowed "to use some of the money they collect from delinquent debts to pay for further debt collection efforts, and to keep a portion of the increased collections" as a form of incentive.[94] The review also recommended the use of private collection agencies in cases where their services would be cost-effective. Private collection agencies may be particularly useful regarding delinquent accounts, but it should be noted that these agencies often charge as much as a 50% commission for what they collect.

The federal government, as discussed in Chapter 7, is attempting to deal with the "hidden liabilities" of federal credit programs. General information on credit is contained in the *Analytical Perspectives* budget document, and more detailed information is available through other documents produced by OMB and the Treasury Department.

OMB Circular A-129, Policies for Federal Credit Programs and Non-Tax Receivables, requires that agencies review their credit programs in terms of the costs and benefits to society. The circular establishes requirements for "sound" credit programs. As noted in Chapter 7, federal agencies must calculate expected credit losses on both direct and guaranteed loans. These losses can reduce the amount of funding available for future loans.

The Debt Collection Act of 1982, the Debt Collection Improvement Act of 1996, and OMB Circular A-129 further require that agencies take steps to improve their credit programs.[95] Loan applications must be examined with an eye toward uncovering the risks that government would take in approving the loans. Delinquent cases can be turned over to collection agencies and can be reported to consumer credit agencies. Salary offsets can be used in the case of federal employees who owe the government, and individuals may have income tax refunds withheld up to the amount owed. State governments also have used this latter technique.

In the mid-2000s, the Internal Revenue Service stirred up a hornet's nest by announcing plans to turn over some tax collection to private firms.[96] The IRS, in trying to head off criticism, announced "safeguards" for taxpayers when dealing with private debt collection agencies.[97] "The private debt collection program [was] expected to bring in $1.4 billion over 10 years, with the collection agencies keeping about $330 million of that, or 22 to 24 cents on the dollars."[98] Congress denied the IRS's request for hiring more agents for delinquent tax collection, which the IRS maintained was more economical than using private debt collection agencies.

In their zeal to extract as many tax dollars as possible from the public, tax administrators must keep in mind that the citizens are ultimately responsible for setting tax laws and for paying the salaries of tax administrators. In other words, administrators are employees of the citizenry. To this end, governments have adopted laws that declare a set of rights for taxpayers.

The Internal Revenue Service Restructuring and Reform Act contains more than 70 provisions that protect taxpayers and give them rights in dealing with the IRS.[99] The law includes such important provisions as altering the burden of proof in taxpayer cases. If the IRS challenges a taxpayer on reported income tax deductions, for example, the taxpayer need only provide some credible evidence, which then shifts the burden to the IRS to disprove the evidence. An important provision is that innocent spouses can be relieved of tax fines and other penalties. Restrictions are imposed on liens and on the seizing of taxpayer property for back taxes. The IRS, as prescribed by the legislation, maintains a taxpayer advocate office, which assists taxpayers in dealing with the agency. States also have taxpayer bills of rights.[100]

The standard view in the field is that taxpayers' privacy needs to be protected, and taxpayers need to be treated equally. As noted earlier, some government workers have been found browsing the tax returns of celebrities and other prominent figures. The response is to restrict access to files to ensure security and avoid record tampering. One problem has been that taxpayer records are sometimes left in open areas of a tax administration office. In such situations, the records can be seen by unauthorized personnel, stolen, or lost.[101] Another concern is that the audit process not be politically motivated.

Cash Management

Cash management is the process of administering monies to ensure that they are available over time to meet expenditure needs and that, when temporarily not needed, they are invested at a minimum risk and a maximum yield. Cash management involves both short- and long-term investments. The latter are used mainly in the case of pension funds that try to build up reserves for future years when employees retire. The state of the art of cash management is necessarily dependent on the state of the larger financial system.

Cash Flow

An essential aspect of cash management is forecasting when revenues will be received and in what amounts and when expenditures will occur and in what amounts over the course of the fiscal year and beyond.[102] A cash management plan will strive to accelerate the receipt of revenues and delay or minimize expenditures. Chapter 11 discusses cash flows statement as one form of financial reporting.

Inflow of Revenues. Enforcement of tax laws is viewed as one means of maximizing inflow. Other techniques involve depositing government receipts as soon as possible into interest-bearing accounts. For example, when tax payments accompany tax returns, these checks can be deposited immediately in banks and processing of the returns can occur later. Governments attempt to minimize the *float time* between when checks and currency are received and when they are deposited. Accounts receivable, involving payments due from citizens, corporations, and other governments, are kept to a minimum. Inflow can be accelerated by prompt invoicing. For example, airlines are invoiced on a monthly basis for their gate space at an airport terminal.

Lockboxes. Another technique used selectively by the federal government and some state governments is the lockbox system, which uses post office boxes that are under the control of banks. Taxpayers send their payments to designated post office boxes that are opened by banking officials, and the receipts are deposited promptly. The process reduces the amount of float time between when a check is written and when government deposits it and begins earning interest.

The Internal Revenue Service learned that some risks are associated with having private contractors operate lockboxes that receive income tax returns. In 2001, employees of Mellon Bank destroyed or misplaced 40,000 returns, with the lost payments estimated at nearly $1 billion. The motivation may have been that workers feared they had fallen behind their quotas in processing returns.[103] Governments also can team up to provide this service for themselves rather than using a financial institution, as in the case of local governments working together.[104]

Governments use a variety of methods for receiving payments. A survey of state and local governments by the Government Finance Officers Association and JP Morgan Chase found that almost all received payments through the mail and by walk-ins into government offices. Over half received funds through drop boxes and automatic bank debit cards. About a third received payments via the telephone, Internet, and lockboxes.[105]

Expenditure Planning and Prompt Payment. Some techniques deal not with inflow, but with outflow. Here the concern is keeping money in interest-bearing accounts until it is needed to cover expenses and avoiding the need to borrow funds to cover expenses when revenues, such as tax receipts, are unavailable in the projected amounts. Cash flow planning is one reason that agencies are required to submit apportionment plans to the central budget office. Agencies may be instructed to shift expenditures in apportionment plans from one month or quarter to another. One rule is to pay promptly—that is, when bills are due and not before or after. This procedure is mandated at the federal level by the Prompt Payment Act of 1982, as amended.[106] Paying bills promptly saves money for the government, such as avoiding payment of late fees, and reduces a common problem encountered by government's suppliers, namely, not knowing when they will be paid. Small businesses are the most severely hurt when government agencies fail to pay their bills on time.[107]

Although the vast majority of the federal government's payments to vendors are on time, that still leaves many millions of other payments that are late.[108] The Financial Management Service within the Treasury Department has a prompt payment web page that provides for simple interest calculations for short-term tardiness and compound interest when a government agency is in arrears by months.[109] For example, in the second half of 2006, the government paid 5.75% interest on late payments. If a payment of $6,000,000 was overdue by 31 days, then the government would owe $29,708 in addition to the principal. The web page also provides a calculator to help an agency decide when to accept a vendor's offer of a discount for early payment.

Of course, another concern is that not only should bills be paid on time, but that they also should be paid to the right party and in the right amount. Lax disbursement systems increase the chances that errors are made in paying vendors and that fraud occurs. Fraud can happen without a government officer being aware of the situation or in conjunction with the officer's assistance.

Borrowing. If forecasted expenditures cannot be adjusted downward to be no greater than expected revenues, then short-term borrowing becomes an important option. State and local governments borrow from banks for up to one year in cases where expenditures are considered essential and funds are unavailable to cover the expenses. The backing of these bank notes consists of future receipt of revenues, and the instruments are known as BANS, RANs, and TANs—*bond, revenue,* and *tax anticipation notes* (see Chapter 13).

Governments also may spend from their own reserves and borrow from themselves. *Unrestricted fund balances,* which are in effect contingency funds, may be drawn upon to meet unanticipated expenditure needs. Short-term borrowing from one fund to meet the cash needs of another also occurs, as in the case of a local government's borrowing from its pension funds. State laws, however, may greatly restrict such borrowing as a protection against depleting the funds.

Some governments have established *rainy day funds* or *budget stabilization funds* that can be used during years when revenues decline. Statutes or state constitutional provisions require that monies be placed in these funds when the economy improves and revenues rise and that monies may be withdrawn only when revenues decline by some set percentage. It is common for governments to have in these funds something in excess of 5% of their general funds, although the appropriate amount needed depends on many factors that vary across different units of government.[110] These funds can reduce fiscal stress during recessions, such as occurred in the early 1990s and the early 2000s.[111] A state that dipped heavily into its rainy day fund in one year to balance its budget might then face major problems in the following year if the economy had not recovered, perhaps forcing decision makers to increase taxes. The use of budget stabilization monies also implies the replenishment of these funds when the budgetary environment becomes more favorable, as was the case in 2006 for many governments.

Investment Planning

When forecasts show periods during the year when revenues will exceed expenditures, plans are made for investment. Virtually all governments encounter this situation. Often there are spurts in revenue receipts, such as when local property taxes are due or when state sales tax receipts are paid following the Christmas shopping period.

At least seven factors must be taken into account when devising an investment strategy:

1. *Security.* Financial institutions insure some deposits up to only $100,000.

2. *Maturity date.* Some instruments mature in a few months, while others mature in 30 years.

3. *Marketability or liquidity.* If cash is needed before the maturity date, may an instrument be sold to a third party or will the issuer convert the instrument to cash?

4. *Call provisions.* May the issuer repay the investor before the date of maturity?

5. *Denominations.* Minimum amounts for investing range from $1,000 to $100,000 or more.

6. *Yield or return on investment.* Yield is measured in terms of a percentage of the investment and often expressed as an interest rate.

7. *Legal authority.* State laws may prohibit the state government and local governments from making some types of investments.

Since the collapse of many savings banks in the 1980s, the security of investments has been a prominent concern of cash managers. When a government deposits funds with a bank, a typical requirement is that the bank set aside funds as collateral on the deposits as a means of protecting the investment in the event that the bank fails. An alternative that was developed in the 1990s is for the bank to purchase private deposit insurance. This insurance is available through the Municipal Bond Investors Assurance Corporation, the largest insurer of municipal bonds.[112]

Investment Instruments

The instruments available for state and local investments consist of three general types: federal government securities, corporate securities, and money market instruments. Any government must decide to what extent it wishes to invest in each type.

Federal Securities. Fully guaranteed federal securities include Treasury bills (T-bills), notes, and bonds. T-bills mature in 4, 13, 26, and 52 weeks. They are sold at a discount by auction and consequently have no set percentage return. Treasury notes and bonds, which range in maturity from 1 to 30 years, have coupons that mature every six months. In 2002, the Treasury Department eliminated the sale of 30-year bonds, opting for securities with shorter maturities, such as 25 years. However, previously issued 30-year bonds remained in circulation. In 2006 in response to demand for long-term investment instruments, the Treasury Department began once again to issue 30-year bonds.

Other securities issued by the federal government may or may not be guaranteed. Bonds issued by the Small Business Administration and participation certificates issued by the General Services Administration are guaranteed, unlike bonds issued by the Tennessee Valley Authority and the Postal Service.

In the 1990s, the Treasury Department launched two instruments that are sensitive to inflation. When inflation occurs, the yield rate increases. Treasury inflation-protected securities, known as TIPS, have their interest rate set at the time of auction. Their principal rises or falls based upon the U.S. city average of the consumer price index. If the consumer price index rises in a time period, the value of the note rises and then the interest is calculated based on the new principal. If deflation occurs, investors at the time of maturity are guaranteed the original purchase price.

The other inflation-sensitive instrument is the Series I savings bond. I bonds are purchased at face value, which ranges between $50 and $10,000, and have a fixed rate of return. Inflation rates, then, are added to the calculations. TIPS and I bonds have yield rates that are somewhat lower than instruments that lack the inflation protection.

Series EE/E savings bonds are guaranteed by the government, can be cashed after six months, and earn interest up to 30 years. These bonds issued before May 1, 2005, pay interest at current market rates. Bonds issued May 1, 2005, and after pay interest at a fixed rate. EE bonds come in paper and electronic form.

Cash management bills are short-term instruments, sometimes for as little as one day. They have been used when expenditures substantially exceeded income and normal borrowing through the above named instruments was unable to take up the gap. The Treasury's use of these bills has been criticized because of the higher interest that is paid on them.[113]

Federal securities largely are sold at auction and are then made available for purchase through financial institutions. It is possible, however, to purchase some bills, notes, and TIPS directly from the Treasury, thereby saving broker fees. This program is known as Legacy Treasury Direct.[114]

Other Federal-Related Securities. Other securities are issued by credit institutions created by the federal government and may have full, limited, or no backing or ambiguous backing of the government. Instruments backed by the federal government include insured notes of the Housing and Community Facilities Programs within the Agriculture Department and Ginnie Maes of the Government Home Loan Mortgage Corporation. Instruments that do not have the expressed guarantee of the federal government but could be backed in emergency situations include Federal Home Loan Bank bonds, Federal Land Bank bonds, and Federal Intermediate Credit Bank bonds. Many of these federal-related securities involve mortgages, including mortgages on homes, farms, cooperatives, and overseas investments (Asian Development Bank notes and bonds and Export Import Bank debentures).

Corporate Securities. Corporations are another possibility for the investment of state and local monies. Corporate bonds are essentially loans made to the issuers. Stocks, in comparison, represent ownership of the corporation. In the event that a corporation goes into bankruptcy, creditors such as bondholders are paid first. If any assets remain, they are then distributed among stockholders.

Money Market Instruments. Financial institutions provide numerous investment opportunities. Interest is paid on *negotiable order of withdrawal* (NOW) checking accounts and on savings accounts. Not only can government earn interest on these deposits, but other benefits also may be negotiated through *linked deposit agreements*. In these situations, banks, as a condition of receiving government deposits, may agree to make available more loans for housing in a community or for industrial development in a targeted area.

Monies also can be invested in money market instruments, with *certificates of deposit* (CDs) being one of the most popular. Issuers include banks, offshore subsidiaries of U.S. banks, and U.S. branches of foreign banks. The latter two issue what are known as *Eurodollars* and *Yankee CDs*, respectively, which are not guaranteed by the federal government. Some, but not all, CDs are negotiable. Issuers may charge interest penalties for early withdrawal of monies.

Other instruments include *bankers' acceptances, commercial paper*, and *repurchase agreements*. Bankers' acceptances are agreements to purchase a bank's agreement to loan money on a short-term basis to a corporation (one usually involved in international trade). The largest banks in the nation issue these instruments. Commercial paper, also available through banks, is a corporate promissory note. A repurchase agreement (repo) is a pool of U.S. government securities held by a financial institution and sold temporarily to state and local governments and other purchasers. The institution agrees to repurchase the securities at a later date.

Repurchase agreements are controversial because a few major firms specializing in repos went bankrupt in the mid-1980s. Some governments, including the local governments of Beaumont, Texas, and Toledo, Ohio, lost many millions of dollars. In response, Congress passed the Government Securities Act of 1986 that brought these securities dealers under the regulation of the Treasury Department and the Securities and Exchange Commission.[115]

State and local governments may purchase combinations of various money market instruments. One technique is to invest in a money market fund that is a pool of securities. The Securities and Exchange Commission regulates these funds in an attempt to reduce the risks undertaken by investors. Despite these regulations, however, laws preclude many governments from investing in money market funds because they often include higher-risk investments such as Eurodollars.

Derivatives. One of the most controversial financial instruments is known as a derivative.[116] Derivatives are highly complex devices that often are poorly understood by both those who sell them and the state and local governments that buy them. A derivative's value depends upon some underlying security or a market index. In other words, the derivative is a bet on what future interest rates will be. Governments purchase swaps that trade in variable rates for fixed rates, with the underlying gamble by the government being that the return on investment will be better with the fixed rate. Some derivatives take the form of collateralized mortgage obligations, that entail investing in a pool of mortgages with the return being based on changes in interest rates and changes in mortgage prepayment rates. Some governments have lost large sums of money in these investments.

Investment Pools. Another money management technique that has become popular is for jurisdictions to combine their investments into a state-authorized investment pool.[117] By pooling resources, smaller jurisdictions can take advantage of higher-yield investments that require larger investments than passbook savings or CDs. Liquidity is improved in that jurisdictions often can withdraw some of their monies from these pools without the financial loss that would be involved if they held securities themselves and had to liquidate them.

Yield Rates. **Table 10–3** provides a snapshot of yield rates for some of the instruments discussed here. As can be seen from the table, the rates varied considerably between the two years reported. Rates increase with risk, with higher risk instruments paying higher rates. The federal inflated-indexed securities paid decidedly less than other securities, indicating a price that purchasers pay for being protected from possible inflation. Bonds usually pay a higher rate than notes, and notes pay a higher rate than bills, because of the time factor involved, but this pattern does not happen to show up in the years sampled.

Use of Investment Instruments. Most of the money (more than 90%) in state and local government trust funds, such as employee retirement systems and workers' compensation, is invested and little is kept on hand. In contrast, the money for the rest of state and local governments is kept much more fluid (one-third in cash and deposits and two-thirds invested). Retirement systems invest mainly in corporate stocks and bonds (53%), federal securities (8%), and foreign and international securities (15%).[118] In 2006, the California investment pool had 22% of its funds in certificates of deposit, 19% in commercial paper, 16% in federal securities, 12% each in federal agency discount notes and bank time deposits, and 10% in corporate bonds.[119]

As noted earlier, legal constraints affect investment programs. Illinois law, for example, bars the state from depositing funds with financial institutions that have specific ties with Sudan. The purpose of that provision is to avoid using public monies to perpetuate the atrocities prevalent in Sudan.[120] Illinois may not invest in derivatives and reverse repurchase agreements.

Table 10–3 **Yield Rates of Selected Investment Instruments, August 2001 and 2006 (in Percent)**

Instrument	2001	2006
Federal Securities		
4-week bills	3.48	5.06
3-month bills	3.36	4.97
6-month bills	3.29	4.98
Inflation indexed		
5-year	N.A.	2.32
10-year	N.A.	2.36
20-year	N.A.	2.39
Constant maturities		
5-year	4.57	4.89
10-year	4.97	4.96
20-year	5.58	5.14
30-year	5.48	5.05
Other Deposits and Securities		
3-month certificates of deposit	3.48	5.43
3-month commercial paper, financial	3.44	5.34
3-month Eurodollars	3.47	5.45
1-year derivatives	4.27	5.54
Moody's corporate bonds, Aaa rating	7.02	5.76

N.A.—Not Available

Source: Compiled from Federal Reserve Board (2001 & 2006). *Selected interest rates*. Retrieved August 28, 2006, from http://www.federalreserve.gov/releases/h15/20010917/h15.htm & http://www.federalreserve.gov/releases/h15/20060807/h15.txt.

In many emerging market economies, newly developing pension systems impose generally strict regulations on investment instruments. It is common to require that at least 50%, and sometimes as much as 80%, of pension funds be invested in central government securities. Restrictions limiting investments outside the country are often tight, with no more than 10% being a common limitation. The motivations are partly to protect pension funds that have not previously existed from investing in too risky a portfolio as a result of inexperience, and partly to ensure a flow of investment funds into central government securities.

Investment Risks

Investments are not risk-free. One type of risk involves the creditworthiness of the issuer of a security. Bonds issued by the federal government are nearly risk-free in this sense, and bonds issued by major corporations, such as General Electric, are low risk. Another aspect of risk, however, is whether a particular instrument is volatile in terms of the yield it may produce. In this context, fixed-rate, long-term government bonds are risky investments. If a government's portfolio contains high-yield securities at a time when yield rates are declining, then the situation is generally positive. If trends reverse and yield rates climb above those in the portfolio, however, the government may have difficulty selling low-bearing securities. In that situation, a government's investments might fail to keep pace with inflation. Derivatives often are singled out as one of the most high-risk investments due to their volatility, even though the issuers of the derivatives may be creditworthy. Orange County, California, in the 1990s, was embroiled in a massive problem involving derivatives. **Exhibit 10–2** discusses that situation.

The Governmental Accounting Standards Board (GASB) has issued important directives regarding investments of government monies.[121] Statement No. 3, Deposits with Financial Institutions, Investments (including Repurchase Agreements), and Reverse Repurchase Agreements, mandates that governments report high-risk investments in their comprehensive annual financial reports (CAFRs). Statement No. 9, Reporting Cash Flows of Proprietary and Nonexpendable Trust Funds and Governmental Entities that Use Proprietary Fund Accounting, as its title suggests sets rules for reporting cash flows for those activities within a government that are run like businesses, such as a municipal transit system or parking garage.

While an annual report showing such investments is helpful, more short-term reporting is needed. One option is to mark or report the value of each item in a portfolio on a daily basis. GASB Statement No. 31, Accounting and Financial Reporting for Certain Investments and for External Investment Pools, specifies that governments account for and report "fair value" for their investments in (1) interest-earning investment contracts; (2) external investment pools; (3) open-end mutual funds; (4) debt securities; and (5) equity securities, option contracts, stock warrants, and stock rights.

Federal Cash Management

The federal government's cash management system is considerably different from those of state and local governments. Federal monies are kept with the Federal Reserve System (see Chapter 15), which pays a form of interest for deposits, and

Exhibit 10–2   Derivatives and the Case of Orange County, California

Orange County, California, the home of Disneyland and the fifth largest county in the United States, experienced a painful lesson in the risks of investing when it filed for bankruptcy protection in 1994.[1] The county had been hailed as a shrewd investor, earning close to double the rate of return on investments compared with other governments and investment pools. The county had been so successful that 180 other local governments had deposited money with Orange County with the expectation of reaping the benefits of an investment policy that was more aggressive than the typical one. In 1994, reality hit hard. This approach resulted in a loss of nearly $2 billion.

What went wrong in Orange County? First, heavy investments were placed in derivatives, that as noted earlier are gambles on what will happen to interest rates. When rates went in the opposite direction than expected, the county was in trouble. Second, the situation was exacerbated by the use of reverse repos. A repurchase agreement, or repo, is an instrument for investing money, while a reverse repo is a means for a government to borrow against securities that it holds. The instrument is a form of temporary debt for the issuer. Orange County used reverse repos to obtain additional money that was used in turn to purchase additional risky instruments. Subsequently, the Governmental Accounting Standards Board (GASB) issued Interpretation No. 3, Financial Reporting for Reverse Repurchase Agreements, which is intended to force governments to disclose their dealings in reverse repos and presumably rein in their use.

The Orange County debacle underscores the need for careful management of risk in developing a portfolio of investments. Derivatives may be a hedge against other investments that have low yields, but the derivatives themselves clearly entail substantial risks. As of the mid-2000s, Orange County operated two investment pools but with considerable caution such that the county's standards were stricter than those dictated by the State of California.[2]

[1]Kearns, K. P. (1995). Accountability and entrepreneurial public management: the case of the Orange County investment fund. *Public Budgeting & Finance, 15, Fall*, 3–21.

[2]County of Orange, California (2006). *Notes to comprehensive annual financial report for year ended June 30, 2005*. Retrieved August 19, 2006, from http://www.ac.ocgov.com/2005CAFR/NOTES.pdf.

banks, which also pay interest. The Financial Management Service (FMS) of the Treasury Department handles transactions. FMS provides extensive information on its website about the overall aspects of cash management and about specific operations. For example, the FMS "Green Book" provides detailed instructions to financial institutions as to how they are to process federal monies using automatic clearing houses (ACH).[122] The agency's "Gold Book" gives specifics on how federal checks are to be reclaimed as when they have been forged or have been issued to persons no longer eligible for payment.[123] Other departments and agencies handle many cash management transactions in accordance with instructions issued by the Treasury Department.

The inflow of federal receipts comes from taxes and other payments and from the sale of T-bills and other instruments discussed earlier. These sales are handled through the Federal Reserve and are limited according to the total debt ceiling set by Congress (see Chapter 9). T-bills are auctioned off weekly and other instruments are sold less frequently. There is, of course, a secondary market for these securities.

Like state and local governments, the federal government is concerned about having needed cash on hand and minimizing the costs of money, such as avoiding late payment fees on government purchases and avoiding paying out funds any earlier than required. An additional consideration at the federal level is that the government's cash operations affect markets (see Chapter 15).[124]

The federal government operates under the Cash Management Improvement Act of 1990 in making payments to state and local governments, particularly grant payments.[125] FMS lists three objectives of the law:

1. Efficiency—to minimize the time between the transfer of funds to the states and the payout for program purposes.
2. Effectiveness—to ensure that federal funds are available when requested.
3. Equity—to assess an interest liability to the federal government and/or the states to compensate for the lost value of funds.[126]

Another important consideration is that the federal government must meet its cash needs on a global basis. Sufficient amounts of money must be available at specific times in specific countries. For example, the Defense Department must handle large sums of foreign currency and, in doing so, exposes itself to potential problems in the value of such currency, particularly in the currency's devaluation.[127]

Currency and Coins. Since the 1990s, the federal government has been introducing redesigned currency.[128] The bills use color-shifting ink, security threads, watermarks, large off-center portraits, low-vision features, and microprinting that greatly deter counterfeiting. Nevertheless, counterfeiting remains a concern, given the sophistication of contemporary photocopying equipment.

The U.S. Mint in the Treasury Department has used coinage literally as a "money-making" business.[129] By making coins that are collected and therefore taken out of circulation or never put into circulation, the government in effect makes money. The 25-cent pieces (quarters) that commemorate each state are examples. The Treasury was selling two quarters from the first day of mintage for $19.95, when the face value was only $0.50. The $1 golden Sacagawea coin was similarly marketed but in addition was available as a holiday ornament, a bolo tie, a key fob, and a chain pendant. In 2002, the Mint even had a clearance sale, its first ever.

There have been some issues over how the Mint and the US Bureau of Engraving and Printing report their costs for creating coins and currency. Part of the confusion stems from the fact that the Federal Reserve system purchases currency at the cost of its printing but buys coinage at face value.[130]

Checks. In addition to redesigning currency and introducing a redesigned $1 coin, the government redesigned its checks. The punch-card checks that had been used for decades were replaced by checks that have counterfeiting protections and can be read by high-speed processing equipment. Despite advances made in checks and their processing, Congress decided in 1996 to phase out most check writing by January 1, 1999 (Debt Collection Improvement Act of 1996). Nevertheless, the government continues to issue many millions of checks every year—about 250 million a year out of one billion payments. The Treasury Department was concerned that the reduction in check-writing had slowed in the mid-2000s. This was troubling in that millions of baby-boomers were starting to retire and were they increasingly to expect to receive checks, the goal of eliminating such would not be met. The Treasury launched a program called "Go Direct" to try to encourage people to use direct deposits rather than checks.[131]

Electronic Fund Transfers. Advances in computer technology have made possible extensive use of electronic fund transfers (EFT). Through EFTs monies are moved via computer communication from bank to bank and from account to account. Monies received at one bank through a lockbox system, for instance, can be moved to other accounts in distant banks. Another advantage of electronic fund transfers is that they can be used for recurring payments, such as making direct deposits of Social Security payments into retirees' bank accounts. A form of electronic fund transfer is the electronic benefit transfer, which can be used to transfer funds through automatic teller machines. Some governments use electronic benefit transfers to make payments to welfare recipients. EFTs also are used by governments to transfer funds for alimony and child support in cases of divorce. The transfers, which are processed nationally by a few large banking systems, cost much less per transaction than do conventional checks.

Letters of Credit. An important cash management technique, especially for the federal government, is the use of letters of credit. As mandated by the Cash Management Improvement Act of 1990, these letters are provided to governments and nonprofit corporations that are awarded grants and contracts. The letters allow recipient organizations to establish credit at banks without the federal government having to provide money until it is needed. Funds then are transferred electronically into these accounts by the federal government.

The letter of credit may be thought of as a middle ground on how grants are paid. On the one hand, recipient governments prefer to have the full funding of their grants up front, even though money may be spent over the course of one or more years. Upfront payment would draw down federal reserves and needlessly benefit recipients who could earn interest on unspent federal dollars. The other alternative is for the federal government to pay recipients only when billed after they have incurred expenses. That would put them in the situation of footing the bill on expenses until grant monies were received as reimbursement. The letter of credit procedure, then, allows the government to delay until the last moment the transfer of funds, thereby saving it money as compared to paying in advance. Recipients benefit because they can draw down on their letters of credit as soon as payments are due. The University of Massachusetts, for example, reports that most federal dollars it receives come through this mechanism.[132]

Other Cash Management Considerations

Computer Usage. New computer technology has greatly altered how financial institutions operate and how governments handle cash. As already noted, electronic fund transfers have greatly modified how government does business. The Internet, which was in its infancy in the early 1990s, is today a commonly available source of information about investment opportunities.[133] Another example of computer applications involves municipal water systems. Electronic water meters allow readers to check readings outside of buildings rather than entering them.[134] Readings can be gathered by simply driving through neighborhoods. Some communities have installed electronic water meters that telephone their readings to a central office at specified intervals.[135] At the national level, automated clearing houses (ACH) are used for high-speed clearing of electronic payments.[136]

Intergovernmental Relations. Cash management has important intergovernmental aspects. States, as noted earlier, have passed laws setting standards for their local governments, which often view these laws as unnecessarily restrictive. Several states have established *investment pools* for their local governments. Some states provide assistance to local governments in the development of cash management plans. One important issue is the timing of grant payments that the federal government makes to state and local governments. The federal government, for cash management reasons, attempts to provide grant installments at the last possible moment. The Cash Management Improvement Act of 1990 provides that states are to pay interest on federal grant monies if the monies are received earlier than required and that the federal government must pay interest if it is tardy in providing promised grant monies.

Cash and Investment Managers. As is obvious, cash management involves a complex set of interdependent activities that require extensive expertise. For that reason, governments do not attempt to operate solely with their own capabilities. A state or local government will select one or more financial institutions to provide a range of services. Banks will receive checks, clear them, and deposit them in government accounts. A government may have a bank concentration account into which monies are first entered and then disbursed to others. Each day the bank will move money into accounts requiring deposits to cover checks, and any remaining funds will be placed in overnight interest-bearing instruments. Banks offer EFT services, lockbox services, armored cars, safety deposit boxes, lines of credit, and more. These institutions can provide a wide range of investment services and can handle the registration of government bonds and payments to bondholders. A preferred method for selecting a bank for everyday transactions or a securities dealer for managing an investment portfolio is to request bids from competing institutions.

▌ Procurement

Procurement entails the acquisition of resources required in providing government services.[137] While this function is not at the core of budgeting, it has major budgetary implications. In fiscal year 2004, the federal government spent $328 billion (or roughly 13% of its budget) on contracted goods or services.[138] Of course, state and local governments each year also spend billions on contracts. Some government agencies, such as the Defense Department and the National Aeronautics and Space Administration (NASA), spend a majority of their resources on contracted products and services rather than delivering services directly on their own. In addition, most other federal agencies accomplish their missions through the actions of other parties, usually through grants and other transfers of funds. The U.S. Department of Education, for example, delivers little direct education but provides grants to state and local education agencies in support of congressionally approved federal education objectives. State departments of education similarly spend little directly but grant billions to local school districts for the delivery of specified services.

Contracting, while fundamental to the operations of government, is not always handled well in budgets. Some local governments exclude contracts from their budgets and others only report them in lump sum. With the growing emphasis on results-oriented budgeting, governments have been forced to report contracts in their budgets.[139]

Procurement is extremely big business. The top five companies in federal contracting in fiscal 2004 were Lockheed Martin, Boeing, Northrop Grumman, General Dynamics, and Raytheon. All of these companies play major roles in defense and the aerospace industries. However, also included in the top 50 were the University of California (ranked 11th), California Institute of Technology (14th), and Johns Hopkins University (44th). Perhaps coming as somewhat of a surprise, the Government of Canada was ranked 55th.[140]

Organizational Configurations

Most jurisdictions have procurement systems that blend centralized and decentralized services. A central purchasing agency may be responsible for acquiring commonly used materials, such as office furniture and supplies, while line agencies have authority to purchase items used primarily by themselves. Centralization, at least in theory, has the advantage of providing overall controls to ensure that appropriate procedures are followed, resulting in fair competition among government suppliers and the purchase of quality goods and services at the lowest possible prices. Decentralization, on the other hand, presumably reduces red tape, allowing individual agencies to make purchases as needed and to custom-tailor purchases to their specific needs. The National Performance Review, in recommending greater decentralization in federal procurement, cited instances where buying in bulk through central purchasing cost the government more than it would have spent purchasing smaller quantities on a decentralized basis.[141]

At the federal level, several major organizational units are responsible for procurement. The General Services Administration (GSA) provides overall support to departments by procuring buildings, equipment, motor vehicles, computer systems, telephone systems, supplies, day care centers for employees' dependents, and the like. Its operations are immense. In any given year, the agency operates a fleet of more than 200,000 vehicles, spends several billions of dollars every year on construction, manages more than 300 million square feet of building space (excluding parking), and keeps many thousands of items on hand in its warehouses.[142]

Although GSA has numerous components, the main ones are the Public Buildings Service and the Federal Acquisition Service (FAS). FAS was formed in 2006 when the Federal Supply Service and the Federal Technology Service (FTS) were merged.[143] The Public Buildings unit operates with appropriated funds, while FAS operates with revolving funds by buying goods and services and then selling them to federal agencies.[144]

All federal line departments and agencies carry out procurement, with the Department of Defense having one of the largest procurement operations. Defense hires the equivalent of 700,000 workers through its contracting operations.[145] The Defense Logistics Agency purchases many items centrally for the department, while the individual services also have purchasing authority.[146]

Having many procurement offices can result in a hodgepodge of operations, each with its own peculiar set of regulations. In 1974, Congress attempted to deal with this problem by creating the Office of Federal Procurement Policy (OFPP) within the Office of Management and Budget.[147] President Clinton strengthened the OFPP's role in 1994 by issuing Executive Order 12931, which charged the unit with providing "broad policy guidance and overall leadership" in procurement. The OFPP, while not conducting purchasing activities, is responsible for coordinating the activities of purchasing offices. The General Services Administration issues the Federal Acquisition Regulation (FAR) that sets standards for basically all federal acquisitions. The Defense Department and other agencies have regulations that supplement FAR.[148]

The Services Acquisition Reform Act (SARA) of 2003 provided for the designation of high-ranking procurement officers in departments and agencies.[149] These chief acquisition officers (CAOs) meet periodically as the CAO Council to work on problems of common concern.[150]

Besides a central procurement office and individual agency offices, there are other possible arrangements. In some instances, one agency may piggyback on a contract issued through another agency. At the federal level, the Department of Defense is the largest user of contracts by other agencies.[151] Another approach is for agencies to jointly work together on acquisitions. This has the advantage of increasing buying power over what any one agency would have but has the drawback of requiring that the procurement regulations of both agencies be met. OMB has created a working group to further interagency acquisitions and resolve some of the inherent problems with the process.[152]

Procurement Objectives. A procurement program has several objectives. One chief concern is having the materials and supplies available when needed and avoiding stock outages. Every agency must keep focused on its mission and use procurement as a means of meeting that mission in a timely fashion.

Keeping unit costs as low as possible is another objective. Often the lowest costs for acquiring items are obtained by ordering large quantities, whether large amounts of office stationery or entire fleets of automobiles. Ordering large quantities, however, conflicts with another concern: keeping stocked items to a minimum. Procurement specialists strive to determine *economic ordering quantities*, or when to purchase particular types of items and in what quantities. Some purchasing offices have shifted to *just-in-time ordering*, in which items are received from vendors when needed, thereby eliminating the cost of warehousing these items. The widespread use of computer systems has greatly increased the ability of organizations—both public and private—to implement just-in-time ordering.

Another objective is creating some flexibility in decision making. For example, if all personnel in a city government are on continuing appointments, then difficult choices will need to be made about possibly laying off workers during economic recessions. On the other hand, if some employees are on fixed-term contracts and expenditures need to be reduced, then these contracts simply need not be renewed when they expire. The same can be done with auxiliary services. When budget cuts are required, auxiliary contracts may not be renewed or at reduced levels.[153]

Procurement objectives often conflict with one another. On the one hand, procurement policies may include numerous specific requirements that are viewed as red tape and unnecessarily hinder executives in managing their operations. On the other hand, such red tape may be important in preventing fraud and waste.

Choices also must be made between purchasing, leasing, and privatizing. In some instances, there may be financial and other advantages to leasing a building rather than purchasing it. The federal government, however, may rely too heavily on leasing office space, as ownership presumably is less expensive in the long run. A wide range of equipment can be leased, including photocopying machines, computers, and dump trucks. The Defense Department even has considered leasing rather than buying its most expensive weapons systems.[154] *True* or *operating leases* are those in which the government pays for the specified period and gains no ownership of whatever is being leased, whereas *lease-purchase agreements* provide for ownership after a specified period. Leasing and other forms of contracting out are not necessarily an avenue for reducing costs. One survey of state governments found that only one-third reported reduced service costs.[155]

Outsourcing, as discussed earlier, is another option and may involve contracting with a private firm to use its facilities, personnel, and other resources to deliver a service. In many cases, private contractor employees and government employees work side by side to produce services in government facilities. Federal agencies must follow the guidance in Circular A-76 that covers contracts for commercial (nongovernmental) activities.[156] While many services can be contracted out, policy making is regarded as a core activity that cannot be privatized. This possibility becomes a concern in situations where government relies heavily on consulting firms to the extent that they seem to be responsible for setting policy or conducting other inherently governmental functions. A blurring of organizational boundaries occurs when a government agency works not with just one but two or more contractors on a particular program or project. In making a choice among these options, a paramount concern must be to use tax dollars efficiently.

The process prescribed by Circular A-76 is a complicated one.[157] OMB provides a "Supplemental Handbook" detailing the procedure to be used. Each year OMB issues guidance on cost figures to be used in calculating anticipated pay raises and changes in the costs of supplies and equipment. An agency must identify an activity that can be contracted out, must establish a process for accepting bids from both private entities and the public organization that currently is providing the service, must review the bids and select the winner, and must implement the outcome. In the Defense Department, this process often takes 18 months or longer. These competitions tend to result in cuts in the federal work force either because the work is contracted out or because the government unit won the bid by being more cost-effective—namely, operating with fewer workers.[158]

In fiscal year 2004, there were 217 competitions under A-76, and according to OMB, the effort netted a savings or cost avoidance of $1.4 billion over five years. The Federal Aviation Administration moved to consolidate its stations from 58 to 20, which was expected to save $1.7 billion over 10 years.[159]

Part of the Circular A-76 process involves setting performance targets or standards so that it is clear what work is to be accomplished. At issue has been the fact that sometimes the same people who set the standards were the ones who prepared the in-house bids to retain operations within the government. The General Accounting Office (now Government Accountability Office) ruled that this situation involves a conflict of interest and that the two functions need to be performed by different individuals.[160]

In addition to Circular A-76, the Federal Activities and Inventory Reform (FAIR) Act of 1998 gives priority to outsourcing. Each year federal agencies, under OMB's guidance, must report what activities are "not inherently governmental in nature."[161] Upward of 50% of all jobs analyzed have been identified as potentially being outsourced. The law does not require that some or all of these jobs actually be contracted out, but certainly there is an implication that maybe they should be contracted out. The lists can be challenged, however. Contractors usually contend that jobs that should have been included were not. Employees and unions typically contend the opposite.

The George W. Bush administration, in its *President's Management Agenda*, identified "competitive sourcing" as one of its five government-wide initiatives.[162] The administration has used FAIR to further that initiative.

In 2005, Congress passed a law limiting the use of outsourcing. A section was included in an appropriations act limiting outsourcing only to proven cases that would yield a savings of at least $10 million or a savings of 10% of the personnel required to operate the activities.[163]

By the mid-2000s, there was growing concern that competitive sourcing had become too narrowly focused and that a broader approach was needed at all levels of government and in the private sector. *Spend analysis* became popular as a method for *strategic sourcing*. The underlying idea here is that careful study of existing spending patterns can provide insights into improving the efficient and effective acquisition of services and products. Both OMB and GAO have called on federal agencies to make use of spend analysis.[164] New York State has a spend analysis program for information technology acquisition that is available to state agencies and local governments.[165]

Contracting Process

Steps. Standard procedures are normally followed when contracting for products or services. Specifications for what is to be purchased are determined. For example, a truck might be required to have a specified ground clearance, load capacity, passenger capacity, and the like. Then, bidding procedures begin through the issuance of *invitations for bid* (IFBs), *requests for proposal* (RFPs), and *requests for quotation* (RFQs). An IFB is used when a government has a reasonably detailed conception of what is to be purchased, such as the painting of the exterior of a building. An RFP or RFQ is used in a situation where some latitude exists on the part of the bidder in terms of what is to be offered. Once bids are received, they are analyzed and, in the case of IFBs, awards are made to the lowest responsible bidder. In a competition involving an RFP, an award might be made to a higher bidder, one that was thought to have the best approach to dealing with a problem.

Contracting officers are required to perform a *best value* analysis so that the lowest technically qualified bid is not necessarily the best value. The life cycle cost of a truck including expected maintenance costs over the life of the truck, fuel efficiency, and so forth would generally be included in the best value analysis. For technical services, as opposed to physical items such as a truck, the best value analysis might take into account which bid offers the most inputs for a given price, and the award could go to a higher bidder in order to obtain better value. The Office of Management and Budget has pushed agencies to use the best value approach in competitive sourcing between public and private bidders.[166]

When the government selects a firm using an RFQ, bilateral negotiations are required before a final selection may be made. In contrast, with an RFP, the government may select a firm without further negotiations. The receipt of a product or service follows the signing of a contract or the award of a grant. Additional steps include inspecting the product or service received and paying the contractor.

Not all spending is handled through the bidding process. As discussed later, many small purchases can be handled through government credit cards and no bids are required. Although restricted to small purchases, the credit card transactions amount to many billions of dollars each year and pose major challenges for auditors.

In some situations, contracts are awarded not to one company but to several firms. The federal government, because it serves the entire nation, finds it advantageous to contract with several suppliers in the same industry. This *multiple-award schedule system* makes goods and services available on a standby basis, allowing agencies to order them when needed.[167] All forms of construction, ranging from simple repair and maintenance to the construction of an entire building, can be handled through a job order contracting mechanism in which suppliers agree to provide services at specified costs when needed. For example, a painting firm might sign a contract agreeing to charge a set amount per square foot. Any agency could then hire the firm for painting services.

The federal government has experimented with *reverse auctioning*. This technique allows bidders during the open bidding period to see the bids made by competing firms but not the identities of the firms themselves. If a company finds its bid has been undercut by another bidder, then the first bidder may consider lowering its bid to meet the competition.

Another feature of some procurement programs is specification of performance in terms of timeliness and quality. For example, a contract for a state highway construction project may stipulate that the project must be completed by a specified date, with financial penalties being imposed for each day beyond the deadline.

The 1994 Federal Acquisition Streamlining Act instructs federal agencies to develop *results-oriented* or *performance contracts* for acquisitions other than standardized commercial items.[168] In other words, when an agency buys a service, such as using a firm to process grant applications from local governments, standards should be set for evaluating the firm's performance. Measurable performance is increasingly a part of federal contracts for research and development. These contracts may contain award fee incentives in which contractors can achieve higher or lower fees or profits based on their performance. To engage in such contracting, agencies must be able to specify what work to accomplish, at what time, and with what degree of quality. That has been the rub of the matter. When agencies cannot precisely define their expectations of contractors, then accountability for performance is an elusive matter. The Services Acquisition Reform Act Advisory Panel found that to be the case at the federal level.[169]

One form of performance contracting is known as *share-in-savings*. Share-in-Savings (SiS) allows for government to contract with a private firm that takes on much of the risk of the endeavor with the promise of financial rewards later through cost savings. For example, contracting-out some aspects of debt collection, as noted earlier, can enhance revenue to a government and a contractor can be paid with some of that newly generated revenue. The E-government Act of 2002 authorizes selective use of share-in-savings contracting for information technology.[170]

Competition. Competition in procurement is considered one of the best means of ensuring quality products or services at minimum cost. Lack of competition may result from blatant favoritism in awarding contracts or from somewhat more subtle ploys, such as specifying a named product brand and model in the IFB. At the state and local levels, corporations have become more aggressive in challenging contract awards when they seem to violate legal requirements for competition.

Not all awards are made on a competitive basis. **Exhibit 10–3** discusses *noncompetitive* or *no-bid contracting*.

Exhibit 10–3 No-Bid Contracting

No-bid or noncompetitive contracting has generally been considered anathema to contemporary procurement, but with important exceptions. The bidding process is defended as saving taxpayers' dollars by seeking out the vendors or contractors that offer the best products and services at the best prices. Without bidding, so the argument goes, government pays top dollar and often for inferior goods and services.

No-bid contracting creates opportunities for favoritism. For example, the fact that Vice President Cheney was a former head of Halliburton was the grounds for speculation that any no-bid awards going to Halliburton and its subsidiaries were based on favoritism.[1] The fact that defense contractors donate *millions* of dollars to political campaigns and then reap *billions* of dollars in no-bid defense contracts raises questions about whether these contracts were "bought" by the companies.[2] Questions were raised in 2005 when the Department of Homeland Security (DHS) announced it would enter into a no-bid contract for an intelligence analyst certificate program with a small college in Pennsylvania that just happened to have ties with Tom Ridge, the first DHS secretary and former governor of Pennsylvania.[3]

If noncompetitive contracting is considered faulty, then why use it? There are at least two main factors. One is that sometimes there is only one possible bidder, such as when government needs the services that only one company can provide. Then, going with a "sole-source" contract is the only option. The other reason is that of speed. In times of emergency, there may be no time to allow for a lengthy bidding process. A particular project needs to get underway, as in recovering from a flood or tornado.

What governments enter into no-bid contracts? Basically all of them, and basically all are challenged from time-to-time on their decisions to use such contracts. For example, a community college in Alabama was investigated in 2006 over its decision to hire a painting contractor without using the standard bidding process.[4] That same year, California entered into $51 million of no-bid contracts for sending prison inmates out of state to other facilities.[5]

Federal no-bid contracting received widespread attention with spending on the wars in Afghanistan and Iraq and for recovery from Hurricane Katrina.[6] The Department of Homeland Security awarded most of its Katrina funds with contracts valued at less than $500,000, and 55% of those awards were no-bid. Only 19% were full-and-open competitions, with the remainder falling in other categories.[7] The Government Accountability Office studied Iraq reconstruction spending between 2003 and 2006 and found that only 10% of State Department contracting was awarded competitively compared with 99% for the U.S. Agency for International Development and 82% for the Defense Department.[8] Of course, State Department spending in total was small compared with Defense Department spending.

Other federal no-bid contracting has been controversial. In 2006, both the Federal Aviation Administration and the National Aeronautics and Space Administration were roundly criticized for their no-bid contracting.[9] Senator Charles E. Grassley (Republican of Iowa) said, "It's just outrageous how the FAA was not looking out for the taxpayers' dollars. Three words would sum this up: absolutely no accountability."[10]

continues

Exhibit 10–3   No-Bid Contracting (continued)

No-bid contracting is based on negotiations.[11] A government worker or team of workers is responsible for hammering out the details of a contract with a sole-source vendor. This process can be done in a matter of minutes or if time allows, can extend to months. During the negotiations, there can be bargaining over prices and services. Oftentimes no-bid contracts may involve situations in which the quantity of services is yet unknown as is the timeline for such services.

Cost-plus award-fee (CPAF) provisions are standard. Since the work to be done is uncertain at the outset of the contract, the award simply provides that the vendor's costs will be covered plus the vendor will receive a fee or profit on top of the costs. These provisions often are controversial, since there may seem to be few incentives for vendors to keep costs down. Governments normally have procedures that allow for challenging the costs submitted by vendors.

Governments set thresholds for no-bid contracting, often with some dollar amount as a cutoff above which contracts must be awarded competitively. When a no-bid contract is to be awarded, the agency typically must prepare documents justifying the decision, and contracts exceeding some thresholds may require special approval. For example, no-bid Army contracts worth more than $50 million must be approved by the Assistant Secretary for Acquisition, Logistics and Technology.[12] Companies owned by Native American tribes are sometimes exempt from dollar limits. These companies received no-bid contracts worth $100 million and more from the U.S. Department of Interior, even though the usual threshold was $3 million.[13]

The immensity of no-bid contracting in the mid-2000s has resulted in some key recommendations. Both the Government Accountability Office (GAO) when looking at the experience with Hurricane Katrina and the Special Inspector General for Iraq Reconstruction (SIGIR) when looking at the war situation have recommended better prior planning for emergencies.[14] SIGIR recommended the creation of an enhanced Contingency Federal Acquisition Regulation (CFAR) that would be developed on an interagency basis and eventually enacted into law. When planning for emergencies, contracting staff needed to be included. The contracting staff should not be brought into a situation after the fact. Another recommendation was that responsibilities needed to be specified within agencies and across agency lines.

Adequate numbers of qualified government contracting staff are needed in all aspects of procurement but particularly in no-bid situations, where it is important to have staff alert to possible contractor failures and mismanagement. One observer said that the lack of adequate staff led to extensive waste in Iraq: "People were blowing cash around Iraq like they had leaf-blowers."[15] SIGIR recommended creation of a reserve contracting corps that could be deployed to wherever it was needed in the world.

There were two other important recommendations regarding no-bid contracting in defense. One was that contractors should pre-compete and pre-qualify for reconstruction

continues

Exhibit 10-3 No-Bid Contracting (continued)

work prior to an emergency. The other was that information systems should be devised specifically to deal with contingency operations. On this last point, it was found that Army Corps of Engineers had resorted to entering the code of "dummy vendor" in its information system in order to allow the recording of planned contracts.[16]

[i] Morris, D. (2003). Criticism grows of no-bid work for Iraq reconstruction. *Govexec.com*. Retrieved October 22, 2006, from http://www.govexec.com/dailyfed/0403/0417-3cd1.htm; Avery, A. H. (2006). Weapons of mass construction: the potential liability of Halliburton under the False Claims Act and the implications to defense contracting. *Alabama Law Review, 57*, 827–852.

[2] Strohm, C. (2004). Major defense contractors reap billions in no-bid contracts, report finds. *Govexec.com*. Retrieved October 22, 2006, from http://www.govexec.com/dailyfed/0904/092904c1.htm.

[3] Williams, B. (2005). No-bid contractor has deep ties to Ridge. *Center for Public Integrity*. Retrieved October 22, 2006, from http://www.publicintegrity.org/report.aspx?aid=671.

[4] No-bid contract being examined (2006). *SunHearald.com* (Associated Press), *October 15*. Retrieved October 22, 2006, from http://www.sunhearald.com/mld/sunhearald/news/state/15763692.htm.

[5] California to transfer inmates out of state (2006). *NewYorkTimes.com* (Associated Press), *October 21, 2006*. Retrieved October 22, 2006, from http://www.nytimes.com/aponline/us/AP-California-Prisons.html?_r=1&oref=slogin.

[6] Miller, T. C. (2006). *Blood money: wasted billions, lost lives, and corporate greed in Iraq*. New York: Little, Brown and Company.

[7] Office of the Inspector General, U.S. Department of Homeland Security (2006). *9th PCIE Hurricane Katrina Report*. Retrieved October 22, 2006, from http://www.dhs.gov/xoig/assets/katovrsght/OIG_PCIE_033106.pdf.

[8] U.S. Government Accountability Office (2006). *Rebuilding Iraq: status of competition for Iraq reconstruction contracts*. Washington, DC: GAO.

[9] Wong, K. (2006). The rocket science of technology procurement. *Cadalyst.com*. Retrieved October, from http://management.cadalyst.com/cadman/article/articleDetail.jsp?id=376788.

[10] Grassley, C. E. as quoted in Wilber, D. Q. (2006). Probe of FAA contracting finds waste. *Washingtonpost.com, September 23*. Retrieved October 22, 2006, from http://www.washingtonpost.com/wp-dyn/content/article/2006/09/22/AR2006092201547.html.

[11] See Office of the Under Secretary of Defense for Acquisition Technology and Logistics, U.S. Department of Defense (2006). *Contracting pricing reference guides: noncompetitive negotiations*. Retrieved October 22, 2006, from http://www.acq.osd.mil/dpap/contractpricing/vol5chap4.htm.

[12] Office of the Special Inspector General for Iraq Reconstruction, U.S. Department of Defense (2006). *Attestation engagement concerning the award of non-competitive contract DACA63-03-D-0005 to Kellogg, Brown, and Root Services, Inc.* Retrieved October 22, 2006, from http://www.sigir.mil/audits/sigir_audit_05-019-non-competitive-kbr.pdf.

[13] Palmer, K. (2006). Alaska Native firms capture up to $700 million in no-bid contracts. *Govexec.com*. Retrieved October 22, 2006, from http://www.govexec.com/dailyfed/0106/011506k1.htm.

[14] U.S. Government Accountability Office (2006). *Agency management of contractors responding to Hurricanes Katrina and Rita*. Washington, DC: GAO; Special Inspector General for Iraq Reconstruction, U.S. Department of Defense (2006). *Iraq reconstruction: lessons in contracting and procurement*, 2. Retrieved October 22, 2006, from http://www.sigir.mil/reports/pdf/Lessons_Learned_July21.pdf.

[15] Miller, T. C., as quoted in Mandel, J. (2006). Iraq reconstruction failures tied to contracting breakdowns. *Govexec.com*. Retrieved October 22, 2006, from http://www.govexec.com/dailyfed/1006/101306m1.htm.

[16] Special Inspector General for Iraq Reconstruction, U.S. Department of Defense (2006). *Interim audit report on improper obligations using the Iraq Relief and Reconstruction Fund (IRRF 2)*. Retrieved October 22, 2006, from http://www.sigir.mil/reports/pdf/audits/06-037.pdf.

The Competition in Contracting Act of 1984 was passed to encourage greater competition in federal contracting and specifically enhanced the powers of losing bidders to mount legal challenges to the awards.[171] In addition to filing a protest with the contracting agency itself or with the Government Accountability Office, a losing bidder may be able to appeal to the General Services Board of Contract Appeals, the Court of Federal Claims, or a federal district court.[172] Cooperative agreements and grants awarded as the result of a competitive process are not subject to protest, and task orders within a master task order contract are not subject to protest. The original master award for the task order contract may be protested, but not subsequent task awards.

The 1994 Federal Acquisition Streamlining Act contains important provisions that limit bid protests that often are perceived as needlessly delaying the awarding of contracts. President Clinton's Executive Order 12979 of 1995 instructs agencies to devise *alternative dispute resolution* (ADR) procedures, such as the use of neutral third parties.

Several factors discourage competition among would-be contractors. Lack of knowledge about how contracts are awarded and how to prepare a bid excludes some companies from bidding, although that problem is somewhat mitigated today given the vast amounts of information on contracting available on government websites. The Defense Department has established Procurement Technical Assistance Centers in many states. These centers assist business firms in understanding the process by which they can sell their goods and services to the government.[173] Many procurements are so large and complex that companies would have to make major investments in personnel and technology just to become competitive in the bidding process. *Design-and-build contracts,* in which several contract awards may be made for the design phase, with the best design being selected for the build or implementation phase, enable more firms to compete for much larger, more complex contracts.

Competition is restricted in other ways as well. A close and long-term relationship between a government agency and a contractor can develop over time. When a contract is to be rebid for a new time period, the company already holding the contract usually has a decided advantage.

Contract bundling tends to prohibit smaller companies from competing for contracts, whether this be at the local, state, or federal level.[174] In contract bundling, several would-be small contracts are put up for bid as a single, large contract. The advantages to government are at least twofold. First, the administrative costs of handling the bidding and contracting processes are reduced. Second, the item or service being purchased often is less expensive when it is ordered in bulk as in a bundled contract than when it is purchased in several smaller contracts. Combining efforts into larger and larger contracts often is an agency response to budget cuts or cuts in personnel complement. Fewer procurement officers and fewer government staff to oversee contracts increase the pressure on the agency to make fewer but larger awards. However, such bundled contracts can involve a diverse set of products and services, many of which are beyond the scope of a single small company, thereby excluding the company from the bidding process. OMB has instructed agencies to limit their use of the bundling procedure and said it would rate agencies on their efforts to avoid the practice.[175]

Companies become reluctant to participate in competitions when, if they win, they might have to wait for weeks or months to receive the money owed them. Delays in payments can bankrupt a small firm. Even when payments occur promptly, small firms may face other problems. If payments are made but then later the funding agency demands greater documentation on transactions, the small firm may be unable to comply due to weak recordkeeping. Whatever the situation, it will be costly from the standpoint of the time consumed in trying to comply with the government's requests.

Government contracting also opens up contractors to liability over their compliance with various employment laws, such as equal employment opportunity based on race, gender, and the like. The Rehabilitation Act of 1973 requires affirmative action in government hiring of people with disabilities, and this law is extended to private companies when they become government contractors.[176] Similarly, affirmative action is required in the hiring and promoting of veterans under the Vietnam Era Veterans' Readjustment Assistance Act of 1974.[177] Requirements such as these may discourage companies from bidding on federal contracts, not because the companies oppose equal opportunity or hiring veterans but because they fear lawsuits or the threat of lawsuits.

The widespread use of the Internet beginning in the 1990s has posed major challenges in the procurement arena. Expectations have developed that procurement should be an essential component of E-government. Governments at all levels have worked diligently to convert their paper-based processes for procurement to ones that include electronic processing. These efforts are complicated by the massiveness of procurement programs in large governments, by statutory restrictions that specify processes to be used, and by rapidly changing technology.

At the federal level, several websites are relevant.

- *Business.gov* is a site intended to service all aspects of the business community and not just contracting. The site provides information on such topics as business law, taxes, and international trade as well as government procurement.[178] The Small Business Administration maintains the site in cooperation with more than 20 other agencies.

- *Acquisition Central* is focused specifically on procurement and provides links to a variety of government websites. This site is hosted by the E-government initiative.[179]

- *Fed Biz Opps*, according to its own self-description, is the single government point-of-entry for federal government procurement. The site is hosted by the General Services Administration. Federal agencies have begun to post reverse auctions on this site (see above).[180]

- *FPDS* is the Federal Procurement Data System. It provides access to a wealth of information about government awards.[181] The system is managed by a team of agencies led by the General Services Administration.
- *GSA e-Buy* is a website that allows federal buyers to post RFQs and RFPs (see above) and vendors to respond electronically.

Increasingly, federal agencies that issue research grants have implemented online grant application systems. The National Science Foundation and the National Institutes of Health were early leaders. Once grant applications are received, agencies forward through electronic means the relevant portions of the applications to extramural panels that review the proposals. The review process in which the extramural panels evaluate proposals also is conducted online.

State and local governments and the private sector have become deeply involved in information technology as a vehicle for communicating between the business community and government procurement. For example, California maintains a website for state, federal, and local contracting.[182] One example of a commercial site is *GovCB.com*, Government Contract and Bid, which provides "access to thousands of active counties, schools, hospitals, airports and state bid listings matched to your business profile."[183]

Computer technology is as important to government agencies that consume products and services as it is to firms that sell to government. The General Services Administration operates GSA Advantage!, an online shopping center.[184] Agencies not only can compare prices on products and place orders, but also can configure products and add accessories. GSA offers to agencies similar services in the information technology realm.

Contract management is another critical component of the procurement process.[185] What good is a contract if government procurement officers fail to follow up to be sure that a business met its obligations under the contract? One problem has been for contractors to meet their obligations but for government to overpay the contractors. Congress has required agencies to use recovery auditing to identify overpayments and recoup money that was misspent.[186]

Reforms. Procurement procedures become increasingly complex as additional, well-intended requirements are imposed. Executive Order 13101 is instructive. It requires agencies to buy "environmentally preferable products." Agencies must consider whether the products they purchase may be recycled and the extent to which waste can be prevented. Also, Executive Order 13279 requires agencies to ensure that faith-based and community organizations are treated the same as all other entities when contracts are awarded.

One prescription might be to simplify the government procurement process. Off-the-shelf purchasing of commercial items may be less expensive than specifying items that then might require special designs and types of construction. As an example of the rigidity in government purchasing, the General Services Administration once had elaborate specifications for the design and durability of "ash receiver[s], tobacco (desk type)" when commercially available ashtrays probably would have been suitable, especially given that smoking is banned in most government buildings. Simplification was one of the chief objectives of the 1994 Federal Acquisition Streamlining Act and Executive Order 12931. The law eliminated many contracting procedures for purchases amounting to less than $100,000 and, in purchases of commercial items, waived more than 30 laws that required bidders to collect and submit detailed information of limited utility as part of their bids. The Federal Acquisition Reform Act (FARA) or Clinger-Cohen Act of 1996 broadened the definition of commercial services, bringing more purchasing activities under the simplified procedures.[187] Ten year's experience with the law found that the expected cost savings was not realized.[188]

Work force quality. Another reform frequently mentioned is a move to upgrade the quality and sometimes quantity of the procurement work force. The argument is that upgrades are necessary to reflect the increasing size of contracting and its complexity. The ongoing California Performance Review found the state's procurement work force to be "inadequate." The review called for new civil service classifications and new training programs.[189] New York's Citywide Training Center (CTC) offers procurement classes that are recognized by the Universal Public Purchasing Certification Council and the Institute for Supply Management.[190] The City of Atlanta prides itself on being "best in class" in procurement, a designation awarded by Procurement and Supply Chain Benchmarking Association.[191]

At the federal level, efforts are underway in dealing with perceived acquisition work force problems. One concern is work force turnover and retirements. One report found that 32% of contracting employees would be eligible for retirement in 2010 and 54% in 2015.[192] Another concern is that the work force has shrunk from over 460,000 employees in 1990 to less than 300,000.[193] Shortages in staff may result in procurement officers devoting their time almost exclusively to the awarding of contracts at the expense of overseeing the implementation of the awards.[194] The Federal Acquisition Institute, a branch of the General Services Administration, was established in the 1970s to further the development of the procurement work force. It delivers online and classroom training as well as serves as a link to other training providers. The Office of Management and Budget has instructed agencies to give particular attention to acquisition work force development in their human capital plans, which are part of the *President's Management Agenda*.[195]

Fraud, Waste, Abuse, and Scandals. Despite sustained efforts to improve procurement practices, the field has been plagued with scandals involving fraud, waste (as in the case of toilet seats that cost the military hundreds of dollars), and abuse (as in the case of the Federal Emergency Management Agency having hundreds of trailers sitting unused and exposed to potential flooding after Hurricane Katrina). The acquisition function at several federal agencies appears on the Government Accountability Office's high-risk list, meaning that the government is exposed to the possible loss of large sums of resources.[196]

Fraud comes in many forms. Frauds involving state highway contracting occur in such ways as:

- Specifications that are written by government workers to favor particular contractors and suppliers;
- Conflicts of interest, such as acquisition officials having financial interests in road construction companies;
- Collusive bidding and price fixing, such as some contractors not bidding on a contract so as to swing the award to a favored company;
- Questionable documentation from contractors, such as altering or modifying critical information—the contractor's bond and pre-qualifications;
- Production substitution, such as mismarking and mislabeling products and materials; or
- Cost mischarging for materials and labor, such as consistent cost overruns due to intentional underestimating or underbidding.[197]

Safeguards against such practices exist. Federal agencies have inspectors general offices to ferret out corruption, and similar units exist at the state and local levels. Sometimes governments cooperate with one another, as in the case of FEMA working with New York State to combat fraud related to regional flooding in 2006.[198] The Procurement Integrity Act of 1996 prohibits federal employees from releasing "contractor bid or proposal information" that in some way would unfairly benefit competitors.[199] Many acquisition employees are prohibited from receiving compensation from contractors for one year after they leave government service. While working for government, they are to report any employment offers by contractors. Federal agency personnel in positions other than procurement often are precluded from representing their new private employer with their old agency for one year after leaving government service, although this does not prohibit their being employed by a company that does business with their old agency.

Contracting employees who commit wrongdoings may be reprimanded, suspended, demoted, fired, or prosecuted. There were nearly 3,000 such cases in the federal government in 2005, a concern, but still small compared with the total number of acquisition workers.[200] The Federal Bureau of Investigation in the early 2000s was able to identify about 20 GSA workers engaged in corrupt practices in the Chicago area alone.[201] The accounting giant PricewaterhouseCoopers was found in 2005 to have defrauded federal agencies by nearly $42 million in inflated travel expenses.[202] Sometimes members of Congress get caught up in bribery schemes.[203]

One of the most notorious fraud situations in recent times involved David Safavian, who was chief of the Office of Federal Procurement Policy within OMB. Prior to joining OMB, he had been chief of staff at the General Services Administration. He was indicted and convicted for obstructing a GSA investigation into possible illegal business relations with lobbyist Jack Abramoff. He was convicted in 2006, but filed for a retrial.[204]

Contractors can be sanctioned. They can be suspended from government contracting for a fixed period or barred permanently. Short of these measures, they can have restrictions imposed on them on bidding on contracts and executing them.[205] Nevertheless, abuses are all too frequent. The Government Accountability Office reported that one of the most widespread abuses of contractors was failure to pay federal taxes owed.[206] In the mid-2000s, Boeing Company engaged in bribing an Air Force contractor over tanker procurement and paid $615 million to settle the case. This largest defense contracting scandal in decades resulted in people from the Air Force and Boeing going to prison.[207] In the aftermath of the scandal, the Justice Department created a special task force against fraud in defense and homeland security.[208]

Problem Areas and Innovations

Procurement is undergoing extensive changes too numerous to discuss here, but a few can be noted. One major change is the growing importance of contracting for services as distinguished from acquisition of products. The field has grown to such an extent that there is a professional association known as the Contract Services Association (CSA). The association promotes private contracting by government, creates opportunities for networking between companies and government agencies, and provides training for contractors in how to work with governments at all levels. Service contracting presents special challenges of determining what services of what quality and what quantity are to be delivered and then monitoring the process to assure that the contract requirements are met and that only appropriate expenses are charged for those services.

Measuring the costs of services is particularly troublesome due to variations in accounting rules used in the private and public sectors. This situation complicates efforts to compare the costs of producing a service by a corporation with those of a government agency. Further, when such service contracts are awarded to nonprofit entities, important problems may arise over how government expects operations to be managed and how the nonprofits normally manage themselves.

Credit Cards and ID Cards. Government-issued credit cards have become standard components of acquisition systems. Some governments now provide employees with credit cards so that they may charge their travel expenses and be reimbursed later rather than use travel advances or their personal funds to cover costs until being reimbursed. Credit cards also are being used for small purchases, such as $2,500 or less. The cards in the federal government are helpful in remote areas that lack ready access to General Services Administration supply centers. Today's technology allows credit cards to work or not work for specified sales. For example, the cards can be programmed not to work for liquor sales where bar code systems are used. GSA reported $17.1 billion of card purchases for fiscal year 2004 and claimed it saved nearly $54 on every transaction due to reduced processing costs.[209]

With more than 17 million cards in circulation in the federal government, abuse can be expected. The Defense Department was sharply criticized when it came to light that employees had used the cards to purchase hundreds of dollars worth of cosmetics and compact discs.[210] GAO and the Inspector General of the Department of Homeland Security found that DHS employees had purchased "a beer brewing kit, a 63" plasma television costing $8,000 which was found unused in its original box 6 months after being purchased, and tens of thousands of dollars for training at golf and tennis resorts."[211]

As part of an effort to increase security over all aspects of operations, governments are enhancing their identification systems for employees and the contractors who work for them. As required by Homeland Security Presidential Directive 12, all federal employees and contractors who regularly work in government buildings commenced receiving new *smart card identifications*.[212] These cards, which use integrated circuit chips, will be used in limiting access to government buildings, data files, and specifically purchasing. The cards are referred to as "end-to-end," suggesting that they are comprehensive in their approach to providing secure identification of individuals. Bearing Point was one of the first companies to receive a GSA contract to provide these cards.[213]

Affirmative Action. A continuing problem is the extent to which procurement should support affirmative action to assist minority-owned businesses, women contractors, and other special groups. In 1995, the Federal Acquisition Streamlining Act set nonbinding goals of contracting with minority-owned businesses, and Executive Order 12928 called upon agencies to develop methods for encouraging minority businesses and historically black colleges and universities to bid on contracts with the government. Executive Order 13360, issued by President George W. Bush, expects agencies to create opportunities for service-disabled veterans to contract and subcontract with the government. To avoid charges of reverse discrimination, agencies do not use quotas but rather pursue outreach and other programs to help make minority businesses aware of contracting opportunities and provide advice on how to prepare procurement proposals.

The Supreme Court has ruled that set-aside programs for minority businesses in state and local procurement are permissible only when there is documentation of discrimination against such businesses.[214] That ruling was later extended to the federal government.[215]

Acquisition programs often are expected to provide special opportunities to small businesses that otherwise might be locked out of selling to the government by large corporations. Executive Orders 13169 and 13170 require federal agencies to increase opportunities for small businesses, especially disadvantaged ones.[216]

Labor-Management Relations. In the contracting process, labor–management issues may arise, such as whether a contractor will enter into agreements with labor unions. Executive Order 12871 established the National Partnership Council and required federal agencies to work cooperatively with unions. In 2001, President George W. Bush revoked this order by issuing Executive Order 13202. The new order called for "neutrality towards government contractors' labor relations on federal and federally funded construction projects."

Other Problems. Other procurement problems involve energy, the environment, and immigrants. Agencies are expected to purchase equipment that is efficient in the use of energy and minimizes pollution. Although federal agencies are expected to take into account their purchases' impact on the environment, a study by the General Accounting Office found that they did poorly in determining whether their purchases were "environmentally friendly."[217] Executive Order 12989 of 1996 prohibits agencies from contracting with companies that the Attorney General has determined to have violated immigration laws by hiring illegal alien workers.

Security has emerged as a vast new area of purchasing. Although security-related purchasing has long existed, the attacks of September 11, 2001, dramatized the need to reevaluate security in all aspects of government. All levels of government are concerned with increasing the level of security for buildings, other structures such as bridges and dams, computer networks, and the like. Other security issues involve requiring that all contractors with the federal government ensure that none of their subcontracted activities go even indirectly to terrorist organizations.

Contracting of services is an important form of intergovernmental relations. *The Lakewood Plan* in Los Angeles County, California, is probably the oldest and most extensive such program in the United States.[218] Cities within the county may contract with the county for virtually all of their services that are provided at cost and at the same level of quality as the county provides to unincorporated areas.

Some states contract with each other, as when one state contracts to have another state house some of its prisoners.

International interests have always been of concern, and with economic threats to the U.S. economy has come renewed interest in requirements to "buy American." Congress from time to time has required federal agencies to report on their purchases of products made abroad but has stopped short of blocking such purchases. The purchase of defense components from overseas suppliers has been particularly sensitive.[219] In 2006, there was a brouhaha when the federal government announced plans to award a contract to manage six seaports to Dubai Ports World of the United Arab Emirates.[220] Considerable alarm was expressed over whether port security was being turned over to a Middle Eastern company given terrorism and unrest in that part of the world. Dubai Ports World in facing the furor withdrew from the proposed contract.

Procurement During Crises. The war in Iraq in the mid-2000s and Hurricanes Katrina and Rita in 2005 demonstrate how procurement programs can be challenged under extreme circumstances. Contracts for Iraq's reconstruction worth billions of dollars were awarded to be carried out in extraordinarily difficult situations. In simple terms, how can contractors be held accountable for results when shells are literally falling around them? Additionally, there were charges of favoritism in awarding contracts and just plain simple mismanagement. Congress created the Office of Special Inspector General for Iraq Reconstruction to audit the government's activities.[221] One of the audits found "millions of reconstruction dollars stuffed casually into footlockers and filing cabinets, an American solider in the Philippines who gambled away cash belonging to Iraq, and three Iraqis who plunged to their deaths in a rebuilt hospital elevator that had been improperly certified as safe."[222]

The 2005 hurricane season unquestionably overloaded disaster services and especially contracting systems for the federal, state, and local governments. Just like the Iraq War, the Katrina situation is much too complex to discuss fully here, but some lessons do flow from the hurricane situation. At the federal level, the key players were the Federal Emergency Management Agency (FEMA), the Army Corps of Engineers, and the General Services Administration (GSA). With more than 1 million people displaced by the hurricanes, government offices were under extreme pressure to act quickly, resulting at the federal level in $8.1 billion in contracts being awarded in the first 90 days after the disasters.[223] FEMA awarded some contracts without following required bidding procedures and after many protests in the media and from Congress, announced it would re-bid the awards.[224] Agencies had difficulty acting promptly and meeting the Stafford Disaster Relief and Emergency Assistance Act requirement that local contractors be given preference.[225] GAO found such weaknesses as overall inadequate planning and preparation for disasters and lack of adequate numbers of personnel to oversee the execution of contracts.[226] FEMA was criticized as not understanding what amounts of items to order, such as ordering twice the amount of ice needed. A survey of hurricane victims a year later gave poor marks for all levels of government. Only 30% found the federal government had done a good or excellent job. Comparable numbers for the states and local governments were 33% and 40%. Especially dismaying was that 15% of the respondents said FEMA or the government in general had victimized them after the hurricanes.[227]

Risk Management

To provide services, governments must have property and personnel. Arising from this simple fact are a series of exposures or risks, such as the risk of property being damaged or lost owing to natural disasters, employee error, and fraud by employees and others. Property damage can lead to major repair or replacement costs and to loss of income (e.g., structural problems in a municipal stadium may force its closing). The Chicago flood of 1992, in which water from the Chicago River entered buildings throughout the downtown area, is an example of how inattention to a problem—in this case, leakage into a tunnel system caused by faulty construction under government contract—can have disastrous consequences.

In 2006, Washington, DC, experienced localized flooding, unrelated to any construction contracts. The flooding severely damaged the Internal Revenue Service's headquarters, causing a shut-down of the building. The situation posed a threat to continued generation of revenue, the IRS' main task.[228]

Risk management considers what threats exist, the probability of each happening, and the likely consequence if the threat or disaster materializes. Until September 11, 2001, the probability of commercial aircraft being used as devices to destroy major landmark buildings would have been considered quite low. Since then, risk managers have had to reexamine the vulnerability of food supplies, water systems, nuclear power plants, ports, and the like to deliberate acts of terrorism. Anthrax in powder form was shipped in the mails in 2001, causing a shut-down of delivery to many offices, especially government offices. As of the mid-2000s, many federal agencies had systems in place to help safeguard against future anthrax attacks. Electronic government by which much of government's work is done today has the advantage of avoiding the anthrax threat but faces the disadvantage of malicious computer hacking.

Other risks pertain to financial guarantees. As discussed in Chapter 7, the federal government strives to identify the extent of its exposure in loan programs and other activities, such as mortgage guarantees.

Liability

Governments are vulnerable to suits brought by employees or by corporations and private citizens. Negligence is often the basis of suits in which government is alleged not to have acted the way a "reasonable" person would and inflicted harm as a result. Local governments have been sued for allowing the leakage of harmful chemicals from landfills into privately owned water wells. Governments also may be sued for violating antitrust legislation, as in the instance where a city favors one cable television operator over another. Court-awarded financial settlements can be extraordinarily large. In some suits against local governments, the awards have been greater than the governments' total annual budgets.

Laws govern liability cases. The federal government may be sued only in federal court. One of the most important federal laws is the Federal Tort Claims Act of 1946, which selectively permits suits against the government in cases not arising out of contract.[229] State and local governments sometimes may be sued in federal courts as well as in state courts. Antitrust cases against local governments, for example, are the domain of federal courts. Discrimination cases can be filed in federal and state courts.

Managing Risks

Governments need a management strategy for dealing with exposures. Risk management planning begins by identifying risks and, where possible, eliminating them. A faulty woodworking machine in a school shop should be repaired. The repair will improve the safety of the machine, thereby eliminating some risk when students use it. A road intersection widely known to be dangerous can be redesigned. A community that is subject to hurricanes obviously cannot avoid these fierce storms, but it can take steps to be prepared for such emergencies.

Having eliminated or reduced risks, governments must be prepared to deal with the remaining areas of exposure. Commercial insurance is used by governments and awarded through a bidding process similar to any other purchasing arrangement. Another option is self-insurance, where a government sets aside funds on a regular basis to cover awards or simply expends funds from the current budget to cover abnormal expenses (for example, the costs of repairing police cars damaged in the line of duty). In some instances, governments help cover each other's risks through self-insurance pooling.

Insurance premiums for liability coverage have become extremely expensive, sometimes so expensive that insurance is beyond the reach of governments—if it is available at all. Costs are a function of the nature of a policy. Salient factors include the number of employees and officials of a government, the services covered, the deductibles included, and the loss experienced. The latter is not just the experience of a particular government. A given city might have had no major suits filed against it, but because some cities have encountered major legal problems, as in cases involving landfills, all cities pay heavily for coverage.

The costs of risk management are typically handled centrally. That is, the costs of insurance premiums, court-mandated awards to injured parties, out-of-court settlements, and the like are handled by the central government budget and not charged to department budgets. Were line agencies charged for these costs, managers would be more aware of the costs of their operations and would have greater incentives to reduce risk. Faced with staggering insurance premiums, a government may choose to discontinue a service, such as operating a community swimming pool.

The Governmental Accounting Standards Board (GASB) has several pertinent statements:

- Statement No. 10, as amended by Statement No. 30, covers risks associated with torts, thefts, business interruptions, errors or omissions, job-related illnesses or injuries of employees, and acts of God.
- Statement No. 27 requires governments to report pension plan risks.
- Statement No. 31 covers the reporting of investment risks.
- Statement No. 40 requires reporting of deposit and investment risks.
- Statement No. 42 expects governments to report impairment of capital assets and insurance recoveries for situations such as when a building becomes unexpectedly unusable.[230]

The federal government has taken steps toward integrating risk management into its overall system of management. The Office of Management and Budget drafted a proposed risk assessment bulletin that, if adopted, would establish ground rules for agencies in evaluating the risks they face.[231] The Government Accountability Office has recommended that risk assessment be used to prioritize threats and that it be used in conjunction with performance budgeting for the allocation of scarce resources.[232]

The field of risk management requires special expertise. The Public Risk Management Association is a focal point for the professional development of this field. The organization has identified a wide set of core competencies that every risk manager needs.[233]

Summary

Execution is the conversion of plans embodied in the budget into day-to-day operations. At stake are factors such as interpreting and complying with legislative intent as prescribed in appropriations and providing the services that have been authorized. Control over line agencies is exercised through apportionment planning and preauditing of expenditures.

Since the 1980s, there has been a resurgence of interest in achieving economy and efficiency. Outsourcing of services has been used as one means of increasing the efficiency of operations.

Budget offices are involved in a host of activities other than preparing budgets. On the federal level, OMB exercises major powers related to information collection and dissemination and to agencies issuing regulations.

Tax administration and cash management, which usually are under the direction of a secretary of treasury, are processes aimed at maximizing revenues and minimizing costs. Numerous mechanisms are used to enforce tax laws, ranging from offering assistance in preparing tax returns to prosecuting delinquent taxpayers.

Cash management is the process of administering monies to ensure that they are available to meet expenditure needs and that monies, when temporarily not needed, are invested at a minimum risk and a maximum yield. Many instruments exist for investing state and local funds. The U.S. Treasury Department handles federal cash management through the Federal Reserve System.

Procurement entails the acquisition of resources required in providing government services, while risk management is concerned with protecting those resources. Governments often have a central purchasing office but allow individual departments some independence in purchasing products and services. A procurement program attempts to purchase only what is needed, avoid stock outages, and keep unit costs low.

Risk management attempts to eliminate or reduce risk exposure and to prepare for such events as damage to government property and liability suits arising out of government operations.

Notes

1. Hildreth, W. B. & Khan A. (Eds.) (1999). Symposium on budget execution. *Journal of Public Budgeting, Accounting and Financial Management, 11*, 230–310; Cain, C. et al. (2004). Turnover, trust, and transfers: an examination of local government budget execution. *International Journal of Public Administration, 27*, 557–576.

2. U.S. Government Accountability Office (2006). *Principles of federal appropriations law*, 3rd ed. Washington, DC: GAO.

3. U.S. Office of Management and Budget (2006). *Preparation, submission, and execution of the budget*, OMB Circular A-11, section 20. Retrieved August 12, 2006, from http://www.whitehouse.gov/omb/circulars/a11/current_year/a_11_2006.pdf.

4. Dougherty, M. J. et al. (2003). Managerial necessity and the art of creating surpluses: the budget-execution process in West Virginia cities. *Public Administration Review, 63*, 484–497.

5. Coe, C. K. (2003). Usefully engaging local budget analysts during budget execution. *State and Local Government Review, 35*, 48–56.

6. Douglas, J. W. & Franklin, A. L. (2006). Putting the brakes on the rush to spend down end-of-year balances: carryover money in Oklahoma state agencies. *Public Budgeting & Finance, 26, Fall*, 46–64.

7. National Performance Review (1993). *From red tape to results: creating a government that works better and costs less.* Washington, DC: U.S. Government Printing Office, 19.

8. President's Private Sector Survey on Cost Control (1984). *War on waste.* New York: Macmillan; U.S. General Accounting Office (1985). *Compendium of GAO's views on the cost saving proposals of the Grace Commission.* Washington, DC: U.S. Government Printing Office.

9. Peckenpaugh, J. (2002). OMB to manage Homeland Security reorganization. *Govexec.com.* Retrieved August 13, 2006, from http://www.govexec.com/dailyfed/071702p1.htm.

10. U.S. Office of Management and Budget (2002). *President's management agenda.* Washington, DC: U.S. Government Printing Office, 11–12.

11. Batley, R. (Ed.) (2006). Symposium on non-state provision of basic services. *Public Administration and Development, 26*, 193–278; Block, W. (2006). *The privatization of roads and highways: human and economic factors.* Lewiston, NY: Edwin Mellen Press; Lukemeyer, A. & McCorkle, R. C. (2006). Privatization of prisons. *American Review of Public Administration, 36*, 189–206.

12. Savas, E. S. (1982). *Privatizing the public sector.* Chatham, NJ: Chatham House; Savas, E. S. (2005). *Privatization in the city: successes, failures, lessons.* Washington, DC: CQ Press.

13. Sinn, W. & Whalley, J. (Eds.) (2006). *Privatization experiences in the European Union.* Cambridge, MA: MIT Press.

14. Scheil-Adlung, X. (Ed.) (2001). *Building Social Security: the challenge of privatization.* New Brunswick, NJ: Transaction; Beland, D. (2005). *Social Security history and politics from the New Deal to the privatization debate.* Lawrence, KS: University Press of Kansas.

15. Avery, G. (2000). Outsourcing public health laboratory services: a blueprint for determining whether to privatize and how. *Public Administration Review, 60*, 330–337; Michel, R. G. (2004). Make or buy: using cost analysis to decide whether to outsource public services. *Government Finance Review, 19, August*, 15–21.

16. Minow, M. (2005). Outsourcing power: how privatizing military efforts challenges accountability, professionalism, and democracy. *Boston College Law Review, 46*, 989–1026.

17. City of Phoenix (2006). *Contracting with the city.* Retrieved August 14, 2006, from http://phoenix.gov/business/contract/index.html; Dantico, M. K. (2005). Reworking relationships in the face of privatization: the case of the Phoenix Water Services Department. *State and Local Government Review, 37*, 242–249; City of Fort Lauderdale (2006). *Website.* Retrieved August 4, 2006, from http://ci.ftlaud.fl.us/ cityhall.htm.

18. Inspector General Act (1978). P.L. 95-452; President's Council on Integrity and Efficiency (2006). *Website.* Retrieved August 15, 2006, from http://www.ignet.gov.

19. President's Council on Integrity and Efficiency (2006). *Oversight of Gulf Coast recovery: a semiannual report to Congress.* Retrieved August 15, 2006, from http://www.ignet.gov/pande/hsr/hksemi0406.pdf.

20. Federal Managers' Financial Integrity Act (1982). P.L. 97-255; Robert, N. & Candreva, P. J. (2006). Controlling internal controls. *Public Administration Review, 66,* 463–465.

21. Gauthier, S. J. (2006). Understanding internal control. *Government Finance Review, 21,* February, 10–16.

22. Sarbanes-Oxley Act (2002). P.L. 107-204.

23. U.S. Office of Management and Budget (2002). *President's Management Agenda.*

24. Proposed Managerial Flexibility Act (2001). S. 1612, 107th Cong.; Proposed Freedom to Manage Act (2001). S. 1613, 107th Cong.

25. U.S. Council on Environmental Quality (2006). *Website.* Retrieved August 15, 2006, from http://www.whitehouse.gov/ceq/; Bolton, J. (Director, OMB) & Connaughton, J. (Chairman, CEQ) (2006). *Next steps in successfully meeting Executive Order requirements for effective environmental management.* Retrieved August 15, 2006, from http://www.whitehouse.gov/omb/memoranda/fy2006/m06-11.pdf.

26. Federal Advisory Committee Act (1972). P.L. 92-463.

27. Paperwork Reduction Act (1980). P.L. 96-511; Paperwork Reduction Act (1995). P.L. 104-13.

28. Chief Information Officers Council (2006). *Website.* Retrieved August 15, 2006, from http://www.cio.gov.

29. U.S. Office of Management and Budget (2006). *Information collection budget of the United States Government, Fiscal Year 2006.* Retrieved August 15, 2006, from http://www.whitehouse.gov/omb/inforeg/icb/fy2006_icb_report.pdf.

30. U.S. Office of Management and Budget (2006). *Information collections under review.* Retrieved August 15, 2006 from http://www.reginfo.gov/public/do/PRAMain; jsessionid=0a65171430d6931555c2945f4f8d96a3cf8da48df2a2.e38Nch4NbhuNa40 Qc3uLaxyMbO1ynknvrkLOlQzNp65In0.

31. U.S. Office of Management and Budget (2006). *Questions and answers when designing surveys for information collections.* Retrieved August 15, 2006, from http://www.whitehouse.gov/omb/inforeg/pmc_survey_guidance_2006.pdf.

32. U.S. Government Accountability Office (2006). *Paperwork Reduction Act: new approaches can strengthen information collection and reduce burden.* Washington, DC: GAO.

33. Treasury and General Government Appropriations Act for Fiscal Year 2001 (2000). P.L. 106-554; U.S. Government Accountability Office (2005). *Information Quality Act: National Agricultural Statistics Service implements first steps, but documentation of Census of Agriculture could be improved.* Washington, DC: GAO.

34. U..S. Office of Management and Budget (2002). *Guidelines for ensuring and maximizing the quality, objectivity, utility, and integrity of information disseminated by federal agencies.*

Retrieved August 23, 2006, from http://www.whitehouse.gov/omb/fedreg/ reproducible2.pdf.

35. Government Paperwork Elimination Act (1998). P.L. 105-277.

36. Government Information Security Reform Act (2000). P.L. 106-398.

37. Federal Information Security Management Act (2002). P.L. 107-347.

38. U.S. Office of Management and Budget (2005). *Federal Information Security Management Act, 2004 Report to Congress.* Retrieved August 16, 2006, from http:// www.whitehouse.gov/omb/inforeg/2004_fisma_report.pdf.

39. U.S. Government Accountability Office (2006). *Information security: continued progress needed to strengthen controls at the Internal Revenue Service.* Washington, DC: GAO; Pulliam, D. (2006). OMB steps up data security reporting requirements. *Govexec.com.* Retrieved August 17, 2006, from http://www.govexec.com/dailyfed/0706/ 071406p1.htm.

40. Committee on Government Reform, U.S. House of Representatives (2006). *Staff report: agency data breaches since January 1, 2003.* Retrieved October 20, 2006, from http://reform.house.gov/UploadedFiles/Agency%20Breach%20Summary% 20Final%20(3).pdf.

41. U.S. Office of Management and Budget (2000). *Management of federal information resources, Circular A-130.* Retrieved August 16, 2006, from http://www.whitehouse.gov/omb/circulars/a130/a130trans4.html.

42. U.S. Office of Management and Budget (2004). *Federal enterprise architecture: enabling the vision of E-government.* Retrieved August 16, 2006, from http://www.whitehouse.gov/omb/egov/documents/FEA_Overview.pdf.

43. U.S. Chief Information Officer Council (2006). *Federal enterprise architecture: security and privacy profile.* Retrieved August 16, 2006, from http://www.cio.gov/ documents/Security_and_Privacy_Profile_v2.pdf.

44. Electronic-Government Act (2002). P.L. 107-347; U.S. Office of Management and Budget (2005). *Expanding e-government: improved service delivery for the American people using information technology.* Retrieved August 20, 2006, from http:// www.whitehouse.gov/omb/budintegration/expanding_egov_2005.pdf.

45. Seifert, J. W. (2006). *Federal enterprise architecture and e-government: issues for information technology management.* Washington, DC: Congressional Research Service, Library of Congress.

46. Brown University (2006). *Texas and New Jersey are best states for American e-government.* News release. Retrieved August 18, 2006 from www.brown.edu/Administration/News_Bureau/2006-07/06-006.html.

47. Brown University (2006). *South Korea climbs to top rank in global e-government.* News release. Retrieved August 18, 2006, from http://www.brown.edu/Administration/News_Bureau/2006-07/06-007.html.

48. Perera, D. (2006). OMB: competition key to consolidating financial systems. *Govexec.com.* Retrieved August 21, 2006, from http://www.govexec.com/ dailyfed/0406/042806d1.htm.

49. Bush, G. W. (2005). Improving agency disclosure of information, Executive Order 13392. 70 *F.R.* 75373; Freedom of Information Act (1966). P.L. 85-619.

50. Office of the U.S. Attorney (2006). Attorney General's report to the president pursuant to Executive Order 13392, entitled "improving agency disclosure of information." Retrieved October 21, 2006, from http://www.govexec.com/pdfs/AGReporttoPresidentEO13392.pdf.

51. Federal Funding Accountability and Transparency Act (2006). P.L. 109-282.

52. Mandel, J. (2006). Congress approves federal spending database bill. *Govexec.com.* Retrieved October 22, 2006, from http://www.govexec.com/dailyfed/0906/091306m1.htm.

53. West, W. (2005). Administrative rulemaking: an old and emerging literature. *Public Administration Review, 65,* 655–668; Teske, P. (2004). *Regulation in the states.* Washington, DC: Brookings Institution.

54. Card, Jr., A. H., (2001). Regulatory review plan, memorandum. Retrieved August 16, 2006, from http://www.whitehouse.gov/omb/inforeg/regreview_plan.pdf.

55. U.S. Office of Management and Budget (2003). *Regulatory analysis, Circular A-4.* Retrieved August 16, 2006, from http://www.whitehouse.gov/omb/circulars/a004/a-4.pdf.

56. Regulatory Right-to-Know Act (2000). As contained in Treasury and General Government Appropriations Act for Fiscal Year 2000, P.L. 106-58.

57. U.S. Office of Management and Budget (2006). *Draft 2006 report to Congress on the costs and benefits of federal regulations.* Retrieved August 16, 2006, from http://www.whitehouse.gov/omb/inforeg/reports/2006_draft_cost_benefit_report.pdf.

58. U.S. General Services Administration & U.S. Office of Management and Budget (2006). *RegInfo.gov.* Retrieved August 16, 2006, from http://www.reginfo.gov/public/reginfo/Regmap/index.jsp; West, W. F. (2004). Formal procedures, informal processes, accountability, and responsiveness in bureaucratic policy making: an institutional policy analysis. *Public Administration Review, 64,* 66–80.

59. Unfunded Mandates Reform Act (1995). P.L. 104-4.

60. Wiley, R. E. (2005). The "ins and outs" of rulemaking: lessons from government and K Street. *Administrative Law Review, 51,* 951–962.

61. Negotiated Rulemaking Act (1990). P.L. 101-648; Selmi, D. P. (2005). The promise and limits of negotiated rulemaking: evaluating the negotiation of a regional air quality rule. *Environmental Law, 35,* 415–470.

62. U.S. General Services Administration & U.S. Office of Management and Budget (2006). *RegInfo.gov.*

63. U.S. Environmental Protection Agency (2006). *Regulations.gov.* Retrieved August 16, 2006, from http://www.regulations.gov.

64. Coglianese, C. et al. (2005). Unifying rulemaking information: recommendations for the new Federal Docket Management System. *Administrative Law Review, 57,* 621–646.

65. Shulman, S. W. et al.(2005). E-rulemaking. *Public Administration and Public Policy, 111,* 237–254; U.S. Government Accountability Office (2005). *Progress made in developing centralized e-rulemaking system.* Washington, DC: GAO.

66. Regulatory Flexibility Act (1980). P.L. 96-354; Small Business Regulatory Enforcement Fairness Act (1996). P.L. 104-121.

67. U.S. Government Accountability Office (2006). *Regulatory Flexibility Act: Congress should revisit and clarify elements of the act to improve its effectiveness.* Washington, DC: GAO.

68. Congressional Review Act (1996). P.L. 104-121.

69. U.S. Government Accountability Office (2006). *Perspectives on 10 years of Congressional Review Act implementation.* Washington, DC: GAO.

70. Truth in Regulating Act (2000). P.L. 106-312.

71. Internal Revenue Service Restructuring and Reform Act (1998). P.L. 105-206.

72. Internal Revenue Service, U.S. Department of Treasury (2006). *Today's IRS organization.* Retrieved August 17, 2006, from http://www.irs.gov/irs/article/0,,id=149197,00.html.

73. Internal Revenue Service, U.S. Department of Treasury (2005). *Modernizing America's tax agency.* Retrieved August 17, 2006, from http://www.irs.gov/irs/article/0,,id=98170,00.html; Riccucci, N. M. et al. (2006). Leadership and the transformation of a major institution: Charles Rossitti and the Internal Revenue Service. *Public Administration Review, 66,* 596–604.

74. U.S. Internal Revenue Service Oversight Board (2006). *Website.* Retrieved August 17, 2006, from http://www.treas.gov/irsob/.

75. U.S. Government Accountability Office (2005). *Tax administration: systematic information sharing would help IRS determine the deductibility of civil settlement payments.* Washington, DC: GAO.

76. Gruber, A. (2006). IRS plan to close service centers based on faulty data. *Govexec.com.* Retrieved August 17, 2006, from http://www.govexec.com/dailyfed/0306/0324961.1.htm.

77. U.S. Government Accountability Office (2005). *Tax administration: IRS can improve its productivity measures by using alternative methods.* Washington, DC: GAO; Klun, M. (2004). Performance measurement for tax administrations: the case of Slovenia. *International Review of Administrative Sciences, 70,* 567–574; Sera, P. (2005). Performance measures in tax administration: Chile as a case study. *Public Administration and Development, 25,* 115–124.

78. Hackbart, M. & Ramsey, J. R. (2001). Estimating tax evasion losses: the road fund case. *Public Budgeting & Finance, 21, Spring,* 58–72.

79. U.S. Government Accountability Office (2006). *Tax compliance: challenges to corporate tax enforcement and options to improve securities basis reporting.* Washington, DC: GAO.

80. Inspector General for Tax Administration, U.S. Department of Treasury (2006). *The electronic fraud detection system redesign failure resulted in fraudulent returns and refunds not being detected.* Retrieved October 21, 2006, from http://www.treas.gov/tigta/auditreports/2006reports/200620108fr.pdf.

81. Internal Revenue Service, U.S. Department of Treasury (2006). *IRS updates tax gap estimates.* News release. Retrieved August 17, 2006, from http://www.irs.gov/newsroom/article/0,,id=154496,00.html; U.S. Government Accountability Office (2005). *Tax compliance: reducing the tax gap can contribute to fiscal sustainability but will require a variety of strategies.* Washington, DC: GAO; U.S. Government Accountability Office (2006). *Tax gap: making significant progress in improving tax compliance rests on enhancing current IRS techniques and adopting new legislative actions.* Washington, DC: GAO.

82. U.S. General Accounting Office (2001). *Tax administration: millions of dollars could be collected if IRS levied more federal payments.* Washington, DC: U.S. Government Printing Office.

83. U.S. Government Accountability Office (2006). *Tax compliance: opportunities exist to reduce the tax gap using a variety of approaches.* Washington, DC: GAO; U.S. Government Accountability Office (2006). *Individual income tax policy: streamlining, simplification, and additional reforms are desirable.* Washington, DC: GAO.

84. California Franchise Tax Board (2005). *California tax amnesty.* Retrieved August 17, 2006, from http://www.ftb.ca.gov/amnesty/index.html; Indiana Department of Revenue (2005). *Indiana tax amnesty.* Retrieved August 17, 2006, from http://www.in.gov/dor/amnesty/; Rhode Island Division of Taxation (2006). *RI tax amnesty information.* Retrieved August 17, 2006, from http://www.tax.ri.gov/amnesty/amnesty.htm.

85. Internal Revenue Service, U.S. Department of Treasury (2006). *Electronic Federal Tax Payment System.* Retrieved August 23, 2006, from http://www.eftps.gov.

86. Pulliam, D. (2006). IRS gives teleworkers high-speed access to networks. *Govexec.com.* Retrieved August 17, 2006, from http://www.govexec.com/dailyfed/0306/032206p1.htm.

87. Internal Revenue Service, U.S. Department of Treasury (2006). *Electronic Federal Tax Payment System.* Retrieved August 17, 2006, from http://www.irs.gov/efile/article/0,,id=98005,00.html.

88. U.S. Government Accountability Office (2006). *Internal Revenue Service: assessment of the interim results of the 2006 filing season and fiscal year 2007 budget request.* Washington, DC: GAO.

89. Pulliman, D. (2006). Tax filers use IRS web site in record numbers. *Govexec.com.* Retrieved August 17, 2006, from http://www.govexec.com/dailyfed/0406/042606p1.htm.

90. U.S. General Accounting Office (1997). *Tax systems modernization: IRS needs to resolve certain issues with its integrated case processing system.* Washington, DC: U.S. Government Printing Office.

91. Taxed by Technology (1999). *Govexec.com.* Retrieved August 17, 2006, from http://www.govexec.com/gpp/0299irs.htm.

92. U.S. General Accounting Office (2000). *Tax systems modernization: results of review of IRS' August 2000 interim spending plan.* Washington, DC: U.S. Government Printing Office.

93. Perera, D. (2006). Rules of the road. *Govexec.com.* Retrieved August 17, 2006, from http://govexec.com/dailyfed/0406/042606mm.htm.

94. Perera, D. (2006). Failure of digital detection system allows millions in tax fraud. *Govexec.com*. Retrieved August 17, 2006, from http://www.govexec.com/dailyfed/0706/071406d1.htm.

95. National Performance Review (1993). *From red tape to results*, 107.

96. Debt Collection Act (1982). P.L. 97-365; Debt Collection Improvement Act (1996). P.L. 99-578.

97. Mandel, J. (2006). IRS announces first contracts for debt collection work. *Govexec.com*. Retrieved August 17, 2006, from http://www.govexec.com/dailyfed/0306/030906m1.htm.

98. Internal Revenue Service, U.S. Department of Treasury (2006). *Safeguards included in private debt collection initiative*. Retrieved August 17, 2006, from http://www.irs.gov/newsroom/article/0,,id=155065,00.html.

99. Johnston, D. C. (2006). I.R.S. enlists help in collecting delinquent taxes. *New York Times, August 20*. Retrieved August 20, 2006, from http://www.nytimes.com/2006/08/20/business/20tax.html; Mandel, J. (2006). IRS readies to start private debt collection next week. *Govexec.com*. Retrieved August 31, 2006, from http://www.govexec.com/dailyfed/0806/083106m1.htm.

100. Internal Revenue Service, U.S. Department of Treasury (2006). *Taxpayer rights*. Retrieved August 17, 2006, from http://www.irs.gov/advocate/article/0,,id=98206,00.html.

101. U.S. Government Accountability Office (2006). *Management report: improvements needed in IRS' internal controls*. Washington, DC: GAO.

102. Dropkin, M. & Hayden, A. (2001). *The cash flow management book for nonprofits: a step-by-step guide for managers, consultants, and boards*. San Francisco, CA: Jossey-Bass; Fight, A. (2005). *Cash flow forecasting*. Boston, MA: Elsevier.

103. Bank fires workers for hiding returns and tax payments (2001). *New York Times, September 6*. Retrieved August 23, 2006, from http://select.nytimes.com/gst/abstract.html?res=FB0E12F8395D0C758CDDA00894D9404482.

104. Payne, J. et al. (2004). A public alternative to commercial lockbox services: Clark County's joint remittance processing center. *Government Finance Review, 20, April*, 41–45.

105. Michel, R. G. & MacKenzie, M. (2005). Cash management technology in state and local government: Results of a GFOA/JP Morgan Chase survey. *Government Finance Review, 21, October*, 10–15.

106. Prompt Payment Act (1982). P.L. 97-177.

107. U.S. Government Accountability Office (2006). *DOD payments to small business: implementation and effective utilization of electronic invoicing could further reduce late payments*. Washington, DC: GAO.

108. Pulliam, D. (2006). Pentagon late payments hurt small contractors. *Govexec.com*. Retrieved October 21, 2006, from http://www.govexec.com/dailyfed/0506/052206p1.htm.

109. Financial Management Service, U.S. Treasury Department (2006). *Prompt payment*. Retrieved August 18, 2006, from http://fms.treas.gov/prompt/index.html.

110. Joyce, P. G. (2001). What's so magical about five percent? A nationwide look at factors that influence the optimal size of state rainy day funds. *Public Budgeting & Finance, 21, Summer,* 62–87.

111. Hou, Y. (2004). Budget stabilization fund: structural features of the enabling legislation and balance levels. *Public Budgeting & Finance, 24, Fall,* 38–64; Marlowe, J. (2005). Fiscal slack and counter-cyclical expenditure stabilization: a first look at the local level. *Public Budgeting & Finance, 25, Fall,* 48–72; Schunk, D. & Woodward, D. (2005). Spending stabilization rules: a solution to recurring state budget crises? *Public Budgeting & Finance, 25, Winter,* 105–124.

112. Municipal Bond Investors Assurance Corporation (2006). *Website.* Retrieved August 18, 2006, from http://www.mbia.com.

113. U.S. Government Accountability Office (2006). *Debt management: Treasury has refined its use of cash management bills but should explore options that may reduce cost further.* Washington, DC: GAO.

114. Financial Management Service, U.S. Treasury Department (2006). *Treasury direct.* Retrieved August 18, 2006, from http://www.treasurydirect.gov/indiv/myaccount/myaccounty_legacytd.htm.

115. Government Securities Act (1986). P.L. 99-571.

116. Strong, R. A. (2005). *Derivatives: an introduction,* 2nd ed. Mason, OH: Thomson/South-Western; Hinkelmann, C. & Swidler, S. (2005). State government hedging using financial derivatives. *State and Local Government Review, 37,* 127–141; McDonald, R. L. (2006). *Derivatives markets,* 2nd ed. Boston: Addison-Wesley.

117. Office of the State Treasurer, State of Wisconsin (2006). *Local government investment pool.* Retrieved August 18, 2006, from http://www.ost.state.wi.us/home/lgip.htm; Treasury Department, Tennessee (2006). *Local government investment pool.* Retrieved August 18, 2006, from http://www.treasury.state.tn.us/lgip/index.htm; Sims, R., King County Executive (2006). King County investment pool receives highest rating from Standard & Poor's. *King County, Washington website.* Retrieved August 18, 2006, from http://www.metrokc.gov/exec/news/2006/0109investmentpool.aspx.

118. Census Bureau, U.S. Department of Commerce (2006). *Cash and security holdings of major public employee-retirement systems, 2001–2006.* Retrieved August 19, 2006, from http://ftp2.census.gov/govs/qpr/table1.txt.

119. Angelides, P., California State Treasurer (2006). *Pooled money investment board report.* Retrieved August 19, 2006, from http://www.treasurer.ca.gov/pmia-laif/reports/mnthly/0606.pdf.

120. Illinois State Treasurer's Office (2006). *Website.* Retrieved August 18, 2006, from http://www.state.il.us/treas/.

121. Governmental Accounting Standards Board (2006). *Summaries/status of statements.* Retrieved August 19, 2006, from http://www.gasb.org/st/index.html.

122. Financial Management Service, U.S. Department of Treasury (2006). *Green book: guide to federal ACH payments and collections.* Retrieved August 19, 2006, from http://fms.treas.gov/greenbook/index.html.

123. Financial Management Service, U.S. Department of Treasury (2006). *Gold book: the check reclamation guide.* Retrieved August 19, 2006, from http://www.fms.treas.gov/goldbook/index.html.

124. U.S. General Accounting Office (2001). *Federal debt: debt management actions and future challenges.* Washington, DC: U.S. Government Printing Office; U.S. General Accounting Office (2004). *Debt ceiling: analysis of actions taken during the 2003 debt issuance suspension period.* Washington, DC: U.S. Government Printing Office.

125. Cash Management Improvement Act (1990). P.L. 101-453.

126. Financial Management Service, U.S. Department of Treasury (2006). *Cash Management Improvement Act: common questions.* Retrieved August 19, 2006, from http://fms.treas.gov/cmia/questions.html.

127. Groshek, G. M. (2000). Foreign currency exposure in the Department of Defense. *Public Budgeting & Finance, 20, Winter,* 15–35.

128. Bureau of Engraving and Printing, U.S. Department of Treasury (2006). *Website.* Retrieved August 19, 2006, from http://www.moneyfactory.gov/.

129. U.S. Mint, U.S. Department of the Treasury (2006). *Website.* Retrieved August 19, 2006, from http://www.usmint.gov/index.cfm?flash=yes.

130. U.S. General Accounting Office (2004). *Coins and currency: how the costs and earnings associated with producing coins and currency are budgeted and accounted for.* Washington, DC: U.S. Government Printing Office.

131. Cabral, A. E., U.S. Treasurer (2005). *Remarks of U.S. Treasurer Anna Escobedo Cabral.* Retrieved August 20, 2006, from http://www.treas.gov/pres/releases/js2319.htm.

132. Controller's Office, University of Massachusetts (2006). *Research receivables and letter of credit.* Retrieved August 20, 2006, from http://www.umass.edu/aco/ra/lcr.htm.

133. See Investors Business Daily (2006). *Website.* Retrieved August 20, 2006, from http://www.investors.com; Wall Street Journal (2006). *Website.* Retrieved August 20, 2006, from http://www.wsj.com.

134. City of Rochester, New York (2006). *Water meters.* Retrieved August 20, 2006, from http://www.ci.rochester.ny.us/des/index.cfm?id=275; Denver Water, Colorado (2006). *Automatic meter reading.* Retrieved August 20, 2006, from http://www.denverwater.org/custserve/residential/amr.html.

135. Sioux City, Iowa (2006). *Sioux City automatic meter reading.* Retrieved August 20, 2006, from http://www.sioux-city.org/customer_service/automatic_meter.asp.

136. NACHA—The Electronic Payments Association (2006). *Website.* Retrieved August 20, 2006, from http://www.nacha.org.

137. Cooper, P. J. (2003). *Governing by contract: challenges and opportunities for public managers.* Washington, DC: CQ Press; Seddon, N. (2004). *Government contracts: federal, state, and local,* 3rd ed. Annandale, New South Wales, Australia: Federation Press; Emanuelli, P. (2005). *Government procurement.* Markham, Ontario: LexisNexis Butterworths; Brown, T. L. et al. (2006). Managing public service contracts: aligning values, institutions, and markets. *Public Administration Review, 66,* 323–331.

138. Guarded Growth (2005). *Govexec.com.* Retrieved August 21, 2006, from http://www.govexec.com/features/0805-15/0805-15s2.htm; see U.S. Government Accountability Office (2006). *Highlight of a GAO forum: federal acquisition challenges and opportunities in the 21st Century.* Washington, DC: GAO.

139. Rubin, I. (2006). Budgeting for contracting in local government. *Public Budgeting & Finance, 26, Spring,* 1–13.

140. Top 200 federal contractors (2005). *Government Executive Magazine, August 15.* Retrieved August 20, 2006, from http://www.govexec.com/features/0805-15/0805-15s2s1.htm.

141. National Performance Review (1993). *From red tape to results,* 26–31.

142. U.S. General Services Administration (2006). *About GSA.* Retrieved August 20, 2006, from http://www.gsa.gov/Portal/gsa/ep/home.do?tabId=6.

143. Pulliam, D. (2006). GSA finalizes merger of contracting organizations. *Govexec.com.* Retrieved October 21, 2006, from http://www.govexec.com/dailyfed/1006/1013206p1.htm.

144. Harris, S. (2002). GSA lacks hard data on inter-agency competition. *Govexec.com.* Retrieved August 20, 2006, from http://www.govexec.com/dailyfed/0402/041102h1.htm.

145. Cahlink, G. (2001). Pentagon says it uses 700,000 service contractors. *Government Executive, March 30.* Retrieved August 20, 2006, from http://www.govexec.com/dailyfed/0301/033001g1.htm.

146. Defense Logistics Agency, U.S. Department of Defense (2006). *Website.* Retrieved August 20, 2006, from http://www.dla.mil/.

147. Office of Federal Procurement Policy Act (1974). P.L. 93-400.

148. U.S. General Services Administration (2005). *Federal acquisition regulation.* Retrieved August 21, 2006, from http://acquisition.gov/far/index.html; Office of Under Secretary of Defense Acquisition Technology and Logistics, U.S. Department of Defense (2006). *Defense federal acquisition regulations supplement.* Retrieved August 21, 2006, from http://www.acq.osd.mil/dpap/dars/dfars/index.htm; Mandel, J. (2006). GSA launches review of acquisition rules. *Govexec.com.* Retrieved August 21, 2006, from http://www.govexec.com/dailyfed/0206/022206m1.htm.

149. Services Acquisition Reform Act (2003). P.L. 108-136; U.S. Government Accountability Office (2005). *Progress in implementing the Services Acquisition Reform Act of 2003.* Washington, DC: GAO.

150. Chief Acquisition Officers Council (2006). *Website.* Retrieved August 21, 2006, from http://cao.gov/.

151. U.S. Government Accountability Office (2005). *Interagency contracting: franchise funds provide convenience but value to DOD is not demonstrated.* Washington, DC: GAO; Mandel, J. (2006). Competition levels in interagency contracting are murky. *Govexec.com.* Retrieved August 21, 2006, from http://www.govexec.com/dailyfed/0806/081006m1.htm.

152. U.S. Office of Management and Budget (2005). Establishing of interagency acquisition working group, memorandum. Retrieved August 21, 2006, from http://

www.whitehouse.gov/omb/procurement/publications/
interagency_work_group.pdf; Palmer, K. (2006). Shopping together. *Govexec.com.*
Retrieved August 23, 2006, from http://www.govexec.com/dailyfed/
0206/021506mm.htm.

153. Pallesen, T. (2006). The politics of contracting out in school districts: the case of
Washington State. *State and Local Government Review, 38,* 34–40.

154. Wilson, G. C. (2002). Rent-a-weapons. *Govexec.com.* Retrieved August 21, 2006, from
http://www.govexec.com/dailyfed/0202/020502db.htm; Smith, R. J. (2005). E-mails
detail Air Force push for Boeing deal. *Washington Post, June 7.* Retrieved August 21,
2006, from http://www.washingtonpost.com/wp-dyn/content/
article/2005/06/06/AR2005060601715_pf.html.

155. Brudney, J. L. et al. (2005). Exploring and explaining contracting out: patterns among
the American states. *Journal of Public Administration Research and Theory, 15,* 393–419;
Nemec, J. et al. (2005). Contracting-out at local government level: theory and selected
evidence from the Czech and Slovak Republics. *Public Management Review, 7,* 637–648.

156. U.S. Office of Management and Budget (2003). *Performance of commercial activities,
Circular A-76.* Retrieved August 21, 2006, from http://www.whitehouse.gov/omb/
circulars/a076/a76_incl_tech_correction.html.

157. U.S. Government Accountability Office (2005). *Review of OMB Circular A-76 health
benefit cost factor needed.* Washington, DC: GAO.

158. Peckenpaugh, J. (2001). A-76 competition may not hurt federal workers' pay. *Govexec.com.*
Retrieved August 21, 2006, from http://www.govexec.com/dailyfed/
0401/041801p1.htm.

159. U.S. Office of Management and Budget (2005). *Competitive sourcing: report on competitive
sourcing results, fiscal year 2004.* Retrieved August 21, 2006, from http://
www.whitehouse.gov/omb/procurement/comp_sourcing_results_fy04.pdf.

160. Peckenpaugh, J. (2001). Conflict-of-interest rules to apply only to new A-76 studies, says GAO. *Govexec.com.* Retrieved August 21, 2006, from http://
www.govexec.com/dailyfed/0602/060302p1.htm.

161. Federal Activities and Inventory Reform Act (1998). P.L. 105-270.

162. U.S. Office of Management and Budget (2001). *President's Management Agenda.*
Retrieved August 21, 2006, from http://www.whitehouse.gov/omb/
budget/fy2002/mgmt.pdf.

163. Transportation, Treasury, Housing and Urban Development, the Judiciary, the
District of Columbia, and Independent Agencies Appropriations Act, fiscal year 2006
(2005). P.L. 109-115.

164. U.S. Office of Management and Budget (2005). Implementing strategic sourcing,
memorandum. Retrieved August 21, 2006, from
http://www.whitehouse.gov/omb/procurement/comp_src/implementing_strate-
gic_sourcing.pdf; U.S. General Accounting Office (2004). *Federal acquisition: increased
attention to vehicle fleets could result in savings.* Washington, DC: U.S. Government
Printing Office; U.S. General Accounting Office (2004). *Best practices: using spending
analysis to help agencies take a more strategic approach to procurement.* Washington, DC:
U.S. Government Printing Office.

165. New York State Office of General Services (2005). *2005 Cronin Club Classic Innovation Award: aggregated IT procurement program.* Retrieved August 21, 2006, from http://www.naspo.org/awards/2005awards/NY_ClassicBronze.doc.

166. U.S. Office of Management and Budget (2006). *Competitive sourcing: report on the use of best value tradeoffs in public-private competitions.* Retrieved October 21, 2006, from http://www.whitehouse.gov/omb/procurement/comp_src/ cs_best_value_report_2006.pdf.

167. U.S. Government Accountability Office (2005). *Contract management: opportunities to improve pricing of GSA multiple award schedules contracts.* Washington, DC: GAO; Romzek, B. S. & Johnston, J. M. (2005). State social services contracting: exploring the determinants of effective contract accountability. *Public Administration Review, 65,* 436–449.

168. Federal Acquisition Streamlining Act (1994). P.L. 103-355.

169. Mandel, J. (2006). Panel finds performance-based contracts poorly implemented. *Govexec.com.* Retrieved August 21, 2006, from http://www.govexec.com/ dailyfed/0606/062906m1.htm.

170. U.S. Government Accountability Office (2005). *Federal contracting: share-in-savings initiative not yet tested.* Washington, DC: GAO; U.S. General Services Administration (2006). *Frequently asked questions: share-in-savings.* Retrieved August 21, 2006, from http://www.gsa.gov/Portal/gsa/ep/contentView.do?contentType=GSA_OVERVIE W&contentId=13402&faq=yes&noc=T.

171. Competition in Contracting Act (1984). P.L. 98-369, Title VII.

172. U.S. Government Accountability Office (2006). *Bid protest decisions.* Retrieved August 20, 2006, from http://www.gao.gov/decisions/bidpro/bidpro.htm.

173. U.S. Department of State (2006). *Procurement technical assistance centers.* Retrieved August 21, 2006, from http://www.dla.mil/db/procurem.htm.

174. Rubin, I. (2006). *Budgeting for contracting in local government.*

175. Mandel, J. (2006). OMB to rate agencies on efforts to break up large contracts. *Govexec.com.* Retrieved August 21, 2006, from http://www.govexec.com/ dailyfed/0806/081806m1.htm.

176. Rehabilitation Act (1973). P.L. 93-112; U.S. General Services Administration (2006). *Section 508.* Retrieved August 22, 2006, from http://www.section 508.gov.

177. Vietnam Era Veterans' Readjustment Assistance Act (1974). P.L. 93-508; Committee on Veterans Affairs, U.S. House of Representatives (2006). *NASA extends contract proposal deadline for service-disabled veteran-owned small businesses.* Retrieved August 21, 2006, from http://veterans.house.gov/news/109/8-3-06.html.

178. U.S. Small Business Administration (2006). *Business.gov.* Retrieved August 21, 2006, from http://www.business.gov.

179. Integrated Acquisition Environment (2006). *Acquisition Central.* Retrieved August 21, 2006, from http://www.arnet.gov.

180. U.S. General Services Administration (2006). *FedBizOpps.* Retrieved August 21, 2006, from http://www.fedbizopps.gov.

181. U.S. General Services Administration (2006). *Federal procurement data system—next generation.* Retrieved August 21, 2006, from http://www.fpds.gov.

182. Department of General Services, State of California (2006). *State, federal, and local contacts.* Retrieved August 21, 2006, from http://www.pd.dgs.ca.gov/publications/state_federal_local_contacts.htm.

183. GovCB.com (2006). *Website.* Retrieved August 21, 2006, from http://www.govcb.com/.

184. U.S. General Services Administration (2006). *GSA Advantage!* Retrieved August 21, 2006, from http://www.gsaadvantage.gov/advgsa/advantage/main/start_page.do.

185. Romzek, B.S. & Johnston, J. M. (2005). *State social services contracting: exploring the determinants of effective contract accountability.*

186. National Defense Authorization Act for Fiscal Year 2002 (2001). P.L. 107-107.

187. Federal Acquisition Reform Act/Clinger-Cohen Act (1996). P.L. 104-106, section 4001.

188. Andrues, W. (2006). The Clinger-Cohen Act, 10 years later: measuring efficiency. *Govexec.com.* Retrieved August 22, 2006, from http://www.govexec.com/dailyfed/0706/071806cc.htm.

189. California Performance Review (2006). *The state needs to professionalize its state procurement workforce.* Retrieved August 22, 2006, from http://cpr.ca.gov/report/cprrpt/issrec/stops/proc/so61.htm.

190. New York City (2006). *Citywide Training Center.* Retrieved August 22, 2006, from http://www.nyc.gov/html/dcas/html/resources/ctchome.shtml.

191. City of Atlanta (2006). *Department of Procurement.* Retrieved August 22, 2006, from http://www.atlantaga.gov/Government/Procurement.aspx; Procurement and Supply Chain Benchmarking Association (2006). *Website.* Retrieved August 22, 2006, http://from www.pasba.com.

192. Federal Acquisition Institute (2006). *Annual report on the federal acquisition workforce, fiscal year 2005.* Retrieved August 22, 2006, from http://www.fai.gov/pdfs/FAWF2005.pdf.

193. Schooner, S. L. (2006). Keeping up with Procurement. *Govexec.com.* Retrieved August 22, 2006, from http://www.govexec.com/features/0706-01/0706-01advp.htm.

194. Mandel, J. (2006). Panel agrees OMB needs official dedicated to acquisition workforce. *Govexec.com.* Retrieved August 22, 2006, from http://www.govexec.com/dailyfed/0706/071406m1.htm.

195. U.S. Office of Management and Budget (2005). *Developing and managing the acquisition workforce, Policy Letter 05-01.* Retrieved August 22, 2006, from http://www.whitehouse.gov/omb/procurement/policy_letters/05-01_041505.html.

196. U.S. Government Accountability Office (2005). *Framework for assessing the acquisition function at federal agencies.* Washington, DC: GAO.

197. Compiled from Federal Highway Administration, U.S. Department of Transportation (2006). *The reporting and detecting of fraud.* Retrieved August 22, 2006, from http://www.fhwa.dot.gov/programadmin/contracts/fraud.htm.

198. Federal Emergency Management Agency, U.S. Department of Homeland Security (2006). *FEMA and state alert to fraud.* News release. Retrieved August 22, 2006, from http://www.fema.gov/news/newsrelease.fema?id=28298.

199. Procurement Integrity Act (1996). P.L. 104-106.

200. Mandel, J. (2006). Punishments stemming from IG probes on the rise. *Govexec.com.* Retrieved August 22, 2006, from http://www.govexec.com/dailyfed/0806/081606m1.htm.

201. Pulliam, D. (2005). GSA corruption case. *Govexec.com.* Retrieved August 22, 2006, from http://www.govexec.com/dailyfed/0705/072205lb.htm.

202. Palmer, K. (2005). Accounting giant pays $42 million to settle dispute over travel expenses. *Govexec.com.* Retrieved August 22, 2006, from http://www.govexec.com/dailyfed/0705/072505k1.htm.

203. Bribery probe going beyond elections (2006). *Washington Post, August 21.* Retrieved August 22, 2006, from http://www.washingtonpost.com/wp-dyn/content/article/2006/08/21/AR2006082101020.html.

204. Palmer, K. (2005). Former OMB official indicted. *Govexec.com.* Retrieved August 22, 2006, from http://www.govexec.com/dailyfed/1005/100505k1.htm; Palmer, K. (2006). Ex-procurement chief argues for new trial. *Govexec.com.* Retrieved August 22, 2006, from http://www.govexec.com/dailyfed/0806/081706k1.htm.

205. U.S. Government Accountability Office (2005). *Federal procurement: additional data reporting could improve the suspension and debarment process.* Washington, DC: GAO.

206. U.S. Government Accountability Office (2005). *Financial management: thousands of civilian agency contractors abuse the federal tax system with little consequence.* Washington, DC: GAO.

207. Smith, R. J. (2006). Tanker inquiry finds Rumsfeld's attention was elsewhere. *Washington Post, June 20.* Retrieved August 22, 2006, from http://www.washingtonpost.com/wp-dyn/content/article/2006/06/19/AR2006061901090.html.

208. Cahlink, G. (2005). Justice forms procurement fraud task force. *Govexec.com.* Retrieved August 22, 2006, from http://www.govexec.com/dailyfed/0205/022305g1.htm.

209. U.S. General Services Administration (2006), *Charge card program statistics, fiscal year 2004: executive summary.* Retrieved August 22, 2006, from http://www.gsa.gov/Portal/gsa/ep/programView.do?pageTypeId=8199&ooid=11490&programPage=%2Fep%2Fprogram%2FgsaDocument.jsp&programId=10137&channelId=-13503.

210. Ballard, T.N. (2002). Defense task force aims to clean up charge card abuse. *Govexec.com.* Retrieved August 22, 2006, from http://www.govexec.com/dailyfed/0302/032702t2.htm.

211. U.S. Government Accountability Office (2006). *Purchase cards: control weaknesses leave DHS highly vulnerable to fraudulent, improper, and abusive activity.* Washington, DC: U.S. GAO.

212. Bush, G. W. (2004). *Homeland security presidential directive 12.* Retrieved August 22, 2006, from http://www.whitehouse.gov/news/releases/2004/08/20040827-8.html; see U.S. Government Accountability Office (2006). *Electronic government: agencies face challenges in implementing new federal employee identification standard.* Washington, DC: GAO.

213. Pulliam, D. (2006). GSA awards contract for end-to-end ID card services. *Govexec.com.* Retrieved August 22, 2006, from http://www.govexec.com/dailyfed/0806/082106p1.htm.

214. *City of Richmond v. J.A. Crosson Company* (1989). 488 U.S. 469.

215. *Adarand Constructors v. Pena* (1995). 515 U.S. 200.

216. Gangemi, J. (2006). Winning the federal contracting game. *Businessweek Online, July 26.* Retrieved August 21, 2006, from http://www.businessweek.com/smallbiz/content/jul2006/sb20060726_724414.htm?chan=search.

217. U.S. General Accounting Office (2001). *Federal procurement: better guidance and monitoring needed to assess purchases of environmentally friendly products.* Washington, DC: U.S. Government Printing Office.

218. City of Lakewood (2004). *The Lakewood story: history, tradition, values.* Retrieved August 22, 2006, from http://www.lakewoodcity.org/civica/filebank/blobloadasp?BlodID=3160.

219. Scully, M. (2006). Negotiators pressured to resolve "Buy America" dispute. *Govexec.com.* Retrieved October 22, 2006, from http://www.govexec.com/dailyfed/0906/091206cdam1.htm.

220. Bumiller, E., & Hulse, C. (2006). Panel saw no security issue in port contract, officials say. *New York Times, February 23.* Retrieved August 22, 2006, from http://www.nytimes.com/2006/02/23/politics/23port.html?ex=1298350800&en=507c0dd1d3a708e4&ei=5090&partner=rssuserland&emc=rss; Cloud, D. S. & Sanger, D. E. (2006). Dubai company delays new role at six ports. *New York Times, February 24.* Retrieved August 14, 2006, from http://select.nytimes.com/gst/abstract.html?res=F10912FC345AOC778EDDAB0894DE404482.

221. U.S. Office of the Special Inspector General for Iraq Reconstruction (2006). *SIGIR: independent & objective oversight.* Retrieved August 22, 2006 from www.sigir.mil/; see U.S. General Accounting Office (2004). *Contract management: contracting for Iraq reconstruction and for global logistics support.* Washington, DC. U.S. Government Printing Office.

222. Glanz, J. (2006). New U.S. audit describes misuse of funds in Iraq projects. *New York Times, January 25.* Retrieved August 22, 2006, from http://select.nytimes.com/gst/abstract.html?res=F00F16FC3B5B0C768EDDA80894DE404482.

223. Pulliam, D. (2006). Report sheds light on hurricane fraud investigations. *Govexec.com.* Retrieved August 22, 2006, from http://www.govexec.com/dailyfed/0106/011206p1.htm; President's Council on Integrity and Efficiency and the Executive Council on Integrity and Efficiency (2005). *Oversight of Gulf Coast hurricane recovery: A*

90-day progress report. Retrieved August 22, 2006, from http://www.dhs.gov/interweb/assetlibrary/OIG_90DayGulfCoast_Dec05.pdf#search=%22%22oversight%20of%20gulf%20coast%20hurricane%20recovery%22%22.

224. Weisman, J. & Witte, G. (2005). Katrina contracts will be reopened. *Washington Post, October 7.* Retrieved August 22, 2006, from http://www.washingtonpost.com/wp-dyn/content/article/2005/10/06/AR2005100600854.html.

225. Stafford Disaster Relief and Emergency Assistance Act (1988). P.L. 100-707.

226. U.S. Government Accountability Office (2006). *Hurricane Katrina: improving federal contracting practices in disaster recovery operations.* Washington, DC: GAO.

227. USA Today/Gallup Hurricane Katrina survivors follow-up poll (2006). *USA Today, August 20.* Retrieved August 22, 2006, from http://www.usatoday.com/news/polls/tables/live/2006-08-20-katrina-poll.htm.

228. Internal Revenue Service, U.S. Department of Treasury (2006). *IRS headquarters will remain closed for months; tax administration operations continue as employees relocate.* Retrieved August 22, 2006, from http://www.irs.gov/newsroom/article/0,,id=159959,00.html.

229. Federal Tort Claims Act (1946). Ch. 753, 60 Stat. 842.

230. Governmental Accounting Standards Board (2006). *Summaries/status: statements.* Retrieved August 22, 2006, from http://www.gasb.org/st/index.html.

231. U.S. Office of Management and Budget (2006). *Proposed Risk Assessment Bulletin.* Retrieved August 22, 2006, from http://www.whitehouse.gov/omb/inforeg/proposed_risk_assessment_bulletin_010906.pdf.

232. U.S. Government Accountability Office (2005). *Risk management: further refinements needed to assess risks and prioritize protective measures at ports and other critical infrastructure.* Washington, DC: GAO; U.S. Government Accountability Office (2005). *Strategic budgeting: risk management principles can help DHS allocate resources to highest priorities.* Washington, DC: GAO.

233. Public Risk Management Association (2006). *Website.* Retrieved August 22, 2006, from http://www.primacentral.org.

Chapter 11

FINANCIAL MANAGEMENT: ACCOUNTING, REPORTING, AND AUDITING

The term "creative accounting" perhaps originated with the 1968 Mel Brooks movie, *The Producers*, which was later turned into a highly successful Broadway musical and a big budget movie.[1] Both "creative accounting" and the older term of "cooking the books" refer to deliberate manipulation of accounting systems and accounting reports in order to hide the actual financial condition of an entity. In the case of *The Producers*, the lead characters deceive the backers of a play by selling many times over the total value of the enterprise. The assumption is the play will flop, the backers will expect no financial gain, and the producers will net a hefty ill-gained profit. Chaos ensues when the play unexpectedly becomes a sensation.

The Producers has provided great fun to viewers over the years, but it is not great fun when people lose their life savings in investments in companies that have used fraudulent accounting and when taxpayers must pay-up through higher taxes due to accounting bad practices and fraud in their governments. For example, an accounting error that simply failed to recognize in advance that not all taxes owed will be collected can throw a budget badly out of balance, forcing stringent measures on spending and possibly giving decision makers no choice but to adopt a tax increase in order to correct the mistake.

Budget execution requires accounting systems that track projected and actual revenues and expenditures during the budget year. Accounting is the process of recording all financial transactions—revenues and expenditures—according to clear and usually precise rules, in such a manner that all transactions can be audited independently. As will be seen in the following sections, accounting serves a variety of purposes, but one of the most important has always been maintaining honesty and integrity. Accounting also is important to the functions discussed in the preceding chapter—namely, tax administration, cash management, procurement, and risk management. Accounting systems provide the financial information components of more comprehensive management information systems.

This chapter has three sections. The first is devoted to accounting systems, and the second, to reporting, that is the types of documents that flow from accounting data. The third section discusses the auditing of accounting systems.

▮ Governmental Accounting

"A standard definition of accounting is the art of analyzing, recording, summarizing, evaluating and interpreting an organization's financial activities and status, and communicating the results."[2] Accounting is one type of information system, one which contains mostly financial information on transactions involving the receipt of funds and their expenditure.

In this section, we explore several aspects of accounting systems, beginning with the purposes and standards of accounting and the organizations that shape accounting systems. Fund accounting, the structure of accounting systems, the classification of expenditures, and the bases for accounting are considered.

Organizational Responsibilities and Standards

Purposes. Accounting systems have been devised for a variety of purposes. **Exhibit 11–1** lists the main ones, including the ever-present one of insuring honesty in the handling of public monies—keeping the rascals honest. As will be seen, accounting systems are based on details, but those who operate accounting systems should never lose sight of the main purposes. This is the old familiar problem of losing sight of the forest because of all of the trees. It has been said that the Department of Defense "uses a magnifying glass to check a Tootsie Roll purchase and misses the million-dollar problems."[3] Accounting systems, in meeting the purposes noted here, are valuable tools in running the government rather than simply being additional costs of government operations.[4]

Federal Government Accounting Organizations. For accounting systems to serve these purposes, certain conventions or standards must be established, or else chaos would reign as each government or department within a government estab-

Exhibit 11–1   Purposes of Accounting

Here are some of the main purposes of accounting:

- Perhaps the primary purpose is the maintenance of honesty. Through accounting, people who have wrongly intercepted monies being paid to government or have channeled expenditures to their own advantage can be detected. Accounting, then, serves as a deterrent to fraud and corruption as well as prevents inadvertent loss.

- A related purpose is to prevent expenditures from straying beyond legal parameters. Illegal expenditures can occur that do not involve graft, as in the case of agency expenditures that exceed an appropriation or are used for purposes other than those permitted in authorizing legislation. Accounting serves to control agencies so that they act in accordance with policy and administrative directives as well as appropriation legislation.

- Accounting systems are intended to provide complete, timely, and accurate information concerning receipts and expenditures. The information is used in billing taxpayers and receiving tax payments, paying employees, ordering goods, receiving goods, and paying vendors or contractors. Accounting systems help control inventory by providing accurate records of what items have been purchased.

- Another important purpose is to report on the management of funds that are held in custody or trust. For example, accounting systems are used to handle contributions to employee retirement funds and outlays to beneficiaries.

- Decision making is facilitated by accounting systems, which report historical data on revenues and expenditures that are essential for forecasting financial transactions. Without accurate information from an accounting system, decision makers are unable to determine whether a gap exists between proposed spending for the budget year and available revenue. Accounting information is important in determining whether a budget deficit exists and in what amount. Data are used in determining the size of the government's total debt, including those debts that are part of credit programs. Accounting data can help identify historical trends and current costs, and this information is essential in the funds required for proposed changes in service levels and service quality.

- Accounting is used internally to help managers increase efficiency and effectiveness in delivering services. The utilization of resources is monitored so as to avoid waste and to help ensure that desired programmatic outcomes are achieved. Managerial accounting focuses on calculating the costs associated with providing services to citizens. These derived costs also can be used for setting schedules for service charges. Office of Management and Budget (OMB) Circular A-123, Management's Responsibility for Internal

continues

Exhibit 11–1	Purposes of Accounting (continued)

Control, emphasizes that management should be held accountable for achieving results and not just for using resources efficiently and honestly. One of the five government-wide initiatives in President George W. Bush's Management Agenda was to integrate budgeting and performance. Another was to improve financial management, focusing on the quality of accounting systems and the sufficiency of agency controls against fraud and over-spending.[1]

- Information from accounting systems is used in communication between a government and its citizens, investors, and other governments. Financial reports derived from detailed accounting information can help citizens gain confidence that the government's resources are well supervised. The federal government, in making grants to state and local governments, wants to be assured that the recipient governments have accounting systems that will protect the assets being invested.

- Accounting in the public sector is being increasingly used to identify financial condition or the relative fiscal health of a government and the environment in which it operates. Investors in such commodities as state and local bonds and federal Treasury bills use accounting-based information to understand the financial condition of governments.

[1]U.S. Office of Management and Budget (2001). *President's management agenda.* Retrieved August 26, 2006 from http://www.whitehouse.gov/omb/budget/fy2002/mgmt.pdf.

lished its own standards and practices. Numerous organizations establish the ground rules for accounting.

Both the Government Accountability Office (GAO), which is an agency of Congress, and the Office of Management and Budget (OMB), which is an arm of the Executive Office of the President, set guidelines for federal agencies and to some extent compete with one another over control of accounting.[5] The Federal Managers' Financial Integrity Act of 1982, amending the Accounting and Auditing Act of 1950, requires that each executive agency establish internal accounting and administrative controls in accordance with standards prescribed by GAO and that the agency conduct annual reviews to determine the extent of compliance with those standards.[6] However, since the Supreme Court has ruled that GAO cannot be in a position of instructing agencies in what they must do (see Chapter 9), OMB has the upper hand in establishing financial management practices.

OMB's deputy director for management oversees the Office of Federal Financial Management, which is headed by the controller. The Chief Financial

Officers Act of 1990 created similar offices and chief financial officer (CFO) positions within the major agencies of the government.[7] Agency CFOs have responsibility for all financial operations, including budgeting, and the CFOs, along with OMB's deputy director for management, the controller, and the fiscal assistant secretary of Treasury, meet periodically as the Chief Financial Officers Council for the purpose of coordinating their activities.[8] OMB and the council, in accordance with the law's instructions that a government-wide financial plan be developed, have launched an ambitious program to improve internal controls, lines of business, debt collection, asset management, payments to contractors and state and local governments, and the like.[9]

In addition to the Chief Financial Officers Act, 1990 also brought the formation of the Federal Accounting Standards Advisory Board (FASAB).[10] As its title suggests, this entity is strictly advisory, but its recommendations have indeed had major impacts on federal accounting. The board consists of representatives of GAO, OMB, and the Treasury Department plus a representative from the Congressional Budget Office, representatives from civilian agencies and the Department of Defense, and nonfederal members. Its mission is to develop consensus on accounting standards that can then be adopted by GAO, OMB, and the Treasury Department. FASAB has issued numerous *standards*, such as ones pertaining to the accounting of assets and liabilities, the first standard that it adopted, to others dealing with inventory, managerial cost accounting, and social insurance accounting. OMB reviews each standard issued and in effect incorporates them into government policy through Circular A-134, Financial Accounting Principles and Standards.

Chief financial officers are to some extent in competition with another set of key officers, namely chief information officers (CIOs). The latter were established by the Clinger-Cohen Act (Federal Acquisition Reform Act) of 1996 and have overall responsibility for information technology in their respective organizations.[11] The catch arises in that accounting systems are necessarily part of information technology operations, which creates issues over who is in charge whenever any accounting matter is at hand.[12]

The General Services Administration (GSA) is another player in the accounting game at the federal level. GSA, as described in Chapter 10, is the federal government's central purchaser for buildings, materials and supplies, vehicles, and computers. In 2006, GSA had responsibility for preparing, under OMB's supervision, the Common Government-wide Accounting Code, which was expected to be the foundation for future accounting systems.[13] This effort is part of the Financial Management Line of Business (FMLoB) Consolidation being driven by OMB. The plan is for agencies to migrate toward shared accounting systems and in many instances share in the use of private vendors for their accounting needs. That same year OMB issued migration planning guidance as to how agencies were to make the transition.[14]

State, Local, and Related Organizations. State and local accounting systems are influenced by several sources. State auditors and comptrollers general set standards for their state and local systems as do individual state legislatures. These systems also are influenced by GAO and OMB, which determine how federal grant monies are handled.

Professional organizations have periodically attempted to establish standards of accounting in the public sector. The former National Council on Governmental Accounting consisted of representatives of such bodies as the Government Finance Officers Association, the American Institute of Certified Public Accountants, and the American Accounting Association. It produced what was known as the "blue book" or GAAFR (*Governmental Accounting, Auditing, and Financial Reporting*). Although the National Council on Governmental Accounting no longer exists, GAAFR continues to be published by the Government Finance Officers Association and is designed to assist governments at all levels achieve what are considered the standards in the field.[15] The Government Finance Officers Association issues a variety of policy statements not only on accounting, auditing, and financial reporting, but also on budgeting, cash management, debt management, and retirement and benefits administration. For example, it issued a revised statement in 2006 on Using the Comprehensive Annual Financial Report to Meet SEC Requirements for Periodic Disclosure.[16]

In 1984, a government counterpart to the Financial Accounting Standards Board (see below) was established. The Governmental Accounting Standards Board (GASB, usually pronounced "gas-bee") speaks for accounting practices by government entities.[17] Both the Financial Accounting Standards Board and GASB are under the umbrella of the Financial Accounting Foundation. GASB issues accounting standards, known as statements, first as exposure drafts available for public comment and then in final form. The organization also issues technical bulletins that provide guidance on the implementation of the standards. The Governmental Accounting Standards Advisory Council (GASAC) provides advice to GASB.

Private Sector Accounting Organizations. The private sector has long had a well-established standards-setting organization. The Financial Accounting Standards Board issues authoritative pronouncements on accounting for profit and non-profit organizations.[18] Also, private accounting firms have major input into determining what constitutes good accounting. The Big 4 accounting firms are Deloitte Touche Tohmatsu, Ernst & Young, KPMG, and Pricewaterhouse-Coopers.[19]

There had been the Big 5 that included Arthur Andersen, but it was brought down by scandal. Energy giant Enron went bankrupt in 2001 when it came to light that the company had been cooking the books, making the firm's financial situation look far better than it actually was. Enron officials were eventually convicted. Andersen was involved, because it had been Enron's auditor. The company was found guilty of shredding key documents about Enron, and since a felon cannot be an auditor, the company was forced to relinquish its certified public accountant licensure.[20] That was effectively the end of Andersen as an accounting firm, although the consulting arm of Andersen continued as a company known as Accenture.[21]

The Enron situation and other major scandals involving accounting practices and major corporations' auditors led to widespread criticism of companies who performed both an auditing function and served as financial consultants to the corporations. At the time of the Enron collapse, Andersen was receiving more payments from Enron for consulting and financial advice than for auditing. Such situations may create conflicts of interest in which the consulting arm of a company is eager to see that the auditing arm finds no serious problems in the manner that accounting is conducted by the client. The Securities and Exchange Commission has authority in this area. The Sarbanes-Oxley Act, discussed later, limits greatly this cozy relationship between consulting and auditing. None of the major management consulting firms now has management and financial consulting practices.

One of the most troubling revelations of the scandal was the seeming attitude of Enron and Andersen officials. That can be summed up as "Show me where it says I can't."[22] Accountants often are criticized as blocking "creative" accounting practices that are fraudulent or border on it. In the Enron situation, executives seem to have said that unless something could be shown that a particular accounting practice was prohibited, then it could be used and indeed would be used if it improved the financial outlook of the company.

The vanishing of Andersen from the accounting and auditing arena has left the field with one less competitor. The result may be higher fees that companies must pay the remaining Big 4 who themselves are smaller after selling off their consulting practices. Worldwide there are complaints about the fees these and other accounting and auditing companies charge. An Australian newspaper summed up a situation in New South Wales: "Bankers, lawyers, and accountants 'feasted' on more than $12 million in NSW taxpayers' money," and then the project for which they were being paid was scrubbed.[23]

Of course, Enron is not the only relatively recent accounting scandal. In the early 2000s, telecommunications behemoth WorldCom was force to reveal that it had overstated its financial health through the use of inappropriate accounting practices to the tune of approximately $15 billion.[24] In 2006, the U.S. Justice Department decided against prosecuting Fannie Mae, a giant mortgage company that once was a government-sponsored enterprise and had been spun off as a private company. Fannie Mae was the center of a scandal involving hundreds of millions of dollars in accounting errors that extended over many years.[25]

Standards and Principles of Accounting. While GAAFR is useful to state and local governments in evaluating their accounting systems, it is not regarded as an authoritative document. In contrast, GASB issues annually a document that is authoritative regarding the standards to be used in public accounting: *Codification of Governmental Accounting and Financial Reporting Standards*.[26] The Government Finance Officers Association's "blue book" includes discussions of how it is related to GASB's pronouncements. For example, the 2005 book covers all pronouncements through No. 45.

GASB and its predecessors have recognized what are considered *generally accepted accounting principles* (GAAP). While space limitations do not allow a discussion of each of the 12 principles, it should be noted that they are intended as guides to establishing and modifying accounting systems. The first principle provides the foundation for the other 11 by requiring that accounting principles should be followed and that the legal requirements of a government should be met. Adhering to this first principle can be difficult in that laws can require accounting practices that are contrary to the generally accepted principles.

At the federal level, the generally accepted accounting principles are established by the Federal Accounting Standards Advisory Board (FASAB), having been granted this authority by the American Institute of Certified Public Accountants (AICPA).[27] AICPA's statement No. 91, the Federal GAAP Hierarchy, determines what is GAAP for the federal government.[28] From that statement, FASAB has promulgated numerous statements and interpretations that constitute the first tier in the hierarchy, technical bulletins that are second, and the other documents that make up third and fourth tiers. Together, these constitute GAAP for the federal government.

Organizational Arrangements and Fraud. Creating organizational arrangements that deter fraud is of paramount interest in accounting. Fraud can be committed by workers handling receipts. An employee might hold taxpayer A's money for personal use and use taxpayer B's money to cover A's taxes and subsequently C's money to cover B's taxes. Employees may steal from petty cash or from inventory. Employees may pay vendors who are due nothing or provide travel reimbursement checks to employees who are due nothing. In Michigan, a county official was caught having filed false travel expense claims for years. What was significant was that he was the finance chairman for the county government commission, the very person who should have been alert to possible financial wrong-doings.[29] Financial control systems rely upon the principle of segregation of authority such that a person who can authorize a financial transaction cannot also approve of paying out the actual cash when it is time. So a county official should not have been able to approve incurring a travel expense for himself and then approving its payment. But segregation of duties is not always complete.

Frauds can involve one or two individuals or can be systemic. The Accountant General of the Federation of Nigeria has complained about public servants systematically looting the treasury, particularly through the payroll systems. He said this is done in part with the cooperation of the international community in that stolen funds are transferred overseas to international financial institutions that readily accept new deposits regardless of their source.[30]

One prescription is that accounting systems need to be *transparent.* How they operate and the products of their operations, specifically their various reports, need to be available to interested parties and the public in general. This is of wide-spread concern ranging from highly developed countries to less developed ones. The International Monetary Fund uses its Code of Good Practices on Fiscal Transparency in working with developing nations.[31] United Way International has adopted Global Standards that include Financial Accountability and Transparency as a key requirement when working with participating nongovernmental organizations.[32] Simply getting officials to make public their accounting reports can be controversial, as has been the situation in Uganda, for instance. Officials there when called to testify about their reports sometimes switched off their phones so as not to be reached or claimed they had gone to burials.[33] Australia's Auditor-General has called for bringing governmental accounting in line with private-sector accounting. Special rules in that country's accounting allows, for example, that missiles be classified as either inventory or property, resulting in confusion over financial statements and possible opportunities for misdeeds in the handling of funds.[34]

To prevent fraud and to reduce other losses due to errors and the like, internal controls that specify organizational arrangements and procedures are established. OMB Circular A-123, for example, "provides guidance to federal managers on improving the accountability and effectiveness of federal programs and operations by establishing, assessing, correcting, and reporting on internal control."[35] Responsibility needs to be assigned to individuals, and any delegations of responsibility need to be detailed in writing. One standard practice is to segregate duties, so that one individual may have only limited authority over monies and two or more people may be required to approve some financial transactions. The presumption is that if two or more individuals are part of a particular process, they will monitor each other's behavior and limit various abuses. For example, two or more signatures may be required in approving the issuance of checks or in transferring money through electronic fund transfers.

Employees are trained in how to enter transactions properly in accounting systems and what their ethical and legal responsibilities are in handling public resources. Individuals who handle funds may be subject to more extensive background checks before hiring and may be bonded. Downsizing can force the elimination of personnel and increase the risk that funds are vulnerable to theft or accidental loss due to the reduced oversight of financial operations.

Auditing bodies are important in preventing and detecting fraud. GAO selectively conducts financial as well as program audits and on occasion finds losses in the billions of dollars. GAO audits the financial statements for the government as a whole, for departments (for example, the Treasury Department), independent commissions (for example, the Securities and Exchange Commission), and for federally chartered corporations (for example, Boys Scouts of America). The heavyduty workload of auditing at the federal level is handled by the inspector general offices in their respective departments and agencies. When discrepancies are identified through audits, follow-up is necessary to determine their causes and corrective measures need to be initiated.

Fund Accounting

One of the main differences between public and private sector accounting is the definition of the accounting entity. For the typical private sector organization, the entity is the organization itself, since accounts are designed to reflect its entire resources. Governments, in contrast, separate financial resources into distinct accounting entities called funds. Each fund is set up to record and account for the uses of a specific group of assets or sources of revenue or collection of specific type of costs. As provided for in generally accepted accounting principles 2, 3, and 4 and as modified by GASB, there are three general classes of public sector funds and 11 different particular types of funds.[36] These are the funds that state and local governments use.

1. *Governmental Funds* consist of five types.
   - The *general fund* is the most important governmental fund. Several revenue sources may flow into a government's general fund, such as property tax and income tax receipts at the local level. The resources in the fund are available for expenditure for virtually any purpose that the jurisdiction is legally empowered to pursue. Most municipalities, for instance, may use

general fund receipts for police and road services but not schools, since the latter are the domain of independent school districts. The other fund types within the governmental class are available for what are thought of as normal government operations, but these types have receipt and/or expenditure restrictions.

- *Special revenue funds* receive monies from special sources and are earmarked for special purposes. Gasoline taxes are typically accounted for in a special revenue fund, with expenditures limited to transportation, especially roads and highways.

- *Capital projects funds* account for receipts and expenditures related to projects, such as construction of a new park or city hall, or for major pieces of equipment, such as vehicles for a city fire department. Monies may come into these funds from bond sales that will be paid for with general fund tax receipts.

- *Debt service funds* are used to account for interest and principal on general-purpose long-term debt. The revenue received by this type of fund usually is from the general fund.

- *Permanent funds* are used in cases where only the earnings may be expended and the principal may not. These funds earlier were part of what were called trust and agency funds.

2. *Proprietary Funds*. The second class of funds consists of those that are proprietary or business-like in nature.

   - *Enterprise funds* operate as businesses whose customers are external to government. Such funds are established for toll roads, bridges, and local water systems. Numerous proposals have circulated recommending that various federal operations be converted to government corporations that would be run as enterprises.[37]

   - *Internal service funds* operate as businesses whose customers are internal to government. A central purchasing office or a vehicle maintenance garage may operate as an internal service fund, with revenues coming from other departments as services are rendered. When bonds are sold to support the activities of a proprietary fund (for example, bond proceeds might be used to renovate a city sewage system), capital expenditures and payment of debt are handled through the proprietary fund, not through a capital project or debt service fund.

3. *Fiduciary Funds*. The third class, known as fiduciary funds, has four types. This class, often called *trust and agency funds,* consists of accounts that are dedicated to a third party.

   - *Pension trusts* for government employees are often the largest set of fiduciary funds.

- *Investment trust funds* are used for tracking and reporting the external portion of local government investment pools.
- *Agency funds* pertain to government acting as a conduit for another party, such as a city government collecting taxes for the local school district.
- *Private purpose trust funds* cover all other trust-type arrangements of the government in which principal and earnings may be expended. An increasingly large set of fiduciary funds at the state level are monies held in trust for savings when children grow up and enroll in college or university.[38]

Account Groups. According to generally accepted accounting principles 5 through 7, governmental funds use account groups to report fixed assets and long-term liabilities, whereas proprietary and fiduciary funds report these resources and debts within the funds themselves. Governmental funds include only financial assets—namely, assets that will be converted to cash—and therefore the general fixed asset account group (GFAAG) is used to report assets that will not be converted to cash, such as buildings, swimming pools, aircraft hangars, and airport terminals. The GFAAG is simply a reporting of assets and does not involve transactions. Fixed asset account groups are increasingly important to the description and analysis of the financial health of government agencies and entire government jurisdictions (see Chapter 12).

The second account group is the general long-term debt account group. This group reports government debt that is not part of proprietary or fiduciary funds. In other words, the account group reports liabilities of the entity as a whole, as distinguished from specific funds. This account group and the fixed assets group in effect are memoranda that report assets and liabilities that otherwise would not be reported.

Structure and Rules of Accounting Systems

Ledgers. Accounting systems use ledgers as a means of organization or structure. Each fund has a general ledger and subsidiary ledgers. The general ledger records the overall status of revenues and expenditures, while subsidiary ledgers are established for each revenue source and type of expenditure. In a general fund having several tax sources of revenue, a subsidiary revenue ledger is used for each source. The Office of Management and Budget and the Treasury Department have established a U.S. Government Standard General Ledger that indicates how agencies are to organize their ledgers.[39] A large users manual is available online (37,131 KB). OMB Circular A-127 requires agencies to comply with the standards of the general ledger.[40]

Expenditure subsidiary ledgers control expenditures by appropriation, organizational unit, object of expenditure, and sometimes purpose or activity.

Accounting systems are used to track expenditures according to provisions in appropriations. Often these appropriations are specific to organizations, as in the case of $2 million appropriated to a city housing department. The appropriation also may contain limitations on how funds will be spent, such as expenditures for personnel or equipment. This aspect of accounting is explained later. Some jurisdictions track expenditures by program or activity (this is done if a government's program budget structure does not match its organizational structure).

Accounting Formula. Accounting systems use equations that allow systematic recording of transactions and double-checking that the transactions have been properly recorded. The basic equation that is used is:

$$assets = liabilities + fund\ balance$$

In the formula, *assets* can be the revenue in a fund. *Liabilities* are the monies owed others, such as suppliers of office equipment and tires for police cars. The *fund balance* comprises the residual, uncommitted monies. Specific accounts are established for each of the three components of the formula. Asset accounts, for example, can include those showing cash on hand as well as monies owed by taxpayers (taxes receivable). FASAB has recommended standards for assets and liabilities.

In the mid-2000s, the Governmental Accounting Standards Board (GASB) began work not to revise this fundamental formula but to revise its components. It developed a draft concept statement on Elements of Financial Statements. If the draft is adopted, the concept of *resources* will become part of state and local government accounting. As the draft states:

> A *resource* is an item with a present service capacity. The essential characteristic of a resource in the government environment is its present capacity to provide, directly or indirectly, services. A resource may be tangible and have physical form, such as buildings and equipment; may be intangible, such as the right to use intellectual property or the right to use public waters or airspace; or may even be embodied in the skills of individuals.[41]

Other terms defined are:

- *Assets* are resources that the entity presently controls.
- *Liabilities* are present obligations to sacrifice resources or future resources that the entity has little or no discretion to avoid.
- An *outflow of resources* is a consumption of net resources by the entity that is applicable to the reporting period.
- An *inflow of resources* is an acquisition of net resources by the entity that is applicable to the reporting period.

- A *deferred outflow of resources* is a consumption of net resources by the entity that is applicable to a future reporting period.
- A *deferred inflow of resources* is an acquisition of net resources by the entity that is applicable to a future reporting period.
- *Net assets* [fund balance] are the residual of all other elements presented in a statement of financial position.[42]

Why go through all of this work simply defining the elements to be used in accounting? The answer is simple: unless terms are defined, there is no consistency from jurisdiction to jurisdiction and even from department to department within a jurisdiction. As a result, financial statements, to be discussed later, become largely worthless in that they are unclear as to how transactions have been recorded. Further, the lack of consistency makes pointless any efforts to draw comparisons across departments and across jurisdictions. For example, it is important to handle separately resources flowing immediately into a jurisdiction as distinguished from resources that are deferred and presumably will flow into the jurisdiction at some later reporting period. Also, the inflow concept means that the resources are coming into the government and are not merely being transferred from one fund to another within the government. The latter activities are known as transfers and are discussed later.

In addition to its work on the Elements of Financial Statements, GASB in 2006 issued an invitation to comment (ITC) on its draft Fund Balance Reporting and Governmental Fund Type Definitions.[43] This document was the result of concerns over inconsistencies across jurisdictions as to how they were treating fund balance. An outside observer when looking at the fund balance of a jurisdiction could not be certain of its significance, since governments treated fund balance differently. Differences in the application of basic concepts across jurisdictions greatly complicate the need for investors in bonds issued by those jurisdictions to understand the financial condition of the bond issuer (see Chapter 13).

Double-entry accounting, in which any single transaction is recorded twice (at a minimum), is used as a cross-check. For instance, if taxes are received and no additional obligations are incurred, then both assets and the fund balance increase, and the accounting system will record these two events. The double-entry approach also can be used within one portion of the overall formula. If taxes are received but were already noted in an asset account called taxes receivable, then that account would be reduced while another asset account for cash would be increased. That particular set of transactions would not affect liabilities or the fund balance.

Transactions are recorded in a T in which the left side of the T constitutes *debits* and the right side constitutes *credits*. The terms debits and credits refer only to the left and right sides of the T. Contrary to everyday conversation, debits are not negative in the sense of expenses or debts owed, and credits are not positive in the sense of receipts or money to be paid to government. Rules exist as to when an account should be debited and when credited. In any transaction, the amount debited to one or more accounts must equal the amount credited to other accounts.

Specified Procedures. Flowing out of accounting standards and principles are procedures that determine how transactions will be recorded and in what accounts. These procedures are typically specified in manuals or handbooks so that employees involved in whatever aspects of accounting know how to meet their responsibilities. Manuals may begin with such basics as how to log onto the computer system and proceed to explain the handling of receipts and purchases, including, for example, overall purchasing policy, purchase orders, contract payments, and emergency purchases. Payroll procedures will be specified in some detail in a manual and are likely to require the approval of specific individuals, possibly including written signatures confirming which employees are to be paid what amounts.

The typical accounting cycle is as follows.[44] An event occurs and a source document is prepared. The event might be a decision to tax property and the document might be a tax bill sent to a citizen. When the citizen pays the bill, another transaction occurs, and the accounting system needs to reflect such. On the expenditure side of the budget, one event might be placing an order for office supplies and a later event might be receipt of the supplies and the invoice. These types of transactions will first be posted in a *journal*, which is a chronological listing of events or transactions. The journal entry indicates both the credits and the debits involved in the transaction. For example, tax monies received would increase a cash account and decrease a taxes receivable account. Entries once recorded in the journal are posted to ledgers, and from time to time the debits and credits of these accounts are totaled to obtain *trial* and *final balances*. The balances are used in preparing financial reports (which are discussed later).

Classification of Receipts and Expenditures

Receipts and expenditures are classified in a variety of ways, and elaborate coding systems are used to monitor and control financial transactions. Such coding devices help hold government officials responsible for honestly managing the government's business.

Receipts. The monies that government receives need to be recorded according to the source. The money derived from each tax source, such as property and income taxes, needs to be recorded separately and in distinction from user fees, such as charges for using a municipal golf course. The federal government treats user fees as *offsetting collections*. Money derived from fees, as in the case of the Tennessee Valley Authority, is used to offset expenditures for Tennessee Valley Authority operations. The net differences in such transactions are reported in the budget. The practice of netting receipts against expenditures in the budget for enterprise operations, while perfectly appropriate, means that one cannot use the government budget alone to gauge the size of government.

GASB has had to deal with a relatively recent phenomenon in the realm of revenues. Some governments strapped for cash have borrowed against outstanding receivables, such as taxes owed, and have actually sold such receivables, an act known as *securitizing* a stream of receivables (see Chapter 13). GASB has issued an exposure draft that would require these governments to report such transactions as liabilities in that they have pledged collateral against borrowed resources.[45]

Fund and Appropriation. Expenditures are accounted for in a variety of ways. One set of characteristics is the fund and appropriation. An appropriation is a legislative approval to spend from a specific fund. Since several bills may be passed that appropriate out of the general fund, the dollar stipulations in each of these bills must be observed vis-à-vis the total assets available in the general fund. Even if a jurisdiction uses only one appropriation bill, each of the expenditure limits in the bill must be observed and consequently must be monitored by the accounting system. When an expenditure is made, it is charged against the appropriated amount and the remaining available balance is shown. In this way, an accounting system can be used to keep agency expenditures within budgeted figures.

If the legislative body earmarks expenditures in detail, then the accounting system becomes increasingly complex. For example, Congress in its annual foreign assistance appropriation bill typically imposes detailed figures on the level of funding for programs within the Agency for International Development and amounts to be available in each country receiving aid. The accounting system, therefore, must monitor expenditures by program (e.g., child survival) and by country to adhere to the stipulations in the appropriation bill.

Organizational Unit. Expenditures are made by organizational units, and accounting systems must track expenditures accordingly. Appropriation bills usually are specific to agencies so that, instead of the government simply being authorized to spend an amount on forest preservation, a specific unit within a department is granted the money. Large governments, then, account for expenditures not only at the department level but also at the bureau, office, division, or regional unit level.

Objects of Expenditure. Accounting systems invariably account in terms of the objects acquired or the objects of expenditure. Broad groupings of objects are called major objects, and their subdivisions are called minor objects. **Exhibit 11–2** illustrates the object classes used by the federal government. The object series beginning with the number 11, for example, covers all personnel-compensation expenditures, while the 12 series covers personnel benefits. The other major classes are contractual services and supplies, acquisition of assets, grants and fixed charges, and other.

Accounting systems can become unwieldy in their use of minor objects. For instance, travel as a major object can be subdivided in numerous ways:

- Mode (personal automobile, government automobile, commercial airline)
- Type of person traveling (elected official, political executive, career executive, employee, client)
- Purpose (meeting, conference, training, inspection)
- Location (in state, out of state, out of country)
- Type of expense (lodging, meals, transportation)

The number of possible permutations is great. When an accounting system uses such detail, the entry of many transactions may be delayed due to classification ambiguities.

Despite the administrative problems of detailed minor objects, legislative bodies often incorporate such details in appropriation bills. These line items in an appropriation allow control when there is concern that funds may be abused. Restrictions may be inserted regarding the purchase of newspaper subscriptions, the number of automobiles, and government employee travel. When minor object restrictions are embedded in appropriations, the limits are legally mandated, and the accounting system must ensure compliance.

Executives also use object classifications in an attempt to control agencies and increase their efficiency. Executive Order 12837 requires federal agencies to reduce their administrative costs, especially travel and other selected objects that often are viewed as luxuries. Of course, many administrative expenses are central to the missions of agencies. Travel is essential for inspectors of meat and poultry processing plants, mines, and workplaces, for example.

Purpose and Activity. Program-oriented budgets that focus decision-making attention on specific program goals and objectives also require accounting-based information on how much each program costs. The federal government uses broad functional categories, such as national defense, energy, and income security, which are divided into subfunctions. For example, energy is subdivided into supply and energy information, policy, and regulation.[46] If a budget based on program classifications cuts across agency lines, then the accounting system needs to cut across agency lines to accumulate the costs according to program. Similarly,

Exhibit 11–2   Federal Objects of Expenditure Classification

Code	Classification Title
10	**Personnel Compensation and Benefits**
11	Personnel Compensation
11.1	Full-Time Permanent
11.3	Other than Full-Time Permanent
11.5	Other Personnel Compensation
11.7	Military Personnel
11.8	Special Personal Services Payments
11.9	Total Personnel Compensation
12	Personnel Benefits
12.1	Civilian Personnel Benefits
12.2	Military Personnel Benefits
13	Benefits for Former Personnel
20	**Contractual Services and Supplies**
21	Travel and Transportation of Persons
22	Transportation of Things
23	Rent, Communications, and Utilities
23.1	Rental Payments to General Services Administration
23.2	Rental Payments to Others
23.3	Communications, Utilities, and Miscellaneous Charges
24	Printing and Reproduction
25	Other Contractual Services
25.1	Advisory and Assistance Services
25.2	Other Services
25.3	Other Purchase of Goods and Services from Government Accounts
25.4	Operation and Maintenance of Facilities
25.5	Research and Development Contracts
25.6	Medical Care
25.7	Operation and Maintenance of Equipment
25.8	Subsistence and Support of Persons
26	Supplies and Materials
30	**Acquisition of Assets**
31	Equipment
32	Land and Structures
33	Investments and Loans

continues

Exhibit 11–2	Federal Objects of Expenditure Classification (continued)

40	**Grants and Fixed Charges**	
	41	Grants, Subsidies, and Contributions
	42	Insurance Claims and Indemnities
	43	Interest and Dividends
	44	Refunds
90	**Other**	
	91	Unvouchered
	92	Undistributed
	93	Limitation on Expenses
	94	Financial Transfers
	99	Subtotal Obligations
	99.5	Below Reporting Threshold
	99.9	Total New Obligations

Source: Adapted from U.S. Office of Management and Budget (2006). *Preparation, submission, and execution of the budget, Circular No. A-11.* Washington, DC: OMB, sec.83, 4-23. Retrieved August 25, 2006, from http://www.whitehouse.gov/omb/circulars/a11/current_year/a_11_2006.pdf.

preparing a budget that allocates funds according to detailed work activities requires an accounting system that tracks expenditures by those activities. The problem of accounting for finances by program or activity is discussed more fully in the next section in regard to cost accounting.

Performance Measurement. While practitioners and academics in the field of budgeting have long been concerned about how to measure the results of government programs, accountants only became particularly concerned starting in the 1980s.[47] They came to recognize a need for measuring outputs, outcomes, efficiency, effectiveness, and the like (see Chapter 6). What is significant here is that accountants now back the notion that financial accounting should be tied to performance measurement. If one wishes to determine the efficiency of an organization in delivering a service over time, then there needs to be a measurement of the service provided (outputs) and the costs (obtained through accounting).

GASB is moving toward adopting an accounting statement that may require *service efforts and accomplishments* (SEA) reporting as part of *general-purpose external financial reporting* (GPEFR). The accounting body's action is slow and deliberate, since SEA reporting as a requirement would bring about radical and costly changes in state and local government accounting systems. In 1994, it issued Concept Statement No. 2 as an exposure draft.[48] In 2005, it issued a guide to understanding SEA reports.[49]

Accounting for performance and then auditing for it require going beyond the boundaries of the organization to where results are produced. In contrast, traditional accounting systems have been structured to capture financial transactions within organizations. Once the accounting system has to take measurements outside the organization, as it must with performance accounting, major problems arise over how to collect information and how to audit it. Measurement errors inevitably occur in such systems, raising issues about their accuracy and utility.

The federal government has taken major steps in the direction of greater utilization of performance measurement. The Chief Financial Officers Act of 1990 instructs agency CFOs to develop reporting systems that provide for "the integration of accounting and budgeting information and the systematic measurement of performance." The Government Performance and Results Act of 1993, as explained in Chapter 6, requires federal agencies to develop annual performance plans that are integral to the budget.[50] Of course, one should keep in mind that achieving change is different than simply mandating change. Efforts to include performance measurement within accounting systems face major challenges.

Perhaps equally difficult is the direct challenge that connecting performance and the budget creates for accounting systems themselves. Connecting performance information and cost information implies the ability to appropriately measure both. Proper cost measurement requires a level of accounting sophistication that has proved difficult for governments to achieve. They have attempted to remedy this problem through greater attention to cost accounting, as discussed later.

Basis of Accounting

The *basis of accounting* refers to the timing of transactions, or when a revenue item is recorded as received by the government and when an expenditure is recorded as having occurred. There are several methods for determining when a revenue or expenditure item is recorded, and each has a different purpose.

Cash Accounting. The oldest system is cash accounting, which is still used today, particularly in small governments. In general, all governments have a cash aspect to their accounting systems. In a cash accounting system, tax receipts are recorded when they are actually received by the government and expenditures are recorded when payments are made. Minor variations exist. Some systems record expenditures when checks are written, but others record expenditures when checks clear the banking system. The major advantages of the cash system are that it is simple in comparison with alternatives and that it presents an accurate picture of cash on hand at any point in time.

The major disadvantage of the cash system is that it does not provide information about the future—namely, anticipated receipts and expenditures.[51] The cash on hand may seem to suggest that one's financial situation is reasonably secure, but a different picture may emerge when considering obligations that must be met, such as payrolls.

Encumbrance Accounting. A step in the direction of anticipating future transactions is encumbrance accounting. Expenditures are recorded when purchase orders are written or contracts are signed. Some of the cash on hand, then, is said to be encumbered and not available for covering other expenditures. In the case of a multiyear contract, all of the expenditures for a year may be encumbered at the outset of the fiscal year, or amounts may be encumbered each month as work is completed by the contractor. An encumbrance system helps ensure that a government unit will not overspend its appropriation.

Accrual Accounting. In accrual systems, financial transactions are recognized when the activities that generate them occur.[52] Revenues are recorded when the government earns the income, as when a local government sends tax bills to property owners. Expenditures are recognized when the liabilities are incurred, regardless of when payment for those goods or services might actually be made during the year.

The accrual basis has been required of federal agencies for more than 30 years, but few federal accounting systems actually use accrual accounting.[53] The obstacle has been the diversity of accounting systems. Large departments such as the Department of Defense, for example, have many different accounting systems. Where accrual accounting is used in government, it is normally on a modified accrual basis. Not all transactions are accrued and some remain on a cash basis. Under modified accrual accounting, revenues are recognized when they are "measurable and available" for obligation, and expenditures are recognized when an obligation to spend has occurred. Full accrual, however, is recommended for proprietary funds (enterprise and internal service funds) and pension trusts.

Despite the obstacles to implementation, the accounting profession continues to endorse strongly the accrual basis of accounting. GASB's Statement No. 11, Measurement Focus and Basis of Accounting: Governmental Fund Operating Statements (MFBA, pronounced "muff-bah"), provides for extending the accrual process to cover items previously not covered.[54] For instance, the costs of employees' vacations are to be recognized when employees earn their vacation time.

When employees are allowed to accumulate vacation leave, the accounting system needs to recognize that government's liabilities have increased. Particularly controversial is the provision that employee pension funds should recognize future payments owed future retirees by recording them in the governmental funds rather than as normally reported in the general long-term debt account group. These provisions are controversial in that they negatively affect fund balances, pushing some governments into negative balances.

However, not recording those future obligations in the accounting system gives a false picture of the financial condition of the governmental entity. In the private sector, future pension payouts must be accounted for now to control for the possibility that the company will not have the funds to pay out the pension obligations when members of its workforce retire. Government presumably is in a somewhat different situation in that at least in principle, government can use its taxing power in the future to obtain the funds necessary to meet pension fund payout obligations.

Cost Accounting. While the cash, encumbrance, and accrual bases of accounting focus attention on resources coming into government and being expended, cost accounting is concerned with when resources are used in the production of goods and services.[55] For example, gasoline purchased for a state highway department could be accounted for when the order is made (encumbrance), when the goods are received (modified accrual method), or when the vendor is paid (cash method). The cost approach, in contrast, records the transaction when the gasoline is consumed.

Managerial cost accounting can be viewed as providing key information needed by managers in conducting their operations and, in addition to this internal function, providing information to external parties such as the legislative body, taxpayers, and investors in governmental securities.[56] In a cost accounting system, costs of providing services are matched with measures of those services. For example, a school district might want to know the average cost of graduating someone from the general population compared with the average cost of graduating a student with special needs — for instance, a student with physical disabilities.

Activity-based costing and *activity-based management* concentrate on collecting costs of delivering services to citizens.[57] The costs of delivering services can be monitored over time, thereby giving an impetus for increased efficiency of operations. Such accounting can determine the costs of producing activities, outputs, and outcomes.

The incentives for using cost accounting are different in the private and public sectors. To determine their profitability, corporations need to know the cost of providing each product or service. The costs of production can be subtracted from sales receipts to determine a corporation's profit or loss, something that every investor wants to know about a company. Governmental programs, such as police and fire departments, obviously do not seek a profit and consequently may see less need for cost accounting. Contemporary public safety managers want to know whether desired outcomes are being achieved and want to know from their accounting systems what the costs are for outputs and work (Chapter 6).

Other programs, particularly enterprise and internal service funds, while not seeking a profit, do endeavor to break even and consequently have an incentive to know the costs of their services. For example, a centralized office supplies agency has an incentive to calculate its costs so as to set appropriate fee schedules for charging departments for products. A central maintenance garage for city vehicles needs an accurate understanding of its costs for maintaining garbage trucks, police cars, and buses. Keeping costs down in each of these areas is important in linking the production of services with costs. Cost accounting systems should be able to provide insight into marginal costs, such as the extra expense of repairing each additional police car damaged in the line of duty.

Cost accounting is especially important in the public sector in an era of privatization. In particular, "managed competition," where government agencies and private firms compete to provide services, necessitates the ability to make appropriate cost comparisons between public agencies and private firms. As a means of cutting costs, for example, a police department might be eager to contract out for patrol car repairs rather than use a city maintenance facility. Bureaucratic politics are rampant in such situations.

Besides the reduced incentives to use cost accounting in government, several other impediments to its implementation exist. One such obstacle is that purposes and objectives are not neatly compartmentalized into organizational units, resulting in situations in which one organization may be serving multiple purposes and another organization may be serving some of those same purposes. To resolve this problem, *cost centers* must be used in which the accounting system records financial information for each activity performed within an organizational unit. In a bureau that engages in three activities and that has its personnel working at various times on the three activities, records must be maintained regarding the amount of time each worker spends on each activity. Other bureau costs, such as those for supplies, telephones, and furniture, must be distributed among the cost centers.

Other impediments to cost accounting being used in government pertain to how various financial transactions are currently conducted. Government agencies sometimes provide services to one another at no charge, resulting in a form of subsidy to the recipient agencies and a consequent understatement of the costs of the services that those agencies provide. Salaries, wages, and other personnel expenses, such as pension contributions and health benefits for employees and retirees, often appear in central budgets and not in the budgets of units that deliver services. Likewise, other support services involving budgeting, legal assistance, janitorial services, and computer support may not be charged to line agencies. The result is that organizational budgets typically fall short of fully reflecting the costs of activities.

Cost accounting requires that special attention be given to the acquisition and utilization of *fixed assets*—land, structures, and major pieces of equipment. Fixed assets sometimes are financed centrally and, as a consequence, do not appear in the budgets of the organizational units that actually use these assets. Additionally, the purchase of fixed assets or capital goods should not be considered costs in the year of purchase but rather should be depreciated over the life span of the goods. From a cost standpoint, the cost of police patrol cars might be spread over three years. From a cash standpoint, the purchase will be recorded in the first year when the purchase is made. Buildings and vehicles then are depreciated over time, showing a truer picture of the cost of services than the cash method does.

The life cycle of an asset needs to be considered—that is, how long an asset has utility. Federal law and OMB Circular A-131 instruct agencies to use value engineering as a management technique in determining how long assets will be of use. The circular defines *value engineering* as "an organized effort directed at analyzing the functions of systems, equipment, facilities, services, and supplies for the purpose of achieving the essential functions at the lowest life-cycle cost consistent with required performance, reliability, quality, and safety."[58]

Depreciation is essential in cost accounting, and depreciation rules need to be applied differently according to the assets involved. FASAB has identified four types of *property, plant, and equipment* (PP&E).[59]

- The *general PP&E* category includes buildings for which a market value can be derived, such as the value of an office building.
- The category of *federal mission PP&E* is for the uniquely federal functions of defense and space exploration. Depreciating these assets is extremely difficult because it requires estimating the assets' useful lives. How long will a weapons system be of use, or how long will a space satellite continue to operate?
- The *heritage PP&E* category includes education, culture, and artistic endeavors.[60] The Washington Monument and the White House are in this grouping, as they have special significance and are not just ordinary government buildings.
- The last category, *stewardship PP&E*, covers government holdings that are entrusted to the government for safekeeping. It includes federal land held by the National Park Service and the U.S. Forest Service.

In addition to fixed assets, other investments pose major challenges for the use of cost accounting in government. When a government bureau pays for several of its workers to attend a training program, is it an investment and, if so, what is the life of that investment? When a state government provides a grant to a local government for construction of a sewage treatment plant, how should the state record the investment given that the new plant will belong to the local government and not to the state?

Given the complexities of cost accounting, one can readily see why it is used in only limited cases in government. It is an open question whether FASAB and its participating agencies will be successful in moving the federal government toward the use of cost accounting. The Government Accountability Office studied efforts to implement managerial cost accounting in a variety of federal agencies. One fundamental conclusion of these studies was that when leadership from the top was missing, implementation of cost accounting was spotty at best. This was the case at the Department of Health and Human Services and the Department of Education. In contrast, the Department of Transportation and the Social Security Administration were singled out as having strong leadership that fostered development of cost accounting throughout their respective component units.[61]

Project-Based Accounting. Another option that is not as elaborate as cost accounting is project-based accounting. Accounts can be established on a temporary basis to track costs for selected activities. Private firms, both for-profit and nonprofit, keep detailed accounting records for contracts, including costs at task or subtask levels. If a consulting firm has been awarded a government contract, a separate set of accounts is established showing which personnel worked on which tasks for what length of time within a given reporting period (weekly, biweekly, or monthly). Accounts of this type are important for reimbursement purposes. Federal cost accounting standards require strict adherence to project cost accounting. Charging time or other costs to a project when that time or other resources were not actually contributing to the project, if determined to be deliberate and significant, can result in severe penalties including debarment from future government contracting.

Project-based accounting also is used for monitoring internal operations. If a corporation is developing a new product or group of products, separate accounts can be established to gauge the developmental costs of the project. In the quasi-governmental arena, the World Bank uses account codes and employee time reporting systems to account for project costs, enabling management to evaluate the cost of preparing, negotiating, and supervising a specific loan to a country.

Cost Finding. In some instances, governments may be satisfied with something less than a complete cost accounting system or even project-based accounting. Rather than having an ongoing cost information system, governments sometimes selectively study costs of specific activities that may be contained within a single organization or spread across several units. The cost of delivering family planning services to teenagers might be derived through analysis of expenditure records and a sampling of employee time commitments. A far more elaborate cost-finding endeavor would be to try to derive the costs of HIV/AIDS to a state government. The analysis would attempt to determine the costs of prevention and treatment activities that most likely are not encoded in the accounting system. For example, AIDS may well increase health care costs for prisoners, but such costs would not routinely be segregated in the accounting system.

The analysis of cost data can be useful in identifying *fixed costs* and *variable costs*. There may be a minimum or fixed cost for providing a given service up to some particular level, above which costs increase as units of service increase. For example, a preschool program for disadvantaged children begins with a fixed set of costs for essentials such as a school room, a teacher, and some supportive services—costs that are incurred whether one or ten children are taught. As the number of children in the class increases, variable costs increase, such as those for teaching materials and supplies, and perhaps teacher aides. Fixed costs, however, do not rise unless the number of children grows to a level that another classroom, another teacher, and so forth are required.

Allowable Costs. In the awarding of grants and contracts, governments need to determine what costs are allowable. The federal government's Cost Accounting Standards Board, located within OMB's Office of Federal Procurement Policy, has attempted to set parameters for costs in defense and related contracts.[62] OMB Circular A-87 specifies in great detail what costs are allowable in grants to state and local governments.[63] Unallowable costs include entertainment, alcoholic beverages, interest on debt (such as working capital borrowings), and donations, as in the case of volunteer services.

Risk and Credit Accounting. Public sector officials have come to recognize that risks arise in carrying out public duties. Not only are revenues raised and expenditures made, but other factors create conditions that can result in major financial loss and/or expenditures. Risk management involves assessing the risk exposure of a government (see Chapter 10). On the one hand, in making and guaranteeing loans, the federal government assumes risks that can have major financial consequences, as evidenced by the forced bailout of failed savings and loan associations. On the other hand, credit programs can yield savings or negative subsidies, particularly at some point in the future. Estimating such savings poses considerable technical problems, plus agencies that administer such programs may be biased in favor of forecasting such savings.

State and local governments are expected to follow the instructions for reporting risks as prescribed by several GASB statements. These were discussed in Chapter 10.

The Office of Management and Budget, as prescribed by the Federal Credit Reform Act of 1990, oversaw a thorough revamping of how the government accounts for credit programs and how decisions are made about these programs. The law was intended to "place the cost of credit programs on a budgetary basis" so that they compete with all other programs for scarce resources.[64] Prior to the enactment of the Credit Reform Act, the budget "charged" costs based on the cash that would flow out of the budget in a given year. This meant that direct loans appeared to be the budgetary equivalent of grants, even though many of the funds would be repaid in later years. Loan guarantees, on the other hand, appeared to be cost free because third parties were disbursing the funds in the budget year, even though the federal government was liable for (sometimes substantial) costs in future years when loan recipients defaulted on their obligations. By focusing on the long-term costs to the federal government from both kinds of programs, the Credit Reform Act put them on an equivalent budgetary basis.

OMB requires agencies to supply data on direct loans, loan subsidies, guaranteed loans, and guaranteed loan subsidies as part of the agencies' budget submissions (Circular A-129). Prior to passage of the Federal Credit Reform Act, many federal agencies could borrow from the Federal Financing Bank, but they now must borrow from the Treasury Department to finance their direct and guaranteed loan programs. When the law was implemented in the 1990s, federal agencies encountered considerable difficulty in complying, because their existing accounting systems and supporting staff often were inadequate.[65]

Generational Accounting. Of growing interest are the potential effects of government finances on different generations.[66] Expenditures for elementary and secondary education obviously help children, whereas alcohol programs help adults and programs such as Medicare help the elderly. Generational accounting is important in considering future benefits or costs imposed on different age groups. Although accounting systems have not been devised for identifying the costs or the benefits of government activities for different age groups, some reporting of such effects occurs.

Need for Different Bases. These different approaches to the basis of accounting are not substitutes for one another. Rather, each satisfies a different type of need.

- From the standpoint of a treasury department, a cash basis for recording receipts and expenditures is necessary because the department has the legal responsibility to receive revenue and issue checks to cover expenses. This responsibility extends to determining that there are sufficient funds to cover checks to be issued.

- The encumbrance basis is important in showing the current status of assets and liabilities, including liabilities that will place a demand on cash in the future.
- Cost accounting is valuable in identifying resources consumed, as distinguished from resources acquired and placed in inventory.
- Risk accounting provides a more comprehensive overview of obligations than is available through accounting systems that cover only revenues and expenditures.
- Generational accounting provides insights into the implications of government finances for different generations, from the elderly to the young and to those not yet born.

Private Sector Reforms in Accounting and Implications for Government Accounting

The discussion has shown that government accounting has been undergoing considerable reform, but there are two possible reforms that deserve special attention—the possible extension of the Sarbanes-Oxley Act to privately held companies, nonprofit organizations, and governments, and the reform of state and local government pension accounting and funding.

Sarbanes-Oxley. The Sarbanes-Oxley Act, formally the Public Company Accounting Reform and Investor Protection Act and commonly referred to as *SOX*, was passed in 2002 in the wake of the financial scandals involving Enron and WorldCom.[67] As its official title indicates, it was aimed at upgrading accounting practices in publicly traded companies in order to protect investors.

SOX's complex provisions include:

- Created the independent Public Company Accounting Oversight Board (PCAOB), which sets standards and oversees the accounting profession.
- Required chief executive officers and chief financial officers of companies to take personal responsibility for the content of financial statements.
- Prohibited ongoing use of lead auditors and instead required that they be rotated at least every five years.
- Imposed internal controls and required such structure of controls be audited by the company and assessed by auditors and reported to the Securities and Exchange Commission.
- Heightened penalties for fraud in terms of fines and imprisonment.
- Provided protection to company employees who report wrongdoing (whistleblowers).

- Made illegal the destruction of documents that are routinely needed in investigations and legal actions.

In response to Sarbanes-Oxley, the Office of Management and Budget launched a review of federal financial management. This process already was ongoing as required by the Federal Financial Management Improvement Act of 1996.[68] Circular A-123, dealing with internal controls, was revised in 2004 and subsequent guidance was released by OMB and the Chief Financial Officers Council in 2005 and 2006.[69]

Of interest is whether the law or a variation of it should be extended to state and local governments, nonprofits, and privately held companies.[70] A law that outright dictated changes in state and local auditing would certainly be contested in court and most likely would be overturned on the grounds of infringing on the independence of the states and their political subdivisions. However, Congress could pass such a law through a backdoor as it has done in other situations. A law similar to Sarbanes-Oxley could be imposed on state and local governments as a condition of accepting federal grant monies.

Proposing such a law would stir up a hornet's nest of vast proportions. Besides the line of argument that the federal government should not dictate financial management to state and local governments, the argument would be raised that adequate safeguards are already in place. These governments already have independently elected auditors that check for wrongdoing, and legislative bodies perform many of the same roles.

While some advocates would extend Sarbanes-Oxley's coverage, others would scale back its scope. Efforts have been made to reduce the liability of accounting firms in cases of wrongdoing, to direct prosecutions toward corporate wrongdoers rather than their corporations, and to reduce the scope of shareholder lawsuits. Some of these changes require congressional action but others could be implemented through the regulatory process of the Security and Exchange Commission.[71]

Reforms in Private Sector Pension Plans and Implications for Government Plans

The other major topic for possible reform is that of state and local pension plans. There are approximately 200 state-administered plans, some of which include local government employees as well as state employees, and about 2,000 locally administered plans.[72] In addition, there are thousands of other small plans involving annuity policies with private insurance carriers.

Retirement systems—both public sector and private sector—must comply with federal laws. The Employee Retirement Income Security Act (ERISA) of 1974 governs private sector plans.[73] Sections 415 and 457 of the Internal Revenue Code exert major controls over public retirement systems. In 1996, Congress amended these provisions to allow greater flexibility on the part of state and local systems in complying with federal law.[74]

Retirement systems generally are based on an assumption that a person will use a variety of measures to cover living expenses during retirement besides pension checks. First, living expenses may decline as the individual becomes less active and has fewer demands on income, such as support for dependents. Second, savings are used to cover expenses. Third, many government workers are covered by Old-Age and Survivors Insurance, disability insurance, and health insurance (Medicare) of the Social Security Administration.

Defined Benefit and Defined Contribution Plans. Pension systems in the public sector historically have used *defined benefit plans*, in which benefits normally are determined according to some combination of years of services, wages or salaries (for example, average salary of the last three years of service), and age at time of retirement. The longer one has worked for a government and the higher one's salary, the higher pension benefits will be. State and local government retirement systems historically have used the defined benefit plan.

In addition to initial retirement benefits, *cost-of-living allowances* (COLAs) are usually assigned to pensioners, in some cases on an automatic basis according to an economic barometer, such as the consumer price index, and in other cases on an ad hoc basis. In the latter instance, a government might decide one year to increase retirement benefits by the same percentage as salary increases being awarded current employees. Other benefits are provided for disability retirement (for people who retire early because of poor health) and for survivors' benefits (covering family members who continue to live after the death of retirees). The vast majority of benefits paid each year go to elderly retirees, with the remainder divided between disability retirees and survivors.

Defined benefit plans coupled with cost-of-living allowances provide income security to employees and retirees and place investment risks on employers. Since benefits are determined in advance of retirement, employers must take steps necessary to ensure that sufficient funds will be available when employees retire. Cost accounting standards require that private sector companies "fund" the future liabilities created by these defined benefit programs. If projected earnings from investments of a company's pension fund are less than projected payouts, then the company must take an accounting adjustment, generally a write-down of profits, to cover the projected difference.

An alternative to defined benefits is the *defined contribution plan.* Under this plan, benefits are not defined in advance of retirement, but rather the employer commits to contributing regularly to an employee's retirement account (usually a percentage of compensation). The benefits received at the time of retirement are a function of the employer's and employee's contributions plus investment earnings on these contributions. 401(k) plans (named after the section of the Internal Revenue Code that defines their tax treatment) are the most common examples of defined contribution plans. 403(b) plans are the nonprofit company equivalent. Both involve employer and individual contributions. Private companies also may have plans that are based solely on employer contributions. Most private employers use defined contribution plans, and while public employers are shifting to defined contribution plans, many still use defined benefit plans. A key advantage of a defined contribution plan for an employer is its predictability. All that need be done each year is to set aside a percentage of salaries and wages for depositing into retirement accounts.

Funding. Pension plans are funded by a combination of contributions from government and employees and investment earnings on those contributions. In some cases, the retirement program is financed exclusively by government, but that practice is an exception to the rule.

There are basically two methods of financing retirement programs: *pay-as-you-go* and *advance funding.* With the pay-as-you-go method, all that is required in any one budget year is to raise sufficient revenue to cover retirement benefit checks. This method is generally discouraged because it allows for the accumulation of debt. Persons in the future will be owed benefits, and taxpayers at that time will be forced to meet those costs.

The preferred method is advance funding, in which monies are accumulated for workers while they are working and those monies generate income through investments while workers are on the payroll and during retirement as well. If using this method, a retirement system must invest prudently but effectively to avoid any unfunded actuarial accrued liability so that the system is "actuarially sound." Advance funding uses the concept of *present value.* That is, future receipts, particularly contributions and investment earnings, are compared with anticipated costs (benefits) in terms of current dollars.

Liabilities. Until the 1970s, many public retirement systems were woefully underfunded. Over the years, governments had made pension plan commitments to employees but had failed to follow through by contributing sufficient funds to the plans. For those governments that do have underfunded pension plans, serious problems loom. Meeting current operating needs and covering the costs of retiree benefits can easily put a budget out of balance and force a tax increase. Where jurisdictions are at their legal or political limits on tax rates, severe program cuts may be the only alternative. Pension fund liabilities can increase the cost of doing business, as interest rates may be higher for jurisdictions that have large outstanding pension debts.

Several options are available for improving the funding situation of retirement systems:

- An obvious option is to increase government and employee contributions.
- A jurisdiction can take advantage of economies of scale by combining systems. This technique may reduce administrative costs and make possible more lucrative investments.
- Retirement systems can pool their funds for investment purposes.
- A jurisdiction can make investments that are riskier but also have higher rates of return. The stock market crash of 1987 and the Orange County, California, bankruptcy of 1994 (see Chapters 10 and 13), however, are sobering reminders of the loss that can result from nonguaranteed investments. Models are available that suggest how to balance high returns with acceptable levels of risk.
- Some jurisdictions have sold bonds to obtain the funds needed to cover retirement liabilities.
- A pension system can have its creditworthiness rated in terms of the system's ability to meet its financial obligations. This rating then can be used to back other entities for fees, consequently increasing the revenue for the pension system.

Accounting and Reporting. Three statements and a technical bulletin issued by the Governmental Accounting Standards Board are the governing documents for accounting and reporting of state and local pension systems:

- Statement No. 25, Financial Reporting for Defined Benefit Pension Plans and Note Disclosures for Defined Contribution Plans
- Statement No. 26, Financial Reporting for Postemployment Healthcare Plans Administered by Defined Benefit Pension Plans
- Statement No. 27, Accounting for Pensions by State and Local Governmental Employers
- Technical Bulletin 96-1, Pension Disclosure Requirements for Employers

Overall, these documents require an annual reporting of assets, changes in assets from year to year, and actuarial information on the long-term prospects of pension funds.

So what is the issue? In 2006, it became woefully obvious that despite ERISA protecting private sector workers, private pension plans were underfunded. For example, giant Delphi Corporation, which was General Motors' primary parts supplier and once had been part of GM, went into bankruptcy and left in doubt the pension plans of current workers and those already retired. In the first half of the 2000s, more than 700 pension plans went belly up. This caused substantial losses for the federal Pension Benefit Guaranty Corporation (PBGC), which insures private pension plans, eventually creating a PBGC deficit of $23 billion. With private pension systems perhaps underfunded by as much as $450 billion, the fear was that a massive collapse of plans would occur, leaving the government and ultimately the taxpayers to foot the bill.

Congress passed the Pension Protection Act of 2006 in response to this situation.[75] In general, the law gave private companies seven years to get their pensions up to a standard of being fully funded. The financially troubled airlines were given longer to comply. Plans that are deemed "at risk" have tougher funding standards to meet. Workers were given new incentives to save on their own through individual retirement accounts (IRAs) and 401(k) plans. The law can be seen as a balancing act of being tough with companies about their pension funding but not being so tough as to have them eliminate traditional pension systems.[76] Future funding of guaranteed health insurance benefits also has been an issue for private companies. Accounting reforms require private companies to fund through accrual the estimated costs of these health insurance payouts.

The question arises whether such a law in some form is needed for state and local governments, providing there are means of getting around the constitutional protections that the states have against the federal government. Despite efforts to bring state and local pension plans into full funding, many remain underfunded. San Diego suffered through a massive scandal that began in 2004 and continued into 2006. It was revealed that the city's pension plan was underfunded by about $1.4 billion. This seventh largest city in the nation was nicknamed "Enron by the Sea."[77] A team of experts was hired to assess the situation and had this to say:

> The evidence suggests that at root San Diego City officials fell prey to the same type of corruption of financial management and reporting that afflicted municipalities such as Orange County and such private sector companies as Enron, HealthSouth, and any number of other public corporations. That is, San Diego officials cultivated and accepted a culture of financial management and reporting premised upon non-transparency, obfuscation, and denial of fiscal reality. Under the pressure of short-term needs, City officials gave expedience a higher priority than fiscal responsibility and came to view the law as an impediment to be circumvented through artful manipulation.[78]

In 2006, New York City reported it could be in arrears by as much as $49 billion in funding for its pensions.[79] The situation involving state and local pension plans has been described as "a ticking time bomb set to explode."[80] Some states are moving away from defined benefit plans to head off crises by switching to defined contribution plans. The question remains whether legislation is needed to force change.

Successful and Unsuccessful Reforms

The Government Accountability Office, which has a long history of studying accounting systems and their reforms, concluded that three factors were important in determining success or failure of reform efforts.[81] First, there needed to be "disciplined processes" for introducing reforms. For instance, new processes needed to be carefully and systematically designed, installed, and tested for their efficacy. Second, attention needed to be paid to human capital management. There was need to have the right number of people with the right skills in the right jobs. Third, information technology was critical. Enterprise architecture and information security were seen as fundamental. A fourth factor comes to mind when considering state and local pension plans and that is funding. No matter how fine the accounting system is, if the pension plan is underfunded, then there are problems of raising the required resources.

Reporting

Accounting systems generate reports that are used by managers, policy makers, and people outside of government. In state and local governments, generally accepted accounting principle 12 calls on jurisdictions to prepare both interim and annual reports (see above). Interim reports, such as daily and weekly reports, serve internal purposes, as in the case of checking on appropriated funds that are neither spent nor encumbered. These reports are useful in monitoring budget execution and anticipating situations in which agencies might lack sufficient funds to operate their programs throughout the fiscal year. A fundamental expectation of all financial reports is that they can be audited, meaning that accounting records back up the data in the reports.

Annual reports are particularly useful to people and organizations outside of government. They can show taxpayers how revenues have been used to support services, for example. Annual reports of local governments are helpful for businesses that are considering locating, relocating, or expanding existing facilities. Such reports are used to help discover the financial condition of governments and decide whether to purchase their bonds. The Government Finance Officers Association issues certificates of achievement for excellence in financial reporting.

The association also issues awards for outstanding *popular annual financial report-ing* (PAFRs). These reports are prepared for use by the general public and not accountants and budgeters.[82]

Financial Reports

GASB prescribes a *comprehensive annual financial report* (CAFR) that has three sec-tions: introduction, finances, and statistics.[83] The first section includes a letter of transmittal and general information about the government. It lists the principal officials and provides an organization chart indicating lines of authority and responsibility.

The second section contains a variety of financial statements. As governments make extensive use of funds, several different types of statements may be provid-ed on each fund. These statements by themselves can be confusing in that they do not provide an overall perspective on the finances of the government. For this rea-son, GASB and other professional accounting organizations prescribe the use of condensed statements that offer a comprehensive picture of a jurisdiction and omit some of the confusing detail.

One particularly troubling aspect of these statements is the use of *transfers* among funds. Monies can be moved from one fund to another without affecting the overall assets of a jurisdiction, but if transfers are not carefully noted, they may appear as expenditures in one fund and as new assets or receipts in another fund. These transfers need to be clearly identified not only to avoid confusion but also to provide important information about a government's operations. Transfers may indicate that enterprises are subsidizing general government operations, as when proceeds from a city airport are used in part to support a city's general fund. This type of transfer may be welcome relief to local taxpayers but may raise con-cern among holders of airport bonds. Good financial reports clearly label trans-fers—showing the source of receipts and the recipient of transfers—so that false impressions of asset creation or usage are avoided.

The third section of a financial report contains statistical data. Some tables present trend data assembled from earlier financial reports, such as general rev-enues by source over the most recent ten-year period. Other tables provide demo-graphic data and indicate the principal taxpayers in the jurisdiction.

Balance Sheets

Of the numerous types of financial statements, balance sheets are one of the most common. A balance sheet can be thought of as a snapshot of a government's finances at a point in time, such as at the end of a quarter or fiscal year.

A balance sheet is organized according to the accounting formula discussed earlier. Assets are first listed, showing cash on hand (bank deposits) and taxes receivable. For proprietary funds and fiduciary funds, fixed assets (buildings, land, and so forth) are also reported as assets. The balance sheet then indicates liabilities—namely, accounts that are payable and bonds outstanding—followed by the fund balance, showing items such as monies that are encumbered. **Table 11–1** is an example of a balance sheet from the State of Colorado. The table is just for the general fund, but the state supplies information about all other funds as well. Colorado's highway users tax fund is nearly as large as the general fund.

GASB's Statement No. 11 on measurement focus and the basis of accounting (MFBA, or "muff-bah") requires governments to recognize items as liabilities that were previously excluded. As a result of complying with this requirement, balance sheet bottom lines went from positive to negative for many governments. When numerous governments complained about the potential political and economic harm of such balance sheets, GASB allowed governments to use the term *fund equity* for the difference between revised assets and liabilities. The term *fund balance* can be used for calculating balance sheets in the format that preceded Statement No. 11.

While a compelling case is often made that governments should operate like private businesses, a balance sheet for the federal government modeled strictly on the basis of that used for private corporations would be incomplete in that important resources and needs of the nation as a whole would be excluded. As can be seen in **Figure 11–1**, the U.S. government's statement on financial condition consists of three components. It begins with the familiar listing of assets and liabilities. The second component consists of resources/receipts and responsibilities/ outlays. This section of the statement projects long-run receipts (based on the expected growth of gross domestic product) and outlays (notably, those for entitlement programs). The third component reports the assets that have been developed and national needs that require the expenditure of monies.

Rather than preparing one massive table for the government as a whole, OMB provides separate tables on the items shaded in **Figure 11–1**. **Table 11–2** is for the first shaded box, Assets and Liabilities. Net assets for 2005 are reported at $-5,694 billion or the equivalent of a debt of $19,163 per capita. In the *management's discussion* and analysis (MDA) portion of the budget, explanation is provided that the government pursues the nation's needs and is not exclusively concerned with its balance sheet. The explanation goes on to state that the government is not insolvent and has the ability through its taxing power to obtain the resources that it needs.

Table 11–1   General Fund Balance Sheet, State of Colorado, Fiscal Year Ended June 30, 2006 (in Thousands of Dollars)

	General Fund
Assets	
Cash and Pooled Cash	$ 793,790
Tax Receivables, net	914,327
Other Receivables, net	60,707
Due from Other Governments	257,082
Due from Other Funds	20,772
Due from Component Units	56
Inventories	7,514
Prepaids, Advances, and Deferred Charges	21,382
Restricted Cash and Pooled Cash	
Restricted Investments	
Restricted Receivables	
Investments	4,539
Other Long-Term Assets	91
Land and Nondepreciable Infrastructure	
Total Assets	$ 2,080,260
Liabilities	
Tax Refunds Payable	450,166
Accounts Payable and Accrued Liabilities	389,151
TABOR Refund Liability (Note 8B)	2,917
Due to Other Governments	72,832
Due to Other Funds	8,748
Deferred Revenue	140,008
Compensated Absences Payable	48
Claims and Judgments Payable	1,631
Notes, Bonds, COPs Payable	415,000
Other Current Liabilities	6,472
Deposits Held in Custody for Others	7
Total Liabilities	$ 1,486,980

continues

Table 11-1 **General Fund Balance Sheet, State of Colorado, Fiscal Year Ended June 30, 2006 (in Thousands of Dollars) (continued)**

	General Fund
Fund Balances	
Reserved for:	
Encumbrances	$ 12,233
Noncurrent Assets	91
Debt Service	
Statutory Purposes	251,704
Risk Management	32,851
Emergencies	
Funds Reported as Restricted	
Unreserved, Reported in:	
General Fund	296,401
Special Revenue Funds	
Capital Projects Funds	
Nonmajor Special Revenue Funds	
Nonmajor Permanent Funds	
Total Fund Balances	$ 593,280
Total Liabilities and Fund Balances	$2,080,260

Source: Reprinted from State Controller's Office (2006). *State of Colorado basic financial statements for year ended June 30, 2006 (unaudited)*. Denver, CO: State of Colorado, 8. Retrieved August 29, 2006, from http://www.colorado.gov/dpa/dfp/sco/BFS/FY%202005%20BFS. pdf.

Operating Statements

A second major type of financial statement is the operating statement, which shows the monies received and expended during a specified period of time. State and local governments refer to these as "statements of revenues, expenditures, and changes in fund balance." Revenues can be reported by source—sales tax and income tax. Expenditures can be reported by major objects, organizational units, or other means. **Table 11–3** is an operating statement for the State of Missouri. Data are provided for two years for comparison purposes. Tables such as this one and others shown in the chapter typically have notes that explain what is included and excluded in specific entries in the statements. These notes are essential components of the statements.

Figure 11–1 The Financial Condition of the Federal Government and the Nation

Assets/Resources		Liabilities/Responsibilities

Federal Assets
Financial Assets
  Monetary Assets
  Mortgages and Other Loans
  Other Financial Assets
    Less Expected Loan Losses
Physical Assets
  Fixed Reproducible Capital
  Defense
  Nondefense
Inventories
Non-Reproducible Capital
  Land
  Mineral Rights
	Federal Governmental Assets and Liabilities	**Federal Liabilities**
		Financial Liabilities
		  Debt Held by the Public
		  Guarantees and Insurance
		    Deposit Insurance
		    Pension Benefit Guarantees
		    Loan Guarantees
		    Other Insurance
		  Federal Retiree Pension and
		    Health Insurance Liabilities
		  Miscellaneous
		  Net Balance

Resources/Receipts Projected Receipts	Long-Run Federal Budget Projections	**Responsibilities/Outlays** Projected Outlays Surplus/Deficit
	Actuarial Deficiencies in Social Security and Medicare	Actuarial Deficiencies in Social Security and Medicare

National Assets/Resources
Federal Owned Physical Assets
State & Local Government
  Physical Assets, Federal
  Contribution
Privately Owned Physical
  Assets
Education Capital,
  Federal Contribution
R&D Capital,
  Federal Contribution
	National Wealth
	
	Social Indicators
		National Needs/Conditions
		Indicators of economic, social, educational, and environmental conditions

Source: Reprinted from U.S. Office of Management and Budget (2006). *Analytical perspectives, budget of the United States Government, fiscal year 2007.* Washington, DC: U.S. Government Printing Office, 177.

Table 11–2 United States Government Assets and Liabilities, Fiscal Year 2005 (in Billions of Dollars)*

	2005
Assets	
Financial Assets:	
Cash and Checking Deposits	$ 23
Other Monetary Assets	2
Mortgages	76
Other Loans	117
Less Expected Loan Losses	-41
Other Treasury Financial Assets	338
Subtotal	608
Nonfinancial Assets:	
Fixed Reproducible Capital	1,106
Defense	697
Nondefense	408
Inventories	272
Nonreproducible Capital	1,774
Land	729
Mineral Rights	1,045
Subtotal	3,152
Total Assets	$ 3,760
Liabilities	
Debt Held by the Public	$ 4,590
Insurance and Guarantee Liabilities:	
Deposit Insurance	1
Pension Benefit Guarantee	82
Loan Guarantees	48
Other Insurance	16
Subtotal	147
Pension and Post-Employment Health Liabilities:	
Civilian and Military Pensions	2,169
Retiree Health Insurance Benefits	1,125
Veterans Disability Compensaion	1,123
Subtotal	4,416
Other Liabilities	
Trade Payables and Miscellaneous	183
Benefits Due and Payable	117
Subtotal	301
Total Liabilities	$ 9,454
Net Assets (Assets Minus Liabilities)	$ -5,694
Addenda	
Net Assets Per Capita (in 2005 dollars)	$ -19,163
Ratio of GDP (in percent)	$ -45.2

* This table shows assets and liabilities for the government as a whole excluding the Federal Reserve System. Data are extrapolated in some cases.

Source: Reprinted from U.S. Office of Management and Budget (2006). *Analytical perspectives, budget of the United States Government, fiscal year 2007.* Washington, DC: U.S. Government Printing Office, 182.

Table 11–3 State of Missouri Receipts, Expenditures, and Transfers, December 2004 and 2005

	December 31, 2005	December 31, 2004
Receipts and Transfers In		
Receipts		
Taxes	$ 840,924,020	$ 785,034,774
Licenses, Fees, and Permits	54,347,982	52,373,140
Sales, Services, Leases, and Rentals	63,337,437	47,532,105
Bond Sale Proceeds		
Contributions and Intergovernmental	639,492,539	583,234,642
Interest, Penalties, and Unclaimed Properties	13,320,103	7,507,078
Refunds	14,544,666	15,744,243
Interagency Billings/Inventory	11,370,576	9,860,793
Miscellaneous Receipts	19,145,443	26,871,711
Total Receipts	1,656,482,766	1,528,158,486
Transfers In	635,335,825	454,664,214
Total Receipts and Transfers In	$ 2,291,818,591	$ 1,982,822,700
Expenditures and Transfers Out		
Expenditures		
Personal Service	231,196,822	232,334,007
Expense and Equipment	124,003,695	120,996,297
Capital Improvements	61,742,196	45,040,580
Program Specific	1,189,077,022	1,076,411,985
Refunds	41,208,464	38,380,909
Court Ordered Desegregation Payments		
Total Expenditures	1,647,228,199	1,513,163,778
Transfers Out	635,335,825	454,664,214
Total Expenditures and Transfers Out	$ 2,282,564,024	$ 1,987,827,992
Excess Receipts and Transfers In (Expenditures and Transfers Out)	$ 9,254,567	$ 14,994,708

Source: Reprinted from Division of Accounting (2006). *Comprehensive annual financial report, fiscal year ended June 30, 2005.* Columbia, MO: State of Missouri. Retrieved August 29, 2006, from http://oa.mo.gov/acct/pdffiles/finsum_allfunds123105.pdf#search=%22missouri%20receipts%2C%20expenditures%22.

The *pro forma operating statement* represents a particular type of statement. Although used routinely in the private sector, the pro forma is rarely used as such in the public sector. It commonly is prepared in the private sector when a company is considering a capital investment. The statement has three component forecasts: demand and prices, variable expenses, and fixed expenses. The pro forma is used to determine whether a potential capital project, such as the expansion of a hotel, would add to the company's bottom line.[84] Columbus, Ohio, has prepared versions of pro forma operating statements selectively for its internal service funds, such as for fleet and technology acquisitions.[85]

Cash Flows Statements

A third form of financial statement details cash flows. The purpose is to show how cash entering and leaving a fund affects an entity's operations. These statements cover cash and cash equivalents, such as short-term investments (U.S. Treasury bills; see Chapter 10). Controversy exists over how these statements should be organized and whether they should be extended from just covering enterprise funds to include basically all funds. **Table 11–4** is a cash flows statement for the Commonwealth of Pennsylvania, covering the enterprise and internal service funds. Not shown in the table is Pennsylvania's detailed presentation on specific enterprise funds, which include unemployment compensation, state workers' insurance, state lottery, tuition payment, and other funds.

Other Reports and Reporting Requirements

In addition to balance sheets, operating statements, and cash flow statements, governments issue other important financial reports (e.g., disclosures on securities). Governments provide statements when issuing bonds and other securities that are intended to help would-be purchasers understand what is being offered for sale in terms of the backing of the securities and what risks are involved. Some governments, such as Bellevue, Washington, and Des Moines, Iowa, have issued *annual performance reports*.[86] These reports are intended to cut through the morass of data characteristic of financial reports so as to provide useful information to policy makers and the citizenry. These reports commonly include findings from citizen surveys about satisfaction with government services and perceived needs.

GASB Statement No. 34, issued in 1999, has imposed dramatic changes on state and local government financial reporting, including the following:

- Statements must have *management's discussion and analysis* (MDA) indicating in an objective way the current financial situation in understandable English.
- Government-wide financial statements must be provided and must show the current and prior year.

Table 11–4	Commonwealth of Pennsylvania Combined Statement of Cash Flows, Proprietary Funds, Fiscal Year Ended June 30, 2005 (in Thousands of Dollars)

	Enterprise	Internal Service
Cash Flows from Operating Activities		
Receipts from employers	$ 2,218,125	$
Receipts from customers	3,971,251	89,466
Receipts from borrowers	(12,373)	
Payments to programs for the elderly	(467,026)	
Payments to prize winners	(1,346,401)	
Payments to participants	(61,797)	
Payments to claimants	(2,056,459)	
Payments to borrowers	(707)	
Payments to suppliers	(1,539,894)	(76,595)
Other receipts	90,044	57
Net Cash Provided by Operating Activities	794,763	12,928
Cash Flows from Non-Capital Financing Activities		
Net borrowings under advances from other funds	479	
Transfers in	16,068	
Transfers out	(357,300)	
Net Cash Used for Non-Capital Financing Activities	(340,753)	
Cash Flows from Capital and Related Financing Activities		
Acquisition and construction of capital assets	(4,874)	(8,630)
Loss on disposition of capital assets	64	963
Net Cash Used for Capital and Related Financing Activities	(4810)	(7,667)
Cash Flows from Investing Activities		
Purchase of investments	(20,720,888)	(291,857)
Sales and maturities of investments	20,393,553	281,176
Investment income	149,184	1,867
Change in securities lending obligations	(30,545)	(792)
Net Cash Provided by (Used for) Investing Activities	(208,696)	(9,606)
Net Increase (Decrease) in Cash	240,504	(4,345)
Cash at July 1, 2004	873,742	8,401
Cash at June 30, 2005	$ 1,114,246	$ 4,056

(continues)

Table 11–4   Commonwealth of Pennsylvania Combined Statement of Cash Flows, Proprietary Funds, Fiscal Year Ended June 30, 2005 (in Thousands of Dollars) (continued)

	Enterprise	Internal Service
Reconciliation of Operation Income (Loss) to Net Cash Provided by (Used for) Operating Activities		
Operating income (loss)	$824,038	$ 4,233
Depreciation and amortization	5,057	9,055
Provision for uncollectible accounts	20,295	
Non-operating revenues	(1,252)	(685)
Reclassification of investment income	(183,458)	
Changes in Assets and Liabilities		
Accounts receivable	(103,406)	222
Unemployment compensation assessments receivable	(30,741)	
Inventory	5,622	(185)
Due from other funds	(151)	2,287
Due from component units	460	289
Due from other governments	3,610	(66)
Due from political subdivisions	2,084	80
Other current assets	(5,520)	(46)
Accounts payable and accrued liabilities	(46,221)	(4,243)
Tuition benefits payable	124,226	
Due to other funds	1,138	9
Due to political subdivisions	(2,089)	
Due other governments	(1,024)	16
Unearned revenue	9,597	
Insurance loss liability	145,121	
Other liabilities	27,377	1,962
Total Adjustments	(29,275)	8,695
Net Cash Provided by Operating Activities	$ 794,763	$ 12,928
Increase (decrease) in fair value of investments during the fiscal year	$ 83,254	$ 243

Source: Reprinted from Comptroller Operations (2006). *Comprehensive annual financial report for the fiscal year ended June 30, 2005.* Harrisburg, PA: Commonwealth of Pennsylvania, 48.

- Full accrual accounting for all government activities is mandated.
- All capital assets must be shown and depreciated, including infrastructure assets.
- Analysis must be shown of significant changes in fund balance for the various governmental, proprietary, and fiduciary funds.
- Note disclosures are required to show important accounting policies. Disclosures must show changes in long-term liabilities and in capital assets.
- GASB No. 34 reconfigured the types of funds to be used. The new configuration was presented earlier when we discussed governmental, proprietary, and fiduciary funds.[87]

GASB has gone on to issue several other statements since No. 34 and has others in the pipeline.

- No. 37 is a major amendment clarifying earlier statements and dealing with among other matters the use of management's discussion-and-analysis portions of reporting.
- No. 39 specifies how jurisdictions are to go about determining whether an organization is a part of the government and needs to be included in financial statements.
- No. 41 requires reporting of budgeted and actual dollar figures so as to show whether the jurisdiction was accurate in revenue projections and kept its expenditures within budgeted figures.
- No. 42 requires that impairment of capital assets be reported.
- No. 44 specifies how governments are to report their economic conditions.
- No. 45 imposes the requirement that governments report their financial commitments in providing benefits in post-employment, exclusive of pensions. Health care benefits for retirees are important here.[88]
- No. 46, mentioned above, requires reporting how the use of net assets is restricted by enabling legislation.
- No. 47 necessitates reporting on termination benefits, such as employees retiring early in response to offers of special benefits.

As of 2006, GASB had the following exposure drafts in circulation:

- The important draft on Elements of Financial Statements, discussed above.
- Accounting and Financial Reporting for Derivatives.
- Reporting for Pollution Remediation Obligations, such as pollution from government operated landfills.[89]

Federal Reports

As noted above, the Office of Management and Budget issues annually a series of tables that together report on the financial condition of the government. **Figure 11–1** shows how the various components of reporting fit together.[90]

In addition, OMB works with federal agencies in their preparation of agency-specific reports. The Chief Financial Officers Act of 1990 and the Government Management Reform Act of 1994 required agencies to prepare a series of *auditable* financial statements by March 1, 1997, and every year thereafter.[91]

Circular A-136, which OMB updates annually, is the governing document in this process.[92] Federal entities are required to prepare annual *performance and accountability reports* (PARs). MDA is required at the outset of the report, discussing such matters as mission, organizational structure, and performance goals, objectives, and results. Next is the performance section, which provides program information. Then a financial section follows, covering balance sheets and several other types of financial statements. The circular also provides for quarterly and interim financial statements.

The 2005 PAR for the National Aeronautics and Space Administration is illustrative.[93] The management's discussion and analysis begins with addressing the question of why explore space? Out of this report of about 240 pages, about 100 are devoted to performance. The report carefully documents annual performance goals (APGs) that are designed to cover the past three years. However, these pages are largely narrative discussions complete with colored photographs but lacking in any data.

Government financial reporting has clearly become much more extensive in recent decades, but this expansion has come at a cost. Questions arise regarding whether accounting systems have become overloaded and whether some of the resources spent on financial reporting might be better spent on the delivery of services to citizens. Demands for the streamlining of financial reports are increasing. To date, Congress has authorized OMB to waive some reporting requirements imposed on federal agencies. The accounting profession itself has shown some awareness that reporting requirements can create overwhelming burdens.

Governmental Auditing

Auditing serves a variety of functions and consequently exists in many different forms, although regardless of its forms, it exists all over the world.[94] One distinction made is between *preaudits* and *postaudits*—that is, between reviewing transactions before and after they occur. The preaudit occurs before the government commits itself to a purchase and is used to verify, for example, that the police department has sufficient funds to purchase a piece of equipment and that the department is authorized to have that equipment. Not only the budget office but also an accounting department may be involved in preaudits. If personnel are to be hired, a personnel office may have some preaudit responsibility. Often at the state and local levels, independent comptrollers, controllers, or auditors general have preaudit responsibilities.

Postaudits generally involve more extensive procedures and often more participants. The following discussion concerns the function of postaudits in government budgeting and finance. This form of auditing has been defined as "a systematic collection of the sufficient, competent evidential matter needed to attest to the fairness of management's assertions in the financial statements, or to evaluate whether management has efficiently and effectively carried out its responsibilities."[95]

Audit Objectives and Organizational Responsibilities

Purposes. Auditing in the private sector is used largely to ensure that the financial statements issued by a firm fairly reflect its financial status, and this same concern exists in the public sector. Auditing provides some assurance to investors in both the private and public sectors that their investments are secure and are being well managed.

Another purpose of auditing is ensuring that funds are not subject to fraud, waste, and abuse, or subject to error in reporting. When financial reports cannot be verified by checking accounting records, the opportunities for dishonesty, waste, or just poor management of funds may exist. GAO has been highly critical of the Internal Revenue Service for being unable to reconcile its account records, but in 2002, the agency was lauded for its "extraordinary efforts" so that the financial statements for fiscal 2000 and 2001 received unqualified opinions. These efforts were necessary in part because the IRS, along with many other federal agencies, lacked automated accounting systems that produced timely and accurate financial information. Instead, agencies relied on cumbersome manual systems to produce information necessary to generate unqualified opinions (see discussion of types of opinions on p. 460).[96]

Auditing in government is used for *compliance* purposes as well. As has been noted, accounting systems track receipts and expenditures to ensure that they are handled in conformance with restrictions contained in revenue and appropriation bills. Auditing helps ensure that an agency does not spend funds on an activity that, while beneficial to society, simply has not been authorized. Compliance auditing can include ensuring that an agency has accomplished programmatically what it was instructed to do. Another form of compliance auditing involves grants and contracts. The federal government, for example, needs to check that only appropriate charges have been made by a state government in the case of a federally funded project or program, such as Medicaid, or by a university in the case of funded research. Similarly, government contracts are audited regularly for compliance with financial provisions of the contracts to ensure that billed costs are within the scope of the contracts and that adequate records exist to support the legitimacy of these billed costs.

Auditing Organizations. Nationally, several organizations influence the practice of governmental auditing. The American Institute of Certified Public Accountants (AICPA) issues *generally accepted auditing standards* (GAAS).[97] AICPA's Attestation Standards (SSAE No. 10) instructs auditors on what records to keep and for how long. GASB, in the process of identifying standards for accounting, inevitably becomes involved in auditing. GASB Statement No. 34, discussed earlier, created several issues about auditing in state and local governments.

The Public Company Accounting Oversight Board (PCAOB), the body that was created in response to the Enron scandal and others, issues auditing standards that the federal government applies to itself.[98]

FASAB, which regulates federal accounting, has a role in federal auditing. For example, its standard SFFAS No. 29 covers Auditing Heritage Assets and Stewardship Land.

The Government Accountability Office issues *Government Auditing Standards* (GAS, known as the "yellow book"). The standards are applied to federal agencies and may be applied to state and local governments that receive federal financial assistance.[99] GAO uses an Advisory Council on Government Auditing to assist in reviewing and revising the yellow book. The council's members come from all levels of government, the private sector, and academia. GAO and the President's Council on Integrity and Efficiency issue the *Financial Audit Manual*, which provides a methodology for federal auditing.[100]

The Office of Management and Budget is deeply involved in auditing, a relatively new role for the organization. The key documents are Circular A-123 on internal controls, Circular A-136 on reporting requirements, and Bulletin No. 06-03, Audit Requirements for Federal Financial Statements.[101] A-123 was revised in 2004 to bring federal standards in line with those for the private sector as required by SOX.[102] The circular began taking effect in fiscal 2006. The bulletin is designed to bring federal auditing in line with private sector auditing as prescribed by the PCAOB. For example, the bulletin defines *material weakness* as "a significant deficiency, or combination of significant deficiencies, that results in a more than remote likelihood that a material misstatement of the financial statements will not be prevented or detected." Circular A-123 provides that agencies must give annual assurances on the accuracy and effectiveness of their internal controls for financial reporting. Agencies eventually will be required to undergo audits of their internal controls.

The Treasury Department, as noted earlier, is working with agencies in a multiyear project to develop a government-wide accounting system. That necessarily brings the department into the auditing picture. The process is known as auditing "fund balance with treasury" (FBWT).

Auditing within a government often is performed by several organizations. Audits are conducted periodically by officers within an agency to provide information to management. These internal audits help maintain managerial control over operations. Other audits are conducted by external officers, who can be from a unit answerable to the legislative body (such as GAO being answerable to Congress), a unit headed by an independently elected officer, or an independent private corporation that has a contract to conduct an audit.

The federal government ratcheted up the auditing function during the 1970s and 1980s by creating *inspectors general* in major federal agencies. Appointed by the president with the advice and consent of the Senate, inspectors general are located within agencies but can only be removed by the president. According to the Inspector General Act of 1978 and the Chief Financial Officers Act of 1990, inspectors general are responsible for conducting audits and for investigating possible cases of fraud, waste, and abuse of government resources.[103] Most of the burden of federal auditing rests with these IGs rather than the GAO. The Government Accountability Office, formerly the General Accounting Office, has had its mission shift over recent decades from conducting financial audits to performance audits. GAO issued a report in 2005 underscoring that the vast majority of executive branch entities were required under law to have their financial statements audited.[104]

The Chief Financial Officers Act, by creating CFOs in major agencies, greatly increased the attention that agencies devote to sound accounting practices and to the auditing of accounts. Agencies have redesigned their central staff units, consolidating considerable powers under the CFOs. Other federal agencies not covered by the 1978 legislation also have inspectors general.

Executive Order 12993 provides a process for dealing with instances of possible wrongdoing by inspectors general and their deputies. The Federal Bureau of Investigation is authorized to investigate such matters, and the President's Council on Integrity and Efficiency (PCIE) reviews the FBI's findings. The PCIE consists of department inspectors general and selected central administrators, such as representatives from OMB and the Office of Personnel Management.

All levels of government use the Big 4 and other accounting firms to conduct or assist in auditing. Depending on the state, a local government may have a choice of paying either the state auditor or a private firm for audit services. State services may be less expensive, but private services may perform audits in a more timely fashion. When a private firm is to be used, a government will employ a bidding process to give competing firms an opportunity to indicate what services they can provide, in what time frame, and at what cost.

A practice often recommended for the public sector is the use of independent *audit committees*. These bodies typically consist of administrators, legislators, and financial experts from outside of the government. The committees can serve as useful interfaces between finance offices and auditors. The Sarbanes-Oxley Act required such committees of publicly traded corporations, but the committees are used only on a limited basis in the public sector.

Sometimes the number of organizations involved in auditing in a given situation can seem overwhelming. An agency may have two or more auditors. In the Department of Defense, for instance, audit functions are performed by the Defense Contract Audit Agency (which audits contractors), the inspector general, the comptroller, and the CFO. Large state and local agencies may have similar internal auditors, and all levels of government have their central auditors, such as the Auditor General of Illinois. As noted, private accounting firms may have responsibilities as well. Additional auditing occurs because of intergovernmental financial transactions. State government agencies, for example, may be audited by federal funding agencies and GAO, although this level of auditing has changed since passage of the Single Audit Act of 1984 (see below).

Types of Audits and Standards

Audit Types. As already noted, there are preaudits and postaudits, and internal and external audits. Another means of categorizing audits is by considering the purposes to be served. The definition of auditing provided earlier suggests that audits can be directed toward finance and performance.

Financial audits focus on whether financial statements prepared by a government accurately reflect financial transactions and the government's or agency's status. The standards of auditing provide a framework for conducting an audit.

Financial audits also review how financial matters are handled or whether suitable internal controls exist to protect resources. Auditors are concerned with the vulnerability of a financial management system to potential fraud. Are organizational lines of responsibility clearly established to ensure that whoever is in charge has the authority to protect the government's or agency's finances? Are policies and procedures established for maintaining records, and are those policies and procedures adhered to in practice? Are computer systems that handle financial transactions protected against potential fraud?

Identification of risks is the first step in eliminating problems. Auditors make risk assessments to determine which accounting activities or operations to audit, as only a sample of financial activities can be audited, given the auditors' limited resources. The risk assessment determines which activities are most vulnerable to fraud, waste, and abuse and therefore should be audited.

As of 2005, the GAO's list of high-risk situations included 25 items, with some items having been on the list for many years, such as defense weapons systems acquisition. Other items have been removed because of progress made, such as student financial aid programs and Forest Service financial management.[105]

The other major auditing function served is performance or program auditing, which deals with whether resources are being used efficiently and whether results or objectives are being achieved (see Chapter 6). In GAO's case, it has moved largely away from financial audits and conducts mostly performance audits. According to the Government Performance Project, several states are actively engaged in program audits. These include Florida's Office of Program Policy Analysis and Government Accountability (OPPAGA), Missouri's Auditor's Office and the Oversight Division of the Committee on Legislative Research, Pennsylvania's Department of the Auditor General and the Legislative Budget and Finance Committee, and Virginia's Joint Legislative Audit and Review Commission (JLARC).[106]

Any audit agency faces the difficult choice of deciding how much effort and resources should be devoted to the competing functions of financial and performance auditing. If major emphasis is given to performance auditing, fraud and other abuses may become more prevalent. Conversely, placing greater emphasis on financial auditing may keep government honest but do little to encourage agencies to fulfill their missions.

Auditing Standards. The federal Government Auditing Standards provide overall guidelines as well as standards for conducting fieldwork and preparing audit reports. Overall standards call for auditors to be independent of the agencies under review and to be fully trained in the auditing function. The Securities and Exchange Commission oversees accounting firms to ensure that private auditors are independent of the entities that they audit. Fieldwork is to be planned adequately in advance and sufficiently staffed to meet the requirements of the work plan. Auditors must keep accurate records of their fieldwork to answer questions that may arise at a later time.

Field auditing involves verifying sample transactions to ensure that transactions did occur as recorded. For example, an expense report of a trip taken by a city employee to a national conference, among numerous expense reports, might be selected for review. The auditor may (1) call the travel agent or airline to verify the ticket price, (2) check that the trip was an authorized budget expenditure, (3) interview the employee to verify unreceipted miscellaneous expenses, and (4) review other receipts and documents to determine the accuracy of the report. The purpose of this fieldwork is not particularly to find cases of fraud, waste, and abuse but rather to verify that the jurisdiction has procedures in place to protect against them.

The Single Audit Act. A concern of the federal government for many years has been the large volume of federal financial transfers to state and local governments and to nongovernmental organizations, and verification of whether these transfers are being suitably audited. The Office of Management and Budget has six circulars that detail how these organizations are to arrange their accounts:

- A-21, Cost Principles for Educational Institutions (2000)
- A-87, Cost Principles for State, Local and Indian Tribal Governments (1995)
- A-102, Grants and Cooperative Agreements with State and Local Governments (1994)
- A-110, Uniform Administrative Requirements for Grants and Agreements with Institutions of Higher Education, Hospitals, and Other Non-Profit Organizations (1993 with 1999 amendments)
- A-122, Cost Principles for Non-Profit Organizations (1998)
- A-133, Audits of States, Non-Profits, and Local Organizations (1997 with revisions and supplements in 2003 through 2006).

The Single Audit Act of 1984, as amended, requires recipients of federal assistance amounting to $500,000 or more in a fiscal year must undergo a single audit of their accounting systems and the way federal funds are handled.[107] Audits must be submitted within nine months of the audit period's close. The law applies to state and local governments as well as to nonprofit organizations. It has had the effect of requiring tens of thousands of audits annually. These audits, normally conducted by private firms, are intended to help ensure that recipients use federal resources in accordance with federal laws and regulations. The act is implemented through OMB Circular A-133. The Single Audit Act has undoubtedly improved the handling of federal financial assistance, but it may have had only a limited impact on overall financial management in these governments.

GAAS, GAS, and the Single Audit Act set standards for audit reporting. Of course, one of the chief concerns with regard to any report is that financial statements be in accordance with generally accepted accounting principles. Audit reports are expected to indicate deficiencies, such as inconsistent use of accounting procedures. Reports indicate whether internal controls exist to protect against fraud, waste, and abuse.

Four types of conclusions can be drawn by the auditing body:

1. The audit might be *unqualified*, providing an unqualified or "clean" opinion—that is, the accounting system meets all standards.
2. The report may be *qualified*, indicating there are problems but that the system generally meets standards. A qualified audit of a local or state government might be interpreted unfavorably by would-be investors in the government's bonds.
3. A *disclaimer audit* indicates that the accounting system is inadequate and that conducting an audit is impossible.
4. An audit can be *adverse* or *negative*, indicating that the financial statements fail to provide an accurate report of the entity's finances.

For fiscal year 2005, the federal government as a whole received a disclaimer of opinion from the Government Accountability Office's audit of consolidated financial statements.[108] This was the ninth year of such disclaimers, covering every year since GAO carried-out these audits. Treasury, which compiled the statements, was faulted for not being able to insure that the information it received from agencies was tied to verifiable accounting data. Treasury could not show that the data between 2004 and 2005 were comparable. In another report, GAO concluded that Treasury lacked any disciplined process for implementing the government-wide financial reporting system, putting at risk the project's future and whether it would eventually be able to resolve existing endemic auditing problems.[109] These findings were particularly disturbing considering that the government needed to address its fundamental budgetary imbalance.[110]

The audit news out of departments has been encouraging. For fiscal year 2005, unqualified opinions were issued for all federal departments, with the important exceptions of the Departments of Defense, Energy, and Homeland Security.[111] Defense had the highest number of material weaknesses at the end of the year, 33, but that was an improvement over the 46 with which it began the year. Homeland Security was second with 12 material weaknesses. One should keep in mind that the Defense budget is much larger and more complex than the budget for the Department of Homeland Security. As for state governments, the Government Performance Project for 2005 reported that 36 received unqualified opinions on their comprehensive annual financial reports (CAFRs) and many on all of their financial statements as well.[112]

While the overall auditing results for federal agencies are encouraging, one should keep in mind that there is much room for improvement. In mid-2006, the budget office on its management scorecard for financial management assigned a code of red, indicating serious flaws with financial criteria, for most departments: Agriculture, Defense, Energy, Health and Human Services, Homeland Security, Housing and Urban Development, Interior, Justice, Transportation, Treasury, and Veterans Affairs. OMB even gave itself a red score.[113]

Improper Payments. Erroneous or improper payments have been one of the biggest problems detected through auditing. Correcting these problems was identified as part of President George W. Bush's Management Agenda in 2001. According to the Management Agenda report, "Federal agencies recently identified $20.7 billion in erroneous benefit and assistance payments associated with just 13 programs. That amount represents more than the total annual expenditures of seven states."[114] The governing legislation at the federal level is the Improper Payments Information Act of 2002.[115] The law requires federal agencies to (1) conduct risk assessments, gauging the possibility and likelihood of making improper payments, (2) estimate the annual amount of such payments, and (3) report recouped funds. This information is to be included in the agencies' performance and accountability reports (PARs, see above).

The extent of the improper payments problem at the federal level is yet to be determined, since agencies have not been fully compliant with the law in assessing risks and estimating wrongful payments. GAO reviewed 18 PARs that discussed improper payments and found that the estimate was $38 billion in just one year. Perhaps alarming was that some major agencies, accounting for $228 billion of annual expenditures, had not provided estimates of their improper payments.[116]

The monumental disaster spawned by Hurricanes Katrina, Rita, and Wilma in 2005 was perhaps the cause of the greatest single set of improper payments in the history of the federal government. The Government Accountability Office estimated the problem at between $600 million and $1.4 billion.[117] The Federal Emergency Management Agency has been rightfully criticized for failing to prepare adequately for such a catastrophic disaster, but it must be recognized that the pressures on FEMA to move quickly were immense, namely to get aid to hundreds of thousands of displaced people. Between August 2005 when Katrina struck and February 2006, FEMA made about 2.6 million payments. Inevitably, some of those payments had to have been made in response to fraudulent claims. One problem was that some people had fled and lacked proper identification to be able to prove that they were from the afflicted areas in the Gulf Coast, but FEMA proceeded to make payments even when the claims were patently fraudulent, such as people listing as their home address post office boxes and even cemeteries. GAO tested FEMA's vulnerability to fraud by using an undercover agent to apply for assistance and using a vacant lot as an address. Both FEMA's inspector and an inspector from the Small Business Administration reported that the property had not been a residence, but FEMA proceeded to pay $6,000 for this patently fraudulent claim.

Of course, the federal government is not the only government subject to wrongful spending. A county treasurer in Iowa was accused, for example, of making hundreds of dollars of phone calls at government expense to a lonely-hearts telephone service.[118] State auditors check on both state spending and state grants to local governments. GAO has criticized states for not having adequate procedures for auditing against improper payments that use federal monies, such as food stamps and unemployment insurance.[119] The federal government cannot get a handle on the extent of overpayment of federal money if such overpayments go undetected in state programs administering federal money. When state auditors find improper payment errors in the administration of state money by local governments, the grant payments can be halted. As an example, this happened to a Florida opportunity council that provided services to the poor and had poorly organized accounting records so that the auditor could issue no opinion.[120] In extreme cases, when local governments' finances are in disarray, states have the authority to take over the jurisdictions on a temporary basis.

Follow-up after an audit is essential to ensure that weaknesses are corrected. Without such follow-up, auditing is an empty exercise. OMB Circular A-50, Audit Followup, sets guidelines for checks to be made after audits have been completed at the federal level.

Summary

Governmental accounting is characterized by procedures intended to prevent fraud and to guarantee agency conformance with legal requirements. Information from accounting systems is used in decision making and can help improve the efficiency and effectiveness of services. The Governmental Accounting Standards Board was established to help improve state and local government accounting systems, and the Federal Accounting Standards Advisory Board has similar responsibilities at the federal level. Generally accepted accounting principles allow the use of several different types of funds, with the general fund usually the most important for any government.

Accounting systems are structured by having a general ledger and subsidiary ledgers. They follow a relatively simple formula: assets equal the total of liabilities and fund balance. Within the ledgers, expenditures are accounted for in a variety of ways, including major and minor objects of expenditures.

Bases of accounting include cash, encumbrance, accrual, and cost. Some jurisdictions use project-based accounting and cost finding instead of the more comprehensive cost accounting methods. Regardless of the basis for accounting, reports summarizing transactions are prepared at specified intervals. Three of the most common types of reports are balance sheets, operating statements, and cash flows statements.

Auditing attempts to determine whether financial statements accurately reflect the status of accounts and/or whether an organization is operating efficiently and effectively. It is used for compliance purposes—namely, to ensure that financial transactions are in accordance with revenue and appropriation legislation. Generally accepted auditing standards constitute the guidelines for auditing in the public sector.

The field of public sector accounting, reporting, and auditing is undergoing rapid change. The stimuli for reform generally center around patent cases of fraud and waste, some on a small scale and others of huge magnitude.

Notes

1. Brooks, M. (1968). *The Producers.* MGM Studios.

2. Norvelle, J. W. (1997). *Introduction to fund accounting,* 5th ed. Eaton Rapids, MI: RIA Professional Publishing; see Harris, J. (2005). The discourse of governmental accounting and auditing. *Public Budgeting & Finance, 25, Supplement 1, Winter,* 154–179.

3. Harkin, T., U.S. Senator (Dem., Iowa) (1997). As quoted in Report faults accounting at Defense Department. *Washington Post, No. 159, May 13,* A4.

4. U.S. General Accounting Office (2000). *Executive guide: creating value through world-class financial management.* Washington, DC: U.S. Government Printing Office.

5. Mosher, F. C. (1984). *A tale of two agencies.* Baton Rouge, LA: Louisiana State University Press.

6. Federal Managers' Financial Integrity Act (1982). P.L. 97-255; Accounting and Auditing Act (1950). Ch. 946, Title I.

7. Chief Financial Officers Act (1990). P.L. 101-576.

8. U.S. Chief Financial Officers Council (2006). *Website.* Retrieved August 26, 2006, from http://www.cfoc.gov.

9. U.S. Office of Management and Budget (2006). *Federal financial management report, 2006.* Retrieved August 26, 2006, from http://www.whitehouse.gov/omb/financial/2006_report.pdf#search=%22federal%20financial%20management%20plan%2C%202006%22.

10. Federal Accounting Standards Advisory Board (2006). *Website.* Retrieved August 26, 2006, from http://www.fasab.gov.

11. Clinger-Cohen Act (Federal Acquisition Reform Act) (1996). P.L. 104-106.

12. Palmer, K. (2005). Chief financial officers highlight their job challenges. *Govexec.com.* Retrieved August 26, 2006, from http://www.govexec.com/dailyfed/0205/020805kl.htm.

13. Mitchell, M., Deputy Associate Administrator, U.S. General Services Administration (2006). *GSA's role in implementing FMLoB government-wide.* Retrieved August 26, 2006, from http://www.gsa.gov/Portal/gsa/ep/contentView.do?contentType=GSA_BASIC&contentedId=212628noc=T; Mosquera, M. (2006). Financial LOB moves to standardize rules. *GCN.* Retrieved August 26, 2006, from http://www.gcn.com/print/25_25/41730-1.html.

14. U.S. Office of Management and Budget (2006). *Competition framework for financial management lines of business migrations.* Retrieved August 26, 2006 from www.whitehouse.gov/omb/financial/ffs/competition_framework_fmlob.pdf.

15. Gauthier, S. J. (2005). *2005 governmental accounting, auditing, and financial reporting.* Chicago, IL: Government Finance Officers Association.

16. Government Finance Officers Association (2006). *Using the comprehensive annual financial report to meet SEC requirements for periodic disclosure.* Retrieved August 26, 2006, from http://www.gfoa.org/services/rp/documents/cafrfordisclosure.pdf; see

Christensen, P. (2006). Celebrating 100 years of GFOA. *Government Finance Review, 21, April*, 24–30.

17. Governmental Accounting Standards Board (2006). *Website.* Retrieved August 26, 2006, from http://www.gasb.org.

18. Financial Accounting Standards Board (2006). *Website.* Retrieved August 26, 2006, from http://www.fasb.org.

19. Deloitte Touche Tohmatsu Global (2006). *Website.* Retrieved November 7, 2006, from http://www.deloitte.com/dtt/home/0%2C1044%2Csid%25253D2000%2C00.html; Ernst & Young (2006). *Website.* Retrieved August 26, 2006 from www.ey.com; KPMG (2006). *Website.* Retrieved August 26, 2006, from http://www.kpmg.com; Pricewater-houseCoopers (2006). *Website.* Retrieved August 26, 2006, from http://www.pwcglobal.com.

20. Andersen guilty in Enron case (2002). *BBC News, June 15.* Retrieved August 26, 2006, from http://news.bbc.co.uk/2/hi/business/2047122.stm; Brown, R. E. (2005). Enron/Andersen: crisis in U.S. accounting and lessons for government. *Public Budgeting & Finance, 25, Fall*, 20–32.

21. Accenture (2006). *Website.* Retrieved August 26, 2006, from http://www.accenture.com.

22. Weil, R. L. (2002). Fundamental causes of the accounting debacle at Enron: show me where it says I can't (testimony before U.S. House Committee on Energy and Commerce). Retrieved August 26, 2006, from http://gsb.uchicago.edu/pdf/weil_testimony.pdf#search=%22%22show%20me%20where%2C%22%20weil%22.

23. Benson, S. (2006). Advisers drain the Snowy dry. *Daily Telegraph, August 26.* Retrieved August 27, 2006, from http://www.news.com.au/dailytelegraph/story/0,22049,20249129-5006009,00.html.

24. Report: WorldCom's problems worsen (2002). *Associated Press, August 8.* Retrieved August 9, 2002, from http://news/findlaw.com/ap_stories/f/1310/8.../2002080815401_04.htm.

25. Hilzenrath, D. S. & Johnson, C. (2006). Fannie Mae avoids criminal charges over accounting. *Washingtonpost.com, August 25.* Retrieved August 26, 2005, from http://www.washingtonpost.com/wp-dyn/content/article/2006/08/24/AR2006082400639.html.

26. Governmental Accounting Standards Board (2006). *Codification of governmental accounting and financial reporting standards.* Norwalk, CT: GASB.

27. American Institute of Certified Public Accountants (2006). *Website.* Retrieved August 27, 2006, from http://www.aicpa.org.

28. American Institute of Certified Public Accountants (2000). *Federal GAAP hierarchy, SAS No. 91.* Retrieved August 27, 2006, from http://www.cpa2biz.com/CS2000/Products/CPA2BIZ/Publications/Sub+2/Federal+GAAP+Hierarchy+-+SAS+No.+91.htm?cs_catalog=CPA2Biz&pagetype=product&cs_category=statements%5Fon%5Fauditing%5Fstandards.

29. Smith, J. L. (2005). Lapeer official says "sorry." *Flint Journal, December 2*, A1, A2.

30. Abuja, F. M. (2006). How public servants loot treasury—accountant general. *AllAfrica.com, August 25*. Retrieved August 27, 2006, from http://allafrica.com/stories/printable/200608250483.html.

31. International Monetary Fund (2001). *Code of good practices on fiscal transparency.* Retrieved November 7, 2006, from http://www.imf.org/external/np/fad/trans/code.htm.

32. United Way International (2006). *Global standards for United Way organizations.* Alexandria, VA: United Way International.

33. Odyek, J. Accounting chiefs warned. *New Vision, August 21*. Retrieved August 27, 2006, from http://www.newvision.co.ug/PA8/13/516501.

34. Gettler, L. (2006). Push to get government accounting into open. *The Age, August 3*. Retrieved August 26, 2006, from http://222.theage.com.au/news/business/push-to-getgovernment-accounting-into-open/2006/08/02/1154198206453.html.

35. U.S. Office of Management and Budget (2004). *Management's responsibility for internal control, Circular A-123.* Retrieved August 27, 2006, from http://www.whitehouse.gov/omb/circulars/a123/a123_rev.html.

36. Norvelle (1997). *Introduction to fund accounting,* 16–18.

37. U.S. General Accounting Office (1995). *Government corporations: profiles of recent proposals.* Washington, DC: U.S. Government Printing Office; Bunch, B. S. (2000). Changes in usage of enterprise funds by large cities. *Public Budgeting & Finance, 20, Summer,* 15–29.

38. McCoskey, M. G. et al. (2003). Trust, trusts, and accountability: the role of states in college saving plans. *Public Budgeting & Finance, 23, Fall,* 49–63; College Savings Plan Network (2006). *Website.* Retrieved August 27, 2006, from http://www.collegesavings.org.

39. Financial Management Service, U.S. Department of Treasury (2006). *USSGL: standard general ledger.* Retrieved August 27, 2006, from http://www.fms.treas.gov/ussgl/index.html.

40. U.S. Office of Management and Budget (1993). *Financial management systems, Circular A-127.* Retrieved August 27, 2006, from http://www.whitehouse.gov/omb/circulars/a127/a127.html.

41. Governmental Accounting Standards Board (2006). *Elements of financial statements, exposure draft.* Norwalk, CT: GASB, 2.

42. Governmental Accounting Standards Board (2006). *Elements of financial statements,* v.

43. Governmental Accounting Standards Board (2006). *Invitation to comment: fund balance reporting and governmental fund type definitions.* Retrieved November 7, 2006, from http://www.gasb.org/exp/ITC_Fund_Balance_Reporting.pdf.

44. Norvelle (1997). *Introduction to fund accounting,* 43.

45. Governmental Accounting Standards Board (2005). *Sales and pledges of receivables and future revenues, exposure draft.* Retrieved August 27, 2006, from http://www.gasb. org/project_pages/12-05_sales&pledges_article.pdf.

46. U.S. Office of Management and Budget (2006). *Historical tables, budget of the United States government, fiscal year 2007, 55.* Retrieved August 27, 2006, from http://www. whitehouse.gov/omb/budget/fy2007/pdf/hist.pdf.

47. Roberts, A. (1999). Accounting for results, 1997: government-wide performance plan, fiscal year 1999. *Journal of Policy Analysis and Management, 18,* 187–191; Cunningham, G. M. & Harris, J. (2005). Toward a theory of performance reporting to achieve public sector accountability: a field study. *Public Budgeting & Finance, 25, Summer,* 15–42; Berman, B. J. (2006). *Listening to the public: adding the voices of the people to government performance measurement and reporting.* New York: Fund for the City of New York.

48. Governmental Accounting Standards Board (1994). *Service efforts and accomplishments reporting, Concept Statement No. 2.* Retrieved August 27, 2006, from http://www.gasb. org/st/index.html; see Governmental Accounting Standards Board (2006). *Performance measurement for government (website).* Retrieved August 27, 2006, from http://www.seagov.org/index.shtml.

49. Governmental Accounting and Standards Board (2005). *Government service efforts and accomplishments performance reports: a guide to understanding.* Retrieved August 27, 2006, from http://www.seagov.org/sea_gasb_project/sea_guide_summary.pdf.

50. Government Performance and Results Act (1990). P.L. 101-576.

51. Musso, D. (2006). Social Security: reliance on cash flow accounting and projections disguises an inherent upside cash flow bias. *Public Budgeting & Finance, 26, Spring,* 143–156.

52. Van der Hoek, M. P. (2005). From cash to accrual budgeting and accounting in the public sector: the Dutch experience. *Public Budgeting & Finance, 25, Spring,* 32–45; Caridad, M. (2006). Accrual budgeting: accounting treatment of key public sector items and implications for fiscal policy. *Public Budgeting & Finance, 26, Summer,* 45–65.

53. U.S. General Accounting Office (2000). *Accrual budgeting: experience of other nations and implications for the United States.* Washington, DC: U.S. Government Printing Office.

54. Governmental Accounting Standards Board (1990). *Measurement focus and basis of accounting: governmental fund operating statements, Statement No. 11.* Retrieved August 27, 2006, from http://www.gasb.org/st/index.html.

55. Kinney, M. R. et al. (2006). *Cost accounting,* 6th ed. Mason, Ohio: Thomson/South-Western; Brock, H. R. et al. (2007). *Cost accounting: principles and applications,* 7th ed. Boston, MA: McGraw-Hill.

56. Rivenbark, W. C. (2005). A historical overview of cost accounting in local government. *State and Local Government Review, 37,* 217–227.

57. Activity-based costing and activity-based management symposium (1999). *Public Budgeting & Finance, 19, Summer,* 3–58; Kaplan, R. S. & Andersen, S. R. (2004). Time-driven activity-based costing. *Harvard Business Review, 82,* 131–140; Rozlocki, N. (2006). *Introduction to activity based costing (ABC): internet ABC online presentation.* Retrieved August 27, 2006, from http://www.pitt.edu/~roztocki/abc/abctutor/.

58. U.S. Office of Management and Budget (1993). *Value engineering, Circular A-131.* Retrieved August 27, 2006, from http://www.whitehouse.gov/omb/circulars/a131/a131.html.

59. Federal Accounting Standards Advisory Board (1995). *Accounting for property, plant, and equipment, Statement of Federal Financial Accounting Standards 6.* Retrieved August 27, 2006, from http://www.fasab.gov/pdffiles/vol1v4.pdf.

60. Federal Accounting Standards Advisory Board (2005). *Heritage assets and stewardship land, Statement of Federal Financial Accounting Standards 29.* Retrieved August 27, 2006, from http://www.fasab.gov/pdffiles/sffas_29.pdf.

61. U.S. Government Accountability Office (2005). *Managerial cost accounting practices: leadership and internal controls are key to successful implementation.* Washington, DC: GAO; U.S. Government Accountability Office (2005). *Managerial cost accounting practices: Departments of Education, Transportation, and the Treasury.* Washington, DC: GAO; U.S. Government Accountability Office (2006). *Managerial cost accounting practices: Department of Health and Human Services and Social Security Administration.* Washington, DC: GAO.

62. U.S. Office of Management and Budget (2006). *Cost Accounting Standards Board.* Retrieved August 27, 2006, from http://www.whitehouse.gov/omb/procurement/casb.html.

63. U.S. Office of Management and Budget (2004). *Cost principles for state, local and Indian tribal governments, Circular No. 87.* Retrieved August 27, 2006, from http://www.whitehouse.gov/omb/circulars/a087/a87_2004.html.

64. Federal Credit Reform Act (1990). P.L. 101-508, Title XIII.

65. U.S. General Accounting Office (1993). *Federal credit programs: agencies had serious problems meeting credit reform accounting requirements.* Washington, DC: U.S. Government Printing Office.

66. Collard, D. (2004). Generational accounting and generational transfers. *Ageing Horizons, no. 1.* Retrieved August 27, 2006, from http://www.ageing.ox.ac.uk/ageinghorizons/thematic%20issues/pension%20reform%20and%20social%20justice/papers%20pensions/pdf%20files/GENERATIONAL%20ACCOUNTS%20David%20Collard.pdf#search=%22generational%20accounting%22; Eschker, E. (2005). Generational accounting and the saving rate decline, 1960–2000. *Public Budgeting & Finance, 25, Spring,* 46–65.

67. Sarbanes-Oxley Act (Public Company Accounting Reform and Investor Protection Act) (2002). P.L. 107-204; McCarthy, E. (2004). *Tips for the Sarbanes-Oxley learning curve.* Retrieved August 29, 2006, from http://www.aicpa.org/PUBS/jofa/jun2004/mccarthy.htm; *Sarbanes-Oxley 101: information guide to the Sarbanes-Oxley Act of 2002.* Retrieved August 29, 2006, from http://www.sarbanes-oxley-101.com.

68. Federal Financial Management Improvement Act (1996). P.L. 104–208.

69. U.S. Chief Financial Officers Council (2005). *Implementation guide for OMB Circular A-123, management's responsibility for internal control; appendix A, internal control over*

financial reporting. Retrieved August 29, 2006, from http://www.cfoc.gov/documents/Implementation_Guide_for_OMB_Circular_A-123.pdf; U.S. Office of Management and Budget (2005). *OMB circular A-123, appendix C, requirements for effective measurement and remediation of improper payments.* Retrieved August 29, 2006, from http://www.whitehouse.gov/omb/memoranda/fy2006/m06-23.pdf.

70. McGladrey & Pullen, CPAs (2006). *The Sarbanes-Oxley Act may impact state and local governments.* Retrieved August 29, 2006, from http://www.mcgladrey.com/Resource_Center/Audit/Articles/SOX_SLG.pdf#search=%22sarbanes%2C%20government%accounting%22; Gentry, J. (2006). *Sarbanes-Oxley impact extends far beyond public companies.* Retrieved August 29, 2006, from http://www.business journalism.org/pages/biz/2006/06/sarbanesoxley_impact_extends_f/.

71. Labaton, S. (2006). Businesses seek protection on legal front. *New York Times, October 29.* Retrieved October 29, 2006, from http://www.nytimes.com/2006/10/29/business/29corporate.html?hp&ex=1162184400&en=9358599aad440557&ei=5094&partner=homepage.

72. Census Bureau, U.S. Department of Commerce (2004). *Employee retirement systems of state and local governments: 2002.* Washington, DC: U.S. Government Printing Office.

73. Employee Retirement Income Security Act (1974). P.L. 93-406.

74. Small Business Job Protection Act (1996). P.L. 104-188.

75. Pension Protection Act (2006). P.L. 109-280; BNA Tax Management (2006). *Pension Protection Act of 2006.* Retrieved August 29, 2006, from http://hwww.bnatax.com/tm/pension_protectionact.htm; CCH (2006). *Pension Protection Act of 2006.* Retrieved August 29, 2006, from http://tax.cchgroup.com/Legislation/2006-Pension.pdf.

76. Freed, J. (2006). Bill may speed traditional pensions' end. *BusinessWeek.com.* Retrieved August 29, 2006, from http://www.businessweek.com/ap/financialnews/D8J9RNU00.htm?chan=search.

77. Ritter, J. (2004). San Diego now "Enron by the sea." *USA Today, October 24.* Retrieved August 29, 2006, from http://www.usatoday.com/news/nation/2004-10-24-sandiego-_x.htm.

78. Audit Committee, City of San Diego (2006). *Kroll Report.* Retrieved August 30, 2006, from http://www.sandiego.gov/mayor/news/breakingnews.shtml#report.

79. Walsh, M. W. & Cooper, M. (2006). City gets a sobering look at possible pension trouble. *New York Times, August 20.* Retrieved August 29, 2006, from http://select.nytimes.com/gst/abstract.html?res=F10D13F63E5A0C738EDDA10894DE404482.

80. Fabry, S. (2005). State, local pension plans are "a ticking time bomb set to explode." *Budget and Tax News.* Retrieved August 29, 2006, from http://www.heartland.org/Article.cfm?artId=17833; Walsh, M.W. (2006). Costly promises: public pension plans face billions in shortages. *New York Times, August 8.* Retrieved August 29, 2006, from http://select.nytimes.com/gst/abstract.html? res=F70713F6355B0C7B8CDDA10894DE404482.

81. U.S. Government Accountability Office (2006). *Financial management systems: additional efforts needed to address key causes of modernization failures.* Washington, DC: GAO.

82. Government Finance Officers Association (2006). *Popular annual financial reporting.* Retrieved August 29, 2006, from http://www.gfoa.org/services/awards.shtml#PAFR.

83. Governmental Accounting Standards Board (2006). *Codification of governmental accounting and financial reporting standards.*

84. Andrew, W. P. et al. (2007). *Financial management for the hospitality industry.* Upper Saddle River, NJ: Pearson Prentice Hall.

85. Department of Finance and Management, City of Columbus, Ohio (2005). *2006 City of Columbus budget, internal service funds.* Retrieved August 29, 2006, from http://finance.columbus.gov/Asset/iu_files/2006_Budget/29_Internal_Service_Funds.pdf#search=%22%22pro%20forma%20operating%20statement%22%2C%20government%22.

86. Walter, J. (2006). The fine art of reporting results. *Governing, August.* Retrieved August 29, 2006, from http://www.governing.com/manage/pm/perf0806.htm.

87. Governmental Accounting Standards Board (1999). *Basic financial statements—and management's discussion and analysis—for state and local governments, Statement No. 34.* Retrieved August 29, 2006, from http://www.gasb.org/st/index.html; Kravchuk, R. S. & Voorhees, W. R. (Eds.) (2001). Governmental Accounting Standards Board (GASB) Statement No. 34 symposium. *Public Budgeting & Finance, 21, Fall,* 1–87.

88. Wisniewski, S. C. (2005). Potential state government practices impact of the new GASB accounting standard for retiree health benefits. *Public Budgeting & Finance, 25, Spring,* 104–118; Voorhees, W. R. (2005). Counting retirement expenditures before they hatch: GASB and the new reporting requirements for other postemployment benefits. *Public Budgeting & Finance, 25, Winter,* 59–71.

89. Governmental Accounting Standards Board (2006). *Exposure documents.* Retrieved August 29, 2006, from http://www.gasb.org/exp/.

90. Government Accountability Office (2005). *Understanding the primary components of the annual financial report of the United States Government.* Washington, DC: GAO.

91. Government Management Reform Act (1994). P.L. 103-356.

92. U.S. Office of Management and Budget (2006). *Financial reporting requirements, Circular A-136.* Retrieved August 29, 2006, from www.whitehouse.gov/omb/circular/a136/a136_revised_2006.pdf.

93. U.S. National Aeronautics and Space Administration (2006). *Fiscal year 2005 performance and accountability report.* Retrieved August 31, 2006, from http://www.nasa.gov/pdf/138910main_FY_2005_PAR.pdf.

94. Carlos, S. (2006). Banking on accountability? Strengthening budget oversight and public sector auditing in emerging economies. *Public Budgeting & Finance, 26, Summer,* 66–100.

95. Government Finance Officers Association (1994). *Governmental accounting, auditing, and financial reporting.* Chicago, IL: Government Finance Officers Association, 314.

96. U.S. General Accounting Office (2002). *Financial audit: IRS's fiscal years 2001 and 2000 financial statements.* Washington, DC: U.S. Government Printing Office.

97. American Institute of Certified Public Accountants (2006). *Generally accepted auditing standards: SAS No. 95.* New York, NY: AICPA; Dauber, N. et al. (2005). *2006 auditing standards: including the standards of the PCAOB.* Mason, Ohio: Thomson.

98. Public Company Accounting Oversight Board (2006). *Website.* Retrieved August 30, 2006, from http://www.pcaobus.org.

99. U.S. General Accounting Office (2003). *Government auditing standards.* Washington, DC: U.S. Government Printing Office; U.S. Government Accountability Office (2006). *Government auditing standards: 2006.* Retrieved August 30, 2006, from http://www.gao.gov/govaud/d06729g.pdf; Kearney, E. F. et al. (2005). *Federal government auditing: laws, regulations, standards, practices, & Sarbanes-Oxley.* Hoboken, NJ: John Wiley.

100. U.S. General Accounting Office and President's Council on Integrity and Efficiency (2004). *Financial audit manual: checklist for federal accounting, reporting, and disclosures.* Washington, DC: U.S. Government Printing Office.

101. U.S. Office of Management and Budget (2006). *Audit Requirements for Federal Financial Statements, Bulletin No. 06-03.* Retrieved August 30, 2006, from http://www.whitehouse.gov/omb/bulletins/fy2006/b06-03.pdf.; U.S. Chief Financial Officer's Council (2005). *Implementation guide for OMB Circular A-123, management's responsibility for internal control, Appendix A, internal control over financial reporting.* Washington, DC: CFOC.

102. Tierney, C. E. et al. (2006). *OMB Circular A-123 and Sarbanes-Oxley: management's responsibility for internal control in federal agencies.* Hoboken, NJ: Wiley.

103. Inspector General Act (1978). P.L. 95-452.

104. U.S. Government Accountability Office (2005). *Financial audits: the vast majority of executive branch entities included in the federal budget are statutorily required to have their financial statements audited.* Washington, DC: GAO.

105. U.S. Government Accountability Office (2005). *High risk series: an update.* Washington, DC: GAO.

106. Government Performance Project (2006). *Grading the states, 2005.* Retrieved November 7, 2006, from http://results.gpponline.org/States.aspx.

107. Single Audit Act (1984). P.L. 98-502; Single Audit Act Amendments (1996). P.L. 104-156.

108. U.S. Government Accountability Office (2006). *Financial audit: significant internal control weaknesses remain in preparing the consolidated financial statements of the U.S. Government.* Washington, DC: GAO.

109. U.S. Government Accountability Office (2006). *Financial management systems: lack of disciplined process puts effective implementation of Treasury's government-wide financial report system at risk.* Washington, DC: GAO.

110. U.S. Government Accountability Office (2006). *Fiscal year 2005 U.S. Government financial statements: sustained improvements in federal financial management is crucial to addressing our nation's financial condition and long-term fiscal imbalance.* Washington, DC: GAO.

111. U.S. Office of Management and Budget (2006). *Federal financial management report, 2006.*

112. Government Performance Project (2006). *Grading the states, 2005.* Retrieved November 7, 2006, from http://results.gpponline.org/Search.aspx?keyword=unqualified%20opinion.

113. U.S. Office of Management and Budget (2006). *Executive branch management scorecard, June 30.* Retrieved August 30, 2006, from http://www.whitehouse.gov/results/agenda/scorecard.html.

114. U.S. Office of Management and Budget (2001). *President's management agenda,* 19.

115. Improper Payments Information Act (2002). P.L.107-300.

116. U.S. Government Accountability Office (2006). *Financial management: challenges continue in meeting requirements of the Improper Payments Information Act.* Washington, DC: GAO.

117. U.S. Government Accountability Office (2006). *Hurricanes Katrina and Rita disaster relief: improper and potentially fraudulent individual assistance payments estimated to be between $600 million and $1.4 billion.* Washington, DC: GAO.

118. Kompas, K. (2001). Treasurer faces charges for making calls at work. *Des Moines Register, March 16.*

119. U.S. Government Accountability Office (2006). *Improper payments: federal and state coordination needed to report national improper payment estimates on federal programs.* Washington, DC: GAO.

120. Rousos, R. (2006). Agency under fire: a Q and A. *The Ledger, August 25.* Retrieved August 30, 2006, from http://lledit.us.publicus.com/apps/pbcs.dll/article?AID=/20060825/NEWS/608250370/1134.

Chapter 12

CAPITAL ASSETS: PLANNING AND BUDGETING, ANALYSIS, AND MANAGEMENT

This chapter examines systems for planning and budgeting for capital projects, analysis for capital project selection, and managing the government's portfolio of assets. Every year, governments spend resources on the construction of facilities or the purchase of equipment that will continue in use for many years beyond the year of purchase. The construction of a new water treatment plant will serve a community for decades, although the actual construction itself may take less than two years. By constructing the water treatment plant, the community has acquired a capital facility. It has purchased an asset. This chapter focuses on the decision to build that facility or purchase an asset and related systems for managing these long-lived facilities or equipment once they are in place. Decisions on how to finance those asset purchases, often through issuing long-term debt in the form of municipal bonds, is the focus of Chapter 13.

In this chapter, we examine both the rationale for public sector capital budgeting and the general form of capital plans and budgets. We see that it differs for the U.S. federal government, and most national governments, when compared with state and local governments. Further, since the cost of capital projects is large relative to a state or local government's operating budget, capital projects are subject to more detailed analysis, often with formal criteria for determining whether the benefits of the project are worth the cost of the project. The chapter concludes with a section on asset management. This final section focuses on how governments ensure that the capital assets they own (that they have built or purchased) are managed effectively and are maintained so that they achieve the long life cycle for which they were designed.

▮ Capital Planning and Budgeting

In this section we define capital and capital investments, discuss the reasons for considering capital spending separately from operating budgets, describe the general form for a capital investment planning and budgeting process, and discuss the issues involved in separating capital from operating budgets. We focus mainly on state and local governments. Although there is much discussion in annual federal budgets of investments and capital expenditures, the federal government has considered several times adopting a formal capital budget, but each time the arguments against a federal capital budget have outweighed the arguments for it.

Capital Investments Versus Current Expenditures

Capital Investments. The purchase or construction of a long-lasting physical asset or facility is a capital investment. Businesses invest to have new capacity and to replace existing capacity with more efficient methods of production. These investments are intended to increase the businesses' output in the future. Many public sector physical facilities also represent investment in the ability to provide more or higher-quality services in the future. However, public sector assets differ in important respects from private sector assets. In conventional private sector accounting, "assets are defined as economic resources" and they are the accounting counterpart to liabilities that are "amounts owed to outside entities and employees."[1] Current assets may consist of cash, investments, and a variety of items that can be readily converted into cash, such as inventory. Capital assets in the private sector have the capacity to generate future revenues for the enterprise. In the public sector, assets typically do not have as a primary purpose the generation of future revenues.

While a government facility that provides a service to citizens, such as a wastewater treatment plant, may not have as an objective generating future revenues, the facility once built does provide a continuing service through many future years. In that sense, an expenditure on a facility that will provide benefits for many years after its construction is an investment, and the investment creates a long-lasting asset. According to Statement No. 34 of the Governmental Accounting Standards Board (GASB; see Chapter 11), "infrastructure assets are long-lived capital assets that normally are stationary in nature and normally can be preserved for a significantly greater number of years than most capital assets."[2] This long-lived investment aspect helps explain why many governments distinguish capital expenditures for infrastructure from current expenditures and have capital budgeting processes, in addition to budgeting processes for current (operating) expenditures.

For governments, it is useful to distinguish among three types of investments. First, a government may purchase physical assets for its own use over many years in the future—assets such as office buildings, heavy equipment, and machinery. Second, governments may make investments in physical facilities that enhance private economic development and deliver needed public services—for example, roads and water systems. Third, governments may invest in intangibles, such as education and research. Capital budgeting processes deal with the first two. Capital budgets assist in deciding how much of each type of investment is necessary, and assist in evaluating available revenues (including loans) to finance those investments.

With or without a formal capital budget, focusing some attention on the investment component of a government budget is politically useful because it draws attention to the fact that many public spending programs build for the future. Taxpayers should be informed about government spending that occurs in one year, but then has benefits over many future years. There is some evidence indicating that voters are much more sensitive to infrastructure decisions reflected in capital budgets than to operating budget decisions. Bricks and mortar decisions can be decisive in whether incumbents are re-elected.[3] Attention to capital assets also reminds citizens that public assets, like highways, may deteriorate to the point of uselessness if not regularly rehabilitated. Governments with formal capital budgets often draw attention in the operating budget to expenditures that are necessary to preserve the value of a previously constructed or acquired asset.

State and local governments also stress the importance of public capital investment in stimulating economic growth. Not only are obvious facilities such as convention centers or improved water services for water-intensive industries the focal point of economic development-oriented investments, but increasingly state and local governments invest in quality-of-life facilities, such as parks and other recreational facilities, and even open space to attract companies to locate in the area.[4] States and local governments compete with each other in offering facilities, tax concessions, and other inducements to attract economic growth (see Chapter 14), requiring in many cases significant capital investments.

Sometimes it is difficult to draw the line between investment and consumption expenditures. The federal budget's definition of investment is very broad, including such human capital investments as education, research, and development expenditures, but still it does not include many other elements that it logically could. For example, mental health programs, programs for juveniles, and family counseling programs may be considered investments that help prevent future social and economic problems. A major rationale for the Child Health

Insurance Program, which provides federal assistance to states for uninsured children, is that the investment in health helps prevent some future federal expenditures for Medicaid.

While it is useful to think of government expenditures in terms of investment or consumption, for budgeting purposes the more meaningful distinction is that between capital versus current or operating expenditures. Investments in social capital such as health and education do not fall into the capital category in any budgeting system. Since capital expenditures differ from current expenditures, many state and local governments therefore distinguish between capital and current budgets.

Physical Nature and Time Duration. Businesses think of capital expenditures as the purchase of physical assets or the construction of facilities that will be used over a period of several years. Public sector capital expenditures likewise involve the purchase of physical assets whose use extends over a number of years, often 30 to 50 years with proper maintenance, as in the case of sewage treatment plants.

Examples of capital expenditures are easy to find. A school building is physically present and will last for many years. On the other hand, paper, pens, pencils, and staples, although physical, are used up and have to be purchased anew each year. The purchase of the building is easy to classify as a capital expenditure and the purchase of the supplies is clearly a current expenditure. Similarly, water mains extending from a treatment plant to neighborhood lines have a physical presence and will serve for many years. Their construction is a capital expenditure. In contrast, chemicals used in the water treatment process will be used up and need to be purchased again and again. Purchase of these chemicals is an operating or current expenditure.

Conventionally, debt service payments for both principal and interest for long-term bonds or loans also are included in the capital budget, as opposed to the operating budget, when the government has a capital budget separate from the operating budget (see Chapter 13 for discussion of bonds and capital financing). Debt service accounts may be used to segregate these payments (see Chapter 11), but they are regarded as capital budget items.

Classification Problems. These examples illustrate that capital expenditures normally are for purchases of physical assets that have a long life. Other examples, however, show that the distinction between capital and current expenditure is sometimes ambiguous. A big-city police department may purchase more than 50 vehicles per year, and many of them may replace vehicles purchased the previous year. That city may classify the purchase of the police cars as a current expenditure. A small town may purchase two police cars of the same type as the big city's but expect those two cars to last for three to five years. The small town probably would consider purchase of the police cars to be a capital expenditure.

Even within the same city, some classification problems occur. Books and periodicals bought for a library are expected to be used for many years, and their purchase can be treated as a capital investment. On the other hand, purchase of a periodical by a department of public works, if the periodical has a short useful life, would be an operating expense.

Every government and every business establishes some kind of arbitrary cutoff point that distinguishes current from capital expenditures. In most cases, the cutoff is a combination of the size of the expenditure and the useful life of the asset. Purchase of anything expected to be consumed (or destroyed) during one year normally will be a current expenditure, no matter how large it is. In addition, small expenditures, even for goods that will last several years, also are classified as current. But the size of the government's budget usually determines how small is small. A small town may classify expenditures of less than $1,000 as current regardless of the useful life. A larger city may use $25,000 as a cutoff and below that anything is a current expenditure regardless of its useful life. Although some purchases may be classified arbitrarily one way or the other, what constitutes a capital purchase and what constitutes a current one usually is not controversial.

Capital Decisions Versus Current Decisions

Separate Capital Budgets. The size of the expenditure and the longevity of the asset or facility purchased distinguish a capital expenditure from a current one. A third distinction of importance to decision making, the method of financing the expenditure, leads most state governments and a majority of local governments to pay at least some separate attention to capital expenditures in the annual budget decision-making process. Few states fail to distinguish capital from current expenses in the form of either capital improvement plans or budgets or both, and most larger counties and cities as well as some smaller ones make similar distinctions.

Table 12–1 shows state and local capital expenditures for 2002 as a proportion of total expenditures. Considering only direct capital outlays, about 13% of state and local expenditures are for capital purposes. That percentage has remained about the same (10% to 13%) for more than a decade. The actual expenditures do not tell the whole story, however, since most of the capital outlays at the state and local level are financed by borrowing and hence have interest costs. With interest included, the figure is closer to 18%. Local government capital outlays are a higher proportion of total outlays than state government outlays—15% and 10%,

Table 12-1 **Direct Capital Outlays as a Proportion of Total State and Local Outlays, 2002 (in Billions of Dollars)**

Government	Total Direct Outlays (a)	Capital Outlays	Capital as Percentage of Total	Interest on Debt (b)	Combined Capital Outlays	Combined Capital as Percentage of Total
State and Local	2044.3	257.2	13%	120.1	377.3	18%
State	915.5	89.9	10%	33.2	123.1	13%
Local	1128.8	167.3	15%	86.9	254.2	23%

(a) Outlays here exclude duplicative intergovernmental transfers so that the figures shown are for the level of government making the expenditure even if the source of finance is a transfer from another level of government.

(b) Interest on general debt plus interest on utility borrowing is attributed in this table to borrowing for capital investment.

Source: Compiled from Bureau of the Census, U.S. Department of Commerce (2006). *Statistical abstract of the United States: 2006.* Washington, DC: U.S. Government Printing Office, 281–282.

respectively. However, these gross percentages obscure the real nature of the decisions to undertake capital projects. Capital expenditures cluster in only a few government functions. For local governments, school construction; utilities such as electricity, roads, sewage, and water; and housing construction account for most direct capital outlays.

State government capital outlays also cluster in only a few functional categories, and decisions made in one year affect future-year budgets. More than 60% of state public works expenditures in 2002 went to highway construction. That level of capital construction implies significant future-year expenditures for highway maintenance. Combined state and local highway capital expenditures in 2002 were $66 billion, but total expenditures—capital plus operating or current—on highways were $115 billion.[5] An amount almost equal to new capital investments in highways was spent on operations and maintenance of highways built in prior years.

These examples demonstrate that decisions about capital spending at the state and local levels are consequential in the year they are made and can have major consequences for future budgets. As discussed in previous chapters, particularly Chapter 6, it is difficult to incorporate a long-run perspective into budget decisions, especially when the decisions tend to focus in large part on personnel expenditures and only on the current-year implications of starting new programs. The fact that current-year capital budget decisions have significant implications for future operations and maintenance suggests that the effects of capital decisions on future operating budgets must be taken into account in any budgeting process.

For state and local governments, the logic of having some kind of process for examining capital spending decisions in more detail seems compelling. That does not necessarily entail separate capital budgets, however. In the next section, we illustrate a general approach to capital investment planning and budgeting that satisfies both the requirement to examine capital decisions in more detail and the requirement to consider implications for future-year operating budgets.

Capital Investment Planning

Few governmental jurisdictions simply ignore the distinction between capital costs and current. The form in which capital and current costs are planned and budgeted varies greatly across jurisdictions. For most governments, some form of long-term capital investment plan is the starting point. For those without formal capital budgets, capital investment planning is still the norm. Illustrating with examples from different types of institutions, the following discussion focuses on a general framework for capital investment planning that highlights the data that inform capital decisions.

Multiyear Capital Investment Plans. Most governments that distinguish between capital and current budget decisions have an established process for developing a multiyear capital investment plan (CIP) and incorporating elements of that plan into a capital budget. Likewise, governments that do not have a capital budget still have a multiyear investment plan. Five years is a common period for projecting capital expenditures, although a longer period is often included in the statements of long-range programs. For example, the Orange County (North Carolina) Water and Sewer Authority distinguishes between its 15-year capital improvements plan and its five-year capital improvements budget.[6] The long-range plan focuses on the expected needs for water supply and sewage treatment for the next decade and a half, while the capital improvements budget includes detailed cost estimates only for the next five years.

Other jurisdictions focus on the five-year time frame. California and Michigan, for example, have five-year capital investment planning cycles. Michigan's CIP is integrated into an overall asset management system. In order for a project to be included in Michigan's capital budget, it must already have gone through the investment planning process and have been included in the CIP.[7] However, not everything included in a CIP necessarily will make its way into the capital budget as the financial resources simply may not be available to afford every investment that the planning process has identified. Or something in the capital investment plan may be deferred beyond the immediate five-year plan when financing, hopefully, becomes available. **Exhibit 12–1** illustrates the way a capital improvement program typically contains items for which the financing is already secured, and items for which the financing sources are not yet known, and in some cases may never become available.

Exhibit 12-1   City of Durham, North Carolina, Capital Improvement Program, 2006–2012

The City of Durham, North Carolina produces a multiyear capital improvement plan (CIP) that reports on the most recent prior year's capital investments, identifies financing that already has been approved—which could be voter approved bond issues, federal grants, or other sources—and illustrates the difference between a plan and a budget. The following two tables present the plan for FY 2006–07 through FY 2011–12 as well as projects that will still be incomplete in FY 2011–2012, and the revenue sources for those investments. To be included in the Durham CIP, the asset must have a useful life of 10 years or more, and must have an investment value of over $100,000.

CITY OF DURHAM
CAPITAL IMPROVEMENT PROGRAM

FY 2007 - 2012 CAPITAL IMPROVEMENT PROGRAM SUMMARY

SUMMARY BY PROJECT CATEGORY

Category	Prior Year	FY 2006-07	FY 2007-08	FY 2008-09	FY 2009-10	FY 2010-11	FY 2011-12	Future Years	Total Request
Culture & Recreation	71,900,418	580,000	7,889,288	10,640,996	10,511,314	16,612,805	0	0	118,134,821
Downtown Revitalization	70,365,393	935,500	850,000	7,787,154	23,083,723	16,290,719	0	0	119,312,489
General Services	16,985,291	828,877	6,440,061	1,818,157	5,418,330	874,945	0	0	32,365,661
Housing & Neighborhood Revitalization	56,923,657	3,353,000	14,560,000	18,400,000	5,200,000	1,250,000	0	0	99,686,657
Public Protection	22,498,794	435,000	5,709,500	10,978,866	2,429,628	2,812,000	1,000,000	0	45,863,788
Stormwater	2,925,370	1,350,000	1,450,000	950,000	450,000	0	0	0	7,125,370
Technology	6,889,885	0	175,000	1,950,000	1,700,000	0	0	0	10,714,885
Transportation	96,012,474	1,795,000	13,150,000	22,810,000	66,123,465	32,475,000	10,250,000	17,250,000	259,865,939
Wastewater	47,520,513	5,500,000	14,716,000	15,852,000	7,374,000	8,964,400	21,889,600	0	121,816,513
Water	61,530,153	8,000,000	30,281,500	31,248,000	46,584,000	8,045,000	18,175,000	0	203,863,653
	$453,551,948	$22,777,377	$95,221,349	$122,235,173	$168,874,460	$87,324,869	$51,314,500	$17,250,000	$1,018,549,776

continues

Exhibit 12–1 City of Durham, North Carolina, Capital Improvement Program, 2006–2012 (continued)

SUMMARY BY REVENUE SOURCE

Source	Prior Year	FY 2006-07	FY 2007-08	FY 2008-09	FY 2009-10	FY 2010-11	FY 2011-12	Future Years	Total Funds
GOB Authorized	225,153,547	0	0	0	0	0	0	0	225,153,547
GOB Unauthorized	1,181,000	0	8,680,093	10,781,110	38,422,461	30,081,898	1,000,000	0	90,146,562
Impact Fees	28,053,086	1,945,000	7,850,000	19,301,932	21,150,000	12,650,000	0	3,000,000	93,950,018
Installment Sales	48,284,887	685,000	2,512,500	825,248	2,367,000	0	0	0	54,674,635
Intergovernmental	33,021,970	0	4,275,000	6,860,000	7,700,000	750,000	0	0	52,606,970
Other	62,791,011	3,353,000	40,916,756	47,511,432	36,074,447	29,578,571	15,425,000	14,250,000	249,900,217
Pay-As-You-Go	11,764,350	16,144,377	13,353,000	2,438,451	11,322,552	0	0	0	55,022,730
Rev Authorized	41,627,097	0	200,000	200,000	200,000	200,000	200,000	0	42,627,097
Rev Unauthorized	1,675,000	650,000	17,434,000	34,317,000	51,638,000	14,064,400	34,689,600	0	154,468,000
	$453,551,948	$22,777,377	$95,221,349	$122,235,173	$168,874,460	$87,324,869	$51,314,600	$17,260,000	$1,018,549,776

Source: City of Durham: Capital improvement program, reproduced from City of Durham, North Carolina (2006). *City of Durham capital improvement program process.* Retrieved August 15, 2006, from http://www.ci.durham.nc.us/departments/bms/07cip/intro.pdf.

Practices vary considerably from city to city and state to state, but it is possible to outline a general format for a capital investment planning process. One such model for capital investment planning and budgeting, linked to an inventory of existing facilities, consists of eight steps (see **Exhibit 12–2**).

Step 1: Identifying Present Service Characteristics. The first step is to make an inventory of existing physical or infrastructure facilities and to assess the services provided. For a state or local government that has not previously conducted an inventory, this first step is complex and expensive although maintaining the inventory once established need not be burdensome. Such an inventory involves listing all physical facilities and elements of the physical infrastructure and such related information as date of construction, date of last major rehabilitation, type of construction material (such as type of road surface), and, where relevant, characteristics such as size and capacity. For a building, information may be collected on electrical wiring, fiber optics for computer hookups, plumbing, and elevators. All capital asset inventory systems offered by a variety of information technology solutions providers to the public sector contain an asset inventory module.

Quantity of service includes such characteristics as the number of people served, the proportion of total population served, the geographic area covered (area, density, and spatial distribution), and various socioeconomic groupings related to coverage, such as number of clients served by a facility. Different quantity measures are appropriate for different services.

Quality of service in part is a function of the level or the type of service provided. For example, water treatment systems that remove only bacteriological contaminants are qualitatively less effective than those that remove toxins and heavy metals as well as bacteria. Quality also may be indicated by such things as the age of the facility and its condition. The latter may be measured by the frequency-of-repair record. Qualitative measures of service, including records of citizens' complaints and structured citizen satisfaction surveys, are as appropriate as other measures.

Step 2: Identifying Environmental Trends. The next step looks toward the future. Most city and state governments develop long-range planning forecasts to estimate future service requirements. These forecasts, which project population growth, commercial and industrial growth, demographic and economic changes, and so forth, are linked to the capital facilities planning process in order to develop plans for required service expansion or contraction. In addition, more detailed analyses of trends in business locations may predict possible shortages or other problems in critical areas, such as the water supply. The capital facilities planning process can provide a means for the jurisdiction to plan expansion of services in

Exhibit 12–2 **Capital Facilities Planning and Budgeting**

1. Identify present service characteristics (inventory facilities and service levels)

   a. Coverage (quantity)

   b. Quality

   c. Cost per unit of service (efficiency)

2. Identify environmental trends

   a. Population growth projections

   b. Changing regulatory environment

   c. Employment and economic development trends

3. Develop service objectives

   a. Extension of service to new population or area (coverage)

   b. Improvement in quality of service

   c. Opportunities to stimulate economic growth

4. Develop preliminary list of capital projects and cost estimates

   a. Rehabilitation of existing facilities

   b. Replacement of existing facilities

   c. Addition of new facilities

5. Identify financial resources

   a. External assistance

   b. Projected growth in present revenue base

   c. Potential for direct cost recovery for individual projects

   d. Use of credit

6. Select subset of projects for inclusion in five-year capital investment plan (CIP)

7. Identify future recurrent cost impact of CIP on operating budget

8. Include first year of CIP in annual budget estimate

an orderly way and can help convince potential investors that the jurisdiction is anticipating future business and residential requirements.

School buildings serve as a good example. When the school-age population of a community is rising, the school district must plan for having the appropriate number of buildings with the appropriate sizes and in the appropriate locations. When the population is declining, the district must plan for decommissioning school buildings. When buildings are in surplus, should they be sold off to bring in revenue for the district or should they be converted to other purposes? Keeping a building in inventory, even though it is not used as a school, may be advantageous if the district thinks population will increase in coming years and necessitate reopening the building.

Step 3: Developing Service Objectives. The third step is developing service objectives. The process of defining the need for capital investments can take numerous forms. Not only is the technical judgment of government staff important but so are citizens' preferences and willingness to pay. Typical ways to include citizen input include representation on long-range planning groups, open forums to discuss the need for community facilities, and referendums to approve a specific bond issue to finance a capital investment (see Chapter 13). Even in jurisdictions with established channels for citizen input, a special group often convenes every two to three years just to review the current CIP and establish new priorities. Thus a key step is to determine the service objectives that capital investments will need to satisfy.

Step 4: Preliminary Listing of Capital Projects and Cost Estimates. Based on the service objectives established in the previous step, a preliminary list of capital projects can be developed, along with a timetable for completing the projects. Typically, the preliminary list includes the rehabilitation of existing facilities to improve the quality and/or efficiency of service; the replacement of existing facilities, also for the purpose of improving quality and efficiency; and the addition of new facilities or expansion of existing facilities to meet expansion objectives. The preliminary list typically will not be screened for financial feasibility at this stage.

Step 5: Identifying Financial Resources. With a preliminary list of projects and cost estimates in hand, identifying the financial resources potentially available to carry out the preliminary list of capital projects is a critical next step. This step involves analyzing the jurisdiction's overall financial condition and some of the individual capital projects for possible sources of financing specific to them. Since the 1980s, an important aspect of overall financial management has been the evaluation of the financial condition of local governments.[8] In the wake of public pressure to hold steady or to cut back state and local taxes, major new revenue initiatives in the form of tax increases often are not possible, even when the need to build up infrastructure and rehabilitate existing facilities is obvious. However, because of the expansion of tax bases, making long-range projections of tax yield increases and assessing the performance of other ordinary revenue sources sometimes reveal potential revenues that will be available at some point in the future for capital investment financing.

More commonly, state and local governments (and particularly the latter) rely increasingly on revenue sources specific to individual capital projects. User fees and property assessments traditionally have been used to finance the major portion of water and other utility capital investments as well as operating expenses. More recently, cities have exacted special impact fees and other charges from residential and commercial developers to pay for roads, water, and sewer lines and drainage intended to serve new developments (see Chapter 5).

Other sources of revenues tied to particular projects include grants from other levels of government and borrowing (typically involving the issuance of bonds). Although federal funding cutbacks were significant starting in the early 1980s, state aid to local governments has in some cases made up for some of the federal cutbacks, and federal funds are still available on a more limited programmatic basis (see Chapter 14).

Step 6: Selecting Projects for Inclusion in Five-Year Capital Investment Plan. Step 6 involves matching available financial resources with the set of projects included in the preliminary investment plan. Steps 3 through 6 may be iterated to eventually narrow down the list of projects and select a feasible set. Reevaluation of desired service objectives sometimes is necessary during this iterative process, because financial realities can make it clear that some objectives are impossible without major new financial initiatives. For most state and local governments, the application of complex analytical tools such as cost-benefit analysis or rate-of-return analysis plays only a small role in the selection of projects. Further, there is substantial disagreement over the validity of estimates of economic benefits from investments in infrastructure.[9] Instead, the ranking of priorities is often based on the principle that replacing deteriorated facilities should be the first concern, meeting population growth requirements should be the second, and improving quality of services should be last.

Contemporary management tools such as the *balanced scorecard* have been adapted to help in the project selection process.[10] This approach emphasizes balancing selection criteria among four factors—financial information, customer requirements, internal management processes, and innovation and learning— with the notion being that a structured process to balance several criteria in different categories can lead to better choices and more successful implementation than over-reliance on any one set of factors.

Step 7: Identifying Implications for Future Recurrent Costs. Decision makers frequently neglect the recurrent cost implications of capital investments.[11] It is sometimes difficult to anticipate the costs of keeping a facility operating, and the usually valuable public relations aspects of a new project tend to overshadow the longer-run impact on the general fund's budget. The problem is exaggerated by the fact that the operating and maintenance costs of any new project or facility are lower in the early years of operation, and the heavier costs fall outside the range of normal five-year capital planning cycles. Without an analysis that takes into account this fact, a state or local jurisdiction may find itself 10 or 20 years down the road facing the dilemma of either forgoing new capital investments because of the need to budget greater funds for maintenance or neglecting maintenance in favor of more politically popular capital projects.

The analysis of future operation and maintenance costs is not all negative. If the analysis of the current capital facilities base in step 1 has been carried out well, the jurisdiction will have an idea of the present operation and maintenance costs of existing facilities. Replacing some facilities that require expensive maintenance expenditures may produce significant reductions in operation and maintenance costs in the operating budget.

Step 8: Including the First Year of the Capital Investment Plan as the Capital Budget. Once a feasible set of investments has been selected and the short- and long-term costs have been determined, the final step is to incorporate the first year of the CIP into the budget. To this point, the process, which has been one of planning and programming, may have involved input from the legislative body, but no legal appropriation of funds will have taken place. Some jurisdictions submit the CIP to the legislative body (e.g., state legislature, city council) for formal approval, but the CIP rarely includes actual appropriation of funds. Some states appropriate the full costs of capital projects, at least for smaller projects, whereas other states appropriate only the annual costs of each project. In the latter case, only a single year's cost actually shows up in the appropriation act.

The eight steps outlined in this section are a generic process description. Governments may use different names for the various steps, and likely will combine one or more steps. But governments will, to varying degrees of intensity, carry out some aspects of each of these steps. Some may have very involved processes for garnering input from citizens. Others may only hold a public hearing at the end of a process carried out by city staff or merely publish the capital investment plan.

Capital Budgeting

Even though most governments of any size have some formal capital investment planning process, and the results of that process feed into budget decisions, not all governments have a formal capital budget and capital budgeting process. This section discusses capital budgeting as a decision process or budget system.[12]

Much of the argument over the value of capital budgeting at state and local government levels hinges on whether there should be a separate capital budget. There is little argument over the need to examine the full long-term implications of capital spending and not just focus on a single budget year. It is possible to have a comprehensive capital planning process that concludes with a capital investment and financing plan or capital investment statement without a separate capital budgeting process. The amount the city council or state legislature is then asked to appropriate may be for only one year, but the budget request is made in the context of future-year requirements.

Pros and Cons of Separate Capital Budgeting. Capital budgets and statements indicate the extent to which investments are being made with current expenditures. From a political perspective, this gives capital budgets a certain public relations value, since government officials can show citizens that government funds are being used for the acquisition of useful assets and not solely for the payment of bureaucrats' salaries.

On the negative side, capital budgeting can encourage political logrolling, in which various political interests agree to help each other. A capital budget can be a political grab bag, a fund where every interest can find a project. A state capital budget may provide highway projects in every county, even though real need is concentrated in a small number of counties. In providing everyone with something, some important needs will not be met while less pressing needs will be satisfied. Furthermore, if capital costs are presented in a completely separate budget, particularly when financed by borrowing, it may appear as if capital decisions are "costless" in the current year.

On balance, however, the arguments in favor of paying special attention to capital spending, at least at the state and local levels, seem overwhelming. While capital budget decisions are no less political than other budget decisions, the logic of focusing attention on long-run financial and economic consequences of spending or failing to spend for capital facilities is compelling. More than current operating budget decisions, decisions to invest in infrastructure help shape the future direction, location, and extent of private economic investments in the community. Local governments' capital investments may in some cases play a leading role in encouraging future local economic development (see Chapter 15). The combination of strategic planning and capital budgeting at the municipal level has been found in some studies to be positively related to overall financial performance of the municipality.[13] State and local governments compete for location of major facilities, and they sometimes offer large incentive packages comprising infrastructure projects and financial assistance to induce private companies or federal agencies to locate facilities in their jurisdictions.

Once built, major facilities largely will be limited to the uses for which they were designed. Inadequate planning of facilities can result in inadequate services, major financial burdens, or the need for expensive alterations. Excess capacity built into a community sewer system cannot be converted into other uses. Too little acquisition of land for parks in a rapidly growing suburban area may later result in a shortage of recreational opportunities or may force the local government to pay far more for space than it might have earlier.

These arguments do not mandate that capital budgets be separate from operating budgets. While capital spending requires attention to some issues that are not germane to operating budgets, capital and operating expenditures are intertwined. As noted earlier, the mistake governments often make even with separate capital budgets or a distinctive capital planning/budgeting process is not taking into account the much longer-term operation and maintenance costs. And as governments get strapped for funds, as happened in the early 2000s after several years of surpluses at all levels of government, maintenance expenditures begin to be neglected. Capital budgeting, even if formalized and well done, must clearly link back to the operations and maintenance implications in the future for current capital spending.[14]

As we discuss in Chapter 13, the main reason state and local governments formally segregate capital and current into two distinct, formal budgets, is related to the primary means of financing large-scale infrastructure. State and local governments rarely have sufficient revenue to finance large capital items from regular revenues, though a few do operate on a *pay as you go* basis. But to appropriate the entire portion of capital facilities to be built in a given year from current revenue would typically leave insufficient funds for all the recurring expenses of state and local governments. Typically, state and local governments borrow to finance capital infrastructure, and this debt does not "count" in determining budget balance. Further, operating on a *pay as you use* basis, which governments do when they finance capital projects through debt, permits the annual cost of capital to be borne by the specific residents who are benefiting from facilities being used to provide services in a given year.

Federal Capital Budgeting. For the federal government, the logic of capital budgeting is less compelling. First, much of the "capital" side of the federal budget goes toward defense acquisitions—50% in 2005 and an estimated similar 50% in the 2007 budget proposal. The other 50% is for non-defense capital investments, but that estimate is misleading. **Table 12–2** shows the distribution of federal physical capital outlays in the fiscal year 2007 budget proposal. Approximately 35% of the proposed federal physical capital outlays are grants to state and local governments.

If one examines only those physical capital outlays undertaken directly by the federal government, excluding grants to state and local governments, defense

Table 12-2 Federal Physical Capital Outlays, 2005 and 2007 (est.) (in Millions of Current Dollars)

	Total Federal Physical Capital Outlays	Direct Federal National Defense	Direct Federal Non-Defense	Federal Grants to States/Local	Federal Exclusive of Intergovernmental
FY 2005 actual	177.6	89.5	27.3	60.8	116.8
FY 2007 estimate	199.4	99.2	30.3	69.9	129.5
FY 2005 actual Percent of Total		50.4%	15.4%	34.2%	76.6%
FY 2007 estimate Percent of Total		49.7%	15.2%	35.1%	76.6%

Source: Compiled from U.S. Office of Management and Budget (2006). *Budget of the United States Government for 2007: analytical perspectives.* Washington, DC: U.S. Government Printing Office, 55.

physical acquisitions are 77% of the total.[15] These are not investments in the same sense as state and local expenditures for water systems or highways. This statement does not mean that the purchase of nuclear-powered aircraft carriers, for example, has no implications for future operations and maintenance. Rather, the need to replace a weapons system often is generated not by its wearing out, but by its inability to cope with new offensive or defensive systems of a potential enemy or its being destroyed or damaged beyond recovery in a combat or training situation.

Furthermore, the federal government may undertake many non-defense capital expenditures more for macroeconomic policy reasons than for investment purposes. Because of the federal government's role in stimulating the economy, capital spending sometimes has the primary objective of assisting a state or local economy rather than providing a needed facility. Federal grants to state and local governments for non-defense physical capital was proposed to be almost $70 billion in 2007, an important part of total federal physical outlays as noted above.[16] Unfortunately, this use of capital spending often leads to earmarking or pork barrel decisions that place expensive projects in every congressional district.

There have been periodic calls for federal capital budgeting. At the time the unified budget was adopted at the recommendation of the 1967 President's Commission on Budget Concepts, a capital budget for the federal government was rejected.[17] There was a resurgence of calls for capital budgeting at the federal level in the 1980s. In response to General Accounting Office (GAO) recommendations, the federal budget for fiscal year 1996 for the first time included a capital budget presentation in the *Analytical Perspectives* chapter on investment spending.

The Government Accountability Office and others argue that the federal government must adopt more contemporary financial management practices to improve the efficiency of government operations. According to these critics, current federal management practices are inadequate for the task of achieving efficiency or effectiveness in government operations. This does not mean that GAO is in favor of a separate federal capital budget, but rather that much more systematic attention should be given to physical capital investments, to the value of those assets, and to their management.[18]

The second cause for renewed interest in federal capital budgeting is the concern that the nation is not investing sufficiently in basic infrastructure, to the long-run detriment of the economy. Legislation in 1984 established the National Council on Public Works Improvement and gave it the mandate to assess the state of the nation's capital infrastructure and make recommendations for improvement.

Many of those concerned that the level of investment in infrastructure is too low have argued that the federal budget is biased against such capital investments because it must show the full cost of the capital outlays in the construction years instead of showing only the annual depreciation of the investments over their long life.[19] A capital budgeting statement might show only one year's depreciation value in the current year budget, spreading the budget implications of such an investment over the expected years of benefits. This approach would more clearly isolate how much of the federal deficit is due to investments that will pay for themselves through future economic growth and might reduce some concern for the size of the deficit.

The most recent official review of federal capital budgeting was the President's Commission to Study Capital Budgeting, appointed in 1997 by President William Clinton. That commission examined primarily federal capital spending, but also considered the larger question of the nation's total investment in productive capital. The commission concluded that the federal budget process does not give sufficient attention to the long-term implications of capital spending, given that capital investments are expensed in the federal budget in the years in which the costs are incurred. However, the commission also did not recommend the creation of a separate federal capital budget, or a capital budgeting process. The recommendation focused on providing information in the annual federal budget to focus congressional decisions and public awareness on the physical infrastructure stock, the investments proposed in a given year for capital investments, especially non-defense, and the longer-term maintenance requirements implied in proposed investments, as well as the maintenance costs in the budget for previous investments.[20]

For the most part, recent administrations have accepted the arguments and recommendations that federal budgeting must include more focus on capital spending. One section of the federal budget for fiscal year 2003 even used the (new) title Federal Investment Spending and Capital Budgeting in which an illustrative capital budget was presented as discussed in **Exhibit 12–3**. This one attempt to show what a federal capital and operating budget might look like, focusing entirely on capital investments that are physical in nature, has not been repeated in subsequent budgets of the George W. Bush administration.

The 2003 budget also outlined legislation that would have created Capital Acquisition Funds and changed the way agencies that acquire physical assets would show those acquisitions in the agency budget (see below). Instead of the agency showing the full expenditure for the acquisition in the year acquired, the cost would be shown as the first year's depreciation, using straight-line depreciation. For example, if a physical asset had an expected life of 20 years, then 5% of the cost of that asset would show in the agency's budget, as if the agency were borrowing the full amount from the Treasury and repaying it at 5% per year for 20 years. The Treasury, however, would show the full outlay for the building, so the unified budget outlay total would not be affected by this presentation, although some agency budgets would have looked smaller.[21]

Exhibit 12–3 | **Illustrative Federal Capital Budget**

Developing a federal capital budget would not be a simple process. In the 2003 budget, the Office of Management and Budget (OMB) developed a sample capital and operating budget, as shown below. Considerable estimation was required to determine depreciation values. In addition, what should count as investments in a capital statement is controversial, because as discussed previously, one can make a case for including many government expenditures for programs, such as education and health programs, that do not produce any physical asset but do produce future benefits. Naturally, all program advocates would want their programs included in the capital or investment budget, because only the annual amortized value of those programs would appear as an outlay in the operating budget, which typically gets more media attention. Carried to an extreme, the budget might shrink to a small proportion of its present size, covering only obviously current consumption expenditures. Yet the actual cash requirements of the federal government would not have changed. That sample capital and operating budget presentation was dropped after the one-time appearance in the 2003 budget.

Capital, Operating, and Unified Budget Concepts, United States Government, Fiscal Year 2003 (in Billions of Dollars)

Operating Budget	
Receipts	2048
Expenses	
Depreciation	82
Other	2028
Subtotal, expenses	2111
Surplus or deficit (-)	−63
Capital Budget	
Income: Depreciation	82
Capital Expenditures	100
Surplus or deficit (-)	−18
Unified Budget	
Receipts	2048
Outlays	2128
Surplus or deficit (-)	−80

Source: Extracted from U.S. Office of Management and Budget (2002). *Budget of the United States Government: fiscal year 2003, analytical perspectives.* Washington, DC: U.S. Government Printing Office, 148.

The fiscal year 2003 budget discussed again much of the argument and experience with capital budgeting in states, other developed countries, and some developing countries. But the various discussions of improved presentations of capital investments did not portend the adoption of capital budgeting at the federal level. Outlays for acquisition of assets or construction of facilities are still recorded fully in the year acquired or constructed. In contrast, in state and local capital budgets, full investment cost is shown, albeit in connection with the method of financing. So when a state government borrows (typically issues bonds) to finance highways, the bond issuance and construction costs are fully disclosed, but the only impact of the project in the operating or general budget is the cost of debt service—principal and interest payments.

Federal capital budget presentations, by contrast, are not linked to any specific method of financing, and they do record in the budget the full construction or acquisition cost incurred in that year. That is unlikely to change in the near future. The special emphasis in the 2003 budget on capital investments was a one time emphasis, and the illustrative capital budget presentation has not been repeated.

In the *Analytical Perspectives* volume of the annual federal budget, a chapter on federal investments continues to discuss the nature of federal expenditures on physical capital, and other types of investments such as research and development funding and education. But there has been no resurgence of interest in a federal capital budget, or capital budgeting process. **Table 12–3** is the federal investment outlays table, including all types of investments—physical capital, research and development, and education and training—from the fiscal year 2007 budget. After the one capital budget illustration in the 2003 budget, the attention to federal investments once again has taken the broad perspective of **Table 12–3**.

▮ Capital Project Analysis

In this section, we discuss methods for analyzing prospective capital investments. Some of the tools discussed can be used for non-physical capital investments as well. Many social programs, for example, are discussed in terms of the costs of the programs and measures of effectiveness that may be output oriented (the number of participants in a workforce training program, for example) or outcome oriented (the reduction in morbidity and mortality from introducing an immunization program against a specific disease). In this chapter we are concerned with analytical approaches to the investment and return on investment from physical capital expenditures, such as water treatment plants, highways, elementary schools, and so forth. Conceptually, the overall approach is cost-benefit analysis.

Table 12–3 | **Federal Investment Outlays, All Investment Purposes, 2005–2007 (in Billions of Dollars)**

	Actual	Estimate	
	2005	2006	2007
Major public physical capital investment:			
Direct federal:			
National defense	89.5	97.3	99.2
Non-defense	27.3	30.2	30.3
Subtotal, direct major public physical capital investment	116.8	127.5	129.5
Grants to state and local governments	60.8	65.9	69.9
Subtotal, major public physical capital investment	177.7	193.4	199.3
Conduct of research and development			
National defense	70.6	75.6	76.8
Non-defense	49.2	51.8	53.9
Subtotal, conduct of research and development	119.8	127.4	130.7
Conduct of education and training			
Grants to state and local governments	51.6	53.7	52.6
Direct federal:	43.2	50.5	32.9
Subtotal, conduct of education and training	94.7	104.2	85.5
Total, major federal investment outlays	392.3	425.0	415.5

Source: Compiled from U.S. Office of Management and Budget (2006). *Budget of the United States Government: fiscal year 2007, analytical perspectives.* Washington, DC:U.S. Government Printing Office, 55.

Cost-Benefit and Cost-Effectiveness Analysis

We can distinguish between cost-benefit and cost-effectiveness analysis. Both attempt to relate costs of projects or programs to performance, and both quantify costs in monetary terms. They differ, however, in the way they measure the outcomes of programs.

Cost-effectiveness analysis measures outcomes in quantitative but non-monetary form. For example, it might focus on the number of patients served by the construction of a new primary health care clinic, or by the introduction into existing health care facilities of new diagnostic technology. Cost-benefit analysis, by contrast, measures program outcomes in monetary form, thereby allowing for the development of ratios or other measures of the extent to which returns exceed costs, or vice versa. In the case of constructing a multi-lane, divided highway, for example, cost-benefit analysis would estimate the dollar value of reduced wear and tear on vehicles and time saved to travelers and would use that figure to calculate the dollar value of the gains.

Attaching monetary value to some things, however, can be controversial. Some investments in physical infrastructure may have as the primary impact a reduction in morbidity (disease) or mortality (death), or both. For example, controlling or eliminating environmental conditions that breed mosquitoes, such as a major low-lying area drainage program has the aim of reducing illness and death from malaria. A cost-effectiveness analysis of that program might compare the environmental intervention with an indoor residual spraying program or the issuance of insecticide treated bed nets that intend to kill or ward off mosquitoes from being able to infect household residents. The analysis would focus on monetary costs of the various interventions, and non-monetary results such as reduction in the number of malaria cases, deaths averted, reduction in days lost to debilitating disease, and so forth.

A cost-benefit analysis of the same investment comparisons would place monetary value on deaths averted, work days not lost to debilitating illness, and so forth. The potential technical merit of cost-benefit analysis over cost-effectiveness analysis is that the former allows for analysis across subject areas. When the expressed ratio of benefits to costs of a program is 1.0, costs are equal to benefits. As the ratio increases, the benefits accruing have increased. In theory, if government investment in a new high efficiency airplane yielded a ratio of 1.7 and a highway traffic control program yielded a ratio of 2.5, then, based on the standard of economic efficiency (and assuming the difference in the magnitude of the programs was not great), government would be advised to favor the traffic control program over the air transportation program. Cost-effectiveness analysis, in contrast, would not allow such direct comparisons because the effects would be expressed in time saved for one program and lives saved for the other.

For a private sector company, capital projects can be evaluated and choices made in terms of the financial results to the company's owners, such as the stockholders. General Electric (GE) can make choices between investing in the aviation jet engine business and the electric turbine business, and can let the monetary returns relative to the monetary costs guide the decision.

A local government cannot as easily make the same kinds of trade-off decisions. A local government responsible for both water and sewer service cannot just decide that because the economic returns on a water project are greater than they are for the sewer project, it will just not provide sewer service. What the local government typically has to do in this kind of comparison is decide what possibilities exist for redesigning both projects, for changing the timing of when water and sewer projects will be implemented, and what possibilities exist for more favorable financing terms. But even though compromises will be made, the local government cannot simply decide that citizens do not get sewer service the way GE can decide to go into or to exit a line of business. Regulatory matters may be more important that economic decisions. A local government may be forced to install a sewer system or upgrade an existing system because of state and federal regulations.

The following paragraphs discuss the various issues that arise in public sector decision making on capital projects within an overall economic and financial framework. We make the distinction between *economic analysis* and *financial analysis* to emphasize that there are some differences between a project being valuable (generating returns) for economic reasons and being valuable because it generates direct financial returns to the organization making the investment. Every public sector capital project has both kinds of returns. Financial returns are defined as actual cash flow returns that are directly the result of the investment. Economic returns may also be measured in dollar terms, but some economic returns do not come in the form of direct cash flow to the jurisdiction making the investment. Extending the distribution of the water system has direct financial returns in the form of user payments for the water. But it also may make water using commercial activities more efficient than the means they relied upon before they got service from the utility. Economic analysis would attempt to measure the value of those efficiency gains in dollars, but these would not be cash flow to the water utility. The World Bank in appraising a loan for a capital investment program in a developing country would require that both economic and financial returns be measured.

Identifying Costs and Benefits. The first basic issue in an economic or financial analysis of a capital project is the decision as to what counts as a cost and as a benefit. It is usually different for an economic analysis versus a financial analysis. Determining the financial costs of existing programs is often difficult because accounting systems are designed to produce information by organizational unit and not necessarily by program. Only if a program is unique to an organizational unit specified in the accounting system will the financial costs be easy to measure. For capital projects, the acquisition or purchase price and the construction costs are relatively easier in that engineering specifications precede the cost identification process, and then the specifications may be figured out.

Even when the costs are identified in this manner all that is produced are the direct financial expenditures of government rather than costs as would be derived by a cost accounting system (Chapter 11). Indeed, critics often charge that analyses overlook the costs imposed on others. Failure to consider all costs tends to weight the analysis in favor of the proposed project under review. If personal residences have to be acquired and demolished to secure the right of way for a road project, the cost of purchasing those properties can be measured, but subsequent lawsuits may result in larger amounts to the property owners, and those additional costs may or may not ever be attributed back to the construction project. Furthermore, even if they are, they may be too late to influence the decision itself as the suits may not be resolved before the project is finished. Similarly, the money paid to property holders for their condemned property may not fully reimburse them for their purchase of a comparable property and moving, and those additional costs imposed on the property owners never will be measured in the cost analysis.

Externalities. Indirect costs as well as benefits granted to others are called externalities, or *spillover, secondary*, and *tertiary effects*. These costs and benefits affect parties other than the ones directly involved. In the private sector, air and water pollution from industrial plants are externalities. The main concern of a private enterprise is making a profit, but part of the cost of production may be imposed on persons living in the area. Residents of areas downstream and downwind of the plant may pay the costs of discomfort, poor health, and loss of water recreation opportunities. They may also experience an actual decrease in the value of their assets, such as their homes if the pollution is bad enough to make it difficult to sell property. If a municipality downstream has to treat water that has been polluted by the plant, the costs imposed are relatively easy to identify.

Most government capital expenditure decisions involve similar spillover effects. The costs of an urban redevelopment program are not just the financial outlays required for purchasing and clearing land, but also the costs imposed on the families and businesses that must relocate. One government's decision can affect thousands of individuals, businesses, nonprofit organizations such as churches, synagogues, and mosques, and other governments.

Some argue that there are no such things as secondary or spillover effects, that all effects of a program should be part of the explicit benefits and costs of that program. This idea is sometimes expressed as the belief that every affected individual or organization should have *standing* and should thus be taken into account in any analysis of the program.[22] Affected parties are said to be stakeholders in that they have interests regarding the outcomes of the program and any decisions that may change it.[23]

Redistributive Effects. Related to spillover costs and benefits are redistributive effects, which analysts once tended to ignore. Today, consideration of major infrastructure projects encompasses their potential redistributive effects. For example, the federal budget has in some administrations included a summary table of the redistributive effects of taxing and spending decisions as part of the budget presentation. But for infrastructure projects, the question is whether some groups in the society will benefit more than other groups. In the example of the high efficiency airframe investment mentioned earlier, the program presumably would benefit middle- and upper-income groups, who would be the ones more likely to take advantage of this means of transportation. Other criteria for judging redistribution include race, educational level, and occupational class.[24] The effects of programs on different generations in the population have increasingly become a focus of attention.

Common tools exist for analyzing redistributive effects including *Lorenz curves* and *Gini coefficients* of inequality. For capital infrastructure projects, an analysis of the current situation in a jurisdiction before the project is built and after the project is completed could see if the existing Gini coefficient measure of income inequality improves, worsens, or is unaffected. However, it should be cautioned that a project has to be large relative to the population of the jurisdiction undertaking the project to even imagine that income distribution would be affected enough to warrant the analysis. Chapter 15 includes a discussion of redistributive effects analysis more generally including the use of Lorenz curves and Gini coefficients of inequality.

Subjective Information. Analyses often must rely on subjective, attitudinal data as distinguished from data that gauge behavior. One objective measure of a city road program might be the miles of roads resurfaced. An attitudinal measure of the same program might be citizen satisfaction with road conditions. It is indeed possible for citizens (stakeholders) to exhibit no increase in satisfaction even though road conditions may have improved markedly. The same type of situation can develop regarding police protection. Citizens' fear of being burglarized may not decrease despite a decline in the burglary rate brought on by the acquisition of city surveillance technology. In addition to not feeling safer, citizens also may feel that the surveillance system is an invasion of privacy.

Analytical models such as cost-benefit and cost-effectiveness analyses are based on rational behavior models in which individuals are presumed to respond to choices based on the desire to maximize their personal utility. Behavioral research calls into question these underlying assumptions, with the consequence that a supposedly rational result of analysis still may not be the actual preferred result of those affected by the project. Methodologies to take into account these more subjective perspectives involve surveying preferences of stakeholders or those with presumed interests in a potential project and assessing their subjective values.

The generic capital investment planning process discussed in the first section of this chapter, typical of many local governments, incorporates several opportunities for citizen involvement. For some, the CIP itself is the product of a joint government and citizen advisory committee, whereas the government's capital budget is the operationalization of that CIP.

Internal Validity. When costs, benefits, and expected relationships among them are defined, analysis must consider whether other possible variables may influence outcomes. Such influence is a threat to internal validity.[25] For example, the previous example of comparing an indoor spraying program for mosquitoes versus a low-lying area drainage program to combat malaria would be affected by the amount of rainfall after implementation of either choice, and good results may be attributed to a naturally occurring reduction in the number of mosquitoes. Similarly, a school construction program to build facilities for vocational education to increase employment among disadvantaged teenagers may seem to be effective when, in fact, it may have little influence on employment. Any increase in employment might be attributable not to school district investments, but to some other program, such as one operated by a nonprofit agency or church. Whether the analysis of a capital project is rigorously quantitative in economic terms or not, every effort must be made to state clearly the causal relationships between the project(s) and the expected outcomes and then to determine the possibility of variables not related to the capital project are affecting the result.

Problems of Quantification

Even if an ideal model is designed displaying all of the relevant types of costs and benefits or effects of a program, the problem of quantifying them remains. What are the monetary costs imposed on families relocated by urban redevelopment activities? Part of the costs will consist of moving expenses, perhaps higher rents, and greater costs for commuting to work. These measurements go well beyond the physical investment cost of the redevelopment program. While these items can be measured, it is much more difficult to set a dollar value on the mental anguish of having to move and leave friends behind. For the financial analysis of the urban redevelopment project, only the direct payments to families for purchasing their homes, moving expenses and so forth will count. For the economic analysis, the higher rents they will have to pay after the move, their greater commuting costs, and so forth will also count.

Shadow Pricing. Much of the problem of setting dollar values in the analysis stems from the fact that the results of many government investments do not have market prices. Despite various limitations, the private market does provide some standard for measuring the value of goods and services by the prices set for those.

Much of analysis in the public sector, however, must impute the prices or values of programs. One such method is known as shadow pricing.[26]

Suppose an analyst is given the task of predicting the benefits of a proposed outdoor recreation project such as a community swimming facility. The average hourly value (the shadow price) to a person attending the proposed new public facility can be assumed to be what individuals on the average spend per hour for other similar forms of outdoor recreation. This figure multiplied by the number attending will yield an approximate value of the recreational opportunities to be provided by the facility under study.

More detailed approaches can examine each form of outdoor recreation: hiking, swimming, tennis, golfing, picnicking, and so forth. In the case of swimming, the average spent per person for one hour of swimming at a private beach can be imputed to be the value of swimming at a public beach. One danger of such an assumption, however, is that it ignores the possibility that the quality of swimming may be different at the two beaches. If such a difference exists, the shadow price should be adjusted accordingly. Another danger is that building the new public swimming facility will change the overall market value of swimming in the area. With the additional supply—the public swimming facility—people may now be less willing to pay the price charged by the private facility. In that instance, the shadow price must take into account the changes in demand.

Shadow pricing becomes increasingly difficult and the analysis more tenuous when the subject matter for study involves functions that are primarily governmental. There is no apparent method by which a dollar value can be set for the defense capability of killing via intercontinental missiles X million people of an aggressor nation within one hour. Similarly, it is difficult to calculate the dollar value of avoiding one traffic fatality. The calculations employed require assessing what kinds of people are killed in automobile accidents, how old they are, and what income they would have earned in their remaining lifetimes.

Given the sometimes questionable assumptions that must be made in estimating the dollar value of saving a life, the argument can be made that cost-effectiveness analysis is preferable to cost-benefit analysis. The former does not attempt to place a dollar value on life but leaves the estimation of that value to decision makers. The disadvantage is that cost-effectiveness analysis, unlike cost-benefit analysis, seldom will yield a single measure of effectiveness. A traffic safety program might be measured by the number of lives saved and by the dollar value of property damage caused by crashes. Like apples and oranges, these benefits cannot be added together.

Contingent Valuation. The amount the public is willing to pay for a particular benefit or to avoid a particular cost also can be measured by means of formal surveys.

The methodology, known as contingent valuation, describes to survey respondents a particular service or government action and asks through various contingency statements what the respondent would be willing to pay.[27] For example, "Would you be willing to pay a $0.75 per day per family fee to avoid the smoke and other pollution emitted by a nearby power plant?" Depending on the response, subsequent questions would increase or decrease the $0.75 per day until the maximum price the individual would be willing to pay is identified, or how low the price has to go before the respondent says yes (including $0.00, meaning the respondent is not willing to pay anything to avoid the smoke). Guidelines for federal government cost-benefit analysis, contained in Office of Management and Budget (OMB) Circular A-94, recommend willingness to pay as an appropriate concept for measuring costs and benefits.[28] Contingent valuation is used by both government and private industry in the valuation of resource losses due to damages, such as in the Exxon Valdez oil spill, and by government to assess the benefits of projected recreational and natural resource preservation programs.[29] Contingent valuation studies are now almost universally required in designing multilateral donor agency-funded infrastructure construction projects that are predicated on user fees to ensure project financial viability.[30]

Discount Rates. Another problem for analysis involves the diversion of resources from the private to the public sector and from current consumption to investment in future returns. From an economic point of view, investment in a public project is warranted only if the returns are greater than they would be if the same funds were left to the private sector and if the future returns are worth the current sacrifice. Thus, the relevant concept of the cost of a public expenditure is the value of the benefits forgone by not leaving the money in the private sector to be consumed or invested.

A dollar diverted from the private sector to the public sector is not just an equivalent dollar cost or dollar benefit forgone. Presumably, had the dollar not been collected as taxes, it would have been available for the private citizen's use in some enjoyable, immediate consumption. Or it would have been available for the private citizen to invest in some kind of interest-bearing security. If the tax is used to finance a public project that produces a benefit to that citizen, or to citizens in general, then the benefit may offset the sacrifice the taxpayer had to make in private consumption or investment. This is the concept of *opportunity cost*—the public project comes at the expense of other opportunities. How do we analyze that tradeoff? If the tax is used to finance a public project that produces a benefit to citizens, then the benefit may offset the sacrifice taxpayers had to make in private consumption or investment.

The second problem is that the public benefit typically occurs at some future time, whereas the private consumption would have been in the more immediate time period. The future public benefit, even if it could be said to be exactly equal to the benefit of private consumption, will not be as valuable because of the simple fact of its being postponed into the future. People typically are not willing to put their money in a savings account, deferring its immediate use for some future situation, without the financial institution paying interest for the privilege of holding, and using, those savings. In the project analysis situation, the analogue to interest paid to the saver, some charge must be made against the dollars removed from consumption for an investment in order to arrive at the current value of future consumption forgone. This charge is known as the discount rate.

The discount rate addresses both problems: the opportunity cost and the time value of money, two sides of the same coin. First, it is similar to an interest charge that reflects the cost of removing a dollar from private sector use and diverting it to the public sector. If a dollar could earn 6% in the private sector, investment in the public sector would be warranted (in a strictly economic sense) only if the rate of return from the public investment would be at least 6%. Second, the discount rate takes into consideration the time pattern of expenditures and returns. In general, people prefer present consumption to future consumption. A dollar that might be spent for current consumption is worth more than a dollar that might be consumed 10 years from now.

Clearly, the choice of a discount rate has an important influence on investment decisions. Too low a rate understates the value of current consumption or of leaving the money to the private sector. Too high a rate uneconomically favors current consumption over future benefits and results in less investment than is worthwhile. The choice of a discount rate may thus determine the outcome of the analysis.

Selecting appropriate discount rates is difficult. For the GE example, investing in the jet engine business or the power turbine business, the discount rate typically would be the cost of capital to the corporation. Since GE's capital includes both equity (stock values) and debt (loans, bonds), some kind of weighted cost of capital would be ascertained, and that weighted cost of capital typically would be used as the discount rate. GE then would, if evaluating strictly on financial returns, require that the returns (financial only) must exceed the cost of capital. That would be referred to as the *hurdle rate.* But typically a private corporation would have a higher hurdle rate since they would not just be comparing the investment with the cost of capital. They would be comparing the two different investments in many cases, and would more likely select the one with the higher rate of return. Of course many other factors would go into the investment decision.

For the public sector, private market rates are inappropriate because they include calculations of the risks of loss that lenders must consider in making a loan to a private company. On the other hand, interest rates charged governments often are lower because of the presumed lower risk of default (see discussion in Chapter 13 of public sector borrowing costs and risk). Also, interest cost to government often is artificially low because of various guarantees against defaults and sometimes the loan's tax-exempt status. The appropriate discount rate lies between these extremes. OMB annually provides guidance to federal agencies on the discount rates that should be used for federal projects (Circular A-94, Appendix C). In 2006, the discount rate for costs and benefits ranged from 4.7% for a three-year period to 5.2% for a 30-year period, the equivalent nominal interest rate for federal Treasury bonds with three- and 30-year maturities, respectively.[31]

Several discount rates may be applied to program alternatives to determine the sensitivity of the analysis to discounting. If the cost-benefit ratios of a project are well above 1.0 regardless of the discount rate used, little problem occurs. A different situation arises if some plausible discount rates yield results well below 1.0. In other situations, one discount rate might result in a favorable cost-benefit ratio for alternative A and another ratio for alternative B. The point is that an arbitrary choice of a discount rate without consideration of other ranges can produce misleading results. Some evidence also shows that discount rates and net present value calculations are used less frequently by public sector managers than by private sector managers, attributable presumably to the greater influence in the public sector of political variables.[32]

The relationships among costs, returns, and time are depicted graphically in **Figure 12–1**. Most investment projects involve heavy capital costs early on, followed by a tapering off to operating costs. Returns are nonexistent or minimal for the first few years and then increase rapidly. The shape of the return curve after the initial upturn depends on the nature of the particular investment and is drawn arbitrarily for illustrative purposes in the figure. The comparison of costs to benefits over time makes the necessity for discounting obvious. Higher costs occur earlier in most projects. The higher benefits that occur later are valued less because they occur later in time.

Costs and benefits must therefore be compared for each time period (usually each year), and the differences summed over the life span of the project. That is, in essence, what a discount rate accomplishes. The longer it takes for returns to occur, the more their value is discounted. In effect, the situation involves compound interest in reverse. Costs occurring earlier are subject to less discounting. Thus, for a project to be economically feasible, total discounted benefits must exceed total discounted costs. This excess of discounted benefits over discounted costs is known as the *net present value* (NPV). Government expenditures are efficient allocations of a society's resources when the net present value is positive. Any spreadsheet software contains built-in functions for calculating the net present value, the internal rate of return, and similar concepts useful in assessing the value of benefits occurring over time in comparison with the costs of the investment.

Figure 12–1 Relationship of Costs and Benefits to Time

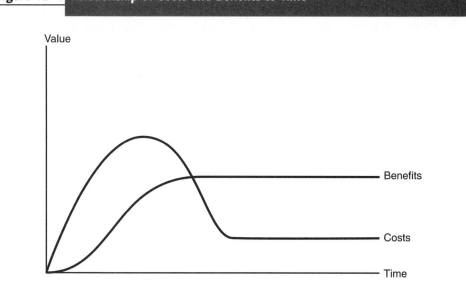

Measuring the Return on Investment (ROI). Two forms of calculating the rate of return on investment are typically used in capital project analysis. If the project is similar to what a private company might do, such as build a parking garage for which customers will pay fees to cover the costs of the facility, then the first analysis will be a financial rate of return (sometimes called a *financial internal rate of return* or FIRR). The full costs of the project are measured on the cost side, and the financial returns in the form of charges to customers over the life span of the garage are the measures on the benefit side. The expectation is that the garage would earn revenues, taking into account the long time period over which those revenues would be earned as exhibited in **Figure 12–1** that would yield a positive FIRR.

Similarly, the extension of water lines into a new neighborhood would yield revenue in the form of hook-up charges and regular charges for water use. A FIRR analysis would inform the decision makers if the planned costs for hook-up fees and regular usage fees would yield a positive financial rate of return. Since private providers build and run parking garages and private companies may provide water services, the financial analysis of a project is important in order to evaluate whether the public investment in either facility pays for itself through future revenue generation. If it does not, then decision makers would in effect need to approve a government subsidy in order for the project to go forward.

The results of the financial analysis, if the financial return is less than an equivalent privately provided option, do not automatically mean the project should not be done. There may be good reasons to go forward anyway including as discussed earlier positive externalities of a non-financial nature or redistributive benefits such as a subsidy element for low-income families. But the strict analysis of financial costs and financial returns makes the value of these other considerations apparent even if they were not directly measured.

Of course not all projects yield direct revenue. Construction of a recreation facility from which the public could not be excluded or regulated through charging fees for use would yield benefits to the community, but if it is open to the public without charge, would yield no revenue. As noted in the discussion of shadow pricing above, imputed prices, the prices people might pay for other recreational opportunities may be used nonetheless to calculate a rate of return. That rate of return would be called an *economic internal rate of return* (EIRR). [33]

These examples might seem as if the distinction between economic and financial rates of return is really just two names for the same thing, that an analyst may use either one or the other indifferently. For some projects, both an FIRR and an EIRR are likely to be calculated, and the results are likely to be different. For example, if the water line extension example includes health benefits to the previously unserved neighborhood whose well water contained some levels of toxic substances, then there would be value to society from the project that would be additional to the financial cash flows from the hook-up and usage fees.

If a reduction in illnesses means fewer days lost to productive work, and fewer costs for health care, then the monetary value of those additional workdays and the reduction in health care costs would be added to the financial returns, even though there would be no attempt actually to *charge* the individuals in their water rates for those health benefits. Similarly, if the project imposed costs on other individuals, or the government as a whole, such as the additional costs to people who had to relocate from their homes, then those costs would be added to the project costs. The economic rate of return analysis typically includes all of the financial costs and benefits, but also adds in economic costs and benefits that are not reflected in the financial structure of the project. The calculation methods are identical. The difference is what is put into the cost stream and the benefit stream.

Asset Management

Asset management historically has not been tied directly to budgeting, not even in the context of capital budgeting. However, the increasingly sophisticated financial management systems that larger governmental jurisdictions employ may blur the lines as comprehensive systems link modules for capital budgeting, asset management, and operating (current) budgeting. Historically, asset management comes into play long after capital budget decisions have been made. Capital projects are implemented, or capital purchases are made, and the resulting physical facilities or equipment then become part of the jurisdiction's inventory of assets, whether the jurisdiction has a formal system or not. These traditionally separate processes are no longer as distinct. Two factors have contributed to the much greater emphasis now given to the role of asset management in public sector organizations—the concern beginning in the 1980s that many state and local governments had allowed critical infrastructure to deteriorate without any adequate planning for its replacement, and the 1999 release of GASB Statement No. 34.

Asset Decline

Asset Decline in the United States. Concern for the condition of America's deteriorating infrastructure base emerged in the early 1980s. Throughout that decade, spectacular incidents, such as the collapse of the Mianus Bridge in Connecticut and detailed studies of investment deficits brought heightened attention to the need to rebuild and maintain the nation's physical infrastructure assets.[34] The concern continues. A study by the American Society of Civil Engineers (ASCE) estimated that the combined public infrastructure deficit in facilities such as water systems, schools, airports, and highways was a staggering $1.3 trillion in 2000.[35] That figure was close to the total amount of municipal debt outstanding that year. The ASCE repeated the study in 2005 and reported that overall public infrastructure conditions continued to deteriorate, estimating the new gap at $1.6 trillion.[36]

The ASCE study defines the infrastructure deficit as facilities that have outlived their usefulness as well as facilities needed to address unmet needs of unserved and underserved populations. For example, some sewer systems still in use were more than 100 years old. An earlier Congressional Budget Office study noted that sewer pipes, for example, have an average asset life of 50 years, and that many systems in major U.S. cities had reached, or were approaching that age.[37] In addition, when governments do not spend adequately for maintenance and rehabilitation, facilities may not come near their useful life span. But budgeting sufficient amounts in the operating budget for repairs and maintenance, in

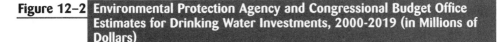

Figure 12–2 Environmental Protection Agency and Congressional Budget Office Estimates for Drinking Water Investments, 2000-2019 (in Millions of Dollars)

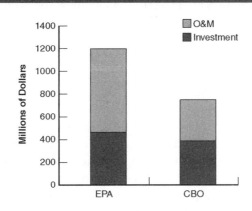

0 & M—Operation and Maintenance

Source: Reprinted from U.S. Congressional Budget Office (2003). *Future spending on water infrastructure: a comparison of estimates from the Congressional Budget Office and the Environmental Protection Agency.* Washington, DC: U.S. Government Printing Office, 2.

order to avoid or reduce capital costs twenty years hence is not easy for elected executive and legislative officials.

Figure 12–2 illustrates the infrastructure deficit in water supply systems, comparing estimates by the U.S. Environmental Protection Agency and the Congressional Budget Office for capital investment and operation and maintenance expenditures needed between 2000 and 2019 for drinking water alone. These estimates are for expenditures to replace systems that have gone beyond their useful life, for major rehabilitation of systems to extend their useful lives, and for systems to address the needs of population growth and quality improvements.

The two agencies' estimates are widely variant for operation and maintenance requirements, but quite close on capital investment requirements. CBO explains the differences in operation and maintenance estimates mainly to timing differences. EPA's assumption in its estimate is that most of the capital investments are needed right away, whereas CBO spreads a similar amount of capital investment over the 20-year period. The earlier capital investments (in EPA's estimate) of course then generate operation and maintenance expenditures over the time period, resulting in a larger EPA cost estimate as the illustration shows.[38] According to the CBO and the EPA, capital investments in drinking water over that 20-year period should be between $360 billion and nearly $500 billion, respectively. If, as the EPA estimates assume, many of the investments need to be now, then operation and maintenance costs over the period evaluated by both agencies exceed the capital investments required.

Asset Decline in Other Countries. Concerns over infrastructure deficits are not limited to the United States, causing similar concern for improved systems for planning and budgeting and then managing the assets once built. European Union countries and especially developing and emerging market countries experience shortages of capital to construct physical facilities, and often also fail to support existing capital facilities with adequate operation and maintenance. The collapse of Asian financial markets in the 1990s and the later scandal-related collapse of Enron has caused continuing problems in attracting capital to investments in power and water, leaving many countries increasingly concerned that public infrastructure cannot keep up with demand for services whether caused by aging infrastructure as in developed countries or inadequate infrastructure in the first place in developing economies.[39] Estimates in 2006 of infrastructure investment requirements in South Asia, for example, indicated that nearly 30% of the investment requirements would be to replace outmoded or deteriorated infrastructure.[40]

The City of Toronto, Ontario, in Canada in its 2005 Water and Wastewater Business Plan gave priority first to addressing renewal needs of aging and deteriorating infrastructure, then to several other objectives. The city had just put in place a relatively new asset management system that allowed them to monitor and evaluate the condition of existing infrastructure. According to the business plan, the system revealed the need is greater to increase investment to replace dilapidated facilities and to increase recurrent operation and maintenance expenditures than to expand the system. The asset management system feeds information into both capital and current budgeting processes.[41]

Spending on Infrastructure. The U.S. physical infrastructure asset base exists primarily because of state and local government investments. As far back as the mid-1950s, state and local capital spending greatly exceeded federal capital spending. In 1956, state and local capital spending on infrastructure amounted to almost $28 billion, whereas federal capital spending was less than $10 billion. A gradual climb in federal spending led to its overtaking state and local capital spending in 1976, and it remained higher until significant federal budget cutbacks affected capital spending in 1986.[42] **Figure 12–3** documents for selected years since 1980 federal, state and local government expenditures for public works facilities specifically. This includes highways, airports, water transport and terminals, sewage, solid waste, water supply, and mass transit.

Figure 12–3 Federal, State, and Local Roles in Public Works Funding, 1980–2002, Selected Years (in Millions of Dollars)

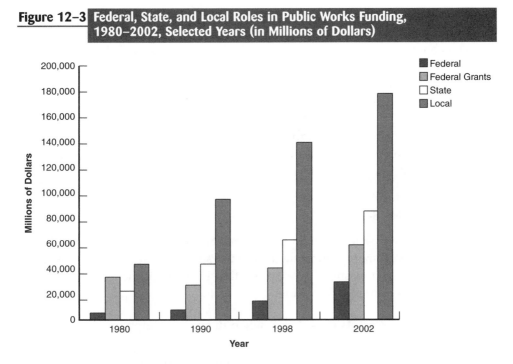

Sources: Compiled from Bureau of the Census, U.S. Department of Commerce (2006). *Statistical abstract of the United States: 2006.* Washington, DC: U.S. Government Printing Office, 282; U.S. Office of Management and Budget (2006). *Budget of the United States, FY 2007: historical tables.* Washington, DC: U.S. Government Printing Office, 167.

This figure gives some indication of the relative roles played by federal, state, and local governments in public works funding. The amounts for the three sources are all for direct spending, both capital investments and maintenance and rehabilitation, other than the specifically identified federal grants. By far, local governments exceed both federal and state governments combined. As can be seen in **Figure 12–3**, over 50% of the total is local government spending in each of the three years after 1980. States are next at around 25%, and federal direct (spent directly by federal agencies on capital projects) is in all the years in the figure less than 10%.

The federal grants figure shows the contribution the federal government makes, for non-defense capital investments only, through intergovernmental grant transfers. Federal grants for physical capital investment historically were a relatively small contribution. Programs introduced in the 1970s caused federal grants to state and local governments for physical capital investments to double between 1975 and 1980, and then remain basically static until the early 1990s. In **Figure 12–3**, federal grants in 1980 for capital projects carried out at the state or local level were just over 30% of total physical capital expenditures. In the other three years depicted, federal grants have been around 15% of the total.

The concern for deterioration of existing physical assets and corresponding inadequate investment levels prompted larger city governments and the more populous states as early as the early 1980s to begin developing, or purchasing from financial information services firms, more sophisticated approaches to planning and managing the infrastructure base. But the introduction of GASB Statement No. 34 in 1999 raised the bar on financial reporting standards for state and local governments, forcing more rigorous attention to the condition of the asset base in reporting on the overall health of the institution.

GASB Statement No. 34

Statement No. 34, issued by the Governmental Accounting Standards Board, requires that governments report their capital assets in a *statement of net assets* and requires that the report show the depreciation in value of those assets. Specific asset reporting requirements include:

- Depreciation of assets must begin when the asset, equipment, or facilities is acquired or put in service;
- Accumulated depreciation for all assets must be reported;
- Assets acquired or built prior to 1980 are not required to be reported, but once a major renovation of an older asset has been carried out, then the rehabilitated asset must be included in the statement of net assets.[43]

The difference that this makes to capital and operating budget practices is substantial.[44] From a budgeting point of view, the cost of a capital project enters the budget in the year in which the cost is incurred whether the governmental entity has a capital budgeting process and a formal capital budget or not. GASB 34 gives visibility to the expected life span of facilities and the depreciation of the assets through the financial reporting process. In turn, citizens may observe the adequacy of the operating budget's provisions for operation and maintenance and provision for future replacement costs. In reality, citizens are unlikely to pay attention to those details unless it becomes an electoral issue. However, bond rating agencies do take into account the adequacy of operation and maintenance programs and provision for timely rehabilitation expenditures to avoid larger capital costs in the future (see Chapter 13). The financial reporting requirements for physical assets more readily expose to financial institutions and bond underwriters the overall health of a jurisdiction's infrastructure and the adequacy of budget planning to preserve those assets. That in turn can affect the bond rating and therefore the interest the jurisdiction will have to pay on a bond issue. (Chapter 13 discusses bond ratings and their effect on the cost of borrowing).

As a result, an increasing number of state and local governments have adopted comprehensive systems for assessing physical asset conditions and linking those conditions to the budgeting process, both capital budgeting and recurrent budgeting. San Diego uses a computerized inventory and mapping system to keep track of maintenance schedules on 3,000 miles of water and sewer pipes.[45]

Requirements similar to GASB 34 in other countries also have produced similar changes. The United Kingdom Accounting Standards Board (ASB) recognizes as a Standard of Recommended Practice (SORP) local government asset accounting that includes asset inventories, depreciation of those assets, and changes in valuation of the assets.[46] Standard accounting practices in New Zealand, noted for its progressive public sector budgeting and financial management practices, "records state highways at depreciated replacement cost based on the estimated present cost of constructing the existing asset by the most appropriate method of construction." [47] Similar requirements have been proposed in Canada. The Sustainable Water and Sewage Systems Act (Bill 175, 2005) would require municipalities to report on the full life cycle costs of water and wastewater service. Toronto's 2005 Water and Wastewater business plan noted: "It is clear that municipalities will be required to implement asset management plans."[48]

Cities throughout developing countries that have underinvested in both maintenance and reconstruction of such critical urban infrastructure assets as paved roadways, water systems, and drainage also have begun to develop more complete systems for taking inventory of existing assets and developing CIPs based on a schedule of needed improvements.[49] These innovations in public sector asset management have begun to alter the ways some cities plan, budget, and manage their finances; capital planning and budgeting are now playing a more important role.[50]

Figure 12–4 illustrates the systems framework for Canada's Ontario Province system for managing the infrastructure planning and budgeting process with the asset management system for the province. Such integration is now common in larger states (or provinces) and cities in the U.S. and other industrialized countries. A capital investment planning process such as that outlined earlier in this chapter links to the budgeting process the capital budget for the investment portion and the operating or recurrent budget for maintenance and repairs. In turn, the infrastructure assets once completed enter into the asset management system that tracks the condition of the infrastructure, shows the depreciated value of the assets as they age, and links back to the recurrent and capital budgets for regular repairs and maintenance expenditures, and major rehabilitation as the infrastructure ages.

Figure 12–4 Framework for Integrating Capital Planning, Budgeting, and Asset Management

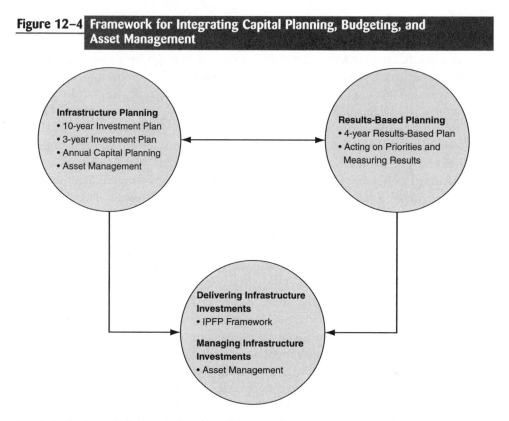

Source: Reprinted from Ministry of Public Infrastructure Renewal (2004). *Building a better tomorrow: an infrastructure planning, financing and procurement framework for Ontario's public sector. Toronto, Ontario: Ministry of Public Infrastructure Renewal.*

Asset management practices are not limited to state and local governments. At the federal level, OMB Circular A-11 was modified in 2006 in Part 300 (focusing on planning, budgeting, acquisition and management of capital assets) to give greater emphasis to the management of federal assets. When proposing in their budget to acquire a new capital asset or significantly improve an existing asset, agencies must include with their budgets a capital asset plan and business case summary.[51] The *business case summary* explains the rationale for the investment in terms of mission, alternatives considered, and provides detailed management information on the acquisition process and subsequent management of the asset. At least three viable alternatives to the asset acquisition must be presented as part of the business case. Operations and maintenance milestones are identified in the business case in order to ensure that there has been adequate planning to preserve the value of the asset once acquired and put into service. A plan for measuring the performance of the asset to be acquired provides the basis for subsequent monitoring to ensure that operations and maintenance activities are taking place to maximize the asset's useful life.[52]

Summary

Governments plan and budget for the recurring expenditures for the myriad of services they provide, and governments plan and budget for major investments in infrastructure systems and equipment. The latter investments are the focus of capital planning and budgeting. Most state and local governments have formal systems for making capital budget decisions and segregate capital investments into separate capital budgets or statements. The reasons are two-fold: state and local capital investments are a major share of their total budget decisions in any given year, and state and local governments generally rely upon various forms of borrowing (discussed in Chapter 13) to finance capital investments. Both reasons make capital budgeting a best practice for state and local governments.

The rationale for federal capital budgeting, despite being evaluated several times in the last three decades, has never been persuasive. Capital investments are a much smaller share of the federal budget, and much of the capital cost incurred by the federal government are for defense expenditures that are not normally considered investments or grants to state and local governments to support their capital investments. Despite not adopting capital budgeting, however, the federal government has continued to adopt financial management and reporting practices to improve upon how capital costs are communicated to Congress and the public, and how they are managed.

Whether it is a formal capital budgeting process or not, federal, state and local governments use formal analysis tools to assist in evaluating capital investments. These tools use both economic and financial measures to assess the value of the investment to the governmental jurisdiction, and take into account that these are long-term investments with long-term pay-off. The analytic tools do not substitute quantitative analysis for judgment in decision making, but they do expose for decision makers and the public the underlying assumptions, costs and benefits so that good judgments can be made.

Also independent of whether capital budgets are employed or not, other pressures since the 1980s have generated demand for better decision making and better reporting on investments. Deterioration of major infrastructure systems that might have lasted much longer before having to be replaced started creating demand in the U.S. for better management of infrastructure systems, and more informed attention to maintenance costs and the depreciating value of infrastructure. Government cost accounting standards, particularly GASB 34, require financial reporting of physical assets that more or less demand more sophisticated and integrated planning, budgeting and financial management systems that include a focus on asset management. This has relegated arguments about whether or not to have capital budgets to the back seat as, regardless of formal capital budgeting, governments must do a better job of managing the entire capital investment process.

Notes

1. Wang, X. (2006). *Financial management in the public sector: tools, applications, and cases.* Armonk, NY: M.E. Sharpe, 116.

2. Governmental Accounting Standards Board (2006). *Statement of governmental accounting standards No. 34, basic statements—and management's discussion and analysis—for state and local government.* Norwalk, CT: Governmental Accounting Standards Board, 11.

3. MacManus, S. (2004). "Bricks and mortar" politics: how infrastructure decisions defeat incumbents; *Public Budgeting & Finance, 24, Spring*, 96–112.

4. Kelly, M. & Zieper, M. (2000). Financing for the future: the economic benefits of parks and open space. *Government Finance Review, 16, December*, 23–28.

5. Bureau of the Census, U.S. Department of Commerce (2006). *Statistical abstract of the United States: 2006.* Washington, DC: U.S. Government Printing Office, 281–282.

6. Orange Water and Sewer Authority (2005). *Capital improvements program for the period 2005–2019 including five year capital improvements budget for the period 2005–2009.* Carrboro, NC: Orange Water and Sewer Authority.

7. Government Performance Project (2005). *State report cards: Michigan State Government's grade for infrastructure management.* Retrieved September 5, 2006, from http://results.gpponline.org/StateCategoryCriteria.aspx?id=114&relatedid=5.

8. Berne, R. & Schramm, R. (1986). *The financial analysis of governments.* Englewood Cliffs, NJ: Prentice-Hall; Nollenberger, K., Groves, S., & Valente, M. (2003) *Evaluating financial condition: a handbook for local government,* 4th ed. Washington, DC: International City/County Management Association.

9. U.S. Congressional Budget Office (1992). *How federal spending for infrastructure and other public investments affects the economy.* Washington, DC: U.S. Government Printing Office, xv; Haughwout, A. (2003). *Public infrastructure investments, productivity and welfare in fixed geographic areas.* New York: Federal Reserve Bank of New York. Retrieved September 5, 2006, from http://www.newyorkfed.org/research/staff_reports/sr104.pdf

10. Germain, C. (2000). Balance your project. *Government Finance Review, 16, August*, 15–20.

11. Duscha, L. (2006). *Managing infrastructure in the 21ˢᵗ century Bureau of Reclamation*, testimony before the Committee on Energy and Natural Resources, U.S. Senate, May 23, 2006. Retrieved August 15, 2006, from http://www7.nationalacademies.org/ocga/testimony/Construction_and_Infrastructure_in_the_Bureau_of_Reclamation.asp.

12. Vogt, A. (2004). *Capital budgeting and finance: a guide for local governments*. Washington, DC: International City/County Management Association.

13. Beckett-Camarata, J. (2003). An examination of the relationship between the municipal strategic plan and the capital budget and its effect on financial performance. *Journal of Public Budgeting, Accounting and Financial Management, 15*, 23–40.

14. Ministry of Municipal Affairs and Housing (2002). *Municipal capital budgeting handbook*. Ontario, Canada: Queen's Printer for Ontario.

15. U.S. Office of Management and Budget (2006). *Budget of the United States Government for 2007: analytical perspectives, federal investment*. Washington, DC: U.S. Government Printing Office, 55.

16. U.S. Office of Management and Budget (2006). *Budget of the United States Government for 2007: analytical perspectives, federal investment*, 55.

17. U.S. Office of Management and Budget (1967). *Report of the President's Commission on Budget Concepts*. Washington, DC: U.S. Government Printing Office, 34.

18. U.S. General Accounting Office (1996). *Budget issues: budgeting for federal capital*. Washington, DC: U.S. Government Printing Office.

19. U.S. General Accounting Office (1995). *Budget structure: providing an investment focus in the federal budget*. Washington, DC: U.S. Government Printing Office.

20. President's Commission to Study Capital Budgeting (1999). *Report*. Washington, DC: U.S. Government Printing Office.

21. U.S. Office of Management and Budget (2002). *Budget of the United States Government: fiscal year 2003, analytical perspectives*. Washington, DC: U.S. Government Printing Office, 12.

22. Whittington, D. & MacRae, Jr., D. (1986). The issue of standing in cost-benefit analysis. *Journal of Policy Analysis and Management 5*, 665–682; Trumbull, W. (1990). Who has standing in cost-benefit analysis? *Journal of Policy Analysis and Management 9*, 201–218; Fuguitt, D. & Wilcox, S. J. (1999). *Cost-benefit analysis for public sector decision makers*. Westbrook, CT: Quorum Books.

23. Steelman, T. & Maguire, L. (1999). Understanding participant perspectives: q-methodology in national forest management. *Journal of Policy Analysis and Management, 18*, 361–388; Walters, L. et al. (2000). Putting more public in policy analysis. *Public Administration Review, 60*, 349–359.

24. Johnson, R. & Pierce, J. (1975). The economic evaluation of policy impacts: cost-benefit and cost effectiveness analysis. In F. Scioli & T. Cook (Eds.), *Methodologies for analyzing public policies*. Lexington, MA: Lexington Books, 131–154.

25. Campbell, D. & Stanley, J. (1963). *Experimental and quasi-experimental designs for research.* Boston: Houghton Mifflin.

26. Tsuneki, A. (2002). Shadow-pricing interpretation of the Pigovian rule for the optimal provision of public goods: a note. *International Tax and Public Finance 9*, 93–104; McKean, R. N. (1968). The use of shadow prices. In S. B. Chase, Jr. (Ed.), *Problems in public expenditure analysis.* Washington, DC: Brookings Institution, 33–65.

27. Brubaker, E. (2004). Eliciting the public's budgetary preferences: insights from contingent valuation. *Public Budgeting & Finance, 24, Spring,* 72–95.

28. U.S. Office of Management and Budget (1992). *Circular A-94 revised: guidelines and discount rates for cost benefit analysis of federal programs.* Washington, DC: OMB.

29. Carson, R. (2002). *Contingent evaluation: a comprehensive bibliography and history.* London: Edward Elgar Publishing.

30. U.S. Department of Agriculture (2006). *Contingent valuation/recreational values.* Retrieved September 15, 2006, from http://www.economics.nrcs.usda.gov/technical/recreate/index.html

31. U.S. Office of Management and Budget (1992). *Circular A-94 revised, appendix C.*

32. Richardson, K. (1998). The effect of public versus private decision environment on the use of the net present value investment criterion. *Journal of Public Budgeting, Accounting and Financial Management, 10,* 21–52.

33. Brighham, E. & Ehrhardt, M. (2004). *Financial management: theory and practice,* 11th ed. Cincinnati, OH: South-Western College Publishing. This is a business-oriented text, as are most texts that provide detailed analysis of rates of return and related concepts, but the analytical framework is the same whether private sector or public sector oriented.

34. National Council on Public Works Improvement (1988). *Fragile foundations: a report on America's public works.* Washington, DC: U.S. Government Printing Office.

35. Kinnander, O. (2001). As infrastructure crumbles, engineers scream for investment, *The Bond Buyer, 335, March 9,* 40.

36. American Society of Civil Engineers (2005). *2005 report card for America's infrastructure.* Washington, DC: ASCE.

37. U.S. Congressional Budget Office (2002). *Future investment in drinking water and wastewater infrastructure.* Washington, DC: U.S. Government Printing Office, 8.

38. U.S. Congressional Budget Office (2003). *Future spending on water infrastructure: a comparison of estimates from the Congressional Budget Office and the Environmental Protection Agency.* Washington, DC: Congressional Budget Office, 1–3.

39. Worenklein, J. (2003). The global crisis in power and infrastructure: lessons learned and new directions. *Journal of Structured and Project Finance, 9,* 7–11.

40. Chatterton, I. & Peuerto, O. (2006). *Estimation of infrastructure investment needs in the South Asia region.* Washington, DC: World Bank, i. retrieved September 15, 2006, from

http://web.worldbank.org/WBSITE/EXTERNAL/EXTABOUTUS/ORGANIZATION/
EXTINFNETWORK/0,,contentMDK:20535909~menuPK:489896~pagePK:64159605~pi
PK:64157667~theSitePK:489890,00.html.

41. Toronto Water (2005). *2005 multi-year business plan.* Toronto, Ontario: City of Toronto, 43.

42. U.S. Congressional Budget Office (1992). *Trends in public infrastructure outlays and the president's proposals for infrastructure spending in 1993.* Washington, DC: U.S. Government Printing Office, 15.

43. Governmental Accounting Standards Board (2006). *Statement of governmental accounting standards no. 34, basic statements—and management's discussion and analysis—for state and local government.*

44. Frank, H. et.al. (2005). Will GASB 34 induce changes in local government forecasting practice? a preliminary investigation. *Journal of Public Budgeting, Accounting and Financial Management, 17,* 557–558.

45. Kittower, D. (2000). Making the most of public assets. *Governing, 14, January,* 58.

46. Ellwood, C. (2002). The financial reporting (r)evolution in the UK public sector. *Public Budgeting, Accounting and Financial Management, 14,* 572.

47. Santiso, C. (2006). Banking on accountability? strengthening budget oversight and public sector auditing in emerging economies, *Public Budgeting & Finance, 26, Summer,* 57.

48. Toronto Water (2005). *2005 multi-year business plan,* 44.

49. Johnson, R. & Barnett, C. (1996). *Urban services delivery in CEE and the NIS,* prepared for U.S. Agency for International Development Zagreb Conference on Local Government. Research Triangle Park, NC: Research Triangle Institute.

50. Fernholz, F. & Fernholz, R. (2006). *Strategic municipal asset management.* Cities Alliance: Municipal Finance Task Force report. Retrieved August 15, 2006, from http://www.mftf.org/resources/index.cfm?fuseaction=index&CatID=67.

51. U.S. Office of Management and Budget (2006). *OMB Circular A-11: capital assets.* Washington, DC: U.S. Government Printing Office, 9–11 of Section 300.

52. U.S. Office of Management and Budget (2006). *OMB Circular A-11: capital assets.* Washington, DC: U.S. Government Printing Office, 27 of Section 300.

Chapter 13

CAPITAL FINANCE AND DEBT MANAGEMENT

In this chapter, we discuss the means for financing capital projects. As noted in Chapter 12, capital investments are *lumpy.* That is, financing a large infrastructure project requires a large amount of capital up front, whereas the benefits and the revenue from that up front investment are spread over many years—20 to 50 years in the case of significant infrastructure such as a sewer system. Not only will present taxpayers, or service charge payers, benefit from the investment, but future generations will too, and they should help pay for the investment. For such large projects, few governments other than national governments have the capital or taxing power to finance the acquisition and construction at one time. The same is true of large private corporations wishing to undertake a major expansion of their production facilities. And the same is true of most households when it comes to purchasing something as large as a home. Few families have the cash on hand to make their first home purchase. Consequently, most governments, corporations, and households look to other sources of funds—investors or lenders—to finance up front the capital investment, and agree to pay a financial return to those investors at a future time or times.

The primary source for governments financing large capital projects is borrowing from investors: individuals and financial institutions. In the United States, state and local governments borrow from individuals and institutions such as banks, capital market funds, and other institutional investors by issuing bonds. At the end of 2006, the outstanding value of municipal securities held by various investors was over $2.3 trillion.[1] That is over 8% of total U.S. domestic debt outstanding, second only to U.S. government treasury securities and corporate bonds. Bonds and bond issuance by governments are a major focus of discussion in this chapter. In other industrialized countries, specialized lending institutions that serve as bankers for municipalities often substitute for bond issues. The second focus in this chapter is on governments' debt management practices, and what happens when the borrower does not or cannot repay.

Even with robust capital markets and governments in sound financial condition, borrowing is not always sufficient nor always the best way to finance infrastructure. The last 25 years has seen an increase in private equity investments in public infrastructure projects. This means of financing has quite different implications for financing and managing public facilities, and is the final topic of this chapter.

▌ Types of Finance

In the private sector, there are three sources of financing capital assets: *debt*, *equity*, and *retained earnings*. Retained earnings are what households think of as *savings*. Debt is available to both public and private institutions, and to households. Equity comes in the form of stock issuance in the case of publicly traded companies. Companies whose stock is traded on one of the stock exchanges—the New York Stock Exchange (NYSE) and the National Association of Securities Dealers Automated Quotations (NASDAQ), for example—sell stock in order to raise capital for investment or operating purposes. Purchasers of stock then literally *own* a fraction of the corporation. They are not entitled to any *repayment* of the money invested in purchasing the stock. Rather, they are entitled to a share of the value of the corporation. They may benefit from that value share if the corporation pays dividends, or they may sell the stock at a later date, and if the company has performed well in the market, the value of the shares sold will have appreciated. Equity investors of course also may experience a decline in value and actually sell their stock for less than they originally invested.

Creditors who have lent money to a public or private enterprise legally have first recourse to being repaid; they have the first claim on the assets of the borrower. Equity investors come in after all debts are satisfied. In some countries, the state owns companies that are listed on that country's stock exchange(s). For example, oil and gas companies in some countries may be owned in part by the state and in part by private investors. Public transportation companies, such as airlines, telecommunications, and some utilities such as electric power generation and water supply may be organized as state-owned enterprises with partial, usually minority, ownership in the hands of private investors.

The other forms of equity capital are owners' equity investments in the case of privately held companies and retained earnings. In a family-owned company in which 100% of the ownership is private, not available for public sale through shares of stock, the investment(s) these private owners have made both initially in founding the company and potentially later as additional capital is required is *owners' equity*. Of course it need not be a family-owned company. Partnerships such as law firms are privately held, and the owners' investments are the source of equity capital. Cargill, an agribusiness company, is the largest U.S. privately held company with revenues in 2004 of over $67 billion.[2] When a privately held company, including a state-owned enterprise that does not offer stock shares for sale, seeks equity investment, it either comes from the current owners inviting additional private owners to put capital into the company, in exchange for partial ownership, or from the existing owners contributing additional capital from their own sources.[3]

Retained earnings, essentially profits not distributed to owners, are the third source of equity capital. For private companies, revenues in excess of cost may be distributed to the owners as their share of the profits, or they may be reinvested in the company for a variety of purposes, including capital facilities expansion. These *retained* earnings, earnings not paid out to owners but kept in the company for investment, are an important source of finance for capital investment. Retained earnings also may be available to public utilities such as water authorities, but typically they are tightly regulated, or even prohibited. That is, a public water authority is not set up to make a profit, and certainly would not be expected to pay dividends to the owners (citizens). But water rates may be set up to generate revenue in excess of operating and depreciation costs in order to build up a capital reserve that then must be reinvested in the water utility. These *excess* revenues often may be referred to as *retained earnings.*

In some countries such as the Philippines, a utility may be *owned* by the municipality it serves, and the municipality may expect dividends to be paid back into the municipal treasury. However, that practice in the 1990s almost decapitalized some water utilities because the *parent* municipality took capital out of the enterprise as dividends, capital that should have been retained to replace depreciating and deteriorating facilities.[4]

All three sources of finance are used by public sector institutions to secure the capital needed to finance investments that may be rehabilitating aging infrastructure or other facilities or building new capacity in order to meet the needs of a growing population, as discussed in Chapter 12. While debt is by far the most prevalent form of capital financing for public sector institutions, the public sector since the 1980s both in industrialized countries and in developing nations has sought private equity investments to help finance infrastructure.

▮ State and Local Debt Financing

State and local governments around the world rely upon debt capital to finance many types of public facilities and infrastructure. In many European countries, borrowing from banks or financing institutions especially created to lend to local governments is the most common means by which local governments secure debt capital. The Municipal Bank of the Netherlands is an example. In the United States, although some local governments borrow from banks for temporary operating funds, the main source of debt finance is the issuance of bonds. Commonly referred to as municipal bonds, bonds are issued by state and local general-purpose jurisdictions as well as many nonprofit public institutions, such as hospitals, and single-service authorities, such as school and water districts. The exemption from federal taxes of the interest earned from many of these bonds is a critical feature of their success and a controversial one that is discussed below.[5]

Types of Bonds

Guaranteed and Non-Guaranteed Bonds. The two main categories of long-term bonds are *full faith and credit bonds* (or *general obligation bonds*) and *non-guaranteed* (or *revenue*) *bonds*. General obligation bonds are generally described as *guaranteed* because they are backed by the full faith and credit of the issuing government. That means that the issuer pledges to repay the debt using its resources (all the assets available to the issuer to satisfy the debt), including the jurisdiction's legal authority to raise taxes if necessary. Non-guaranteed bonds are those that are backed by specifically identified revenue sources and do not have the legal backing of a larger governmental entity with taxing power. If a municipality offers the full faith and credit guarantee, it is obligated to raise taxes or reduce services to pay back the credit. What happens when a municipality refuses to raise taxes or cut services is covered later in the discussion of defaults.

General obligation (full faith and credit) bonds typically are considered safer investments than non-guaranteed bonds because of the full backing of the jurisdiction's resources. These bonds typically carry lower interest rates than non-guaranteed bonds. The interest rate is critical in large bond issues, for which a difference of 0.1% can affect total interest payments by millions of dollars. However, revenue bonds from a well-managed special-purpose authority, such as a water district, with an excellent record of previous borrowing are likely to have a lower interest rate than a general obligation bond from a municipality with a declining property tax base and low personal income.

Bonds not backed by the general revenue resources of a state or local government have become much more common as special districts such as water and sewer authorities, economic development zones, and so forth have grown in number and size. In addition, state limitations on general tax revenues, such as Proposition 13 in California, have forced state and local governments to favor revenue bonds over general obligation bonds. Such non-guaranteed bonds do not have the full backing of the issuing jurisdiction's resources. Whatever security is offered, such as a pledge of the revenues from the services delivered by the new facility, no other resources are available to the creditor/investor. In that case, if the revenues fail to materialize, then the investor has no recourse to other sources of repayment. For both guaranteed and non-guaranteed bonds, the investor is paid, except in the case of default, typically at a fixed rate of interest, although variable rate bonds also are sometimes issued.

Revenue bonds are politically easier to issue, for two reasons. First, voter approval is required in almost every instance of a full faith and credit bond, but typically is not required for revenue bond issues. Second, revenue bonds are repaid by the charges made to only those who consume or benefit from the services provided by the debt-financed facility or infrastructure, so taxpayers not using the service are not required to help pay off the debt. As voter approval has become more difficult to achieve, the proportion of revenue bonds versus general obligation bonds has increased.

Non-guaranteed debt generally is repaid from funds restricted to the revenue earnings of the specific facility created by the investment. Many sources are used to repay these so-called non-guaranteed bonds. In the case of revenue bonds, the most common type, charges to users generate the funds necessary to repay the loans. Other sources include special assessments, in which the properties affected by an investment are assessed charges. For example, property owners might be assessed hook up charges for sewer installations.

Revenue bonds pledging the revenue from a specific tax or fee have the advantage of placing the burden for financing a facility on those who will use it. For example, using the parking fees from a parking garage to finance its construction places the burden on those who park in the garage. From an intergovernmental perspective, the revenue bond device forces nonresidents who use the parking garage or the highways to pay their fair share regardless of where they reside.

Traditionally, municipalities and local utilities issued bonds in a fairly local market with the main purchasers being banks. Bonds issued were mostly plain vanilla. A general-purpose municipal government or school district almost always issued a general obligation bond, backed by the jurisdiction, mainly by property tax proceeds. Water and other utilities issued non-guaranteed revenue bonds backed by the future revenue streams from user charges. Local or nearby banks bought most of the bonds issued. In recent times, these conditions have changed radically. The number of different instruments for debt, while still falling within

Table 13-1   Holders of Municipal Debt, 1940-2005 (in Billions of Dollars)

	Commercial Banks	Housholds	Property and Casualty Insurance
1940	3.6	n.a.	n.a.
1950	7.4	n.a.	n.a.
1960	16.8	n.a.	n.a.
1970	61.2	n.a.	n.a.
1980	148.8	104.5	80.5
1985	231.7	396.3	88.2
1990	117.5	655.7	136.9
1995	93.4	537.5	161.0
2000	114.2	531.2	184.1
2005	157.8	816.8	313.2

Sources: Compiled from Wong, P. C. (1995). *Role of private financial institutions in the development of local infrastructure in Thailand.* Bangkok: U.S. Agency for International Development; The Bond Market Association (2006). *Trends in the holdings of municipal securities: 1980-2006 Q2.* Retrieved December 19, 2006, from http://www.bondmarkets.com/story.asp?id318.

the two general categories, has increased dramatically, and banks are no longer the largest holders of municipal debt.

Table 13-1 demonstrates the shift from commercial banks to households as the predominant holders of municipal bonds. Although data on households' municipal debt holdings are incomplete for the earlier years, the reversal between commercial banks and households as the primary investors in municipal debt is striking. In 1985, commercial banks held 27% of the total outstanding municipal securities. By 2005, commercial banks held only 7%. Property and casualty insurance companies also began to purchase more municipal bonds in the 1990s to diversify their investment portfolios. Mutual funds and money market funds are investing more heavily in municipal bonds too. In 2005, mutual funds and money market funds held approximately 14% and 15%, respectively, of the total outstanding municipal debt.[6] Many of the investors in these mutual funds also are individuals, through their pension programs or their own individual investments. If we could separate out the individual from the institutional investors in these mutual funds, the role of the individual investor in **Table 13-1** would be still more prominent.

Municipal bonds are debt instruments in that the issuer incurs an obligation to repay and the buyer becomes a lender with a claim on future repayments. The buyer, however, has no direct claim on the assets of the issuer. Equity ownership, such as is purchased with corporate stocks, is not a feature of municipal bonds. Private equity ownership is a feature of build-operate-transfer and build-operate-own forms of private financing of public infrastructure facilities as discussed later in this chapter, but the main form of state and local capital financing is likely to continue to be issuance of municipal bonds.

In most industrialized European economies, the banking sector is the primary source of finance to subnational governments. In some countries, such as the Netherlands, municipally owned banks, in addition to managing the accounts and financial transactions of owner municipalities, lend long-term to the municipalities. In other countries, commercial and investment banks are the primary lenders. In still other European countries, specialized financing institutions somewhat similar to U.S. state revolving loan funds, discussed below, have been established to provide credit to municipalities. In many developing countries, such as South Africa, Bulgaria, and Poland, municipalities have emerged as good credit risks and a variety of credit systems have developed or are developing, including bond markets, specialized financing institutions, and direct lending from commercial and investment banks.[7]

Importance of Bond Financing for Infrastructure

Debt Financing Versus Pay-as-You-Go. State and local governments finance a major portion of their capital investment spending through long-term debt instruments. In 2005, state and local governments including special districts issued $409.5 billion in new long-term debt. Of that amount, $146.2 billion was in the form of general obligation bonds and $263.3 billion took the form of revenue bonds.[8] **Table 13–2** illustrates the trend in issuers and type of issues since 1990. Both states and general purpose local governments (municipalities, counties, townships) have declined in terms of total debt issued, with special districts such as water and sewer authorities and school districts having increased from about 62% to about 73% of all new issues. General obligation bonds during that period accounted for about one-third of all debt issues, whereas revenue bonds, at two-thirds of all issues, reflect the trends of the last 30 years for revenue bonds to dominate the issuance market.

Most state constitutions or statutes limit the issuance of long-term debt for both state and local governments to capital investment-type expenditures. Bond financing for infrastructure allows governments to build roads and bridges, schools, hospitals, water and wastewater systems, and numerous other major capital facilities before sufficient capital has been accumulated to pay for these facilities, in much the same way an ordinary consumer often borrows to finance the purchase of a home. The difference between bond financing and a consumer loan

Table 13–2   New Bond Issues by Issuer and Type of Issue: Selected Years 1990–2005 (in Billions of Dollars)

Issuer	1990	1995	2000	2005
State	15.0	14.7	19.9	31.6
Special District incl. School Districts	75.9	93.5	121.2	297.0
Municipality, County or Township	32.0	37.5	39.3	80.9
Type of Issue				
General Obligation	39.5	57.0	64.5	146.2
Revenue	83.3	88.7	115.9	263.3

Source: Abstracted from Bureau of the Census, U.S. Department of Commerce (2006). *Statistical abstract of the United States: 2006.* Washington, DC: US Government Printing Office, 274.

is that state and local governments issue debt instruments called bonds that are sold to various investors, giving the government issuing the bonds the cash to build the infrastructure facility and giving the bond purchaser a claim on that government for future repayment of both the borrowed amount and interest.

Some local governments try to avoid indebtedness as much as possible and work on a pay-as-you-go system. That means saving funds in advance until there is cash sufficient to build the infrastructure facility. These governments are like the car buyers who save money until they have enough funds in the bank to purchase their cars for cash. The motivations are similar: both the government and the consumer avoid the interest costs for borrowing. If the jurisdiction can afford to wait for the facility or can plan far enough in advance to have the funds available when needed, then the prospect of financing without interest costs is attractive. Indeed, as the government is saving funds, it can invest them in interest-earning opportunities, which are becoming increasingly sophisticated for government investors.

Pay-as-you-go local governments tend to be smaller jurisdictions with relatively stable annual capital investment requirements. For example, if a small local government generally needs to spend about $500,000 per year on capital facilities and goods and that figure is not expected to change much from year to year, over time it will need to spend that same amount, plus interest, each year in debt repayment if it borrows for the capital facilities. So if the jurisdiction can plan far enough ahead or can afford to wait for the facility, by establishing a capital investment sinking fund it can accumulate the funds necessary to meet the annual $500,000 per year capital spending requirement. Future citizens of the jurisdiction will then benefit from the services and will not have to pay for the capital costs.

Utilities that operate on a more or less commercial basis—capital and operating costs are financed by fees charged the users of the service—typically include a sufficient depreciation cost in the user charges to accumulate amounts to pay for rehabilitation expenses as the infrastructure wears out. But these utilities, unless small, still require large capital infusions when a major expansion or a major technology change is needed, such as shifting to a more efficient and environmentally friendly energy source. These capital infusions most likely will be through bond issues.

The pay-as-you-go approach does not work as well for larger jurisdictions, which tend to have less predictable requirements, and it does not work well for lumpy investment patterns where large amounts are needed in some years for big construction projects and smaller amounts in other years. Some form of credit financing for most state and local jurisdictions is a necessity and especially in rapidly growing areas where, regardless of size, pay-as-you-go financing cannot keep up with population growth and service demands.

Role of the Tax System and State and Local Bond Financing. A key reason for the attractiveness of bond financing for state and local government capital borrowing is that federal tax law allows deduction from the taxpayer's gross income of interest earned on many government bonds. In addition, most states with income taxes exempt interest earnings from state or local bonds for government entities within that state. Thus an individual who purchases state or local bonds retains the interest earnings tax-free in most cases. For individuals in the highest tax bracket, earning 6% interest on a municipal bond is equal to earning more than 9% taxable interest. Because the tax exemption for interest earnings attracts investors to the state and local bond market, a ready source of capital for infrastructure financing exists for government. The tax-exempt status of the earnings also enables jurisdictions to offer bonds at lower interest rates than they could get by borrowing from commercial lenders or issuing taxable debt securities. Tax exemption for the interest earnings on bonds, then, is the cornerstone of the U.S. system for financing public infrastructure for state and local governments. **Exhibit 13–1** illustrates the value to the investor of federal tax exemption.

Municipal bonds' tax-exempt status is somewhat controversial, however. A wave of expansion in the use of tax-exempt bonds to finance industrial development parks, incubator facilities to woo private developers to invest in local areas, and a wide variety of other essentially private endeavors led to significant curbs on state and local governments' authority to issue tax-exempt bonds in the Tax Reform Act of 1986 (TRA86). Private purpose bonds are discussed in more detail

Exhibit 13–1 | Federal Tax Exemption for Municipal Bond Yields

Municipal bonds are attractive to investors in part because the earnings to the investor on the bond are exempt from federal income taxes. The wealthier the taxpayer, the more valuable the exemption is because generally wealthier taxpayers pay a higher marginal tax rate on their income. In that sense, the tax exemption on municipal bonds is a regressive feature in the federal income tax (see Chapter 4).

Arguments against this tax exemption are its regressive nature that it favors wealthier taxpayers, and the lost federal revenue that must be made up for in the form of either other taxes or higher marginal rates on the individual income tax. Arguments in favor of this exemption are that it enables badly needed public sector infrastructure to be constructed at a lower cost, and that lower cost is of greater benefit to lower-income individuals. That is because the amount lower-income people would otherwise spend on public utilities such as water and sewer would be a higher proportion of their income than it would be to wealthier households.

The table below illustrates the tax advantage using as an example a married couple filing a joint return. For each marginal rate in the 2006 federal income tax, the cells in the table show the return (yield) the couple would have to achieve in a taxable bond to be equivalent to the value of the tax exempt bond. The table does not take into account state taxes. Municipal bonds issued by entities within one's state of residence (state in which one files state taxes) are also exempt from state individual income taxes in almost every state with an individual income tax.

Value to Taxpayer of Federal Income Tax Exemption on Municipal Bond Yields						
Tax-exempt Yield						
3.00%	3.50%	4.00%	4.50%	5.00%	5.50%	6.00%
Marginal Tax Rate, Married Joint Return						
10%						
3.33%	3.89%	4.44%	5.00%	5.56%	6.11%	6.67%
15%						
3.53	4.12	4.71	5.29	5.88	6.47	7.06
25%						
4.00	4.67	5.33	6.00	6.67	7.33	8.00
28%						
4.17	4.86	5.56	6.25	6.94	7.64	8.33
33%						
4.48	5.22	5.97	6.72	7.46	8.21	8.96
35%						
4.62	5.38	6.15	6.92	7.96	8.46	9.23

in a following section. Other features of that tax reform also made municipal bonds a much less attractive investment for commercial banks, accounting in part for the trend noted in **Table 13–1**.[9]

The securities industry clearly recognizes that there is a strong individual/household appetite for municipal bonds, as evidenced by the increasing availability of bonds as part of money market and mutual funds as well as the creation of tax-exempt bond funds. Concern for equity in taxation leads some to question whether interest on government and certain nonprofit bonds should be exempt. It is generally thought that mostly higher-income taxpayers benefit from this exemption, as they are the most likely purchasers of tax-exempt bonds and, therefore, that this exemption unfairly benefits those who can most afford to pay higher taxes. The illustration in **Exhibit 13–1** seems to bear this out, at least in terms of the increasing value of the tax exemption as the marginal tax rate increases. However, the growth of mutual funds in which middle-class individuals are making more investments is mitigating this equity argument.

Challenges to the general philosophy of granting tax-exempt status are unlikely to eliminate this fundamental feature of state and local finance in the United States. At the same time, it is likely that the federal government will continue to increase regulations regarding the issuance of tax-exempt bonds in order to restrict the tax favorability to the essential purposes of financing public infrastructure. The State of South Carolina challenged the constitutionality of any federal regulation of state governments' tax-exempt debt issuance in the 1988 *South Carolina v. Baker* case, questioning a law that denied tax-exempt status to bearer bonds (as opposed to registered bonds; see the discussion of bond features later in this chapter).[10] The Supreme Court ruled that the Tenth Amendment did not prohibit federal regulation of state and local governments and that there is no constitutional right to state and local immunity from federal tax provisions.[11]

Non-Traditional Bond Financing

Securitizing Future Revenue Streams. Securitizing the future revenue stream from some activity or of a set of receivables was an innovation in the private sector in the 1980s. For example, credit card companies often issue a bond or borrow against the stream of receivables that will be flowing in from credit card users. The card company gets immediate revenue instead of waiting for the stream of repayments. This technique is called securitization because the credit card company issues a security (a bond) against the future payments that are already known because the credit card holders have already incurred the debt. Or the securitization may involve a known value for the revenue stream such as outstanding credit card debt, plus estimated additional payments for credit card debt not yet incurred. On a larger scale, banks and housing finance companies may package a group of mortgages and issue a security (a bond) that is repaid by the known stream of revenues from those future mortgage payments. It is somewhat similar to a revenue bond, except that a revenue bond is issued against future revenues that are expected and estimated.

Securitization involves a stream of payments that already are legal commitments, commitments by the credit card holder for charges already made on the card, or for mortgages already held by the institution securitizing that revenue stream. Any assured, meaning legally obligated revenue stream that will accrue to the issuer over future years, is susceptible to securitization. Securitization may involve different risks than straight revenue bonds, and therefore may be priced higher if considered by the market as riskier investments. Or if the revenue stream is clearly known, that security may be considered less risky than a partly speculative future revenue stream.

An example of a securitized revenue stream was the 1996 bond issue by New York City of a $215 million bond backed solely by expected revenues from collection of delinquent taxes on commercial property. The city sold the property liens to a trustee that in turn issued the bonds, contracted with private parties to collect the delinquent taxes, and returned to New York the difference between the amount required to pay off bondholders and the total collected. This bond issue was the first instance of a large tax lien-backed bond.[12] Financial market institutions have followed this individual government's example by issuing bonds against pools of tax liens. A $285 million deal pooled tax liens from Florida and New Jersey allowing the governments holding the liens to capitalize on the value of those liens immediately, with the market issuer acquiring the value of the liens.[13]

New York City also used this market innovation by issuing a $709 million bond in 1999 that entitles the purchasers of the bond to the proceeds the City receives under the tobacco litigation settlement funds.[14] The tobacco settlement funds are payments to states from large tobacco companies as settlement for a class action suit filed by over 40 states to recover the costs the states were incurring for health care for illnesses and chronic conditions attributable to tobacco usage. In 1998, after a few states had won suits in court, the large tobacco companies reached a settlement with the entire class of states. That settlement assured states of a particular revenue stream into the future, and in turn that future revenue set off several securitization deals, such as New York's. The New York securitization of tobacco funds earned a governing "deal of the year" award.[15] Virginia and other states have followed suit. The securitization of the settlement funds allows these governments to enjoy now the use of funds that they would otherwise have been receiving in the future—albeit at a discount. California in 2005 executed a major securitization deal of its tobacco settlement funds to help manage its significant state revenue problems.[16]

Airport Passenger Facility Charges. An invention in the 1990s to finance airport facilities—the pledge of specific charges for use of the airport facility collected from the airlines through increments to ticket prices—is an example of the increasingly innovative ways to use pledged revenue to finance facilities. Airport operators (special authorities, municipalities that own the airport) apply to the Federal Aviation Administration to add a few dollars to the price of the tickets of passengers departing from or terminating their flights at the airport. Lansing, Michigan, and Little Rock, Arkansas, both financed major expansions and renovations through this device.[17]

Broward County, Florida, added another wrinkle to the passenger facility charge instrument. In 1998 and 2001, the airport issued bonds totaling over $150 million secured by passenger facility charges. These were charges added to the price of tickets of passengers emplaning or deplaning at the airport, estimated at a cost of just over $5 per passenger. In 2012, however, the pledged security for the bonds will shift from the passenger facility charge to a lien on total airport system revenues until maturity in 2023. This so-called convertible lien bond device gives added security to the investors, thus presumably lowering the interest rate, and it may enable the airport to reduce the passenger facility charge later if the finances of the airport authority are sound.[18] Since their introduction in the early 1990s, passenger facility charges, both directly and as the revenue to pay off bond issues, have risen to about 16% of the total financing costs for airport expansion.[19]

Tax Increment Financing Bonds. Tax increment bonds combine features of revenue bonds and general obligation bonds.[20] They are used to finance local economic development by pledging future increases in property taxes of areas targeted for development or redevelopment. A city may decide to redevelop an area of the inner city through construction of housing or commercial facilities and may issue a bond to finance that redevelopment. Since the redevelopment will not directly generate revenues, it is not suitable for revenue bond financing. At the same time, the city may not wish to obligate its full resources to repay the bonds, may be at state debt-limit ceilings for full faith and credit bonds, or may wish to confine the repayment obligations to the direct beneficiaries of the redevelopment. A tax increment financing bond will back up the debt issue with the pledge of increased property tax revenue from the area being developed (the property taxes will rise because the property in the redevelopment area will become more valuable).[21]

Private-Purpose Bonds. Starting in the early 1980s, considerable use was made of state and local bonds to finance private construction and ownership of facilities that were then leased back to government entities. Similar use has been made of government bonds for lease and subsequent purchase of privately constructed facilities. In some cases, government bonds have been issued to finance a facility that then is leased to or purchased by the private sector.[22] This last device often has been used to finance industrial development facilities, such as industrial parks and incubator facilities to help small businesses get started. State or local bonds issued for these largely private purposes were quite popular because the interest on the bonds was tax exempt. In 1985, more than half of a record volume in municipal debt issues involved these private-purpose activities.[23]

Pressure for reform arose amid concerns that the intention behind the tax exemption—to assist state and local governments and other eligible entities to build infrastructure for public benefit—was being diverted to benefiting private parties. The Tax Reform Act of 1986 (TRA86) contained several provisions to limit tax exemptions. Interest earned on general-purpose bonds for construction of facilities or infrastructure to provide essential services remains tax exempt. Private activity bonds for construction of facilities such as airports, docks and wharves, hazardous waste treatment plants, and water supply facilities also retain their tax-exempt status, although interest is included in the alternative minimum tax base. But the law removed the tax-exempt status of bonds for construction of industrial parks, parking garages, sports facilities, and convention or trade show facilities. In addition, each state and its local governments are limited in the amount of private-purpose bonds that can be issued in a year, and interest on any otherwise qualified bond issue is subject to tax if the bond issue exceeds the state cap.[24]

Since 1986, the issuance of private-purpose bonds has declined. Some states, however, continue to issue private-purpose bonds to finance facilities tied to economic development promotion, such as industrial parks. These governments consider the economic development benefit to be worth the higher-cost, taxable bond.

Exhibit 13–2 discusses tax credit bonds as an alternative to federal tax exemption on municipal bond interest earnings.

Municipal Minibonds. Most purchasers of municipal bonds are large purchase investors, including financial institutions that develop tax-exempt investment funds that then may be purchased by both large and small investors. Generally it has been more difficult for all but higher-income individuals to get directly involved in purchasing bonds from their own jurisdictions because purchases often involve minimum amounts of $5,000 to $10,000 or more. Mutual funds consisting entirely of municipal bonds have brought them in reach of more investors as smaller investments may be made in these mutual funds. However, tax exemption of the earnings on these mutual funds is tricky.

Some cities have issued bonds in smaller denominations. Denver, Colorado, was one of the first issuers of *minibonds*, a $5.9 million issue in $1,000 denomination bonds in 1990.[25] The minibonds were issued directly by the City without an underwriter (see the discussion later on bond issuance), and purchase was possi-

Exhibit 13–2	Tax Credit Bonds: An Alternative to Federal Tax Exemption on Municipal Bond Interest Earnings

One proposal that could be an additional means of federal assistance to state and local government infrastructure financing is an instrument called a tax credit bond. Tax credit bonds are debt instruments that instead of paying the purchaser interest payments on the bond, allow the investor to subtract the equivalent of interest from the investor's federal income tax liability.[1]

Although considered several times in the 1960s and later, more serious attention was given in the late 1990s and the 2000s. A small pilot program for tax credit bonds was authorized in 1997 as an experiment for school construction. In 2000, it was proposed, unsuccessfully, as a feature of the administration's $25 billion school modernization program. The reauthorization of the Transportation Equity Act in 2003 considered tax credit bonds to finance transportation projects. The Congressional Budget Office (CBO), however, concluded that federally issued tax credit bonds would cost the federal treasury more than appropriating federal funds for transportation, and the idea was dropped.[2]

The concept of a tax credit bond is to deliver more federal support to infrastructure programs. A tax credit to the investor is worth three to four times more than the exemption of interest earnings because the tax credit directly reduces the taxes paid. The interest exemption only reduces taxable income. Of course the cost of the additional benefit to the investor and to the additional infrastructure that might be built, would be borne directly by the federal government in the form of reduced income tax revenue.

Another alternative that leaves investors and state/local issuers whole but eliminates the tax exemption on municipal bond interest is the taxable bond with the federal government in effect reimbursing, from appropriated funds, the state/local issuers for the higher interest they would have to pay investors for purchasing the bonds that do not enjoy the federal tax exemption. For the federal government, the cost of this option is the same as the cost of the foregone revenue from exempting from taxation the bond interest payments. A CBO study in 2004 concluded that it is possible to design a tax credit bond program that could be less costly to the federal budget and still achieve the intended subsidy level of the current tax exemption of earnings on municipal bonds. The problem with this approach, however, is that it disguises the implicit subsidy in that it involves foregone revenues (tax expenditures) rather than more visible direct federal appropriations.[3]

Tax credit bonds were authorized in the Energy Policy Act of 2005 to support nonprofit organizations and cooperatives financing renewable energy sources for power generation. The implementation is a two-year trial, set to expire at the beginning of 2008. As is explained in Exhibit 13–5, Congress allowed for limited tax credit bonds in the aftermath of the 2005 hurricane season.

1 U.S. Department of Education (2000). *School modernization bonds would provide significant support for state and local school modernization projects. Website.* Retrieved December 18, 2006, from http://www.ed.gov/offices/OESE/archives/inits/construction/con_modbonds.html.

2 U.S. Congressional Budget Office (2003). *A comparison of tax-credit bonds, other special-purpose bonds and appropriations in financing federal transportation programs.* Washington, DC: U.S. Government Printing Office.

3 U.S. Congressional Budget Office (2004). *Tax-credit bonds and the federal cost of financing public expenditures.* Washington, DC: U.S. Government Printing Office, 6.

ble only by Colorado residents. Almost 2,000 citizens purchased more than twice the amount initially expected.

Other jurisdictions have followed suit. In 2003, the Bi-State Development Agency for the St. Louis region approved the issuance of $450 million in bonds to support a cross-county metro rail expansion. Among the several purchase options is the ability of investors to purchase mini-bonds in $1,000 increments. The bulk of the issue, however, is in larger denomination conventional municipal bonds.[26] While not appropriate for large-scale bond issues because it becomes uneconomical to sell and track bonds in small denominations, minibonds have proved popular for financing smaller projects that especially interest local residents.

Certificates of Participation. One form of municipal debt issuance that is not legally classified as debt is the use of certificates of participation (COP). Especially popular in California, which has placed severe restrictions on the ability of local governments to borrow, certificates of participation are municipal debt issues to construct facilities that will be operated by private contractors. The government leases the facility from the private operator and the lease payments are used to retire the debt (principal plus interest) from the debt issue. Certificates of participation can be risky investments.

The Richmond County Unified School District, California, and Brevard County, Florida, provide two examples in which the governmental entity was financially unable to make the lease payments (California) and unwilling to make payments (Florida), for a time, because of dissatisfaction with the facility.[27] Richmond County Unified School District subsequently defaulted on the lease payments due on the facility built via the certificates of participation debt issue.

Despite somewhat higher risks, certificates of participation continue to be a popular means of financing facilities. From 1990 through 2002, the State of Oregon sold over $1 billion in new issue certificates for correctional facilities, transportation terminals, public office buildings, and buildings for higher education institutions. These are not full faith and credit bonds. The state legislature biennially approves payment of interest and principal on these certificates. In theory, the legislature could refuse to approve payment, and in that case the state would have to vacate the facilities built with the funds. In practice, that has never happened. However, since somewhat higher risk is involved with COPs, Oregon estimates that the interest it pays on these is about 0.3% higher than for general obligation bonds.[28]

E-trading Municipal Bonds. Just as online trading in the private sector has become a common practice, so securities dealers now offer information about municipal bonds and offer the bonds for sale online. Issuance costs have come down somewhat compared to trading through securities dealers. Fully one-third of the municipal bonds traded publicly on the market by the year 2000 were available on the Internet.[29] Of equal importance to online purchasing is greater access to information for individual investors about possible bond investments that are then purchased through regular securities dealer channels, or sometimes directly from the underwriter.[30] Not just new issues, but the trading prices and detailed information on the issuers, is now regularly available online at sites maintained by regular securities dealers and specialized dealers in the fixed-income municipal securities market.

Bond Banks, State Revolving Funds, and Other Intermediaries

Large cities and state governments, unless there are underlying problems with the jurisdictions' financial status, generally have ready access to the U.S. capital markets to issue their own bonds. However, smaller cities and municipalities, and many municipalities in developing countries where there is only a limited market in fixed-income securities, and generally no track record for municipal debt have greater difficulty issuing debt at competitive prices. Several institutional structures have been prevalent in the United States and industrialized Europe for some decades to assist smaller governments, and have become popular in developing country public finance in the last couple of decades. The most common form is the revolving fund. Other forms include the state bond bank.

Several actions contributed to the invention of and growth in state revolving loan funds and bond banks. The Safe Drinking Water Act of 1974 contained provisions for the Environmental Protection Agency to provide financial assistance to states to set up drinking water revolving funds.[31] A revolving fund is created with some initial capitalization, often grants from the federal government plus state government bond issues, to lend to municipal borrowers. The premise is that the state government can get better credit ratings both because it is in better financial condition and because it can issue debt in larger amounts than individual small local governments. Repayments from the local governments that borrow from the fund keep the capitalization intact, allowing lending and borrowing to continue on a revolving basis.

The original stimulus for many of these funds was federal environmental funding programs for water and sewerage systems. One of the model state revolving loan funds created initially with federal environmental grants is the New York State Environmental Facilities Corporation (EFC). The NY EFC is a state corporation financially independent from the state government. Its transactions are not backed by state budget authority. It operates several state revolving loan funds, the largest of which is the Clean Water State Revolving Fund. Debt outstanding for 2007 was expected to be $6.8 billion, of which approximately $5.9 billion was in the Clean Water Fund.[32]

A bond bank is a variant on the same idea. The state bond bank may pool the borrowing needs of numerous, smaller municipal borrowers into a single state bond issue, and then finance the individual borrower's requirements from the proceeds of the single state issue. Some state bond banks issue bonds to capitalize a fund for lending, which then is a form of revolving fund. Others accumulate individual municipalities' borrowing needs until a sufficiently large amount is reached and then issue a single bond to meet those specific needs. Generally for the smaller municipal borrowers, bond banks reduce the cost of issuance.[33] Many of the state revolving funds and bond banks are used to finance federally mandated water and sewer system improvements.

In 1995, federal legislation—the National Highway System Designation Act—created a pilot program to provide federal grant funding to capitalize *state infrastructure banks* (SIBs) to finance transportation projects.[34] Initially, ten pilot states were authorized, but the program was later extended to all states. Subsequent reauthorizations of the Transportation Equity Act of 1998 (TEA-21) and the Safe, Accountable, Flexible, Efficient Transportation Equity Act: A Legacy for Users of 2005 (SAFETEA-LU) extended a variety of financing tools, including continued support to the SIBs.[35]

Revolving loan funds and special purpose municipal lending institutions have been popular means in developing countries to allow local governments access to debt financing. Beginning in the early 1980s, many developing countries began to decentralize authority and responsibility for many public services from the national to subnational governments. Along with the shift in authority and responsibility, provinces, cities, and towns were given some authority to levy user charges and raise taxes, usually accompanied by significant intergovernmental revenue transfers. To facilitate these newly more autonomous subnational jurisdictions financing capital projects, various types of lending facilities have been created.

Indonesia established in 1987 the Regional Development Account (RDA), an authority within the Ministry of Finance, to make loans on a long-term basis to local authorities, primarily water authorities. Colombia established the Financiera de Desarrollo Territorial (FINDETER) in 1989. Unlike Indonesia's RDA that was established as a separate account within the Ministry of Finance, FINDETER is an autonomous financial institution owned by the Ministry of Finance and regional governments. It operates as a regulated state-owned financial intermediary, channeling various sources of capital organized by the central government to local governments through loans. One study found that over 60 financial intermediaries had been established in the 1980s and 1990s to facilitate subnational governments' access to credit in developing countries.[36]

Problems with repayment rates, the inability to move most of such institutions into lending at market competitive rates, and the overall growth of capital markets in the more advanced developing countries have led since the mid-1990s to a de-emphasis on such financial intermediaries. The favored approach consists of governance and finance reforms that enable local governments to access credit markets through borrowing from banks and issuing municipal bonds.[37]

Overall, the use of bonds to finance state and local investments, both in the U.S. and in other countries, continues to increase as state and local financial conditions improve and federal transfers to assist state and local governments decrease. The distinction between general obligation bonds and limited revenue bonds is less important in practice than the financial condition of the borrowing entity. In fact, many water utilities and other users of more limited revenue bonds are in better financial shape than states and general-purpose local governments. All 50 states have some form of bond bank or revolving loan program.

Bond Issuance Process

The process of issuing municipal bonds involves numerous steps, and the number of participants in these steps is quite large. **Exhibit 13–3** lists the major participants, ignoring some of the minor players (for example, the role of bond printers). More detail on the main actors in the bond issuance process is included in the subsections on the major steps.

Bond Issuance Costs. With so many steps and participants in the process, the costs to the issuing jurisdiction can be high. Numerous legal steps must be followed, numerous documents must be prepared, and numerous transactions with various financial and legal institutions must occur. These transactions require considerable personnel time or the purchase of consulting services. Total costs for these transactions vary widely, from less than 0.3% (District of Columbia) to as much as 1.3% (Alaska). The average is just over 0.6%. Mississippi analyzed bond issuance costs and found for state and local issues in 2000 an average issuance cost of just over 0.5%, but it varied widely with the most expensive issuance cost being over 11% of the issue. The low was 0.3%.[38] Generally, costs in the range of 0.5% are common unless there are unusual characteristics to an issue.

Costs vary by issue based on characteristics of the issue itself—size, complexity, the issuer (financial condition, experience with previous debt issues), market conditions, and general familiarity of investors with the issuer.[39] Variations by state are affected by state policies, the general economic climate, experience with defaults or other financial troubles, and, of course, market conditions. The services of a financial advisor and bond counsel are the largest contributors to transaction costs. For example, an Iowa Board of Regents review of issuance costs for college facility construction bonds found that financial advisory services and bond counsel constituted 50% to 65% of the total issuance costs.[40]

Exhibit 13–3	Participants in the Municipal Bond Market
Issuers:	General purpose municipalities, counties, and states; special purpose governmental entities such as school districts and water authorities; and unique public service entities such as airports and transportation terminals.
Financial Advisers:	Finance specialists increasingly used by bond issuers to structure features of the issue to increase attractiveness to borrowers and/or to address a special need of the issuer—features such as issuer options to call the bond before maturity and structuring debt retirement to match cash flow circumstances of the issuer.
Bond Counsel:	Legal advisors to offer legal opinion on the legal authority of the issuer to borrow, on the tax-exempt status of the issue, and the legal obligation of the issuer to repay.
Dealers (Underwriters):	Investment firms, banks, and other financial institutions licensed to trade in municipal securities who sell the issuers' bonds.
Trustee:	Institution that serves mainly bondholders by securing from the issuers bond repayment cash flows and paying out to bondholders when due.
Investors:	Individuals, investment banks, commercial banks, and other financial institutions.

Issuers typically either secure the services of an underwriter to sell the issue or sell the bonds themselves while relying on a financial advisory service for assistance. Underwriting fees range from 0.5% to 0.75% added to the borrowing cost (usually referred to as 50 to 75 basis points, 100 basis points being equal to 1%).[41] The percentages generally are higher for smaller issues, because some of the costs are relatively fixed. Issuance costs have been declining as the market grows and becomes more competitive.

Voter Approval. In most states, a general obligation (full faith and credit) bond requires a referendum to secure voter approval. Revenue bonds and other forms of limited obligation financing generally do not require voter approval. In some cases, to avoid state limitations on general municipal borrowing, cities have established nonprofit building authorities to issue bonds and construct facilities. Such facilities are then rented to the municipality, and the rental payments secure the bond principal and interest. These special authorities, because they do not legally obligate in a direct way the general revenues of the municipality, can issue bonds without voter approval and without the debt counting as part of the municipality's overall debt. Of course, the source of funds used by the municipality to pay for renting the facility is, in fact, the general revenue fund.

Voters approve far more bond issues than they reject. In the 2006 general elections across all states, voters approved 478 bond issues out of a total of 643 on the ballots. In volume, the amount approved, $67.6 billion, was almost 89% of the value submitted for voter approval. Since 1977 the average voter approval by value of the bonds is 84%.[42]

Underwriting. Typically, the authority issuing a bond will secure the services of an underwriter, whose role is to arrange the actual sale of bonds to financial institutions. The underwriter for a small issue may well be a local bank or a major regional bank. Such firms as Goldman Sachs, Smith Barney Shearson, Merrill Lynch, A.I.G., Morgan Stanley Dean Witter, Citigroup, and other investment bankers and securities dealers typically handle major issues that are marketed nationally (and internationally). Individuals, banks, insurance companies, and mutual and money market funds invest in state and local bonds, as shown in **Table 13–1**. Legal counsel retained by the issuing authority provides a legal opinion on the status of the issue, the legal authority to issue the bond, and the tax-exempt status of the bond.

Most issuers, except those with strong market recognition themselves, such as major cities, rely upon an underwriter. Underwriters have client lists and access to a wide range of investors, and typically are able to sell a borrower's bond issue more quickly than the borrower. The underwriter collects the fee from the issuer by discounting back to the issuer the value of the bonds. For example, an underwriter on a $100 million bond issue, charging 50 basis points as the underwriting fee, will actually pay to the issuer $99.5 million. The underwriter then *owns* the issue. If the market responds favorably to the bond issue, the underwriter may even earn more than the 50 basis points, or in this example $500,000. But if the underwriter has misjudged the market's appetite for the issue, or the market changes while the underwriter is still selling some of the issue, the underwriter may not achieve the planned underwriting fee.

Public Sale Versus Negotiated Sale. Issuers may approach the market to sell their bonds in one of two ways: public competitive bidding and negotiated sale. Historically, bonds have been offered for public sale, with purchasers such as larger financial institutions, which might be purchasing for their own portfolio or for resale, effectively determining the interest rate by their offers. A *public sale* is initiated by a widely published official notice of sale. The notice of sale typically includes information such as the denomination of the bonds, bid conditions and requirements, and provisions for payment. The issuer will have worked with a financial advisor to establish the amount of the issue, the maturity date(s), obtaining (typically) a rating (discussed below), and all other characteristics of the sale. Investors then in effect determine the interest rate through their bids, with the issuer free to choose the investor or potentially several investors who offer the lowest rates. More detailed information is provided in the bond prospectus.

Sealed bids are submitted by interested institutional investors, brokerage firms, and even individuals, although individuals typically purchase through intermediaries. The issuing jurisdiction then is free to accept the lowest bid interest rate or to reject the bid according to the terms and conditions of sale. Jurisdictions with good ratings prefer this method, as they are likely to attract numerous bidders and thus be able to choose lower interest rates.

The *negotiated sale*, however, is becoming increasingly common. Negotiated sales are conducted between underwriters such as the large investment banks and the issuing government. The issuer typically issues a request for proposals (RFP) specifying the objectives of the issue (amount, time period, and so forth). Responders to the RFP present to the issuer their best case for why they should be selected based on track record, fees, and so forth. Once the underwriter, or often several underwriters, is selected, the issuer then works with the underwriter to develop the bond issue. The underwriter acts as a broker between the issuing jurisdiction and the investment community. If the issuer thinks the rates quoted by potential buyers are too high, the issuer is free to reject the bids, as in a public sale.

A key advantage of a negotiated sale is that the bond issue can be spread over a longer period of time. If the interest rates in bids are high but the issuer cannot postpone the project, the issuer may sell only a portion of the total issue to start the project while the underwriter continues to seek additional bids. One disadvantage of negotiated sales is that some investors, including some pension funds, cannot purchase state or municipal securities except through public sale.

Although it has been argued that negotiated sales seem to cost about 30 basis points more than competitive bids, other research has presented evidence that it is more the characteristics of the issuers that determine whether competitive versus negotiated sale is selected by the issuer, and that in turn explains any interest differences.[43] When controlling for issuer characteristics, the research seems to indicate there is little difference in the cost of the issue (the interest rate the issuer will have to pay investors).[44]

Bond Features. Bonds differ from each other in a variety of ways.[45] *Term bonds* may be due and payable to the investors on a single date. *Serial bonds* are due according to a specific schedule of payments over a number of years. In recent years, serial bonds have largely replaced term bonds, in part because of statutory prohibitions against term bonds. Investors holding term bonds obviously must be concerned with whether a jurisdiction is annually setting aside sufficient funds to be able to repay its debt. Underwriters typically require that the issuer establish a *sinking fund* and pay into that fund semi-annually or annually amounts that will be sufficient at maturity to repay the principle on the bonds.

Another difference is between *coupon* and *registered bonds*. Coupon bonds have coupons attached indicating the bond's maturity date and the amount of payment. Whoever presents the mature coupons receives payment. Registered bonds require that the owner register with the government issuing the bonds. The advantage of a coupon bond is that it is easily transferred from one owner to another, whereas a registered bond offers protection against loss or destruction of the bond itself.

States and municipalities historically preferred coupon bonds because the issuing jurisdiction was not responsible for keeping records of the purchasers. However, a provision of the Tax Equity and Fiscal Responsibility Act of 1982 requires that state and municipal bonds be registered to retain their tax-exempt status, and that requirement was upheld in *South Carolina* v. *Baker*. As a consequence, the use of coupon bonds has all but disappeared, although state and local governments continue to lobby for federal legislation that would permit issuing non-registered bonds that are tax exempt.

Another feature of bond sales is *discounting*. A bond is discounted when it is sold at some fraction of its face value. For example, a $10,000 bond may be sold for $9,800. It is thus discounted below par (meaning below face value). When it matures and the principal is paid out, the investor will receive $10,000 in return for the $9,800 investment in addition to the interest payments the investor would have been receiving over the years.

At times, a bond may actually be sold at a premium over its par value. This can happen when a bond whose fixed interest rate was set in a period of high interest rates becomes available for sale after interest rates have fallen. A potential investor will be attracted to the higher interest rate bond, but the seller has less incentive to sell the bond because of the low return offered by other choices now available on the market. So the seller charges the new investor, say, $10,200 for a bond that will repay principal of only $10,000 at maturity. The bond investor must consider both the selling value—discounted, at par, or at a premium—as well as the interest rate in determining the return on investment.[46] The secondary market, in which bonds already sold once are resold to other investors, rarely has bonds that are sold at their face value. Conditions at the time of sales in the secondary market are almost always different from the time of issue, causing the bonds to be valued at either greater or lesser than their face value.

Bonds are becoming increasingly complex in the structure of their terms. Traditionally debt issuers were concerned primarily with the *interest* or *coupon rate* of the bond and the various costs of debt issuance. Today, however, issuers are incorporating detailed features, usually with the help of financial advisory services, to vary the conditions of sale, the conditions under which the issuer may pay off the bond early, and variations in cash flows at different points in the life of the bond. Called *structured finance*, this approach of designing features into a bond issue unique to the cash flow characteristics of the borrower offers ways to tailor a bond issue to its specific situation.[47]

Zero Coupon Bonds. The typical municipal bond pays interest at specified points until the maturity date, when the principal is paid. Zero coupon bonds are growing in popularity, however. The coupon rate, in finance terminology, is the interest rate that the bond will pay. A zero coupon bond pays out no interest until maturity, when both the principal and the interest are paid at once. Attractive to the issuer because they have no annual cash flow requirements, zero coupon bonds naturally require some incentive to attract investors away from the more typical municipal bond, which pays in regular installments through the years until maturity. The usual means of attracting investors to zero coupon bonds is to sell the bonds for much less than their stated value—to discount the bond from face value. Zero coupon bonds typically call for the issuer to set aside funds with a trustee, on a regular basis, sufficient to pay off the debt at time of maturity.

Interest Rates. Interest rates, of course, are one of the most critical elements of bonds for both the issuer and potential buyers. As a hedge against changing interest rates or financial condition, the state or municipal authority may sometimes use a *call feature*. This means the authority may call or repay the bond in part or in full before the maturity date. The issuer can thus take advantage of falling interest rates by paying off all or part of the bond issue. Exercising this feature usually involves the payment of some premium. Callable bonds typically carry a higher rate of interest because investors would otherwise be less attracted to an investment that may be repaid sooner and therefore at a lower profit. A similar feature that favors the bond buyer is the *put option*. It allows the buyer, at specified intervals, to require paying off the bond. For this feature, the buyer agrees to specified discount rates at the different put options.

    Variable interest rate municipal bonds have become common, just as variable rate financing has become standard in the financial industry. Many state and municipal issuers have taken advantage of variable rates both at the time of original issue and to refinance bond indebtedness.

    The actual interest that the jurisdiction will have to pay on a bond issue depends on many factors related to the financial condition of the jurisdiction and the general market for other investments at the time of the issue. The tax-exempt status of the interest earned by state and local bonds means that the interest rate paid will be lower than comparably safe investments that do not enjoy tax-exempt status. If the jurisdiction has a good record of previous debt management, it will be perceived as a lower risk than one that has experienced trouble meeting its financial obligations. Likewise, if the jurisdiction is located in a good regional economy with low unemployment rates and a high tax base, it will be able to sell its bonds at lower interest rates. The issuing jurisdiction also will provide potential investors with information about other long-term obligations, including other debt and also unfunded pension liabilities. A reputation for good financial management is cited as evidence of creditworthiness.

Bond Ratings. Investors rely heavily on standard ratings provided by independent services, such as Fitch Investors Service L.P., Moody's Investor Service, and Standard & Poor's Corporation. Although the rating agencies use somewhat different labels for their ratings, they are quite similar.

The importance of bond ratings is illustrated by an upgrade for the City of Honolulu, Hawaii. In 2006, the city was upgraded by Standard and Poor's from AA- to AA. This seemingly small change would have saved the City over $2.2 million in interest and bond insurance costs on the last two city bond issues, totaling $730 million. The factors cited in the rating change included the City having doubled its rainy day fund, instituted an improved process for regular budget review with all department heads, and other administrative and procedural improvements to the city's basic budget management practices.[48]

A downgrade in rating may come about because of the issuer's own investment practices, as in the case of the Orange County, California, bankruptcy (discussed later in this chapter). State and local governments that invest their own funds, such as pension funds and short-term deposit instruments, can have their borrower status downgraded if they invest too heavily in high-risk derivatives. **Exhibit 13–4** discusses how rating agencies evaluate potential borrowers and potential debt issues.

Credit Enhancement. One device that state and local governments use to control the costs of debt and debt issuance is *insurance.*[49] About half of all new issues are insured by one of the four major bond insurers—Ambac Assurance Corporation, Financial Guaranty Insurance Company, Financial Security Assurance, and Municipal Bond Insurance Association. New York City's debt crisis in the 1970s and the Washington Public Power Supply System (WPPSS) default in 1983 were among the major contributors to the growth of municipal bond insurance. Bond insurance serves to earn the issuer a AAA rating. Usually through the payment of a one-time premium, the bond issuer purchases the guarantee that principal and interest payments will be made and will be made on time. The difference between the insurance cost and the interest costs of an A-rated bond versus a AAA-rated

Exhibit 13–4   **How Do Rating Agencies Evaluate Municipal Bond Issues?**

There are several U.S. financial services firms that rate municipal bond issues in the United States and increasingly the subnational debt issues in developing countries. Moody's, Standard and Poor's, and Fitch are among the most notable. They all use quite similar rating categories, and similar criteria. The lower the grade, the more risky the bond issue, and therefore in general the higher the interest rate the issuer will have to pay to attract investors.

Note that the rating is for an individual bond issue, not the issuer. The same issuer may have a variety of bonds in the market, and they may be rated differently, though since overall financial condition and management of the issuer are important factors in determining a rating, issues with similar characteristics from the same issuer are likely to be rated close to each other.

The table below lists the rating categories for those three major organizations.

Rating Categories from the Three Major U.S. Rating Organizations

	Moody's	Standard & Poor's	Fitch
Best Quality	Aaa	AAA	AAA
High Quality	Aa1	AA+	AA+
	Aa2	AA	AA
	Aa3	AA-	AA-
Upper Medium Grade	A1	A+	A+
	A2	A	A
	A3	A-	A-
Medium Grade	Baa1	BBB+	BBB+
	Baa2	BBB	BBB
	Baa3	BBB-	BBB-

Source: Reprinted from W.M. Financial Strategies (2006). *Website*. Retrieved December 27, 2006, from http://www.munibondadvisor.com/rating.htm.

Other ratings below those depicted in the table are considered speculative or below investment grade quality, although the terminology used by different rating organizations differs. That does not mean the issuer cannot sell the bonds. It means that investors in the view of the rating agency should be cautious and aware of the considerable risk associated with the issue before purchasing. Of course the interest premium will be higher or the issuer may have to sell the issue at below par (below face value).

continues

Exhibit 13–4	How Do Rating Agencies Evaluate Municipal Bond Issues? (continued)

Selling at below par means the issuer will perhaps have to sell the issue at a percentage, illustratively 92%, of the face value of the bond. Discounting below par to 92% on a $100 million issue will net $92 million, but that is not what the issuer receives. Instead, the underwriter possibly might charge $500,000 in fees, netting only $91.5 million for the issuer. But at maturity, the issuer will be expected to repay the full $100 million.

In developing a rating for a specific issue, all rating agencies consider similar quantitative and qualitative information. A long list of basic information requirements from the issuer is common, such as:

1. Several recent years of annual audited financial statements

2. Several years of budget history and forecasts for the next several years

3. Capital improvement program

4. Sources of major revenues if general purpose jurisdiction, and revenue source for the issue if a revenue bond

5. Complete statement of all outstanding debt and terms of debt

6. Basic economic conditions in the region of the issuing jurisdiction, including employment rates, employment by major employers, literacy and other education characteristics, property valuation, sources of regular intergovernmental revenue (determined by formula)

7. Debt management policies

8. Basic institutional characteristics such as background and experience of key administrative and elected (if relevant) officials; mechanisms (electoral, appointment) and frequency for replacing key officials; relevant national or state regulations that affect the operations of the issuer.

These are only examples drawn from the public websites and published materials of the major rating agencies. The processes by which the rating agencies combine the various types of information are proprietary, but generally are relatively transparent to the issuer in that lengthy interviews and time onsite by professionals from the rating agencies explain the information requirements and the way the information is used in constructing a rating. For a rating agency that has previously rated debt from an issuer, a new issue may require only a modest update of the previously submitted information, especially if recent.

Rating agencies periodically review bond issues since conditions may change for the issuer, and/or changes may occur in the markets that affect the outstanding bonds. Since bonds are marketable for secondary resale—original purchasers may elect to sell the bonds before maturity—a regular reconfirmation or change in the rating is necessary to secure continued investor interest.

bond is in the issuer's favor. If the rating without insurance would be below A, the costs of insurance likely will exceed the interest savings as the risk to the insurer requires a high premium.

Another type of credit enhancement is a *bank-issued line of credit*. The line of credit assures the bond buyer that the issuer will not be delayed in meeting payments even if short-term fluctuations in cash flow cause a temporary problem. The line of credit can be accessed if necessary to meet the short-term cash flow problem.

In some developing countries, central governments provide credit enhancements for local government borrowing through the use of an *intercept mechanism*. The central government agrees to intercept, if necessary, a stable source of revenues that otherwise would flow to the borrower, such as a portion of central revenue transfers to local government. This intercept is paid to the lender in the event of default or delayed payment by the local government. The municipal development finance agency of Colombia, FINDETER, relies heavily on the intercept of central government grants/transfers to municipal governments to collect on debt repayments. Some municipal borrowers/bond issuers, rather than repay loans, simply allow the intercept mechanism to make the payments.

Disclosure and Regulation

Municipal bond issuance is subject to the general regulatory functions of the Securities and Exchange Commission (SEC), as are all other public debt and equity issues in the U.S. financial markets. For decades, municipal debt instruments were specifically exempt from SEC regulation. Beginning in the 1970s, however, Congress began to increase the role of the SEC in regulating municipal bond issues. Amendments to the Securities Exchange Act created the Municipal Securities Rulemaking Board (MSRB) in 1975 in the wake of New York City's financial crisis and the revelation that some dealers in state and municipal securities were involved in unethical and "dangerous" conduct.[50]

SEC regulations, for all underwriting and disclosure, focus on the underwriter's role and set disclosure requirements that affect the type and quality of information that underwriters must provide to potential investors. Significant new disclosure rules were adopted in 1990 (SEC Rule 15c-12) that pertain to the consistency and timeliness of an underwriter's release of information provided by the bond issuer. The quality of the information itself and all releases by the bond-issuing jurisdiction are still considered to be the jurisdiction's responsibility. The underwriter does not assume any liability properly borne by the issuer. Evidence suggests that disclosure improves the investor's ability to judge credit, and hence improves credit ratings for creditworthy municipalities.

The Municipal Securities Rulemaking Board (MSRB) was created to provide focus to the SEC's functions in regulating financial institutions in the municipal bond market. MSRB is the standard setting body for all municipal securities dealers. Its authority extends only to dealers and others involved in municipal bond transactions, not to the actual issuing governments themselves. MSRB functions under the general authority of the SEC to ensure that the disclosure information is as accurate and timely as possible. It requires bond dealers to file repository copies of all official documentation on a municipal bond issue so as to make the information more widely available to all potential investors (Rule G-36).

MSRB also makes bond pricing information more widely accessible. Rule G-14 requires securities dealers to report daily to the Transactions Reporting Database all transactions in municipal securities, including both interdealer transactions and retail transactions in municipal bonds. MSRB provides a publicly accessible daily report on pricing and volume of municipal securities, enabling investors to get up-to-date information to guide investment decisions.[51]

A large step in imposing public disclosure requirements on the issuing jurisdictions themselves has been the implementation of Nationally Recognized Municipal Securities Information Repositories. Four national repositories exist, including such financial services organizations as Bloomberg Financial Markets and Standard & Poor's as well as DPC Data and FP Interactive.[52] Several state repositories exist such as Texas and Ohio. Municipal debt issuers must at least annually—and more often if conditions change—report on their financial condition. This reporting requirement extends for as long as the issuer has outstanding debt in the market, providing potentially valuable information to subsequent secondary market purchasers of municipal securities. Also, municipal debt issuers are required to maintain and report regularly on their overall financial condition, not just on the status of specific debt issues.

The additional disclosure requirements initially caused considerable consternation among many of the participants in the municipal bond market.[53] One particular requirement that securities dealers think is too vague is the requirement that brokers and dealers must judge whether a client is capable of understanding the risk involved in an investment before they issue a recommendation to the client. However, the Orange County, California, financial fiasco (see below) has discouraged critics from attempting to reduce disclosure requirements of both issuers and dealers in the municipal securities market.

▌ Debt Capacity and Management

Since the federal government borrows for purposes other than capital investment, we continue in this section to focus on state and local governments, reserving the topic of federal debt for Chapter 15. Media discussions of the federal debt and the size of the federal deficit raise citizens' consciousness of government debt, but locally people are asked officially to approve debt (bond issues) for financing everything from schools to new fire stations. More importantly, citizens are not given the opportunity to vote on an even larger component of state and local debt: debt that is issued by special authorities or that does not involve the pledge of full faith and credit of the jurisdiction. The questions to be addressed in this section involve how much debt can be managed safely and which debt management practices will ensure sound future financial condition.[54]

Size of Debt

The size of debt can be assessed in several ways. The total amount of debt is probably the least meaningful measure. The fact that state and local governments' total outstanding debt at the end of 2006 was nearly $2.3 trillion, although this figure may sound staggering, is not really instructive.[55] Interest payments on general debt in 2006 amounted to $97.6 billion, or only 4.2% of total state and local expenditures, and interest payments have remained relatively constant over recent years at about 5% or less of total expenditures.[56] The fact that this figure is not excessive can be illustrated by considering that individuals commonly devote far more than 5% of their total expenditures on interest payments for home mortgages, car loans, and credit card debt.

Per Capita Debt. Per capita debt figures help put the total government debt in perspective. How much per capita do state and local governments owe? In 2003, they owed $6,234, up almost 50% from 1995, but an increase of less than 17% since 2000. Is that too much, too little, or just about right? Is it growing, declining, or remaining more or less stable? The latter question is easier to answer than the former.

Figure 13–1 charts state and local per capita debt from 1970 through 2003. Per capita debt has risen at both the state and the local government levels with local debt rising somewhat more rapidly than state debt. In addition, the amount of increase in the five-year period 1980–1985 was almost equal to the rate of increase for the preceding 10-year period (1970–1980), and the period 1985–1990 witnessed an even faster rate of growth. The trend since 1995 is a slightly slower rate of growth. Thus, state and local debt is rising faster than population, but is that cause for alarm?

Ratio of Debt to Personal Income. Relating debt to personal income instead of population begins to clear the picture. Calculating total debt outstanding per $1,000 of personal income is one way of assessing whether debt is in danger of becoming an unreasonable economic burden. In 1992, state and local government debt per $1,000 in personal income was $184. These numbers are considerably less alarming. For over a 40-year period, combined state and local debt per $1,000 in personal income has remained stable. Figure 13–2 charts this historical trend. State

Figure 13-1 State and Local Debt Per Capita, 1970–2003

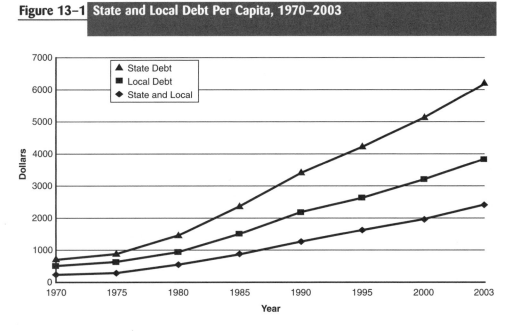

Sources: Compiled from Bureau of the Census, U.S. Department of Commerce. *Statistical abstract of the United States, 1985*, 274; *1996*, 304; *2006*, 271. Washington, DC: U.S. Government Printing Office.

and local debt per $1,000 of personal income in the 1990s, although showing a trend toward increase after a 10-year decline from the 1970s through 1982, was no higher than the previous high of $205 back in 1972 until 2006, and then just slightly over the 1972 high.

Distribution of Debt

Ultimately, whether the size of state and local debt is reasonable is a subjective judgment. The main factors used in making such an appraisal are the financial burden on individual taxpayers and the economy and the perceived value of the facilities and services purchased by the debt. Generally, debt varies somewhat with income and with the amount of state and local services. The state with the highest per capita debt in 2002, Alaska ($13,488), also was ranked fairly high (11th) in personal income per capita ($32,799).[57] Hence, Alaska presumably has the income level to support a higher debt (Alaska's high cost of living tends to inflate all of its statistics, of course). New York ranked sixth in per capita income and second in per capita debt. Connecticut ranked second in per capita income and only fourth in per capita debt, although in recent years it had an opposite pattern— high in personal income per capita and low in debt per capita.

Figure 13–2 State and Local Debt Per $1,000 Personal Income, 1962–2006

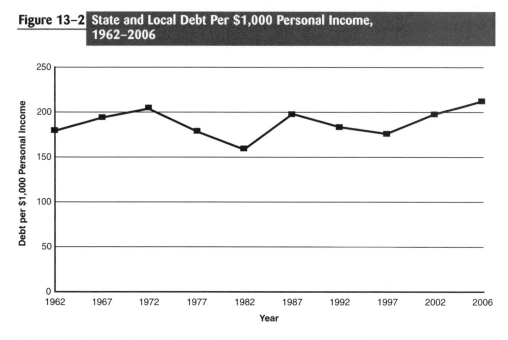

Sources: Compiled from Bureau of the Census, U.S. Department of Commerce (1984). *Historical statistics on governmental finances and employment.* Washington, DC: U.S. Government Printing Office, 113; Bureau of the Census, U.S. Department of Commerce (1988). *Government finances in 1985-86.* Washington, DC: U.S. Government Printing Office,3; U.S. Advisory Commission on Intergovernmental Relations (1992). *Significant features of fiscal federalism, volume 1: revenues and expenditures,* Washington, DC: U.S. Government Printing Office, 245, 286; Bureau of the Census, U.S. Department of Commerce (1996). *1992 census of governments, volume 4, government finances: number 5, compendium of government finances.* Washington, DC: U.S. Government Printing Office, 152; Board of Governors, U.S. Federal Reserve (2006). *Flow of funds accounts of the United States, December 7, 2006.* Washington, DC: Federal Reserve, 16, 59.

Debt Default

It is important to remember that the figures on debt do not reflect the full scope of future financial obligations of governments. Pension programs for public workers constitute a form of debt and often are inadequately funded. Debt defaults are correlated with economic cycles, but it should be noted that there have been few defaults on state or local indebtedness since the Great Depression of the 1930s.[58] In that decade, about 4,800 state and local units defaulted on their obligations. While that number may seem large, the total number of governments then was 150,000. Most of the defaults involved small jurisdictions. Fewer than 50 of these defaulting governments had populations of more than 25,000.[59]

Since that time, the number of defaults has been quite low. By number of issues, from 1980 through 1994, the number of defaults varied from less than 0.2% to 1%. As a proportion of the dollar value of outstanding indebtedness, the average during that period was less than 1%.[60] One study of bond defaults from 1970 through 2002 found that of over 77,000 rating actions for over 28,000 issuers, only 18 defaulted, and 10 of those 18 were in the nonprofit health care sector. That same study was updated through 2005, and found that the default rate for all investment grade bonds in the study (over 80,000) was less than 0.07%.[61]

Averages can mask wide variation. Riskier issues, such as multifamily housing and nonprofit health care organizations such as some hospitals, experience much higher default rates, whereas municipal general obligation bonds and water and sewer and similar revenue-backed bonds experience default rates in the less than 0.05% range. Even more interesting is the fact that, since the Great Depression, no state has defaulted on a debt (even then, only Arkansas postponed payments). Astonishingly, of $300 billion in school district debt issued from 1979 through 1997, only two issues ($10 million) defaulted.[62] The major reason that there are so few defaults relates to the obligation that general purpose governments have to raise taxes to repay debt backed by the full faith and credit of the issuing jurisdictions, and the implicit promise that there will be governmental intervention even for non-guaranteed bonds. Major events such as Hurricanes Katrina and Rita raised the specter of defaults as many jurisdictions had major portions of their tax base (property primarily) wiped out by the storms, and public utility customers in the hundreds of thousands lost the homes that previously were connected to the utilities. But major federal and state intervention averted the defaults that were possible. **Exhibit 13–5** discusses how governments respond to the potential of defaults following these disasters.

Few public bond issuers have faced financial insolvency, although the exceptions have been noteworthy. In 1963, debt service payments on $100 million in revenue bonds for the Calumet Skyway in Chicago were interrupted.[63] In the mid-1970s, New York City came close to bankruptcy as a result of extensive borrowing to meet operating budget requirements and defaulting on some of its short-term debt. As a result, New York City was partially placed under the supervision of a financial control board (see Chapter 14). Only this intervention by the state government and the banking community prevented outright default on several bond issues. Also in the 1970s, Cleveland defaulted on just over $15 million in tax anticipation notes, largely because of poor financial management practices and inadequate accounting procedures.[64]

The largest failure was that of the Washington Public Power Supply System (WPPSS). In 1983, after a more than decade-long program of construction of five nuclear power generating plants, WPPSS defaulted on more than $2 billion in revenue bonds. The revenue bonds were issued in anticipation of the sale of electricity. WPPSS got caught in the situation faced by the power industry in many parts of the country in the 1970s—a combination of slower rates of growth in electricity demand, rapid escalation in the costs of nuclear power plant construction, and rising interest rates.[65] In 1993, WPPSS successfully issued $800 million in bonds to refund the debt.[66] WPPSS was renamed Energy Northwest in 2002 and continues to be operated by a consortium of 20 power companies serving the Pacific Northwest.[67]

In reality, defaults by state and local governments are rare. However, periodic problems arise not as much on individual bond issues but with entire jurisdictions, headlined by the Orange County, California, financial collapse in 1994. Federal legislation in 1934 permitted municipalities to declare bankruptcy, and

Exhibit 13–5   Extraordinary Events Provoke Extraordinary Responses to Prevent Municipal Default

Hurricanes Katrina and Rita in 2005 devastated the Gulf Coast of the United States, causing damages estimated in excess of $140 billion. Losses to government infrastructure alone amounted to between $13 billion on the low end and $25 billion on the high end.[1] At least $16.7 billion in face value of insured bonds were directly affected by the hurricanes, but as of a year after the hurricanes, only a little over $17 million in claims on insured bonds had been paid out, and most of that was thought likely to be recovered as it was mostly late payments as municipalities and special districts struggled to get their records back in order in the immediate aftermath.[2]

The City of New Orleans and other bond issuers faced long-term problems, however, in rebuilding the lost infrastructure by issuing new debt and at the same time meeting payments on previous bonds that financed now destroyed or damaged capital assets. The Gulf Opportunity Zone Act of 2005 (P.L. 109-135) relaxed some of the restrictions on private activity bonds in order to permit tax-exempt issues for housing and other facilities that are not necessarily for public use, and waived other requirements that otherwise would potentially have impeded issuance of new bonds to refund existing bonds or to refinance infrastructure on which existing bonds already were outstanding. One provision of the act also extended authority to the affected states to issue tax credit bonds to pay interest on or to repay debt previously issued, subject to a maximum per state—$200 million for Louisiana—and requiring that the state match the tax credit issue with an equal amount of state resources, financed by debt or otherwise.

The State of Louisiana, for example, in 2006 issued $200 million in tax credit bonds to be used to pay debt service and to repay bonds issued prior to Hurricanes Katrina and Rita in affected areas. The fact sheet from this bond issue shows the debt rated AAA by Fitch and similarly by other rating agencies. While there have been major municipal bond defaults in U.S. history, they are rare, and when significant often result in solutions to work out the losses through a variety of financing options and with extended oversight by regulatory agencies or appointed oversight commissions.

1 Holtz-Eakin, D. (2005). *Macroeconomic and budgetary effects of Hurricanes Katrina and Rita.* Washington, DC: Congressional Budget Office, 3.

2 Hurricane Katrina: One year later the municipal bond market remains resilient (2006). Retrieved December 5, 2006, from http://www.dorseyco.com/documents/GKSTResearch-HurricaneKatrinaOneYearLater_000.pdf .

continues

Exhibit 13–5	**Extraordinary Events Provoke Extraordinary Responses to Prevent Municipal Default (continued)**

Ratings:Fitch: "AAA"
Moody's: "Aaa"
S&P: "AAA"
(CIFG Insured)
(See "RATINGS" herein)

In the opinion of Jones, Walker, Waechter, Poitevent, Carrère & Denègre L.L.P., assuming continuing compliance with certain covenants described herein, the Bonds qualify as Gulf tax credit bonds as described in Code Section 1400N(1)(4) of the Internal Revenue Code of 1986, as amended. Jones, Walker, Waechter, Poitevent, Carrère & Denègre L.L.P. is further of the opinion that, under the laws of the State, the Bonds are exempt from income and all other taxation in the State of Louisiana. See "TAX MATTERS" herein and the proposed form of opinion of Jones, Walker, Waechter, Poitevent, Carrère & Denègre L.L.P. attached hereto as Appendix D.

$200,000,000
STATE OF LOUISIANA
GENERAL OBLIGATION GULF TAX CREDIT BONDS
SERIES 2006-A

Dated: Date of Delivery

Due: July 18, 2008

The State of Louisiana (the "State") is issuing $200,000,000 principal amount of its taxable General Obligation Gulf Tax Credit Bonds, Series 2006-A (the "Bonds") pursuant to Article VII, Section 6 of the Constitution of the State of Louisiana of 1974, as amended (the "State Constitution"), Act No. 41 of the First Extraordinary Session of the Louisiana Legislature of 2006 ("Act No. 41"), and other constitutional and statutory authority, for the purpose of providing funds for the Debt Service Assistance Fund established by Act No. 41 for loans to political subdivisions of the State affected by Hurricanes Katrina and Rita, to insure the timely payment of principal of and interest on their outstanding bonds, notes, certificates of indebtedness or other written obligations for the repayment of borrowed money of local political subdivisions of the State issued prior to August 28, 2005, and to pay debt service on general obligation bonds of the State issued prior to August 28, 2005, as described under "DEBT SERVICE ASSISTANCE PROGRAM" and in "Appendix E-1 – Table of Defeased Bonds of Participating Political Subdivisions" and "Appendix E-2 – Table of Defeased Bonds of the State" attached hereto.

The Bonds are issuable only as fully registered bonds, without coupons, in the denominations of $5,000 or any integral multiple thereof within a single maturity. Except as provided below, principal of the Bonds is payable upon maturity to the registered owners thereof upon presentation and surrender of such Bonds at the designated corporate trust office of Hancock Bank of Louisiana, Baton Rouge, Louisiana, as Paying Agent and Registrar (the "Paying Agent/Registrar"). Hancock Bank of Louisiana is also acting as escrow trustee pursuant to three separate Escrow Deposit Agreements (as hereinafter defined) (the "Escrow Trustee", and, together with the Paying Agent/Registrar, the "Paying Agent").

The Bonds shall not bear interest. See "THE BONDS – Credit Allowance" herein. Initially, the Bonds will be issued in book-entry only form, registered in the name of Cede & Co., as nominee of The Depository Trust Company, New York, New York ("DTC"). DTC will act as securities depository for the Bonds. There will be no distribution of the Bonds to purchasers. Purchases of the Bonds may be made only in book-entry form in authorized denominations by credit to participating broker-dealers and other institutions on the books of DTC, as described herein. Principal on the Bonds will be payable by the Paying Agent to DTC, which will remit such payments in accordance with its normal procedures, as described herein. The State reserves the right to terminate the use of the book-entry only system and issue fully registered certificated Bonds. See "THE BONDS – Book-Entry Only System" herein. Further details of payment of the Bonds are more fully described herein.

The Bonds constitute general obligations of the State and the full faith and credit of the State is pledged to the payment of the principal of the Bonds as and when the same becomes due and payable. The Bonds, together with other general obligations of the State, are payable from monies pledged and dedicated to and paid into the Bond Security and Redemption Fund created and established in the State Treasury, have a first lien and privilege upon all State money deposited into the Bond Security and Redemption Fund, are payable on a parity with all other outstanding general obligation bonds heretofore and hereafter issued by the State under and pursuant to the State Constitution, and are secured by the monies pledged and dedicated to and paid into the Bond Security and Redemption Fund, subject to prior contractual obligations as provided in Article VII, Section 9 of the State Constitution.

The Bonds are not subject to redemption prior to maturity.

CIFG ASSURANCE NORTH AMERICA, INC. has unconditionally and irrevocably guaranteed the full and complete payment by or on behalf of the State of regular payments of principal of the Bonds.

The Bonds are offered when, as and if issued, subject to approval of legality by the Honorable Charles C. Foti, Jr., Attorney General of the State of Louisiana, and Jones, Walker, Waechter, Poitevent, Carrère & Denègre L.L.P., Baton Rouge, Louisiana, Co-Bond Counsel, and certain other conditions. Certain legal matters will be passed upon for the Underwriters by Foley & Judell, LLP, New Orleans, Louisiana, and The Boles Law Firm, APC, Monroe, Louisiana, Co-Counsel to the Underwriters. Government Finance Associates, Inc. serves as independent Financial Advisor to the State. It is expected that the Bonds in definitive form will be available for delivery at DTC in New York, New York, on or about, July 19, 2006 against payment therefor.

This cover page contains certain information for quick reference only. It is NOT a summary of this issue. Investors must read the entire Official Statement to obtain information essential to making an informed investment decision.

MORGAN KEEGAN & COMPANY, INC.

GOLDMAN, SACHS & CO.

Estrada Hinojosa & Company, Inc.   **Loop Capital Markets, LLC**

A. G. Edwards

The date of this Official Statement is July 12, 2006.

during the depression, many did. But it is rare now and usually associated with weak financial management practices.[68]

Financial collapses in both Cuyahoga County, Ohio, in 1978 and Bridgeport, Connecticut, in 1991 preceded Orange County. Bridgeport attempted to declare bankruptcy, although the bankruptcy was not permitted by the courts.[69] The Cuyahoga County and Orange County problems share some similarities. Neither county got into trouble as a result of overextending debt. Both counties became mired in financial difficulties as a result of their investment activities with their own pension funds and other sources of cash, plus those of numerous other local governments for which the counties acted as investment managers. Cuyahoga County lost $114 million on a $1.8 billion investment pool, but subsequently repaid most of the local government co-investors.[70]

Orange County, California, Bankruptcy. The bankruptcy of Orange County, California, set off shockwaves in the finance industry and in the press. Because the county was so wealthy no one imagined bankruptcy was even possible. The county was the investment manager for its own funds and almost 200 other local governmental units.

At the high point, Orange County was investing more than $7 billion. A large proportion of the investments were in derivatives, a hybrid form of financial instrument that depends on changes in the value of other financial instruments. In this case, Orange County invested in instruments that depended for their value on the interest rates on other instruments. In effect, Orange County was betting on a certain directional movement in interest rates (upward) and when interest rates fell, Orange County did not have cash in the pool sufficient to cover the funds invested. The strategy had been successful in previous years. The pool earned rates of return ranging from 7% to 9% from 1991 to 1994.[71]

In late 1994, the county petitioned for bankruptcy under Chapter 9 of the U.S. Bankruptcy Code. Subsequently, the county defaulted on various taxable pension fund and taxable arbitrage notes. Orange County then filed suits of its own against its former auditor KPMG Peat Marwick and the investment firm that managed most of the derivative and other investments, Merrill Lynch. The aftershocks of the Orange County nightmare caused share prices of both insured and uninsured California bonds to drop dramatically, although insured funds rebounded quickly. Partly in continuation of trends toward increasing regulation of municipal debt and investment activities, and partly in response to Orange County's actions, the SEC has continued to increase its regulatory role in this area.[72]

Debt Capacity

Measuring Debt Capacity. Measuring debt capacity is an art rather than a science. In the last couple of decades, the public finance and budgeting profession has paid considerably more attention to improving the level of the art. Three main factors influence debt capacity: expenditure pressures, resource availability, and the commitment of governmental officials to use resources to meet debt requirements.[73] Assessing resource availability involves analyzing all potential sources of revenue including own-source revenues; transfers from other levels of government; and types of self-financing including user charges, special assessments, impact fees, and a variety of other measures to collect fees or revenues sufficient to support the specific project or facility (see Chapters 4 and 5).[74]

Expenditure analysts look at the present and potential future commitments of jurisdictions. Population growth, changing economic conditions, the state of the current capital facilities and infrastructure base, and the socioeconomic characteristics of the population are important influences on potential future expenditures. The willingness of lenders to purchase debt is reflected ultimately in the interest rate they will require to lend. Revenue and expenditure analyses are used by state and local governments to support capital budgeting and debt management. Fiscal capacity analysis, focusing on the ability to generate revenues, and on expenditure needs, is used to determine present fiscal conditions and estimate future conditions. Against that backdrop, the financial requirements and budgetary impact of possible capital investments and debt financing alternatives can be assessed.[75]

Debt Burden. The most common overall measure of debt burden is the *ratio of debt to debt-carrying capacity*, which reflects the extent to which revenues are sufficient to cover debt service, in addition to operating expenses. The World Bank often looks at the ratio of debt service to current revenues, the ratio of capital expenditures to total expenditures, and the excess of current revenues over ordinary operating expenditures as indicators of the ability of a city to incur additional debt. More refined measures focus not on actual revenues but on the revenue base itself. U.S. local governments commonly use the ratio of debt to the assessed value of taxable property, because that assessed value reflects a local government's basic ability to generate revenues. These quick indicators are all useful, but ultimately they are interpretable only in the context of a jurisdiction's overall debt management strategy.

For enterprise-like operations, such as water authorities, conventional ratio measures of debt burden are in common use. The *debt to equity ratio* is a measure of the extent to which a utility is financing itself through debt relative to equity. The higher the ratio, the more risk there is in additional debt issues, as lenders want to see borrowers also making significant commitments of their own resources (equity). Another common ratio, *interest share of operating income*, measures the amount of debt as a percentage, that operating income has to cover.

Debt Management. In general, sound debt management at the state and local levels involves restricting debt primarily to financing long-term investments. A general rule is that borrowing should not be used to meet current operating expenses.

The much-publicized financial crisis experienced by New York City involved short-term borrowing to finance current expenses. Occasionally, short-term borrowing is used to deal with emergencies but often is refinanced as part of a long-term debt issue. Moreover, the payout period of the debt should correspond to the useful life of the facility or infrastructure financed. Poorly maintained road projects built in Africa in the 1970s and 1980s financed through international donor agency credits reached the end of their useful life a decade or more before the debt was paid off, leaving the borrowing countries in the position of having to borrow to rebuild while still paying off the old debt.

The rule to restrict debt to long-term capital financing does not apply to financial emergencies resulting from major flooding or unusually heavy snows during the winter, or the Hurricanes Katrina and Rita instances, for example. But this rule, along with the rule to match the payout period for the debt with the expected life of the facility, should generally be followed. Adherence to these two rules ensures that the jurisdiction will more or less match the benefit flows from capital facilities with the opportunity costs. (See Chapter 12 for a more detailed discussion of cost and benefit streams and the concept of opportunity costs.)

One of the major positive results of the financial difficulties of cities such as New York and the major cutbacks in federal aid in the 1980s has been an increase in the sophistication of the tools used in analyzing the financial condition of governments. Furthermore, in the last two decades, state governments have become quite involved in regulating local government debt, not only by means of the more traditional statutory and constitutional provisions that govern the powers and authority of local governments but also by means of extensive state programs of technical assistance. Effective debt management requires the balancing of competing claims against the current annual budget and future annual budgets. As a consequence, state and local governments increasingly rely on methods to assess overall financial health and place potential bond issues in that context.[76]

Debt Refinancing. From time to time, substantial swings in market conditions bring interest rates down and spur a round of refinancing bonds. In 1998, of $279 billion in new debt issues, nearly $121 billion, or 43%, were refinancings. In 2000, less than 10% of $194 billion in new issues were for refinancing.[77] State and local governments also have become more sophisticated in their transactions in the financial markets. One strategy in use is to swap the interest owed on outstanding bonds for more attractive interest rates. A traditional method for accomplishing that is to call in bonds that have higher interest rates when the market changes and rates fall. That is possible only with bonds having call features.

An alternative that does not require any actual transaction with outstanding bonds is an *interest rate swap*. In this type of transaction, the borrowing authority agrees to pay a third-party financial investor a variable rate of interest over a fixed period of time in exchange for payment of a fixed rate of interest by the third party. This is a synthetic variable rate financing deal in that the bonds themselves remain as they were with the terms and conditions unchanged.

The interest rate swap works by introducing a third party into the transactions between issuers and investors. During a period of high interest rates, for example, bond issuers try several strategies to control the effects of high interest. One strategy is to issue serial bonds, breaking the total issue into several annual *tranches*. If interest rates do fall from the high at the time the choice is made to issue a bond over a series of years, then the later tranches carry lower rates. Another strategy is to issue variable interest rate bonds tied to some short-term rate index. The issuer then may enter into a contract with a third party in which, for a fee, the third party agrees to swap fixed rate payments for the variable rate payments. The issuer elects from time to time whether to take the swap. The issuer "bets" that the fee paid for the swap option over time will be less than what the issuer saves by exercising the swap option.

The Port Authority of New York and New Jersey, for example, in 1991 entered into an agreement with a third party for a 10-year period during which the third party agreed to pay the authority at a fixed rate of 6.5% on a $10 million value. In return, the Port Authority agreed to pay the third party an indexed variable rate. The Port Authority felt, and initial experience bore its expectations out, that the variable rate was likely to remain below the fixed 6.5% rate.[78] Subsequently, the Port Authority entered into a counter swap with the same third party, this time agreeing to pay a fixed rate of 5.32% while receiving from the third party the indexed variable rate. What once had been $10 million in bonds outstanding at 6.5% was converted into the same value at 5.32%.

Wild speculation in interest rate swaps could put a state or local authority into a risky debt position. The Port Authority has a well-established debt management program with formally defined principles. The debt situation vis-à-vis the original bondholders remains unchanged in an interest rate swap. The state or local authority is simply trading in the financial market based on judgments about future interest rates. The original bond issue is not affected, in that investors will be paid according to the original terms. The borrowing authority, through a completely separate transaction, hedges against future interest rate changes and achieves, through a third party, a gain or a loss based on the marginal interest rate differences. The risk analysis focuses on whether the overall portfolio of the borrowing authority has been exposed to higher or lower future interest payments.

Trends in lower interest rates in the mid-2000s made interest rate swaps an attractive possibility for borrowers who had issued long-term debt (bonds) earlier when interest rates were higher. The 2005 comptroller's report on New York

State's financial condition noted that the State had $6 billion in variable to fixed rate swaps and just under $1 billion in fixed to variable rate swaps.[79] This is different from the Orange County, California, strategy for its investments. In the interest rate swap hedges, the party involved negotiates a known risk and return range, and it keeps its maximum risk exposure within bounds of good financial management practice. In the Orange County case, the county's investment manager was in effect borrowing to bet on interest rates rising. When they fell, the county could not pay off the borrowed money.

▪ Private Equity Financing for Public Capital Assets

Traditionally, state and local governments, or subnational governments in other countries, finance infrastructure as described in the preceding sections, with most relying upon access to credit to address the lumpiness of the upfront investment. Since the privatization of the formerly public water authorities in the United Kingdom during the Thatcher administration (1979–1990), there have been waves of private equity investments in a wide variety of what normally have been considered public facilities or public assets. Of course not any one precipitating phenomenon, such as the U.K. water sector privatizations, is *the* causal factor, but what once had been primarily the province of the electric power generation industry—seeking private equity investments to pay for public facilities—spread to a wide range of other public services.

This concluding section examines the options available to governments to attract private equity investment into public service facilities. Not all forms of public-private-partnerships are considered in this section. For example, contracting with private companies to perform a public service, such as contracting out solid waste collection, does not involve private equity capital investment in infrastructure. If an arrangement does involve service contracting plus equity investment, such as contracting for solid waste collection *and* licensing a company to use its own capital to build and operate a solid waste disposal facility, then it is considered in this section. Likewise, if an arrangement involves a contract turning over the assets of an existing infrastructure system or capital asset to a private party, either for a fixed period or permanently, it also is considered in this section.

Figure 13–3 is a schematic depicting the major institutional arrangements for financing infrastructure or other capital facilities. The specifics of contractual provisions embodied in any one category illustrated in **Figure 13–3** may be so varied that some authors would depict the categories somewhat differently. And there is not a universal language in which everyone agrees on exactly what to call a given

Figure 13–3 Capital Finance Options

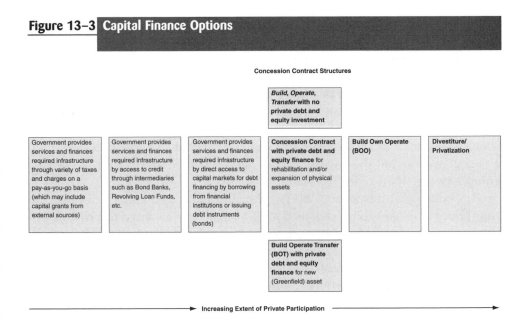

institutional structure. Our illustration focuses on the role of the private sector in bringing debt and equity financing to a public infrastructure project. **Figure 13–3** is illustrative and intended to present the array of options. In the figure, the first three categories involve no direct private participation and were discussed in preceding sections. The figure reads from left to right with the degree of private sector equity participation increasing.

Concession Contracts

Concession contracting involves a substantial change from conventional public sector financing and operation of public service facilities. Concession contracting involves the government awarding a contract with one or more companies to operate a service, such as a water utility, for a fixed concession period. For a major public utility 15 to 30 years is a common time frame.

There are three types of concessions. First is an operating concession in which a new facility or asset is to be constructed, and the private contractor both constructs *and* operates the facility for the contract period. However, in this structure, the contractor is not involved in the capital financing. Second is a concession contract for operating an existing infrastructure system, but also for substantial rehabilitation and expansion of the system. In this, the contractor is responsible for both debt and equity capital finance. The third concession-type contract is similar to the second, except that it involves not an existing facility or capital asset, but the construction and operation of an entirely new facility—a so-called *greenfield* project. In contrast with the first type of concession contract, the private party is responsible for the capital financing requirements, both debt and equity.

In the middle of **Figure 13–3** we show all three concession variants in which the private sector is brought in to operate a facility, such as a water treatment plant or a transit system. The top category is a *Build-Operate-Transfer* (BOT) structure in which a private company is awarded a contract to build and operate a facility for a period of time, but the government or agency that contracts with the private group provides 100% of the financing.

An example of this form of BOT is the Hudson-Bergen Light Rail project in New Jersey. A Phase I contract valued at $1.1 billion was awarded in 1996 to a private consortium to build and operate for a 15-year period the first (9.5 miles) segment of an eventual 25 mile light rail system along the Hudson River in two counties. The private contractor was responsible for designing, building, and operating for the 15-year contract period the entire system including construction of the railway, the stations and provision of the rolling stock. Subsequent contracts were awarded to complete the additional segments with all phases in service in 2005.[80]

The winning private consortia assumed an operating responsibility, but assumed no responsibility for capital finance. The State of New Jersey issued bonds to finance the project, secured by a pledge of future federal transit grants—*grant anticipation note* (GAN) — authorized under TEA-21 (discussed earlier). In the event that these discretionary grants were not awarded, or were insufficient, a secondary pledge of funds in the New Jersey State transportation trust fund secured the bonds.

The Jakarta, Indonesia, water concession contracts first executed in 1997 are examples of the second type of concession contract in **Figure 13–3**. With World Bank and International Finance Corporation assistance, the Jakarta public water authority and the central government of Indonesia began working on a public-private partnership in the early 1990s. Ultimately, Jakarta was split into two geographic areas and competitive bidding resulted in two different consortia of international and Indonesian firms being awarded contracts. The lead international partners in the two concession contracts were Thames Water and Suez Lyonnaise des Eaux respectively. Thames was one of the U.K. private water companies resulting from the divestiture of public water authority assets in the U.K. about a decade earlier, and Suez Lyonnaise was a French private water operator. Both lead international companies started as public utilities and by the time of the Jakarta concession were private, owning in various forms and operating water companies in their home countries as well as other countries.

In 1997, the Metropolitan Manila (Philippines) Water and Sewer Services authority (MWSS) similarly bid out and executed two contracts dividing the metro area roughly in half. The two winning companies were awarded concessions to operate the services for 25 years, and each was required to invest in significant capital facilities improvements including rehabilitation of existing infrastructure, extension of water lines, and building new treatment capacity. The lead international firm was Lyonnaise des Eaux, prior to its merger with Suez Water.

These major water concessions of the late 1990s were not just phenomena in developing countries. Also in 1997, Atlanta, Georgia, entered into a 20-year concession contract for water services. It has been called a privatization, but as we discuss below, it is more accurately characterized as a concession contract as Atlanta never sold or assigned the assets to the concessionaire, United Water, a subsidiary of Suez Water. The Atlanta contract was cancelled after several years.

Characteristics of Concession Contracts

All three water concessions described here reflect similar principles. First, concession contracts were selected in preference to privatization or divestiture, discussed below, largely for country-specific legal reasons and also to avoid the unfavorable perceptions that the governments were selling off the authority and responsibility to the private sector to deliver water services. Public utility concessions generally are competed on the basis of bidders' proposals as to the amount of capital investment they will make, the time period over which that investment will occur, the rates they will charge consumers for the services, and the stipulation that all facilities will be properly maintained so that at the end of the concession period a fully functional utility with fully functional capital assets will remain.

The Buenos Aires water concession awarded in 1993, one of the first major water concessions, illustrates these principles. All bidders were required to invest $240 million per year for the first five years in infrastructure. This compares with only about $10 million per year in capital investments in the preceding several years by the pubic sector utility. The competition was decided on the basis of which bidder offered the largest rate reduction. The winner contracted to reduce water rates by 26.9%, slightly above the 26.1% proposed by the second closest bidder.[81]

Several features of the Buenos Aires concession illustrate the features typically designed to ensure that the public sector's responsibility for the public service is treated by the concessionaire as a *public* responsibility and that consumers' interests are protected by provisions in the contract:

1. Water quality and quantity requirements such as volume and water pressure
2. Operating improvements such as installing a metering system
3. New capital facilities such as building sewage treatment plants
4. Increased population coverage for water and sewerage services

5. Tariffs fixed for five years at a time, and otherwise renegotiable only as a result of situations beyond the concessionaire's control

6. Preservation of employment and negotiation of union contracts

7. Significant capital investment, in the Buenos Aires case at least $4 billion over the life of the concession, over $1 billion of which was to be invested in the first five years.[82]

In this concession-type arrangement, the concessionaire is responsible for all financing, both capital and operating. The public sector is not required to provide capital grants or to raise debt capital for the program. One of the main features, aside from specific contract provisions of the type listed above, is that the concession contract stipulates the minimum amount of the capital investment that must come from concessionaire's equity participation. This has the effect of ensuring the concessionaire's performance over the concession period. The public sector is interested in seeing the concessionaire finance as large a proportion of the cost as can be negotiated as equity investment, whereas the private party typically is interested in minimizing the equity investment. Typical outcomes are 15% to 30% equity investment.

What the public sector gains from the equity investment is that the concessionaire has contributed its own capital, and will not be able to make a profit unless it manages the utility efficiently and effectively to generate the return on equity. The more debt financing, the more *other people's money* other than the concessionaire is in the enterprise, the less incentive there is to maintain the physical infrastructure. And in the worst case, the concessionaire going bankrupt in an all debt financed enterprise would leave the concessionaire without a significant capital loss having no equity in the enterprise and the public holding the bag with a dysfunctional public service.

Concession contracting, and the remaining structures for private equity financing, is not as simple as portrayed here, of course. Major concession contracts typically take three to five years to design, bid, and negotiate. To protect the public interest, the negotiating public entity spends considerable capital on legal and financial advisory fees. The concessionaires of course are sophisticated in the one business of private investment in the specific service, and in operating the business. Developing countries especially, but also smaller jurisdictions in industrialized countries, were at a significant disadvantage in negotiating the earliest contracts. For that reason, for the major developing country initiatives, the World Bank and the Infrastructure Finance Corporation played significant advisory roles.

Most of the earlier concession contracts developed problems, some quickly, and some after several years. The Jakarta concessions were awarded only months before the overthrow of the Suharto Regime and less than a year before the Asia financial collapse that caused the Indonesian rupiah to devalue against the U.S. dollar from about 3,700 to 1 to about 20,000 to 1. Water consumers in Jakarta of course paid their water tariffs in rupiah, whereas much of the debt and equity financing the concessionaires brought to the contracts were denominated in various international currencies, mainly the dollar, pound, and franc. The immediate problem in both the Jakarta and Manila concessions was renegotiating the tariffs to allow at least cost recovery because, as in the Buenos Aires details listed above, events outside the control of the concessionaire were grounds for renegotiation of contract terms.

Build-Operate-Transfer (BOT). A variation in concession contracting illustrated in **Figure 13-3**, involving a still higher degree of private sector investment, is the Build-Operate-Transfer (BOT) structure. Contractual features are quite similar to those already discussed above in connection with the Buenos Aires concession. However, a BOT structure is more common where the intent is to build infrastructure in a geographic area in which no service presently exists, or to extend existing service to a new area, a so-called greenfield project because the contractor is not dealing with an existing system. The BOT contractor is not awarded a concession to improve and operate an existing system or facility, but rather is awarded a contract to create a facility or service where none or minimal services previously existed, or where a new facility will be added into an existing system, but can be built and operated separately from the existing system. In the BOT structure, the private party does not own the capital assets.

The BOT contracts have been common in the electric power generation and bulk water supply industries. Either the existing power supply is inadequate or non-existent. Therefore, a contract is awarded to a private contractor to build, operate, and at the end of the contract period to transfer to the public sector the new facility. In the bulk water supply industry, the BOT contract is used to build and operate for a period of time a new impoundment, a new deep well system, or a new extraction/treatment plant to obtain bulk water from an existing source such as a river. Malaysia has used the BOT mechanism extensively for new bulk water and treatment facilities.

The BOT contracts often are characterized by what is called a *take-or-pay mechanism* for determining payments to the contractor. That is, the contractor agrees to deliver a minimum volume, for instance kilowatts of electricity or cubic meters of water, and the public utility agrees to buy at least that minimum amount. Price per unit is based on that minimum. The public utility will *take* that minimum for which the private contractor likely will be paid by tariffs paid by the consumers. But if the minimum is not actually required by the utility's customers, the utility will nonetheless *pay* the contractor for that minimum. The contractor has the assurance of the minimum, but if demand is there, the contractor may sell more than the minimum.

Other contract features are similar, especially requiring some minimum proportion of the capital investment be the private operator's equity investment.

Again this is intended to protect the public sector against the contractor terminating the agreement early. With no equity investment, the contractor has nothing invested to lose, and the debt suppliers are the ultimate losers, along with the public utility executing the deal in the first place. The BOT structures may involve public funding as well as private funding, or require that the contractor finance the entire project. The contractor needs sufficient assurances of operating the facility for a period of time sufficient to achieve a return on its equity and to repay debt financing. The public agency needs to assure that the prices charged are reasonable in the market, and that the facility is still in operating condition at the time of the transfer. Contract negotiations revolve around these two sets of provisions.

Build-Own-Operate-Transfer (BOOT). The *Build-Own-Operate-Transfer* (BOOT) structure is a variant of the BOT. The distinguishing feature is that the private investor/operator for a period of time actually owns the capital assets. It too has a variant, the *Build-Own-Operate* (BOO). The Enron Corporation became a large multinational corporation by its innovative solutions to power problems in developing countries. One of its early successes was building generating stations on barges and bringing the barges into the metropolitan Manila harbor to add capacity to the existing system. These barges were owned by Enron. At the end of the contract, the barges could be sold to the utility or to other parties, or floated away to be used by Enron elsewhere. The most common practice where the facility is permanently located is that the contract will have provisions for the public entity's buying the facility at a negotiated price at the end of the contract period. Note that this is not a salvage price, the residual value of an asset whose useful life has for the most part been exhausted. The utility is expected to be fully operational, to have been well-maintained, and to be able to provide service continuously into the future. These characteristics will be a primary feature of the concession contract. Telecommunications, transportation, and water are the traditional sectors for large BOOT contract structures for bringing private sector financing into what otherwise would have been a public responsibility.

Divestiture/Privatization

At the end of the spectrum in **Figure 13–3** is divestiture or privatization. A public sector entity may decide upon divestiture of a set of assets because the facility is deteriorating, needs significant investment or is perhaps at the periphery of what the public now thinks of as a "public sector responsibility." In 2006, Chicago sold the Skyway, an expressway connecting Chicago and Indiana, to an international consortium for $1.83 billion and the Skyway was not the only divestiture in Chicago's plan. Morgan Stanley, an investment firm, bought four downtown parking garages for $563 million, and the City as of 2007 was offering Midway

Airport for sale.[83] Similarly, the State of Indiana has sold the Indiana Toll Road and New Jersey has investigated divestiture of a number of assets including the New Jersey Turnpike and the Atlantic City Expressway.[84]

Sales of these types can be controversial in the post-September 11 era, when Americans are wary of international investors owning and/or operating major infrastructure. The Chicago Skyway, for instance, is operated by a group of Australian and Spanish investors. In 2006 a deal by a Dubai ports management firm—Dubai Ports World—to manage six U.S. seaports was killed because of the uproar over a foreign company taking over facilities vital to homeland security.

At the heart of the divestiture decision on the part a of governmental institution is whether or not the assets being divested are a fundamental public sector responsibility that can or should be turned over to the private sector. If a service is considered to be a fundamental public sector responsibility, why bring in the private sector, which lacks traditional public service values? But there is no clear answer in many cases as only a few public sector goods meet the test of a *pure* public good (see Chapter 1). Many public services may have varying degrees of private sector involvement without real consequence to the public one way or the other. Many cities own and operate parking garages, for example. Many other cities have no public parking garages but leave parking entirely in the hands of the private sector. There is no obvious criterion that says parking garages should clearly be public, or clearly should be private. Or at least there is no criterion upon which everyone agrees.

Appraisal of Private Equity Investment Experience

The controversy over privatization or divestiture usually arises when citizens or interest groups feel the city, or other governmental entity, is turning over a fundamental public interest to the private sector, and leaving citizens (especially poorer citizens) unprotected in the aftermath. In every developing country, water sector public-private partnerships of any of the forms above lead to higher prices to some consumers. But this is often in the context of systems that have been previously heavily subsidized with the utility rarely recovering capital costs, and often not even fully recovering operating costs. The utility usually faces a major need for renovation and expansion as a result of urbanization, and the capital is just not available to the public sector.

Typically in these developing country instances, the wealthy and middle income segments have been the only ones receiving direct piped service to their residences, and they enjoy low, subsidized rates. The extremely poor segment of the population pays for bottled water or buys from vendors who travel through impoverished neighborhoods and the price they pay per liter is generally five to ten times more than the per liter cost to a middle income household connected to the public system.

The concession or BOOT type contract then can be quite controversial because current customers may experience rate increases, although the average rate may go down because of the addition of lower income, low volume users. One of the remedies for protecting the lowest income segment is what is sometimes called the *life support* tariff. The first several cubic liters of water service, an amount estimated to be the amount needed to live, is free or billed at a very low cost. Rates then go up as consumption goes up and the middle and upper income groups thus pay more.

In some of the examples cited in this chapter, such as the Buenos Aires case, the concession is for services in which the existing management of the utility has become inefficient, including possibly employing a much larger workforce because the utility was serving not only to provide water, but to provide the social good of employment whether the employees were required or not. In those cases, the concession contract generally lowers the marginal cost of the service.

Certainly there are examples of high expectations not being met.[85] The two Jakarta water concessions have remained controversial, in part because at the time the contracts were awarded, both international lead firms had joint ventures with companies owned and directed by members of the then ruling Suharto family. It has taken more than a decade to work through some of the problems built into the original contracts, and to recover from the effects of the 1997 financial collapse in Indonesia as well as much of the rest of Asia.

Considerable experience has amassed in both the public and private sectors in the last two decades, and sophisticated expertise is available to both sectors to protect the public interest and also to ensure a fair return on investment to the private party. And public interest groups and other watchdogs are actively engaged in informing the public, sometimes dispassionately and sometimes with a strong bias. But we can confidently say that various forms of private equity financing for major capital facilities providing public services will continue to grow. The first driver is capital markets expansion. As capital markets expand, investors such as pension funds look for attractive long-term investments. The second driver is the inability of governments to find enough capital themselves to meet the demand for infrastructure. As governments face pressures to focus on vital public services, they will likely consider divesting themselves of enterprise-like operations that are easily converted to private operations.

Summary

Because of the long life of capital facilities and infrastructure, extensive use is made of long-term financing in various forms. Both the public and private sectors combine debt and equity financing to satisfy capital investment needs, with equity financing for public sector infrastructure a phenomenon that has emerged in the past 25 years. Some local governments still consider it financially prudent to borrow little or not at all, but state governments and virtually all large cities are unable to provide the services demanded by citizens without resorting to some debt financing for capital investments. Although it is generally accepted that future generations should not be saddled with unreasonable debt burdens about which they have no say, most citizens recognize that capital facilities will be enjoyed by future generations. Debt financing provides a means for those future generations to share the costs as well as the benefits.

The municipal debt market has undergone remarkable changes in the last decade. Sophisticated structured financing tools developed for private debt and equity transactions are being applied to municipal debt issues. In addition, municipalities are using increasingly sophisticated money management techniques to minimize their cost of debt and to maximize the returns on their own investments. Occasionally these techniques result in major financial disasters. As a result, the SEC, which once took a hands-off attitude toward the municipal debt market, has adopted increasingly stringent disclosure requirements, and Congress has increased the SEC's regulatory role regarding municipal debt.

Effective debt management requires that the amount of debt incurred not impose hardships on future taxpayers and that it not force future cutbacks in operation and maintenance expenditures necessary to maintain capital facilities. State governments, through constitutional provisions and statutory requirements, regulate their own borrowing as well as that of local governments. These regulations mainly focus on the commitment of the "full faith and credit" of the jurisdiction. Partly because of the restrictions imposed on general obligation bonds and partly because of the efficiency of tying repayment of debt to specific revenues generated by the investment, there has been tremendous growth in the use of a wide variety of debt instruments. Overall, however, state and local debt has grown little over the past 30 years in relation to personal income. State and local governments also have become more sophisticated in their financial analysis of capital investments and debt financing.

Even with innovations in municipal bonds and other means for governments to access the capital markets for credit, debt financing has not been sufficient. Beginning largely with the privatization of the U.K.'s water utilities, the role of public-private-partnerships in financing and operating public infrastructure has become common-place in both industrialized and developing countries. Various forms of concession contracting including structures that feature private operating concessions only to structures that feature significant private debt and equity financing are increasing. This industry has had significant problems with many of the earliest large concession type contracts, but with experience, sophistication on both the private investor and the public sector side has made various forms of private financing more attractive to both investors and public agencies.

Notes

1. Board of Governors, Federal Reserve System (2006). *Flow of funds accounts of the United States: flows and outstandings third quarter 2006.* Washington, DC: Federal Reserve System, 59.

2. Reifman, S. & Wong, S. (Eds.) (2005). America's largest private companies. *Forbes.com website.* Retrieved December 16, 2006, from http://www.forbes.com/2005/11/09/largest-private-companies_05private_land.html.

3. For simplicity's sake, we do not discuss forms of ownership here. A private limited liability company (LLC) also has shares, and additional investors may be allowed to contribute equity capital by purchasing shares. But the shares are not listed publicly and are not available for sale to the public.

4. Johnson, R. (1996). *Capital financing for municipal infrastructure: choices as viewed by the enterprise and the investor.* Research Triangle Park, NC: RTI International.

5. Knepper, D. (2006). Eliminating the federal subsidy in Kelo: restricting the availability of tax-exempt financing for redevelopment projects. *Georgetown Law Journal, 94,* 1635–1665.

6. The Bond Market Association (2006). *Trends in the holdings of municipal securities:* 1985–2006, Q2. Retrieved December 19, 2006 from http://www.bondmarkets.com/story.asp?id=318.

7. Martell, C. & Guess, G. (2006). Development of local government debt financing markets: application of a market-based framework. *Public Budgeting & Finance, 26, Spring,* 88-–119.

8. Bureau of the Census, U.S. Department of Commerce (2006). *Statistical abstract of the United States: 2006.* Washington, DC: U.S. Government Printing Office, 274.

9. Marlin, M. (1994). Did tax reform kill segmentation in the municipal bond market? *Public Administration Review, 54,* 387–390.

10. *South Carolina* v. *Baker.* (1988). 485 U.S. 505.

11. For a discussion of the history of legal actions concerning state and local tax immunity, see Wrightson, M. (1989). The road to *South Carolina*: intergovernmental tax immunity and the constitutional status of federalism. *Publius, 19, Winter,* 39–55.

12. Kittower, D. (1997). Municipal bonds: the deals of the year. *Governing, 11, March,* 56.

13. Resnick, A. (2006). Capital asset seeking to continue success with lien purchasing service. *Website.* Retrieved December 20, 2006, from http://www.lienexchange.com/Tax-Lien-Certificates-Capital-Asset-Seeking-To-Continue-Success-With-Lien-Purchasing-Service.html.

14. Lemov, P. (2000). Tobacco bonds draw a market. *Governing, 14, January,* 54.

15. Kittower, D. (2000). Deals of the year. *Governing, 14, March,* 68.

16. Barrett, K. et. al. (2005). Grading the states '05: the year of living dangerously. *Governing, 19, February.* Retrieved December 20, 2006, from http://www.governing.com/GPP/2005/intro.htm.

17. Kyle, C. (1994). Airport financing: let the passengers pay. *Governing, 7, March,* 18–19; Lemov, P. (1996). A groundbreaking bond takes off in Little Rock. *Governing, 10, July,* 51.

18. Passenger facility charge convertible lien bonds for airport expansion (2002). *Website.* Retrieved December 21, 2006, from http://www.leighfisher.com/pdfs/expertise/FLL10.pdf.

19. Dillingham, G. (2003). *Airport finance: past funding levels may not be sufficient to cover airports' planned capital development.* Washington, DC: U.S. General Accounting Office, 6.

20. Johnson, T. & Scott, J. (2004). A comprehensive approach to the assessment of tax increment financing (TIF) projects. *Journal of Public Budgeting, Accounting & Financial Management, 16,* 394–412.

21. Missouri Economic Development Commission (2006). *Tax Increment Financing (TIF) Commission.* Retrieved December 4, 2006, from http://www.edckc.com/tif/index.htm.

22. Hildreth, W. & Zorn, C. (2005). The evolution of state and local government municipal debt markets over the past quarter century. *Public Budgeting & Finance, 25, Silver Anniversary Edition,* 127–153.

23. Kreps, M. (1993). Ups and downs of municipal bonds' volume and yields in the past century. In J. Lamb. et al. (Eds.), *The handbook of municipal bonds and public finance.* New York: New York Institute of Finance, 114.

24. Internal Revenue Service, U.S. Department of the Treasury (2005). *Introduction to federal taxation of municipal bonds.* Retrieved December 17, 2006, from http://www.irs.treas.gov/pub/irs-tege/tebph1b.pdf.

25. Pohle, L. (1991). Marketing mini-bonds: lessons learned from Denver's successful first issuance. *Government Finance Review, 7, June,* 32–34.

26. MetroLink Cross County (2002). Bi-State Board of Commissioners approves funding structure for MetroLink cross county extension. Retrieved January 18, 2007, from http://www.crosscountymetro.org/news101802.asp.

27. Johnson, C. & Mikesell, J. (1994). Certificates of participation and capital markets: lessons from Brevard County and Richmond Unified School District. *Public Budgeting & Finance, 14, Fall,* 41–54.

28. State of Oregon (2003). *Website.* Retrieved December 17, 2006, from http://www.oregon.gov/DAS/BAM/docs/Capital_Investment/AboutCOPS.pdf.

29. Petersen, J. (2000). The muni e-bond revolution. *Governing, 14, April,* 67.

30. Morgenstern, R. (2000) Electronic bidding for municipal bonds: technology innovations for competitive bond sales. *Government Finance Review, 16, February,* 23–26.

31. Safe Drinking Water Act (1974). P.L. 95-523.

32. New York State Environmental Facilities Corporation (2006). *Proposed 2007–2008 fiscal year budget and financial plan.* Retrieved December 20, 2006, from http://www.nysefc.org/home/index.asp?page=8&recordid=587&returnurl=index%2Easp%3Fpage%3D8

33. Robbins, M. & Kim, D. (2003). Do state bond banks have cost advantages for municipal bond issuance? *Public Budgeting & Finance, 23, Fall,* 92–108.

34. National Highway System Designation Act (1995). P.L. 104-59.

35. Transportation Safety Act (1998). P.L. 105-178; Safe, Accountable, Flexible, Efficient Transportation Equity Act: A Legacy for Users (2005), P.L. 109-59.

36. Peterson, G. (2006). *Using municipal development funds to build municipal credit markets.* Washington, DC: Urban Institute.

37. Martell, C. & Guess, G. (2006). *Development of local government debt financing markets,* 88–119.

38. Bloomberg Financial, Municipal bond investors pay low spreads in Nevada, cited in *Las Vegas Review Online Edition, January 23, 2001.* Retrieved August 15, 2002, from http://www.lvrj.com/lvrj_home/2001/ Jan–23–Tue–2001/business/15271455.html; Mississippi Legislature Joint Committee on Performance Evaluation and Expenditure Review (2001). *Cost of issuance expenses cy 2000 state and local bond issues.* Retrieved December 20, 2006, from http://www.peer.state.ms.us/427.html.

39. Robbins, M. et al. (2000). Maturity structure and borrowing costs: the implications of level debt service. *Municipal Finance Journal, 21, Fall,* 40–64; Kriz, K. (2000). Do municipal bond underwriting choices have implications for other financial certification decisions? *Municipal Finance Journal, 21, Fall,* 1–23.

40. Iowa Board of Regents (2005). *Memorandum: costs of bond issuance.* Retrieved December 23, 2006, from http://www2.state.ia.us/regents/Meetings/DocketMemos/05Memos/feb05/0205_ITEM11.pdf.

41. Marois, M. & Selway, W. (2006). *Oregon taxpayers denied benefits of competitive bids for schools.* Retrieved December 28, 2006, from http://www.bloomberg.com/apps/news?pid=20601015&sid=aY6EMMx6FDc8&refer=munibonds#.

42. National Conference of State Legislatures (2006). *State and municipal bond general elections 2006: voter approval rate exceeds average.* Retrieved December 27, 2006, from http://www.ncsl.org/programs/fiscal/bonds06vote.htm.

43. Simonsen, W. & Robbins, M. (1996). Does it make any difference anymore? competitive versus negotiated municipal bond issuance. *Public Administration Review, 56,* 57–63.

44. Peng, J. & Brucato, Jr., P. (2003). Another look at the effect of method of sale on the interest cost in the municipal bond market — a certification model. *Public Budgeting & Finance, 23, Spring,* 73–95.

45. Temel, J. (2001). *Fundamentals of municipal bonds.* New York: Bond Market Association.

46. Kriz, K. (2004). Risk aversion and the pricing of municipal bonds. *Public Budgeting & Finance, 24, Summer,* 74–87.

47. Tavakoli, J. (2003).*Collateralized debt obligations and structured finance: new developments in cash and synthetic securitization.* New York: Wiley.

48. Honolulu Star Bulletin (2006). *Better bond rating is boon to Honolulu.* Retrieved December 27, 2006, from http://starbulletin.com/2006/12/21/editorial/letters.html

49. Denison, D. (2003). An empirical examination of the determinants of municipal bond issues, *Public Budgeting & Finance, 23, Spring,* 96–114.

50. Doty, R. (1990). The role of the Municipal Securities Rulemaking Board and the central repository for public securities: dealer regulation or market regulation? *Municipal Finance Journal, 11,* 7–51.

51. Municipal Securities Rulemaking Board (2006). *Website.* Retrieved January 2, 2007, from http://www.msrb.org/msrb1/archive/sdpr/text.htm.

52. U.S. Securities and Exchange Commission (2006). *Municipal securities information sources.* Retrieved January 2, 2007, from http://www.sec.gov/info/municipal/nrmsir.htm

53. Lemov, P. (1996). A new investment rule requires "suitable" advice. *Governing, 10 October,* 57.

54. Denison, D. et.al. (2006). State debt limits: how many are enough? *Public Budgeting & Finance, 26, Winter,* 22–39.

55. Federal Reserve System (2006). *Flow of funds accounts of the United States,* 59.

56. Federal Reserve System (2006). *Flow of funds accounts of the United States,* 19.

57. Bureau of the Census, U.S. Department of Commerce (2006). *Statistical abstract of the United States: 2006.* Washington, DC: Government Printing Office, 278 (for per capita debt by state); Bureau of the Census, U.S. Department of Commerce (2003). *Statistical abstract of the United States: 2003.* Washington, DC U.S. Government Printing Office, 434 (for personal income by state).

58. Dickson, S. (1993). Civil war, railroads, and road bonds: bond repudiations in the days of yore. In J. Lamb et.al. (Eds.), *The handbook of municipal bonds and public finance,* 166–173.

59. Mitchell, G. (1975). Statement before the Committee on Banking, Housing and Urban Affairs. *Federal Reserve Bulletin, 61,* 729–730.

60. The Bond Market Association (2002), *Municipal bond defaults: 1940–1994.* Retrieved July 15, 2002, from http://www.bondmarkets.com/Research/defaults.shtml (no longer accessible).

61. *Moody's municipal bond rating scale* (2002). New York: Moody's, 5; *Mapping of Moody's municipal bond rating scale to Moody's corporate rating scale and assignment of corporate equivalent ratings to municipal obligations* (2006). New York: Moody's, 4.

62. Petersen, J. (2000). All hail the dowager queen. *Governing, 14, December,* 74.

63. Dickson, R. (1995). *Civil war, railroads, and road bonds: bond repudiations in the days of yore,* 172; Collin, R. (1995). What the law says about Orange County: creditors' rights and remedies on municipal default. *Municipal Finance Journal, 16, Summer,* 52–89.

64. Cohen, N. (1989). Municipal default patterns: an historical study. *Public Budgeting & Finance, 9 Winter,* 62.

65. Leigland, J. & Lamb, R. (1986). *WPP$$: who is to blame for the WPPSS disaster?* Cambridge, MA: Ballinger.

66. Sitzer, H. (1994). The Washington Public Power Supply System: then and now. *Municipal Finance Journal, 14, Winter,* 59–78.

67. WPPSS no more (2002). *Puget Sound Business Journal, February 1.* Retrieved January 11, 2007, from http://www.bizjournals.com/seattle/stories/2002/02/04/story2.html; Energy Northwest. *Website.* Retrieved January 11, 2007, from http://www.energy-northwest.com.

68. Watson, et al. (2005). Financial distress and municipal bankruptcy: the case of Prichard, Alabama. *Journal of Public Budgeting, Accounting & Financial Management, 17,* 129–150.

69. Park, K. (2004). To file or not to file: the causes of municipal bankruptcy in the United States. *Journal of Public Budgeting, Accounting & Financial Management, 16,* 228–256.

70. Lemov, P. (1995). Two down-and-out localities are back on the fast track. *Governing, 9, December,* 49.

71. Chapman, J. (1996). The challenge of entrepreneurship. *Municipal Finance Journal, 17, July,* 16–32.

72. Halstead, et al. (2004). Orange County bankruptcy: financial contagion in the municipal bond and bank equity markets. *Financial Review, 39,* 293–315.

73. Berne, R. (1993). *Governmental accounting and financial reporting and the measurement of financial condition.* In J. Lamb et. al. (Eds.), *The handbook of municipal bonds and public finance,* 257–315.

74. Brecher, et.al. (2003). An approach to measuring the affordability of state debt. *Public Budgeting & Finance, 23, Winter,* 65–85.

75. Hackbart, et al. (2004). *Debt capacity and debt limits: a state road fund perspective,* Kentucky Transportation Center, University of Kentucky. Retrieved December 4, 2006, from http://www.ktc.uky.edu/Reports/KTC_04_16_TA_5_03_1F.pdf.

76. Brecher, et al. (2003). *An approach to measuring the affordability of state debt,* 65–85.

77. Bureau of the Census, U.S. Department of Commerce (2001). *Statistical abstract of the United States: 2001.* Washington, DC: U.S. Government Printing Office, 275.

78. Haupert, J. (1992). Using interest rate swaps as part of an overall financing and investment strategy. *Government Finance Review, 8, April,* 13–15.

79. Comptroller, State of New York (2005). *2005 State of New York financial condition report.* Albany, NY: Comptroller's Office of Public Information, 15.

80. Federal Highway Administration, U.S. Department of Transportation. *Case study: Hudson-Bergen Light Rail.* Retrieved January 2, 2007, from http://www.fhwa.dot.gov/PPP/hudson.htm.

81. The World Bank (2001). *The Buenos Aires concession: the private sector serving the poor.* Washington, DC: World Bank, 1–2.

82. World Bank (2001). *The Buenos Aires concession,* 3 (all further details of Buenos Aires concession from this source).

83. Swope, C. (2007). Unloading assets. *Governing, 20, January,* 36.

84. Swope, C. (2007). Unloading Assets. *Governing,* 40.

85. Hood, J. et al. (2006). Transparency of risk and reward in U.K. public-private-partnerships. *Public Budgeting & Finance, 26, Winter,* 40–58.

Chapter 14

INTERGOVERNMENTAL RELATIONS

Each level of government has discrete financial decision-making processes that determine matters of revenue and expenditure. Decisions about revenues and expenditures at different levels of government, however, are interdependent. Budgetary decisions made at one level are partially dependent on budgetary decisions made at other levels. Nonbudgetary decisions made at one level also may have dramatic impacts on budgets at another level.

This chapter examines the financial interdependencies among federal, state, and local governments.[1] The first section examines some of the basic economic and political problems that stem from having three major levels of government that provide various services and possess differing financial capabilities. The second section considers the patterns of interaction among the different levels and the third section considers the main types of intergovernmental financial assistance programs. Key topics include devolution of responsibility from the federal government to state and local governments, especially welfare reform and health care for lower-income groups. The chapter concludes with a discussion of current issues and alternatives for restructuring these patterns of financial interaction, including the controversial issue of unfunded mandates.

Structural and Fiscal Features of the Intergovernmental System

For convenience, we have commonly referred throughout this book to the three levels of governments, but at this point this simplification must be set aside. In this section, we consider the problems associated with having multiple levels and types of governments.

Areal and Functional Relations

Multiple Governments. Governments around the world and the organizations that they create constitute an intricate web of interjurisdictional relations. The United Nations, the European Union, NATO, and the like affect their member states and also other states throughout the world. The World Trade Organization (WTO), for example, with about 150 member states, sets ground rules for international commerce and resolves trade disputes among member nations.[2] The WTO's actions impact governments, businesses, and individuals everywhere. These interactions are about diplomacy, trade, and global concerns that extend beyond the scope of this book, but it needs to be recognized that what occurs in intergovernmental relations in the U.S. is within a much broader context of governments relating with one another around the world.

Turning to the United States, governments operate within a federalist system in which power is constitutionally shared between a central or national government and 50 states, which have sovereign status meaning they are (at least technically) independent of the national government.[3] Federal systems include those in Australia, Belgium, Canada, Germany, India, and Switzerland. In contrast is a centralized or unitary system in which all power resides in a national government with some powers then being delegated to regional units. The United Kingdom is an example of this form of government.

In a federal system, the national government and states almost inevitably clash from time to time over their respective powers, and legal remedies are often available. In the U.S., the states may sue in federal court when they allege federal action has abrogated their constitutionally protected powers. In a unitary system, the national government has the power to create and dissolve subunits, which may or may not have any legal recourse against adverse actions taken against them by higher authority. In other words, American states can and often do defend their rights by filing suit claiming the federal government has usurped their powers, whereas in unitary systems, such rights are severely circumscribed at best.

Complicating the federal system in the U.S. is the fact that Native American tribes have independent status. The tribes exist within states but are independent of them and at least theoretically independent of the federal government. This fact has been the source of endless confusion, politicking, and legal wrangling since 1987, when the Supreme Court ruled that Native American tribes could operate gaming facilities. Congress passed the Indian Gaming Regulatory Act of 1988 that allowed for gaming and created the National Indian Gaming Commission to regulate the newly emerging industry.[4] The Supreme Court decision and the 1988 law set the stage for an elaborate set of intergovernmental actions.

Although politicians in many states opposed the introduction of casinos in their jurisdictions, the 1988 law required the states to grant licenses to Native American casinos providing certain requirements were met. Native American casinos are allowed only in states that otherwise allow other specific forms of gaming. In return, states benefit from tax receipts. The law has led to states having to negotiate with tribes over the construction, operation, and expansion of casinos, regardless of whether they wanted such casinos to exist at all.[5] For example, California and the San Manuel Indian Nation in 2006 reached agreement on increasing the number of gaming devices used by the tribe.[6]

Indian gaming has grown dramatically. Revenues were $5.4 billion in 1995 and reached $22.6 billion in 2005.[7] Of the 391 casinos in operation in 2005, 118 were in the region consisting of Iowa, Michigan, Minnesota, Montana, North Dakota, Nebraska, South Dakota, Wisconsin, and Wyoming. Another 93 were in Kansas, Oklahoma, and Texas. Casinos bring employment and perhaps some improvement in Native American health, due to citizens being better able to afford health care, but casinos also yield higher crime rates which impose law enforcement costs on local governments.[8] In other words, actions at the federal level forced state and local governments to interact with tribes, and these interactions produced both costs to governments and revenues.

In addition to the federal government, the 50 state governments and more than 25 Native American tribes, the United States includes almost 88,000 local governments and the District of Columbia.[9] The local "level" is not a single level in that most states have county governments (more than 3,000 nationwide), and within their boundaries exist such general-purpose governments as municipalities and sometimes townships (more than 19,000 municipalities and 16,500 townships). Superimposed over these are numerous independent school districts and special-purpose districts such as irrigation and sewer districts. Special districts, of which there are more than 35,000, are the most numerous. There are more than 13,500 school districts.

These various local governments have a decidedly different legal status from that of the states. While the states created the national government and preserved their sovereignty through the Constitution, local governments are creatures of their respective states. They were created by the states and can be destroyed by the states.

Whether federal or unitary, many countries are granting greater autonomous authority to regional, provincial, or local governments. This autonomy does not necessarily mean shifts from unitary to federal systems. India, for example, enacted in 1991 constitutional reforms to establish certain powers and responsibilities for local governments as a matter of national constitutional authority, effectively removing some aspects of state government control over local government. In the independent republics of the former Soviet Union, central authority over all governmental functions is gradually giving way to increased responsibility at the regional and city levels, and that authority is defined and delimited by the central government. Hence, the degree of decentralization of authority in Russia has waxed and waned since the break-up of the Soviet system with President Vladimir Putin retrieving some authority from oblasts (regions) granted in previous administrations.

Having myriad governments at different levels within a nation can be defended in several ways. By having multiple governments, an omnipotent, despotic type of government may be avoided. Another advantage is that the diversity of governments allows for differing responses according to the divergent needs of citizens in different locales. For instance, some communities may place greater emphasis than others on amenities, such as flower beds and other decorations along city streets, while other communities may prefer more utilitarian, and presumably less expensive, streets. The Federalist framers and advocates for the U.S. Constitution defended a federal structure using three arguments:

- It would promote a sense of community and affinity between citizens and the government.
- It would promote efficiency by assigning functions that had mainly local importance to local governments and functions of national importance to the federal government.
- It would promote liberty by avoiding concentration of power in the hands of a few.[10]

The existence of numerous units of government increases the probability that individuals will be able to find communities to live in that suit them. For example, people may locate in communities that offer desirable mixes of taxes and services. Of course, we do not suggest that such economic calculations are the sole criteria on which people base their location decisions, but the existence of multiple governments enhances that important aspect of quality of life.[11]

Another advantage is that having multiple governments allows the achievement of economies of scale. Functions may be performed by the size of government that is most efficient in carrying out the functions. Just as it may be advantageous from the standpoint of efficient resource use for private, profit-oriented organizations to grow to a large scale, so it also may be advantageous for one unit of government to conduct some government activities on a large scale.

On the other hand, to perform all government functions at the central level might result in inefficient conduct of some activities. Not only did the economic woes of the former Soviet Union demonstrate that overly centralized planning of the productive sector of the economy produced many inefficiencies, but the overly centralized administrative and fiscal systems also left a legacy of weak decision making not well adapted to provision of basic local public services.[12] Lessened flexibility of operations and other diseconomies suggest the need for some functions to be performed by units of government smaller than the central government. Geographically and economically smaller-scale activities are more efficient when carried out by smaller governments. Probably many services can be provided most efficiently at the local level.

No government, no matter what the level, is free to do whatever it pleases. The U.S. Constitution provides for the federal government's powers (especially Article I, Section 8) and reserves all other powers to the states (Tenth Amendment). In some countries, the reverse is true, with the states having enumerated powers and the national government having the remainder. In the U.S., each state constitution provides for the powers of that government. Local governments have fewer constitutional protections, because these governments have been created by their states. Within these constitutional and legal parameters, a higher-level government may impose standards upon lower levels.

Coordination Problems. The existence of thousands of governments results in coordination problems both geographically and functionally. Municipalities in a metropolitan area need some coordinative mechanisms. Road networks, for example, need to be planned in accordance with commuting patterns within a metropolitan area, and such plans should not be restricted to the geographical boundaries of each municipality. Before the federal government became involved in highway programs, many highways did not connect sensibly across state lines. Recreation and parks programs may be provided on a metropolitan or area basis and thereby achieve economies of scale. Numerous regional planning agencies, regional or metropolitan transportation planning groups, and regional economic development programs exist so as to consolidate an otherwise fragmented approach to interjurisdictional overlaps.

The need to avoid excessive fragmentation at the local level in a decentralized system has led some to argue for consolidation of the local governments in a metropolitan area, such as in Miami-Dade County, Florida, and Nashville-Davidson County, Tennessee. However, some studies have shown that the savings expected from metropolitan consolidation have not been achieved. Rather, greater efficiencies seem to result from competition among the various local governments in a metropolitan area.[13] Where coordination is needed among the local governments of a metropolitan area, it seems achievable through cooperation and shared decision making rather than consolidation. Nevertheless, there does seem to be evidence that consolidation has benefits in the case of very small local units of government.

Federal-state, interstate, and interlocal arrangements have been developed for the provision of services (as distinguished from forums for discussion), including metropolitan councils of governments that involve officials from various communities in a region. One of the most successful interstate organizations is the Port Authority of New York and New Jersey, established in 1921 by the two participating states.[14] The authority operates terminals, bridges, and tunnels. It operated the World Trade Center until its destruction in 2001. Subsequently, the Port Authority and the Lower Manhattan Development Corporation approved plans for rebuilding on the site.

At the local level, numerous types of cooperative arrangements exist. Some counties provide services such as water and sewage treatment on a contract basis for municipalities within their jurisdiction. The choice of such an arrangement may be at the discretion of municipalities, as in the case of the Lakewood Plan, whereby communities can contract with Los Angeles County for virtually all city services (see Chapter 10). In some instances, state governments may require city-county cooperation for services, such as police and fire departments having stand-by aid agreements during large civil disturbances or fires.

Functional coordination among different levels is also necessary because the three main levels of government share responsibilities for some of the same functions. Criminal justice, for instance, is a shared function. Some type of police, court, and prison system exists at each government level. The independent pursuit of similar objectives by different governments can result in wasted resources and ineffective services.

Multilevel overlapping and shared responsibility can make it difficult to design federal programs to achieve national objectives. Any given federal assistance program may be a good fit for local governments in one state and not in another state given the differences in how states allocate responsibilities between themselves and their respective local governments. Therefore, emphasis has been given to developing mechanisms for functional integration.[15] While program specialists stress functional integration, however, policy generalists may stress areal integration. This conflict was popularized by Deil S. Wright as "picket fence federalism"—each picket represents a function, such as mental health or education, and all three levels of government make up part of each picket.[16] Another analogy used is that of silos, that program areas are compartmentalized within each of many silos. As with pickets of a fence, silos discourage the crossover of information and integration of services that so often is needed in government operations.

Exhibit 14–1 illustrates how complicated the mosaic of intergovernmental relations can be. The exhibit uses as its focus the efforts made to control air emissions in an intergovernmental context. The particular device illustrated in the exhibit, an interstate compact, is one mechanism that can be used to coordinate efforts by multiple jurisdictions to combat problems that span jurisdictional boundaries. More generally, all problems dealing with the environment, whether they involve air, land, or water, more or less need to be handled on a multijurisdictional basis, including internationally.[17]

The September 11 Disasters. The terrorist attacks of September 11, 2001, dramatically underscore the need for intergovernmental cooperation and coordination. One fact that immediately became painfully obvious was the lack of sharing of information and coordination within federal agencies and among them. Equally important was the weak linkages existing among federal intelligence gathering and law enforcement agencies on the one hand and similar units internationally and at the state and local levels within the U.S.

The federal government responded to its immediate problems by creating a Department of Homeland Security that pulled together a variety of agencies that had been located throughout the federal bureaucracy. Among other things, Homeland Security provided grants for upgrading law enforcement and fire protection at the state and local levels. Noticeably absent, however, from Homeland Security's ranks was the Federal Bureau of Investigation (FBI) that remained within the Department of Justice. The FBI continues to be the federal government's primary criminal investigation and law enforcement unit, including having responsibility for international investigations such as tracking international conduits for funding terrorist activities. The U.S. Treasury Department also has a key role in investigating international financial crimes.[18]

Although a thorough assessment has not been made, it is probably safe to conclude that improvements have been made in intergovernmental cooperation on intelligence gathering but that much work in this endeavor lies ahead.[19] Do local, state, and federal law enforcement organizations routinely share relevant information about possible terrorists? Is such information shared on a timely basis? Is there a system for following up on leads about possible terrorist activities? These are fundamental intergovernmental questions for which there are no simple answers.

Additionally, September 11 made apparent the need for governments to work cooperatively in responding to major national disasters. Fire services, emergency rescue assistance, and law enforcement were called upon to handle situations of

Exhibit 14–1 | Coordinating Air Emissions as a Case Study in Interstate Compacts

Like watersheds, airsheds respect no political boundaries. Emissions from private vehicles, public facilities, and factories within the boundaries of one political jurisdiction effectively go where the winds blow. Unlike water, which has a stable pattern of flows, emissions into the air over time span the full 360 degrees of the map.

In purely self-interested terms, it may not be rational for a local government with a strong "smokestack" industry that is employing a large percentage of the workforce to regulate emissions from that industry, especially if the prevailing winds for the most part blow the polluted air away from the jurisdiction. For this reason, the federal government has for several decades played a significant role in setting limits on emissions. However, federally imposed limits rely on states and localities to develop policies and practices to meet the standards. Increasingly, states and the local jurisdictions within metropolitan areas realize that they cannot act unilaterally to solve the problems if their neighbors are not also taking care of the problems. They then act to create coordinated policies and programs to impose and enforce stronger controls.

One such example is an interstate compact among New England and mid-Atlantic states to control ground-level ozone concentrations.[1] Members of this Ozone Transport Commission (OTC) agree on a "budget" or a total amount of nitrous oxide emissions that would be allowed from sources within the states in the compact.[2] States then allocate the allowable emissions among the major producers/sources, rewarding those that come in "below budget." Individual emitters and even states may trade in these permitted levels. Those falling below the levels may trade for various compensations with those who cannot meet the allocated amount.

Although substantial cutbacks in emissions have been achieved (more than a 50% reduction from 1990 to 1999), the scenario has not been all rosy. Midwestern states did not join the commission, and prevailing winds bring large problems eastward, so the attorneys general of some states have sued coal-burning power plants in several Midwestern states.[3] While the legal steps may take several years to play out, the Ozone Transport Commission has achieved some significant progress on a common problem in intergovernmental relations.

Air quality has improved in the Northeast, although OTC's specific contribution is impossible to determine. Between 1990 and 2003, ozone levels decreased in the Northeast by 13% . Only the West-Southwest did better with a 16% decline.[4]

While interstate compacts can be effective in addressing cross-jurisdictional issues, they are not easy to set up. Article I, Section 10 of the Constitution requires congressional approval of any interstate compact. Despite this step, this approach has proved a useful mechanism for creating interjurisdictional authority to address mutual interests.

1. Arrandale, T. (2000). Balking on air. *Governing, 14, January*, 26–29.

2. Ozone Transport Commission (2005). *Final OTC multipollutant program development strategy*. Retrieved September 27, 2006, from http://www.otcair.org.

3. Arrandale, T. (2000). Trading off summer smog. *Governing, 14, June, 52*.

4. Smog check (2004). *Governing*. Retrieved September 27, 2006, from http://www.governing.com/textbook/graphics/0704p60.htm.

vast proportion. In New York City, the drama was played out in a situation where communications systems were largely destroyed by the collapse of the twin towers of the World Trade Center. Therefore, there was need to coordinate intergovernmental and interorganizational disaster recovery efforts in a context of poor communications links. Police and fire communication units were largely blocked from communicating with one another, underscoring the importance of intergovernmental and interorganizational coordination.

The Katrina-Rita Disaster. September 11 dramatized the need for all levels of government to cooperate in the event of catastrophic disasters. The second major event in this regard was the devastation inflicted in 2005 by Hurricanes Katrina, Rita, and Wilma. This was the worst natural disaster in the history of the U.S. All half-million of New Orleans' residents had to flee the city and tens of thousands more were displaced along the coast. One stark item of evidence that the intergovernmental system failed was that thousands of people arrived at the New Orleans Superdome having nowhere else to go, and federal, state, and local officials were left clueless as to how to get these people out of the city to safety as water broke through the levees and inundated the city. The need to evacuate thousands had been played out in an intergovernmental exercise in the spring of 2005, but plans were not put in place for the disaster that came to pass in August, September, and October.

State and local governments were overwhelmed. First responders, particularly the police, were at a loss to control order. Thousands needed help at a time when the revenue coming into governments was cut off and yet governments were expected to operate on balanced budgets. Roads, sewers, water systems, schools, and other government facilities were destroyed, creating need for massive rebuilding.

The people who were displaced typically sought help from governments other than their own.[20] New Orleans could not help its residents who had been evacuated to other locales in Louisiana, Texas, and other states. People were unable to work and needed cash assistance in the form of unemployment insurance or welfare. People were without housing and were temporarily placed in shelters, some operated by Red Cross, and later in hotels and motels paid for by the Federal Emergency Management Agency (FEMA). Eventually FEMA brought trailers to the area but those themselves were the subject of intergovernmental conflict. Many localities did not want temporary trailer parks set up for fear that there was nothing so permanent as something that is temporary. Thousands of trailers sat unused in vast lots. On the positive side, state and local governments and charitable organizations from areas not ravaged by the storms received evacuees with little expectation of being reimbursed for their expenses.

Health hazards were common.[21] Sewage and industrial pollutants had poured into New Orleans. Wherever houses were flooded and mold grew, posing health dangers to people trying to restore their homes. Meanwhile, many hospitals and clinics were knocked out of operation, while those that remained in operation were overwhelmed with demands on their services. Many of the displaced people were poor and needed Medicaid assistance.

Congress eventually made available $109 billion in relief funding and another $8 billion in tax relief.[22] The money was for use in the five affected states from Texas to Florida and included coverage of damage from Hurricane Wilma in Florida. How effectively the money was spent is to be determined, since there was great pressure to get money to recipients and contractors, a situation that tended to breed waste and fraud.

The Katrina disaster caused a collapse in the intergovernmental system, at least in the short run. "When Hurricane Katrina hit New Orleans, only one thing disintegrated as fast at the earthen levees that were supposed to protect the city, and that was the intergovernmental relationship that is supposed to connect local, state and federal officials before, during and after such a catastrophe."[23] During and after the disaster, accusations flew about as to who was to blame, and surely there were plenty of major blunders on the part of many participants.

One conclusion that emerged from the disaster was that roles needed to be better spelled out in advance before a disaster hits.[24] There is general agreement that in the early hours of a disaster, those on the ground locally—state and local officials and local voluntary groups such as Red Cross and Salvation Army—have primary responsibility. As time passes, the federal government can be expected to step in but in what ways is yet to be determined. For example, one knotty issue is whether the federal government should be able to declare marshal law and bring in regular Army troops or should take command of state National Guard troops. State and local officials, as would be expected, are suspect of federal control, but a counter argument on the Fed's side is that they are likely to get the blame for whatever goes wrong and therefore should have the authority to get the job done, whatever that may require. The argument is that in crisis times, one organization whose authority spans the geographical region, namely the federal government, should have responsibility with state and local governments assuming secondary roles.

FEMA had been an independent agency until it was brought into the newly formed Homeland Security Department in response to the September 11 disasters. Arguments have been made for retaining FEMA within Homeland Security or spinning it off once again as an independent agency, reporting directly to the president. The arguments are not especially persuasive on either side. What is persuasive is the need for a clear role for FEMA. That would seem to be one of a coordinator for all federal, state, and local units when major national disasters occur.[25]

Fiscal Considerations

Vertical Fiscal Imbalance. The conflict between the organizing principles of geographic area and program function plays out within the context of need for services and the corresponding need for revenues, with differences in capabilities existing both within levels of government and among levels.[26] *Vertical fiscal imbalance*, or *fiscal noncorrespondence*, refers to the relative abilities of different levels of government to generate needed revenue and to produce specific public services. The intergovernmental fiscal problem is deciding upon assignment of expenditure responsibilities, and then designing an intergovernmental fiscal system of revenue authority, shared revenue sources, and transfers to match the expenditure assignments. Although one level of government may have a comparative advantage in providing a particular service efficiently, it may not have the same advantage in obtaining revenue. Conversely, another level of government may possess sufficient revenue capability but is not the most efficient unit to provide certain services.

In the United States, it is typically the federal government that possesses the greatest revenue capacity, but not the comparative advantage in providing many government services. State and local governments, on the other hand, have functional expenditure obligations that exceed their ability to raise revenue.

This disparity is due largely to the different revenue sources used by governments. The federal government, relying on personal and corporate income taxes, has a more elastic tax structure in which revenues increase with any increase in economic activity. While state and local revenue sources are relatively more inelastic, the demand for services provided by these governments is quite elastic. For example, the property tax does not change when the economy swings up and down. As discussed in Chapter 4, the property tax is based on the assessed value of the property. Assessments are expensive to carry out, so they are not changed frequently. Hence, we describe the property tax as inelastic with respect to changing economic conditions. When income falls, property taxes still must be paid, but the amount of tax paid on income drops. Of course, when property taxes increase or even remain stable and the economy takes a significant downturn, as happened in 2001–2003, property owners who have lost their jobs may experience extreme difficulty in making their property tax payments.

Superior fiscal capacity can be used by one level of government to entice or persuade another to provide a given service. For example, the federal government used its tremendous fiscal capacity to persuade the states to build an interstate network of freeways. Had the federal government not been willing to pay 90% of the cost of the system, there would be far fewer freeways today. Federal programs created by the Clean Water Act and the Safe Drinking Water Act, discussed in Chapter 13, initially provided grant funding for water and sewer systems, and then after some years of grant funding, provided capitalization funding for state revolving loan funds to lower the borrowing costs for water and sewer systems. Similar federal assistance to capitalize state education loan programs to induce more school construction have been proposed, but not implemented. States also induce local activities through grants and loans.

Horizontal Fiscal Differences. Problems caused by differences in fiscal capacity also exist for governments at the same level. From state to state, there clearly are differences in income and wealth, which are the basic sources of government revenue. For example, U.S. per capita personal income in 2004 was $32,937, but Connecticut's was $45,398, or 138% of the national average, and Mississippi's was $24,650, or only 75% of the national average.[27] Differences in income and wealth lead to differences in revenue-generating abilities, tax burdens, and levels of public services, although no simple correlation exists between income on the one hand and taxing and spending on the other hand.

There is disagreement over whether per capita income differences are a good measure, however, of the differing fiscal capacities of the states. Per capita income has been widely used since the 1930s to differentiate among the states' relative needs for federal assistance. However, this measure does not fully capture ability to pay for services within states. Other measures include retail sales and gross state product. Analysts often use full market property value to assess debt repayment capacity, but this measure reflects accumulated wealth and not necessarily the direct ability to generate revenues.

The ability of a state to raise revenue to meet its spending requirements is called the *fiscal capacity* of the state. The *total taxable resources* (TTR) index, as calculated by U.S. Department of the Treasury, is an estimate of a state's gross state product, similar to the concept of gross domestic product calculated for a national economy, as compared with the nation as a whole (see Chapter 15).The index is set with the national score of 100, and states with scores above that level presumably have high abilities to generate revenues and states with scores below have low abilities. For 2004, Connecticut and Delaware scored high on the index (142 and 162 respectively), while Mississippi was at the bottom (69). Other low states were Arkansas and West Virginia (77 and 72 respectively). Near the middle point of 100 were California, Illinois, Rhode Island, and Washington (in the 105 to 107 range).[28] The TTR is used by the Department of Health and Human Services in distributing community mental health and substance abuse block grant money to the states. Were the index to become widely accepted as an effective measure of states' capacity, it might well be used for a host of grant formulas.

The extent to which a state taps into its available resources is called the *tax burden*. Before it was eliminated in federal budget cutting, the U.S. Advisory Commission on Intergovernmental Relations (ACIR) calculated a measure that estimated the revenues a state would raise if it were to use the average tax system employed throughout the country. This *representative tax system* (RTS) measured tax capacity and, when divided by population, provided a gauge of a state's fiscal effort.[29] The ACIR subsequently added the concept of representative expenditures, including information about costs for public services, to help measure different states' financial abilities.[30]

There has been some reconstruction of the ACIR's work since its demise.[31] Scholars in other countries have shown interest in the concepts of the representative tax system and fiscal capacity.[32]

Several other measures are used to gauge the tax burden in the states. These include total state and local taxes as a share of personal income, as a share of total taxable resources, or as a share of gross state product. Similar measures are derived using state and local own-source revenue. Using the own-source revenue figure as a share of total taxable resources, Alaska in 2004 was ranked first at 19% compared with middle ranked Arkansas and Oregon (13%) and lowest ranked South Dakota (10%).[33] It should be noted that sometimes Alaska is excluded from state comparisons because of its unusual economic conditions.

Overall, although there are plenty of arguments about the adequacy of any one measure or group of measures, the empirical research corresponds to common-sense expectations. Some poorer states in the country have greater needs for spending on services than they have the fiscal capacity to respond, and some richer states have greater fiscal capacity than their expenditure requirements.

Any comparisons among states or localities, whether based on income, wealth, or tax effort, cannot capture an essential feature determining levels of services and levels of taxation. Residents of each state do not make uniform demands for services. Even if the ability to tax or charge for services were distributed evenly across the country, expenditures would differ because citizens desire different levels of services. From a strict demand point of view, a state would provide only those services for which citizens are willing to pay. But willingness to pay for services, as measured by tax effort, still may not solve the problem. The need for many government services is greatest in those states where the fiscal capacity to meet those needs is lowest. Mississippi is a good example of a state that has high needs and falls short despite making a better-than-average effort to meet those needs. The problem is even more acute with respect to different local jurisdictions within the same state. Central city governments within large metropolitan areas face demands for services that increase at a faster rate than does the value of their revenue sources.

Fiscal Responsibilities. Another issue is the extent to which one government with greater revenue-generating capacity should be responsible for aiding other lower-level governments. The issue is whether and to what extent governments should redistribute resources among different segments of the population and geographic areas. Since the 1980s, there seemingly has been less support for redistributive activities, especially at the federal level, than in the decades beginning with the Johnson administration's War on Poverty. The two decades from 1960 through 1980 witnessed the largest effort ever by the federal government to redress disparities among the states and among regions within states.

By 1979, questions had been raised about the ability of the federal government to sustain such a redistributive effort. In response, the New Federalism of President Reagan implemented significant reductions in federal programs to transfer funds to impoverished individuals and low-income states and localities. In the 1990s, balanced federal budgets came at the same time as economic prosperity produced state budget surpluses, so there was no great pressure to increase programs to equalize disparities among the states. The return to federal deficits after 2000 discouraged such efforts, even in the face of severe state budget crises.

One governing principle is that a government should engage in such funding only when the problem addressed corresponds to its level of responsibility—that is, the federal government should deal with national problems and the states with state problems. Oates made this argument in a classic work in the 1970s.[34] The principle was articulated quite clearly by President Ronald Reagan's Executive Order 12612: "It is important to recognize the distinction between problems of national scope (which may justify Federal action) and problems that are merely common to the States (which will not justify Federal action because individual States, acting individually or together, can effectively deal with them)."[35] Though there have been differences in preference for various programs since then, both Democratic and Republican administrations since have tended toward devolution of responsibility. For instance, President George W. Bush created the Interagency Working Group on Federalism, which among other things was responsible for identifying "federal endeavors which may more appropriately be carried out by state or local authorities."[36]

Disparities in fiscal capacity among governments at the same level lead directly to another problem, that of *external costs* and *external benefits* of government functions. People of low income moving from states with low services to states with high services create new burdens on the high-service states. This occurred, for example, with the population migration of the 1930s from impoverished areas to the West Coast and in later migrations from the rural South to cities in the North and West. Proportionately more people who move from lower-income to higher-income states receive welfare payments and generate greater demands on other public services than do those moving from states with similarly high levels of income and services. The flow of illegal immigrants into some states exacerbates those states' difficulties in financing social services and education.

Some of the costs of the failure to provide comparable levels of service across state lines are borne by those outside the low-service states. But the situation has positive aspects as well. Providing services at the most economical level may result in the benefits' spilling over into other areas. The most obvious example is education. Higher levels of education generally yield higher levels of income. Given the mobility of the population, the benefits produced by one local education system may spread far beyond its geographic boundaries.

Economic Competition. Governments compete with each other in trying to attract businesses and industries.[37] Firms locate for a variety of reasons, such as access to markets, a good labor supply, and availability of other resources. Furthermore, they locate where there are clusters of related industries and suppliers. Because businesses seek to minimize production costs, the advantage lies with jurisdictions that have a high service level and low taxes on industry. Whether these are the main reasons businesses actually move or not is irrelevant. As long as governments compete on the basis of taxes and services, the fiscal effects are the same.

Competition for businesses among political jurisdictions can have important consequences, including distortions in revenue and expenditure patterns. When special concessions are granted to firms, needed revenues must be obtained elsewhere or the level of services must be reduced. Devoting resources to special facilities, such as industrial parks, which are frequently financed by long-term debt instruments, may affect a community's ability to finance other capital projects, such as a civic center or a new sewage treatment plant. The package of tax forgiveness and free services that Alabama gave Daimler Benz in return for locating its first U.S. manufacturing facility in the state was a gamble. If one looks at the cost to government for each job created by the plant, the gamble may seem to have been a mistake. On the other hand, Daimler Chrysler has built additional factories in Alabama since the 1993 plant, and other automotive companies such as Honda have located facilities there, although each of these decisions has been accompanied by additional tax concessions.[38]

While intense competition among some states for industrial relocation does cause problems, there are important benefits from this competition. First, it serves as a market-like regulator, preventing state and local governments from over-taxation. Second, it increases the efficiency of the allocation of public sector resources.

States and localities that offer uneconomical incentives to businesses ultimately cannot sustain those incentives. There is a tendency toward equilibrium in the balance of incentives and the taxes and other charges necessary to make services available to support industrial development. Some states have backed away from the use of high-cost incentives.

Overlapping Taxes. The taxes of jurisdictions overlap with each other, and ultimately the same people and firms must pay the various governments. Tax overlapping also occurs when all levels of government tax the same specific source, such as when federal, state, and local governments all tax income. Overlapping or multiple taxation is unavoidable and not necessarily undesirable. It causes serious problems only when a government at one level in effect preempts another government's ability to raise sufficient revenue. This can occur if the state sales tax rate is so high that it discourages local jurisdictions from levying such a tax. Indeed, states may preclude their local governments from having sales taxes but may provide them with alternative sources of revenue. On the other hand, some states have begun allowing local governments to have sales taxes to support transportation but only after obtaining voter approval.[39]

The same kind of crowding-out problem occurs as a result of heavy federal personal and corporate income taxes. State and local governments, while often criticized for failing to raise sufficient revenue to meet needs, may be largely preempted by the federal government from major reliance on income taxes.

One proposal that has been dormant for years would cause a major reallocation of governmental responsibilities among federal, state, and local governments to address tax overlapping directly by introducing a new shared tax—a value-added tax (see Chapter 5)—and sharing corporate income and gasoline taxes. Differences in the latter two taxes among the states would be eliminated.[40] Shared taxes also would reduce tax competition among states. Shared taxes are common in developing countries, where decision makers typically revamp their countries' fiscal systems to support decentralization and devolution.

▮ Patterns of Interaction Among Levels of Government

The structural and fiscal features of the U.S. intergovernmental system ensure that there will be numerous interactions among the different levels of governments. Multiple governments within the same nation interact in numerous ways that directly involve budgetary and other financial decisions as well as each government's fiscal condition. Intergovernmental revenue transfers, such as grants, are a common form of interaction, but they are by no means the only important form. Federal direct expenditures and taxes that occur within a state or local jurisdiction are also important, as is the financial assistance that one level of government gives to another. Finally, regulations, statutes, and other actions that do not directly involve taxing and spending, but nevertheless affect taxing and spending, shape budgetary decisions.

Direct Expenditures and Taxes

Discussions of intergovernmental finance too often concentrate exclusively on financial assistance and neglect the importance of direct expenditures. How much the federal government spends in a state and, in turn how much a state spends in specific local areas have large impacts. Direct federal expenditures have varying geographical impacts, and the same is true for state expenditures.

Nongrant Spending. Locating government-owned or -built facilities in a jurisdiction can substantially affect the jurisdiction's economy. Political considerations are crucial at the state level in regard to the location of highways, state hospitals, prisons, and parks. Local and state governments work actively to obtain federal projects in their jurisdictions as one means of guaranteeing future prosperity. At the federal level, military installations, the awarding of defense contracts to corporations (which are geographically based), and other civilian installations inspire intensive lobbying.

In an attempt to reduce the political bargaining over which military facilities to close during defense downsizing, Congress has several times created temporary commissions to make recommendations on base closings that then must be approved by the president and Congress. The most recent Defense Base Closure and Realignment Commission made 180 such recommendations in 2005. The recommendations were greater than all previous commissions' recommendations combined.[41]

Although some of the political bargaining was reduced in the past by the existence of these commissions, members of Congress still fight to save facilities in their home districts or states. The reality sometimes is that communities benefit more from the base closing than from the previous operations of the base. Facilities and space are turned over to the local community for economic development, and that new activity often proves more valuable. Portsmouth, New Hampshire, for example, turned the former Pease Air Force Base into an industrial park, and more than 10 times the number of people are employed in the industrial park than formerly worked at the Air Force base. Charleston, South Carolina's economy grew after a naval base closing, with new companies occupying old Navy sites. With so many closings and downsizings having occurred, a body of knowledge has developed over how communities can adjust—although painfully—to the loss of defense dollars.[42]

Beyond the physical items are various programs that disburse loans and grants to individuals and corporations. At the federal level, these programs include Social Security, Medicare, support to farmers, and small business loans. Social Security, Medicare, and Medicaid alone accounted for nearly half of all federal expenditures in 2007.[43] States also distribute large welfare and other human services payments among local jurisdictions.

Federal spending other than grants to individuals, organizations, and governments includes significant salaries and wages paid to federal employees and members of the military, most of whom live in one state or another. States having more than 100,000 federal civilian workers include California, Florida, Maryland, New York, Pennsylvania, Texas, and Virginia plus the District of Columbia.[44] Defense payrolls in states ranged in 2003 from as low as $136 million in Vermont to as high as $13 billion in California and $14 billion Virginia.[45] California, which is a major beneficiary of federal defense spending, had 130,500 active duty military troops stationed in the state along with 91,000 Reserve and National Guard people and another 58,000 defense civilian personnel.[46] Contracts with private firms and individuals for defense work totaled $191 billion, with California getting 15% of that very large pie.[47] These contracts, federal salaries, and miscellaneous other small programs are of far greater economic significance than are actual federal grants given to state and local governments.

Tax Collections. In addition to spending, tax collections have varying effects on locales, and the resulting balance between federal tax collections and expenditures has significant effects upon jurisdictions. Generally, federal revenues raised in the Northeast and the Midwest have tended to be greater than the federal expenditures in these regions. The opposite pattern has existed in the South and the West, with the exception of Texas, California, Colorado, Nevada, and Oregon, where the federal tax burden is greater than total federal expenditures.[48] Of course, this discussion in no way suggests that federal taxes should be equal to expenditures in a state and certainly not all states could have higher federal expenditures than taxes (analogous to the suggestion that all kids are above average).

Table 14–1 indicates the states with the highest and lowest ratios of federal spending per dollar of taxes for 2004. New Mexico topped the list. The federal government spent $2.00 in New Mexico for every $1.00 extracted in taxes. New Jersey was at the other extreme. For every $1.00 in taxes, only 55 cents flowed back into the state. Note that despite California being the greatest beneficiary of federal defense spending, the state did not quite recover in total federal spending the money flowing out of it in the form of taxes (for every one dollar flowing out, only 79 cents was returned). Where the balance is less than even, federal finance has a negative impact on a state's economy. This has been the case in the Great Lakes states, which are part

Table 14–1 States with Highest and Lowest Ratios of Federal Spending Per Dollar of Federal Taxes, 2004

Highest Ratios of Spending Per Dollar of Taxes			Lowest Ratios of Spending Per Dollar of Taxes		
Rank	State	Ratio	Rank	State	Ratio
1.	New Mexico	2.00	41.	California	0.79
2.	Alaska	1.87	42.	Colorado	0.79
3.	West Virginia	1.83	43.	New York	0.79
4.	Mississippi	1.77	44.	Massachusetts	0.77
5.	North Dakota	1.73	45.	Nevada	0.73
6.	Alabama	1.71	46.	Illinois	0.73
7.	Virginia	1.66	47.	Minnesota	0.69
8.	Hawaii	1.60	48.	New Hampshire	0.67
9.	Montana	1.58	49.	Connecticut	0.66
10.	South Dakota	1.49	50.	New Jersey	0.55

Source: Compiled from Dubay, C. S. (2006). *Federal tax burdens and expenditures by states.* Washington, DC: Tax Foundation, 2.

of the so-called Rust Belt. Federal tax collections from each of the following Northeastern and Midwestern states exceeded federal expenditures in these states in 2004: Illinois, Indiana, Michigan, Minnesota, New York, and Wisconsin.

Table 14–1 compares federal spending with federal taxing without regard to estimates of need or ability to pay. If one federal responsibility is to redistribute income from wealthier areas of the country to poorer areas, then it should not be surprising that some states send more taxes to Washington than the federal government spends in those states. **Figure 14–1** illustrates the relationship between the net revenue flow of federal expenditures and federal taxes, for all 50 states, and state per capita income. If this net federal flow is generally redistributive, then we would expect the pattern to be generally downward sloping to the right, which indeed is what **Figure 14–1** demonstrates. The lower the per capita income, the greater the net flow of federal funds to the state.

We inserted the overall, linear trend line in the figure. The correlation between net flow and per capita income is -.61, which is consistent with the hypothesis that net federal revenue and expenditure actions are redistributive. Of course, numerous other factors are involved. **Figure 14–1** merely illustrates the general tendency of total federal activities in the states to be redistributive. As we noted previously, per capita income is neither the only nor necessarily the best indicator to try

Figure 14–1 Net Federal Flow to/from State as a Function of State Per Capita Personal Income, 2004

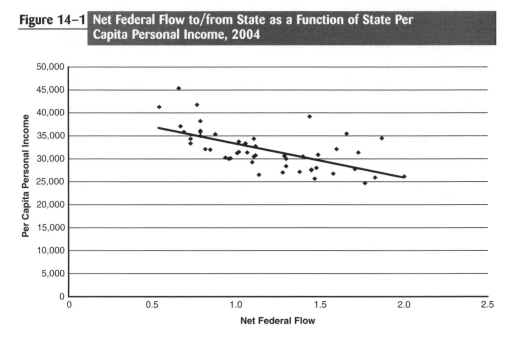

Sources: Compiled from Dubay, C. S. (2006). *Federal tax burdens and expenditures by state*. Wasington, DC: Tax Foundation, 3; Bureau of the Census, U.S. Department of Commerce (2006). *Statistical abstract of the United States, 2006*. Washington, DC: U.S. Government Printing Office, 452.

to estimate the redistributive character of federal spending. **Figure 14–1** is important, however, because it includes not just federal grants, but all federal spending in states. It would appear that total federal spending is more redistributive than federal grants alone.

Intergovernmental Assistance

State Aid. The literature on intergovernmental relations tends to overemphasize federal aid to state and local governments and underemphasize state aid to local government. In 2002, federal aid to states was $318 billion and to local governments was $43 billion. State aid to local governments was $356 billion, about 12% more than what the federal government provided to local governments.[49] State support of local governments for most states is the largest element in the state budget. Of course, state aid probably would be much smaller were states not receiving substantial federal support. As noted in Chapter 2, states receive slightly more than one-fifth of their revenue from the federal government. Local governments receive about 33% of their revenue from state governments and only 4% from the federal government. Except for school districts, each type of local gov-

Figure 14–2 Intergovernmental Sources of General Revenue for Types of Local Governments, 2001–2002

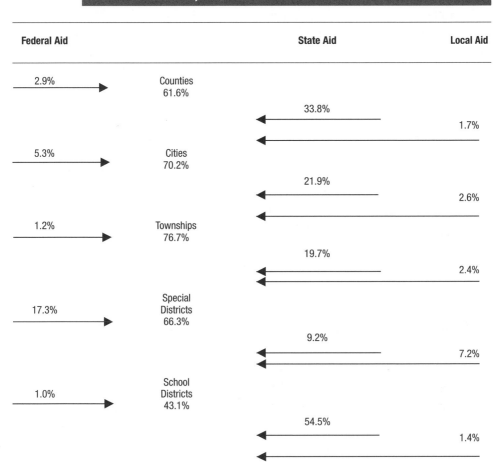

| Federal Aid | | State Aid | Local Aid |

Source: Compiled from Bureau of the Census, U.S. Department of Commerce (2005). *Compendium of government finances, 2002.* Washington, DC: U.S. Government Printing Office, 2.

ernment obtains half or more of its revenue from its own sources. Differences in federal and state support exist among the types of local governments.

Figure 14–2 illustrates intergovernmental revenues provided to the different types of local government entities, as a proportion of those entities' total revenues. In the middle column, county revenues for 2002 were 61.6% from their own sources. The remaining 38.4% came from intergovernmental transfers—2.9% from federal government, 33.8% from states, and 1.7% from other local entities. Similarly, one can see that school districts are the only local entities that receive more than half of their revenue from other governments—state governments provided a majority of the funds that school districts spent (54.5%).

Another way to look at intergovernmental aid is to consider where most of the federal intergovernmental transfers go, and similarly for state and local transfers. As of 2002, about 35% of all federal aid to local governments went to cities, but these monies constituted only about 5% of city revenues. Special districts such as sewer and water districts were the most dependent on federal aid, which constituted 17% of their budgets. Slightly more than half (55%) of state aid went to school districts, with these monies accounting for just over half of school district revenues. Most of the other state aid was divided roughly evenly between counties and cities/townships.[50]

These summary figures, of course, do not convey the great variety in patterns of state aid. Some states provide much greater assistance to local governments than other states. Some states may provide a given service and thereby make direct expenditures, whereas other states may fund local governments to provide the service. Tennessee, for example, provides only 21% of local government general revenues, much less than New Mexico, which provides 48%.[51] Several states provide more than $1,000 per capita to local governments, including Alaska and California. Others provide much smaller amounts, such as South Dakota at $620 per capita and Hawaii at $128.[52] Hawaii is low because it directly operates schools, unlike the other states that funnel elementary and secondary school money to local districts.

State Aid to Education. Aid to elementary and secondary education, as noted, constitutes the largest portion of state aid to local governments. Local school districts have not always depended as heavily on state and federal aid. **Figure 14–3** shows that local sources in the early part of the 20th century accounted for more than 80% of total funding, whereas it had declined to only 43% by 1980. Since then, local financing for education has varied, rising to 48% by the mid-1990s but then falling again to about 44% by 2004. Just as state aid to local governments in general varies considerably from state to state, so too does state aid to education, with Connecticut, Illinois, Nebraska, and South Dakota providing the lowest percentage of funding (low to mid-30% range).[53]

Because of the importance of external—mainly state—funding, the manner in which funds are distributed to local school districts is often a matter of some controversy. States use a formula for distributing these funds. Historically known as the *foundation plan,* such formulas are geared toward guaranteeing a minimum amount of educational expenditures either per pupil or per classroom. The word *foundation* suggests equality of educational opportunity, meaning that every student should have a minimum level of education—a foundation program. Formulas typically have been tied to real estate property assessments, with districts having low assess-

Figure 14–3 Federal, State, and Local Support for Elementary and Secondary Education, 1920–2004 (in Percent)

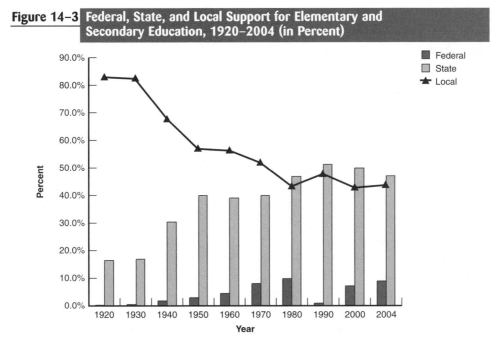

Sources: Compiled from Monk, D. H. (1991). *Educational finance: an economic approach.* New York, NY: McGraw-Hill, 101; Bureau of the Census, U.S. Department of Commerce. *Government finances: 1989-90.* Washington, DC: U.S. Government Printing Office, 7; Bureau of the Census, U.S. Department of Commerce (2002). *Public education finances, 2000.* Washington, DC: U.S. Government Printing Office, 1; Bureau of the Census, U.S. Department of Commerce (2006). *Public education finances, 2004.* Washington, DC: U.S. Government Printing Office, ix.

ments per pupil receiving more aid than districts having high assessments. Although relatively rare, some state formulas even have recapture provisions in which state aid to wealthier districts can be negative, with the funds the state receives from wealthier districts being used to support the poorer districts.[54] Separate formulas may be used for programs serving preschool, disadvantaged, and handicapped children as well as elementary-level children and secondary-level children.

These formulas were attacked in the courts starting in the 1970s as discriminatory. Foundation plans were accused of failing to equalize educational opportunity among jurisdictions. While recognizing the great importance of education, the Supreme Court in 1973 decided in a Texas case, *San Antonio School District v. Rodriquez*, that the allocation of funds for education was a state responsibility and was not controlled by the Constitution.[55] The Court, in that case, was concerned that basing the formula on a macro measure such as the property tax base may not represent circumstances at the micro or individual level (e.g., extremely poor families might live in a wealthy district and not be receiving equal educational opportunity). Thus, the Court ruled that the reliance on the property tax did not create any inequality challengeable on constitutional grounds.

Despite the Court's conclusion in *Rodriquez*, other cases have been won in state courts, so that many states have been required to alter their education financing schemes to minimize disparities in per-pupil expenditures among districts. The California Supreme Court ruled in *Serrano v. Priest* (*Serrano II*) in 1976 that the state's finance system for education violated California's equal protection clause in the state constitution because it created disparities in per-pupil spending.[56]

A National Academy of Sciences study concluded that the foundation plan notion and its emphasis on equity defined as an approximately equal funding amount per pupil is no longer useful in assessing how education is financed and provided.[57] Equal spending does not assure that spending will be sufficient for each child to achieve desired outcomes. Adequacy is a more profound concept that links equity to educational achievement. The No Child Left Behind Act of 2001 reauthorizing the Elementary and Secondary Education Act expresses the philosophy that individuals should have equal chances to educational achievement and mandates individual testing to measure success.[58] The equal opportunity to learn is not necessarily assured by equal funding. Some have argued that student performance is not correlated with funding amounts, calling into question both formula systems and states' attempts to equalize educational opportunity using various measures of equal spending.[59]

Rose v. Council for Better Education, a 1989 Kentucky Supreme Court case, is often considered the landmark case in litigation using the adequacy concept. The court decided that the Kentucky legislature had failed to live up to the state's constitutional requirement to "provide an efficient system of common schools throughout the state."[60] That forced the state to change its school funding scheme. By the mid-2000s, a third to a half of the states were being sued in any given year over their support for education.[61]

Other State Aid. Other state aid programs are comparatively small. Education is followed in size by expenditures for welfare and highways. Aid for these programs is usually handed out based on some type of formula (welfare programs are often per-client reimbursement programs). Virtually all states have some form of motor fuels tax-sharing formula that benefits local government road programs as well as state roads.[62] General local government support, as opposed to specific functional aid, is higher than support for any functions other than education and welfare.

Overall, state assistance has been more predictable than federal aid because of the extensive use of formulas. Formulas facilitate budget planning at the local level because jurisdictions from year to year have some knowledge of what state funds will be. The only major controversies have centered on the factors used in the formulas. Aid to local governments in many states rises and falls depending on the states' economic health. Local governments have shown resiliency in making up for state and federal decreases by drawing on their own resources and by placing greater reliance on user charges and other charges aimed at direct benefi-ciaries of programs (see Chapter 4).

Local governments particularly were at the bottom end of the food chain in 2001–2002 when state budget deficits were redressed in most states at least in part by drastic cuts in aid to local governments. In some cases, states failed to live up to legislated formulas.[63] When state funding, even though it is supposedly guar-anteed, seems threatened, local school districts take various measures in anticipa-tion of possible funding problems. Expenditures may be reduced to some extent, and then later may be boosted when state funds are released to the districts. Districts sometimes may deliberately overestimate their local revenue receipts in order to be able to have a balanced budget, at least on paper.[64]

Federal Aid. Federal grants have been aimed at inducing state and local govern-ments to increase the level of services in specified areas and are not intended to replace state or local spending with federal revenues. The inducement effect is based on the theory that the more separation exists between taxing and spending, the more taxpayers will not perceive the full costs of local services. This is known as the *fiscal illusion hypothesis.*

Matching Requirements, Fungibility, and the Flypaper Effect. Matching provisions are usually required as a means of ensuring that grants will not merely result in a less-ened tax effort by the recipients of the grants. For example, a grant might require that a state government match federal aid dollar for dollar, that a particular proj-ect funded by a grant be funded 50% by each level of government. Without a matching provision, a $1 million federal grant could be offset by an equal reduc-tion in state or local revenues supporting a program, thereby producing no increase in the level of services.

The ability to replace local or state money for a program with grant money is known as *fungibility.* The government providing the grant usually does not want this to occur, since its intent is to increase funding within a targeted area. For example, if grant money is targeted at crime, then the intent is to boost law enforcement expenditures and not to have federal dollars simply supplant some of the state and local money that otherwise would have been spent on law enforcement. The freed up funds then might be used to support other programs, to reduce taxes, or a combination of these. In the case of nonprofits, the issue has arisen over whether grants for housing to nonprofits could be fungible and allow such organizations to shift money to further their political activities.[65]

However, sometimes substituting spending by a recipient government with a grant or transfer from another government may be the goal. States may want local governments to accept state aid and decrease reliance on the property tax. A relat-ed matter is the extent of earmarking of grant money for specific purposes, a topic addressed later in this chapter. When grants are earmarked in detail, flexibility is decreased. In the case of helping small businesses recover from the September 11 disaster in New York City, the New York City Investment Fund found it important to avoid earmarking and to provide small businesses with the flexibility that they needed in the use of the assistance.[66] In the case of donations, for example, people who donated to Red Cross in the wake of the 2005 hurricane season often earmarked their donations specifically for that set of disasters and reduced the flexibility of the agency in meeting its other needs.

Fungibility poses a major threat to analyses of the effectiveness of programs and the use of such analyses in budgetary decision making. If dollars are replaced one-for-one with grant money, then no increase in funding has occurred and any identified change in program results clearly is not associated with funding. This has been the problem with evaluating the federal program for juveniles supported by the U.S. Department of Justice.[67]

The extent to which governments take advantage of possible fungibility relates to another concept known as the *flypaper effect*. When private citizens receive increased funding, say bonuses of $1,000 each, the typical pattern will be to spend some and save some. A family with a tight budget might spend all or almost all of the $1,000, but other families might spend only $700 and put the remaining $300 in savings. The question for state and local governments is whether they tend to do the same or is there a flypaper effect in which the money received gets spent for the intended purpose (that is, whether the money "sticks" to the grant area as planned by the donor government). Research tends to support the flypaper effect. Recipient governments tend to spend the money received and for the intended purpose, and in some cases the governments even spend more of their owns funds than they otherwise would have spent.[68]

One study of state general grants to local education agencies found that grants do induce increased local spending for education, but not by as much as the amount of the grant funds.[69] The fiscal effect, inducing more local spending, is less when the grants are provided without any minimum requirements for tax effort or expenditure requirements. When there is no matching requirement, the greater effect may be on local tax relief—mainly property taxes in the case of education—rather than on increasing spending.

Where the objective is more clearly weighted toward redistributive effects, such as welfare assistance, there is the risk that states with less fiscal capacity may choose to spend less than what is considered nationally desirable. The various low-income assistance programs with which the federal government assists states and localities exhibit a range of federal involvement. Food stamps are fully federally funded. The Supplemental Security Income (SSI) program for the low-income elderly and disabled is mainly federally funded. The Temporary Assistance to

Needy Families (TANF) program is a block grant program with major contributions from both the federal government and the states.[70] State fiscal responses to this package of programs has been somewhat mixed, with apparent reduced efforts for cash assistance programs and overall increased state and local spending for various welfare programs, especially Medicaid.

For grant programs aimed at inducing behavior changes and not necessarily fiscal responses, the task is more difficult. To accomplish changes in program emphasis at the state and local levels with grants, one has to believe that state and local preferences for service modes, such as transportation, are primarily driven by the cost and revenue availability. The Intermodal Surface Transportation Efficiency Act of 1991 (ISTEA) and the Transportation Enhancement Act of 1998 (TEA) were intended in part to encourage development and use of transportation modes other than cars on highways. In reality, states and localities are more likely to choose to repair and rehabilitate deteriorating highways and bridges than to fund mass transit.[71] The federal Children's Health Insurance Program (CHIP) was designed to induce states to implement programs to insure low-income children. It was designed with a punitive "use it or lose it" provision that gave states limited time to meet all the provisions. As a result, most states lost millions in unspent CHIP money—California in the first year forfeited nearly $600 million.[72]

Federal Aid and Functional Areas. During the 1960s, about 80% of all federal aid went for transportation and income security. As can be seen in **Table 14–2**, there have been substantial shifts since that time. Transportation, which accounted for more than 40% of the aid in the 1960s, declined at one point to less than 3%, but with new programs had increased again, to 11% by 2007, due to ISTEA, TEA, and subsequent funding laws. Aid for health programs rose to 47%. Income security accounted for about 21% of the aid. It has fluctuated widely, up in the 1960s, down to the current levels, then spiking in the late 1980s to 1990 and back down again, the last time in part due to welfare reforms limiting the number of years during which an individual can receive assistance (TANF program). Generally, the effects of rapidly rising health care costs and the number of individuals qualifying for income security programs explain most of the shifts that occurred between 1980 and 2007.

The amount of federal aid given to state and local governments varies among federal agencies. As can be seen in **Table 14–3**, the Department of Health and Human Services disburses the most aid by far, accounting for nearly a quarter of all federal grants. A different perspective, however, is gained by looking at the portion of an agency's budget committed to grants. While the Department of Health and Human Services spends about 38% of its funds on grants, the Department of Education spends over half (64%), and the Department of

Table 14-2   Percentage Function Distribution of Federal Grants-in-Aid, 1960–2007

	1960	1970	1980	1990	2000	2007#
Administration of Justice	*	*	1	*	2	1
Agriculture	3	3	1	1	0	*
Community and Regional Development	2	7	7	4	3	5
Education, Employment, Training, and Social Services	7	27	24	19	13	13
General Government	2	2	9	2	1	1
Health	3	16	17	37	44	47
Income Security	38	24	20	30	24	21
Natural Resources and Environment	2	2	6	3	2	1
Transportation	43	19	14	3	11	11
Other	*	1	1	1	*	*
Total	100	100	100	100	100	100

Totals may not equal 100% due to rounding.

Estimated

* 0.5% or less

Source: Compiled from U.S. Office of Management and Budget (2006). *Analytical perspectives, budget of the United States Government, 2007.* Washington, DC: U.S. Government Printing Office, 108.

Transportation and the Department of Housing and Urban Development spend 78% and 86% on grants, respectively.

Regional Differences. Just as total federal outlays are not uniform from state to state, so too do grants vary. In 2005, the national average was $1,169 per capita in federal grants to state and local governments, up from $533 in 1990 and $992 in 2000. The states receiving the highest per capita grants were New York ($1,989), Maine ($1,666), West Virginia ($1,627), and Vermont ($1,615). The group with the lowest per capita grants consisted of Colorado, Nevada, and Virginia ($731, $702, and $698 respectively). Alaska actually was the highest state with $2,472, but it commonly is an outlier and needs to be excluded from comparisons.[73]

These per capita grant figures must not be interpreted simply as revealing which areas are winners and losers in the federal aid game. As noted in the previous section, a state and its local governments might receive comparatively small

Table 14–3   **Federal Agency Outlays and Grants to State and Local Governments, 2007 Estimated (in Billions of Dollars)**

Agency	Total Outlays	Grant Outlays	Grants as Percentage of Total
Agriculture	92.8	26.5	28.6
Commerce	6.6	0.5	7.6
Education	64.5	41.0	63.6
Energy	21.4	0.3	1.4
Health and Human Services	699.6	264.3	37.8
Homeland Security	43.6	13.9	31.9
Housing and Urban Development	44.7	38.5	86.1
Interior	9.4	4.7	50.0
Justice	24.7	4.3	17.4
Labor	53.4	7.0	13.1
Transportation	65.7	51.5	78.4
Treasury	494.3	0.5	0.1
Veterans Affairs	73.8	0.1	0.1
Environmental Protection Agency	7.9	3.7	46.8
Social Security Administration	622.7	0.1	0.0
Other Agencies	755.2	2.1	0.3
Total	3,080.1*	459.0	14.9

* Total does not include allowances and undistributed offsetting receipts (on-budget and off-budget).

Sources: Compiled from U.S. Office of Management and Budget (2006). *Historical tables, budget of the United States Government, 2007.* Washington, DC: U.S. Government Printing Office, 78; U.S. Office of Management and Budget (2006). *Analytical perspectives, budget of the United States Government, 2007.* Washington, DC: U.S. Government Printing Office, 99.

amounts of grants, but extensive economic support as a result of direct federal expenditures. Virginia receives relatively little in grants, but benefits from having a great many federal offices and facilities.

Assuming that the federal graduated income tax has the effect of drawing proportionately greater resources from wealthy states than from less wealthy states, federal aid could amplify or dampen this effect. For example, per capita federal aid to state and local governments might increase as per capita personal income declined, which would amplify the effect. This pattern, however, is not evident. This indicates that federal grant amounts to state and local governments, at least in 2004, were distributed without apparent connection with per capita income. As already discussed, however, a strong relationship demonstrates redistributive effects when the total flows to states from all federal actions and flows of taxes from the states are compared to per capita income. Other factors explaining the distribution of federal grants include the number of Medicaid recipients and the amount of federal land in the state, which brings money from minerals, timber, and grazing rights. Again, caution is necessary when interpreting only one measure of federal economic impact on states. The lack of a clear pattern is explained by the numerous federal grant programs that tend to offset each other in benefiting particular types of states.

Studies that have compared federal aid and state aid to urban areas have concluded that, while both are responsive to need, state aid is more responsive. Cities with greater fiscal problems receive greater per capita state assistance. An important factor in this area is local initiative itself. Some cities are much more aggressive and adept at securing federal and state aid, and this ability is not necessarily correlated with the extent of need. In recent years, state governments have tried to offset some of the decline in federal aid to local governments, particularly by targeting their assistance to cities with the severest problems measured in terms of need, such as prevalence of poverty and low fiscal capacity. However, state budget crises beginning in 2001, as noted above, resulted in serious cutbacks in state assistance to all local governments, both rural and urban.

Within metropolitan areas, fiscal imbalances can cause problems in the pattern of services and the ability to pay for those services. Capital flight out of central cities in the form of wealthier households and businesses moving to the suburbs exacerbates differences, especially in the older cities of the Northeast and the Midwest. One way that some metropolitan areas have combated this problem is to develop metropolitan area tax base sharing and other fiscal equalization strategies, although few governments across the country willingly share their tax bases.[74] Some multiple municipal jurisdictions within the same metropolitan area have begun to see advantages in increased coordination as some city regions look to their potential fate in a global economy.

Federal aid to local communities can be provided directly to these communities or indirectly through the states. In the latter case, state officials are allowed some discretion in distributing federal funds, although federal regulations may require that a given amount pass through to localities and that some of this money be distributed according to set criteria, such as population. State *enabling legislation* often is required before a local government may receive funds directly from the federal government.

Devolution and Future Trends. The dollar volume of federal grants-in-aid continues to climb each year, but federal aid as a percentage of state and local revenues reached a peak in 1980 and is not expected to grow again in the foreseeable future. The decline in federal assistance and the increasing responsibilities of state and local governments are changing the character of intergovernmental relations in the United States. As **Figure 14–4** indicates, federal aid in 1980 was approximately 27% of state and local expenditures. Since then, that percentage has been slipping. On various comparative measures, federal aid is expected to continue to decline. In 2007, it was about 17% of the federal budget, about the same as in preceding years. Federal aid hovered between 2% and 3% of gross domestic product throughout the period covered by **Figure 14–4**.[75]

Figure 14–4, in addition to tracking changes in federal grants vis-à-vis state and local expenditures and total federal outlays, also indicates the substantial change in the character of federal aid to state and local governments. In the 1960s, federal aid focused significantly on physical capital investments. Almost 50% of total grant outlays were for capital investment. By 2007, capital investment outlays had declined to only 15%. During the same period, payments to individuals

Figure 14–4 | **Selected Characteristics of Federal Grants to State and Local Governments, 1960–2007**

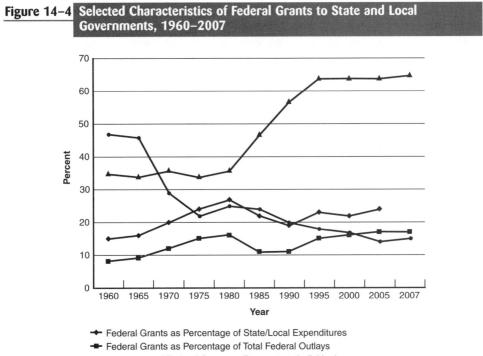

- ◆ Federal Grants as Percentage of State/Local Expenditures
- ■ Federal Grants as Percentage of Total Federal Outlays
- ▲ Percentage of Federal Grants as Payments to Individuals
- ● Percentage of Federal Grants as Physical Capital

Source: Compiled from U.S. Office of Management and Budget (2006). *Analytical perspectives: budget of the United States Government, 2007.* Washington, DC: U.S. Government Printing Office, 208.

went from 35% (1960) of total grants to 65% (2007). This shift toward payments to individuals has meant a change for state and local governments. Rather than serving as active agents in implementing federally funded programs, they now play a role as conduits for channeling federal funds to individuals. During the 1960s, which saw extensive federal assistance to capital infrastructure programs, state governments mainly (but also local governments) were heavily involved in selection, design, and contracting for public works financed by federal dollars. The shift toward payments to individuals channeled by the states has meant hiring more staff to determine eligibility, to verify information, and to track benefits paid to recipients. Prior to welfare reform in the mid-1990s (discussed later in this chapter), the states were not extensively involved in program design.

Federal aid cutbacks in many states have created difficulties for many governments and have proved nearly devastating for others, especially when combined with reductions in revenue due to economic recessions and taxing limitations. The recessionary period of 1990–1992 caused enormous hardships for state and local governments. After almost a decade of prosperity, the recessionary period beginning in 2001 depleted state reserves and forced cutbacks. Prior to the 1960s, state and local governments had primary financing responsibility for domestic programs. Beginning with the 1960s and the antipoverty programs of the Johnson administration, the financial role of the federal government came to equal and, by the mid-1970s, even exceed the financial role of state and local governments. While state and local spending has not yet caught up with federal domestic spending despite the substantial shifts in spending patterns of the last decade, growth in state and local government spending has been more rapid than growth in federal spending. Not only have federal grants for capital declined, but state and local spending for capital investment as a percentage of gross domestic product has declined as well. Thus, states have been forced to scramble to keep services operating and in many situations have had little or no choice but to cut and sometimes eliminate programs. There is limited evidence that as grant levels have declined, states have taken on greater debt to keep their operations going.[76]

The good news may be that state and local governments have responded by improving management and efficiency, increasing their own-source revenue generation, and moving toward employment of user charges and other mechanisms that limit expenditures more to what people are actually willing to pay. This change is yielding greater overall allocative efficiency in the economy that is, producing goods and services that citizens value the most and thereby maximizing net benefits. The change signals a stronger role for state and local governments as determinants of domestic policy, and for many it represents a welcome shift back toward a more decentralized political system in which federal management expertise is no longer seen as significantly greater than that of state and local governments.

Nevertheless, the federal government has been less than satisfied that its grant monies are being well administered. The 2007 budget reported that of the 211 grant programs evaluated under the PART system (see Chapter 7) only 47 were rated moderately effective or effective (accounting for 56% of the $210 billion in the programs). Sixteen were considered ineffective and 86 were rated as "results not demonstrated." These latter two groups accounted for 25% of the money at stake.[77] "On average, grant programs received lower ratings than other types of programs...."[78] Results such as these are the basis for recommendations that various grants be eliminated and others be scaled-back in funding.

Devolution has meant a fundamental shift in responsibility for policy, programs, and financing. Devolution involves outright reductions in federal aid to state and local governments, changes in some programs from matching to non-matching grants, and, of course, greater flexibility. In response to the challenges, state and local governments have taken on much more activist roles in policy formulation, program design, and program implementation in assuming responsibilities that have been determined by federal policy and program design since their origins. States have become more activist in developing and implementing environmental programs, including some that exceed mandatory federal standards.[79] They have also taken the initiative in developing policies and programs in child health insurance, despite some of the disasters initially experienced as a result of rigid federal design.[80]

Some critics point out, however, that devolution will have a negligible impact on the total size of the public sector, even though proponents of devolution often contend that government is bloated and needs to be reduced drastically. One estimate is that if all functions except defense and foreign affairs, debt service, Social Security, and other federal payments to individuals were devolved to state and local governments, and if states proved to be able to carry out the devolved programs for 90% of the previous federal cost, the total cost of government would drop by less than half of 1%.[81]

Exhibit 14–2 discusses welfare reform as an example of devolution. Massive changes were initiated in 1996 with passage of the Personal Responsibility and Work Opportunity Reconciliation Act (PRWORA).[82] The law gave states considerable authority in devising programs for the needy. In the more than ten years of experience under the law, successes have been achieved but problems remain.

Other Elements Affecting Intergovernmental Patterns

Direct expenditures and financial assistance provided by one level of government to another level are not the only factors in the U.S. system of intergovernmental relations that affect budgeting. In addition to restrictions and requirements built

Exhibit 14–2   Welfare Reform as a Case Study in Devolution

The most prominent shift in devolving policy and program design in the last three decades has been the reconfiguring of the nation's welfare system. Several changes in parts of the system were made in the decade leading up to passage of the Personal Responsibility and Work Opportunity Reconciliation Act (PRWORA) of 1996. The earned income tax credit was changed to increase disposable income among low-income, basically welfare-eligible house-holds and individuals. Medicaid coverage was expanded to include adults with dependent children, affecting mainly families with incomes that previously had put them above welfare eligibility.

The big change in the intergovernmental system introduced by PRWORA was the shift of federal responsibility for setting welfare standards and the long-standing approach of federal matching grants to a fixed block grant program.[1] States were given wide latitude in designing programs. From the point of view of welfare recipients, the major change was a maximum lifetime eligibility of five years for public financial assistance. This change involved the replacement of the Aid to Families with Dependent Children (AFDC) program with Temporary Assistance for Needy Families (TANF). Some states, such as North Carolina, chose to take devolution one step further by delegating the administration of TANF to local governments.[2]

PRWORA provided for considerable relaxation in federal requirements through granting states waivers, thereby exempting them from many federal requirements, to develop their own policies and system designs.[3] Some states secured waivers to contract out to private organizations such previously state functions as eligibility determination, job counseling and training, and administration of the program.[4] Others consolidated numerous programs. States were allowed to determine eligibility, set benefit levels, and design their own program administration.

State programs are funded through a combination of federal funds (through the TANF block grant) and state funds. Federal funding exceeded $17 billion in 2007.

The law provided for limitations as to how long people could be eligible for cash assistance. By 2005, welfare rolls were slashed by 50%, bringing the number of recipients down to 2 million people.[5] One continuing problem and one addressed in the 2007 budget is that cash assistance all-too-often goes to people who should have been ineligible for benefits.[6] This is the *improper payments* problem discussed in Chapter 10.[7]

Innovative policy and program reforms in welfare-to-work transition, teen pregnancy reduction, health screening, and single-parent family issues have been developed as a result of the "experiments" conducted across the states. By the standard of intergovernmental reform and devolution, welfare reform by the year 2006 was considered to have achieved large successes, with the recognition that problems remained and more effort was needed in improving the system.[8]

continues

| Exhibit 14–2 | Welfare Reform as a Case Study in Devolution (continued) |

Welfare recipients themselves have had varying experiences. Clearly, some have found productive employment and are unlikely to return to public assistance. Many have experienced frustrations at finding only minimum-wage jobs.[9] A study comparing former welfare recipients in terms of job retention with otherwise similar individuals not previously on welfare found that former welfare recipients were more likely to retain their jobs.[10] To reduce clients' dependence on cash assistance and increase their employability, states have used a variety of programs, including job training, technical post-secondary education, assistance in entrepreneurship through formation of self-owned businesses, and training in money management and savings.[11]

Some states have developed supplemental forms of assistance to address the group of individuals who are no longer on the welfare rolls, are working, but are earning wages that would otherwise qualify them for public assistance. Measuring whether people are working has proved troublesome because of the latitude afforded states by devolution. Some states have been more inclusive in counting people as working. For instance, some states considered people working if they were at home tending to disabled family members.[12] Congress restricted the definition of worker participation, and in 2006 the Department of Health and Human Services, which administers the program, issued regulations dealing with this problem.[13]

Children slipped through the cracks in some instances under TANF. The share of poor children receiving support had dropped from over 60% in the 1990s to about 30% by the mid-2000s.[14]

States in some cases have adjusted their income taxes to benefit poor families. Minnesota, for example, implemented a state earned income tax credit and supplemental programs for child care subsidies and child care credits.[15] Problems persist over how best to assist people with disabilities. These people are eligible for Supplemental Security Income (SSI) and can be eligible for TANF as well.[16]

Congress has reauthorized PRWORA since its inception in 1996 and is expected to continue to do so. One continuing issue is whether Congress should authorize what is called "superwaivers." As noted above, federal officials have authority to waive various requirements at the request of state governments. The superwaiver simply would broaden that authority. The plus side of the argument is that the superwaiver would allow states to have the flexibility they need. The negative side is that state programs would evolve into widely divergent activities, losing any semblance of being a national program. Indeed, were that to happen, some fear that could be the grounds for eliminating or reducing TANF funding.[17]

continues

Exhibit 14–2	Welfare Reform as a Case Study in Devolution (continued)

A continuing problem is obtaining systematic information across the states as to how they are using TANF funding. Since the states have great flexibility in the spending of federal dollars, evaluating the effectiveness of such spending is a challenging endeavor.[18]

1. Personal Responsibility and Work Opportunity Reconciliation Act (1996). P.L. 104-193.

2. Berner, M. (2005). A race to the bottom? Exploring county spending shortfalls under welfare reform in North Carolina. *Public Budgeting & Finance, 25, Winter,* 86–104.

3. Meyer, B. D. & Rosenbaum, D. T. (2000). Making single mothers work: recent tax and welfare policy and its effects. *National Tax Journal, 53,* 1027–1061.

4. Arsnault, S. (2000). Welfare policy innovation and diffusion: Section 1115 waivers and the federal system. *State and Local Government Review, 32,* 49–60.

5. U.S. Government Accountability Office (2005). *Welfare reform: more information needed to assess promising strategies to increase parents' income.* Washington, DC: GAO.

6. U.S. Office of Management and Budget (2006). *Analytical perspectives, budget of the United States Government, 2007.* Washington, DC: U.S. Government Printing Office, 100.

7. U.S. Government Accountability Office (2004). *TANF and child care programs: HHS lacks adequate information to assess risk and assist states in managing improper payments.* Washington, DC: GAO.

8. Walters, J. (2000). The welfare bonanza. *Governing, 14, January,* 34–36; Parrott, S. & Sherman, A. (2006). *TANF at 10: program results are more mixed than often understood.* Retrieved October 3, 2006, from http://www.cbpp.org/8-17-06tanf.pdf.

9. Walters, J. (2002). The flip side of welfare reform. *Governing, 16, March,* 17–20.

10. Gooden, S. T. & Bailey, M. (2001). Welfare and work: job-retention outcomes of federal welfare-to-work employees. *Public Administration Review, 61,* 83–91.

11. U.S. Government Accountability Office (2005). *Welfare reform: more information needed to assess promising strategies to increase parents' incomes.* Washington, DC: GAO.

12. U.S. Government Accountability Office (2005). *Welfare reform: HHS should exercise oversight to help ensure TANF work participation is measured consistently across states.* Washington, DC: GAO.

13. Greenberg, M. & Parrott, S. (2006). *Summary of TANF work participation provisions in the budget reconciliation bill.* Retrieved October 3, 2006, from http://www.cbpp.org/1-18-06tanf.htm; Lower-Basch, E. et al. (2006). *An analysis of new interim final TANF rules.* Retrieved October 3, 2006, from http://www.cbpp.org/7-21-06tanf.htm.

14. Parrott, S. & Sherman, A. (2006). *TANF at 10.*

15. Wilson, P. (2000). Tax implication of welfare reform: the Minnesota experience. *National Tax Journal,* 53, 417–437.

16. U.S. Government Accountability Office (2004). *TANF and SSI: opportunities exist to help people with impairments become more self-sufficient.* Washington, DC: GAO.

17. Nivola, P. S., Noyes, J. L., & Sawhill, I. V. (2004). *Waive of the future? Federalism and the next phase of welfare reform.* Retrieved October 3, 2006, from http://www.brookings.edu/es/research/projects/wrb/pulications/pb/pb29.htm.

18. U.S. Government Accountability Office (2006). *Welfare reform: better information needed to understand trends in states' uses of the TANF block grant.* Washington, DC: GAO.

into most financial assistance, the programs financed by the assistance contain various requirements that influence how state and local governments plan and budget. Another element derives from the fact that state governments are the constitutional authorities for establishing local governments within their jurisdictions and thus have significant roles in determining which revenue sources local governments may use, which services local governments are responsible for providing, and under which circumstances local governments may enter into debt.

Features Associated with Financial Assistance. The preceding sections discussed the targeting aspects of grants provided by one level of government to another level. Additional controls often are built into the assistance arrangement. One of the fastest-growing budgetary components for all levels of government is the Medicaid program, which offers health assistance to the poor. Prior to 1991, some states adopted taxes on health providers as one means to raise the funds required by the state matching provision. In 1991, the Health Care Financing Administration (HCFA), now renamed the Centers for Medicare and Medicaid Services (CMS), prohibited the use of health provider taxes and prohibited counting private donations to health providers as part of the state match.[83] This particular regulation was aimed at increasing the likelihood that state matches would be additive, rather than federal funds substituting for state efforts.

In the early 2000s, Congress clamped down on states manipulating their finances so as to qualify for greater federal Medicaid funds. The states using a variety of accounting techniques were able to circumvent the "upper payment limit" which was supposed to put a cap on federal support.[84] A point not wasted on federal officials—both elected and appointed—is that federal aid is a high stakes game which many states play with great assertiveness so as to maximize their financial benefits. **Exhibit 14–3** provides some basic information about the Medicaid program.

Features Not Directly Associated with Financial Assistance. The federal government's authority under the Constitution has been used to *preempt* or supercede state authority, and state governments frequently preclude local action in various arenas. Since the late 1960s, coinciding with the development of many of the federal assistance programs, federal preemptions of state and local authority have increased at a rapid pace. From 1960 through 1995, more than 800 statutory actions were implemented preempting state policy or action in favor of federal policy or action.[85] Examples include the Clean Water Act amendments in 1987 and the Safe Drinking Water Act amendments of 1996. The former retained the regulatory requirements, but reduced federal financial assistance to state and local governments and shifted it to assisting states to set up revolving loan funds to finance systems. The 1996 amendments to the Safe Drinking Water Act strengthened the regulatory requirements to mandate stronger scientific studies of health risks. The result of those additional requirements has been increased costs to states.

Judicial strengthening of the federal government's preemptive right to regulate is often traced to the 1985 case of *Garcia v. San Antonio Metropolitan Transit Authority*.[86] The case focused on whether the federal Fair Labor Standards Act applied to a local government entity. The Supreme court ruled that since the transit authority had received considerable funding from federal programs (Urban

---

Exhibit 14–3	Features of the Federal-State Medicaid Program

Medicaid is a federal-state program administered at the federal level by the Centers for Medicare and Medicaid Services in the Department of Health and Human Services. The program provides medical insurance to the categorically needy, including people who qualify for cash assistance under the Temporary Assistance for Needy Families (TANF) program, pregnant women and children below the poverty level, children at the poverty level, caregivers of children, disabled people receiving benefits under the Supplemental Security Income (SSI) program, and others.

Beyond the categorically needy are the medically needy who cannot qualify for assistance because their incomes are too high, but who cannot afford medical insurance. Services to the medically needy are only provided in those states that opt for such, amounting to somewhat more than half of the states. States may participate in the State Children's Assistance Program (CHIP or SCHIP) that provides additional support and is intended to expand coverage of children beyond the standard Medicaid program, particularly to children whose families otherwise do not qualify for Medicaid.[1]

Benefits and their administration vary widely among the states. Some states basically combine Medicaid and SCHIP, some have them together within the same unit, and some have separate Medicaid and SCHIP programs. This fact is an outgrowth of allowing states flexibility in administering the health insurance programs.

More than 50 million people are covered by Medicaid.[2] Enrollment patterns and benefit patterns are sharply contrasting under Medicaid. About 75% of enrollees are children and their parents. The major beneficiaries of medical care, as measured in dollars, however, are the elderly and disabled clients—about 70% of expenditures. At the time of patients' discharge from nursing homes, about two-thirds of all patients in the country are on Medicaid.[3]

The federal government was expected to spend about $199 billion on Medicaid and $6 billion on the children's insurance program in 2007.[4] With the federal government providing about 57% of funding and the states, 43%, that put state spending at about $150 billion. Program expenditures are rising rapidly due to the ever increasing costs of health care. A doubling of costs over ten years is likely.

continues

Exhibit 14-3	**Features of the Federal-State Medicaid Program (continued)**

Some observers, such as Tommy Thompson, former Secretary of Health and Human Services, think that states must wrestle with this problem largely on their own, that the federal government is unlikely to face up to this monumental problem.[5] The options are limited. Benefits might be reduced, but that hardly seems justified given the need for health care by Medicaid clients. The clients could be required to contribute to their care through premiums and increased co-pays, but that is an unattractive option considering these people already by definition lack the money needed for health insurance. Another alternative is simply to provide greater tax dollars to support the program, an option that is particularly painful during recessionary periods such as the early 2000s.

1. Centers for Medicare and Medicaid Services, U.S. Department of Health and Human Services (2005). *Medicaid at-a-glance, 2005*. Washington, DC: U.S. Government Printing Office.

2. U.S. General Accounting Office (2004). *Medicaid: intergovernmental transfers have facilitated state financing schemes*. Washington, DC: U.S. Government Printing Office.

3. Marron, D. B., Acting Director, Congressional Budget Office (2006). *Medicaid spending growth and options for controlling costs*. Washington, DC: U.S. Government Printing Office, 1.

4. U.S. Office of Management and Budget (2006). *Analytical perspectives, budget of the United States Government, 2007*. Washington, DC: U.S. Government Printing Office, 115.

5. Walter, J. (2005). Thompson's warning. *Governing.com*. Retrieved October 3, 2006, from http://www.governing.com/articles/11poto.htm.

Mass Transportation Act of 1965), it must adhere to fair labor standards requirements. In this case, the Court narrowly interpreted the extent to which the Constitution protects the powers and authority of the states.

The Court in recent times has not always ruled in favor of preemption, which is welcome on the parts of states and local governments, but is unsettling to all parties involved in that the Court has not delineated any clear doctrine as to when preemption should be upheld and when denied. In *Printz v. United States* (1997), the U.S. Supreme Court ruled that the provision of the Brady Handgun Violence Prevention Act requiring chief law enforcement officers of local jurisdictions to conduct background checks until a national system was in place was an unconstitutional requirement of state officials to enforce federal law.[87] On the other hand, the Court in *Geier v. American Honda Motor Company* (2000) upheld preemption, which had the effect of protecting the automobile manufacturer from tort suits claiming that vehicles should have been equipped with airbags.[88] In 2000 and 2001, the Court ruled that the Age Discrimination in Employment Act and the Americans with Disabilities Act (ADA) did not apply to the states.[89]

The National Conference of State Legislatures regard preemption as such a threat to state sovereignty that it has a project devoted to analyzing proposed federal legislation and working against would-be preemptions. Despite its efforts, preemptions march on. In 2005, Congress passed a law that preempted state courts from hearing lawsuits stemming from alleged injuries caused by defective vaccines. In 2006, Congress preempted the states regarding the registry of sex offenders.[90]

State Control of Local Governments.   These issues are not limited to federal effects on state and local governments. Since state governments have full constitutional authority over local governments, significant limitations on local authority may stem from state actions. Statutory debt limitations, usually expressed as a maximum debt to the property tax base ratio, are common, as are requirements that state legislatures approve through formal legislative enactment some local taxes, such as sales taxes.

A state also may assume direct control of a local government if it cannot exercise the capacity to govern itself. Instances of state takeover of municipal functions have been associated with some aspect or another of financial failure, but not usually bond debt failures. State governments watch local situations to see whether intervention is needed, although they do not consistently use specific indices of financial condition in making their decisions.[91]

State takeovers are not restricted to cities of a certain size. In December 1996, the State of Florida appointed a State Control Board to supervise for a five-year period the City of Miami's budget and finances after the City was unable to balance its budget in two successive years, which is against state law. Although the City experienced considerable political turbulence, including a mayoral election that was invalidated several months after the mayor took office, by the end of the oversight board's commission, in 2002, the City had regained sound financial footing, and even was able to sell $32 million in bonds to refinance bonds sold previously at higher interest rates.[92] Philadelphia, New York, and East St. Louis are among other cities that have had state-appointed oversight or financial control boards.

In 1997, the State of North Carolina took over the small town of Princeville, under a previously never used state statute dating back to 1931. The state's Local Government Commission took over town finances and revenue collections, while the town commissioners continued to govern otherwise. Town officials had been unable, or unwilling, to collect taxes due, and the town sewer system was overflowing into the streets due to neglected maintenance.[93] Under the commission's financial oversight, Princeville began to restore its situation, but hurricanes Dennis and Floyd in 1999 severely flooded the town, overtaking the town's own fiscal crisis.

Somewhat analogous was the situation with the nation's capital, except that it is the federal government that statutorily controls the District of Columbia. Like cities in many states, the District operates under the auspices of a home rule charter that grants considerable autonomy to the District, albeit subject to change by the legislature. In 1995, a financial control board was appointed to supervise the finances of the District of Columbia, similar to one created by the New York legislature to supervise New York City's finances in 1975. As part of the 1997 Balanced Budget Act (see Chapters 9 and 15), Congress also developed a financial assistance package for the District of Columbia. The aid package focused on relieving the District of its unfunded pension liability, a tax credit package, Medicaid, and prison system financial relief. To end the oversight of the Financial Responsibility and Management Assistance Authority, the District had to become current with bond debt service, repay U.S. Treasury loans, restore access to short- and long-term credit, and achieve a balanced budget for four consecutive years. In 2001, the District of Columbia met all four conditions and the assistance authority ceased operations.[94]

State takeover of a general-purpose jurisdiction such as a city or town is not the only kind of state control over substate entities. School systems are a target of state action. Texas passed a law in 1995 that would allow the state to take over schools that failed to meet specified state standards. The law was challenged in the courts, but the Supreme Court determined in 1998 that there was no need for a ruling at the time because no school takeover was imminent.[95] In recent years, school district takeovers have occurred in at least 18 states and the District of Columbia. The reasons for taking over a district are financial, academic, financial and academic, or all encompassing.[96] In 2001, after Philadelphia school system finances spun out of control, Pennsylvania assumed control over the school system. Setting budget policy, managing the system's finances, and contracting out the operations of about 40% of the schools in the system to three private companies were among the financial and operational controls imposed.

By the mid-2000s, takeovers were in operation and others were being considered. Detroit, which had had its schools taken over by a board imposed by the state in 1999, was facing possible takeover of city operations in 2005. In 2006, St. Louis schools, the City of Los Angeles, and the City of San Bernadino were among the governments under pressure to perform or face possible takeovers.[97]

A state's assuming complete control over a city or a school district is a rare event, but it serves as a reminder that local governments are statutorily governed by state governments. Local governments have nothing comparable to the states' protection from the federal government as guaranteed by the Constitution's Tenth Amendment reserving a broad array of powers to states.

Types of Fiscal Assistance

Grant Characteristics

Of the numerous aspects of grants-in-aid, at least four are particularly important: (1) the purpose of the award, (2) the recipient, (3) the amount, and (4) the method of distribution. The purposes of awards will be discussed in some detail in the next subsection, but for the moment it should be noted that purposes range from narrowly defined functions to general support.

Recipients can be individuals or families who receive financial aid, as in the case of welfare payments made directly to clients or Medicaid payments made to medical providers to cover the health needs of the poor and medically needy. When programs provide guarantees of aid to individuals and families, they are referred to as entitlements. Sometimes the term *entitlement* is used for programs providing funds to state and local governments, as in the instance of the Community Development Block Grant program (CDBG), in which entitlement communities receive funds on a formula basis—funds that are predictable by the cities in advance of their receipt.

The third aspect is the amount of aid that is made available. Some programs are open-ended in the sense that aid is provided to all persons who qualify. All persons meeting a needs test based on income, for instance, might qualify for aid. If the number of qualified applicants increases, then the amount of aid available must also increase. This type of grant, of course, complicates budgeting, because administrators do not know in advance the amount of funds that will be needed. An alternative is for the legislature to predetermine an amount that will be available regardless of the number of potential recipients.

The Women, Infants, and Children (WIC) supplemental food program is an example of a program in which the amount that eligible families may receive is determined by a needs test, but funding may or may not be made available for everyone who is eligible. Once the funding limit in a particular state is reached, other eligible candidates are placed on a waiting list. For this program, the Food and Nutrition Service in the U.S. Department of Agriculture must annually estimate the number of eligible individuals so that federal appropriations can cover the number of people who are eligible. Some studies have shown that more people participate than are eligible, leading some in Congress to call for funding cuts, but other evidence indicates that there are more people who are eligible than who participate.[98]

Fourth, various methods are used in deciding whether applicants will receiving funding and in what amounts. In one method, would-be recipients compete for awards by submitting proposals to indicate how funds will be used. This method is common for demonstration grants available to private and nonprofit institutions and several categories of grants available to state and local governments. Another method is to use a formula that allocates funds among eligible recipients. Formulas can be used to help target money where it is needed most. Gaining agreement on specific provisions in a formula among legislators can be difficult. For example, members of Congress evaluate proposed provisions of a formula in terms of how their home districts or states will be affected. Sometimes the distribution is set by the legislative body, particularly in instances in which funds are provided for specified public works projects.

At the federal level, the process of awarding and administering grants is spelled out in OMB Circular A-102, Grants and Cooperative Agreements with State and Local Governments.[99] *Cooperative agreements* are used when "substantial involvement" by federal agencies are planned, unlike *grants* in which activities are carried out primarily by state and local governments.

Categorical Aid

At the federal level, hundreds of grant programs exist. **Table 14–4**, based on data from the 2006 online *Catalog of Federal Domestic Assistance*, provides a count of various grant programs, by type of grant, and an illustration of each type. There are between 1,000 and 2,000 federal domestic assistance programs in the catalog, of which only the grant programs (as opposed to loans and other programs) are listed in **Table 14–4**. It needs to be noted that the listings in the table are not mutually exclusive, that a program is sometimes listed in two or even more categories. Also, not all items listed flow directly through state and local governments; some grants go directly to individuals, businesses, and nonprofit organizations.

Categorical grants are a historically common designation, although not used in the *Catalog*. The meaning of "categorical" was that funds were targeted for expenditure in specified areas. This broad type is now separated into three in the *Catalog*. (1) The category of *project grants*, of which there were 905 in 2006, covers such items as scholarships, research grants, and constructions grants. (2) The category of *direct payments for specified use*, of which there were 144, is for comparatively narrowly defined projects. The category does not include contracts, such as when the federal government contracts with a local government to carry-out an activity on its behalf. (3) The category of *direct payments with unrestricted use*, of which there were 43, is broader than the second grouping. As the table indicates, payments for a broad range of vocational rehabilitation services for veterans falls into this category.

Table 14-4 Federal Grant Programs by Type with Illustrations, 2005

Type of Program	Number of Programs	Example
Formula Grants	177	School Breakfast Program
Project Grants	905	Small Business Innovation Research
Direct Payments for Specified Use	144	Food Stamps
Direct Payments with Unrestricted Use	43	Vocational Rehabilitation for Disabled Veterans
Sale, Exchange, or Donation of Property and Goods	24	Food Donation
Use of Property, Facilities, and Equipment	16	Donation/Loans of Obsolete equipment Department of Defense Property
Provision of Specialized Services	85	Weights and Measures Service

Source: Adapted from U.S. General Services Administration (2006). *Catalog of federal domestic assistance.* Retrieved October 2, 2006, from http://12.46.245.173/cfda/cfda.html.

The last three entries in **Table 14-4** are of a different character. *Sale, exchange, or donation of property and goods* covers such activities as the government donating surplus food to a food bank. *Use of property, facilities, and equipment* includes loaning surplus military equipment (tanks, artillery, and clothing) to state-run military museums. *Provision of specialized services* covers the direct support by federal agencies in pursuit of state and local activities, such as assuring accuracy in weights and measures.

The number of these various types of aid, of course, does not signify the amount of assistance available, but it does indicate the diversity of programs. Indeed, one frequent complaint over the years has been that there are too many specific grant programs and that they should be reduced in number. As a result, various consolidations have occurred from time to time but then later new programs are added, resulting in an ever-fluctuating number of grants.

Categorical programs have a narrow focus and target aid to deal with perceived problems. If rat infestations are seen as a major problem in poor neighborhoods, an aid program can be established to support efforts to eliminate or control rat populations. Categorical programs presumably allow the federal government to target aid to deal with problems that are perceived to be national in scope and allow the state governments to do the same in regard to state problems. Many categorical programs were created during the War on Poverty initiated by

President Johnson in the late 1960s. Part of the motivation for creating categorical programs was that state legislatures, then dominated in many states by politicians from rural areas, were unresponsive to urban needs, especially the problems of large center cities. Many categorical grant programs were intended to channel funds directly to cities, bypassing the state legislatures.[100]

Another reason for creating categorical programs was to target and restrict assistance in various ways in an effort to control the recipients' behavior.[101] For example, assistance for community development projects required extensive community participation to ensure that low-income groups had an influence over program design.

Categorical grants typically require would-be recipients to apply for aid by preparing proposals. These proposals indicate what problems exist, how the problems will be addressed, and what the expected benefits will be. During the application process, applicants must engage in considerable preplanning that is expected to help increase the chances that the money will be spent effectively. Funding agencies, by means of an application review process, presumably can weed out unsound projects.

Criticisms of categorical aid programs abound. Grants may skew local priorities. A jurisdiction might apply for funds for one type of project even though some other project, for which no grant funding was available, would provide greater benefits to the jurisdiction. Another criticism is that much time and energy are consumed in drafting grant proposals. Still another is that some jurisdictions do not obtain their "fair share" of federal dollars simply because they lack adequate staff for proposal writing. Small jurisdictions, in particular, may have little "grantsmanship" capability. Categorical grants make budget planning difficult because proposals may be held pending for months. Another problem is that grants are not coordinated. Furthermore, state legislatures dislike being bypassed, and many grant recipients—whether governmental or private organizations—resent some of the restrictions that are attached to the use of funds.

Critics frequently propose that the application process be simplified. Simplification includes reducing the amount of paperwork involved and standardizing some forms and procedures to make the process more comprehensible to applicants who may wish to seek funds from two or more agencies. OMB Circular A-102 and subsequent legislation reducing duplicative audit requirements have standardized some forms and procedures, but preparing individual grant applications is no less time-consuming. Most federal agencies have automated some or all of their application processes, making it possible for applications to be submitted online. Of course, that step has not eliminated the actual proposal writing, but processing time has been reduced.

Revenue Sharing

A dramatic alternative to categorical grants is General Revenue Sharing (GRS), which at the federal level was created by the State and Local Fiscal Assistance Act of 1972.[102] Under the original legislation, the federal government shared some of its revenue with states, counties, cities, and townships. In subsequent years, the states were dropped from the list of beneficiaries, in part because many had surpluses in their budgets and could hardly claim to be in need of general federal support.

Although general revenue sharing was allowed to expire in 1986, it is worthy to note in that it represents the opposite end of the spectrum from categorical grants. GRS also continues to be proposed from time to time, along with shared tax systems, as more radical overhauls to the intergovernmental fiscal system. The now-defunct program had three key characteristics:

- Preestablished amounts of aid
- Use of formulas for distributing the aid
- Considerable latitude to spend funds in terms of local priorities

When renewing the program, often for three years at a time, Congress set specific dollar amounts to be disbursed in given time periods. Such provisions allowed local governments to plan well in advance as to how GRS monies would be used. Of course, the drawback from the point of view of the federal government was that this portion of the budget was relatively uncontrollable.

The GRS allocations were made by a series of complex formulas. A ceiling was set to limit how much any jurisdiction would receive, as well as a floor to guarantee that most jurisdictions would receive some funds. A distinguishing feature of GRS was that jurisdictions received funds without having to make application for these monies.

GRS attempted to solve some of the problems associated with categorical grant programs. Jurisdictions had great freedom in deciding which functional areas would receive funds. Another benefit was that time and energy were not wasted in proposal writing. Jurisdictions that needed funds but lacked the staff capability to make application for categorical grants still received GRS funds.

On the other hand, there were many criticisms of GRS. The formula was said to provide unneeded monies to some jurisdictions. The floor provision may have propped up basically inefficient jurisdictions that might otherwise have been forced by economics to consolidate their services with those of other governments. The ceiling may have denied needed funds to many deserving jurisdictions, particularly center cities. Communities allegedly were allowed to squander their GRS funds, whereas categorical grants require more planning.

GRS expired because a compelling case could not be made for its continuation. As the federal government faced annual budget deficits in excess of $200 billion, federal officials could convincingly argue that there simply was no revenue to share with local governments. Additionally, proponents faced the difficult task of identifying a national purpose being served by GRS. In the short run, eliminating the program caused serious budgetary problems for municipalities with shrinking tax bases. In addition, many local governments shifted to user charges, which in some cases were regressive (Chapter 5). User charges are typically based on the cost of the service rather than the ability to pay.

While revenue sharing is no longer in operation at the national level, it persists at the state level. Many states provide funds to local governments using formulas based on population and income. Fiscal pressures on state governments in the early 1990s caused many to reduce the amounts allocated to revenue sharing. Then, after almost a decade of surpluses, a return in 2001 to severe state budget pressures again caused states to drastically reduce funding.[103]

Revenue sharing is still the most common means of central government financial assistance to lower level governments in other countries in the wake of major decentralization of governmental responsibilities. For example, the Philippines underwent in the 1990s a major shift from central government responsibilities for almost all services to extensive devolution of responsibility to local governments. Functions such as health and education, which previously were entirely central government responsibilities, were devolved to provincial and various levels of local government. Former central ministry of health and education employees were transferred to province or local payrolls. To equalize the financial impacts, the Internal Revenue Allotment (IRA) was created, allocating almost all of the proceeds of the national income tax to local levels of government.[104]

Block Grants

A form of compromise between GRS and categorical grants is special revenue sharing, or block grants. Under this system, a higher-level government shares part of its revenue with lower-level governments, but the use of funds is restricted to specified functions, such as law enforcement or social services. Sometimes a distinction is made between block grants and special revenue sharing, with the former requiring submission of an application and the latter not. More often, however, the terms are used interchangeably or the term block grant is used to cover both types of revenue sharing. State aid to education, using various formulas, is an example of a block grant, with the funds coming largely from state general revenue. State aid for local roads is another form of block grant, with monies coming from earmarked taxes on motor fuels. The Temporary Assistance to Needy Families program discussed earlier is a federal example.[105]

Block grants at the federal level have been used as a method for consolidating categorical grant programs. These "categoricals" are grouped together so that jurisdictions have greater flexibility within specified program areas. The application process is greatly reduced, because a jurisdiction applies for only one grant instead of several. Early block grant legislation included the Partnership for Health Act of 1966, the Law Enforcement Assistance Act of 1968, and the Comprehensive Employment and Training Act of 1973.

A landmark in block grant legislation was the Housing and Community Development Act of 1974, which created the Community Development Block Grant (CDBG) program.[106] This program provided entitlement funding to medium and large cities through the use of a formula and gave funds to states to award small cities on a discretionary basis. The law phased out programs for open space, public facility loans, water and sewer grants, urban renewal, model cities, and rehabilitation loans. Under the original legislation, entitlement cities were required to submit an application for funding. The process was considerably less detailed than had been required for the previous categorical programs. Later, the application process was dropped for the entitlement cities.

Some federal block grants awards are based on metropolitan areas, which are defined by the Office of Management and Budget. An area that is not classified as metropolitan may be excluded from funding, and the amount of funding to a given area may be dependent on its population size or other key characteristics. Therefore, the definition of an area becomes critical for funding purposes. In 1999, OMB redefined the concept of metropolitan area.[107] The CDBG grants are affected by the metropolitan definition.[108]

Various consolidations of categorical grants into block grants have taken place over recent decades. The first wave started with the Omnibus Budget Reconciliation Act of 1981, which among other things consolidated many existing categorical grant programs and created nine new block grants, four in health-related services, to be administered by the states.[109] The most recent round of consolidation and relaxation of federal control created the Temporary Assistance to Needy Families (1996), the initial major reform of welfare assistance in an attempt to devolve responsibilities from the federal government to states, as discussed earlier. President George W. Bush's 2006 budget called for consolidating 18 community development grants into one and cutting back their funding. The proposal met with opposition from both Democrats and Republicans.[110]

The programmatic feature of federal block grants is that monies are granted in lump sums to states, which determine how the money is to be used and, when it involves local government assistance, how funds are to be divided among governments within each state. This approach has been championed as restoring power to the states. The fiscal feature of federal block grants, each time they are introduced, has been a substantial reduction in funds. These cuts are defended in part in the name of efficiency. Allowing states and localities to select the desired mix of activities and levels of quality and quantity, block grants reduce the costs of "one size fits all" categorical grants, which substitute federal judgments for those at the state and local levels. Further, since the block grants provide more flexibility to state and local governments, fewer federal officials are needed to administer the programs and fewer state officials are needed to oversee local government operations. Given that block grants almost always result in some degree of reduced federal financing because they are consolidating previous categorical programs, state and local governments have to achieve the supposed efficiencies, make up for the losses, or reduce quality or quantity of services.

When federal block grants are cut, local governments often must make difficult choices among apples and oranges. With block grants funding a variety of activities, should one or more be cut or should all experience some funding reduction? For example, a CDBG program might be helping "agencies that build homes for low-income residents, run drug-treatment facilities, organize youth-sports leagues and provide other services."[111] Where, then, should cuts be made if necessary? Decision making is easier with categorical cuts, since where the cuts will occur is set. With block grants, local officials have flexibility in meting out budget reductions, but that means these officials must be prepared to explain to agencies and the public why they chose to impose specific cuts.

Figure 14–5 illustrates that state and local governments have generally maintained their overall revenue growth since 1980, despite relative declines in federal grants. In **Figure 14–5,** state and local total revenues are shown in billions of dollars on the left *y*-axis, and the percentage of state and local general revenues constituted by federal aid is shown on the right *y*-axis. State and local revenues as a whole have steadily increased, making up with their own sources for the drop in federal aid.

Homeland Security—A Case Study

Homeland security is a complex problem that is overseen by a complex federal department and a myriad of other state, federal, and local governments. Following the September 11, 2001, attacks, decision makers in both Congress and the executive branch agreed that a major federal response was required. Not everyone agreed that a separate federal department should be created, but that was the outcome. The U.S. Department of Homeland Security was formed by pulling together a variety of agencies from other executive departments, resulting

Figure 14–5 **Impact of Federal Aid Cuts on State and Local Revenues, 1952–2002**

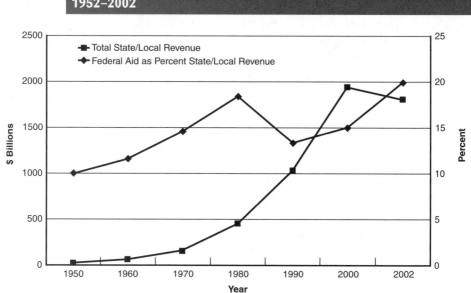

Sources: Compiled from Bureau of the Census, U.S. Department of Commerce (1952). *Statistical abstract, 1952.* Washington, DC: U.S. Government Printing Office, 353; *Statistical abstract, 1962,* 416; *Statistical abstract, 1982,* 275; *Statistical abstract, 2006,* 280.

in what some would consider a hodgepodge organization.[112] Much of the focus of the department is on combating terrorism, but it also is responsible for natural disasters such as floods, hurricanes, and the like.

Focusing on homeland security here is fitting, given its importance in all aspects of daily living and given that it is the most recent major change in the U.S. intergovernmental system. Homeland security illustrates more generally how grant systems work.

Organization of Homeland Security and Intergovernmental Relations. **Table 14–5** shows the main organizational units within the Department of Homeland Security (DHS) and their portions of the department's budget. The table is useful in understanding the diversity within the department, how funds are distributed across a wide variety of activities, and how components of DHS must interact with state and local governments. Indeed, virtually all aspects of DHS have an intergovernmental component.

- The single largest unit in terms of budget (20%) is the U.S. Coast Guard, which during wartime is under the Navy in the U.S. Department of Defense. The

Table 14–5	Organizational Units and Percent of Budget, U.S. Department of Homeland Security, Fiscal Year 2007

Organizational Unit	Percent
Departmental Operations	2
US—VISIT	1
U.S. Customs and Border Protection	18
U.S. Immigration and Customs Enforcement	11
Transportation Security Administration	15
Preparedness Directorate	2
Preparedness: Office of Grants and Training	6
Analysis and Operations	1
Federal Emergency Management Agency	12
U.S. Citizenship and Immigration Service	5
U.S. Secret Service	3
U.S. Coast Guard	20
Federal Law Enforcement Training Center	1
Science and Technology Directorate	2
Domestic Nuclear Detection Office	1
Total	100

Source: Compiled from U.S. Department of Homeland Security (2006). *Homeland Security: budget-in-brief, fiscal year 2007*. Washington, DC: U.S. Government Printing Office, 15.

Coast Guard interacts with state and local governments in terms of harbors and international waters, including the Great Lakes.

- Customs is served by two units—U.S. Customs and Border Protection (18%) and U.S. Immigration and Customs Enforcement (11%).[113] The latter unit is the main investigative arm of the department, but noticeably absent from the department is the Federal Bureau of Investigation, which remains in the U.S. Department of Justice. State and local governments are involved with DHS in terms of investigating illegal smuggling of people, drugs, and other commodities into the nation.

- The Transportation Security Administration (TSA, 15%) is responsible for airport screenings among other duties. State and locally operated airports must interact with TSA.

- The Federal Emergency Management Agency (FEMA, 12%) is responsible for preparing for and responding to disasters. Its handling of the Katrina and Rita Hurricane disasters brought into question it ability to respond effectively to national disasters. Hurricanes and other disasters have underscored the need for FEMA to work with state and local governments.
- Besides these main units, there are other smaller ones in DHS.

The department carries out its functions through a mix of approaches. Unlike some departments, which are mainly in the business of awarding money, such as the Department of Housing and Urban Development, DHS spends a good portion of its own funds. As noted above (**Table 14–3**), about a third of homeland security money is in grants and cooperative agreements. Additionally, DHS is a primary user of contracting (Chapter 10). For example, FEMA and other units contract extensively for both services and products. FEMA has special needs to be able to enter into contracts on a speedy basis.[114]

Grants. The two main series of grants within the department, as shown in **Table 14–6,** are the Homeland Security Grant Program (HSGP) and the Infrastructure Protection Program (IPP). The first entry in the table under HSGP is the state program. All states have counterparts to USDHS and receive federal funding, which is dispersed to state and local units.[115] Law enforcement grants, as the name suggests, go to state and local police and related first-responder departments. All states share in these grants. Similarly, all states share in the Citizen Corps grants which support activities similar to the old Civil Defense. These grant programs vary considerably in magnitude. In 2006, for example, Ohio received $12.6 million in state grants, $9.2 million in law enforcement grants, and only $0.6 million in Citizen Corps grants.[116]

The other two sets of grants under HSGP do not go to every state. The Urban Areas Security Initiative awards in 2006 went to about 30 states, reflecting the fact that some states have urban concentrations of populations and others do not. About 40 states received Metropolitan Medical Response System awards that help support emergency medical organizations in preparing for disasters. Using Ohio as the example, it received $17.6 million in urban grants and $1.4 million in metropolitan medical grants.

The awards for the five subprograms under HSGP in 2006 broke out as follows: (1) state homeland, $544.5 million; (2) law enforcement, $396 million; (3) urban areas, $757.3 million; (4) metropolitan medical response, $29.7 million; and (5) Citizen Corps, $19.8 million.[117]

Besides the Homeland Security Grant Program, there is the Infrastructure Protection Program. As its title suggests, it is aimed at protecting vital facilities, most notably ports and transit systems. Buffer zone grants are used by state and

Table 14–6	Grant Programs Operated by the U.S. Department of Homeland Security, 2006

Program

Homeland Security Grant Program
   State Homeland Security
   Law Enforcement, Terrorism and Prevention
   Urban Areas Security Initiative
   Metropolitan Medical Response System Allocation
   Citizen Corps

Infrastructure Protection Program
   Port Security
   Transit Security
     Intracity Bus
     Intracity Rail
     Ferry
   Buffer Zone Protection
   Chemical Sector Buffer Zone Protection
   Intercity Security Programs
     Intercity Bus
     Intercity Passenger Rail
     Trucking
     Intercity Bus

Other Grants and Contracts

Source: Compiled from U.S. Department of Homeland Security (2006). *Website*. Retrieved October 5, 2006, from http://www.dhs.gov.

local governments to create protection areas around "chemical facilities, nuclear and electric power plants, dams, stadiums, arenas and other high-risk areas."[118] There also is a program for chemical sector buffer zones.

In addition, the department awards grants and contracts in other security areas. For example, it has award programs for radiation detection and information technology.

Awards are made for the Homeland Security Grant Program through a combination of formula and categorical processes. Monies do not flow automatically to state and local governments so therefore they must apply for funding. That is done exclusively online and interestingly through the Department of Justice's website rather than that of Homeland Security.[119] The guidelines for application are extensive—159 pages for fiscal year 2005. In order to apply, therefore, a government needs some savvy in understanding the language and forms of grantsmanship.

Some of the HSGP, as prescribed by Congress, must be distributed among the states at a minimum of 0.75% of total funds. This is akin to the floor that was set under General Revenue Sharing, assuring a minimum amount of funding across governmental boundaries. The remaining money is discretionary and was originally distributed based largely on population. Simply, the more people a state had, the more funding it received.

Critics rightfully contended that threats to security are not evenly divided among the population; therefore, money should not be evenly divided. The National Commission on Terrorist Attacks upon the United States, the 9/11 Commission, in 2004 said that money should be allocated based on "risks and vulnerabilities" and not population. "Such assistance should not remain a program for general revenue sharing or pork-barrel spending."[120]

The catch is finding a method of allocating funds that is defensible. In 2006, the department shifted to a *risk-based awards* system. In the words of DHS Secretary Michael Chertoff, "First and foremost to the extent the law permits, we use risk as the basis for giving money out. And risk is a combination of what the threat is, what the vulnerability is, and what the consequences would be of a successful attack."[121]

This translated in the department cutting back on the number of metropolitan areas eligible for Urban Areas Security Initiative grants from 50 in 2005 to 35 in 2006. Recipients in urban areas eliminated from funding were eligible for continuation awards to complete the projects they had begun but were ineligible for new awards. This was called "sustained" funding. California lost two areas— Sacramento and San Diego. Others eliminated included Phoenix, Arizona; Las Vegas, Nevada; and Toledo, Ohio. Two Florida areas were added—Orlando and Fort Lauderdale.

The change in the funding process met with vociferous opposition from some members of Congress and state and local government officials. Critics challenged Homeland Security's decision making, questioning the basis on which risk was assessed. Las Vegas officials noted that their being a major tourist destination and known around the world made them a likely target for a massive terrorist event. San Diego officials noted that the extensive military installations in the area made that city a target for terrorists. New York City, although not eliminated, was cut back in funding. Critics questioned why the City would be cut when it was the focal point of September 11. Senator Charles Schumer (Democrat of New York) said Secretary Chertoff had "'promised to fight to increase New York's formula, and here it is, we're being whacked with a two-by-four and we don't hear a peep out of Secretary Chertoff.'"[122] DHS in making the urban areas announcement was unable to articulate, at least publicly, its criteria for stripping some areas of funding and adding others to the list.[123]

Homeland Security's 2006 announcements on port grants under the Infrastructure Protection Program met with equal opposition from some political leaders. The U.S. Coast Guard evaluated the risks associated with the 101 top ports in the nation and sorted them into four tiers by risk. The first tier and riskiest consisted of three ports: Houston, Texas; Los Angeles-Long Beach, California; and New York-New Jersey. Funds were awarded to specifically proposed projects in Tier 1 ports, with money trickling down to the other tiers. Obviously, it was advantageous for a port to have a higher tier ranking, but ports needed to propose projects that could be defended on their merits and not duplicate other activities. For example, some ports wanted to create "seaward facing radar systems" that would be alert to all vessels in their vicinity. DHS rejected all of these proposals, regardless of tier level, on the ground that the task was being handled by the Coast Guard.[124] Although New York City was cut back on the urban grants program, it was the biggest "winner" in the ports competition.

Secretary Chertoff warned against thinking of its grants programs as a horse race in which governments seek to dash to the finish line with the largest amount of money possible. "If you want to do a horse race, go to Pimlico."[125] He said that awards would be made on departmental priorities and the strength of grant applications, that the department would select those applications that appeared to yield the greatest return within the parameters of the department's needs. The secretary reasoned that those needs should be expected to vary over time, resulting in variations over time over what ports, what transit systems, what urban areas, and the like would be funded. He promised that the department would post well in advance of application deadlines the priorities for that year's funding. A complaint had been that state and local governments were unsure of the department's priorities and when completing applications were uncertain whether their proposals would be viewed favorably. They might well be proposing useful projects but ones that were considered by DHS to be of low priority in a given funding year.

The criticisms of how DHS handled its grants programs were so blistering that Congress added important restrictions onto the process in 2006. The department was required to post applications within 45 days of the appropriations bill's passing, and governments were given a minimum of 90 days to apply. The department was required to act within 90 days after receiving applications.[126]

Although the department through its review of grant applications attempts to head-off wasteful spending, projects are funded that sometimes raise doubts about priorities. For example, funding Wyoming to buy a bomb-handling robot may seem like wasteful spending, given the seemingly low threat in that state, but the state was vindicated when the robot was used in a highway pipe-bomb incident.[127] Some fire departments have hired clowns and puppeteers under the Law Enforcement, Terrorism and Prevention program.[128] Wasteful? The answer is no if the clowns and puppets impress on children the key dangers of fire and the importance of fire safety. On the other hand, teaching children about fire safety may seem of low priority when there are terrorists to be caught.

Congress as is its rightful role has set funding constraints on homeland security grants, but those priorities are sometimes questioned. One is the 0.75% requirement for each state to receive some funding. Some critics have argued for that provision's elimination.[129] Some of the law enforcement grants have been spent on physical fitness training for law enforcement and the purchase of treadmills and other training machines, seemingly aimed at making law enforcement officers buff. Homeland security officials have winced over such spending but have noted that it is specifically authorized by Congress.[130]

But the biggest concern is that Congress sets priorities on spending by allocating money to the various grant programs independent of what the "experts" in Homeland Security think makes sense. For instance, DHS requested $1 billion for urban areas grants in 2006 but ended up with $765, which was $65 *less* than it received for 2005.[131] Similarly, Congress determines how much money will be spent on ports versus other forms of infrastructure. Congress, as the representative of the people, has the right and responsibility to set priorities and allocate funds, but in the era of the War on Terrorism should greater flexibility be afforded the Department of Homeland Security? Should the department have flexibility in allocating funds among ports, law enforcement, and the like. If yes, how much flexibility? This is the age-old problem of trying to reach an appropriate balance in decision making between the legislative and executive branches.

Restructuring Patterns of Intergovernmental Relations

Tax Laws

Tax Deductions and Exemptions. A substantive change that could be made is to adjust taxes in ways that would reduce the need for financial assistance. By increasing the taxing powers of lower-level governments, the need for grants-in-aid may be reduced. For example, taxpayers currently may deduct many state and local taxes from gross income before computing federal tax liabilities. Included are state and local income taxes, property taxes, and some other lesser taxes. Excluded are state sales, gasoline, and similar consumption and excise taxes. The Tax Reform Act of 1986 (TRA86) is responsible for removing the deductibility of some state and local taxes, such as sales taxes.[132] Since 2004, taxpayers may choose to deduct sales or incomes taxes. Federal tax law could be altered either to increase or decrease deductibility. Such tax policies affect disposable income, affect government revenue, and alter the distribution of taxing power among levels of government.

Economists have been particularly critical of deductions for property taxes in that this benefit is largely enjoyed by middle-income families. Lower-income families are less likely to own homes and therefore are unable to benefit from the deductibility, and higher-income families do not benefit appreciably from such deductions. The importance of the home building industry to the overall economy, however, has been used by lobbyists to argue in favor of property tax deductibility. TRA86 did limit mortgage interest deductions to only two homes, one of which must be a principal residence and the other a vacation or second home.

On the other side of the argument, tax deductions do provide some measure of latitude for state and local taxation. They reduce somewhat the differentials among states and among localities, and they mitigate some of the problems of tax overlapping. At least overlapping taxes may be held to a level that is not confiscatory. The strongest argument in favor of tax deductibility is that the practice is firmly entrenched and that any effort to eliminate deductibility for property taxes, for example, would be politically unacceptable without compensating tax relief.

Some states, such as New York, offer exemptions on property taxes. A state exempts a portion of a taxpayer's bill and then reimburses the local school district for the full amount. The exemptions make homeownership more affordable without denying school districts the money they need for their operations. Some analysis has indicated that when exemptions exist districts are likely to be less efficient in their operations, since they can raise taxes and let the state government foot much of the bill rather than local taxpayers.[133]

Tax Credits. The institution of tax credits would be likely to cause a more substantial shift in revenue sources than would result from changes in tax deductibility. Tax credits would allow individual taxpayers to use taxes paid to one jurisdiction to reduce the tax liability owed to another jurisdiction. As discussed in Chapter 4, a tax credit reduces tax liability dollar for dollar, whereas a deduction of taxes paid to another jurisdiction from one's taxable income is worth only the marginal tax bracket percentage, the highest being 35%. One proposal sometimes made is to allow such credits for the federal income tax. The effect would be to redistribute revenue from the federal government to state and local governments. A tax credit on income taxes could encourage those states without income taxes to adopt them because the taxpayers would be less affected. However, if the tax credit is uniform regardless of income, it would benefit the wealthier states even more than the poorer ones.

Unemployment Insurance. The federal government has enticed or forced states to impose unemployment insurance taxes on employers by providing that most monies from such taxes may stay within each state. In the event that a state did not have an approved system, a tax presumably would be imposed by the federal government. Until TRA86, unemployment benefits were not treated as income under federal tax law, thereby providing an important benefit to individuals and creating a costly tax expenditure for the federal government. These benefits are now taxable. Inheritance taxes are practically forced on states by a federal tax provision deducting 80% of any state inheritance tax paid. Any state that did not adopt an inheritance tax would lose considerable appeal to retirees and other older citizens.

Tax Exemptions on Bonds. Another important benefit afforded state and local governments through federal tax law is the tax exemption on interest earned on bonds issued by these governments.[134] Tax exemption has had the effect of allowing governments to pay lower interest rates to bondholders than if the bonds were taxable. An even more important impact of TRA86 on state and local revenues was the reduction in the types of municipal bonds that are eligible for tax-exempt status, particularly private-purpose activity bonds (see Chapter 13). Some have argued that TRA86 has farther-reaching implications because provisions relating to required registration of tax-exempt municipal bond buyers and state reporting on arbitrage gains from tax-exempt bond proceeds undermine the autonomy of state and local governments within the federal system.

The Internal Revenue Service audits questionable tax-exempt bonds, suspecting that they may not meet the tax-exempt criteria. Some taxpayers have received unwelcome surprises when interest earned on what they thought were tax-exempt sources turned out upon later review by the IRS to be taxable interest.

The state and local government financial crises following the 2005 hurricane season brought forth suggestions for federal policy changes on municipal bonds. One set of proposals would have provided federal backing for existing debt, since some governments in the affected states thought they might need to default.[135] Another set of proposals would have allowed for the issuance of tax-exempt bonds for reconstruction.[136] Congress approved neither of these.

Shared Taxes. Presently, the federal, state, and local governments in the United States have either exclusive or overlapping jurisdiction over various tax sources. Only the federal government may tax imports and exports. The federal government does not have a property tax or general sales tax. Federal, state, and local governments overlap in the use of personal and corporate income taxes. Some states benefit from linking their own personal income tax systems to the federal system. Individuals in North Carolina, for example, can file a state income tax form that bases taxes on the federal taxable income. This simplifies administration of the system and reduces state tax administration costs. When TRA86 expanded the federal tax base, it automatically expanded the base for most states, since their systems are tied in one form or another to the federal system. However, there is no shared link between the two—the federal Internal Revenue Service collects only federal income taxes, and state and local governments collect their own income taxes. State and local governments typically share a sales tax. It is collected by the state, but revenues are allocated to local governments that levy such taxes.

A.M. Rivlin, the first director of the Congressional Budget Office and later the director of the Office of Management and Budget, proposed a value-added tax that would be shared among levels of government.[137] This idea still has currency in intergovernmental fiscal reform discussions in that it would be a major rationalization of the tax system, rather than piecemeal reform.[138] Sharing the tax means that it would be a common tax, eliminating competition between states over the level of taxation. It would also mean shared administration, reducing the collection costs, and it would minimize the ability of one level of government to preempt other levels' use of a particular tax. State and local finance in the German federal system, for example, relies heavily on shared taxation. A national shared sales tax also would resolve the issues around states' inability to develop an effective way to tax e-commerce (see Chapter 4). Any major realignment of responsibilities among levels of government must include changes in revenue systems as well.

Grant Requirements

Strings. State and local officials are all too familiar with the strings that come attached to grants. The solicitation announcements in which governments are encouraged to apply for grants are replete with notifications as to how the money may and may not be used and other requirements. For example, grants must be audited and the audit reports supplied to the funding agency. Other progress and final reports are required. These reporting requirements for the federal government have grown as federal agencies needed to comply with the Government Performance and Results Act and President Bush's PART system.

Grants administration sometimes involves grey areas in which funding agencies say something *should* be done but lack authority to say it *must* be done. Officials of recipient governments are wary of not following such guidance even though they think the funding agency may be stepping out of bounds. No one wants to jeopardize possible future funding by failing to follow unofficial guidance. The situation has been referred to as "soft governance."[139]

Mandates. Other proposals to improve intergovernmental fiscal relations pertain to mandates. For instance, when a state legislature passes a law requiring school districts to adopt certain procedures in dealing with gifted children or children with learning disabilities, a mandate has been established that has budgetary implications. Typically, federal mandates on state and local governments are tied to grants or other forms of federal assistance and contracts, making the stipulation that a government (or private party) must meet specified conditions to qualify for funds.

Notable federal crosscutting mandates—requirements that apply to the work of most federal agencies and grant programs—require recipients to pay locally prevailing wages, meet Americans with Disabilities Act standards for removing architectural barriers for persons with disabilities, and prevent discrimination based on race, gender, and the like. These mandates are at a basic level unrelated to the purpose of the grant or contract or other funding. That is, a local government carrying out an activity funded under the Community Development Block Grant program related to building a community facility would be required to pay minimum wages and would be required to adhere to provisions of the Fair Labor Standards Act and the Davis-Bacon Act. The various requirements imposed have to do with federal policy as stated in legislation and regulation toward work and employment conditions including fair wages. These regulations would apply to the entire local government, not just the particular department involved with the facility. It is possible, however, that challenges in court to the applicability of these labor laws might be ruled in favor of state governments, but the courts generally have not exempted local governments.

Other mandates are directly related to the grant program objectives. As noted earlier, continued TANF funding to states is contingent on their reducing the number of people on their welfare rolls. How the states accomplished that goal was open to wide latitude in this block grant program, but the states were required to achieve a 20% reduction by 2002 (the end of the first five years of the program).

Medicaid is a categorical grant program that is always on the firing line because of the high and increasing costs of health care and because of the state funds that have to be committed along with the federal funds. Federal mandates limit state control of Medicaid by specifying in great detail who is eligible and what costs are reimbursable. As a result of these mandates, states have felt they are less able to make their own budgetary decisions.

Unfunded Mandates. Another category for reform has been eliminating what many term "unfunded mandates." These are federal or state mandates that are not necessarily tied to particular financial assistance programs. For example, federal laws and court rulings have set standards for state prison systems that in many cases require additional prisons to be built without federal assistance. These requirements are not associated with any program of financial assistance, and they are mandatory for all states (in the case of federal requirements) regardless of whether or not the state is a recipient of federal programs related to the justice system. They are a matter of a federal determination that it is in the national interest to require states to meet certain standards, but no help to do so is available from the federal government.

The Disabilities Education Act of 1975 and later known as the Individuals with Disabilities Education Act is implemented by regulations that include detailed requirements for states to accommodate students with disabilities to enable successful educational outcomes.[140] The act promises federal funding assistance up to 40% of the amount states spend. In principle, one might call that a "funded mandate." However, appropriations have never come close in meeting that 40% promise. Hence, the mandate is unfunded.

Clean air and water standards have forced local governments to build new solid waste treatment facilities, substantially change wastewater treatment systems, and adopt numerous other practices. The City of Columbus, Ohio, estimated that thirteen environmental regulations cost the City as much as $1.6 billion between 1991 and 2000.[141] OMB determined in 2006 that over a ten-year period, seven rules imposed costs of greater than $100 million on states, local governments, and tribes. Air emission standards for waste combustors alone cost $320 million per year in constant 1990 dollars.[142] One cannot argue that local governments would otherwise spend nothing and attribute the total spending to federal, unfunded mandates.

State and local officials argue that these mandates should be accompanied by federal funding because they appear to be attempts to achieve goals previously set by the federal government through financial assistance programs and now, with federal aid being cut due to budgetary pressures, have become regulatory means to the same end. The contrary view argues that there are genuine national goals that relate to such public purposes as health and safety, environmental regulation, minimum living standards for every family, and so forth, and that these require federal action. Just because a national purpose exists, it does not necessarily mean there should be a matching federal payment to assist in achieving that purpose. The same line of reasoning is employed by states in their use of mandates for local governments.

In 1995, Congress passed the Unfunded Mandates Reform Act (UMRA), which requires draft legislation to be analyzed as to what unfunded mandates might be imposed on other governments or the private sector.[143] Bills below certain thresholds that are adjusted annually do not fall under the law. For a bill in 2005 to be covered by UMRA, it had to have an impact on state and local governments of $62 million or more and on the private-sector, $123 million or more.[144] The Congressional Budget Office, a staff arm of Congress, prepares the estimates which are attached to committee reports on the bills. If the threshold is reached, a member in the House of Representatives may raise a point of order, which then requires the full house to vote on whether to consider the bill. If a point of order is raised in the Senate, the chamber is barred from considering the bill unless a vote is taken to waive the order or the presiding officer overrules the point of order. Note that this provision only goes into effect when a point of order is raised. Otherwise, the bill's consideration proceeds with the unfunded mandate included.

Three provisions in the law restrict its applicability. First is that of the threshold cost figure. Second, any new conditions imposed on grant programs are excluded. Thus, if the federal government required states to change state law in order to receive federal highway money (as it did by requiring each state to enact a 21-year-old drinking age) this would not count as a mandate. Third, a wide variety of topics are outside of the law, such as national security, constitutional rights, and part of the Social Security program. Included here are the statutory rights protecting against discrimination, such as in voting and employment. Some critics have argued that the law is too restrictive in its application.[145]

President Clinton in 1999 issued Executive Order 13132, Federalism, to implement the law.[146] Federal agencies are required to estimate mandates contained in legislation they wish to see passed and estimate the mandates contained in regulations that they draft. The Government Accountability Office has responsibility for reviewing the regulation estimates.

As might be expected, most proposed federal legislation does not include mandates. In the first ten years of UMRA implementation, 1996–2005, the Congressional Budget Office (CBO) reviewed about 5,800 bills. Of the bills involving intergovernmental relations, 88% had no mandates, 10% had mandates below the threshold, 1% had mandates with costs above the threshold, and 1% had mandates with costs that could not be estimated. The point of order procedures between 1996 and 2004 was used only a dozen times in the House and not at all in the Senate.[147]

Mandates Since Passage of the Unfunded Mandates Reform Act. In the first ten years of experience under UMRA, according to CBO, Congress considered 27 bills with unfunded mandates exceeding the threshold and passed five of them. They were:

- an increase in the minimum wage,
- a reduction in federal funding to administer the Food Stamp program,
- a preemption of state taxes on premiums for certain prescription drug plans,
- a temporary preemption of state authority to tax certain Internet services and transactions, and
- a requirement that state and local governments meet certain standards for issuing driver's licenses.[148]

Not included in the list is the No Child Left Behind Act of 2001, which greatly reconfigured how the federal government relates to state and local governments regarding elementary and secondary education. That law is discussed at length in **Exhibit 14–4.** As that discussion indicates, there has been lengthy and heated debate over whether the law contains unfunded mandates.

The fifth "official" mandate (from the above list) to be passed between 1996 and 2005 was the Real ID Act of 2005.[149] Following the September 11 disasters, there was general consensus that government needed to have better identification of people, but whereas many countries required adults to have passports regardless of any plans to travel overseas, that notion was anathema in the U.S. Instead, the view was that the country would stay with state identification systems, but Congress wanted more careful attention devoted to confirming that people were who they said they were when applying for driver's licenses and identification cards. Congress also wanted more secure state cards in order to thwart counterfeiters.

The 2005 legislation, therefore, required extensive revamping of state driver's license and identification card systems, with the task to be completed by May 2008. Congress did not have authority to require states to comply and indeed some states even voiced interest in rebelling. However, there was considerable clout behind the legislation. If a state did not comply, its licenses and identification cards would be unacceptable by the federal government. In just one simple example, people with such licenses would be prohibited from passing security at airports and boarding aircraft.

The CBO estimated that Real ID would cost $100 million to implement, and Congress appropriated $40 million in fiscal 2006.[150] The states found both the CBO number and the appropriation to be wildly underestimated. Implementation was estimated to cost $11 billion according to a study done by the National Governors Association, National Conference of State Legislatures, and American Association of Motor Vehicle Administrators.[151] The bulk of the cost, $8.5 billion, was expected to come from re-enrolling 245 million people with state licenses or IDs. The law required more extensive documentation on individuals, and the report did not estimate the costs people would encounter in obtaining the needed documents for submission to their respective state licensing offices. The report did not estimate the costs of time applicants would spend in lines waiting their turn.

The report made several recommendations. One was to extend the implementation time to ten years instead of five. Another was to provide full funding. The sum appropriated by Congress was considered a pittance at best. Another recommendation was to allow the states to accept federal identification and thereby detour around the elaborate vetting process that was to be required. If the federal government had done a thorough job in screening individuals and issuing identification cards, such as in the case of millions of federal civilian employees, then

Exhibit 14–4 **No Child Left Behind: Reform or Revolution?**

The No Child Left Behind Act (NCLB) of 2001 is the most important piece of education legislation to pass Congress since the Elementary and Secondary Education Act of 1965.[1] The law dramatically altered the role of the federal government in public education and how the federal government interacts with states and local school districts. The law can be viewed as an experiment in which the outcome is yet to be determined.

Summary of the Law

This complex law, sprawled across more than 1,000 pages, can be summarized as follows:

• The law stresses accountability in the sense that schools are to test children to measure their progress in reading and mathematics. The aim is to have all students at or above proficiency by the year 2014. To determine whether success is achieved, schools are required to engage in annual testing of children from grades 3 through 8.

• Greater flexibility was afforded the states by allowing for shifting of some federal monies among grants so as to further NCLB objectives.

• Since reading is the foundation of most learning, the subject was given priority with the expectation that all children be able to read by the end of third grade. A Reading First initiative was created to this end.

• The quality of teachers was to be increased so as to improve the quality of instruction.

• The law strives to eliminate the "achievement gap" between general population whites on the one hand and minorities, in particular Hispanics, African Americans, and Native Americans.

• Limited English proficient (LEP) students are given priority, namely students whose families routinely speak a language other than English.[2]

• States are required to establish standards of "adequate yearly progress" (AYP) and to impose sanctions when a school fails to meet its objectives two years in a row. In such cases, students may transfer to another school. In some instances, school districts are required to offer children the opportunity to transfer to other school districts, a fact that requires the creation of intergovernmental agreements to accommodate these children.[3]

• Schools not meeting their AYPs for three years are required to provide students with supplemental education services (SES), such as tutoring.[4]

• The law guarantees full funding so that it supposedly contains no unfunded mandates. "Nothing in this Act shall be construed to authorize an officer or employee of the federal government to mandate, direct, or control a state, local education agency, or school's curriculum, program of instruction, or allocation of state or local resources, or mandate a state or any subdivision thereof to spend any funds or incur any costs not paid for under this act."

continues

Exhibit 14–4	No Child Left Behind: Reform or Revolution? (continued)

Measuring Achievement

How best to measure the academic progress of students has long been debated in the education profession, but under the No Child Left Behind Act, two basic models are used. The U.S. Department of Education which administers NCLB presumes states will use the status model unless there is agreement to use the other model. The status model is aimed at determining whether students are meeting AYP. The model is akin to a pass-fail system, that students in any given school are either passing or failing.[5]

The alternative is the growth model that gauges progress that is being achieved from year to year even though some students may remain below the proficiency level. In growth models, schools typically not only look at total progress, but at the progress of subgroups such as minority students and students who have English as a second language. Student achievement in effect can be graded unlike the pass-fail system of the status model.

Besides state-level testing, a national test is administered ever two years on a sample of fourth and eighth grade children so as to be able to compare student academic achievement across state boundaries. This is known as the National Assessment of Educational Progress (NAEP).

So what have the results been? They have been mixed. The Bush White House reported that 9-year-olds made greater gains between 2002 and 2006 than in the previous 28 years.[6] However, the NEAP results for eighth graders found no improvement in average scores for any state between 2003 and 2005, and seven states actually had lower scores.[7] Observers have predicted that the achievement gap will not be closed by the 2014 deadline. One study estimated that "by 2014, less than 25% of poor and Black students will achieve NAEP proficiency in reading, and less than 50% will achieve proficiency in math."[8]

State officials have tended to defend their school operations on the ground that the tests are faulty. The contention is that multiple measures of student learning and progress should be used.

Mandates

The law does expect states and school districts to accomplish a great deal, but this is done through funding and not official mandates in the sense of requiring compliance. State and local governments need not participate, but to do so means forgoing much needed federal dollars. "Bundling" occurs in which governments are told they must comply with NCLB if they want federal funding of any sort.[9] The governments cannot pick and choose among grants.

In reality, the federal government has not provided full funding. One estimate is that administrative costs were increased by 2% and program costs by 27% for a total 29%, but federal increases have come no where close to that.[10] Senator Edward Kennedy (Democrat of Massachusetts) estimated in 2006 that the law to date had short changed schools by $55 billion.[11]

continues

Exhibit 14–4 No Child Left Behind: Reform or Revolution? (continued)

Legal Challenges

Claims that the law unconstitutionally mandates states to act have been unsuccessful, with the federal courts simply holding that no one is putting an NCLB gun to the heads of state and local governments.[12] Indeed, the Republican Policy Committee has insisted that the law is "neither unfunded nor a mandate."[13]

Connecticut, the National Education Association (NEA), and others have filed suit focusing on the NCLB's provision for full funding.[14] The NEA case included several state education associations and school districts in three states as litigants. These cases face an uphill battle considering that they first will have difficulty showing any mandate exists and second, documenting specific costs imposed on the schools.

The Complaints about NCLB

The complaints against the No Child Left Behind Act are far too numerous to list here, but a few should be noted. These are in addition to the repeatedly stated need for full funding of the law.

• Testing is too rigid and states are not given flexibility in designing systems to meet their specific needs.

• While the Department of Education has authority to issue waivers and exempt states in some aspects of the law and 40 states have made such requests, these have been rarely granted, at least in the eyes of critics.[15] Such action, contend the critics, makes a joke of claims that the law is flexible. The counterargument is that were every requested waiver and exemption be granted, the law would be gutted.

• The system tends to emphasize penalties for schools and teachers, who are stigmatized when they fail to meet adequate yearly progress (AYP) standards. One is reminded of the old saw: "The beatings will continue until morale improves."

• Too much emphasis is given to reading and mathematics at the expense of other subjects, such as high level thinking skills, global understanding, and communication skills. Art and music instruction tend to get set aside to make room in the school day for reading and math instruction.

• The program diverts class time away from learning and wastes classroom time with test preparation and testing.

• For Native Americans and others, the law tends to drub out cultural and heritage learning.

• The emphasis on raising test results has led to the encouragement of low-achieving students to drop out of school. The process has been seen as a positive factor in recruiting for the military, especially during the time when troops were needed for combat in Afghanistan and Iraq.

continues

Exhibit 14–4	No Child Left Behind: Reform or Revolution? (continued)

Critics of the law are almost legion. Democrats, who originally voted for passage of the law, have backed away from it. As noted, the National Education Association and state associations have been critical. One poll of Americans who knew about NCLB found 60% of the respondents thought the act had no positive effect or had been harmful.[16] A survey of 2000 literacy educators found that 76% thought the law "had at least a somewhat negative influence on teaching and learning in English/reading classrooms."[17] One estimate was that 47 of the 50 states as of 2006 were in "some stage of rebellion."[18]

NCLB's Uncertain Future

The law was scheduled to expire in 2007, and by 2006 efforts were underway to claim positions over how best to revamp the law.

Secretary of Education Margaret Spellings took a position that was widely criticized. She told reporters, "There's not much needed in the way of change. I talk about No Child Left Behind like Ivory Soap. It's 99.9 percent pure."[19] Despite those comments, President Bush recommended changes in the law. The president endorsed bonuses for high achieving teachers. He wanted more math and science professionals to be working in classrooms. He supported expanding the use of vouchers so that students could move from low achieving public schools to presumably higher achieving private schools. He called for training up to 70,000 advanced placement teachers.[20]

The debate over reauthorization of the law was expected to be heated and protracted, with the outcome uncertain.

1. Elementary and Secondary Education Act (1965). P.L. 89-10; No Child Left Behind Act (2001). P.L. 107-110.

2. U.S. Government Accountability Office (2006). *No Child Left Behind Act: assistance from education could help states better measure progress of students with limited English proficiency.* Washington, DC: GAO.

3. Illinois State Board of Education (2002). *Many schools off list requiring school choice under No Child Left Behind.* Retrieved October 8, 2006, from http://isbe.state.il.us/news/2002/july 15-02a.htm.

4. U.S. Government Accountability Office (2006). *No Child Left Behind Act: education actions needed to improve implementation and evaluation of supplemental education services.* Washington, DC: GAO.

5. U.S. Government Accountability Office (2006). *No Child Left Behind Act: states face challenges measuring academic growth that education's initiatives may help address.* Washington, DC: GAO.

6. George W. Bush (2006). Fact sheet: the No Child Left Behind Act: challenging students through high expectations, Press Release. Retrieved October 8, 2006, from http://www.whitehouse.gov/news/releases/2006/10/20061005-2.html.

7. U.S. Department of Education (2006). *Reading results: executive summary for grades 4 and 8.* Retrieved October 8., 2006, from http://nces.ed.gov/nationsreportcard/nrc/reading_math_2005/s0002.asp?printver=.

8. Lee, J. (2006). *Tracking achievement gaps and assessing the impact of NCLB on the gaps.* Cambridge, MA: The Civil Right Project at Harvard University, 11.

9. No Child Left Behind and the political safeguards of federalism (2006). *Harvard Law Review*, 119, 885–906.

continues

Exhibit 14–4   No Child Left Behind: Reform or Revolution? (continued)

10. Mathis, W. J. (2005). The cost of implementing the federal "No Child Left Behind Act:" different assumptions, different answers. *Peabody Journal of Education, 80, No. 2,* 90-19; see Imazeki, J. (2006). Does No Child Left Behind place a fiscal burden on states? Evidence from *Texas. Education Finance and Policy,* 1, 217-246.

11. Kennedy, E. as cited in Basken, P. (2006). *Bush seeks better teachers, more transfers with "No Child" law. Bloomberg.com, October 8.* Retrieved October 8, 2006, from http://www.bloomberg.com/apps/news?pid=20601103&sid=aNueuaaDd58s&refer=us.

12. *School District of the City of Pontiac v. Spellings* (2005). 2005 U.S. Dist. LEXIS (E.D.Mich) 29253.

13. Republican National Committee (2004). *The "No Child Left Behind Act": neither unfunded nor a mandate.* Retrieved October 8, 2006, from http://rpc.senate.gov/_files/Ap2104UnfundedJG.pdf.

14. Dillon, S. (2006). Connecticut lawsuit is cut back. *New York Times, September 28*, 18; National Education Association (2005). *NEA stands up for children and parents, files first-ever national lawsuit against administration for not paying for education regulations.* Retrieved October 8, 2006, from http://www.nea.org/newsreleases/2005/nr050420.html.

15. Civil Society Institute (2006). *NCLB left behind: understanding the growing grassroots rebellion against a controversial law.* Retrieved October 8, 2006, from http://www.nclbgrassroots.org/landscape.php.

16. Phi Delta Kappa/Gallup poll reveals public and NEA in Sync about No Child Left Behind (2006). Retrieved October 8, 2006, from http://www.nea.org/newsreleases/2006/nr060822.html.

17. National Council of Teachers of English (2006). *Literacy educators and the public deeply concerned about NCLB.* Retrieved October 8, 2006 from http://www.ncte.org/pubs/chron/highlights/125383.htm?source=gs.

18. Civil Society Institute (2006). *NCLB left behind: understanding the growing grassroots rebellion against a controversial law.*

19. Margaret Spellings, Secretary of U.S. Department of Education, as quoted in Dillon, S. (2006). As 2 Bushes try to fix schools, tools differ. *New York Times, September 28.* Retrieved October 8, 2006, from http://select.nytimes.com/gst/abstract.html?res=F60C13FC3D540C7B8EDDA00894DE404482.

20. Labbe, T. (2006). Bush: No Child Left Behind closing achievement gap. *Washington Post, October 5.* Retrieved October 8, 2006, from http://www.washingtonpost.com/wp-dyn/content/article/2006/10/05/AR2006100500973.html.

their identification cards should be acceptable for issuance of state cards. Another annoyance for the states was that as the end of 2006 approached, the Department of Homeland Security had yet to issue implementation regulations. The states rightfully complained that they were being expected to implement something for which the details had not been worked out in Washington.

One team of researchers suggested that the War on Terrorism by forcing cooperation among the levels of government has had a surprisingly positive effect on intergovernmental relations.[152] That may be correct, but the Real ID Act works against cooperation.

The Courts. The courts also have become somewhat involved in addressing federal mandates, although in cases not involving significant state and local financial issues. In 1995, in *U.S. v. Lopez*, the Supreme Court struck down a federal statute that regulated possessing a gun in a school zone. In 1997, it ruled that the provisions of the Brady Handgun Act requiring state and local law enforcement officers to conduct criminal background checks on persons applying to purchase guns were not enforceable.[153] Other court rulings noted earlier suggest that the Supreme Court will not allow Congress to abrogate states' rights without documented evidence of a compelling need.

Civil Rights. One area of controversy concerns the extent to which a jurisdiction's operations must comply with civil rights stipulations. In 1984, the Supreme Court ruled in *Grove City College v. Bell* that only that portion of an organization affected by federal dollars had to comply with standards protecting against discrimination based on race, gender, age, and handicapping condition.[154] In that instance, the college's only federal support was for student-aid activities, so only those activities had to comply. In 1988, Congress reversed that decision by passing the Civil Rights Restoration Act, which provides that all operations of a recipient government must meet federal standards.[155] The law was passed despite a veto by President Reagan.

Title IX of the Education Amendments of 1972 addressed the same issue: the applicability of the prohibitions against discrimination in educational institutions on the basis of gender to all activities of an institution, whether or not those activities received any federal funding.[156] Title IX is applicable across the entire institution, without regard to specific links to federal funding. If a university, for example, participates in a federal student financial aid program or receives funding directly from the federal government or indirectly from state government agencies for construction of a library, then the university may not discriminate on the basis of gender in any program.

Thus, women's sports programs have to be supported if men's sports programs are funded by the university. Sometimes schools have had to eliminate some sports due to funding constraints, such as James Madison University announcing in 2006 the elimination of ten teams. Critics usually contend that valuable sports would not have had to be eliminated had Title IX not existed.[157] The Title IX impact on women's sports has received the most publicity, but it really was aimed at more fundamental equal opportunities for education such as prohibitions on admission of married women.[158]

Streamlining and Paperwork Reduction. Related to mandates are various reporting requirements that create paperwork and thereby create costs. Reporting requirements may be associated with a single federally funded program, or often identical information is required for many programs funded by the same federal agency. States require local governments to submit numerous reports each year and the federal government requires the same of state and local governments.

The Paperwork Reduction Act, a 1995 revision of the 1980 statute, regulates agency requests for information from state and local governments, and from private corporations and individuals (see the discussion in Chapter 10). Office of Management and Budget approval is required for any information form that is to be administered to ten or more individuals or institutions. OMB reports to Congress periodically on progress in meeting the targets in the reduction of paperwork (see Chapter 10).

The Regulatory Flexibility Act of 1980 and Executive Order 12866 of 1993 require agencies to conduct regulatory impact analyses to determine the effects of proposed rules or regulations, including the effects on state and local governments. Agencies are required to develop annual regulatory plans that must be submitted to OMB, which in effect has a veto power over regulations. The Clinton administration and the George W. Bush administration emphasized the importance of cost-benefit analysis in the regulatory process.

The Single Audit Act of 1984, amended in 1996, is an additional paperwork reduction device (see Chapter 11).[159] Implemented through OMB Circular A-133, the act allows a state or local government receiving funds through numerous different federal programs to comply with those programs' audit provisions by using a single financial compliance audit.[160]

The 1990 Cash Management Improvement Act introduced prompt payment provisions that require the federal government to pay interest to the recipient when a transfer is late. A related provision requires states withdrawing federal funds early to pay interest to the federal government. Streamlining cash flow has been achieved through the provisions of this act.

The Federal Financial Assistance Management Improvement Act of 1999, among other things, was passed to "simplify federal financial assistance application and reporting requirements."[161] The act and its implementing regulations aim to create a standard format for applications for federal financial assistance. These are analogous to the National Science Foundation's and National Institutes of Health's online research grant applications. The Financial Assistance Management Improvement Act of 1999 involves the work of 26 agencies in developing a unified plan.

An outgrowth of these efforts is the creation of the website *Grants.gov*.[162] The purpose of the site is to provide one-stop shopping for grants. The site is searchable for possible grants, and application can be made online. In order for a state or local government agency to apply, it must obtain a DUNS number, which stands for "Data Universal Number System," and must file with the Central Contractor Registry. The Department of Health and Human Services is the contact point for Grants.gov and all federal agencies are required to post their grant announcements and other solicitations on the site. OMB, in accordance with the Federal Funding Accountability and Transparency Act of 2006, is directing the development of a search engine and data base on government grants, contracts, and loans.[163] The system is to be running by 2008.

Another useful tool is the *Catalog of Federal Domestic Assistance* that was mentioned earlier. The *Catalog*, which gives capsule descriptions of grant programs, can help a local government determine whether it might be able to secure federal funding for a contemplated project, even though applications may not be being received at that particular time.

Grant Coordination.   Another concern is how to coordinate federal grants at regional and statewide levels. If a community is applying for a federal grant to assist elderly citizens, how would that grant complement other programs for the elderly in the region and how would it relate to state-level programs?

In response to this type of question and as an outgrowth of the Intergovernmental Cooperation Act, the Bureau of the Budget (now OMB) in 1969 issued Circular A-95, which provided for the establishment of area-wide and state clearinghouses responsible for reviewing and commenting on proposed projects. The review and comment process offered the potential for eliminating waste in the use of federal funds. Jurisdictions applying for these funds were expected to respond to any objections made by the clearinghouses and, where appropriate, to modify the proposed projects. Circular A-95 was later rescinded and replaced by various executive orders. Ultimately, the state- and area-wide reviews proved slow and cumbersome. Only about half of the states established a state-wide clearinghouse.[164]

Awarding Grants and Grants Administration.   All too often applicants for grants worry about possible bias on the part of those responsible for making awards. The fear is that regardless of the merits of grant proposals, awards will be made based on favoritism.

Nightmares along this line became reality in 2006. The Inspector General Office in the U.S. Department of Education issued a scathing report about the handling of the Reading First program, part of the No Child Left Behind program.[165] The report stated that people chosen to serve on review panels for state applications were often biased, that they especially favored particular textbook publishers and curriculum vendors. With a billion dollars at stake annually, the Bush Administration vowed to improve the situation.

All governments experience problems in administering grants. Communication problems are routine, for example between what a local government thinks it needs to report to its funding agencies at the state and federal levels and what they think needs to be reported. As time passes during a grant, recipient governments frequently need to make adjustments to accommodate changes in their environment, but these adjustments may not meet with approval of funding agencies.

Management Capacity. With the increasing emphasis on block grants, greater attention has been focused on the abilities of state and local governments to manage themselves. Devolving to these governments decision-making authority over the use of federal funds has been accompanied by a concern that they improve their management capabilities. There have been suggestions that the federal government should assume responsibility for management capacity building, but the federal government has shown only a limited inclination to accept any such obligation. In fact, management improvements and other innovations at the state and local levels in recent years have led many to look to them as a source of management ideas for the federal government.

The Clinton administration under the leadership of Vice President Gore undertook a major review of government performance and established a performance improvement reform program. As discussed in other chapters, Congress became engaged in the same effort with the Government Performance and Results Act. The George W. Bush administration's management agenda focused on five strategic initiatives: strategic management of human capital, competitive sourcing, E-government, financial management, and budget and performance integration, and created a new scorecard to measure performance. Improving grants management received special attention throughout the bureaucracy. Washington, nevertheless, does not necessarily have superior management capabilities that, if only transferred to the state and local levels, would produce quick results.

Summary

Fundamental issues arise in regard to the question of how to structure intergovernmental relations. Functional integration results in picket fence arrangements that may deter geographic integration. Fiscal capacities differ among and within levels of government, so that the government that perhaps should provide services often lacks the necessary funding capability. Failure to provide services results in externality problems.

Both direct spending and grants-in-aid are important for intergovernmental relations. Decisions by federal and state agencies on the location and expansion of capital facilities affect the economic viability of local jurisdictions. Despite more extensive attention often being devoted to federal aid programs, state aid to local government is actually larger. Some states provide much of their local governments' revenue while others provide little, a point that should be stressed to avoid unwarranted generalizations. Aid to education constitutes the largest portion of state aid, with monies typically allocated on a formula basis. Federal aid is concentrated in the areas of education, income security, health, and transportation.

Major changes are occurring in the intergovernmental fiscal landscape, with substantial responsibilities for welfare reform already having been devolved to state governments, and numerous other proposals up for consideration. Furthermore, substantial concern has prompted legislative and executive action to mitigate the impacts of unfunded federal mandates. The fiscal impact of these changes however, has been small, because they affect only newly proposed mandates.

Intergovernmental grants have at least four aspects: their purpose (narrow, broad, or general), the type of recipient, the amount, and the method of distribution. Categorical grants are criticized as deterring coordination, skewing local priorities, and needlessly wasting time in their proposal preparation. On the positive side, these grants are said to force planning in the preparation of their proposals and to allow for screening out poorly conceived projects. General revenue sharing supported local priorities and provided funds to jurisdictions that did not have staff available to apply for categorical grants. It was criticized as not targeting any national purpose and giving funds to many undeserving jurisdictions. Ultimately, the program was terminated at the federal level, but some states continue to engage in revenue sharing with their local governments. Block grants, a cross between categorical grants and GRS, have the advantages and disadvantages of both.

In addition to grant programs, numerous other intergovernmental devices are employed. They include provisions in federal tax law that benefit state and local governments and review and comment processes for grant proposals. Proposals have been made for major reconfiguring of program responsibilities among the federal, state, and local governments. Since the 1980s, many state and local governments have shown a resurgence in this area, resulting in what many see as a healthy redress of balance between the federal level and the state and local levels.

Notes

1. Tannewald, R. (1998). Devolution: the new federalism—an overview. *New England Economic Review, May/June*, 1–12; Dilger, R. J. (2000). The study of American federalism at the turn of the century. *State and Local Government Review, 32*, 98–107.

2. World Trade Organization (2006). *Website.* Retrieved September 28, 2006, from http://www.wto.org; Roberts, A. (2004). A partial revolution: the diplomatic ethos

and transparency in intergovernmental organizations. *Public Administration Review, 64*, 410–424.

3. Nivola, P. S. (2005). *Why federalism matters.* Washington, DC: Brookings Institution; Conlan, T. (2006). From cooperative to opportunistic federalism: reflections on the half-century anniversary of the Commission on Intergovernmental Relations. *Public Administration Review, 66*, 663–676; McGuire, M. (2006). Intergovernmental management: a view from the bottom. *Public Administration Review, 66*, 677–679.

4. Indian Gaming Regulatory Act (1988). P.L. 100-497; National Indian Gaming Commission. *Website.* Retrieved September 28, 2006, from http://www.nigc.gov.

5. Mays, G. L. (2005). Intergovernmental relations and Native American gaming. *American Review of Public Administration, 35*, 74–93.

6. Tribe, governor come to agreement to amend tribal-state gaming compact (2006). *Native American Casino.* Retrieved September 28, 2006, from http://www.nacasino.com/inbrief.php.

7. National Indian Gaming Commission (2005). *Growth in Indian gaming, 2004.* Retrieved September 28, 2006, from http://www.nigc.gov/TribalData/GrowthinIndian Gaming Graph19952004/tabid/114/Default.aspx; National Indian Gaming Commission (2006). *Tribal gaming revenues (in thousands) by region, fiscal year 2005 and 2004.* Retrieved September 28, 2006, from http://www.nigc.gov/Portals/0/NIGC%20Uploads/Tribal%20Data/2005vs2004gmgrevbyregn.pdf.

8. Evans, W. N. & Topoleski, J. H. (2002). The social and economic impact of Native American casinos. *NBER.* Retrieved September 28, 2006, from http://papers.nber.org/papers/w9198.

9. Bureau of the Census, U.S. Department of Commerce (2006). *Statistical abstract, 2006.* Washington, DC: U.S. Government Printing Office, 272.

10. Walker, D. B. (1995). *The rebirth of federalism: slouching toward Washington.* Chatham, NJ: Chatham House.

11. Tiebout, C. M. (1956). A pure theory of public expenditures. *Journal of Political Economy, 44*, 416–424; Epple, D. et al. (1999). *The Tiebout hypothesis and majority rule: an empirical analysis.* New York: National Bureau of Economic Research.

12. Ter-Minassian, T. (1997). *Fiscal federalism in theory and practice.* Washington, DC: International Monetary Fund.

13. Conley, J. P. & Wooders, M. H. (1997). Equivalence of the core and competitive equilibrium in a Tiebout economy with crowding types. *Journal of Urban Economics, 41*, 421–440; Wood, C. (2006). Scope and patterns of metropolitan governance in urban America: probing the complexities in the Kansas City region. *American Review of Public Administration, 36*, 337–353.

14. Port Authority of New York and New Jersey (2006). *Website.* Retrieved October 9, 2006, from http://www.panynj.gov/.

15. Arrandale, T. (2000). Four states agree on the basics of a save-the-salmon strategy. *Governing, 14, October*, 66.

16. Wright, D. S. (1988). *Understanding Intergovernmental Relations*, 3rd ed. Pacific Grove, CA: Brooks/Cole, 83–86.

17. Sapat, A. (2004). Devolution and innovation: the adoption of state environmental policy innovations by administrative agencies. *Public Administration Review, 64*, 141–151; U.S. General Accounting Office (2004). *Columbia River Basin: a multilayered collection of directives and plans guide federal fish and wildlife activities.* Washington, DC: U.S. Government Printing Office; Intergovernmental Panel on Climate Change (2006). *Website.* Retrieved September 28, 2006, from http://www.ipcc.ch/.

18. U.S. Government Accountability Office (2006). *International finance crime: Treasury's roles and responsibilities relating to selected provisions of the USA PATRIOT Act.* Washington, DC: GAO.

19. U.S. General Accounting Office (2004). *Homeland security: federal leadership and intergovernmental cooperation required to achieve first responder interoperable communications.* Washington, DC: U.S. Government Printing Office; Eisinger, P. (2006). Imperfect federalism: the intergovernmental partnership for homeland security. *Public Administration Review, 66*, 537–545.

20. Winston, P. et al. (2006). *Federalism after Hurricane Katrina.* Retrieved September 28, 2006, from http://www.urban.org/UploadedPDF/311344_after_katrina.pdf.

21. U.S. Government Accountability Office (2005). *Hurricane Katrina: providing oversight of the nation's preparedness, response, and recovery activities.* Washington, DC: GAO.

22. Fellowes, M. & Liu, A. (2006). *Federal allocations in response to Katrina, Rita and Wilma: an update.* Washington, DC: Brookings Institution.

23. Walters, J. & Kettl, D. (2005). The Katrina breakdown. *Governing, December.* Retrieved September 28, 2006, from http://www.governing.com/articles/12disast.htm.

24. U.S. Government Accountability Office (2006). *Catastrophic disasters: enhanced leadership, capabilities, and accountability controls will improve the effectiveness of the nation's preparedness, response, and recovery system.* Washington, DC: GAO.

25. Dickey, B. et al. (2005). Clean sweep. *GovExec.com.* Retrieved September 28, 2008, from http://www.govexec.com/features/1005-15/1005-15s3.htm.

26. Rodden, J. et al. (Eds.) (2003). *Fiscal decentralization and the challenge of hard budget constraints.* Cambridge, MA: MIT Press; Wildasin, D. E. (2004). The institutions of federalism: toward an analytical framework. *National Tax Journal, 57*, 247–272; National Academy of Public Administration (2006). *Financing governments in the 21st century: intergovernmental collaboration can promote fiscal and economic goals.* Washington, DC: National Academy of Public Administration.

27. Bureau of the Census, U.S. Department of Commerce. *Statistical abstract, 2006*, 452.

28. Office of Economic Policy, U.S. Department of Treasury (2005). *Total taxable resources, 2004.* Retrieved November 9, 2006, from http://www.ustreas.gov/offices/economic-policy/resources/2006est.pdf.

29. U.S. Advisory Commission on Intergovernmental Relations (1992). *Significant features of fiscal federalism, vol. 2, revenues and expenditures: 1992.* Washington, DC: U.S. Government Printing Office.

30. U.S. Advisory Commission on Intergovernmental Relations (1990). *Representative expenditures: addressing the neglected dimension of fiscal capacity.* Washington, DC: U.S. Government Printing Office.

31. Wong, J. D. (2004). The fiscal impact of economic growth and development on local government revenue capacity. *Journal of Public Budgeting, Accounting, and Financial Management, 16*, 413–423.

32. Neumann, R. (2002). *Equalization in Canada: reform of the representative tax system or move to a macro approach?* Retrieved September 28, 2006 from http://www.iigr.ca/conferences/archive/pdfs2/Neumann2.pdf#search=%22representative%20tax%20system%22; Sobarzo, H. (2004). *Tax effort and tax potential of state governments in Mexico: a representative tax system.* Retrieved September 28, 2006, from http://www.nd.edu/~kellogg/publications/workingpapers/WPS/315.pdf#search=%22representative%20tax%20system%22.

33. Nagowski, M. (2006). Measures of state and local tax burden. *Federal Reserve of Boston.* Retrieved September 28, 2006, from http://www.bos.frb.org/economic/neppc/memos/2006/nagowski071306.pdf#search=%22federal%20reserve%2C%20representative%20tax%20system%22.

34. Oates, W. E. (1972). *Fiscal federalism.* New York: Harcourt Brace Jovanovich.

35. Reagan, R. (1987). Federalism, Executive Order 12612. *Federal Register, 52*, 41686.

36. Bush, G. W. (2001). *Memorandum: Interagency Working Group on Federalism.* Retrieved September 29, 2006, from http://www.whitehouse.gov/news/releases/2001/02/print/200010226-13.html.

37. Porter, M. (2000). Competition and economic development: local clusters in a global economy. *Economic Development Quarterly, 14*, 15–34.

38. McCracken, J. (2000). Mercedes to build 2nd plant in Alabama. *Auto.com.* Retrieved August 2002, from http://www.auto.com/industry/merc26_20000826.htm.

39. Goldman, T. & Wachs, M. (2003). A quiet revolution in transportation finance: the rise of local option transportation taxes. *Transportation Quarterly, 57*, 19–32; Crabbe, A. E. et al. (2005). Local transportation sales taxes: California's experiment in transportation finance. *Public Budgeting & Finance, Fall*, 91–121; Green, A. D. (2006). Life in the fast lane: transportation finance and the local option sales tax. *State and Local Government Review, 38*, 92–103.

40. Rivlin, A. M. (1992). *Reviving the American dream: the economy, the states, and the federal government.* Washington, DC: Brookings Institution, 126–152.

41. Defense Base Closure and Realignment Commission (2005). *Report.* Retrieved September 29, 2006, from http://www.brac.gov/docs/final/Volume1BRACReport.pdf; see U.S. Department of Defense (2006). *BRAC: base realignment and closure.* Retrieved September 29, 2006, from http://www.dod.mil/brac/.

42. Crock, S. (2004). A tale of two military bases. *BusinessWeek.com.* Retrieved September 29, 2006, from http://www.businessweek.com/bwdaily/dnflash/dec2004/nf2004128_9707_db056.htm?chan=search.

43. U.S. Office of Management and Budget (2006). *Budget of the United States Government, 2007.* Washington, DC: U.S. Government Printing Office, 332.

44. Bureau of the Census, U.S. Department of Commerce (2006). *Statistical abstract, 2006,* 330.

45. Bureau of the Census, U.S. Department of Commerce (2006). *Statistical abstract, 2006,* 340.

46. Bureau of the Census, U.S. Department of Commerce (2006). *Statistical abstract, 2006,* 499.

47. Bureau of the Census, U.S. Department of Commerce (2006). *Statistical abstract, 2006,* 340.

48. Dubay, C. S. (2006). *Federal tax burdens and expenditures by state.* Washington, DC: Tax Foundation.

49. Bureau of the Census, U.S. Department of Commerce (2006). *Statistical abstract, 2006,* 291, 297.

50. Bureau of the Census, U.S. Department of Commerce (2005). *Compendium of government finances, 2002.* Washington, DC: U.S. Government Printing Office, 2.

51. Bureau of the Census, U.S. Department of Commerce (2006). *Statistical abstract, 2006,* 297.

52. Bureau of the Census, U.S. Department of Commerce (2006). *Statistical abstract, 2006,* 21, 297.

53. Bureau of the Census, U.S. Department of Commerce (2006). *Public education finances, 2004.* Washington, DC: U.S. Government Printing Office, 1.

54. Benson, E. D. & Marks, B. R. (2005). "Robin Hood" and Texas school district borrowing costs. *Public Budgeting & Finance, 25,* Summer, 84–105.

55. *San Antonio School District v. Rodriquez* (1973). 411 U.S. 1.

56. *Serrano v. Priest (Serrano II)* (1976). 557 P.2d 929 (Calif.).

57. Ladd, H. F. & Hansen, J. S. (Eds.) (1999). *Making money matter: financing America's schools.* Washington, DC: National Academy of Sciences; Ladd, H.F. et al. (Eds.) (1999). *Equity and adequacy in education finance: issues and perspectives.* Washington, DC: National Academy of Sciences.

58. No Child Left Behind Act (2001). P.L. 107-110.

59. Hanushek, E. (2001). *After the bell: education solutions outside the school.* Retrieved September 30, 2006, from http://www.nyu.edu/fas/cassr/conf01.htm.

60. *Rose v. Council for Better Education* (1989). 7090 S.W.2d 186 (Ky.).

61. Smith, S. (2005). *Education finance litigation: overview, research & trends.* Retrieved September 30, 2006, from http://www.statetaxes.net/NTC%20Presentations%2005/Smith.ppt#7; West, M. R. & Peterson, P. E. (Eds.) (2006). *School money trials: the legal pursuit of educational adequacy.* Washington, DC: Brookings Institution.

62. See Federal Highway Administration, U.S. Department of Transportation (2006). *Highway statistics, 2004.* Retrieved September 30, 2006, from http://www.fhwa.dot.gov/policy/ohim/hs04/index.htm.

63. Greenblatt, A. (2002). Enemies of the State. *Governing, 16, June,* 26–31.

64. Reschovky, A. (2004). The impact of state government fiscal crises on local governments and schools. *State and Local Government Review, 36,* 86–102; Vanylos, I. (2005). Fiscal reaction to state aid uncertainties: evidence from New York State. *Public Budgeting & Finance, 25, Winter,* 44–58.

65. Nonprofit gag passes in House, has uncertain future in Senate (2005). *OMB Watch.* Retrieved October 1, 2006, from http://www.ombwatch.org/article/articleview/3158.

66. New York City Investment Fund (2003). *Lessons learned: an analysis of the New York City Investment Fund's financial recovery fund for small businesses affected by 9/11.* Retrieved October 1, 2006, from http://www.nycif.org/RECOVERYFUND/LessonsLearned_FRF.pdf.

67. Detailed Information on the Juvenile Accountability Block Grants Assessment (2005). *ExpectMore.gov.* Retrieved October 1, 2006, from http://www.whitehouse.gov/omb/expectmore/detail.10000172.2005.html.

68. U.S. General Accounting Office (1996). *Federal grants: design improvements could help federal resources go further.* Washington, DC.: U.S. Government Printing Office; Deller, S. C. & Maher, C. (2005). Categorical municipal expenditures with a focus on the flypaper effect. *Public Budgeting & Finance, 25, Fall,* 73–90; Deller, S. C. & Maher, C. S. (2006). A model of asymmetries in the flypaper effect. *Publius, 36,* 213–230.

69. Fisher, R. C. & Papke, L. E. (2000). Local government responses to education grants. *National Tax Journal, 53,* 153–168.

70. Chernick, H. (2000). Federal grants and social welfare spending: do state responses matter? *National Tax Journal, 53,* 143–152; Rodgers, H. R. & Tedin, K. L. (2006). State TANF spending: predictors of state tax effort to support welfare reform. *Review of Policy Research, 23,* 745–759.

71. Walters, J. (2002). The TEA generation. *Governing, 16, May,* 70–76; Wolf, J. F. & Farquhar, M. B. (2005). Assessing progress: the state of metropolitan planning organizations under ISTEA and TEA-21. *International Journal of Public Administration, 28,* 1057–1080.

72. Walters, J. (2000). CHIP on their shoulders. *Governing, 14, November,* 12; Fossett, J. & Thompson, F. J. (2006). Administrative responsiveness to the disadvantaged: the case of children's health insurance. *Journal of Public Administration Research and Theory, 16,* 369–392; Johnson, T. J. et al. (2006). The effects of cost-shifting in the state children's health insurance program. *American Journal of Public Health, 96,* 709–75.

73. Bureau of the Census, U.S. Department of Commerce (2006). *Statistical abstract, 2006,* 23; U.S. Office of Management and Budget (2006). *Analytical perspectives: budget of the United States Government, 2007.* Washington, DC: U.S. Government Printing Office, 120.

74. Altshuler, A. et al. (Eds.) (1999). *Governance and opportunity in metropolitan America*. Washington, DC: National Academy Press; Miller, D. (2000). Fiscal regionalism: metropolitan reform without boundary changes. *Government Finance Review, 16, December*, 7–12.

75. U.S. Office of Management and Budget (2006). *Historical tables: budget of the United States Government, 2007*. Washington, DC: U.S. Government Printing Office, 312.

76. Martell, C. R. & Smith, B. M. (2004). Grant levels and debt issuance: is there a relationship? Is there symmetry? *Public Budgeting & Finance, 24, Fall*, 65–81.

77. U.S. Office of Management and Budget (2006). *Analytical perspectives: budget of the United States Government, 2007*. Washington, DC: U.S. Government Printing Office, 106.

78. U.S. Office of Management and Budget (2006). *Analytical perspectives*, 99.

79. Arrandale, T. (2002). The pollution puzzle. *Governing, 16, August*, 22–26.

80. Buntin, J. (2001). The increasingly expansive Medicaid machine. *Governing, 15, October*, 30–32.

81. Donahue, J. D. (1997). The disunited states. *Atlantic Monthly, 279, May*, 18–22.

82. Personal Responsibility and Work Opportunity Reconciliation Act (1996). P.L. 104–193.

83. Eckl, C. L. et al. (1991). *State budget and tax actions: 1991*. Washington, DC: National Conference of State Legislatures, 13.

84. U.S. General Accounting Office (2004). *Medicaid: improved federal oversight of state financing schemes is needed*. Washington, DC: U.S. Government Printing Office; U.S. General Accounting Office (2004). *Medicaid: intergovernmental transfers have facilitated state financing schemes*. Washington, DC: U.S. Government Printing Office.

85. Walker, D. B. (1996). The advent of an ambiguous federalism and the emergence of New Federalism II. *Public Administration Review, 56*, 271–280.

86. *Garcia v. San Antonio Metropolitan Transit Authority* (1985). 469 U.S. 528.

87. *Printz v. United States* (1997). 521 U.S. 98.

88. *Geier v. American Honda Motor Company* (2000). 529 U.S. 861; Andrews, J. L. (2006). Saving preemption: a conflict preemption quandary resolved in *Geier v. American Honda Motor Co., Inc. Transportation Law Journal, 32*, 221–284.

89. *Kimel v. Florida Board of Regents* (2000). 528 U.S. 62; *Board of Trustees of Alabama v. Garrett* (2001). 531 U.S. 356.

90. National Conference of State Legislatures (2006). *Preemption Monitor*. Retrieved October 3, 2006, from http://www.ncsl.organ/sclaw/PreemptionMonitor_Index.htm; see Galligan, T. C. (2006). U.S. Supreme Court tort reform: limiting state power to articulate and develop tort law—defamation, preemption, and punitive damages. *University of Cincinnati Law Review, 74*, 1189–1264; Kaulukukui, K. L. (2006). The brief and unexpected preemption of Hawaii's humpback whale laws: the authority of the states to protect

endangered marine mammals under ESA and MMPA. *Environmental Law Reporter News and Analysis, 36,* 10712–10725.

91. Kloha, P. et al. (2005). Someone to watch over me: state monitoring of local fiscal conditions. *American Review of Public Administration, 35,* 236–255.

92. Dluhy, M. J. & Frank, H. A. (1999). Miami's fiscal crisis: two years later. *Municipal Finance Journal, 20, Spring,* 1–19; Once in financial straits, Miami sells $32.5 million in bonds (2002). *Naples Daily News.* Retrieved August 2002, from http://www.naplesnews.com/02/03/florida/d755883a.htm.

93. Kirkpatrick, C. (1997). State seizes town drowning in debts, failed infrastructure. *Durham Hearald-Sun, February 5,* 1, 8.

94. *The District of Columbia Financial and Responsibility Management Assistance Authority will suspend operations.* Retrieved August 2002, at http://www.cdfra.gov.

95. *Texas v. United States* (1998). 523 U.S. 296.

96. Wong, K. K. & Shen, F. X. (2002). Do school district takeovers work? Assessing the effectiveness of city and state takeovers as a school reform strategy. National Association of State Boards of Education. Retrieved October 3, 2006, from http://www.nasbe.org/Standard/9_Spring2002/Takeover.pdf; Burns, P. (2003). Regime theory, state government, and a takeover of urban education. *Journal of Urban Affairs, 25,* 285–303.

97. Heath, B. et al. (2005). Mayor: fix Detroit or risk takeover. *Detroit News, January 13.* Retrieved October 3, 2006, from http://www.detnews.com/2005/metro/0501/13/A01-58735.htm; Fisher, R. (2006). State still has option to takeover St. Louis schools. *Missouri Digital News.* Retrieved October 3, 2006, from http://www.mdn.org/2006/STORIES/NODLER12.HTM; Kennedy-Ross, S. & Vivanco, L. (2006). City takeover talk irks school officials. *San Bernardino County Sun, September 21.* Retrieved October 3, 2006, from http://www.sbsun.com/search/ci_4371038.

98. VerPloeg, M. & Betson, D. M. (Eds.) (2003). *Estimating eligibility and participation for the WIC program: final report.* Washington, DC: National Academies Press.

99. U.S. Office of Management and Budget (1997). *Grants and cooperative agreements with state and local governments, Circular A-102.* Retrieved October 4, 2006, from http://www.whitehouse.gov/omb/circulars/a102/a102.html.

100. McDowell, B. D. (1991). Grant reform reconsidered. *Intergovernmental Perspective, 17, Summer,* 8–11.

101. Givel, M. (1991). *The War on Poverty revisited: the Community Services Block Grant Program in the Reagan years.* Lanham, MD: University Press of America; U.S. Government Accountability Office (2006). *Community Services Block Grant Program: HHS should improve oversight by focusing monitoring and assistance efforts on areas of high risk.* Washington, DC: GAO.

102. State and Local Fiscal Assistance Act (1972). P.L. 92-512.

103. Greenblatt, A. (2002). Enemies of the State. *Governing, 16, June,* 26–31.

104. Philippines Institute for Development Studies (1992). *LGUs slice of internal revenue allotment from the national pie.* Retrieved November 9, 2006, from http://serp-p. pids.gov.ph/details.php3?tid=2913.

105. Golden, O. (2005). *Assessing the new federalism—eight years later.* Washington, DC: Urban Institute; Waller, M. (2005). *Block grants: flexibility vs. stability in social services.* Washington, DC: Brookings Institution.

106. Housing and Community Development Act (1974). P.L. 93-383; U.S. Government Accountability Office (2006). *Community Development Block Grants: program offers recipients flexibility but oversight can be improved.* Washington, DC: GAO; U.S. Government Accountability Office (2006). *Community Development Block Grants: options for improving the targeting of funds.* Washington, DC: GAO.

107. U.S. Office of Management and Budget (1999). *Revised statistical definitions of metropolitan areas (MA) and guidance on use of MA definitions, Bulletin 99–14.* Retrieved October 5, 2006, from http://www.whitehouse.gov/omb/bulletins/b99-04.html.

108. U.S. General Accounting Office (2004). *Metropolitan statistical areas: new standards and their impact on selected federal programs.* Washington, DC: U.S. Government Printing Office.

109. Omnibus Budget Reconciliation Act (1981). P.L. 97-35.

110. Gruber, A. (2005). Hanging on. *GovExec.com.* Retrieved October 5, 2006, from http://www.govexec.com/features/0505-01/0505-01na1.htm.

111. Walker, J. (2005). Possible grant cuts pain localities. *Richmond Times-Dispatch, May 31.* Retrieved October 5, 2006, from http://www.timesdispatch.com/servlet/Satellite?pagename=RTD/MGArticle/RTD_BasicArticle&c=MGArticle&cid=1031783011556.

112. Homeland Security Act (2002). P.L. 107-296.

113. Office of Inspector General, U.S. Department of Homeland Security (2005). *An assessment of the proposal to merge Customs and Border Protection with Immigration and Customs Enforcement.* Retrieved October 5, 2006, from http://www.dhs.gov/interweb/assetlibrary/OIG_06-04_Nov05.pdf.

114. U.S. Government Accountability Office (2006). *Department of Homeland Security's use of special streamlined acquisition authorities in Section 833 of the Homeland Security Act of 2002.* Washington, DC: GAO.

115. See Governor's Office of Homeland Security, State of California. *Website.* Retrieved October 5, 2006, from http://www.homeland.ca.gov.

116. U.S. Department of Homeland Security (2006). *FY 2006 HSGP allocations.* Retrieved October 5, 2006, from http://www.dhs.gov/interweb/assetlibrary/grants_st-local_fy06.pdf.

117. U.S. Department of Homeland Security (2006). *DHS announces $1.7 billion in homeland security grants.* Retrieved October 5, 2006, from http://www.dhs.gov/dhspublic/display?content=5667.

118. U.S. Department of Homeland Security (2006). *Website.* Retrieved October 5, 2006, from http://www.dhs.gov/dhspublic/display?content=5724.

119. U.S. Department of Homeland Security (2004). *Fiscal year 2005 Homeland Security Grant Program: program guidelines and application kit.* Retrieved October 5, 2006, from http://www.ojp.usdoj,gov/odp/docs/fy05hsgp.pdf.

120. National Commission on Terrorist Attacks upon the United States (2004). *Final report.* Washington, DC: U.S. Government Printing Office, 20.

121. Chertoff, M., Secretary of the U.S. Department of Homeland Security (2006). *Press briefing, September 25.* Retrieved October 5, 2006, from http://www.dhs.gov/dhspublic/display?content=5932.

122. Schumer, C., as quoted in Bohn, K. (2006). Homeland Security grants rile DC, NYC. *CNN.com.* Retrieved October 5, 2006, from http://edition.cnn.com/2006/US/05/31/homeland.grants/index.html.

123. Fiorill, J. (2006). Major metro areas found ineligible for anti-terror grants. *GovExec.com.* Retrieved October 5, 2006, from http://www.govexec.com/dailyfed/0106/010406gsn1.htm; California governor concerned about changes to DHS grant program (2006). *GovExec.com.* Retrieved October 5, 2006, from http://www.govexec.com/dailyfed/0106/011206tdpm2.htm.

124. Chertoff, M., Secretary of the U.S. Department of Homeland Security (2006). *Press briefing, September 25.*

125. Chertoff, M., Secretary of the U.S. Department of Homeland Security (2006). *Press briefing, September 25.*

126. Strohm, C. (2006). Homeland Security grants overhaul to begin as key official departs. *GovExec.com.* Retrieved October 5, 2006, from http://www.govexec.com/dailyfed/1006/100406cdpm1.htm.

127. Kersten, D. (2005). Accounting for Risk. *GovExec.com.* Retrieved October 5, 2006, from http://www.govexec.com/features/0305-01/0305-01s1s5.htm.

128. Hudson, A. (2006). Homeland Security grants spent on clowns and gyms. *Washington Times, April 21.* Retrieved October 5, 2006, from http://www.washingtontimes.com/national/20060420-110852-8296r.htm.

129. Carafano, J. J. & Metzl, J. (2006). Homeland Security grant reform: congressional inaction must end. *Heritage Foundation.* Retrieved October 5, 2006, from http://www.heritage.org/Research/HomelandDefense/bg1971.cfm.

130. Hudson, A. (2006). Homeland Security grants spent on clowns and gyms. *Washington Times, April 21.*

131. Strohm, C. (2006). Homeland Security unveils 2006 strategy for awarding urban grants. *GovExec.com.* Retrieved October 5, 2006 from http://www.govexec.com/dailyfed/0106/010306c1.htm.

132. Tax Reform Act (1986). P.L. 99-514.

133. Eom, T. H. & Rubenstein, R. (2006). Do state-funded property tax exemptions increase local government inefficiency? An analysis of New York State's STAR program. *Public Budgeting & Finance, 26, Spring,* 66-87.

134. Marron, D. B., Acting Director, Congressional Budget Office (2006). *Economic issues in the use of tax-preferred bond financing.* Retrieved October 5, 2006, from http://www.cbo.gov/showdoc.cfm?index=7080&sequence=0.

135. Mysak, J. (2005). Katrina bond bailout no sure thing, Snow reminds us. *Bloomberg.com.* Retrieved October 5, 2006, from http://quote.bloomberg.com/apps/news?pid=10000039&refer=columnist_mysak&sid=aqaCQWGYdCss.

136. Petersen, J. E. (2005). Muni bonds to the rescue? *Governing.com.* Retrieved October 5, 2006, from http://www.governing.com/articles/11fin.htm.

137. Rivlin, A. M. (1992). *Reviving the American dream.*

138. Tannenwald, R. (1998). Come the devolution, will states be able to respond? *New England Economic Review, May/June,* 53–73.

139. Bradson, T. et al. (2006). Soft governance, hard consequences: the ambiguous status of unofficial guidelines. *Public Administration Review, 66,* 546–553.

140. Disabilities Education Act (1975). P.L. 94-142; Individuals with Disabilities Act (2004). P.L. 108-446; National Education Association (2006). *Special education and the Individuals with Disabilities Education Act.* Retrieved October 9, 2006, from http://www.nea.org/specialed/index.html.

141. Hicks, R. C. (1992). Environmental legislation and the costs of compliance. *Government Finance Review, 8, April,* 7–10.

142. U.S. Office of Management and Budget (2006). *Draft 2006 report to Congress on the costs and benefits of federal regulations.* Retrieved November 9, 2006, from http://www.white-house.gov/omb/inforeg/reports/2006_draft_cost_benefit_report.pdf.

143. Unfunded Mandates Reform Act (1995). P.L. 104–4; see Gullo, T. (2004). History and evaluation of the Unfunded Mandates Reform Act. *National Tax Journal, 57,* 559–570.

144. U.S. Congressional Budget Office (2006). *A review of CBO's activities under the Unfunded Mandates Reform Act, 1996 to 2005.* Washington, DC: U.S. Government Printing Office.

145. U.S. Government Accountability Office (2005). *Unfunded mandates: views vary about reform act's strengths, weaknesses, and options for improvement.* Washington, DC: GAO.

146. Clinton, W. J. (1999). Federalism, Executive Order 13132. *Federal Register, 64,* 43255–43259.

147. U.S. Congressional Budget Office (2005). *Identifying intergovernmental mandates.* Retrieved October 9, 2006, from http://www.cbo.gov/showdoc.cfm?index-6052&sequence=0.

148. U.S. Congressional Budget Office (2006). *A review of CBO's activities under the Unfunded Mandates Reform Act, 1996 to 2005,* 2–3.

149. Real ID Act (2005). P.L. 109-13.

150. U.S. Congressional Budget Office (2006). *A review of CBO's activities under the Unfunded Mandates Reform Act, 1996 to 2005,* 5.

151. National Governors Association, National Conference of State Legislatures, and American Association of Motor Vehicle Administrators (2006). *The Real ID Act: national impact analysis*. Washington, DC: National Governors Association.

152. Caruson, K. & MacManus, S. A. (2006). Mandates and management challenges in the trenches: an intergovernmental perspective on homeland security. *Public Administration Review, 66*, 522–536.

153. *U.S. v. Lopez* (1995). 514 U.S. 549; *Printz v. U.S.* (1997). 521 U.S. 898.

154. *Grove City College v. Bell* (1984). 465 U.S. 555.

155. Civil Rights Restoration Act (1988). P.L. 100-259.

156. Education Amendments (1972). P.L. 92-318.

157. Redden, E. (2006). Gender equity or finances? *Inside Higher Ed*. Retrieved October 9, 2006, from http://www.insidehighered.com/news/2006/10/03/jmu.

158. U.S. Department of Education (1997). *Title IX: 25 years of progress*. Washington, DC: U.S. Government Printing Office; Munro, N. (2006). Title IX: not just for athletes. *National Journal, 38*, 50–51.

159. Single Audit Act (1984). P.L. 98-502.

160. U.S. Office of Management and Budget (1997). *Audit of states, local governments, and non-profit organizations, Circular A-133*. Retrieved October 9, 2006, from http://www.whitehouse.gov/omb/circulars/a133/a133.html.

161. Federal Financial Assistance Management Improvement Act (1999). P.L. 106-107.

162. U.S. Department of Health and Human Services (2006). *Grants.gov*. Retrieved October 9, 2006, from http://www.grants.gov.

163. Federal Funding Accountability and Transparency Act (2006). P.L. 109-282.

164. U.S. Office of Management and Budget (2004). *Intergovernmental review (single point of contact list)*. Retrieved October 9, 2006, from http://www.whitehouse.gov/omb/grants/spoc.html.

165. Office of the Inspector General, U.S. Department of Education (2006). *The Reading First program's grant application process: final inspection report*. Washington, DC: U.S. Government Printing Office.

Chapter 15

GOVERNMENT, THE ECONOMY, AND ECONOMIC DEVELOPMENT

The sheer size of the government sector in the U.S. economy guarantees that government action will have a major impact on overall economic performance. Total government expenditures as a percentage of gross domestic product (GDP)—a measure of the size of the economy—are more than 31%, and the federal share alone exceeds 20%.[1]

This chapter focuses on the impact of government budgets—primarily the federal government's budget—on the overall economy. The first section introduces basic concepts in measuring the economy. These concepts are used throughout the chapter. Section two considers the U.S. economy and its interdependence with the economies of other nations. Other governments and private individuals in other countries react to actions taken by the U.S. federal government, and actions taken by these external parties sometimes cause economic changes within the United States. To understand government and the economy, one first has to understand the conditioning factors of the world economy.

The third section summarizes the major objectives sought by U.S. government economic policy. Included is a discussion of deficit control and management of the federal debt. In contrast to state and local borrowing that basically is used as a means to finance capital investment, federal deficit spending, and subsequent borrowing function more as macroeconomic policy tools.

The fourth section briefly discusses how governments and businesses attempt to forecast the economic future, and the fifth examines the principal tools used to influence the economy. For the federal government, these tools conventionally include fiscal and monetary policy. For state and local governments, they include infrastructure investments and taxing or spending decisions that are intended to affect the local and state business climate. The final section focuses on the role of government in securing equity through influencing the distribution of income and other social goods in society.

◼ Measuring the Size of the Economy

Economists measure the economy in many ways. Two basic concepts, production and income, characterize the economy in terms of the total value of goods and services produced and the income derived from the production of those goods and services. These two concepts are at the base of all the size measures discussed in this section. In principle, these two concepts are the same. The costs of goods and services sold (the value of the output) are equal to the receipts received by the producers (the value of the income). In practice, there are imperfections in the measurement whether one is measuring production costs including costs of goods purchased, cost of labor, and so forth or one is measuring firms' and households' incomes.

Gross Domestic Product. Gross domestic product (GDP) is the basic measure of economic output. It is the value of the total goods and services produced by the nation. Gross domestic product is the aggregate of personal consumption expenditures, gross private domestic investment, net exports of goods and services, and government purchases of goods and services.

Gross National Product. An indicator similar to GDP, gross national product (GNP), for many years was the common indicator of total production. In 1992, the federal government and most analysts switched to GDP for comparison purposes, since most other countries report production in terms of GDP. The main difference between the two is that GDP excludes the earnings of U.S. businesses and residents abroad, and excludes earnings of foreign workers in the United States that are remitted abroad. Thus GDP reflects production within the U.S. economy as opposed to production by U.S. economic entities.

For the U.S., GDP and GNP typically do not differ much because income earned abroad and income remitted abroad tend to balance. For some economies, especially developing economies, remittances from citizens working abroad is a significant source of national income. In 2005, remittances from the U.S. and many other economies to Central and South America totaled over $56 billion.[2] For example, net remittances for El Salvador amounted to over 15% of national income in 2005. For Guatemala, it was over 10%.

Net National Product and National Income. Two related indicators, both derivatives of GDP, are net national product (NNP) and national income (NI). Gross domestic product includes all capital investment, some of which does not produce new productive capacity but instead replaces capacity that has been used up, such as obsolete equipment no longer capable of producing. Net national product measures only capital investment net of depreciation. Capital replacement expenditures do not count in NNP. In 2005, the U.S. GDP was $12.4 trillion while the U.S. NNP was $10.8 trillion, meaning that approximately $1.6 trillion of GDP represented no new production capacity.[3] Tracking NNP provides clues about future production since if the economy is using up capital stock and not replacing it, the production of goods and services that depends on that decreasing capital stock will decline, or grow at a slower rate.

National income is derived from NNP by eliminating indirect business taxes included in the price of goods sold and business transfer payments. The table contained in **Exhibit 15–1** summarizes the relationships among GDP, GNP, NNP, and NI of the United States economy from 1960 through 2005. Note that beginning in 2004, the statistical tables prepared by the President's Council of Economic Advisers lumped indirect business taxes, business transfer payments, and net surpluses of government enterprises into *statistical discrepancy*, masking somewhat the underlying differences among the measures. The text in the illustration assesses some of the underlying changes in the U.S. economy revealed by evaluating GDP, GNP, NNP, and NI over a 45-year time period, 1960–2005.

▮ The United States and the World Economy

Cross-Border Economic Shocks

Most U.S. citizens after World War II thought of the United States as not only the most significant contributor to, but also the economic controller of, the world economy. The U.S. economy's dependence on imported oil was of little note until the Organization of Petroleum Exporting Countries (OPEC) curtailed oil production in 1973 and 1974, and U.S. citizens for the first time in the post-war era realized the significant effects of other actors in the world economy on U.S. prices. High gasoline prices again in 2005–2006, brought on by higher consumption worldwide and various turbulent events in many oil-producing regions, re-emphasized the interconnectedness among economies.

Similarly, economic growth in several nations once considerably smaller than the U.S. economy, including Japan and Germany, and the emergence of the Indian and Chinese economies as major economic participants in the world economy,

Exhibit 15–1 Relationships Among GDP, GNP, NNP, and NI

There are several measurements of the size of the U.S. economy. They are all based on the value of production in the US economy, or the income derived from that production. Production and income are the opposite sides of the coin. Accurate measurement is complicated, and beyond the scope of this book. But understanding how the different measures relate to each other is important because as discussed in the text, each basic measure of the size of the economy captures somewhat different concepts. The following table shows how each measure is derived from gross domestic product.

Year	GDP	+ Receipts from rest of world	- Remittances Abroad	= GNP	- Consumption of fixed capital			= NNP	- Statistical discrepancies	= NI
					Total	Private	Government			
1960	526.4	4.9	1.8	529.5	55.6	40.5	15.0	473.9	-0.9	474.9
1965	719.1	7.9	2.6	724.4	69.4	50.5	18.9	655.0	1.6	653.4
1970	1038.5	12.8	6.4	1044.9	106.7	80.0	26.7	938.2	7.3	930.9
1975	1638.3	28.0	15.0	1651.3	187.7	147.8	40.0	1463.6	17.7	1445.9
1980	2789.5	79.1	44.9	2823.7	343.0	281.1	61.8	2480.7	41.4	2439.3
1985	4220.3	112.4	85.9	4246.8	506.7	414.0	92.7	3740.1	16.7	3723.4
1990	5803.1	189.1	154.3	5837.9	682.5	551.6	130.9	5155.4	66.2	5089.1
1995	7397.7	233.9	198.1	7433.4	878.4	713.4	165.0	6555.1	101.2	6453.9
2000	9817.0	382.7	343.7	9855.9	1187.8	990.8	197.0	8668.1	-127.2	8795.2
2005*	12605.7	520.8	476.6	12650.0	1863.8	1603.6	260.2	10786.2	66.5	10718.6

*2005 data is 3rd quarter

Source: Extracted from U.S. Council of Economic Advisers (2006). *Economic report of the president: 2006*. Washington, DC: U.S. Government Printing Office, 312.

continues

Exhibit 15–1 Relationships among GDP, GNP, NNP, and NI (continued)

The adjustments to gross domestic product (GDP) to derive several other measures of the size of the economy reveal changing characteristics of the U.S. economy. For most of the years represented in the table, national income (NI) is about 10% to 11% larger than GDP, whereas gross national product (GNP) and GDP are within 1% of each other for all the years. Income earned abroad by U.S. concerns and income earned in the U.S. and remitted abroad by non-U.S. entities balance each other out. Beginning in the 1980s, GDP is a decreasing percent of NI. This is caused by increases in the consumption of fixed capital by both the private sector and government. Phrased differently, neither the private sector nor government is investing in fixed assets, meaning the kind of assets that will yield future production, at the same rate relative to the existing capital stock as in earlier years. Discussion of gross and net savings rate later in the chapter reveals that the U.S. in recent decades saves less from within the economy and relies more on investments in capital from abroad to finance private sector capital investment and the government budget deficit mean that the U.S. share, although still a major component of the world economy, is merely one among several important national economies.[4]

Since that first OPEC production cut and the subsequent strengthening of other economies relative to our own, citizens have become more attuned to how much U.S. economic well-being depends on the economic behavior of billions of individuals around the world and on the economic policy decisions of dozens of other governments. The Asian financial crisis that started in 1997 caused economies first throughout Asia, then other emerging markets, to tumble. Investors rapidly sold off their emerging-market portfolio holdings, and many reinvested in the U.S. and other Western industrial markets, contributing to temporarily soaring market values in the United States. Since that 1997 shock, despite the strengthening of several emerging market economies formerly classified as underdeveloped, investors in developing economy stocks and bonds react rapidly by selling off their holdings if there is any hint that economic conditions are declining. These portfolio investments, as opposed to longer-term investments in fixed assets such as factories and other capital intensive industries, can allow for wide, rapid swings in emerging economy stock markets.

Contributing to further entwining among economies is investment in productive assets such as factories and retail establishments across borders.[5] *Foreign direct investment* (FDI) is the largest source of capital inflow to developing economies. Foreign direct investment accounts for nearly one-third of the GDP of developing economies, up from less than ten percent in 1980.[6] Unlike portfolio investments in stocks and bonds, FDI flows directly create productive assets and are not easily divested during downturns in the target economy. Changes in FDI flows thus tend to reflect investors' predictions about long-term trends in the target economies.

Another economic variable interlinking economies across the world is the simple purchase of goods and services across borders. If you buy a vehicle manufactured in another country, or your business sells pumps to oil companies in other countries, the result is a cash flow inward or outward from one's own economy. The value of international trade—exports plus imports—grew from 16% of U.S. GDP in 1975 to more than 26% in 2005.[7]

The notion that there is now a global economy, and that the United States is a part of that global economy but not the controlling agent, is accepted by most people, albeit for some quite uncomfortably. Of course, the United States is also vehemently criticized for its size and the influence of its economy in some other countries.

The United States as a Debtor Nation

A second major factor influencing today's world economy involves the debt of U.S. individuals, corporations, and governments. Citizens notice price increases in gasoline and other products dependent on imports and dramatic political conditions such as terrorism. Not as obvious are the credit flows among nations and how the U.S. is both actor and reactor to worldwide economic forces. In 1985, for the first time, the United States became a net debtor nation. Formally, that means that the value of foreign investments in the United States for the first time exceeded the value of U.S. investments abroad. In 2005, the value (measured at current market price) of foreign investments in the United States was approximately $13.6 trillion and U.S. investments abroad were valued at $11.1 trillion, both more than doubled since the mid-1990s.[8] The net difference, about $2.1 trillion, reflects a long-term pattern. Investments in the U.S. continue to be more attractive to foreign investors than investments abroad are to U.S. investors, although economic and stock market fluctuations affect the short term from time to time. For example, when the U.S. stock market tumbled in 2001, foreign investors sold off relatively more of their U.S. assets than did U.S. investors, and the proportionate value of foreign holdings in the U.S. dropped.

Generally though, the claims of foreign investors, both private and governmental, on assets in the United States regularly exceed the claims of U.S. investors, private and governmental, on assets in other countries. Since 1985, the United States has remained a net debtor, with the cumulative value of foreign-owned assets in the United States exceeding the value of assets in other countries owned by U.S. investors.

Foreign asset holdings in the United States in descending order are in: (1) debt and equity securities of U.S. companies through portfolio investment; (2) fixed assets including resorts, factories, and even public utilities such as water companies through direct foreign investment; and (3) U.S. government Treasury securities through portfolio investment. The order has changed in the last few years as more foreign investments are going into the U.S. stock market plus fixed assets and less into U.S. government securities such as Treasury bills (Chapter 10). That change is in part due to the U.S. federal budget surplus of the late 1990s that substantially reduced federal borrowing needs. Rising federal budget deficits of course require federal borrowing, much of it from foreign investors, so the trend since 2001 has been for relative growth in foreign purchases of U.S. government debt.

The inflow of foreign capital has helped keep U.S. interest rates low because it fills part of the demand for borrowing created by federal budget deficits, and it finances high levels of consumption, including imported products, by U.S. households. In addition, foreign investment produces jobs in the United States. On the other hand, when the net inflow of foreign capital replaces domestic capital for investment, it makes the economy even more linked to the rest of the world's economies. The U.S. savings rate is too low to finance all the demand for investments, leaving the economy increasingly dependent on the confidence of foreign investors in the U.S. economy. U.S. households' high consumption patterns that include huge purchases of imported goods, and government budget deficits, require importing foreign capital to finance consumption and debt.

As long as foreign investors are confident in the U.S. economy, then these patterns may not be a problem. Major threats to foreign confidence, such as the stock market drop in 2000–2002, the disasters of September 11, 2001, and ongoing problems with the wars in Afghanistan and Iraq, have caused some concerns, but it is relative to other opportunities. The U.S. economy relative to other investment possibilities in other countries remains attractive. If confidence in the U.S. economy were to wane significantly, then interest rates in the U.S. most likely would have to rise to attract investors. Such rates would be guided by monetary policy actions (discussed later in this chapter) taken by the Federal Reserve Board.

Value of the U.S. Dollar in the World Economy

The third phenomenon relates to changes in the value of the dollar in the world economy. When relatively few citizens traveled abroad, and trade accounted for less than 10% of the U.S. economy, most Americans never thought about the value of the dollar against foreign currencies.

Americans now travel extensively abroad and have for the last thirty years or more, and most Americans purchase imported goods. Changes in the value of the dollar relative to other currencies now are quite visible to most consumers and travelers. Early in the 1970s, the dollar purchased a lot of goods and services in or from other countries, as the dollar value was high relative to most major currencies.

Late in 1987, U.S. residents watched the flood of tourists reverse as European and Asian visitors came to the United States while prices for comparable trips for U.S. residents abroad climbed to new highs. Imported cars, stereos, and televisions that had been bargains a year before became unaffordable for many. This reversal occurred for two reasons. Per capita incomes grew faster in several other countries that increased their purchasing power and drove up prices for goods produced in those economies. Also, in an effort to increase the foreign purchase of U.S. goods and services, deliberate actions were taken by the U.S. government to lower the value of the dollar relative to other currencies making foreign goods and services relatively more expensive for U.S. consumers.

One of the major factors affecting the value of the dollar has been the introduction of a common currency in most of Europe—the euro. Initially the dollar and the euro varied within about 10% of each other. The U.S. economy was booming and there were federal budget surpluses. In recent years, the euro has appreciated against the dollar in part because of cyclical economic changes, but also because the prices of goods and services in the various former European country currencies now have settled into clear value in euro terms. Economists now understand that the value of the dollar fluctuates with changes both within the influence range of the U.S. private economy and government action and with changes in other economies. Since the mid-1980s, the dollar no longer dominates world currencies, but is merely one of several dominant currencies.

Competitiveness of the U.S. Economy

A fourth key economic phenomenon to note is the competitiveness of the U.S. economy relative to other emerging industrial powers. Ordinary Americans first took note of this competitiveness issue on a large scale in the 1980s. Although "cheap foreign labor" had been considered a threat by many traditional U.S. industries, such as textiles, for more than two decades, the 1980s saw problems in industries in which innovation and technology had constituted the U.S. competitive edge. For the first time, the United States encountered competitors in computer design, electronics, and other high-technology areas, who began to produce not only cheaper but, in the minds of many consumers, better products.[9]

A surge in the 1990s in U.S. productivity, led by significant private sector restructuring and manifested in part by downsizing of the work force in many industries, helped move the issue of government stimulation of U.S. competitiveness further off the national agenda. Aided by private sector restructuring and a balanced budget, by the middle of the 1990s the U.S. economy experienced both overall growth and strong competitiveness with other economies. A significant factor at that time was the massive investment in computer software and hardware to avoid some problems associated with old software that would not recognize dates beyond the year 1999 (the year-two-thousand, Y2K, problem) and overall growth in the information and communications technology sector. Investment in new computer technology after the Y2K scare of 1999–2000 slowed. Nonetheless, relative to other advanced economies, the U.S. economy is generally more productive, with the gap widening between the U.S. and the European Union economies in recent years.[10] The major factors contributing to U.S. competitiveness and productivity levels are the openness of the economy to world trade, investment in education, health of the financial sector, infrastructure, and technological innovation.

The preceding phenomena indicate that the U.S. economy is so interdependent with those of other nations that no significant actions that the United States takes lack repercussions around the world. Likewise, no significant economic events in other major industrial nations or groups of developing nations fail to have repercussions in the United States. As populous countries like China and India continue to industrialize, demand for resources, especially oil, becomes a major variable in every economy in the world. Understanding the role of the government in the U.S. economy thus means casting a wider net and considering also the actions and reactions of the country's major trading partners and major creditors.

Objectives of Economic Policy

The role of the federal government in the economy consists of several interrelated functions. First, the government provides the legal framework in which economic transactions take place. Second, it directly produces services and some goods, and it regulates private production. Also, it purchases significant quantities of goods and services and redistributes income among individuals and groups. Although the idea is not as widely accepted as these functions, some also argue that governments should promote their countries' economic competitiveness in the global marketplace, though there is a major divide between those that argue that government should invest directly in economic promotion and those that argue the more appropriate government role is creating the right economic climate for growth.[11]

One goal of the government's regulation of economic transactions through setting the legal framework is sometimes described as maintenance of a "level playing field"—making sure that all economic actors play by the same rules and succeed or fail solely on the basis of their own strengths and weaknesses. The stock market scandals in which companies such as Enron and WorldCom apparently inflated earnings by using unacceptable accounting practices resulted in major civil and criminal prosecutions and significant federal legislation, notably Sarbanes-Oxley (see Chapter 11). Setting the legal framework is the subject of texts on regulation, business, and constitutional law. This section and the following one focus on the government's effects on the economy's overall performance.

Although Franklin D. Roosevelt's 1932 election platform promised to involve the federal government in the solution to economic problems brought on by the Great Depression, it was not until after World War II that the overall role of the government in stimulating the economy became formalized through legislative enactment. The Employment Act of 1946, later amended by the Full Employment and Balanced Growth Act of 1978, set several macroeconomic policy objectives for the federal government.[12] Primary among these were full employment, price stability, and steady economic growth. Though not formalized in legislation, two additional objectives are accepted in policy now—equilibrium in the balance of transactions between the U.S. economy and other economies and debt management.[13]

Most industrial nations share these objectives, whether they rely primarily on the private market, central planning, or a mix of central control and market activity to achieve them. Less industrial, developing, and emerging market countries also share these objectives, but the most prominent economic policy objective for these nations is the promotion of economic development. The mood in most industrial economies has consistently favored a less activist role for government, but the success of Japan's economy through the 1980s and the apparent causal role played by the Japanese government's activist production and trade promotion policies intensified the debate on the proper role of the government in promoting development. The U.S. economy's outstanding performance for decades without significant government stimulation quieted (at least in the United States) the call for government intervention to stimulate competitiveness with key exceptions discussed below.

The first three objectives of the federal government are primarily domestic in nature. In many respects, they can be summarized in a single prescription: achieve a level of economic growth that produces full employment without unacceptable inflation. Economic growth is the engine that drives demand for employees. However, running that engine too fast or with too rich a fuel mixture may cause prices to rise unacceptably. The reformulation of these objectives into a single statement brings out the causal connection that exists between economic growth and employment. It also brings into the discussion two key value-laden terms: full employment and unacceptable inflation.

Full Employment

Definition of Full Employment. As a measure of economic performance, employment is the number of civilians over age 16 outside of institutions who are working in formal income-producing jobs. About 60,000 households, statistically representative of the country, are surveyed each month. The survey asks the respondent about his or her activities during the preceding week. If a person responds that he or she worked at a job for pay, or in a family enterprise without being paid, or was on vacation or some other similar situations, the individual is employed. If a person did not work in any of these situations or is not temporarily ill, on vacation, and so forth, and is looking for a job, he or she is unemployed. All others are considered not in the labor force.

The most commonly used measure of employment is unemployment. The unemployment rate is the proportion of the workforce not employed at a given time. To be considered unemployed, one must be seeking employment as measured in the survey by such activities as sending out resumes, visiting unemployment offices, calling about employment, placing ads, and so forth. The definition of seeking employment was refined in 1994 to exclude individuals who reported they were discouraged by failure to find work, but who had not looked for work in the last 12 months. Merely looking at want ads or online employment opportunities do not count. Individuals who have taken no active steps such as the above during the four weeks prior to the interview are not counted in the labor force.

There is no legislated definition of full employment, although an unemployment rate of 3% to 4% was often cited as the criterion of full employment after the 1946 Employment Act. Until the 1980s, the thinking was that about 3 to 4% of the work force at any given time will be between jobs or otherwise temporarily unemployed, thus we can never achieve unemployment below that threshold. Some members of the work force are considered at least temporarily unemployable because of changes in the nature of jobs and skill requirements. Some economists do not count these "structurally" unemployed as part of the base for calculating full employment. Homemakers returning to the workforce, young people voluntarily switching jobs, and fluctuations in demand in the global economy also make it difficult to achieve a 3% to 4% target.

The unemployment rate has been around 4% or below only 12 times in the 58 years from 1948 to 2005, and it was not better than 4.9% from 1970 until 1998, when for four consecutive years the unemployment rate ranged from about 4% to 4.7%.[14] Until that late-century boom period, most in the United States had come to accept an unemployment rate higher than 4% as consistent with the term "full employment."

The adoption of a higher unemployment rate as the criterion of full employment is connected to the fact that the U.S. economy is much more susceptible to external events than it once was. As external economic shocks occur and consumer tastes change more rapidly, U.S. businesses simply cannot react as quickly as once they could, leading at times to downturns and unemployment. When unemployment dropped below 5% in 1997, coupled with low inflation rates and an unexpectedly high rate of growth in GDP, the U.S. economy had reached its strongest point in decades and it was sustained for almost five years. During that period, debate centered on whether the United States had entered a new era of lower unemployment accompanied by low inflation, fueled by the greater value-added contribution of knowledge to production and a decline in the physical capital contribution to total production. However, some of that prosperity was the paper wealth associated with the stock market boom, especially in Internet, telecommunications, and related industry stocks. It also was apparent that at least some of the late 1990s spending on information technology was a concentrated spurt that would not be sustained annually. Post September 11, 2001, with wars in Afghanistan and Iraq and renewed, large federal budget deficits, unemployment rates returned to the 5% to 6% range. The economic downturn that caused unemployment to hit 6% by 2002–2003 reinforced the old notion of 3% to 4% as unsustainable.

Political Acceptability of Unemployment. The political system has a varying capacity to accept unemployment. A nationwide unemployment rate of 9% or 10%, a rate reached in the early 1980s, is clearly unacceptable by current standards but is substantially lower than the peak of 24% unemployment during the Great Depression of the 1930s. As the rate declines toward 5%, acceptance increases. The extent to which society tolerates unemployment is partially dependent on who is unemployed. Although there may be a tendency to accept high unemployment among low-skilled, minority group, or younger workers, tolerance for unemployment quickly dissipates when it reaches middle-income, white-collar workers.

Politically, the unemployment rate is not the only important issue. Since the late 1980s, with the rate generally hovering around 5%, citizens have been more concerned with the types of new jobs that are being created. The concern is that many new jobs have been either service jobs that pay only the minimum wage or part-time jobs that pay few or no benefits. That certainly was a criticism of the 1990s boom, but the greater media attention paid to the number of instant millionaires generated as a result of one phenomenal new stock issue after another muted scrutiny of the types of jobs more ordinary people were obtaining. The presidential and congressional campaigns of 2004 focused on this issue of job quality with Democratic candidates arguing that job creation numbers cited by Republican candidates were misleading because job growth was largely in low-paying service industry jobs.

Another issue is the controversy over part-time work. Many people choose part-time work, but companies also have increased the number of workers they hire either as part-time workers or as temporary workers in order to reduce total wage costs by not paying fringe benefits to temporary or part-time workers. As companies downsize their workforces during downturns, an increasing percentage of the national labor force has begun to work part-time and in temporary activity. Although their total employment often amounts to full 40-hour or more weeks, these workers lack the job security of regular employment and the benefits of health insurance and pension plans. Major auto industry companies in downsizing their North American operations during the 2000s have replaced thousands of full-time workers with part-timers who are paid only a fraction of the hourly wages of former employees.

Controlling Inflation

Relationship Between Unemployment and Inflation. The more the unemployment rate declines, the more difficult it becomes to find workers. As a result, wage rates may be bid up, creating inflationary pressures. Certainly through the mid-1960s the traditional assumption that rising employment leads to price increases and declining employment to price decreases seemed to hold up. However, the mid-1970s recession saw both rising unemployment and rising prices. At the peak, 1974 prices rose 11% over those of the year before, and 1975 prices rose another 9%. During that time, unemployment peaked at more than 8%. **Figure 15–1** illustrates this heretofore unconventional relationship. During the 1980s, the more conventional pattern held, with inflation and unemployment moving in opposite directions until the sustained growth period of the 1990s. By 2000, the economy was achieving both the lowest inflation rates in 40 years and low unemployment rates, as **Figure 15–1** illustrates. Subsequent increases in inflation and unemployment have tracked together, both increasing.

The 1990s experience had economists reestimating the natural rate of unemployment and the *nonaccelerating inflation rate of unemployment* (NAIRU). The latter was proposed as the rate of unemployment below which excess demand for labor is thought to set off wage and price inflation. That rate was previously considered to be in the 5 to 6% range. Unemployment below this range presumably would set off wage-led inflation. Milton Friedman in 1968 proposed to the American Economic Association that there is a natural rate of inflation on which

Figure 15–1 **Changes in Consumer Prices and Unemployment, 1960–2005**

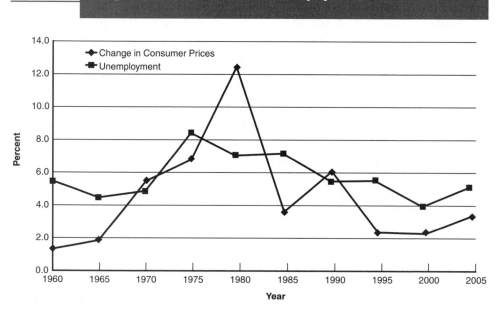

Source: Calculated from U.S. Council of Economic Advisers (2006). *Economic report of the president: 2006.* Washington, DC: U.S. Government Printing Office, 332, 356.

the economy stabilizes for any given unemployment rate. At this natural rate, a rise in employment will set off no inflation, or a fall in employment will bring no price reductions.[15] The NAIRU concept particularly gained currency in the 1990s. **Figure 15–1** illustrates that a lower rate of unemployment (at or below 5%) did not result in wage-induced inflation between 1960 and 2000. If the natural rate or nonaccelerating inflation rate (they are different but related concepts) can be calculated accurately, then monetary policy actions to control inflation need be taken only when the actual unemployment rate falls below the NAIRU. There is no exact measure of NAIRU and various methods yield ranges of plus or minus 1% to 2%.

The natural and noninflationary rates can change over time. For instance, severe drought conditions or a hard winter freeze in major citrus growing regions can cause food prices to increase, contributing to overall higher consumer prices, unrelated to wage pressures. Increased worker productivity can increase output without setting off price deflationary pressures, and more workers can be hired as long as the productivity rate remains constant or increases without putting pressure on wages. This balance is one of the explanations for the recent ability of the U.S. economy to have low inflation and low unemployment. In addition, greater pressure on jobs from foreign competition holds wage rates down regardless of what is happening in the domestic economy. If wage demands grow too high too rapidly, companies may intensify their search for foreign production sources.

Economic Growth

Economic Productivity. Unemployment is not the only—and perhaps not the best—measure of the economy's health. Even if the rate of unemployment and the rate of inflation are both at acceptable levels, the overall productivity of the economy could be seriously declining. The change in GDP is sometimes used as an indication of economic productivity, and to norm for population differences, GDP per capita is preferred. For the United States, the average annual growth rate in productivity or GDP from 1980 through 2005 was 2%. For Japan, the comparable figure was identical—2%. **Figure 15–2** compares the U.S., Canada, Japan, and the United Kingdom for several periods between 1980 and 2005. The figure adjusts for inflation by displaying *real GDP per capita*. By 1980, Japan's economy had reached mature status, yielding growth rates similar to the U.S. and other advanced economies. Japan had much higher growth rates in the 1960s and much of the 1970s when its economic base was much smaller.

During the 1980 through 2005 period, the U.S., Canada, and the U.K. generally outperformed most of the countries of the European Union. Higher labor productivity and technological innovation are generally cited as explaining the U.S. and U.K. advantage. Being more open to international trade was another factor

Figure 15–2 Percent Change in Real GDP Per Capita: Selected Countries, 1980–2005

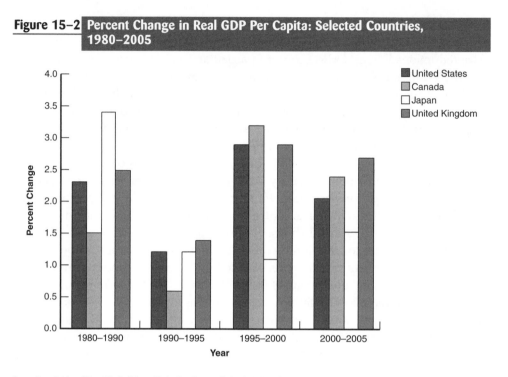

Source: Compiled from Office of Productivity and Technology, Bureau of Labor Statistics, U.S. Department of Labor (2006). *Comparative real gross domestic product per capita and per employed person, fifteen countries, 1960-2005.* Washington, DC: Bureau of Labor Statistics, 14.

explaining higher U.S. and U.K. productivity, and being more open to international trade was a favorable factor for all three. [16]

Beginning in 1996, the U.S. Commerce Department adopted a new method to calculate real GDP. Previously, real (inflation-adjusted) GDP was measured by comparing each year with the base year of 1987. Subsequent years' total production was adjusted for price changes using an index constructed on the base year, yielding real GDP growth rates. The problem with this methodology was that it implicitly assumed that all components of production changed prices by the same amount and in the same direction, although particularly since the 1970s that was not the case. The new methodology computes price changes annually using a rolling average, called a *chain-weighted measurement.*[17] Historical series reported by the Commerce Department and used by other agencies were revised to reflect the new methodology.

Although not illustrated in **Figure 15–2**, inflation varied in the countries illustrated during the period covered by the graphic. Japan's measured GDP per capita growth was largely unaffected by inflation during that time, whereas the U.S.

and Canada experienced more inflation, demonstrating the importance of looking at real GDP in order for the measure not to appear larger than warranted. Clearly different economies can experience differences in inflation during the same period, and therefore to compare those economies, adjustments are made to remove the effects of that inflation on the measures.

Impact of Government on Productivity. Most economists think that the primary impact of the government on economic productivity and long-term growth is due to influences on knowledge development and investment in productive capacity. President George W. Bush and President Clinton before him both emphasized the importance of government support for knowledge development. In his 2006 State of the Union message, President George W. Bush proposed an *American Competitiveness Initiative* " to increase investments in research and development (R&D), strengthen education, and encourage entrepreneurship and innovation."[18] The proposal would have more than doubled federal R&D investments supported through several key federal agencies with an aim of producing technological breakthroughs and indirectly supporting private investment in R&D. In addition, the initiative recommended renewing the federal tax credit program for private sector companies for their qualifying R&D expenditures. Earlier, Congress in 1981 passed a temporary stimulative measure to encourage more private R&D and renewed it regularly until 2005. Congress considered a proposal in 2001 to make the R&D tax credit permanent, but the measure failed, although the tax credit was extended to 2004. Late in 2006, Congress again extended the credit temporarily, through December 31, 2007, and made the provisions retroactive to the expiration of the last temporary extension.

The impact of the direct and indirect actions of government on improving the productivity of the economy can be measured only in the long run. For example, even if businesses substantially increase their expenditures for R&D as a result of government incentives, the payoff in productivity terms will show up only years into the future. Thirty-one states offer a variety of general tax credit programs. A few additional states have more targeted tax credit programs for R&D investments in specific geographic areas of the state, or for specific industries or technologies, such as encouraging the growth of the biotechnology industry.[19]

Worldwide, the focus is somewhat more on the factors that make an economy attractive for foreign direct investment and that facilitate domestic investment than on direct stimulative activities. **Exhibit 15–2** describes research on measuring the ease of doing business in economies around the world as a way of evaluating the effects of government regulations and interventions, or lack

Exhibit 15–2   **The Ease of Doing Business Around the World**

Greater emphasis in the last decade has been placed on reducing the barriers to private economic investment and activity than to direct promotional activities of government. The World Bank produces an annual report on Doing Business that ranks 175 countries on the ease of doing business. Ten subjects are the basis for the measurement:

1. Starting up a business (how long it takes, how much red tape, how many actors must be involved)

2. Dealing with licenses (permitting, renewals, inspections)

3. Employment (hiring rules, firing rules and costs, working hour mandates)

4. Commercial property registration (time it takes, cost, clarity on property rights)

5. Access to credit (legal/regulatory practices, access to information about credit)

6. Investor protection (shareholder suits, disclosures on company transactions)

7. Taxes (complexity/time taken to file, total taxes as percent of income)

8. Export/import regulations (transactions and permits required, duties, ease of movement of goods and capital across borders)

9. Enforceability of contracts (effectiveness of legal system, cost of enforcing, sanctity of contract)

10. Closing a business (costs, bankruptcy rules)[1]

The five top-ranked economies, in order, are Singapore, New Zealand, the United States, Canada, and Hong Kong (China). The five lowest-ranked economies are Republic of Congo, Chad, Guinea-Bissau, Timor-Leste, Democratic Republic of Congo.[2] The World Bank effort is aimed at transforming economies by in part transforming the rules and conditions in which economic activity takes place. Looking at the entire set of rankings, it is not just that overall level of economic development measured by size matters, but government actions and failure to take action to create a favorable climate has a great influence on the productivity of the economy.

1. World Bank (2007). *Ease of doing business.* Retrieved January 19, 2007, from http://www.doingbusiness.org/Documents/DB07Easeofdoingbusinessrankmethod.pdf.

2. World Bank (2007). *Doing business: economy rankings.* Retrieved January 19, 2007, fromhttp://www.doingbusiness.org/EconomyRankings/.

thereof for some issues, in order to target changes that would improve the business climate.

A Government Technology Policy. The question of whether the government should be more active in protecting and promoting critical high-technology industries first emerged in the late 1980s when the U.S. economy began to lose ground in all areas, not just markets dominated by inexpensive labor. The concept has persisted through the current decade as a key policy issue. The George H. W. Bush administration was widely criticized for not protecting critical industries such as microelectronics, and President Clinton made stimulation of high-technology development an economic policy priority. The George W. Bush administration designated corporate tax reduction, repeal of taxes on dividends, and the R&D tax credits as the most important tools with which to support economic development. Congress has been reluctant to support these initiatives, though as noted above in 2006 the George W. Bush White House proposed another package of credits, support to particular technology sectors, and education investments.

The problem with providing more support to one segment of the economy than to another is that government rather than the marketplace "picks winners and losers," and there is little evidence that governments are good in that role. The decades of Japan's double-digit growth seemed to many observers sufficient evidence that government-led development was the proper path, but the last two decades have altered that view considerably. Singapore is sometimes held up as an example of successful and significant government intervention, but as **Exhibit 15–2** notes, Singapore ranks first in the world in ease of doing business, brought about more by the climate created by government than by government choosing and directing industry targets for growth. The federal government has difficulty determining what particular elements in a volatile industry such as electronics will be the most important determinants of U.S. global competitiveness in high-technology markets five or ten years from now.[20] The more widely accepted view is that government actions, rather than overtly promoting particular industries, should be directed toward improving the human and capital base, should encourage savings and investment, and should promote the international exchange of ideas, goods, and services.

There has been an ebb and flow over time to arguments that government should develop a technology policy.[21] The first major federal programs for higher education, focusing on science and math, were launched in the year immediately after the Soviet Union launched the first satellite, Sputnik. Anxiety over Japan's remarkable growth in the 1970s spurred concern about the government not doing enough to ensure U.S. competitiveness in the world economy. More recently, the rapid growth of India and China stimulated debate, and the 2006 State of the

Union address of President George W. Bush, as noted earlier, sounded a call to increase federal support to spur competitiveness.

Equilibrium in International Financial Flows

Important elements of government policy in this era of the global marketplace are actions designed to affect the balance of trade and other financial transactions between nations. Related to this balance is U.S. reliance on world capital markets to finance its budget deficit. The U.S. financial position vis-à-vis the rest of the world is discussed in this section. A discussion of the overall deficit situation and debt management follows.

As noted earlier, since 1985, more capital has flowed into the United States in the form of investments in U.S. private assets and U.S. government Treasury debt than the U.S. has invested in other economies. This means that there are more foreign demands on U.S. assets than there are U.S. claims on assets in other countries. It does not mean that the U.S. government is in debt to other countries, although institutions and individuals do purchase U.S. Treasury securities. Rather, companies and individuals in the United States purchase more abroad than is sold to other countries (creating a trade imbalance). That is one contributing factor for the United States. The other major factor, as noted earlier, is the net balance of investments abroad and foreign investments in the United States. It is of concern to government economic policy in part because the larger the government budget deficit, the more the government borrows from the capital markets, potentially driving up interest rates. It also is of concern to government economic policy because it means an imbalance in payments to investors abroad versus payments from investors abroad.

Balance of Payments.   Balance of payments refers to the value of goods and services and the financial assets and liabilities flowing between the United States and other countries. Historically, the balance of payments policy objective was to avoid a situation in which imported goods and services plus financial transactions created the potential for drawing down on the U.S. gold reserve. Today, with the rate of exchange between the U.S. dollar and other currencies freely set by the market and unrelated to gold reserves, the balance of payments objective is primarily a matter of maintaining equitable trade relationships between the United States and other countries. Trade negotiations between the United States and Japan or between the United States and China, for examples, are contentious because of the much larger value of goods that U.S. businesses and citizens purchase from those two countries than customers in those countries purchase from the United States.

The balance of payments consists of several components or measures. The net balance of goods purchased abroad versus goods sold abroad is the simple trade balance. It is called the *current account surplus* or *current account deficit*. In 2004, for example, the current account deficit was at an all time high of $668 billion.[22] A current account deficit has been the pattern for the U.S. for most years since 1980. To remedy an excess in net imports via trade in goods and services, the U.S. economy would have to (1) produce and sell more goods and services abroad, that would mean an increase in GDP; (2) consume less of the goods currently produced in the U.S. so they could be sold abroad, assuming there is demand for them; (3) reduce consumption of goods from abroad; or (4) achieve some combination of the first three.

Besides the trade balance, financial transactions help determine the current account surplus or deficit. The net flow of capital investments (debt and equity investments, purchases of assets) is called the *capital account surplus* or *deficit*. By definition, if there is a current account (trade flows) deficit, then there must be a capital account (financial flows) surplus to pay for the value of goods and services imported in excess of goods and services exported.

Between 1990 and 2005, the total value of exports from the U.S. to the rest of the world doubled, whereas the value of imports from the rest of the world to the U.S. tripled.[23] There is no universal agreement, however, on the extent to which a long-term current account deficit and its counterpart capital account surplus is a problem. On the down side, it can mean that consumer purchases of goods from abroad exceed the ability of the economy to produce goods and services demanded abroad. In other words, an economy may be unable to produce the goods and services that its residents desire, at a price its residents are willing to pay. The funds that flow abroad for those purchases are not available therefore for investment in the U.S. economy for increased production. To some extent, that is the case. U.S. consumers do purchase large quantities of consumer goods from other countries, and of increasing importance, the U.S. purchases an ever larger proportion of total fuel consumed in the U.S. from other countries.

The imbalance in trade of goods and services, however, has not been the main issue for the United States. As noted earlier, the U.S. capital markets are attractive to foreign investors, and they were especially attractive after the Asian and emerging-market collapses of the late 1990s. Thus, the inflow of investments from abroad is a more important explanation for the current account deficit than is the purchase of goods from abroad. There is a demand in other countries to invest in assets in the U.S. independent of our trade position with the rest of the world.

The danger in the volume of capital account surplus lies in its role in financing investment in future growth that otherwise would have to come from savings in the U.S. To the extent that our future economic growth can be financed only from abroad, because of low savings in the U.S. (discussed below), then a major shock to the U.S. economy that causes investors from abroad to pull out large amounts of funds would both decrease the funds available for investment and decrease current consumption. The post–September 11 period initially did lead to some pull back from the U.S. capital market, but that was short-lived, in part due to actions by the Federal Reserve Board (discussed later in this chapter) to hold down interest rates. As some foreign investments pulled out of the stock market and the decline in the value of the dollar against major foreign currencies decreased consumer purchases from abroad, the current account deficit shrunk marginally.

Financing the U.S. Economy. The flows of capital across international boundaries and the financing of investment will continue to be major focal points of both economists and governments. Globalization, while widely discussed, is still not entirely understood. Historically, investments made in other countries were substantially in productive capacity. When a company or an investment banking group invested in a factory abroad, the productive capacity in that country increased, and it is no easy matter for the investors to take their investment out quickly. Since the late 1980s, international transactions in financial instruments, such as stocks and bonds as opposed to physical capital, have substantially increased. One of the main reasons for the rapidity of the Asian and emerging-market collapses was the amount of foreign investment in tradable financial instruments that allowed investors to pull their funds out quickly.[24]

The importance of these movements in the trade balance lies in their implications for how the economy is financed. From the mid-nineteenth century until the mid-1980s, the U.S. economy was financed domestically. National saving was sufficient to provide funds for national investment, with the surplus national saving being invested abroad. To the extent that households spend heavily on consumer goods and save little, and the government budget is in deficit, investment has to be financed from sources outside the economy. A substantial part of the U.S. economy has been financed not by domestic savings but rather by foreign investments in the United States. These foreign investments represent a future claim on U.S. assets that are not matched by equal U.S. claims on foreign assets.

Concern about this situation is not chiefly motivated by nationalistic pride. Foreign investments in the U.S. economy represent foreign confidence in the economy. Foreign investors have found U.S. Treasury notes an attractive investment because of the interest rates offered and because of their safety. Were the same foreign investments made in U.S. industry's stocks and bonds, financing would be available for economic expansion. To the extent that the investment in U.S. government debt does not produce expansion of domestic U.S. production capacity, the government's need for this financing competes with industry's need for investment finance. In macroeconomic terms, this external financing of the deficit creates a situation in which a greater quantity of U.S. goods and services has to be sold abroad in the long term to meet payments to foreign holders of U.S. debt. That quantity then is not available for U.S. consumption. Thus the trade balance, as well as the overall balance of payments disequilibrium, is intertwined with the federal government budget deficit.

The late 1990s boom in the U.S. economy illustrates this point. The federal budget achieved balance in fiscal year 1998. Not only did the U.S. government not need to issue long-term securities to finance a deficit, but for three years the Treasury actually bought back higher-denominated debt with part of the budget surplus. By the end of the century, foreign borrowing to finance the deficit was becoming less of an issue, but a return to large federal deficits starting in 2002 again spotlighted the role foreign investors play in financing federal budget deficits. The situation further highlighted the comparatively low savings rate of U.S. households.

The Decline in National Savings. Except for the four budget surplus years from 1998 to 2001 (see Chapter 9), the U.S. economy has generated falling amounts of savings to finance investment in the economy, relative to the size of the economy. National savings represent the source of funds for new investment in equipment, plants, and other physical facilities that allow total production to grow. Economists generally measure savings as gross and net national savings as a percent of GDP. *Gross national savings* is the sum of household saving, corporate saving, and government saving. Household saving may be literally in the form of savings accounts or more likely in investment in securities through individual investments and individual and corporate contributions to pension plans. Government saving may be in the form of investment in fixed assets such as roads and bridges, or though rare, a budget surplus. Corporate saving is investment in fixed assets such as factories, equipment, land improvement, and so forth, plus net changes in inventory. These government and corporate investments, financed by purchases of equity and debt in companies or taxes in the case of government, create the economy's capacity to produce goods and services.

Not all investments by governments and corporations actually produce an increase in productive assets, of course, because they must replace older facilities and equipment that are no longer useful. Machinery purchased to replace obsolete equipment would not result in an increase in productive capacity. Chapter 12 discusses capital investment by federal, state, and local government. *Net national savings* captures the difference between investment in productive capacity, whether government or corporate, that adds to new production by subtracting out the value of fixed assets replaced.

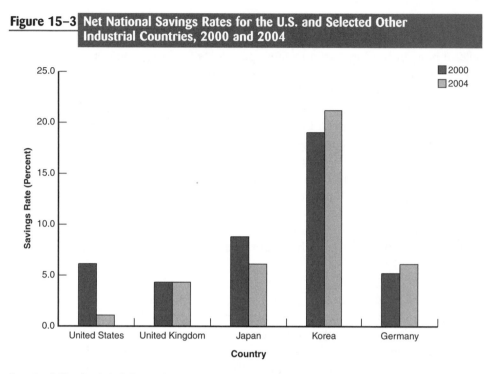

Figure 15–3 Net National Savings Rates for the U.S. and Selected Other Industrial Countries, 2000 and 2004

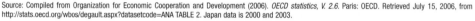

Source: Compiled from Organization for Economic Cooperation and Development (2006). *OECD statistics, V. 2.6.* Paris: OECD. Retrieved July 15, 2006, from http://stats.oecd.org/wbos/degault.aspx?datasetcode=ANA TABLE 2. Japan data is 2000 and 2003.

The U.S. gross national savings rate hovered between 15% and 18% from 1995 through 2004.[25] But as **Figure 15–3** illustrates, the net national savings rate of the U.S. was only 6% in 2000, and fell to just over 1% in 2004. Overall, most of the capital formation that occurred in the U.S. economy was absorbed by replacing obsolete or unusable assets. The substantial decline in U.S. net national savings has been relatively unique as the small sample in **Figure 15–3** illustrates. Even countries such as the United Kingdom that run a capital account surplus typically have higher savings rates than the U.S. In the economic boom of the 1990s, net national savings was relatively high in part because of substantial investment in the U.S. capital markets and in part because of low government budget deficit, including some years of budget surplus.

The compensating factor that offsets some of the problems that might otherwise be created by sustained low savings rate is in the technology advantage that the U.S. economy enjoys relative to most of the rest of the world. The measures of savings discussed in this section capture those elements in the economy that are investments in fixed assets (i.e., physical or tangible objects). Classically, land, labor, and capital were the three elements that combine to produce goods and services. But increasingly, the main factor that enables the U.S. to have the highest gross domestic product, and one of the highest levels of GDP per capita, is the role that technology plays.

Typically when a company replaces an obsolete piece of equipment, the new equipment is highly likely to be much more productive than what it replaced. Net national savings would not capture this increased productive capacity due to the more sophisticated knowledge built into the new equipment. If one were able to measure the production of the old equipment, when it was operating at full capacity, and the production of the new piece of equipment operating at full capacity, then one would not fully subtract the cost of the new equipment from gross national savings. But in the total economy, the measurement problems in trying to capture the value of technology are currently insurmountable. So to the extent that new technology built into new fixed assets is not measured in terms of contribution to productivity, net national savings understates the ability of the economy to continue to produce goods and services. The value of knowledge generated within the economy and the attractiveness of the U.S. economy are what have enabled the U.S. economy despite lower savings rates and despite frequent government budget deficits to continue to enjoy higher standards of living than almost any other country in the world.[26]

Deficits and Debt Management

Chapter 13 described state and local debt primarily as a tool for financing long-term investment in physical infrastructure and other capital assets. It is therefore prudent for state and local governments to use short-term borrowing only for meeting the demands of short-term contingencies and to ensure that long-term borrowing is linked to the expected life of the investments financed. Federal debt policy, on the other hand, relates more to macroeconomic policy considerations than to capital investment requirements. Deficits in the federal budget accumulate as spending exceeds revenues, regardless of whether the spending finances investments in long-term growth, meets operating expenses, pays interest on previous debt, provides transfer payments, or pays the costs of war. While it is possible to make a numeric comparison between the investment levels in the federal budget and the size of the deficit, federal budget deficits have not been the result of conscious investment planning.

Developing-Country Debt Management. For developing countries, prudent debt management is more comparable to that of U.S. state and local governments.

Developing countries as a rule have excess or idle labor capacity. The long-run economic strategy is to invest in education to improve the productivity of labor and in physical infrastructure to facilitate the production and flow of goods and services produced by the private sector. Typically, a shortage of physical infrastructure, such as transportation and communications facilities, retards the economic investment that would employ the excess labor capacity. Governments in developing countries borrow from donor agencies, such as the World Bank, and from banks in industrial countries to increase their physical infrastructure and other capital investments. If they are economically sound, the investments will produce long-run economic growth sufficient to repay the indebtedness.

More often than not, however, developing countries encounter debt troubles when borrowing finances current consumption rather than investment and when physical infrastructure assets that have been built are not maintained. The economy then does not maintain a sufficient level of growth, revenues do not increase as expected, and debt exceeds capacity to repay.

U.S. Government's Use of Debt. In the post-Depression era, the federal budget deficit was used as an overt tool to influence total demand in the economy and thus overall economic performance. According to the prevailing economic theory of that era, deficits should be managed to stimulate the economy without creating inflationary pressure. However, by the 1980s the size of the deficit had reached proportions that were out of step with economic policy objectives. In actuality, the federal budget achieved a surplus in 1998, in part due to deliberate management, but largely due to tax receipts increasing with rapid economic growth. As already noted, 2002 marked a return to a federal deficit with an economic downturn and the short-run effects of September 11. The subsequent wars in Afghanistan and Iraq, financed by supplemental defense and non-defense appropriations that do not fall within self-imposed balanced budget guidelines, made a return to surplus or even low levels of annual deficit unlikely. Furthermore, independent of these presumably short-term, albeit intractable, problems, the federal budget has a built-in deficit for the foreseeable future unless major changes are made in expenditures and/or revenue sources.[27]

Size of the U.S. Federal Debt. To understand the debate about government debt in recent years, it is first important to understand the relative size of the federal debt and then to consider its origins and implications. **Figure 15–4** shows the debt as a percentage of GDP, a useful measure for comparing the growth of the debt with the growth of the overall economy. Total federal indebtedness in 1950 equaled 94% of GDP, reflecting the financing of World War II. That figure steadily declined until it reached post war lows around 35% between 1970 and 1980. Rapid increases after that brought federal debt up to 70% of GDP in 1995, the highest level since

Figure 15–4 Federal Debt as a Percentage of Gross Domestic Product, 1950–2007 (2007 projected)

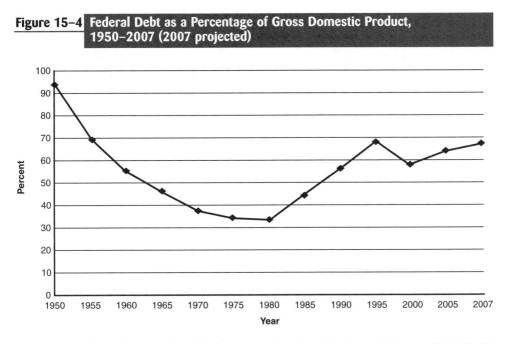

Source: Calculated from U.S. Council of Economic Advisers (2006). *Economic report of the president: 2006*, Washington, DC: U.S. Government Printing Office, 280, 375.

1955.[28] Debt relative to the total economy then fell during the late 1990s surplus period, but as **Figure 15–4** shows, steady increases have characterized the 2000s.

Effects of Economic Performance on the Size of the Federal Debt. Two circumstances explain the rapid rise in the federal government's debt in the 1980s after a long period of decline. First, the federal budget, in terms of both revenues and expenditures, is affected by the overall performance of the economy. Oil price shocks and high inflation led to unbalanced federal budgets throughout the 1980s. Overall growth in the economy in real terms was virtually zero for the decade. This lack of growth created pressure on the budget because of automatic increases in expenditures for some social welfare programs that expand as unemployment goes up. It also caused a decline in federal revenues. The reverse occurred in the mid-1990s, as low unemployment and increased production combined to produce decreased demand for federal social welfare assistance and increased tax revenues. Two simultaneous wars, high prices for imported oil, and rising costs for some federal programs such as Medicare continued the longer term trend to higher deficits into the mid-2000s.

Effects of Tax Cuts on the Size of the Federal Debt. The second set of circumstances affecting the deficit are tax policy decisions beginning with the administration of

President Ronald Reagan. On taking office, President Reagan with approval by Congress initiated a sweeping set of economic reforms, including a major series of tax cuts beginning in 1981 and significant budget reductions in non-defense spending. However, as the program evolved, it proved politically impossible to reduce non-defense spending sufficiently to match increases in defense expenditures, and overall spending remained at prior levels or even went higher than before the tax cuts.

The theory behind the tax cuts was that the funds not collected by the government would be better invested by the private sector, yielding a future revenue dividend in the form of increased tax yields from the heightened economic activity. In reality, the fiscal dividend never materialized. Federal revenue levels grew more slowly than at any time since the 1960s, while defense spending, entitlement program outlays, and interest on the debt soared to new heights.

Since those initial tax cuts, annual increases in federal revenue have fluctuated between 5% and 10%, with only a couple of years below 5% or above 10%. The tax cuts adopted in 1997, unlike those of 1981, were accompanied by offsetting expenditure reductions so there was not as much of a reduction in federal revenue. There was no appreciable dividend in higher productivity and therefore federal revenues did not increase. The exceptions were three economic boom years already attributed in this chapter to an unusual stock market expansion in high technology stocks. The Economic Growth and Tax Relief Reconciliation Act of 2001 has made it more difficult to once again achieve a budget surplus. In fact, total federal revenues declined in dollar terms for each of the fiscal years after fiscal year 2000. This decline in revenues largely explains the movement of the budget from surplus into deficit over that period.[29] Since that time, the costs of the wars in Afghanistan and Iraq have made it even more difficult to move the budget back into surplus.

Anticipating Economic Conditions

Both the private and public sectors need tools to measure economic change and anticipate economic trends. If businesses are to make sound investment decisions (including the decision to hire new workers or build new plant capacity), they have to anticipate future economic developments. If interest rates are expected to fall, it is not the time to borrow to buy new production equipment. If a tax incentive that reduces overall tax liability when funds are invested in new productive capacity is about to expire, it is a good time to make new investments. Some of these events can be predicted with relative certainty. An investment tax credit may have a specific expiration date, as did the R&D tax credit, and it was pretty clear that Congress was not going to renew it. On the other hand, it may not be as easy to predict how much change will occur in interest rates. Forecasting tools are a vital ingredient in business economic planning.

If the federal government is to achieve its economic policy objectives, it also needs sensitive and valid measures with which to predict the direction of the economy. Likewise, it needs models of change that predict what will happen if specific policy changes, such as a change in the maximum corporate income tax rate, are enacted. Although forecasting techniques are beyond the scope of this text, some familiarity with the measures that are watched closely by business and government and with the analytical models used by forecasters is important for understanding government economic policy.

Business and government forecasters watch closely a number of individual economic indicators. Some indicators are related to the labor force, including unemployment, average weekly hours worked, and average hourly earnings. Other indicators reflect financial conditions, such as interest rates and new starts in home building. Businesses, forecasters, and public policy makers examine such indicators to understand current economic conditions and to predict turning points when the economy will begin to move up or down from its current state.

Of particular importance for anticipating economic turning points are cyclical indicators, also known as *leading, coincident, and lagging indicators*.[30] Leading indicators presumably show in advance what the economy will do, revealing the turning points, whereas lagging indicators report what already has occurred. Formerly, the Bureau of Economic Analysis of the U.S. Department of Commerce released the cyclical indicators monthly. In October, 1995, the Department of Commerce awarded a contract to the Conference Board, a private, not-for-profit economics research and business membership organization to maintain the Business Cycles Indicators database. Since 1996 the Conference Board has served as the official source of the indices.

Coincident Indicators

Coincident indicators, those that report what the economy is doing now, are the ones that most commonly reach the public's attention. They include measures of industrial production, personal income, and manufacturing and trade sales.

Prices. In section one, *Measuring the Economy*, we described the basic measures of national product and income that indicate what is happening to the levels of production and income. Prices are another measure of what is happening. Wholesale prices may provide an earlier warning of potential problems than measures of national product because they indicate probable changes in prices about to be paid by consumers. The wholesale or producer price index covers about 2,800 commodities.

The *consumer price index* (CPI) is based on the cost of goods and services bought by urban wage and clerical workers. It is estimated from three data sources—a periodic sample survey of about 50,000 housing units and 23,000 retail establishments in 87 urban areas around the country to determine buying habits, and monthly calls and visits to retail establishments and other vendors to collect price information on most commodities. The household sample includes two population groups—all urban consumers and urban wage earners and clerical workers.[31] Change in the CPI is widely cited as an indicator of inflation. One of its most important uses is to adjust various government benefit programs, most prominently Social Security, for the effects of inflation. Social Security payments are automatically increased based on increases in the CPI.

How the CPI is constructed is controversial, largely because of the effect it has on the government budget and the deficit. The actual household survey of buying habits can take place as long as four or five months prior to the publication of the index. A one-point decrease in the CPI in 1997 would have reduced government expenditures by $6 billion.[32] A National Academy of Sciences panel in 2002 made a series of recommendations for improvement in CPI methods, some of which were adopted.[33] Of course changes in the CPI are not the major variables that affect budget forecasts. The Congressional Budget Office's focuses on changes in real GDP growth, interest and inflation rates, and wage and salaries share of GDP in its long-term (ten year) budget projection.[34]

Unemployment. Two other measures provide good indications of the current state of the economy—unemployment and industrial production. Unemployment, a percentage measure of the people within the labor force who are not employed as discussed in a previous section, is a common public policy target indicator. This measure is politically charged. A change in the unemployment rate of half a percent up or down is enough to send the president before the news media to announce significant economic progress or to have opposition leaders charge that the economy is failing. However, unemployment is subject to wide seasonal fluctuations, and the measurement of unemployment is subject to manipulation. Some job seekers may become discouraged and fall out of the count altogether. Women and members of ethnic minority groups may not be well represented in the count of job seekers because they may be convinced there are no jobs to seek or no jobs worth seeking. Therefore, unemployment data always have to be interpreted with some care.

Unemployment figures can vary widely among regions of the country, states, and substate regions. For instance, rural areas may be hard hit economically while urban areas are less harmed. State economies dependent upon tourists traveling by automobile may feel the effects of higher gasoline prices and the result may be higher unemployment.

Industrial Production. The industrial production index, prepared by the Federal Reserve System, is a measure of the manufacture of durable and nondurable goods. The durable portion of manufacturing is watched closely, particularly key industries such as steel. Sales of steel and other hard inputs into manufacturing reflect future intentions of manufacturing concerns. Rising sales may indicate the possibility of future investments in capital facilities. Falling sales may indicate lack of confidence in the economy and attempts by firms to keep inventories low. The value of this index has declined somewhat as the size of the manufacturing segment of the economy relative to the services segment has declined.

Leading Indicators

Although the coincident indicators are useful measures of the current or recent state of the economy, they often do not provide the lead time necessary to devise intervention strategies. The forecaster as a result turns to the leading indicators. Leading indicators include such items as average duration of unemployment, commercial and industrial loans, change in the consumer price index for services, and inventories to sales ratios in manufacturing and trade.

Employment-Related Indicators. A key leading indicator is the *average weekly hours in manufacturing*. Its usefulness is based on the practice of most manufacturers of cutting back on the length of the workweek rather than laying workers off if the demand for production starts to decline. A somewhat later indicator is the *average weekly initial claims for unemployment insurance*. This indicator provides evidence of the extent to which layoffs are increasing or decreasing. Both measures indicate employers' estimates of the direction of change in the economy.

Housing Starts. Private, non-farm housing starts, measured by the number of building permits issued for new private housing units, provide a measure of the faith of builders and financial investors in the health of the economy. A decline in the number of starts can signal future economic decline. Housing is thought to be sensitive in that it reflects willingness to tie up investment dollars for several months to a year in an expensive commodity for which there may be no buyer at the time construction begins. For example on a substate basis, Flint, Michigan, was heavily hit by cutbacks in automobile manufacturing employment, resulting in a major downturn in housing construction particularly in the mid-2000s. The situation was so dire that not only were housing construction workers out of jobs, but so were government housing inspectors, since they lacked anything to inspect.

Housing starts are also extremely sensitive to mortgage rates. During periods of extremely high rates, such as the early 1980s, many potential buyers were forced out of the market. In both the 1990s and again in 2001–2002, mortgage rates fell to their lowest points in nearly 40 years, and housing starts increased, even after September 11, 2001. A significant portion of 2001–2002 financing activity, however, was in refinancing existing mortgages as opposed to financing newly constructed homes. A steady planned set of increases in interest rates set by the Federal Reserve, discussed later in this chapter, caused home mortgage rates to increase again after 2003, and in some parts of the country, housing prices started to fall.

In recent years, housing starts have become a somewhat less reliable leading indicator. Growth in the use of adjustable rate mortgages allows home buyers to hedge against cyclical swings in interest rates, which in turn keeps demand for housing higher in the initial stages of rising interest rates.

Stock Markets. Stock markets are watched closely by the business community and government analysts, but their volatility makes them difficult to use as leading indicators. The New York Stock Exchange (NYSE) historically was the market most carefully watched. The NASDAQ (National Association of Security Dealers Automated Quotation), where the large majority of technology stocks are traded, later became as important—and to some more important—due to the substantial increase in the information and communications technology sector's share of the economy. The Tokyo and London markets are watched as well. A substantial increase in investments in emerging markets and the swings in these markets have given prominence to several other markets, especially after the volatility of the late 1990s. The Hang Seng (Hong Kong) stock market index is reported daily, for example.

Several composite indexes of stock exchange transactions are used with the most notable being the Dow Jones Industrial and Standard and Poor's indexes. Changes are infrequent in the stocks listed in these indexes, although they became more frequent in the late 1990s as stock values for some of the companies included in these indices fell to near zero and some went out of business. For example, until a major change of dropping four stocks and adding four others occurred in 1997, the 30-stock Dow Jones Industrial Average had remained largely intact since 1980 and includes such giant firms as Walt Disney Company and ExxonMobil Corporation. Enron was dropped after the scandal of its inflated and fraudulent earnings came to light. As the U.S. economy continues to rely upon service industries and technology industries, more frequent additions/deletions are necessary. For example, Wal-Mart was added to the index to capture more of the services component of the economy, and companies like Microsoft and Hewlett-Packard represent information technology in the economy.

Stock transactions are useful as leading indicators in that they reflect the faith of investors in the stocks traded on the open market and thus in the companies whose stocks are traded. Stock transactions may be helpful as a barometer of investor confidence. In principle, the value of a stock reflects the health of the firm. In reality, stocks may surge or decline wildly as a result of corporate takeover attempts and fights to prevent takeover or as a function of irrational investor behavior showing faith in unlimited growth potential in stock prices. Criticism of stock analysts recommendations abounded after the market crash of 2000–2001. To the extent that stock prices reflect factors other than the economic health of the corporations, prices will be misleading as an economic indicator.

Composite Indexes. A variety of combined indexes are used to gauge economic changes and trends. As noted earlier, the private Conference Board took over the database and calculations of leading, lagging, and coincident indicators. The Conference Board's indicators and composites reflect the overall economy. Composite indices are published by the Board monthly, and combine several individual indices.

One type of composite is a *diffusion index*. It measures the proportion of individual components of the index that are moving in the same direction. The numerical value of a diffusion index is equal to the percentage of components of the index that are moving in the same direction. For example, the diffusion index of the leading composite index assigns values of 1, 0.5, or 0 to each component based on change of 5% or more, less than 5%, or no change or drop, respectively.[35] Stock analysts and trade publications also compute and publish indices of the major markets.

Forecasting

Despite the availability of a wide range of indicators and extensive historical series, forecasting remains a risky business. It is common to find two or more major federal organizations in substantial disagreement over expected economic trends. Rarely do the Office of Management and Budget (OMB) and the Congressional Budget Office (CBO) agree, for example, on the forecast of the federal deficit. However, the CBO calculated that the mean percentage error in forecasts of over a dozen economic indicators was rarely more than 1% for the CBO, administration forecasts, and private economic forecasters. CBO did observe that its estimates were (barely) more accurate than administration forecasts. In addition, the CBO notes that its forecasts compare favorably to a consensus survey of private forecasters, called the *Blue Chip Consensus*.[36] Of course, the longer the forecast period, the greater the variances that might be expected among forecasters and the greater inaccuracy of the forecasts.

To the extent that discrepancies arise, forecasts by the president's advisers, reflected in the annual budget, have tended to overestimate economic performance so that government receipts fall short of original estimates and expenditures tend to be higher due to programs such as unemployment benefits that kick in automatically. The CBO also has been optimistic but often is more accurate than OMB.[37]

Economic forecasts are based on informed judgment or a combination of judgment and sophisticated econometric models (see the discussion of forecasting revenues in Chapter 4). Several private organizations employ econometric models that include numerous variables—from around 100 to as many as 1,200. Among the more famous private models is DRI-WEFA (a merger of Data Resources, Inc. and the former Wharton Econometric Forecasting Associates). Several organizations, including the Institute for Survey Research at the University of Michigan, conduct surveys of ordinary consumers and expert analysts to obtain estimates of economic trends. Judgment regularly is used to adjust the sophisticated mathematical models.

Not surprisingly, during major economic changes both business and government are sometimes criticized for not having anticipated the degree of change or sometimes even the direction of change. The recession year of 1982 had been predicted in 1981 to be a year of modest economic growth. The recovery in 1983 was predicted to be a period of slow growth, whereas actual growth in GDP turned out to be more than twice the growth that had been forecast. The recession that plagued the last two years of the George H. W. Bush administration was reputed to be momentarily ending, but the Clinton campaign was able to make the case that recovery had not yet begun. Some economists, especially in Europe, forecasted annually from 1995 through 2000 that the American economic bubble would burst. Finally, in 2001, they were right. Models seem to fail when major structural changes are occurring, such as OPEC's gain of control over oil production in the early 1970s or the rapid rise in fuel prices in 2006. When the economy is stable, various models are fairly successful, and popular opinion then generally agrees with the expert forecasts.

Given the conflicting interpretations possible even with sound information, economic forecasters as well as political leaders interpret the data from their own perspectives. The technical problems involved are great, but inevitably forecasting succumbs not to technical problems but to political resolutions. The president and his staff may attempt to focus attention on one set of indicators that show signs of progress, while members of Congress from the opposing party may focus on another set of indicators. State and local political leaders are just as susceptible to coloring judgment with hope by trying to appear confident in the economic future while sometimes failing to address serious underlying economic and fiscal weaknesses. We return to the issues involved in conflicting theories of economic behavior and the implications for government economic policy in the next section.

Tools Available to Affect the Economy

Automatic Stabilizers

Government actions intended to achieve economic policy objectives can be either discretionary or automatic. In the case of discretionary actions, policy makers discuss alternatives and reach a decision as to how to intervene in specific circumstances. Automatic or built-in stabilizers, in contrast, do not require policy makers to take any special steps. Some government revenues and expenditures rise or fall automatically with changes in the economy. Revenues are especially sensitive to economic performance with tax revenues falling due to falling incomes.

Figure 15–5 shows the relationship between the change in GDP and the change in federal revenues from 1978 through 2005. With few exceptions, GDP declines are matched by declines in revenues, and vice versa, though not always at the same

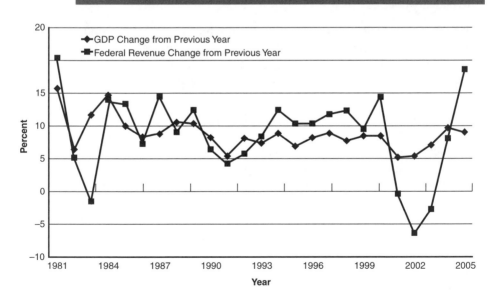

Figure 15–5 **Changes in Gross Domestic Product and Federal Revenue, 1978–2005**

Source: Calculated from U.S. Council of Economic Advisers (2006). *Economic report of the president: 2006*, Washington, DC: U.S. Government Printing Office, 312, 375.

rate. For example, the slight increase in GDP from 1987 to 1988 was exceeded by a much larger increase in federal revenue. Similarly, the drop in GDP from 2000 to 2001 was accompanied by a much larger drop in federal revenue. That latter is accounted for partly by some lag effect as federal revenues did not start to drop as fast as the overall economy at the end of the late 1990s boom, and September 11 largely did not affect GDP whereas federal revenue declined substantially. In most of the years illustrated in the series, the directional changes occur in the same year. There is little lag between a declining GDP and a decline in federal revenue since much of federal revenue derives from taxes on components of GDP (corporate and personal income). Government expenditures, at least at the federal level, do not automatically fall with declining economic performance. In fact, they tend to increase. The combined tax revenue declines and expenditure increases have an automatic, stimulative effect tending to encourage economic growth.

The progressivity of the tax structure is an example of a built-in or automatic stabilizer. As the economy declines, corporate profits decline and workers' salaries decrease. Both corporate and personal taxes go down with the result that proportionately more funds are left available to the private sector for investment, stimulating demand. Similarly, tax revenues rise as the economy expands, providing some brake on growth so it does not lead to inflationary pressures. Unemployment insurance is another example of an automatic stabilizer.

Discretionary Policies

Nongovernmental stabilizers are also an inherent part of the economy and individual economic behavior. Recessions are resisted by individuals and corporations that use savings to maintain established levels of activities. Conversely, expansionary trends are resisted. As income rises, greater proportions of income are placed in savings rather than being used for consumption.

Discretionary interventions vary widely. They are based on economic theories of behavior, both micro- and macro-economic, that anticipate the economy's responses to government actions involving taxing and spending and alterations in the flow of funds through the monetary system. The former actions are called fiscal policy. The latter are dubbed monetary policy. Fiscal policy and monetary policy are first reviewed separately, and then their integration into an overall strategy is discussed. A separate section is devoted to the public investment role of government—a role that is particularly important for developing countries and for U.S. state and local governments.

Fiscal Policy Instruments

The essential tools of fiscal policy are revenues, expenditures, and the implied surplus or deficit. Their use evolved during the twentieth century and continued into the twenty-first, changing as different views of the role of government in the economy have held sway. The prevailing view had been that little government intervention was necessary. If the economy seemed to be faltering, the government's role should be limited to an incremental increase in expenditures over revenues to "prime the pump." During the Great Depression of the 1930s, demand fell so rapidly and to such a depth, however, that small actions by the government had virtually no effect. It was only the extraordinary production demands of World War II that stimulated sufficient growth to pull the economy out of its freefall. The immediate post-war period rode on the demand for consumer goods that had been in short supply during the war, and there seemed to be little for the government to do for the economy one way or the other.

Keynesian Economics. Ideas about what the government should do in the event of a downturn have not stood still. John Maynard Keynes had argued in 1936 that the main cause of downturns was lack of demand.[38] According to this view, the government's aim should be to stimulate demand by spending, thereby ensuring that idle productive capacity is used. By 1946, the federal government had assumed a formal role in the economy and that role was guided by the prescriptions of Keynesian economics. Keynes focused on the problem of cuts in production in response to declining demand. Such cuts result in less purchasing power for consumers, which further reduces demand for goods and services. This still further decline in demand results in further reductions in production levels. The emphasis, according to Keynesians, should be on maintaining demand levels. The way to maintain demand levels, in their view, is for government to spend at a level higher than revenues—in other words, to incur a deficit whenever economic fluctuations threaten to reduce demand to levels that will generate unemployment and general economic decline.

Supply-Side Economics. Keynesian economics was widely accepted until the 1970s, when a contrasting view of the basic problem in a fluctuating demand cycle was given wide circulation. Some economists began to argue that the basic problem lay, not on the demand side, but on the supply side.[39] So-called supply-side economics became the dominant viewpoint of the Reagan and George W. Bush administrations. The supply-side view has held that high tax burdens are the major contributor to reduced economic performance. The more taxes are collected, the less money is available for private investment and the less incentive there is to produce. If taxes are cut, production presumably will be stimulated and additional workers will be hired. Although the tax rates are lower, the actual revenue yield will be higher because of increased corporate profits and increased take-home pay for workers. Furthermore, the increased supply of goods and services available should have a dampening effect on inflation.

The more extreme version of the supply-side view provided the basis for the 1981 tax cuts (Economic Recovery Tax Act of 1981). However, the expected revenue windfall did not materialize. The prevailing explanation of why it did not is consistent with the theory that tax cuts generally stimulate growth. The accepted view is merely that tax revenues from that growth are usually less than necessary to offset the government revenue loss. Generally the periods during which large tax cut packages were introduced have coincided with economic downturns so that federal revenues fell not only as a result of the tax cuts, but also the general decline in economic activity, as **Figure 15–5** illustrated. Furthermore, the economic period of the George W. Bush administration was dominated much more by the September 11 attacks and the subsequent wars in Afghanistan and Iraq. It is impossible to guess whether the federal budget deficit would have just been smaller without the wars, or would have headed toward at least short term balance. That guess largely would have to be based on a guess about the receptiveness of Congress to the aggressive tax cuts proposed by the president and the willingness or political ability to reduce expenditures and to address major long-term issues in financing Social Security and Medicare.

The differences between the demand-oriented economists and the supply-oriented economists have moderated. The middle-of-the-road view is that specific and directed tax decreases or reductions in tax liabilities can be helpful, such as investment tax credits to encourage businesses to invest in capital facilities and an R&D tax credit to encourage private expenditures on research. A major multiplier effect, in which tax reductions yield tax revenue increases, is unlikely, however. Capital gains tax changes seem to produce the greatest level of response. Prevailing views tend to emphasize somewhat more the supply-side view than efforts to stimulate demand.

Contemporary Fiscal Policy. The contemporary view of fiscal policy is more pragmatic than theoretical. Budget deficits have overwhelmed incremental fiscal adjustments in the 1980s, the early 1990s and again since 2002, and these circumstances have overshadowed debate among fiscal policy theorists. The current approach to fiscal policy calls for moderate fiscal efforts on the tax or expenditure side to counter trends rather than massive tax cuts or expenditure increases, although the George W. Bush administration pushed hard in 2001 for much larger tax cuts. Modest increases in government expenditures during periods of economic decline are expected to stimulate demand, which in turn will stimulate a higher level of production. Modest tax reductions, especially those designed to stimulate business investment, should have a similar stimulative effect on the supply of funds available to individuals.

Multiplier Effects. Extracting taxes from the economy or adding expenditures will have not only immediate effects but also multiplier effects, as any transaction will generate several other transactions. For each government expenditure resulting in payments to industry or an individual, part is taxed while the remainder is divided between consumption and investment. The private citizen or firm spends, and in doing so places dollars in the hands of others. Some of those dollars will in turn be taxed and the rest spent or invested. Therefore, an increase of $100 in government expenditures will be multiplied in its effect on the economy.

Expenditures have a stimulative effect when they exceed revenues. An initial government expenditure financed by the deficit puts money in the hands of producers and consumers, who in turn pay a portion in taxes, save a portion, and spend a portion. An excess of revenues over expenditures has a dampening effect. An extremely large federal deficit, however, confounds the fiscal policy effects.

Response Lags in Fiscal Policy. One problem with implementing a modest fiscal policy is the gap between the time a revenue or expenditure response is seen as necessary and the time it actually can occur. The lack of complete information about the economy produces a *perception lag*, the period of time that elapses between an event—such as the beginning of an inflationary period—and its recognition. The perception lag contributes to a *reaction lag*, the time between recognition and the decision to act. Pluralistic or decentralized political systems are often unable to avoid substantial reaction lags. For example, in January 1967 President Johnson proposed a surtax on income to dampen the inflationary effects of Vietnam War spending. The proposed legislation was not introduced in Congress until August and, though finally approved, was not signed into law until July 1968. To close this reaction gap, several presidents have attempted to gain congressional approval for moderate discretionary authority to raise or lower taxes. However, Congress has jealously guarded its prerogative to initiate and approve tax actions.

After the reaction lag is the *implementation lag*, the time required before the action taken actually affects the economy. Tax measures clearly are felt within a short period of time. The introduction of a new tax does require time to establish the specific regulations and mechanisms for collection. Once the tax is established, however, comparatively little time is required to make the necessary adjustments to the tax rate.

In contrast, extended implementation lags are likely when expenditures are adjusted for fiscal policy purposes. In the short term, the apportionment process that allocates funds to agencies may have some marginal influence on spending patterns during the various quarters of the fiscal year (see Chapter 10). Potentially more powerful tools include budget impoundments, which, within certain limits, allow the president to defer or rescind expenditures (see Chapter 9). Many expenditures, however, are basically uncontrollable in the immediate future because of previous commitments (for example, entitlement programs that provide assistance to the elderly and the poor). Furthermore, a large component of the federal budget is now devoted to meeting interest payments on the debt or to refinancing previous debt, expenditure commitments that must be met.

Capital construction has been suggested on occasion as one discretionary area where government expenditures could be used for fiscal policy purposes. The Clinton administration proposed grants to state and local governments for capital projects but failed to secure their passage in Congress. Construction would be initiated during slack periods and curtailed during periods of high employment. To some extent, public construction has been used for this purpose, particularly by the federal government during the Great Depression. The central government in a developing country, which typically has a much larger role in public infrastructure construction, is often in a better position to use this type of discretionary expenditure control. The short-term use of "stockpiled" capital projects that can be implemented when needed for their stimulative effects should not be confused with the role of government investment in long-term economic growth, discussed later.

Effects of Global Capital Flows. As noted at the outset of the chapter, in the United States, changes in world markets were of little consequence for most of the twentieth century. Changes in the U.S. economy, such as the Great Depression and other serious recessions, rippled through other economies, but economic declines in other countries had less effect on the U.S. economy. We have already discussed the current interdependencies among the U.S. and other economies. The Asian and emerging-market financial crisis of the late 1990s has an additional demonstration value with respect to business cycles.

With hindsight, it is relatively easy to explain what happened in Indonesia and Thailand and in turn in other Asian nations. The Indonesian economy had been booming throughout the late 1980s and 1990s. Towering buildings under construction dotted the Jakarta landscape, as was the case in Bangkok, Thailand. The values of the Indonesian rupiah and the Thai baht were both carefully controlled and pegged to the value of the U.S. dollar. Manufacturing and property investments were fueled by substantial lending from overseas investors, eager to participate in the Asian economic miracle. Portfolio investments in the Thai and Indonesian capital markets fueled the debt and equity markets.

Then in 1996–1997, vacancy rates in luxury hotels and office buildings began to climb. Lenders in turn began to reduce the volume of lending, putting pressure on the local currencies, which had to be converted to foreign currencies such as the Japanese yen and the U.S. dollar to pay for consumer goods imports and to pay debt service on some of the prior lending. The government of Thailand was unable to maintain the pegged value of the baht against the dollar, and ultimately devalued the baht. That meant that lenders who had lent yen or dollars and had not denominated the repayments in yen or dollars found their loans almost worthless. A majority of the loans extended by Japanese banks were denominated in local currencies rather than yen. Within weeks of the pressure in the Thai markets, Indonesian capital markets experienced the same pressures, and the value of the rupiah fell from around 3,500 to the dollar to nearly 20,000 to the dollar. Banks stopped lending and started calling in loans, investors rapidly sold their debt and equity holdings in Thai and Indonesian capital markets, and the bubble burst.

The economist Paul Krugman notes that it is too simplistic to describe the situation as purely a debt and equity market bubble.[40] He has argued that the boom in Asian economies was mainly fueled by population growth and consumer demand as opposed to an especially productive set of proactive government economic policies. Once the pressure started on currencies, and Thailand and Indonesia were unable to defend those currencies, a vicious circle began. It consisted of loss of confidence in those economies, plummeting currency values along with rising interest rates, and financial problems for banks, households, and other institutions. Neither fiscal nor monetary policy tools were sufficient to address the issues, and, at least in Indonesia, the political will to take the necessary steps was nonexistent. Ultimately, the collapse forced a regime change in Indonesia in 1998, ousting President Suharto who had been in office since the coup that replaced President Sukarno 32 years before. An important part of the problem for the world economy, and especially for Japan, was that there was no market information about the extent of exposure of foreign banks to losses due to lending in Thailand, Indonesia, and other emerging market countries in local currencies.[41]

A similar worldwide financial market event has not occurred since that Asian financial collapse. The burst of the U.S. technology market a few years later was thought at the time to perhaps be a similar event, but the U.S. economy recovered rapidly led largely by consumer spending. The extreme drop in net national savings to an historic low and very large government deficits led to substantial increases in U.S. government borrowing from world markets.

U.S. government borrowing from the central banks of several nations including Japan and China has caused some concern. Reliance on borrowed dollars from central banks of other countries that hold large dollar reserves is unprecedented in modern U.S. economic history. Most analysts continue to argue that the underlying strength of the U.S. is still very attractive. Those countries whose central banks hold large dollar reserves are willing to continue to lend because their economies depend substantially on purchases by the U.S. economy.[42] Some other analysts argue that this unprecedented borrowing from central banks cannot be assumed to be just like any other time in which the U.S. budget deficit has been high as there is no historical base from which to understand what could make those central banks lose confidence and reduce their levels of lending to the U.S. government.[43] Were that to happen, either federal borrowing from the U.S. markets would have to increase, causing interest rates to rise, or of course dramatic tax increases and/or expenditure decreases would have to occur to reduce the deficit.

Monetary Policy

Control of the Money Supply. Both demand-side and supply-side economists focus on the role of taxing and spending in the economy. Although fiscal policy economists did not launch a major critique of demand-side theories until the late 1970s, other economists since the 1950s have argued that the government's main effect on the economy should not come through fiscal policy at all. Led by Milton Friedman, these economists argue that the main effects of government policy on the private sector should come through control over the money supply. In a simple economy, a government controls the money supply through its monopoly power over the printing of money. As the economy expands, the demand for money increases and ultimately government meets this demand by printing more money. In a sense, the government literally can print currency and use that currency to meet its spending requirements.

The increase in the money supply (over and above printing replacements for worn currency) is called *seignorage*. Clearly, if the government resorts to printing money without regard to demand, the value of the currency printed declines. U.S. news media in the early 1980s showed film footage of individuals in Bolivia actually pushing carts full of currency to pay for a few dollars worth of goods as the annual inflation rate reached several thousand percent. Inflation affected currencies so much in Russia and Poland shortly after the demise of the Soviet Union that the governments issued new currency, eliminating three zeros to ease the use of currency in ordinary transactions. Indonesia followed suit after the financial collapse in the 1990s. In the early 1990s, Ukraine suffered a period of hyperinflation as the economy opened up, and Zimbabwe in 2006 experienced hyperinflation.

To the average citizen, money is cash—paper money and coinage—and the amount of that is strictly controlled by the government. In the U.S., only the federal Treasury Department may print currency or mint coins. But in any complex economy, paper money and coinage in circulation are not the major component of the money supply. In the United States, a little over 50% of the readily circulating money supply takes the form of paper money and coinage. The remaining slightly less than 50% consists mainly of demand deposits in banking institutions. Together, currency, coinage, demand deposits such as checking accounts, traveler's checks, and small time deposits constitute the principal money supply called M1. In 2006, M1 represented about 10% of the total money supply. Paper money and coins thus are about 5% to 6% of total money supply exclusive of debt. Total money supply in 2006 was approximately $13.7 trillion.[44]

Most ordinary financial transactions are conducted with checks, other paper documents, and by electronic means (ATM and debit card transactions) that transfer bank account balances from one individual or institution to another. The other main components of total money supply are M2 and M3 with M2 consisting of individual money market and mutual fund deposits, and time deposits of less than $100,000, and M3 consisting mainly of long-term deposits such as individual retirement accounts (IRAs), and institutional mutual fund, pension fund deposits, and longer-term deposits.

The banking deposit component of the money supply expands through credit or borrowing. When an individual borrows to purchase a new car, the bank increases the individual's bank balance, which allows a check to be written to the car dealer. When corporations borrow from financial institutions, or issue debt in the stock market, they secure funds for investment. In this case, the money supply grows by the amount of the loan. If interest rates are low, both consumer and business borrowing is encouraged, and the economy expands. Similarly, banks can borrow from the Federal Reserve System, which also adds to the money supply. Deregulation of the banking industry and the growth of various stock and bond funds have further increased the number and types of negotiable instruments that constitute the money supply. Influencing the money supply thus grows ever more complicated.

Role of the Federal Reserve System. In the United States, control over the money supply and interest rates, and hence monetary policy, is exercised by the Federal Reserve System, a quasi-public institution.[45] The system is headed by a board of governors consisting of seven members appointed by the president with the advice and consent of the Senate. The chairperson and vice chair are designated by the president, also with the advice and consent of the Senate. The Federal Reserve Bank and its 12 branches are augmented by all national banks and by state banks and trust companies that wish to join the system.

The Federal Reserve serves as a bank to the banking community. Financial transactions among banks and other financial institutions are cleared through the Federal Reserve. The system lends money to the member banks, which the banks can then relend to their customers. In setting its lending rates to banks, the Federal Reserve influences the direction and magnitude of interest rates in the entire economy, in turn dampening or stimulating the credit system. The system also buys and sells government bonds ranging from short-term Treasury notes to long-term bonds (open market operations). In addition, the Federal Reserve controls the reserve requirements

for member banks—the amount of money a bank must have available as a proportion of the total demand deposits of customers. Using these three tools—lending,
open market operations, and control of reserve requirements—the Federal Reserve
controls the money supply. In this way, it attempts to moderate demand that might
lead to inflationary pressures by reducing the growth in the money supply, or to stimulate demand when the economy is faltering by allowing the money supply to grow.

Discount Rate. The Federal Reserve's means to influence directly the level of borrowing is through its lending rate to member institutions (the banks). Called the
discount rate, this tool has increased in prominence as a monetary tool. Banks borrow from the Federal Reserve to meet customers' demands for money. As the
Federal Reserve increases the interest rate, the rate charged to final borrowers
increases, which in turn decreases the demand for funds. Since the 1980s, these
operations have become the main focus of Federal Reserve actions to control inflation in rapid-growth periods such as the late 1990s and again in 2004–2006. In the
boom of the 1990s, until the stock market decline of 2000–2001, the Federal
Reserve was quite successful in using small adjustments in the discount rate to
control inflation while not depressing the economy.

In 2004, the Federal Reserve, or Fed as it is often called, began in June raising
interest rates to slow the rate of growth in the economy out of concern that inflation would get out of control, mainly because of increased consumer spending
and borrowing by the government to finance the deficit. The first increase in June
2004 was followed by regular quarterly increases ending only in August 2006, the
longest period of consecutive increases in recent history. The rate at that point in
August 2006 was at 5.25%, meaning that banks borrowing from the Fed to meet
their obligations and maintain required reserves repaid the Fed at an annual rate
of 5.25%. These actions by the Fed to adjust the interest rate are watched closely
by the stock markets. How the Fed chairman announces a rate change or
announces that there will be no rate change at this time can create rapid reaction
in the markets.

Open Market Operations. Open market operations do not get as much citizen attention, but are highly visible to the financial community because they occur daily.
Open market operations means the Federal Reserve buys or sells government
bonds (or less frequently gold or foreign currency) on the open market. As the
Federal Reserve purchases bonds, it increases the reserve holdings of the member
institutions selling the bonds and hence increases the supply of money available
to be lent. This increase in turn stimulates economic activity, because more investment funds are made available. As member banks buy bonds from the Federal
Reserve, their cash reserves decrease, reducing the total supply of funds available
to the economy.

Reserve Requirement. Changing the reserve requirements of member institutions is done infrequently. For every dollar in customer deposits, member banks are required to retain a specific percentage. By increasing this percentage, the Federal Reserve can immediately curtail the amount of money available. Historically changed only every few years, the reserve requirement in the 1980s became a more prominent feature of monetary policy, with adjustments often occurring on an annual basis. Since the 1980s, however, the Fed has returned to infrequent changes in the reserve requirements.

Putting these monetary tools together, the government's monetary policy is described as *loose* or *tight* (or as *expansionary* or *contractionary*). Loose monetary policy usually involves lowering the prime rate, purchasing securities from member banks, and perhaps lowering reserve requirements. These actions increase the money supply, which permits banks to lend more to customers. As a result, private investment goes up and unemployment falls. The side effects are lower interest rates and higher prices.

A tight monetary policy entails the reverse: the prime rate increases, the Federal Reserve sells securities, and reserve requirements may increase. These actions reduce the ability of banks to lend. Tight monetary policy is pursued generally to dampen inflationary pressures and to slow down a speeding economy. In contrast, loose monetary policy is pursued to stimulate growth and reduce unemployment.

Role of the Chairperson of the Federal Reserve Board. For much of the history of the Federal Reserve, it seems unlikely that many Americans ever knew the name of an incumbent or former chair. However, former Chairman Alan Greenspan became almost a household name in the 1990s, especially to the millions of Americans who became first-time investors in the stock market or started paying attention for the first time to the value of their company pension fund investments in the market. As chair of the Federal Reserve, Greenspan appeared regularly on the news networks and was widely quoted in the press. When he described in 1996 investors' attitudes toward growth in the value of stocks as "irrational exuberance," stock prices plummeted the same and following days.[46] When he stepped down in 2005, replaced by Ben Bernake, it was almost as if an icon had retired, leaving difficult shoes for Bernake to fill.[47]

While the chair clearly is the spokesperson for the Federal Reserve, it is more likely that the news media and the investing public are now highly sensitive to actions by the Federal Reserve, and hence the chair is watched carefully for indications of where the Federal Reserve is going. Internally, the chair presides over a seven-member group and wields his or her influence through personality, force of argument, and relative prestige. The chair and the Federal Reserve are not synonymous.

Political Criticism of the Federal Reserve Board. Although the Federal Reserve Board is protected from direct coercion from the president because its members' terms are fixed without threat of removal, the board is periodically criticized for appearing to respond to political pressure. While there is little evidence of overt behavior in support of incumbent presidents, some evidence indicates that the Federal Reserve Board has done less than it could in some periods (for example, in the 1960s and 1970s) to offset cyclic movements in the money supply and that this lack of action coincided with the interests of incumbent administrations. [48] Until the stock market boom of the 1990s, the Federal Reserve was seen in a loose sense as somewhat more Republican Party–oriented mainly because of its role in managing monetary policy, with the association between monetarists such as Milton Friedman and more conservative public policies focusing on lower levels of federal spending, tax cuts, and balanced budgets. The achievement of a balanced budget during the Clinton administration, though obviously a cooperative result from both political parties and more the result of a sustained economic boom, put the Democratic Party in the mainstream of monetary and fiscal policy, apparently diminishing some of the previous partisan differences over economic policy.

Combining Fiscal and Monetary Policy

Although economists differ on the emphasis given to fiscal versus monetary policy, the two sets of tools operate at the same time, whether deliberately or not. Sometimes they are complementary. At other times the effects of fiscal policy actions are offset by monetary policy actions. Many analysts are wary of advocating frequent changes in fiscal or monetary policy in response to changing economic conditions. The inability to predict economic change sufficiently far in advance and the slow response of governments suggests to many economists that fiscal policy should be oriented toward long-term economic objectives and that monetary policy should be used for effecting short-term adjustments. Although fiscal and monetary policy advocates disagree vigorously, most economists agree that the budget deficits of the 1980s, early 1990s, and after 2002 have been harmful.

Who Is in Charge?

When it comes to fiscal and monetary policy, different organizational entities are involved, sometimes raising the question, "Who is in charge of overall economic policy?"

Monetary policy is somewhat clear cut in that the Federal Reserve System is in charge. The tools that were discussed are under the control of the board with the leadership of the chair.

Fiscal policy is more complicated. The president is responsible for recommending policy and Congress for setting it. The Council of Economic Advisers as well as other key advisors provide input into the president's decision making as to what to recommend to Congress. About the only time Congress looks at the total picture of the budget and economic policy is through the annual budget resolution (Chapter 9). Target revenue and spending levels are set along with a projected deficit (or occasionally, surplus). Tax rates are set by law periodically, with continuing debate over whether they should be adjusted upward or downward. The Treasury Department, then, has responsibility for administering the taxes (Chapter 10). Spending, as was seen in Chapter 9, is set by a series of appropriation bills handled by separate appropriation subcommittees, with each executive agency being responsible for carrying out the mandates specified in these bills. OMB has some influence on spending patterns through the apportionment process (Chapter 10).

Recognizing the importance of the federal government's role in economic affairs, President Clinton created the National Economic Council (NEC) in 1993. The NEC is responsible for coordinating economic policy, and its parallel organization, the National Security Council (NSC) for national security concerns. The NEC serves as a coordinator among the numerous cabinet and Executive Office of the President agencies advising the president, including the Council of Economic Advisers (CEA), the Office of Management and Budget, and the Department of the Treasury.[49] The NEC functions to ensure that actions of the executive branch affecting the economy are consistent with the president's economic policy.   The NEC has been retained during the George W. Bush administration.

Public Investment Role of Government

Government Investment in Infrastructure. Fiscal policy and monetary policy are basically tools of central governments. State and local governments typically have balanced budget requirements, making it inadvisable to incur debt strictly for fiscal policy reasons, and neither type of government has a major influence on the overall money supply. However, state and local governments have significant impacts on regional economies, and increasingly state and local governments are adopting explicit economic development strategies. In this regard, state and local governments pursue strategies to create an effective economic climate to foster economic growth.

Also, these governments inevitably change taxes and spending in response to general economic conditions, which, whether deliberate or not, has at least regional economic effects. Since state and local budgets typically need to be balanced, these governments must respond to economic trends. During the 1990s, 44 states cut taxes.[50] When an economic downturn leads to reduced revenues, expenditures need to be reduced and possibly taxes need to be increased. As a consequence, citizens may find services they need are no longer available or are in scarcer supply. In the case of local governments, one of their biggest problems is that many people during recessions fall in arrears on paying their property taxes. For state governments, economic downturns often lead to decisions to raise tax rates at a time when people can least afford tax increases, though in 2001–2002, less than ten states raised tax rates. More took other temporary revenue measures such as using rainy day funds, securitizing tobacco settlement revenue (see Chapter 13), and postponing temporarily expenditures.[51] This tax raising (or expenditure reducing) imperative has been moderated somewhat in recent years by the common practice of maintaining "rainy day" funds, into which funds are deposited during periods of relative prosperity so that they can be accessed during more difficult economic times.

One of the major strategic elements available is public sector investment in the physical infrastructure necessary for business expansion. As discussed in Chapter 12, serious concern emerged in the United States during the early 1980s regarding the loss in economic productivity due to the deterioration in the infrastructure base of roads, bridges, streets, water and sewer systems, and other public facilities. According to some, fewer technological innovations, decreases in labor productivity, and inadequate capital investment in infrastructure were the major contributors to an overall worsening of the U.S. economy.[52] In developing countries, inadequate operation and maintenance of existing facilities has in many cases led to deterioration of physical facilities long before their expected depreciation. This deterioration has in turn created a decline in economic production.[53]

State and Local Incentives for Private Sector Investment. Governments are a major source of total capital formation in many developing countries. Public sector investment in infrastructure including state-owned enterprises historically accounted for most of the capital formation in developing countries. With privatization of state enterprises and growth of the private sector, however, the public sector role in capital formation has diminished. Although state and local governments in the United States do not invest as high a proportion of their finances in infrastructure, their role in creating a favorable economic climate is important. Some state employee pension funds, for example, have been used as sources of venture capital and to capitalize industrial development funds to attract new business. Federal policies, such as giving municipal bonds tax-exempt status, also influence state and local investment spending (see Chapter 13).[54]

Similarly, even in the face of reduced federal financial assistance and difficult fiscal circumstances, state and local governments have over the last several decades increased both their relative share of infrastructure financing and the absolute amounts spent on public infrastructure. This stimulative effect, of course, required state and local tax increases.

State and local governments also actively compete with each other over the location of major industrial facilities.[55] However, to the extent that state and local governments offer special incentives, such as tax breaks and below-market-cost facilities for industrial expansion, little national economic growth is stimulated. Certainly it may be possible to induce a business to relocate or to locate a planned expansion by offering special incentives, but such a move represents for the national economy as a whole only a relocation of economic activity rather than net new economic growth. Of course, from a national point of view, attracting firms from other countries, such as the Daimler Benz plant in Alabama discussed in Chapter 14, results in net growth within the national economy, albeit at the potential expense of some other country. Matters are not really that simple. The Daimler Benz investment, for instance, was in new productive capacity, contributing to net growth in the world economy wherever that investment eventually turned out to be located.

Similarly, when public investment creates possibilities for new investment, not only the local economy but also the total economy expands. A joint public–private venture, for example, participated in the redevelopment of the Baltimore harbor area that created conditions in which net new economic investment was attracted. Similar ventures have occurred in Portland, Oregon, and Seattle, Washington. Riverfront revitalization projects in San Antonio, Texas, stimulated downtown economic growth and have been emulated elsewhere. The Federal Express (FedEx) location of its worldwide central shipping point was a coup for the City of Memphis, Tennessee. Memphis offered many attractions related to such things as location, weather conditions, and volume of air traffic. The City also invested easily more than $100 million in airport runway and other facilities expansion. This was not a case of moving productive investment from one part of the country (or world) to another part with no net gain to the economy. Rather, FedEx was introducing a new business model of central hub air shipment, a major new investment in economic productivity that subsequently paid off handsomely for both the private and public sector investments.[56]

Link Between Public Infrastructure and Economic Growth. The causal link between public infrastructure investment and real economic growth depends on two conditions. The lack of facilities or infrastructure has to be a barrier to investment, and the costs of the investment have to be in principle recoverable through economic gains. For example, if poor road conditions slow the movement of goods and services, then the costs of those goods and services increase. In addition, firms may hold back on new investments because of the expected difficulty in transportation. Investment in road improvements under these conditions reduces transportation costs, which in turn either provides additional funds for investment or is passed on in savings to consumers, who can subsequently increase either savings or investment. If the economic returns on the road improvements exceed their costs, the result is a net economic gain to the economy. Conversely, if there are insufficient centers of production and consumption linked by those roads, then the volume of transportation will not be sufficient to yield enough economic gain, and the investment will not have been warranted.

Unfortunately, determining when an investment will yield a sufficient economic return is often difficult. Many local governments in the United States have invested in downtown revitalization, business incubator facilities, industrial parks, and other facilities without appropriate analysis of the local economy and have been disappointed with the returns. Some investments that seem to have substantial benefits initially turn out later to be white elephants when the business some years later decides to relocate elsewhere. Charlotte, North Carolina, lost its National Basketball Association team because it would not build a new stadium, though other factors such as less-than-full arenas were cited by the owners. An expansion team was later awarded to Charlotte, but Charlotte first had to promise to build a new facility. One study of U.S. highway investments suggested that instead of significant new capital investment in highways, greater economic impact could occur from decreasing congestion and other planning improvements—for little more spending than current levels. Other studies have reached similar conclusions about a wide range of infrastructure investments.[57] In developing countries inadequate consideration of whether there are genuine economic opportunities to be stimulated by an infrastructure investment at times has led to indiscriminate construction of roads where there were no real market and production centers to link.

Cities competing to host the Olympics (and their national governments) gamble hundreds of millions in investments if selected against an uncertain return on that investment. Most observers agree that the competition is more about the symbolic recognition of the city and country that are expected to pay off forever than the more immediate returns from hosting an Olympics.[58]

▮ Equity and Government Economic Policy

The formal, legislatively mandated objectives of government economic policy for the United States include only full employment, price stability, and steady economic growth as discussed earlier in this chapter. Except in the indirect results of employment policy, the distribution of economic gain is not a formal economic policy objective for the U.S. In many other countries, however, economic growth *and* equity are formal objectives of government policy.[59] Specific and intentional steps to improve the distribution of wealth are matters of formal policy. Whether a policy objective or not, however, government economic policy actions have redistributive effects. The World Bank's 2006 world development report, *Equity and Development*, defines equity as "equal opportunity...and...avoidance of deprivation in outcomes."[60] People should have equal chances at achieving similar life goals, and outcomes produced by society and government should not result in deprivation of some in favor of others.

Unintentional Redistributive Effects

To this point, we have been concerned with the overall performance of the economy. Government involvement in the economy also has consequences for specific subsectors or individuals. Fiscal and monetary policy actions taken to control overall economic growth and price stability are not necessarily neutral in their effects on individuals and industries. If the government lowers corporate tax rates to stimulate business investment but increases other taxes to neutralize the effects on the budget balance, then those for whom taxes are raised are paying for the economic benefits whether they share in those benefits or not. Many developing country governments have attempted to address problems of the urban poor by imposing price controls on agricultural products. While the short-run effect may be to lower food prices in urban areas, the longer-run effect is to decrease agricultural production. In the short run, economic costs are imposed on one group, rural producers, for the benefit of another group, urban consumers. In the long run, overall economic performance declines. Developing country budgets, operating often in conditions of instability and uncertainty, frequently have difficulty achieving any specific policy objective, such as poverty alleviation, through the budgeting process.[61]

Economic policies aimed at stabilization also can have unintentional redistributive effects. Under inflationary conditions, persons on fixed or relatively fixed incomes lose purchasing power. This is especially true for retired persons living on pensions, but it is also true for workers who cannot command increases in wages. If the government takes no action to slow the rate of inflation, its inaction "redistributes" income from those on fixed incomes to those whose wages or other income rises with inflation. Higher interest rates favor income earnings from investments, usually held by upper-income families. Large federal deficits, which ultimately impose repayment costs on future generations, also may create intergenerational inequity (see Chapter 11).

Addressing Inequality

Equity as a concept of "equal chances" as defined above is easy to describe, but difficult to measure directly. Inequality in absolute terms is somewhat easier to measure and therefore is often used in discussions of equity and inequity, such as inequality in the distribution of income. Since the 1960s, the degree of inequality of income distribution in the United States has increased significantly. There was a sharp increase in inequality during the 1980s, attributed by many to a significant cut in federal corporate and personal income taxes, benefiting mainly the already wealthy, and cuts in programs of assistance to the poor.[62] The stock market boom of the 1990s substantially widened the gap between the top and the bottom, though the subsequent crash did convert many of the instant millionaires to ordinary income earners. Some economists, especially in Europe, who are critical of the "monetary policy only" view of the government's economic role, argue that the government should mitigate the negative distributional effects of economic growth that leaves only the middle- and upper-income classes better off. According to these economists, policies such as aggressive employment subsidies to reduce the number of unemployed should be implemented as direct measures to lower the nonaccelerating inflation rate of unemployment.[63]

Exhibit 15–3 illustrates the concept of equity, its measurement, and compares income inequality and education inequality for several nations. The idea is to measure the extent to which an inequity exists, and then devise deliberate government policies to reduce the inequity.

Income Stabilization Policies. Income stabilization policy addresses the problem of economic inequality, with the most deliberate approach being a negative income tax. This would involve determining an appropriate income guarantee, a benefit reduction rate, and a break-even income. The income guarantee is the amount of the transfer when the family income is zero, the benefit reduction rate is the rate at which the amount transferred is reduced as family income increases, and the break-even income is the point where family income reaches a level beyond which the family no longer qualifies for a transfer. The United States has no negative income tax, but its principles are incorporated to varying degrees in several income-related transfer programs.

Transfer Programs. Several transfer programs (food stamps; Supplemental Feeding Program for Women, Infants, and Children; Medicaid) provide a minimum or floor level of benefits comparable to the income guarantee. Major reforms in the welfare system, however, have severely curtailed benefits by imposing lifetime limits on the amount individuals may receive and imposing strict work requirements (see Chapter 14).

Tax Policies. Expenditure programs are not the only form of income redistribution. As noted in Chapter 4, different taxes have different impacts on various groups. In addition, the overall structure of the entire tax system may operate to redistribute income among different groups. The Tax Reform Act of 1986 was in one basic aspect almost exclusively a redistributive act.[64] Throughout consideration of various possible changes, the basic principle followed was that the act had to be rev-

| **Exhibit 15–3** | **Measuring Income Inequality and Selected Country Results** |

For governments that endorse an overt policy to reduce inequality, or advocate for decreasing inequality at the macro level, how does one best characterize the degree of inequality? One approach is to use the Gini index.

The Gini index concept is illustrated graphically in what is called a Lorenz curve as the area between a line that depicts perfect equality and a line (curve) that depicts the actual measured distribution in a specific society or economy.

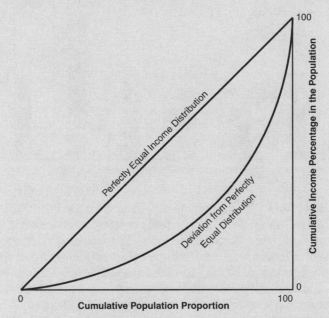

A Lorenz curve plots the cumulative percentage of income (or other valued good) held by income groups against the cumulative percentage of income groups. For example, in a perfectly equal distribution of income, the lowest population decile in income would have 10% of the income, the first and second lowest deciles would have 20% of the income, and so forth. That perfectly equal distribution would plot as a straight 45-degree line on an x, y graph. The difference between the actual plotted Lorenz curve and the perfectly equal distribution is measured as the area between the two curves—the Gini coefficient of inequality.

The graphic below looks at a selected group of countries in terms of two measures of inequality, one for income distribution and one for education attainment. The Gini indices reported essentially measure the distance between a theoretically perfect distribution of income and education. The higher the index number, the greater the deviation from a perfectly equal distribution.

continues

| Exhibit 15–3 | Measuring Income Inequality and Selected Country Results (continued) |

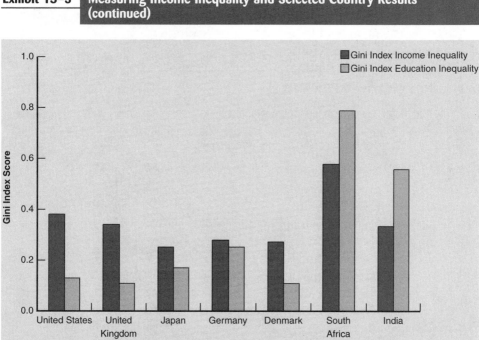

The graph is helpful in understanding the differences among countries. South Africa and India have higher Gini indices of inequality on both measures than the selected industrialized countries, as one might expect. Among the industrialized countries in the figure, the U.S. has the highest index of income inequality, with the U.K. close behind. Japan, Germany, and Denmark show similar indices for both education and income, whereas unlike the income score, the U.S. has a much lower education index score. Thought for discussion: what tools might policy makers use to address inequalities as reflected in such measures?

Source: Calculated from World Bank (2006). *World development report 2006: equity and development,* New York: Oxford, 280–281 and 284–285.

enue neutral. In the face of huge budget deficits, neither political party was prepared to support a tax reform that reduced revenues, as the Economic Recovery Tax Act of 1981 had. As a consequence of the 1986 law, lower-income groups benefited from sharply reduced taxes, middle-income groups benefited from modest reductions, and upper-income individuals and corporations faced tax increases. In 1993, there were sharp increases in the top tax bracket. In 1997, tax decreases focused on both ends of the income spectrum. The 2001 tax changes and subsequent proposed changes such as making the capital gains tax cuts permanent, and eliminating the inheritance tax substantially benefit upper-income groups.

Tax expenditures, discussed in Chapter 4, are often redistributive in effect. Not taxing interest on municipal bonds redistributes income toward the purchasers of municipal bonds, who tend to be retirees either directly or through pension fund investments. Allowing interest on mortgages, including second homes, to be deducted from taxable income has a redistributive effect toward middle- and upper-income individuals. The problem with the redistributive effects of tax expenditures is that they are much less transparent as a policy instrument. A tax expenditure does not appear plainly as an expenditure, nor does it appear directly as a tax reduction.

While economic policy affects the distribution of income, it cannot be expected to address structural features of the labor market. For example, workers with minimal or obsolete skills will have difficulty finding employment even during periods of rapid growth. Economic policy also is of limited assistance in coping with readjustments in the economy, such as might occur with changes in homeland security and defense operations in the U.S. and overseas. Other policies, of course, are designed to deal with more basic structural problems. Expenditures on education, both academic and vocational, are expected to increase the overall human resource base for the economy. Regulatory policies are expected to reduce private incentives to pollute the environment, a problem that imposes an eventual economic cost when the environmental damage is repaired.

No redistributive policy is neutral in its economic impact. Indeed, no economic act, no matter what its intended effects, is automatically neutral with regard to distribution of income. Designing redistributive policies should take into account the potential reduction in economic efficiency and try to mitigate any losses. During a recessionary period, both the labor force and total plant capacity are underemployed, so that government action to stimulate the economy may do just that without causing significant unintended redistributive effects. But since recession is not the normal state of the economy, we have to assume for starters "that if the government expands its purchases of goods and services or provides additional benefits so that some group of private citizens can consume more goods and services, somewhere else in the economy purchases of goods and services for consumptionary investment, exports, or other government programs will have to be reduced."[65]

Summary

Representing more than 31% of total economic activity in the United States, federal, state, and local government budgets have a tremendous combined effect on the economy. The federal government acts deliberately to intervene in the economy to achieve aggregate economic objectives. The major economic policy objectives of most central governments include economic growth, full employment, stable prices, and balance in the flow of funds into and out of the economy. Increasingly, as national economies become more interdependent, governments, including the U.S. federal government, are including specific competitiveness objectives as part of national economic policy. Because federal budget deficits sometimes soared to unacceptable (politically and economically) heights, management of the deficits and the overall government debt also has been added as a major economic policy objective in the United States. For some countries, achieving some degree of equity in income and social status is a formal policy objective, though not in the U.S.

Fiscal policy and monetary policy are the main tools used to influence macroeconomic performance. Fiscal policy encompasses the use of the government's taxing and spending powers to stimulate or dampen economic activity. An excess of expenditures over revenues (a deficit) stimulates demand and thus employment. A possible consequence, however, may be inflation. An excess of revenues over expenditures (a surplus) has a dampening effect on the economy. Monetary policy affects economic activity through control over the money supply. By changing interest rates and reserve requirements and by buying or selling bonds, the Federal Reserve can speed up or slow down the pace of economic activity. In the latter half of the 1980s, debates over the theory and detail of fiscal and monetary policy were overshadowed by the huge federal budget deficit. Several years of balanced budgets, with a surplus for 1998 through 2001, somewhat shifted the focus to delicate adjustments in interest rates to sustain economic growth.

Although state and local governments do not exercise fiscal and monetary control, their role in providing the basic infrastructure required for private sector business activity is important to regional economic performance. In this respect, state and local governments and developing country governments pursue similar ends. For developing country governments, their effective use of borrowed funds from donor agencies and commercial banks depends on putting the funds to use in increasing economic productive capacity.

Government policy interventions also have consequences for income redistribution. Changes in tax policy and increases or decreases in expenditures are almost never neutral as regards income distribution. In addition, there is general agreement that some level of redistribution of income is appropriate to address the problems of individuals with very low incomes. How extensive these programs should be, however, remains perennially controversial.

Notes

1. U.S. Council of Economic Advisers (2006). *Economic report of the president: 2006.* Washington, DC: U.S. Government Printing Office, 375, 376, 379. Note: state and local expenditures available for 2005 only in National Income and Product Accounts.

2. Inter-American Development Bank (2005). *Remittances to select LAC countries in 2005.* Retrieved August 7, 2006, from http://www.iadb.org/Mif/remittances/index.cfm.3.

3. U.S. Council of Economic Advisers (2006). *Economic report of the president: 2006,* 312.

4. Friedman, T. (2006). *The world is flat: a brief history of the twenty-first century,* expanded ed. New York: Farrar, Straus & Giroux.

5. World Bank (2004). *The world development report 2005: a better investment climate for everyone.* New York: Oxford.

6. United Nations Conference on Trade and Development (2006). *Foreign direct investment.* Retrieved July 31, 2006, from http://www.unctad.org/Templates/StartPage.asp?intItemID=2527&lang=1

7. U.S. Council of Economic Advisers (2006). *Economic report of the president: 2006,* 310, 312.

8. Nguyen, E., Bureau of Economic Analysis (2006). *The international investment position of the United States at yearend 2005.* Retrieved August 5, 2006, from http://www.bea.gov/bea/ARTICLES/2006/07July/0706_IIP.pdf

9. Executive Office of the President (1993). *Technology for America's economic growth: a new direction to build economic strength.* Washington, DC: U.S. Government Printing Office.

10. McGuckin, R. & van Ark, B. (2006). *Performance 2005.* New York: The Conference Board.

11. The World Bank (2004). *World development report 2005: a better investment climate for everyone.*

12. Employment Act (1946). P.L. 79-304; Full Employment and Balanced Growth Act (1978). P.L. 95-253.

13. Musgrave, R. A. & Musgrave, P. B. (1989). *Public finance in theory and practice,* 5th ed. New York: McGraw-Hill.

14. U.S. Council of Economic Advisers (2006). *Economic report of the president: 2006,* 332.

15. Federal Reserve Bank of San Francisco (1998). Economic Letter 98–28: *The natural rate, NAIRU, and monetary policy.* San Francisco: Federal Reserve Bank of San Francisco. Retrieved August 2003, from http://www.frbsf.org/econrsrch/wklyltr/wklyltr98/el98–28.html. Discussion and examples of NAIRU in this paragraph rely on this source. See also Ball, L. & Mankiw, N. (2002). The NAIRU in theory and practice. *Journal of Economic Perspectives, 23,* Fall, 115–136.

16. McGukin, R. & van Ark, B. (2006). *Performance 2005: productivity, employment and income in the world's economies.* New York: Conference Board.

17. Executive Office of the President (1995). *Economic report of the president: 1995.* Washington, DC: U.S. Government Printing Office. The 1995 report contains a detailed description of the methodology. Data in all subsequent government economic series use the revised concept, and historical tables have been adjusted.

18. President George W. Bush (2006). *State of the union: American competitiveness initiative.* White House press release, January 31.

19. Federal Reserve Bank of San Francisco (2005). *The rise and spread of state R&D tax credits.* Retrieved August 24, 2006, from http://www.frbsf.org/publications/economics/letter/2005/el2005-26.html

20. Grossman, G. & Helpman, E. (1992). *Innovation and growth: technological competition in the global economy.* Cambridge, MA: MIT Press.

21. Samuelson, R. (2006). Cooling off about keeping up. *Washington Post.* Retrieved August 12, 2006, from http://www.realclearpolitics.com/articles/2006/08/experiencing_another_competiti.html.

22. U.S. Council of Economic Advisers (2006). *Economic report of the president: 2006,* 125.

23. U.S. Council of Economic Advisers (2006). *Economic report of the president: 2006,* 311.

24. Krugman, P. (1999). *The return to depression economics.* New York: W.W. Norton.

25. U.S. Council of Economic Advisers (2006). *Economic report of the president: 2006,* 140.

26. Walsh, D. (2006). *Knowledge and the wealth of nations: a source of economic discovery.* New York: Norton.

27. U.S. Government Accountability Office (2006). *Fiscal year 2005 U.S. government financial statements: sustained improvements in federal financial management is crucial to addressing our nation's financial condition and long-term fiscal imbalance.* Washington, DC: GAO.

28. Executive Office of the President (2002). *Economic report of the president: 2002.* Washington, D.C.: Government Printing Office, 406.

29. U.S. Congressional Budget Office (2006). *The budget and economic outlook: fiscal years 2007–2016.* Washington, DC: U.S. Government Printing Office.

30. The Conference Board (2000). *Business cycles indicator handbook.* New York: Conference Board.

31. Bureau of Labor Statistics, U.S. Department of Labor (2004). *Understanding the consumer price index: answers to some questions,* revised. Washington, DC: U.S. Government Printing Office.

32. Norwood, J. (1997). The consumer price index, the deficit, and politics. *Government Finance Review, 13, February,* 32–33.

33. Schultze, C. (2003). The consumer price index: conceptual issues and practical suggestions. *Journal of Economic Perspectives, 17, Winter,* 3–22.

34. U.S. Congressional Budget Office (2006). *Budget and Economic outlook: fiscal years 2007–2016,* 129.

35. The Conference Board (2002). *Business cycles indicators.* Retrieved August 5, 2002, from http://www.tcb-indicators.org/methodology/di_computation.cfm.

36. U.S. Congressional Budget Office (2005). *CBO's economic forecasting record: an evaluation of the economic forecasts CBO made January 1976 to January 2003.* Washington, DC: U.S. Government Printing Office.

37. The CBO's annual analysis, *The economic and budget outlook: fiscal years* [ten year period], always contains a chapter explaining the differences between CBO and OMB estimates. A mid-year publication, *The economic and budget outlook: update*, reflects changes in the months since publication of the *Outlook*. U.S. Congressional Budget Office, *The economic and budget outlook: update*. Washington, DC: U.S. Government Printing Office, annually.

38. Keynes, J. M. (1936). *The general theory of employment, interest and money*. New York: Harcourt Brace.

39. Laffer, A. & Seymour, J. (Eds.). (1979). *The economics of the tax revolt: a reader*. New York: Harcourt Brace Jovanovich.

40. Krugman, P. (1999). *The return to depression economics*, 93–96.

41. Fuhrer, J. & Schuh, S. (1998). Beyond shocks: what causes business cycles? an overview. *New England Economic Review, November/December*, 3–24.

42. Levey, D. & Brown, S. (2005). The overstretch myth. *Foreign Affairs, 84*, 2–7.

43. Setser, B. et al. (2005). How scary is the deficit? *Foreign Affairs, 84*, 194–200.

44. Federal Reserve Board (2006), *Federal Reserve statistical release: money supply*. Retrieved August 25, 2006, from http://www.federalreserve.gov/releases/h6/Current/h6.pdf.

45. Federal Reserve Bank of Atlanta (2006), *Federal Reserve: structure and functions*. Retrieved August 27, 2006, from http://www.frbatlanta.org/invoke_brochure.cfm?objectid=883843FC-AB84-11D5-898400508BB89A83&method=display_body

46. Greenspan lets things simmer (1999). *The Economist, 346, July 1*. Retrieved August 23, 2006, from http://economist.com/displayStory.cfm?Story_ID=218974.

47. Big Ben strikes gold (2005). *The Economist, 352, October 29*. Retrieved September 4, 2006, from http://economist.com/opinion/displaystory.cfm?story_id=E1_VDRQGVV.

48. Beck, N. (1991). The Fed and the political business cycle. *Contemporary Policy Issues 9*, 25–38.

49. President William J. Clinton (1983). Executive Order 12835: establishment of the National Economic Council. *Federal Register, 58*, 6189–6190.

50. Johnson, N. & Filipowich, B. (2006). Tax cuts and continued consequences: states that cut taxes the most during the 1990s still lag behind. *New Republic Online, December 19*. Retrieved January 14, 2007, from http://www.cbpp.org/12-19-06sfp.htm

51. National Governors Association & National Association of State Budget Officers (2002). *Fiscal survey of the states*. Washington, DC: National Governors Association and National Association of State Budget Officers.

52. Kinnander, O. (2001). As infrastructure crumbles, engineers scream for investment. *The Bond Buyer, 335, March 9*, 40.

53. The road to hell is unpaved (2002). *The Economist, 349, December 19*. Retrieved September 4, 2006, from http://www.economist.com/displaystory.cfm?story_id=E1_TQRSVRP.

54. Miller, M. & Glick, M. (1999). The resurgence of federalism: the case for tax-exempt bonds. *Municipal Finance Journal, 19*, 46–73.

55. Ulbrich, H. (2002). Economic aspects of business tax incentives. *Public Policy and Practice, 2, October.* Retrieved January 16, 2007, from http://ipspr.sc.edu/ejournal/businesstax.asp.

56. Fulton, W. (2000), The FedEx story. *Governing, 14, April,* 68.

57. Small, K. et al. (1989). *Road work.* Washington, DC: Brookings Institution; Krohl, R. (2001). The role of public capital in the economic development process. *International Journal of Public Administration, 24,* 1041–1060.

58. London pips Paris at the finishing line (2005). *The Economist, 352, July 6.* Retrieved September 1, 2006, from http://economist.com/agenda/displaystory.cfm?story_id=E1_QTQGSNG.

59. The World Bank (2005). *World development report 2006: equity and development.* New York: Oxford.

60. World Bank (2005). *World development report 2006,* vii.

61. Lee, Jr. R. D. (1992), Linkages among poverty, development and budget systems. *Public Budgeting & Finance, 12, Spring,* 48–60.

62. Niggle, C. (1989). Monetary policy and changes in income distribution. *Journal of Economic Issues, 23,* 809–822.

63. Up the NAIRU without a paddle (1997). *The Economist, 344, March 8,* 92.

64. Birnbaum, J. & Murray, A. (1988). *Showdown at Gucci gulch: lawmakers, lobbyists, and the unlikely triumph of tax reform.* New York: Vintage.

65. Schutze, C. (1992). Paying the bills. In Aaron, H. & Schultze, C. (Eds.). *Setting domestic priorities: what can government do?* Washington, DC: Brookings Institution, 300.

Concluding Remarks

Public budgeting, because it involves allocating scarce public resources, will always be at the center of debates about government. While any predictions about the future should always be attempted with some humility, recent experience leads us to conclude that the field of public budgeting and finance in the coming years will be characterized by sustained or increased attention given to several areas:

- Disagreements about the level and type of taxes, who pays them, and the viability of various revenue sources
- Integration of planning, budgeting, accounting, performance measurement, and evaluation systems
- Financial management and financial reporting, including accounting rules for governments and nonprofit agencies
- Legislative–executive conflict over budgetary roles
- Setting priorities for the nation within the intergovernmental system, including the continuing need to consider the tradeoffs between the costs of security versus other pressing needs
- Promotion of economic growth within an international context
- Coming to grips with the fiscal implications of an aging society and with the consequences of promises that have been made to the elderly.

In concluding the book, we would like to give brief attention to each of these areas in order to encourage readers to follow these debates for themselves.

Financing Public Services

The financing of services is one of the most controversial aspects of government. The resources that finance government do not just appear. In a democratic society, decisions must be made by the populace and their elected leaders to provide these resources. In a country founded in response to concerns about "taxation without representation," however, even taxation *with* representation has proven to be controversial.

There are many sources of this controversy. First, there is the question of the level of taxation. This question, while difficult, often is driven by consensus over how much money would be necessary to raise in order to finance the desired level of services. This decision itself is quite difficult and controversial. Even after the decision about "how much" has been resolved, it does not tell us which taxes will be employed by a given government. The individual income tax and the property tax have provoked the most hostility, which has taken the form of specific limitations on the level of taxation and how taxes are administered. It is likely that these kinds of movements will continue, with the "taxpayer bills of rights" (TABORs) as perhaps the most prominent current example of efforts to limit government revenues.

Second, the question of who will pay what level of tax will remain the subject of great debate. Disagreements about whether a given tax should be progressive or proportional, or even how progressive it should be, are really debates about how the tax burden will be distributed across the population. If tax increases are part of the federal government's solution to its current fiscal imbalance, this will lead to questions about whether the deficit should be reduced by taxing mainly higher-income people or whether there should be relatively equal sacrifice among income groups.

Third, there is the question of the viability of certain revenue sources, particularly the state and local sales tax. The popularity of Internet sales has threatened the sales tax, as states and localities find it difficult to collect the tax on items sold over the Internet and through mail-order catalogs. As more sales shift from traditional "bricks and mortar" venues, states and localities that rely heavily on the sales tax will find their revenue streams increasingly at risk. This may eventually put pressure on these governments to turn to alternative revenue sources. Other taxes, such as those on certain forms of gambling and on corporations, may be somewhat risky as well, because the tax base for these sources is a bit less stable than for some other sources of revenue.

Integrating Planning, Measurement, Accounting, and Budgeting

While budget reform, focused on better integration of budget and performance data, has been a hardy perennial over at least the past 50 years, it seems obvious to even the most casual observer that the trend in government has been toward greater availability of information that will permit elected officials and citizens to evaluate the success of public services. The next logical step, already in evidence in many governments, is that budgetary decision systems will have increased capabilities to use this program information when resources are allocated. Whether the use of program information is desirable has been a moot question for years. The issue today is how to use program information, not whether to use it.

Advancements in computer technology—both hardware and software—will help strengthen the trend toward use of program data. Where 30 years ago the impediments to wider use of program data were both conceptual and technical, the technical limitations (for developed countries anyway) have largely disappeared. Wider accessibility to computer technology also is spurring the rapid growth of tools that can help decision makers use the technology. Knowledge management systems and decision support systems will increase the capacities of decision makers to consider information even under tight deadline pressures.

Increasingly, the conceptual framework for the use of performance information for budgeting is becoming more widely accepted as well. Most governments recognize the need for some enterprise-wide strategic planning effort, informed by the desires of program or agency stakeholders. Further, the development of performance and cost measures that are directly related to the programs or activities listed in these plans is viewed as essential to understanding how well these programs or agencies are functioning.

The integration of planning and budgeting, with the goal of informing the budget process with data on expected performance, is recognized as the crucial last step in making budgeting more performance-focused. It is fair to say that many—perhaps the majority—of governments have made substantial progress in planning and in the supply of relevant measurements, but many still fall short when it comes to the use of those measures for budgeting and management. The trend toward using performance measures does not mean that political realities will be removed from budgetary decision making, as some critics have contended. Rather, a greater array of information will be more readily available than in the past, and decision makers will have the options of considering that information in determining what positions to take on difficult problems. The desire—quite attainable—is not to have resource allocation driven by performance information in some kind of automatic sense, but to have more resource allocation decisions *informed* by considerations of performance.

Regardless of exactly how these connections are made, the movement toward performance-informed budgeting is unlikely to abate, largely because it focuses on the major budgeting question: Does the value that society receives from the public expenditure match or exceed the cost of the program or service? Growth in government programs will be accepted grudgingly, if at all, by taxpayers, who remain skeptical of the ability of governments to do many things well.

Increasingly, this will mean that justifying government spending requires demonstration that "value for money" is being delivered.

Financial Management and Financial Reporting

Financial management—defined as the stewardship of public resources after they are received—can hardly avoid being an important focus for the budget process. Particularly because these are public resources, the accountability for their use is even more important. Economic problems at the local, state, and federal levels have continued to make for "tight" budget situations that call for frugal measures. Frequently governments need to engage in midyear "rebudgeting" in response to unanticipated spending pressures or inadequate revenues. Budget execution, therefore, will receive greater attention in the future. Can savings be achieved through closer monitoring of program spending? Can improvements in accounting systems lead to savings? What alternative financial arrangements hold promise for reducing costs? To what extent should governments pursue contracting out of services, privatization, and leasing arrangements?

The past 25 years have seen major additional requirements for accounting and financial reporting for state and local governments. In large part, these have been spurred by the need for those external to government to have a better understanding of government's financial position. For example, potential investors in municipal bonds desire to understand the underlying fiscal health of a given state, locality, or government enterprise. Prior to the institution of common accounting standards by the Governmental Accounting Standards Board, it was difficult to draw any valid conclusions about the fiscal health of these jurisdictions based on information contained in their financial statements. Overall performance of the entire jurisdiction, such as the local government, in maintaining and preserving the assets that have been the result of previous capital investment, much of it debt financed is viewed by citizens and bond purchasers as vital.

At the federal level, successive presidential administrations since 1990 have made improving federal financial management and reporting a priority, even without the same kinds of accounting standards. Complying with these rules and guidelines, however, can be complicated and costly for governments at all levels. For example, the requirement under GASB 34 that states and localities report the full accrued cost of employee benefits may ultimately cost these governments significant resources not in reporting costs, but in order to fund these benefits more fully in the interest of improving their stated financial position.

Legislative and Executive Roles in Budgeting

Executives and legislative bodies will continue their struggles with one another over their relative roles in budgetary decision making. Both executives and legislatures may be less than assertive in dealing with the most intractable problems. Gridlock existed largely from 1981 to 1993 when Republican Presidents Reagan and Bush controlled the White House and Democrats largely controlled Congress. Gridlock developed again in 1995 when the president was a Democrat, Bill Clinton, and Congress came under the control of Republicans. During the first part of the George W. Bush administration, the Republicans controlled the White House and the House of Representatives while the Democrats controlled the Senate.

In the 2006 election, Democrats regained control of the Congress after 12 years out of power. They have pledged to reinvigorate the "power of the purse" and to exercise much more vigilant oversight over the activities of the executive branch. Faced with an unpopular war in Iraq that has an uncertain path to resolution, President Bush and the Congress faced challenges in working together to find some way out of the conflict. This was particularly true given the focus of both parties on the 2008 election, which will represent the first time since 1920 that there will be no sitting President or Vice President even attempting to gain the nomination for President. In such an environment, there will be numerous members of Congress in both parties—especially in the Senate—with their eye on the White House in 2008.

State and local governments have their own share of legislative–executive conflict. These conflicts are made more or less important in a given jurisdiction by the relative budgetary power of the branches. While some state governments have strong legislatures similar to the Congress, in other cases the legislatures are weaker because of short legislative sessions, term limits, limited staff, or a combination of all of these. It is probably the trend toward term limits that has weakened state legislatures the most. It remains to be seen whether this trend will continue into the future or whether the appeal of term limits has ebbed. In addition, the 2006 election saw substantial gains for the Democratic party both in control of legislatures and governorships. Similarly, the local "legislative branch" differs in power from government to government, especially between those governments which are council–manager versus strong mayor systems.

Priority Setting Within an Intergovernmental System

Governments will continue to be confronted with competing programmatic needs that must be met within a context of limited resources and intergovernmental relationships. Homeland security and the global fight against terrorism are likely to have the highest priority on limited resources for the foreseeable future. Small and larger scale wars also seem likely to continue putting pressure on the federal budget. Programs for the elderly (especially Social Security) and health care will continue to demand the attention of the federal government (see more on this below), while all levels of government will be called upon to deal with such intractable problems as HIV/AIDS and other infectious diseases, drug trafficking and drug abuse, and poverty and related conditions, such as homelessness. If the new Democratic majority in the Congress makes good on its pledge to reduce the federal deficit, this may squeeze the funding available for all levels of government.

State and local governments, on the other hand, will continue to find that financing elementary and secondary education will require new approaches as traditional sources of finance decline or are limited by taxpayer resistance. The pressures to improve the quality of education are likely to continue, both because of federal initiatives like the No Child Left Behind Act and because of similar state-level accountability efforts. While there is not necessarily a direct relationship between spending more money and education quality, it is nonetheless true that these efforts will put more pressure on the budgets of state and local governments. Difficult choices must be made over how other programs will operate and how they will be financed. Presidents, governors, and mayors may all lament the afflictions of AIDS and drug dependency, but where are funds to be obtained for dealing with these problems? Local governments may be willing to provide programs for the poor, but only if state and federal funds are available to support these efforts. The intergovernmental finance system will come under increasing scrutiny as the different levels of government vie for the same tax dollars.

Continued conflict among national, state, and local levels of government may be expected as new problems emerge that challenge existing intergovernmental divisions of authority and responsibility. Nowhere are the intergovernmental roles more complex than in attempting to ensure homeland security. How are security agencies at the federal level best able to relate to state and local agencies, especially given the long-standing tension that has existed among the levels of government? The budget systems of all governments allocate large sums of money to security efforts, but how are agencies to be held accountable for results when buck-passing for any failures can easily be done in such a decentralized environment? Other continuing intergovernmental concerns include preemptions of authority by the federal government over areas claimed by state and local governments and mandates by the federal government to state and local governments and by states to local governments.

Promoting Economic Growth in an International Context

Promoting economic growth for the nation will continue to be a priority. In addition, Rust Belt states will continue their struggle to reorient their economies in search of new industrial niches. Other regions, such as those dependent on the price of petroleum, will continue through periods of boom and bust as petroleum supplies and prices fluctuate. The extent to which state and local governments can affect their economic futures will remain uncertain, since all governments are subject to the ups and downs of the business cycle.

One of the most important sources of the uncertainty in promoting economic growth by all levels of government is the interdependence of the U.S. economy with the international economy. What the U.S. economy makes and sells is intimately influenced by the economies of other nations. Perhaps none of these will have a greater impact on the U.S. and the world than the rapid changes in the Indian and Chinese economies. The industrial mix of the U.S. economy and its labor force will inevitably change. These changes will arise at a time when the U.S. labor force is growing older as a whole due to the aging of the baby boomers. In addition, to the extent that more manufactured goods are produced abroad, the number of higher wage U.S. manufacturing jobs will continue to decline. How budget systems will be able to respond to these challenges is unknown.

Dealing with the Budgetary Implications of an Aging Society

The U.S. population is getting older. As this happens, it will place pressure on the entire society—public, private, and nonprofit sectors—to deal with the budgetary implications of an older population. The most obvious implication for public budgets is at the federal level, where both Social Security and Medicare face mounting financial pressures. These pressures largely result from the nature of these programs, which transfer resources from current workers (through payroll taxes) to current retirees (through benefits). As the baby boomers retire and begin receiving benefits, the ratio of workers paying into these systems to individuals receiving benefits will decline. For Social Security, dealing with this imbalance is conceptually easy, but politically difficult. That is, because the federal government controls both sides of the Social Security equation—the taxes paid and the benefits received. A wide variety of fixes is possible, including tax increases and benefit cuts, but each of these is politically difficult because of the popularity of the program.

Medicare is a different story. The financing problems of Medicare are driven in part by the aging of the population, but a more important factor affecting the future fiscal imbalance for the program is the generally high level of medical care inflation across the entire economy. This, in turn, is driven by factors such as increased life expectancy and the availability of often expensive drugs and procedures to prolong life. Medicaid—the shared federal/state/local program providing health benefits for the poor—is also substantially affected by the cost of health care. The solutions for both Medicare and Medicaid are also politically difficult, but perhaps the larger problem is that they are analytically insoluble. Simply put, it is hard to know how to bring down the cost of medical care without sacrificing other things that Americans hold dear, such as the choice of doctors and unfettered access to procedures.

These themes do not capture all that is likely to transpire over the coming years. Based on history, the thing that is the surest is that the budgetary conflicts and decisions will mirror the conflicts and debates about priorities within the society. This is both appropriate and inescapable, because the budget represents the priorities of the government expressed in dollar terms.

Bibliographic Note

This bibliographic note is intended to assist the reader in finding materials for further reading on public budgeting systems. Because the preceding chapters have extensive endnotes, we make no attempt here to recapitulate everything cited. Readers will find the index to be a handy guide to endnote references. This bibliographic note is meant as an aid in identifying general references as well as sources that have produced and can be expected to continue to produce literature on public budgeting.

Numerous periodicals provide information about the theory and practice of administration in general, and budgeting and finance in particular. Researchers frequently have a choice today of locating journal articles in print or on the web. While many journals are available online, they are seldom free. Publishers commonly will provide only a free sample or abstact online, and then researchers must rely upon print or electronic subscriptions. Online databases such as EBSCOhost or ProQuest Direct offer full-text access to collections of journals for subscribers. Researchers need to check with their local libraries for access to these or other full-text databases or for print copies of the journals described below.

Periodical indexes, once available in print and on CD-ROM, are now generally available online. Researchers may still need to rely on print indexes when searching for topics in older issues. As with the journals themselves, these online indices are not free. Researchers should check with local libraries for access or may be able to pay a per-search fee individually for some databases. Periodical indices include *Current Contents* (Philadelphia, PA: Institute for Scientific Information), *Economic Literature* (Pittsburgh, PA: American Economic Association), *Ingenta Connect* (Providence, RI: Ingenta), *Public Affairs Information Service* (PAIS) International (New York, NY: OCLC Public Affairs Information Service), and *TOC Premier* (Ipswich, MA: EBSCO Publishing). *Current Contents* and *TOC Premier* provide table of contents information for academic journals. *EconLit* is the American Economic Association's electronic bibliography of economics literature, containing abstracts, indexing, and links to full-text articles in economics journals. PAIS, as its title suggests, indexes journal articles in the field of public administration and public affairs. Ingenta is a subscription service that provides for searches and full texts of articles.

Some of the most important journals that produce articles on budgeting and finance include the following. *Public Administration Review* (American Society for Public Administration) often publishes scholarly articles on budgeting. *Policy Studies Journal* (Policy Studies Organization) includes occasional articles related to budgeting in its regular issues and in special symposia issues. *State and Local Government Review* (University of Georgia) frequently includes budget-related articles that are particularly helpful to practitioners as well as scholars. *Public Budgeting & Finance* (Blackwell Publishing for the Association for Budgeting and Financial Management and the American Association for Budget and Program Analysis), *Journal of Public Budgeting, Accounting, and Financial Management* (PrAcademics Press), *OECD Journal on Budgeting* (Organization for Economic Cooperation and Development), and *Public Finance and Management* (Southern Public Administration Education Foundation) focus especially on financial management and budgeting. *Government Finance Review* (Government Finance Officers Association) provides brief analytic pieces and news items on budgeting and finance.

Numerous journals cover the fields of public finance, policy analysis, and policy evaluation. Although occasional articles related specifically to budgeting systems appear in these journals, their usual focus is on specific budgetary subtopics. *National Tax Journal* (National Tax Association), and *Public Finance Review* (Sage) publish empirical and theoretical analyses of economic policy concerns, including government growth and size, tax policy, and fiscal and monetary policy, as well as economic analysis. Numerous journals are devoted to policy analysis and policy evaluation. In addition to *Policy Studies Journal*, the journals *Evaluation Review* (Sage), *Evaluation and Program Planning* (Elsevier), *Journal of Policy Analysis and Management* (Wiley for the Association for Public Policy Analysis and Management), and *Public Performance and Management Review* (M.E. Sharpe) all share that focus.

Besides the periodicals concentrating on budgting or related topics, other professional journals publish occasional articles of relevance. These include *Administration and Society, Administrative Science Quarterly, American Economic Review, Americal Political Science Review, Journal of Public Administration Research and Theory, Management Science*, and *Public Management Review*. The Washington-based *National Journal* (http://nationaljournal.com) and *Government Executive* (http://www.govexec.com) provide news and analysis of the federal government, including budgetary events, and the *C. Q. Weekly Report* (Washington, DC: Congressional Quarterly, http://www.cq.com) covers congressional actions in particular. Most of the journals listed have annual or occasional indices to facilitate general searches.

Another major source of up-to-date analysis and data consists of government publications. An excellent reference work that explains various types of documents and their sources is Joe Morehead's *Introduction to United States Government Information Sources*, sixth edition (Englewood, CO: Libraries Unlimited, 1999). An annual index to many local, state, and federal documents is *Bibliographic Guide to Government Publications*—U.S. (Boston, MA: Hall). Federal documents can be located through the Government Printing Office and its Government Information Locator Services website (http://www.access.gpo.gov) and through the federal government's main web portal, *USA.gov* (http://www.usa.gov). For statistical information, refer to the *American Statistics Index* which indexes federal documents, and the *Statistical Reference Index*, which indexes state government publications. Both indices are published by the Congressional Information Service owned by LEXIS/NEXIS (Washington, DC).

Congressional documents can be identified and obtained through a variety of sources. A useful index is the *CIS Index to Publications of the United States Congress* (Washington, DC: Congressional Information Service, LEXIS/NEXIS). Many congressional documents are available through the Thomas database of the U.S. Library of Congress's website (http://thomas.loc.gov). The Government Accountability Office, which is an arm of Congress, has its reports available online as well (http://www.gao.gov).

Congress in 2006 passed the Federal Funding Accountability and Transparency Act that provided for the creation of a federal spending database. The system once developed was to be a central entry point for obtaining information about all aspects of federal government spending.

There are numerous online subscription databases related to government. One of the most valuable is LEXIS/NEXIS (Reed Elsevier). Four major databases that are part of LEXIS/NEXIS are Congressional Universe, for information about Congress; Academic Universe, for legal research; State Capital Universe, for information about state governments; and Statistical Universe, for data searches. Westlaw (St. Paul, MN: West Publishing) is comparable to LEXIS/NEXIS Academic Universe.

Students of budgeting and finance will find themselves returning regularly to several key governments sources. The Office of Management and Budget (http://www.whitehouse.gov/omb), Council of Economic Advisers (http://www.whitehouse.gov/cea), Treasury Department (http://www.treasury.gov), Congressional Budget Office (http://www.cbo.gov), Government Accountability Office (http://www.gao.gov), and the Federal Reserve (http://www.federalreserve.gov) produce publications and data of major import to the field. Reports from these agencies are available in print and on the web. Data related to international budgeting and economic issues are found in a variety of sources, including the World Bank (http://www.worldbank.org), the Organization for Economic

Co-operatiuon and Development (http://www.oecd.org), the International Monetary Fund (http://www.imf.org), and the International Finance Corporation (http://www.ifc.org).

Several annual volumes from various agencies contain basic data on revenues and expenditures for local, state, and federal levels and intergovernmental transfers among levels. Considerable care must be exercised when working from more than one source, as the figures do not always agree. For instance, some sources dealing with government and the economy use national income as a measure whereas others use gross domestic product. In other words, users must be cautious when data are combined from two or more sources. The Census Bureau in the Department of Commerce publishes the annual *Statistical Abstract* and a host of materials on government finances. The Census of Governments is conducted every five years and contains not only financial data but also a wealth of organizational information. State and local government budget information is almost always three to four years out of date, except right after the Census of Governments. The Census Bureau is located on the web at http://www.census. gov. Publications in print and online of the Federal Reserve contain more up to date information on state and local government, but these publications do not disaggregate local from state.

Besides the Census Bureau, other providers of statistical information are located on the web. They include Statistical Resources on the Web, maintained by the University of Michigan (http://www.lib.umich.edu/govdocs/stats.html) and the Government Information Locator Service, maintained by the U.S. Government Printing Office (http://www.access.gpo.gov/su_docs/gils/index.html).

Analyses of federal budgeting and finance are published by private organizations such as the American Enterprise Institute (Washington, DC, http://www. aei.org), the Committee on Economic Development (New York, NY, http://www.ced.org), the Heritage Foundation (Washington, DC, http://www. heritage.org), the National Bureau of Economic Research (New York, NY, www.nber.org), the Conference Board (New York, NY, http://www.conference-board.org), and the Tax Foundation (New York, NY, http://www.taxfounda-tion.org). The Brookings Institution (Washington, DC, http://www.brook.edu) publishes numerous books on budgeting and taxation.

Books, of course, are an important source of information. Five of the classics in public budgeting, no longer subject to revision and updating, are:

- W. F. Willoughby (1918). *The Problems of a National Budget.*, New York, NY: Appleton.
- A.E. Buck (1919). *Public Budgeting,* New York, NY: Harper and Brothers.

- Smithies (1955). *The Budgetary Process in the United States.* New York, NY: McGraw-Hill.
- J. Burkhead (1956). *Government Budgeting.* New York, NY: Wiley.
- A. Wildavsky (1984). *The Politics of the Budgetary Process.* Reading, MA: Addison-Wesley.

Histories of budgeting include:

- V. J. Browne (1949). *The Control of the Public Budget.* Washington, DC: Public Affairs Press.
- B. M. Gross (1969). The New Systems Budgeting, *Public Administration Review.* 29, 113–137.
- C. W. Lewis (1989). History of Federal Budgeting and Financial Management from the Constitution to the Beginning of the Modern Era. *Public Budgeting and Financial Management 1*, 193–213.
- A. E. Meyer (2002). *Evolution of the United States Budget*, rev.ed. Westport, CT: Praeger.
- I. S. Rubin (1993). Who Invented Budgeting in the United States? *Public Administration Review 53*, 438–444.
- C. Webber & A. Wildavsky (1986). *A History of Taxation and Expenditure in the Western World.* New York, NY: Simon & Schuster.

Works on budgeting with a special focus, such as on the federal government, state governments, budget theory, and budget politics, include the following:

- Richard Allen and Daniel Tommasi's *Managing Public Expenditure: A Reference Book for Transition Countries* (Paris: Organisation for Economic Co-operation and Development, 2001)
- Robert L. Bland and Irene S. Rubin's *Budgeting: A Guide for Local Government* (Washington, DC: International City/County Management Association, 1997)
- Dall W. Forsythe's *Memos to the Governor: An Introduction to State Budgeting*, 2nd ed. (Washington, DC: Georgetown University Press, 2004)
- James L. Gosling's *Budgetary Politics in American Governments*, 4th ed. (New York, NY: Routledge, 2005)
- Steven G. Koven's *Public Budgeting in the United States* (Washington, DC: Georgetown University Press, 1999)
- Jerry L. McCaffery and L. R. Jones' *Budgeting and Financial Management in the Federal Government* (Greenwich, CT: Information Age, 2001)
- R. Gregory Michel's *Organization and Design of an Effective Budget Function* (Chicago, IL: Government Finance Officers Association, 2002)

- John L. Mikesell's *Fiscal Administration*, 7th ed. (Belmont, CA: Wadsworth, 2006)
- David C. Nice's *Public Budgeting* (Belmont, CA: Wadsworth, 2002)
- B. J. Reed and John W. Swain's *Public Finance Administration*, 2nd ed. (Thousand Oaks, CA: Sage, 1996)
- Irene Rubin's *Balancing the Federal Budget* (New York, NY: Chatham House, 2003)
- Irene Rubin's *The Politics of Public Budgeting: Getting and Spending, Borrowing and Balancing*, 5th ed. (Washington, DC: CQ Press, 2005)
- Allen Schick's *The Federal Budget: Politics, Policy, and Process*, rev. ed. (Washington, DC: Brookings Institution, 2000)
- Robert W. Smith and Thomas D. Lynch's *Public Budgeting in America*, 5th ed. (Upper Saddle River, NJ: Pearson Prentice Hall, 2003)
- Kurt M. Thurmaier and Katherine G. Willoughby's *Policy and Politics in State Budgeting* (Armonk, NY: M.E. Sharpe, 2001)
- Alan Walter Steiss and 'Emeka O. Cyprian Nwagwu's, *Financial Planning and Management in Public Organizations* (New York, NY: Marcel Dekker, 2001)
- A. John Vogt's *Capital Budgeting and Finance: A Guide for Local Governments* (Washington, DC: International City/County Management Association, 2004)
- Aaron Wildavsky's *Budgeting and Governing*, edited by Brendon Swedlow (New Brunswick, NJ: Transaction, 2001)
- Aaron Wildavsky and Naomi Caiden's *The New Politics of the Budgetary Process*, 5th ed. (New York, NY: Longman, 2001).

Edited volumes provide reprints of journal articles and originally prepared pieces. Among these are *Budgeting Formulation and Execution*, edited by Jack Rabin, W. Bartley Hildreth, and Gerald J. Miller (Athens, GA: Carl Vinson Institute of Government, University of Georgia, 1996); *Case Studies in Public Budgeting and Financial Management*, second edition., edited by Aman Khan and W. Bartley Hildreth (New York, NY: Marcel Dekker, 2003); *Evolving Theories of Public Budgeting*, edited by John R. Bartle (New York, NY: JAI, 2001); *Government Budgeting: Theory, Process, and Politics*, third edition, edited by Albert C. Hyde (Fort Worth, TX: Harcourt College Publishers, 2001); *Handbook of Government Budgeting*, edited by Roy T. Meyers (San Francisco, CA: Jossey-Bass, 1999); *Management Policies in Local Government Finance*, fifth edition., edited by J. Richard Aronson and Eli Schwartz (Washington, DC: International City/County Management Association, 2004); *Managing Local Government Finance: Cases in Decision Making*, edited by James M. Banovetz (Washington, DC: International City/County

Management Association, 1996); and *Public Budgeting and Finance*, fourth edition, edited by Robert T. Golembiewski and Jack Rabin (New York, NY: Marcel Dekker, 1997).

A variety of simulations is available to assist students in appreciating the dynamics of decision making. Numerous simulations, directly or indirectly related to budgeting and finance, are listed on the website of the Association for Budgeting and Financial Management (http://www.abfm.org). The *Public Budgeting Laboratory* is a comprehensive set of materials prepared by Jack Rabin, W. Bartley Hildreth, and Gerald J. Miller. It consists of a book of readings, noted above, by Rabin, Hildreth, and Miller, plus a *Workbook*, a *Data Sourcebook*, and an *Instructor's Manual* (Athens, GA: Carl Vinson Institute of Government, University of Georgia, 1996).

For literature on decision making, program budgeting, zero-base budgeting, accounting, economic policy, personnel management, program evaluation, and the like, the reader is encouraged to turn to the endnotes for each chapter.

Happy reading.

INDEX

A